For Suzanne and Zoë —
my protection in the wilderness.

CLOSE-UPS

INTIMATE PROFILES OF MOVIE STARS BY THEIR COSTARS, DIRECTORS, SCREENWRITERS, AND FRIENDS

EDITED BY DANNY PEARY

A FIRESIDE BOOK   PUBLISHED BY SIMON & SCHUSTER INC.

NEW YORK   LONDON   TORONTO   SYDNEY   TOKYO

ACKNOWLEDGMENTS

I am extremely pleased that Fireside/Simon & Schuster is publishing this tenth anniversary edition of *Close-Ups: The Movie Star Book*. I particularly want to thank my Fireside editor, Tim McGinnis, for getting this project off the ground before its eleventh anniversary. And I again thank Chris Tomasino, whom I sought as an agent in 1977 after she gave me such a hard time while representing an author on this book. (I got her back by badly misspelling her name.) Gratitude also goes to Cathy Hemming, Laura Yorke, and Joe Smith.

I would again like to acknowledge those people who helped me when the book was first published in 1977 by Workman Publishing Company: Peter Workman, Bob Fitzpatrick, Paul Hanson, Karyn Kay, John Bloom, Jim Harrison, Jane Elliot, Robert Knutsen, Debra Weiner, John Kremitske, Paul Brenner, John Cocchi, Lee Eisenberg, Doug McClelland, Gail MacColl, Norine Doherty, Gail Liss, Howard Mandelbaum, Paula Klaw, Ira Kramer, *Movie Star News*, the Directors Guild of America, the Writers Guild of America, Trade Composition, Charles Champlin, Kathy Hintz, Lou Valentino, John Springer, Judith M. Kass, Cory Gann, Jenifer Smith, Jennifer Rogers, Roberta Beck, William Dufty, Esther Cohen, Jonathan Roberts, Lawrence Siegel, Paul Bartel, Anthony Slide, Jewel Smith, Debbie Getlin, Gerarld Peary, Ina Weisser, Jerri Buckley, Stanley Kramer, John Randolph, Sam Jaffe, Howard Gelman, Cori Wells Braun, Douglas Heyes, Douglas Marshall, Melissa Sutherland, Bill Condon, Charles Kreloff, Shaun Johnston, my wife Suzanne Rafer, my daughter Zoe Weaver, and my parents Joseph and Laura Peary. I would like to single out my Workman editor, Sally Kovalchick, who deserved and took a long vacation.

Finally, I'd like to acknowledge those contributors to *Close-Ups* who have helped me on subsequent projects: John Landis, Robert Bloch, Robert C. Cumbow, Pat McGilligan, Michael Wilmington, Michael Crichton, John Springer, Charles Bennett, Paul Bartel, Richard Schickel, Joel McCrea, Joseph H. Lewis, David Thomson, and Stanley Kramer.

CONTENTS

I. THE COMICS

II. THE ENTERTAINERS

III. THE GREAT STAGE ACTORS

IV. THE SEX SYMBOLS

V. THE CULT FIGURES

VI. BOX OFFICE CHAMPIONS FROM 1932 TO 1977

VII. HOLLYWOOD MISFITS

VIII. HOLLYWOOD CASUALTIES

IX. CHARACTER ACTOR AS STAR

X. ACADEMY AWARD WINNERS FROM 1927 TO 1977

XI. LADIES AND GENTLE MEN

XII. THE VIOLENT MEN

XIII. THE PROFESSIONALS

XIV. THE INSTITUTIONS

XV. STARS OF THE SEVENTIES

XVI. APPENDIXES

INTRODUCTION

Close-Ups was conceived in the fall of 1976, exactly a year before it was first published. It was a time when almost everyone "serious" about film had broken away from evaluating movies in terms of stars and acting and had cast eagle eyes at directors, their styles, and their themes. I wanted to buck the *auteurist* tide a bit and assemble an anthology—at the time I envisioned a scrapbook or photo album with text—that would pay tribute, or at least give proper consideration, to the suddenly underappreciated performer. My inspiration was, in part, the Winter 1972/73 "Actor" issue of *The Velvet Light Trap*, a Madison, Wisconsin–based film quarterly for which I wrote in the early and midseventies. Only instead of having all the essays written by film critics, I also wanted contributions from novelists, playwrights, directors, actors, producers, screenwriters, costume designers, composers, agents, publicists, and so on. Such a diverse group of authors would guarantee the kind of crazy-quilt quality I was after. Although it often turned out to be the exact opposite, I figured that most of the critics would write serious pieces about the screen personas of individual stars, their key roles, and their contributions to film history, while most of the celebrity authors would write more subjective, more intimate pieces about stars they knew personally. At the time I intended that celebrity authors should write about 15 percent of the articles; in fact, they would write the vast majority.

For my previous animation book, Elliott Gould's promised essay on Popeye turned out to be a bad one-verse poem. So, except for the critics, screenwriters, and a select number of directors and actors, I didn't expect the celebrity contributors to turn in penetrating analyses of their subjects. On the contrary. But this didn't worry me. I believed it would add to the book's charm to have lightweight tributes and "valentines" (Irene Dunne on Cary Grant, Edith Head on Grace Kelly, Mervyn LeRoy on Clark Gable, Joseph H. Lewis on Barbara Stanwyck) interspersed with serious criticism. Many celebrity contributors had no pretensions about their writing ability, so I greatly appreciated their willingness to put themselves on the critical line to take part in what they considered a worthwhile project (many helped me out simply because they were flattered to be asked). I assured them that it was less important how well they wrote than that they wrote at all, especially about someone they cared about. I think today, ten years later, the value of such pieces can better be seen; in many instances, these articles remain the only published material by certain celebrities, some of whom have passed away. However, I don't want to imply that all the celebrity-written pieces are skimpy. In fact, most have substance, style, fascinating insight, and humor. Many reluctant authors revealed untapped writing talent—and I take pride in having convinced them to contribute.

I have been asked many times how I was able to get so many well-known people to write for a small fee, on a strict deadline, at a time when many were involved in major film projects, for someone they didn't know. Well, many joined the project because they saw that I had already assembled a number of illustrious contributors. (After about three months, by the time word got around Hollywood about this book, people actually started contacting me to offer their services.) But the real key was that I allowed everyone to choose the particular stars about whom they would write. (It helped that I wasn't after gossip or dirt about the stars' personal lives.) In several instances, I made suggestions (usually ignored) about whom a particular author might choose, but I didn't demand that anyone write about a specific star. When I contacted prospective writers (in the pre–word processor days, my staff and I sent out a couple of hundred personally typed letters), I mailed a list of about three hundred actors and actresses from which to choose, along with a list of committed contributors and the stars they were writing about. As various stars were selected over the eight months in which I assembled the book, I removed their names from the master list. In some cases, the authors chose subjects not on the list: for instance, Academy Award–winning screenwriter Harry Brown said he was no longer interested in human actors, but was passionate about the cartoon comedy team the Road Runner and Wile E. Coyote; William Saroyan contributed only because it gave him the opportunity to reveal his longtime crush for B-actress Phyllis Brooks (who was delighted and surprised to read his tribute). I had no objections. Many choices made perfect sense: Tony Roberts on Woody Allen, Garson Kanin on Ruth Gordon, Ann Rutherford on Mickey Rooney, Buddy Rogers on Mary Pickford. Others were intriguing surprises: James Dickey on Charles Bronson, Robert Bloch on Buster Keaton, John Landis on Laurel and Hardy.

Several years after *Close-Ups* was published, a disgruntled reader called long-distance to demand a refund because the book didn't contain an article on Tyrone Power. Well, at no time did I intend the book to include essays on every major star. From the start, I was more interested in obtaining particular writers than I was in making sure certain stars were assigned. It was only because I was able to get many more acceptances than the seventy-five I projected (Workman Publishing generously accommodated 130 original pieces and ten reprints) that so many major stars were covered in the book . . . making it seem that those few major stars that still were not included were mistakenly left out. That wasn't the case. But for the record, I'm still waiting for promised, ten-years-overdue essays on William Powell, Bruce Dern, Audrey Hepburn, Margaret Sullavan, Natalie Wood, Burt Lancaster, Dustin Hoffman, and yes, Tyrone Power. (Among the unreliable authors were an equal number of critics and celebrities.)

My intention when assembling authors was to combine famous writers (I got chills when I picked up the ringing phone and it was Gloria Swanson!) with those who hadn't achieved fame or had never received proper recognition. I wanted to give equal space to young and established filmmakers, little-known critics (who wrote for the type of specialized film journals I did) and those who were recognized by the mainstream movie audience (like Roger Ebert, Richard Schickel, and Bosley Crowther). I was particularly interested in tracking down old-time screenwriters, whose contributions have pretty much been neglected by film-history books. So little was known about what happened to them that I wrote to one who had been dead, his annoyed widow informed me, for ten years. Yet I got hold of Casey Robinson, who scripted Errol Flynn swashbucklers, living in Australia; Charles Bennett, who had been Hitchcock's top screenwriter in England; Allan Scott, who scripted many Astaire-Rogers films; Irving Brecher, who had written films for the Marx Brothers; and others who wrote some of our favorite movies. I was especially happy to get contributions from William Tunberg, who scripted *Old Yeller*, and Ted Sherdeman, who scripted *Them!*, because their films were so special to me in my youth. In some cases it was as hard to find well-known contemporary filmmakers as those who had retired years ago. I was delighted to find John Boorman in Ireland, Sergio Leone (a coup!) in Italy (his Henry Fonda piece, written in Italian, arrived on deadline day); Paul Almond in Canada. Even American Michael Crichton was away in England filming *The Great Train Robbery*. I am still grateful to the Writers and Directors Guilds for forwarding mail all around the world.

Yes, there were authors who got away, who wanted to contribute but couldn't beat the book's deadline: Deborah Kerr, Eric Ambler, Pandro Berman, Virginia Mayo, and others. Ronald Reagan wrote that he was "flattered by your request. However, I must decline as my schedule is just too hectic to permit me the luxury of projects such as this." Those who would have written on Patricia Neal and a rising star named Meryl Streep demanded more money than I could afford. But I have no regrets: a remarkable and extremely cordial group of authors did contribute and make *Close-Ups* a one-of-a-kind film book.

I am thankful to Workman Publishing for having published *Close-Ups* in 1977. And I am delighted that Fireside/Simon & Schuster has seen fit to rerelease the book on its tenth anniversary. I do think the book has added meaning today. An unfortunate number of the stars written about have died since 1977: Fred Astaire, Cary Grant, John Wayne, Gloria Swanson, Ruth Gordon, Richard Burton, Mae West, Rita Hayworth, Rock Hudson, Louise Brooks, Buster Crabbe, Orson Welles, Steve McQueen, Ingrid Bergman, Grace Kelly, Lee Marvin, Mary Pickford, James Cagney, Henry Fonda. A number of my authors have also passed away, including: Edith Head, Bosley Crowther, William Saroyan, Alvah Bessie, Leonard Spigelgass, Harold Clurman, Herman Weinberg, Mervyn LeRoy, Casey Robinson, and Barry Brown, whose tragic suicide occurred less than a week after he turned in his essay for the book. Several authors have become much better known than they were when they were contributors: John Landis and James Ivory have emerged as two of our most successful directors; Horton Foote won another Academy Award for his *Tender Mercies* script and is now one of our most in-demand scenarists and playwrights; David Thomson and Kenneth Turan have become best-selling authors; and critics Bill

Condon, Stuart Kaminsky, and my coeditor Karyn Kay have had screenplays produced. As for me: *Close-Ups* gave me the opportunity and the desire to edit and write other conceptually unusual film books, which I have been doing for ten years. That's why it still gives me special pleasure to flip through its pages. . . .

Danny Peary

—Danny Peary,
Fall 1987

THE
COMICS

6

CHARLES CHAPLIN: EMINENT TRAMP

HAROLD CLURMAN

"Chaplin was always a true artist. He made himself into a great artist and a whole person."
— *H. C.*

IN HIS LIFETIME (1889–1977) almost everything was said about Chaplin. Claude Debussy recognized the "true artist" in him when Chaplin was still a youth on tour in Paris. The great Nijinsky in 1917 saw him as a dancer. He was sometimes thought of as a roué, while some reproached him for being mean in monetary matters. During the 1950s, a great many considered him subversive. At the time, the noted German-born novelist Lion Feuchtwanger remarked, "You are the one artist in the theater who will go down in American history as having aroused the political antagonisms of a whole nation." Today he is universally acknowledged to have been the supreme, perhaps the only, genius of acting our film industry has produced.

Whether we accept or dispute any of these diverse judgments, the hindsight afforded me by my contacts with Chaplin convinces me that the contradictions found in the opinions just cited are more apparent than real. If we trace his career back to its source — his native London — we discern the natural logic of his development and discover unity.

He was born to vaudevillian parents. His father died of alcoholism at the age of thirty-seven, having abandoned Charlie's mother and gone to live with another woman.

Charlie's mother was a singing soubrette. (When she once lost her voice in the middle of one of her numbers, Charlie, then five, was forced to complete the act by singing in her stead.) When he was twelve he played the page boy in *Sherlock Holmes,* touring in it for forty weeks. At the time he could hardly read. Charlie never acquired a proper education. And "to gauge the morals of our family by common standards," he was to write, "would be as erroneous as putting a thermometer in boiling water." In other words, he had been no better than he needed to be.

HAROLD CLURMAN *was a founding director of the Group Theater. He has edited drama anthologies and has written several books, including* Ibsen, All People Are Famous *and* On Directing.

His early years were marked by abject poverty. His mother would go insane from malnutrition. During her confinement to a mental hospital, he and his brother Sydney were consigned to a poorhouse. These facts alone indicate some of his enduring preoccupations. The down-and-out and the derelict peopled his environment from the day of his birth.

The Outsider. Chaplin's Tramp was apart from the rest of society.
It was by choice.

It was not altogether an accident that Charlie's signal creation was the Tramp, and that his major themes were destitution and hunger. A person whose first recollections are of penury grows keen about the acquisition of money. He learns the value of a penny. Chaplin embarked on his career as an actor not with any conscious artistic purpose, but from a desperate need to earn a living.

Charlie first won recognition as a clown. A clown is a licensed fool, and it is the fool's privilege to say the right thing at the wrong time, and vice versa. The fool punctures hypocrisy, complacency, and stale custom, thoughtless prejudice, and bigotry. In a word, he is "subversive." In a lie-infected world he summons the truth.

It was because the Tramp epitomized the core of his personal experience that Chaplin was so universally acclaimed. The vices he mocked are prevalent; they are the cause of suffering or, to use a fancy term, of the "alienation" visible everywhere. His Tramp was a tragic figure that provoked uncontrollable laughter.

The Tramp's position in society makes it impossible for him to be a conformist. Charlie was never, could not be, a conformist. The low-born and the lonely flocked to see him; there was consolation in the Tramp's persistent efforts to rise above adversity. There was encouragement

in his lucky escapes. And, above all, the Tramp exemplifies the will to live. He puts up a brave front in the face of oppression and superior forces. He employs every wile to forge a place for himself and perhaps — despite all — to achieve safety or fortune. This lends the Tramp an unexpected dignity.

There are few really great actors in the history of the stage or films. Chaplin was one of them. He was *all* actor. His body was flexible and fleet, his movement had a certain asymmetrical grace, responsive to his every emotion, to every physical hazard. That made him "the dancer," poignantly expressive in the very pose of awkwardness. His props and costume (cane, hat, trousers), presumably discovered by chance, were the choice of a profound intuition. They projected an almost mythical meaning: the human atom lost and yet spontaneously defiant in the cosmos. It is this which gives Chaplin's Tramp its universal dimension.

Think of his large, dark eyes. We can perceive his shyness in them, his perplexity, his dismay at the callousness of power, his yearning for love. Underneath the mask there is a gravely handsome face, unusual in a comedian.

Chaplin's voice was not an effective dramatic instrument; it is nevertheless a mistake to underestimate the films in which he spoke. There is the scene of memorable pathos in *Limelight* (1952) when, as a former star and now a has-been, he enters a manager's office to seek an engagement of any sort. What disguised anguish! And the same actor's mortal discouragement as he removes his makeup after a flop.

And there was something more to Chaplin's preeminence as an actor than the attributes I have mentioned. They all point to the special distinction of his work. True artists are not to be identified so much by their versatility as by their individual personal vision. Chaplin's art is grounded in a central idea. He knew that life entails conflict and pain, and that humankind achieves worth and stature in confronting this pain with resolute courage and love. It is the rebellion of the "little man" (and in the light of the universe we are all "little men" — and women) against everything which conspires to crush him. It is this which lends grandeur to the human struggle, and gives nobility to Chaplin's clown.

At first, Chaplin himself hardly understood this. He was just a funny man, whose antics brought him fame and fortune. In 1919 Waldo Frank, a New York critic and essayist, in his book *Our America* called attention to the symbolic meaning of Chaplin's comedy, and it was not until then that the actor became aware of himself as an artist and of the social significance of his artistry.

His images grew clearer. The eating-contraption sequence in *Modern Times* (1936), for example, is a visual metaphor for the horrors of latter-day "efficiency." In the same vein the little man's sliding like a bolt in the works of the factory's engine is a summation of the machine age.

The early twenties mark Chaplin's coming of age as a knowing citizen as well as the fabulous actor. At about this time, and in the following years, he achieved full

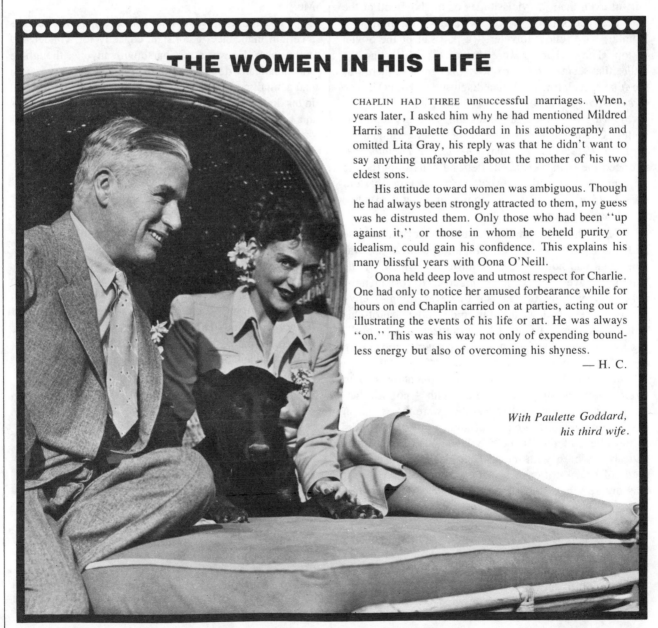

THE WOMEN IN HIS LIFE

CHAPLIN HAD THREE unsuccessful marriages. When, years later, I asked him why he had mentioned Mildred Harris and Paulette Goddard in his autobiography and omitted Lita Gray, his reply was that he didn't want to say anything unfavorable about the mother of his two eldest sons.

His attitude toward women was ambiguous. Though he had always been strongly attracted to them, my guess was he distrusted them. Only those who had been "up against it," or those in whom he beheld purity or idealism, could gain his confidence. This explains his many blissful years with Oona O'Neill.

Oona held deep love and utmost respect for Charlie. One had only to notice her amused forbearance while for hours on end Chaplin carried on at parties, acting out or illustrating the events of his life or art. He was always "on." This was his way not only of expending boundless energy but also of overcoming his shyness.

— H. C.

With Paulette Goddard,
his third wife.

independence as actor, director, writer, producer. He was now fully prepared to deliver his message to the world. These were the years of his most conspicuous celebrity and the prologue to his most arduous trials.

He had become immensely wealthy, and had built a sumptuous mansion in Beverly Hills. Yet apart from Douglas Fairbanks and several of his coworkers, he had few real friends in the movie colony. For a while he was close to William Randolph Hearst, whom he described to me as ''a monster, a fascist, and a great man.'' His intimates when I got to know him in the late thirties were Clifford Odets, the composer Hanns Eisler, Salka Viertel (frequently Garbo's scenarist), Bertolt Brecht — all of them outsiders in the Hollywood community. Whatever their profession or job, he was devoted above all to people of genuine gifts and sound character.

The hardest thing Chaplin had to endure, more hurtful even than the vicissitudes of his boyhood or the silly sex accusations, were the attacks on him as a ''pinko,'' a ''fellow traveler,'' a partisan of the Soviet Union. These charges were due to his addressing the rallies that seemed to be pro-Soviet. Then, too, there was the final speech (the little man disguised as Hitler) in *The Great Dictator* (1940).

During the hysterical fifties many things were forgotten: Chaplin's contribution to the Liberty Bond drive in 1917–1919; the fact that *The Great Dictator* denounced the twin menaces Hitler and Mussolini (before we went to war with them). It mattered little that our president had been of the same mind and that Russia had then been our ally.

Hearst thought Chaplin was anti-Hitler only because he (Charlie) was Jewish. Chaplin's response to this was that ''that had nothing to do with it'' — which, by the way, still leaves the question of his ''racial'' origin in the dark. The real point of all this is that everything — envy of his success and wealth, his independent spirit, his failure to become a United States citizen, his ''sinful'' sex life — served to foment hostility against him among the gullible and the crypto-fascists.

Insofar as the speeches and the implications of *The Great Dictator* may be equated with ''political activities'' we can now realize that they were the extension of Chaplin's interest in public affairs. A constant witness to the plight of the ''underprivileged,'' his sympathies had always been with them. That his art contained the seeds of social criticism had gone unnoticed because it was dressed in a clown's apparel. *The Great Dictator* and, to a certain extent, *Monsieur Verdoux* (1947) complete the Chaplin cycle.

What is to be emphasized now — something which became fully apparent long before his death — is that, in the respect just discussed, he had always been right. This was not due to any political acumen; he had very little — or of any other kind of knowledge through formal study. He was led by his instincts, rooted as they were in personal experience.

Yes, Chaplin was a rebel — especially against mediocrity, officiousness, lack of humaneness. But his was a gentle rebellion. There was hardly ever a note of aggressiveness, malice, or bitterness. For instance, one can hardly call *A King in New York* (1957) a vindictive picture.

Charlie was essentially modest. He was determined above all to maintain the integrity of his own being. It has been captiously remarked that in his autobiography he bragged of all the ''greats'' — scientists, statesmen, churchmen, artists — he got to know and who had paid tribute to him. I judge this to be the opposite of conceit: In fact, it's a form of humility. ''Imagine,'' he told me, ''Churchill expressed disappointment because I had not replied to a fan letter he had written me. Think of Churchill even remembering that I had failed to answer him. Me!''

For all his shrewdness in business, there was always a certain innocence, a constant capacity for wonder and enthusiasm. He was rarely harsh with anyone, though he was fanatically demanding of his pictures. An actor who had a small part in *Monsieur Verdoux* once told me that in his directorial passion Chaplin once yelled instructions at a baby in a crib! He may have been a ''bad father,'' as one of his sons complained, because he demanded of them the same discipline and enterprise he had manifested himself. He feared their becoming spoiled.

At the 1972 Oscar awards, when Chaplin was greeted by thunderous applause, he murmured, ''Beautiful people!'' and wept. It was as much Chaplin's fortitude as his accomplishments that were being hailed.

During the days of Charlie's worst troubles in the United States, Europeans remained loyal to him. In a long letter from the president of the French Society of Authors we find the following lines: ''. . . you have wanted to spare others the harm you suffered or at least you have wanted to give everybody reason for hope.''

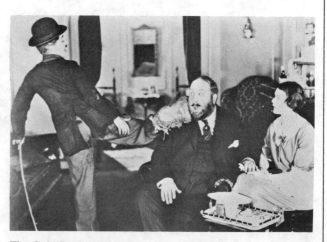

The Gold Rush, *with Mack Swain and an extra.*

BUSTER KEATON: STONE-FACED OPTIMIST

ROBERT BLOCH

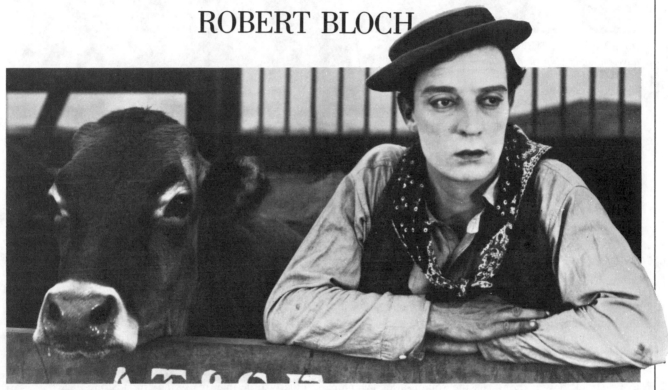

The Friendless One (R) . . . and friend. The well-remembered moment from Go West.

I T WAS 1922, in a Chicago theater. He was up on the screen, and I was in the audience. He didn't, of course, see me — but I saw him and I gave him the greatest tribute a five-year-old could possibly bestow on a comedian: I laughed so hard I wet my pants.

The film was one of his classic two-reelers, *The Boat* (1921). I didn't know it was a classic — for that matter, neither did Buster Keaton, for unlike Chaplin, he was never concerned with his own status or image. He wanted only to make us laugh.

ROBERT BLOCH *has written the screenplays for many films dealing with the macabre, including* Strait-jacket, The Night Walker, The Deadly Bees, The Torture Garden, *and* The House That Dripped Blood. *He is the original author of* Psycho.

In the years that followed I made it a point to see Keaton's movies again and again. My trousers remained dry, but I never stopped laughing.

His great short subjects were superseded throughout the twenties by his great silent features. With the coming of the talkies he gained a voice but lost his independence. A combination of studio interference and domestic difficulties ruined his career and his private life; comedy gave way to tragedy.

Almost any Hollywood hack could have written the rest of the script. The dialogue is obvious:

BUSTER: Please, Mr. Jennings — you've got to help me!
PRODUCER: Sorry, kid. We just can't use you.
BUSTER: Look — all I'm asking for is a

Boiling an egg in The Navigator. *Soon he will have an entire ship running automatically.*

Poster for College. *A son any* mother would be proud of.

chance — a chance to make people laugh again.

PRODUCER: It's too late for that now. You're through, Buster — washed up! Don't you understand? You're not funny anymore!

The rest of the story line is also obvious: bouts with the bottle; an endless round of humiliations and rejections; and then — God and scriptwriter willing — a final opportunity for a comeback, out of the blue. For one brief moment the hero again takes center stage, only to be struck down, dying, as the sought-after laughter echoes in his ears.

Come to think of it, Chaplin used such a script for *Limelight* (1952). But Keaton would never have played it; he wasn't one for self-pity or even audience sympathy in his films. And he didn't play it that way in real life.

The humiliations and rejections were there, and for a time he used drink as a weapon against them. But like the indomitable little man he played on screen, he never succumbed to defeat, and in the end his sheer perseverance brought salvation. It took twenty-five years of cheap two-reelers, sleazy foreign features, brief cameo appearances in American films, summer stock, gag-writing for other comedians, European circus performances, television guest shots — but he never gave up. Somewhere along the line he won the girl — his third wife Eleanor Norris — and discarded the bottle. By 1960 he was again economically secure and on the verge of fresh acclaim from a new generation.

It was then, thirty-eight years since I saw him on the screen, that I met Buster Keaton in the flesh. I'd been working on scripts in Hollywood for a few months when a Writers Guild strike was called. During this period of unemployment, friends invited me to Griffith Park to play in a baseball game between writers and actors. There, warming up on the field, was the actors' star pitcher: Joseph Francis Keaton III — Buster himself.

I did a double take. Was this pudgy, baldheaded, elderly little man really the Great Stone Face?

The game began. The pudgy little man disappeared, and in his place was a superbly controlled athlete, leaping into the air for difficult catches, running bases at championship speed, doing comic slides, backflips, and pratfalls with dazzling timing.

He struck me out.

Later, after I was introduced by mutual friends, Mr. and Mrs. Keaton drove me to their Woodland Hills home. Somewhere along the way they became Buster and Eleanor.

Over several years I came to know something of the face behind the stoic mask. Buster loved to laugh. The man who played The Friendless One in *Go West* (1925), was, in fact, gregarious — fond of card playing, group sports, entertaining. At parties he reminisced with a ukulele, reproducing with amusing accuracy the songs and routines of vaudeville performers he'd met through his parents' act, ''The Three Keatons.''

In private moments, he enjoyed recalling summer vacations at Muskegon, Michigan, where he led the everyday life of a Midwestern boyhood. Only when urged would he talk about the bad times — candidly but without bitterness. Once I was bold enough to ask what had sustained him through the long years of decline. His reply was revealing: "No matter how tough things got, I could still walk into a restaurant anywhere in the world and get a good table. Even when Hollywood forgot me, the audiences remembered."

What they remembered has been analyzed in detail by film historians. His astonishing mechanical ingenuity, the love-hate relationship with machinery, is immortalized in films built around a boat (*The Navigator,* 1924) and a train (*The General,* 1926). His camera tricks are dazzling in *The Playhouse* (1921), in which the entire cast of a vaudeville show, the orchestra in the pit, and the audience consist of Buster himself in scores of disguises, including Buster made up as a trained chimpanzee and nine members of a blackface minstrel troupe. His virtuosity is even more brilliant in *Sherlock, Jr.* (1924); as a motion picture projectionist, he walks into the screen and becomes a part of the film itself. He had unerring timing and sheer perfection in his routines, the sudden, unexpected bite of his mordant humor, the amazing range of emotional nuances he conveyed without a smile.

But the real secret of his genius is simple. Unlike other great silent screen comedians, Buster Keaton was inimitable.

Charlie Chaplin's imitators were legion, and some, like Billy West, almost defied detection. Harold Lloyd's go-getter or coward-turned-hero roles were duplicated by Johnny Hines and Douglas MacLean. Harry Langdon's simpleton was a stock figure of the day, paralleled by Lloyd Hamilton and other innocents; his white clown makeup was reminiscent of Larry Semon's. Raymond Griffith's sophisticate echoed Max Linder.

But no one ever imitated Buster Keaton. Lloyd was a fine athlete; Keaton, a great one. Griffith's unflappable fop was in no way superior to Keaton's portrayals in *The Navigator* or *Battling Butler* (1926). Lloyd and Chaplin were masters of the sight gag, but Keaton equaled or surpassed them. And his use of gags was more ethical. Unlike Lloyd or Chaplin, he was not petty or malicious; yes, he would use a gag to outwit an enemy, but he never stooped to revenge. At times Keaton seemed to be as confused and gullible as Langdon, but he was more resourceful. Once he sized up the situation, he took direct and (usually) effective action.

Battling Butler. *Keaton made films that highlighted his amazing athletic prowess.*

The General, *Keaton's masterpiece. With co-stars Marian Mack and train.*

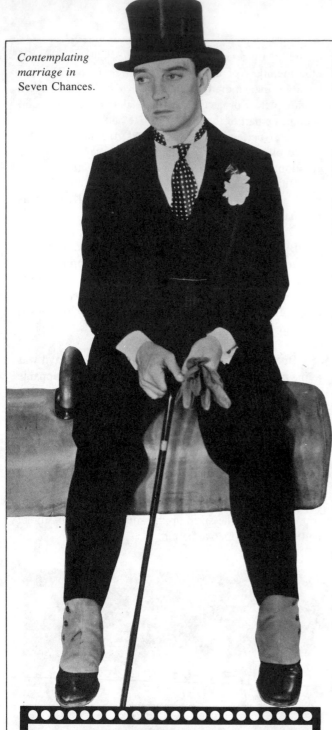

Contemplating marriage in Seven Chances.

Chaplin's mastery of mime involved exaggerated mugging to indicate reaction; Keaton's pantomime made its point without facial acrobatics. And while Chaplin was shameless in his plea for audience sympathy — witness the mawkish, interminable death scene in *Limelight* — Keaton met indignity with dignity.

Only Keaton was versatile enough to incorporate elements of many comedic styles into a broader and deeper characterization which stands unequaled to this day.

The ridiculous little figure in the pancake hat, slap-shoes, and baggy trousers may have resembled a knock-about vaudeville performer. The resemblance ended there. Inside that costume was Buster himself.

Chaplin was a supreme clown, Griffith a deft caricature, Langdon a baby, Lloyd the eternal boy — but Keaton, combining their roles and adding the dimension of his own attitude toward life, was a man. The motionless face surmounting the busy body represents a mature approach to the problems of life — a combination of thought and action. And though both thoughts and actions are comic, the element of recognition is always apparent. Buster Keaton used the screen as a mirror. And in that mirror, the Great Stone Face we see is always our own.

GODOT'S BEGINNINGS?

MANY PEOPLE WONDER where Samuel Beckett got his inspiration for his play *Waiting for Godot*. Beckett was a great fan of Keaton's and wrote his short *Film* (1965) with Keaton in mind, and Keaton did star. Is it possible that Beckett saw Keaton in a minor role in a film called *The Lovable Cheat* (1949)? In that obscure movie, a man waits for the return of his partner who has their fortune in his possession. He waits and waits, but his partner never comes. The partner's name? Godot.

Keaton and Elsa Lanchester wasting their talents in Pajama Party. *Keaton's rediscovery by movie fans in the late sixties rescued him from films such as this — and elevated him once again to star status.*

HAROLD LLOYD: HIGH-FLYING GENIUS

RICHARD KOSZARSKI

A YOUNG MAN in a business suit, straw hat, and horn-rims hangs from the hands of an oversized clockface. It is 2:45 in the afternoon, twelve stories above the streets of Los Angeles. This surreal image, a frozen moment from a 1923 screen comedy, says one thing to millions of people: Harold Lloyd. Many of these people have never seen the film in question or, for that matter, *any* of Lloyd's two hundred film comedies. But they know this single image. Why should it be so compelling?

RICHARD KOSZARSKI *wrote the screenplays for the documentary films* Roger Corman: Hollywood's Wild Angel *and* The Man You Loved to Hate. *He is the author of* The Rivals of D.W. Griffith; Hollywood Directors 1914–40; Hollywood Directors 1941–76; Universal Pictures: 65 Years, *and articles in many film publications.*

Lloyd did all his own stunts, which usually meant risking injury from a fall. Sometimes he would do something simple like flying into a moving streetcar, but he could be really spectacular, as demonstrated in Safety Last *(top left), and* Feet First *(top right).*

It's no accident that in this most familiar silent comedy still there is neither a flying pie nor an obese policeman. There are just two simple, everyday elements: man and clock. Lloyd's genius was to discover that the more mundane the elements, the more outrageous the laugh — in fact, he built an entire style of comedy around the average. He developed a prototypical middle-class character and created for that character an instantly recognizable middle-class world. This world was the raw material for two decades of exceptional screen comedy.

When Lloyd started out in movies, he was far from being exceptional. He arrived with only a minimal background in theater, a handful of roles played at backwater stock companies. But as fate would have it, Lloyd fell in with another bit player, Hal Roach, who, with the aid of a modest inheritance, was about to set himself up as a film producer. Roach's budget was equal to the demands of Lloyd's salary, and Harold became a featured comedian. Lloyd observed the comedians around him and saw that screen comedy meant clown comedy: ill-fitting clothes, grotesque makeup, a physical quirk or two, a useful prop. Borrowing as much as he could from Chaplin, Lloyd pulled together a character of his own and named him Lonesome Luke. When he reached the screen in 1915, the movies were already awash with Chaplin imitators, but fueled by Lloyd's inner demon, Luke caught on through sheer force of effort. There is little grace, pathos, or even wit in a typical Lonesome Luke subject, but the man works so hard he *makes* us laugh. These brutal knockabouts have a direct appeal which audiences found outrageous and invigorating. Hardly in the same league with ''Fatty'' Arbuckle or Chaplin, but on their own terms quite acceptable. Unfortunately, seen today, Lonesome Luke has not aged well.

It is to Lloyd's eternal credit that he ultimately became fed up with Luke and his clown getup and his bag of tricks, despite the Roach studio's urging him to continue with Luke. In 1917 Lloyd introduced a new personality, a character who was not funny in dress, makeup, or mannerism: We just saw an ordinary fellow in the glasses. Lloyd implied that the funny thing about this fellow was interior rather than exterior. The laugh would come not from baggy pants or skittering gait, but from a way of thinking, acting, and behaving — from personality alone.

To deal in terms of personality meant abandoning much of the stylized shorthand of early silent screen acting. These conventional gestures were tremendously helpful in conveying moods, thoughts, or intentions, and practically obligatory for the brief one-reelers of the earliest days. No time was wasted on developing characterizations, which were accepted by the audience as a given. Instead, attention was given to plot manipulations that could cram as much action as possible into twelve minutes. But gradually the early screen dramas began to

Professor Beware *(L) and* Lloyd's most-heralded film The Freshman *(Below) were typical in that they emphasized activities in which men in glasses usually don't participate. Jerry Lewis, donning glasses at times, and Woody Allen would carry on the tradition.*

In Hot Water, *the only passenger with packages — and a turkey — must stand.*

demonstrate a growing awareness of psychological realism. Under the guidance of men like D. W. Griffith, films grew longer, plots more satisfying, and complex characters appeared for the first time. While this evolution was an accomplished fact in the screen drama by the time Lloyd appeared on the scene, comedy was still dealing in the most primitive clichés and archetypes. It was Lloyd who forged two traditions, uniting the movement and energy of the clowns with the psychological realism of the dramatic tradition. The comedy of Woody Allen, and of all those like him, stems directly from Lloyd's decision to replace the grotesque Luke with the innocuous character who hung from the clockface.

Why Lloyd took this step is a matter of some interest. It has often been pointed out that Lloyd was not "funny in himself" — by which is meant, apparently, that he lacked a natural comic impulse. Put a truly great comedian on a bare stage, so the idea goes, with no props and no prepared material, and he will be able to conjure comedy out of the air. One can easily imagine this of, say, Chaplin or Jonathan Winters. But with Lloyd the idea doesn't work. Yet he certainly made funny films; the best of his silent features can still reduce an audience to hopeless hysteria — as a pure laugh provoker Lloyd had no rivals. (But it has to be admitted that even his top comedies do not have the resonance of a good Chaplin or Keaton.)

Lloyd's method of constructing his comedies takes the blame here as well as the credit. Most of the screen's classic comedians had a retinue of assistants and hangers-on, a staff that contributed what they could to story line and gag construction. But Lloyd's devotion to collaborative filmmaking far exceeded that of his rivals. Lloyd held on to his team with obvious pride, unlike Harry Langdon. He seems to have had no ego, and once

he realized that Fred Newmeyer, Ted Wilde, and the rest of the boys were as tuned into the "glasses" character as he was, he gladly moved along with the consensus. The personality of the character had been established early on by Lloyd in almost instinctive fashion — young, eager to please, often naive, but blessed with unparalleled self-assurance when the need arose. Each of his films turned a variation on this model, but there was a finite limit to the number of variations. Even at the height of his popularity Lloyd felt no shame in admitting that the "bag of tricks" for this character could be exhausted in only three films, and that much of his creative effort was going into keeping the character from growing stale. Turning out these variations was the job of Lloyd's production staff.

Lloyd himself was an unspectacular fellow with few apparent qualifications for success as a screen comedian. While his rivals carried with them to the screen the polish that only years of prior stage experience could guarantee, Lloyd was forced to make up his own comedy rules as he went along. He made many more short comedies than Keaton or Chaplin, learning not just to be a comedian, but a *movie* comedian as well. The added realism of character, incident, and setting that Lloyd introduced to screen comedy is a function of his understanding of the camera's peculiar relation to reality. Lloyd learned what made the camera tick, and it was easy for him to discard the borrowed conventions of the baggy-pants tradition.

He gave us an eager young man whose fortitude and initiative more than made up for any lack of special talent or ability. He simply took off the makeup and put himself on screen. And it worked.

THE EARLY LAUGH MACHINE

HAROLD LLOYD'S FILMS were audience-tested in a sophisticated fashion, and their success at laugh-getting was plotted on charts and graphs in hopes of polishing them to ultimate perfection. (One of these graphs is reprinted in Adam Reilly's *Harold Lloyd, King of Daredevil Comedy*—Lloyd and his people were so proud of it that they issued it at the time for publicity purposes!) Such mechanistic methods were certainly successful in creating the type of comedy Lloyd and his crew were after; however, this machine-made quality has built-in limitations. Not only do the contrivances sometimes show through, but the films seem to lack a true human center; often one feels that the character is *too* ordinary, and that his lack of extraordinary qualities means that the films themselves never get beyond the ordinary.

— R. K.

LAUREL AND HARDY: BROTHERLY ANTICS

JOHN LANDIS

O F ALL THE COUNTLESS movie comedians, only Charles Chaplin and the team of Stan Laurel and Oliver Hardy were capable of working with equal success in both silent and sound movies. I think the reason for this is that they dealt with a universal theme — the Brotherhood of Man — and words, while (arguably) beneficial to them, did not alter the *essence* of their comedy.

JOHN LANDIS *is the director of* Kentucky Fried Movie, National Lampoon's Animal House, *and he was the director and the title character of* Schlock.

Most movie comedy teams are funny, but much of their humor is derived from their internal friction: They lash out at one another with verbal, and in some cases physical, abuse. But Laurel and Hardy have a special sweetness about them, a gentle politeness to each other, and it is that which makes them the equals of Chaplin in winning audience affection.

The relationship between Laurel and Hardy is on the surface very simple: Oliver is the dominating parent, Stanley the child. Time and again anger, suspicion, greed, lust, and revenge come between them. Yet, no matter how violent the conflict, we remain secure that ultimately Laurel and Hardy will remain together, united in their struggle for survival in an often hostile world.

For many years, critics claimed that Laurel, who wrote all the teams gags and received a larger salary than his partner, was responsible for the duo's success. Lately, Hardy has been given his due praise as well.

Classic scene in Two Tars *finds the boys involved in the demolition of numerous cars in massive traffic jam.*

In *A Chump at Oxford* (1940) Stanley is struck on the head and undergoes a complete personality change. Not only is he transformed into a superior athlete and scholar, but he totally forgets who Ollie is! At the conclusion of the picture Stan is once again conked on the head and becomes his former self.

When Stan does not acknowledge Ollie as his friend, one feels in him the panic of a small child who is separated from his parent in a crowded department store. When Stan regains his memory, Ollie's joy is equal to that of the child reunited with the parent. We too feel safe, protected and whole again when Ollie cries as he embraces him, "Stan, you know me!"

A Chump at Oxford is not a great movie — maybe not even a good movie. The direction and screenplay are uninspired and the production clearly did not have a high priority. However, the ending is powerful stuff and never fails to make me cry.

The magic of Laurel and Hardy is their love for each other. Bud Abbott ditches Lou Costello in a second when the chips are down. Groucho Marx gleefully cheats Chico and Harpo — and vice versa. And there is no doubt that Dean Martin clearly thinks Jerry Lewis is a moron. But between Laurel and Hardy there is a loyalty that transcends all their trials. While it often seems that other comedy teams are together purely out of convenience, Stan and Ollie are an organic whole from the first frame of every picture. You never question their oneness. There is an intangible strength, something "thicker than water," in their relationship.

Charlie Chaplin's films are always moralistic; Good is rewarded and evil punished. In the Laurel and Hardy films, even when their endings are triumphant, there always seems to be one more brick to fall on Ollie's head, or one more wall for Stanley to walk into. In *Towed in a Hole* (1933) Stan and Ollie are fishmongers who drive through the streets of Beverly Hills hawking their wares. Stanley comes up with the idea that if they had their own boat and caught their own fish, they would eliminate the middleman and make more money. So the two of them buy a beat-up boat and proceed to repair it. For their honest labor and good intentions, Ollie gets a black eye and their boat and truck are totally destroyed.

The world of Laurel and Hardy is chaotic, and the boys are often forced to endure great hardship. What audiences appreciate — and what especially appealed to audiences during the Depression — is that they never waver from their optimistic nature. Laurel and Hardy are the best, the nice guys of the comic screen. And that is the secret of their lasting rapport with their audience.

Getting into big trouble in Brats.

Stan is about to shut car door on Jean Harlow's dress in Double Whoopee.

Putting Pants on Philip, *their initial film as a team, includes Hardy's first "fine mess."*

Ready to pick up women in Men O' War.

W. C. FIELDS:
THE GENTLE SIDE

JAMES M. CAIN

William Claude Dunkinfield.

COMEDIANS, AS A CLASS, are a notoriously churlish bunch who smile when paid to smile. Maurice Chevalier pops into my mind. He was in California at Paramount when I was, and for six months I ate lunch within twenty feet of him. He always ate alone. Never once in that time did I see him smile, or say one agreeable word to those faceless men who surrounded him or one word to anyone else. He was sour, scowling, and ill-humored, as well as a notorious tightwad.

JAMES M. CAIN'S *novels include* Mildred Pierce, Double Indemnity, *and* The Postman Always Rings Twice. *He died in 1977.*

But if Chevalier's behavior clashed with his public image, and confirmed the notion of comedians as a grumpy breed, I found that the outstanding exception to this rule in those days was the very man whose public image was the most churlish, W. C. Fields.

I met him in 1930, through Philip Goodman, who had more to do with Fields' success than anyone else — a close personal friend, of mine as well as of Fields. Goodman, father of Ruth Goodman Goetz, the playwright, also my close friend, started out in the advertising business, grew bored with it, and turned to publishing. He put out one book, Mencken's *In Defense of Women*, and then switched again, to theatrical producing. He became convinced that Fields could talk. Fields . . . was highly dubious, and Goodman had a battle on his hands. The difficulty was the principle that Tilden later plugged so indefatigably: Don't change a winning game. Fields' game, until then, was winning and winning big. He was a headliner in vaudeville, in nightclubs, [and] in the Follies, but always in pantomime — as a comedy juggler, magician and actor, he never said a word. So when Goodman began arguing with him, Fields listened, but had no intention of giving up something sure for something that might be a fiasco. However, Goodman could dangle one piece of bait like no other. Talking, Fields could star, not merely be featured. He could star on Broadway, something they all dream about. Then, little by little Fields began to listen, and by a funny coincidence, Goodman had a script, called ''Poppy,'' which would do very well for a vehicle.

My contribution was that the character Little Eva would be cast as a post-teenager, small enough to wear a tot's clothes and go to heaven in Act III, but actually quite a sexpot. I knew, of course, that before we got done with it she would wind up as Fields' daughter and look exactly like Poppy, but at least I didn't make her like that. So, I was introduced to Fields, he in his car, an open roadster, in which he had a girl I won't name, as she may still be living, a girl in her twenties, though Fields was now close to fifty. (It was not Carlotta Monti,

The Barber Shop,
an early Fields short.

In the hours we would spend at Goodman's, Fields told many more stories, all of the same kind, once speaking of "that pest of a woman, always with something to tell you, who hangs on and digs her chin in your shoulder." I was startled but then realized this was a completely original conception, that he wasn't cribbing from *Alice In Wonderland*, and in fact, had probably never heard of *Alice In Wonderland* or Lewis Carroll. But these harassments were only a part of the talks that went on at my place, before we would walk over to Goodman's.

Often he would get off on something that had happened that day, and have to tell me about it. Once, he was struck by the harangue of a masseur he had had at the turkish bath he patronized, and sat there reciting it, working on himself, kneading his leg as he did and becoming so wrapped up in his tale as to be transformed. Actually, I sat there staring at him, asking myself, "Is that Fields?" He didn't look like himself at all, but exactly like a masseur. And I remembered things I had read, for example about Coquelin, the celebrated French actor, and how *"Son visage, ça change,"* and so on — how his face became different with every part that he played. It was that way with Fields, and I woke up that night to the realization I was beholding one of the great actors of all time.

who wrote the book about him.) Then, for the rest of that summer, Fields and I would talk, at my apartment on East Nineteenth Street, and then perhaps around ten o'clock, walk around to Goodman's apartment, on Tenth Street, to pick up the girls, and also for an hour or so of talk.

I quickly found out that on story, on plot, on structure, Fields drew a complete blank — and in fact, could hardly make himself get his mind on it. He thought in terms of gags, which followed a set pattern: annoyances of one kind or another. In *Million Dollar Legs* (1932), as president of Klopstokia, he was constantly being interrupted, at cabinet meetings, by a member who had to sneeze. Paramount hired Joe Sneeze for the job, and the moments while Fields, his white-gloved hands opening and closing, waited for Joe to complete the project were funny — I still remember them.

Then there was Kadoola-Kadoola, as he called it, I never knew why. In this, halfway through "Poppy," he would come out with a skeleton cello, sit down with it after putting his silk hat on the floor, and start "Pop Goes the Weasel." But he would barely play three notes before the silk hat would start to roll, and continue around the back of the chair, to stop on the other side. He would put it in place again, again, again, and have to stop again. That was the whole sketch, but it was sheer delight, and I don't know anyone who ever figured out how he did it — how he made the silk hat roll, I mean, on cue, in exactly the right way.

Disguised as female trick-shot artist in You Can't Cheat an Honest Man.

A POPULAR "UNPOPULAR" IMAGE

With small look-alike on the set of My Little Chickadee. *This tot did not cause him the misery that Baby LeRoy did.*

PUBLICITY ON W. C. Fields usually pointed out that he hated kids, chased women, and preferred drinking something stronger than water. Many claimed that Fields was jealous of the scene-stealing Baby LeRoy (seen in inset relaxing with a goat). Speculation increased following the time Fields spiked LeRoy's orange juice.

While many people doubted he was really a womanizer or a child-hater, few questioned that this was his reaction to non-alcholic beverages.

Lucky number.

Performing his remarkable cane-hat juggling routine.

Goodman, when I'd see him alone, was satisfied with the progress I was making on my end, so when Fields would come, I could lean back, let him talk, and enjoy something memorable. But all things come to an end, and so it turned out with him. Paramount got into the act, with an offer he couldn't refuse, and so he had to back out of Goodman's venture. He did so with obvious regret, and before leaving for Hollywood, gave us a little dinner at a speak in the forties — an Italian place that he frequented, that had fairly good wine, for this, of course, was in the middle of Prohibition. The Goodmans, Phil, Lily, his wife, and Ruth, whom I've already mentioned, and I were the guests — the girl wasn't with him that night. We had hardly sat down when the proprietor's son, a boy of perhaps ten, "that nauseous brat," as Ruth always called him, planted himself before Fields and piped: "Hi, Big-Nose."

"Hi," said Fields.

That was all, or would have been all, except that a waiter heard and Judased to the proprietor. So, this tall Italian, white with rage, breathing through his nose, appeared from nowhere, seized the boy by the arm, and dragged him back out of sight. Then, [in time] to his shrieks, we would hear the hairbrush, or whatever was being used. Fields leaned close to me and half under his breath mumbled: "Jim, that's all for my benefit. What kind of imagination is it that thinks I will get pleasure, or satisfaction, or whatever I'm supposed to get, at hearing a boy punished? I have a big nose, and I suppose to him it's fact of life like the Grand Canyon or Niagara Falls or some other natural wonder. . . ."

He went on, while the spanking went on, but I was within inches of the nose, and for the first time had a good look at it. And I suddenly became aware there was something wrong with it. It was just the least bit lumpy, as though it was not sound tissue. Then I knew this nose had once been frozen, and that's why it looked as it did. I thought of Bill Dukinfield, the boy who had to sleep in the stable, and there practiced his juggling, and what must have happened one bitterly cold night. Compassion for him swept over me — why? I'm not sure I know. At $5,000 a week, which was what Goodman said he would get in Hollywood, he needed no compassion from me. Just the same it was how I felt.

But that night there was more. The proprietor appeared pretty soon, leading the boy by the arm. "I'm sorry, Mr. Fields," came the snuffling apology. "I didn't mean it, honest, I didn't."

"Come here, son," said Fields, ignoring the father. And then, for twenty minutes, this man, already celebrated for his line "The man who hates dogs and small boys can't be all bad," gave a show for this small boy, which, had it been put on film, would have been played over and over for years. In addition to being a juggler, he was also a master magician, and he made half dollars come out of the boy's nose, letting him keep the coins. He stuck toothpicks into the dinner rolls and made them dance on the table. He came up with a yapping dog between the boy's feet then, and went tearing into the boy's pocket when the dog took refuge there, finally fishing him out (a two-inch thing of red flannel) and letting the boy keep him, too. It went on and on, with the boy utterly entranced, Ruth utterly disgusted, and Lily, Phil, and I fascinated.

So it turns out, that in spite of McGargle's pomposity, his cynical viewpoint on life, that Fields himself had a heart of gold. Well, so be it — but I saw the scene with the boy. And it occurs to me that this heart of gold may have more to do than might at first be suspected with the greenness of his legend, here now thirty years later.

THE THREE STOOGES: SLAPSTICK MASTERS

JEFF LENBURG

THE THREE STOOGES' knockabout comedy style entertained movie audiences for more than forty illustrious years, concluding in 1970 when Larry Fine, the frizzy-haired Stooge, suffered a paralyzing stroke. Ironically, it was in their last year that these veteran comics switched from their time-honored muscle-bound brand of humor to rollicking situation comedy.

From the beginning to the end, Larry and Moe Howard had been part of the trio. Their deaths in 1975 were very sad to me, since I had enjoyed a close relationship with them for many years. Larry was the more personable of the two. Even after his stroke, he continued to answer all letters from fans and to fulfill requests for autographed pictures. Larry was a completely natural comic; on film, his character was never forced.

Moe Howard was a "Jekyll and Hyde" character. On stage or before the cameras he would open himself up and let his nervous energies flow, but on a personal level, he was very protective of himself; his true feelings never surfaced. While Larry was gregarious, Moe was an introvert. Yet Moe was the businessman of the group and did well for himself investing in real estate.

Over the years, four other men joined Moe and Larry at different times to fill out the trio. The first was "Curly" Howard, Moe's youngest brother. Curly suffered a stroke in 1947 and was replaced by another brother, Shemp. When Shemp Howard died in 1955, Joe Besser took his place. In 1959, the Three Stooges made a comeback with ex-burlesque comedian "Curly-Joe" De Rita filling the void.

What is interesting and indicative of the Stooges evolution as screen comedians is that their scripts were adapted differently for each new trio.

The team of Moe, Larry, and Curly poked fun at the upper classes during the time when America was plagued by the Depression. Audiences identified with the lower-class Stooges as they conquered the high hurdles of soci-

The best Stooge trio: (L–R) Curly, Larry, and Moe.

ety, working as plumbers in a ritzy mansion, seeking employment, spoofing United States involvement in World War II.

Slapstick abounds. Moe was always the tormentor of the group. To keep his ruffian partners in line he would holler at them or bang them on the head or poke them in the eye. Curly was the total nitwit. He would bark, nudge his weight against Moe's body with an enormous growl, and wave at his brother in response to the violent actions being directed toward him. Larry was the common man who had somehow become mixed up with half-witted, bald Curly and the not-so-bright-but-intelligent-in-comparison Moe. His main role was to offset his partners' brutish comments with even more reserved stupidity:

Moe: You're an ignoramus.

Larry: Yeaaaah, and that goes for my whole family, too!

JEFF LENBURG *is an agent whose clients include Joe Besser, once a member of The Three Stooges.*

When Shemp joined the team, the scripts became weaker, and the quality of production decreased. It was hard to adapt the Stooges formula to each new member of the group. Shemp was a versatile character actor-comedian. His style had no resemblance to Curly's, and he would outsmart Moe or guard himself from menace by using something that would hurt Moe's hands. He always had to have the last laugh.

Joe Besser was the only Stooge to hit Moe back — not accidentally, but in self-defense. His feisty little-kid character had to be parlayed into stories agreeable to his type. Stooge films in the Joe Besser days were more like situation comedies.

With Curly-Joe De Rita, the major overhaul was that the violence, the slapping, and hitting was toned down, and the pictures became more family-oriented. Unfortunately, because of this revamped style, the Stooges' tempo faltered slightly at times. This final group made several feature films based on timely news events, or famous characters (Hercules) or classic tales.

The Three Stooges, whatever the combination, were different from the other major comedy teams. They were the best at what they did — slapstick. They were "quick-laugh" artists and, as such, deserve to rank

Joe Besser (Top) replaced Shemp.

among the great comedy teams. They made contributions equal to those of Abbott and Costello, Laurel and Hardy, and the Marx Brothers, in winning the hearts of fans throughout the world.

Shemp Howard (R), who had been with group when they were part of Ted Healy and His Stooges in the early thirties, replaced Curly.

Curly-Joe DeRita (L) joined Moe and Larry to form final trio.

THE MARX BROTHERS: UTTER CONFUSION

IRVING BRECHER

Launching their movie career in The Cocoanuts. *(L–R) Zeppo, Groucho, Chico, and Harpo.*

UNLESS YOU WERE AN EYEWITNESS, you cannot possibly imagine the collision when the Marx Brothers and the movie audience slammed into each other in the early thirties. The millions that found much to laugh at in the silent screen antics of Buster

---

IRVING BRECHER'S *screenplays include* Shadow of the Thin Man, Best Foot Forward, DuBarry Was a Lady, Yolanda and the Thief, Summer Holiday, Bye Bye Birdie, Meet Me in St. Louis, *for which he received an Academy Award nomination, and two Marx Brothers movies. He also wrote and directed* The Life of Riley, Somebody Loves Me, *and* Sail a Crooked Ship.

Keaton, Harold Lloyd, et al., and boundless joy from the work of the master, Charles Chaplin, were either shocked, nonplussed or outraged by the on-screen words and deeds of four nihilists named Groucho, Harpo, Chico, and Zeppo. To audiences accustomed to watching comedians taking pratfalls, or being chased by an irate farmer whose buckshot *never,* in a thousand films, hit the leading man, the Marx Brothers approach to dismantling the Establishment smacked of another Marx — Karl (no relation). Those less politically aware simply thought the Marx Brothers were crazy. And some — their numbers are now legion — realized that a fresh well of marvelously original comedy had been tapped. I didn't analyze why they were funny back then — I was too busy laughing — but now when I think back, I know why.

They were totally uninhibited in their confrontations with authority — fearlessly contemptuous. And in those days we plain folks simply didn't dare to be that irreverent of the high-ups. At that time, young people ''behaved.'' As for the established screen comics, most of the story lines were designed for a poor schnook like Lloyd or Keaton, who spent six or seven harrowing reels in heartbreaking efforts to get the girl. What those bumblers, who would spend ten minutes just trying to insert a key in a keyhole, will do *after* they get the girl, one wonders. (Except Chaplin, the genius — Groucho's opinion too — who touches you, makes you laugh, makes you cry, but he rarely gets the girl.)

The Marxes were radically different in their approach. When Groucho made a verbal pass at a pretty woman, he wasn't proposing marriage, simply a brief honeymoon. And Harpo, who tooted his own horn as he chased a different blonde in every film, was clearly not interested in commitment. Only those in the movie who *dealt* with Harpo believed in commitment — commitment of Harpo. In an institution!

And Chico? He had little free time to court a young beauty. Aside from bungling any nefarious scheme that Groucho was promoting, Chico was kept busy trying to remember to add the letter *a* to the end of words in his futile efforts to sound like an Italian. If the nation of Italy had been paid a dollar for every time Chico said ''At's-a fine, boss,'' or ''At's-a no good,'' it would have had a huge financial harvest — and well justified, considering the damage Chico did to its beautiful language.

CHICO MARX THE BUSINESSMAN

AFTER ZEPPO'S RETIREMENT, it was Chico who handled the trio's business matters and engineered a fabulous deal at MGM. The brothers got a big salary and a piece of their movies' profits, which had never before been granted at Metro. How did this happen? With a deck of cards.

An executive at Metro had been playing gin rummy with Chico and constantly winning. He became convinced that he was a better player than Chico. Since the Marxes were free of any contracts, the sharp exec thought it would be nice to have Chico on the lot, on salary, thus making it convenient to shear Chico at gin rummy. So the man sold his boss, Irving Thalberg, on signing the Marxes to a five-film pact. Chico's demands were unheard of, however, and Thalberg rejected them. But Chico the gambler was fearless. He held out, and got the deal. The day after the contract was signed, the studio exec started to lose to Chico, steadily and heavily. Until the day he died, Chico would tell me that ''losing to that schmuck was the best acting I ever did.''

— I. B.

But more than anything, Chico's role was to protect and big-brother the elfin, deliciously manic, mute Harpo. And he, grateful for Chico's devotion, did something no

Animal Crackers.   *For the Marx Brothers, Margaret Dumont played ''straight man.''*

The Marx Brothers usually brought chaos with them, but in At the Circus, *zany characters, such as Peerless Pauline (L) and a mean midget (Above) had already turned things topsy-turvy.*

other character ever did — he actually *believed* Chico was a real Italian.

Only Zeppo, the youngest and the straight man, was romantically involved. In their Paramount films, Zeppo eventually got the girl, but who cared? How could you root for this handsome young man who *voluntarily* hung around with three creatures who collectively wore a phony burnt-cork mustache, a fake blonde wig, and a fraudulent Italian accent?

No, the early Marx films — *The Cocoanuts* (1929), *Animal Crackers* (1930), *Monkey Business* (1931), *Horse Feathers* (1932), *Duck Soup* (1933) — were not designed to touch the heart. Unlike the perennial loser Chaplin, the Marxes always won, hilariously destroying fat cats and pompous bores. Whether in the military, university, art world, or opera, no one with whom they came into contact would be the same at fadeout. Nor would any screenwriter be quite the same after long-term close encounters with them.

I was fifteen, and living in Yonkers, New York, when I saw a preview of *The Cocoanuts* at the Strand

Theatre. It changed my life. Though much younger, and taller and thinner than Groucho, when I parted my wavy hair, wore my wire-rimmed eyeglasses, applied a square burnt-cork mustache, wiggled a rubber cigar, I was almost a clone of Groucho. Our voices had a remarkable similarity, so, by stealing some of his routines, aping his nasal-incisive delivery, I leered and crouch-loped to the laughs of multitudes — sometimes as many as six or seven other kids. Romping over beds and couches, I never dreamed, even in my most Mittyish moments, that one day I would be brought to Hollywood, by Mervyn LeRoy, to write films at Metro-Goldwyn-Mayer, which was then home to my idols, Groucho and *frères!*

I added comedy scenes to Judy Garland's *The Wizard of Oz* (1939), met Gable, rode an elevator once with Garbo, had my car fender dented by John Barrymore. . . . I had had all but the greatest of thrills: I never saw the Marx Brothers in person. Then one fateful day, the studio tapped LeRoy to produce the follow-up to the Marx Brothers' two MGM comedy classics *A Night at the Opera* (1935) and *A Day at the Races* (1937). The background, I read in *Variety,* would be the circus. And just like in the movies, I was assigned to write it. When I came down to earth, LeRoy added: ''But first, I want you to meet Groucho. He's the only one of the brothers who worries about the script, but don't be nervous!''

Approaching my first meeting with my god, I was not nervous. Just petrified. He was lounging in LeRoy's swivel chair, feet up on the producer's desk. My champion, LeRoy, was generous in his praise. ''Groucho, this is Irv Brecher; he's only twenty-three,

In Go West, *Harpo shows his usual restraint around authority figures and women.*

not much experience, but believe me, he's a brilliant writer.''

Groucho eyed me, puffing on his cigar for what seemed an eternity. (He could be sadistic at times.) Then: ''Hello, brilliant writer.''

''Meeting you is like a dream come true,'' I blurted out.

Groucho turned to LeRoy. ''You told me he was brilliant! What kind of comedy line is that — 'meeting you is like a dream come true'? We need a writer with originality!''

I was hurt and embarrased. ''I admit it's not original, Mr. Marx,'' I managed to say. ''It's a line you used in *Horse Feathers*, which I assumed you ad-libbed. You didn't get a laugh with it either.''

Groucho's stern expression dissolved into a small smile. ''C'mon, sonny, I'll buy you lunch . . . *if* you're a light eater.''

★ ★ ★ ★

The next two years are still exciting to recall. They were frustrating, exhausting, pressure-packed, stimulating, and finally rewarding. I achieved something of a record, being the only writer ever to receive ''solo screenplay credit'' (or debit?) on a Marx Brothers' film. Actually, on two: *At the Circus* (1939) and *Go West* (1940). This achievement may well be a tribute more to my stamina than to talent. Making any movie is difficult, but more so are comedies, and toughest of all, Marx Brothers' movies. I learned a great deal about writing.

To get Chico to read a script, it would have been necessary to slip the pages into his racing form. He was, until shooting began, at the racetrack or at a card table, being an expert at bridge and gin rummy, and a dedicated gambler.

Harpo never knew the story line. He would ask me to explain what comedy business I had in *his* scenes, and we would kick it around, and he would often add brilliant touches.

Groucho, younger than Chico and Harpo, did the worrying. To successfully judge what will arouse that mercurial commodity, laughter, requires a gift all too

When Groucho was too sick to pose for Go West *promotion posters, Irving Brecher took his place.*

rare. Though the great comics had it, they all had insecurity, fear of "guessing wrong," and Groucho had it too. Not in regard to *his* dialogue, but relative to the overall story. He would often challenge me, in our story conferences, but never with the ridicule of his on-screen character. He never forgot that he, too, was a writer, as his several books amusingly confirm.

Groucho was a very critical man, cynical about producers, most of whom he considered curses of nepotism. But Irving Thalberg's decisions regarding their first two films at MGM had won Groucho's hard-to-get respect.

But Thalberg had died, and Groucho felt his absence. He would occasionally vacillate in his opinions, and this uncertainty would pervade the thinking of the studio brass. But slowly I won his trust, and eventually I found him defending my work against the criticisms of executives he considered unqualified. If he thought you were good, he let the world know it. Being a very funny man, he was not afraid to acknowledge others were funny too. Other writers, before and after my two films, were also grateful for Groucho's outspoken appreciation of the writers' importance to movies — "ninety percent," he said.

During my two years of writing for the Marx Brothers, I valued Groucho and Harpo as close, loyal friends. The two brothers, though fond of each other, socialized in different arenas. Harpo was adored by

musicians, writers, artists such as Salvador Dalí (Harpo *was* surrealistic!), and was the adopted puppy of the literati in New York, even though he never read anything.

I was lucky to be accepted in Harpo's circle, but it was with Groucho that I spent most of my time. One reason: Harpo had a perfect married life, but Groucho was usually separated or divorced, and had more time to be lonesome. I had priceless experiences with him, on coast-to-coast trains, on ships, in posh hotels. I even seduced him into a trip into the wildest woods of Wyoming, the first time in his life he had gone fishing. I can still see this giant of funnymen eyeing me with hostility, as he sat in misery in the saddle of a pack mule in the deerfly-infested Grand Teton Mountains. "Brecher," he groaned, "how could you do this to me, a star? A man lionized by the greats of the civilized world, who just threw up his lunch, which was Spam! I could be at '21' right now, insulting a waiter! If I get out of this jungle alive, I'll have my revenge on you, you s.o.b. I'll make you write our next picture!"

In every situation, Groucho was amusing. The more harrowing, the funnier. He could be cruel too, to bores, pests who invaded his privacy, and bigots, whether political or religious. And he never left a room, a dinner table, or an office conference, without a good exit line. To be Groucho, he just had to have the last word.

Now Chico and Harpo are gone. Last year there was a rumor, in the media, that Groucho had also died. I don't believe it. I know my friend Groucho. If he were leaving, he would have spoken some memorable exit line. So I think he just stepped out for a moment, and he'll be right back . . .

The inimitable Groucho Marx.

CAROLE LOMBARD: BLITHE SPIRIT

SIDNEY SALKOW

I CROSSED PATHS with Carole Lombard in 1933, but her wacky antics, lilting voice, and whooping laugh — together with a reputation for having the filthiest mouth in Hollywood — had made her a legend long before I met her.

Born Jane Peters in Fort Wayne, Indiana, in 1908, she debuted in 1921 in Allan Dwan's *The Perfect Crime*, playing a tomboy. It was perfect typecasting. From early childhood, she had rejected the company of girls her own age to box with her two brothers, become first baseman on their team, and run faster and jump farther than any classmate at Fairfax High. She had medals to prove it.

As a young teenager, she would win a closetful of dance trophies at Hollywood's Cocoanut Grove and attract enough attention to earn a meager contract with Twentieth Century-Fox. At eighteen her burgeoning career was interrupted by a car accident that left a slight facial scar. Carole would never lose her self-consciousness about this almost unnoticeable blemish.

Nor did she lose her will to become Hollywood's number one star, its premier comedienne. Let go by Fox, she became one of the youngest and loveliest inmates of Mack Sennett's "pie-throwing academy." Her uninhibited spirits made her a natural follower of Charlie Chaplin, Marie Dressler, Chester Conklin, Mabel Normand — just to name a few of the many stars who graduated from the ranks of Sennett's comedies. With a baptism of custard pies, she developed one of her rarest qualities: She could take it. Besides the name Carole Lombard which she adopted while at Sennett's, the actress also acquired a reputation for indulging in endless slapstick offscreen. Carole moved to Paramount, where she quickly established herself as the most beloved artist on the lot.

I was assigned to work with director Erle C. Kenton as associate director on *From Hell to Heaven* (1933).

SIDNEY SALKOW *has directed numerous features since 1937, including* Girl Overboard, The Adventures of Martin Eden, Scarlet Angel, Chicago Confidential, Sitting Bull, *and* The Great Sioux Massacre.

Paramount's madcap.

My stage experience, it was assumed, would help me shape the dialogue passages. I was twenty-one years old, full of self-esteem, and exceedingly serious. Carole must have sensed my dedication to the film because she treated me with a respect that neither my experience nor my age warranted. Ruthless in her self-criticism, she welcomed my honest suggestions. I watched her each day with growing disbelief and heightened respect. This dynamic golden girl enchanted me with her vibrant personality, wildly energetic drive, fantastic sense of humor, excellent mind, and forthright talent. I fell in love with her, and realized why everyone else in the crew had succumbed to her charms.

Years before his mustache and their marriage, Gable and Lombard co-starred in No Man of Her Own.

She was easily the most diverting and unpredictable member of our troupe, ready to concoct a dozen gags a day to enliven the tediousness of the schedule. Even when her services were not required, she haunted the set, saucily offering advice to the other actors if she felt a scene was lagging, shooting pictures with the still photographer's camera, or even displacing the motion picture camera operator and making skillful pan shots.

I worked with her once more, on her next picture, a horror film called *Supernatural* (1933). She read the script, met the director Victor Halperin, and then promptly threatened to kill herself, Halperin, and everyone in Paramount's front office in order to avoid the assignment. Finally, worn out by her agent and Paramount's threats to suspend her, Carole acquiesced. I was thrown in at Carole's request to serve as a minor mediator.

Carole bridled at Halperin's every suggestion and offered only mild resistance to my pleadings and entreaties to face the cameras. Matters were not helped much when Halperin, a sweet mild-mannered gentleman, consistently managed to place Carole on the wrong side of the camera, revealing her scar. Poor Victor, subject to Carole's pithy and never-ending verbal assaults from morn till night, seemingly could no longer tell her right side from her left. Each time he bumbled, Carole would erupt. As Carole girded herself to deal shot by shot with the absurd story, her profanities came more regularly and her appeals for help wracked the stage walls.

Particularly painful for both Victor and Carole were those times when facial transformations had to be filmed. It was a painstaking process that required Carole to remain motionless for what seemed an eternity while the transformation was achieved with makeup and stop-frame photography. For Carole, whose internal combustion machine was never at rest, this was the final indignity. She came down hard on Victor. ''God, this bastard's trying to paralyze me. Victor, God'll punish you for this . . . ,'' she moaned.

And maybe God was listening. At 5:10 P.M., March 10, 1933, the set suddenly started to rumble; a deep roar drowned out the clatter of lights, props, furniture, and sets rattling and crashing while the ground swayed and the earth buckled and writhed. In panic everyone ran shrieking from the set in wild flight.

To all of us it was the Long Beach earthquake (it took fifty-two lives). To Carole it was "Lombard's Revenge." I watched her, mindless of everyone's preoccupation with the moment, stride to Victor Halperin huddled outside the still-swaying stage and point a finger at him, "Victor — *that* was only a warning!"

Despite such failures as *Supernatural,* Carole by the mid-thirties would assume the unrivaled position as Hollywood's highest-paid artist. While Carole was delighted to be considered cinema's screwball comedy queen, she often passed up prize comedy parts to fight for roles that would prove her credentials as an equally adept dramatic actress. *In Name Only* (1939), *Vigil in the Night* (1940), and finally her appearance with Charles Laughton in *They Knew What They Wanted* (1940) were prized landmarks in her life.

Her light blond hair, ivory complexion, and voluptuous body combined to make her one of Hollywood's top glamour girls. Certainly, Carole could have emerged a greater sex symbol than Jean Harlow or Marilyn Monroe, but her own sense of fun prevented it. I can remember our still man trying to get her to smile and "look sexy" in a pose. She kept frowning. He sweet-talked her, "C'mon, Carole, smile! Sex is fun!" Carole summed it up: "I'd rather play tennis."

Lady By Choice. *With May Robson.*

Publicity shots emphasized Lombard's sex appeal.

A DEMAND FOR EQUALITY

IT WAS MIDWINTER and the weather was freezing when we sought to film a scene for *From Hell to Heaven* at the stables at Santa Anita racetrack. The script called for summer clothes, and Carole was dressed in a light silk nothing, shivering and uttering a stream of profanities. The rest of us, crew and all, looked on swathed in heavy, warm jackets. After a dozen scenes, Carole, a mass of goose pimples, erupted, "All right, you warm, bloody bastards, what's good for one is good for all! I'm not shooting till I see every one of you down to your jockey shorts." And, believe it or not, we stripped, while Carole howled with glee. Years earlier, Joseph Kennedy had rescued her from the Sennett harness and offered her a contract with his Pathé Studios, but on one condition. "I'd say you can stand to lose twenty pounds," he told her. "You're not so slim yourself," she countered. "I'll lose it if you lose it." He accepted the challenge.

The great director Ernst Lubitsch also became part of the Lombard legend. Carole wanted Lubitsch to direct her film *Love Before Breakfast* (directed by Walter Lang in 1936). He had reservations. Puffing on his big black cigar, a fixture of his, he told her, "I don't think it's going to be a success." Carole pleaded, "Let's do this picture. . . . if it turns out to be a stinker you can have your way with me." Lubitsch's face beamed with interest as Carole snatched the black cigar from his mouth and added, "But if it's a hit, I'll shove this black thing up your ass."

— S. S.

With ex-husband William Powell in My Man Godfrey.

On and off screen her romantic involvements were tempestuous. Her marriage to William Powell was short-lived. Powell, a moody intellectual with an innate respect for social proprieties, found no match in Carole's casual, spontaneous temperament. But they remained close friends and would form a perfect team in *My Man Godfrey* (1936), a screwball comedy classic.

When Russ Columbo, her "greatest and truest love," fell victim to a bizarre gun accident in 1934, she sought relief by pushing herself even harder into her film career. Yet her shenanigans and capers, wisecracks and playful profanity did not stop. In 1935, Carole arrived at a party thrown by writer Donald Ogden Stewart in an ambulance. Hired interns bore her, grinning from ear to ear, into the house on a stretcher. Clark Gable was there as a guest. He became her ardent suitor. Gable was everything she wanted. They were married in 1939.

Although Gable cured Lombard of her swearing, she never lost her madcap sense of humor. Gable recalled a moment once at their San Fernando Valley ranch, looking out at the valley below: " 'It's beautiful,' I said to Carole, 'we're awfully lucky, you and I — all this and each other — anything you want we haven't got?' You know what she said? She said, 'Well, I could do with another load of manure for the south forty.' "

★ ★ ★ ★ ★

In January 1942, six weeks after Pearl Harbor, Carole accepted the honorary national chairmanship of a drive to sell war bonds. It was while serving in this job that on January 16, 1942, her plane crashed into the side of a Nevada mountain. There were no survivors. No performer in the media would be so deeply mourned or so lovingly remembered. President Franklin D. Roosevelt spoke for all Americans when he wired Gable, "She brought great joy to all who knew her and to the millions who knew her as a great artist. She gave unselfishly of her time and talent to serve her government in peace and in war. She loved her country. She is and always will be a star. We shall never forget nor cease to be grateful to her."

But I think Carole would have been more pleased by the reception *To Be or Not To Be* (1942), her last film, received from a unanimous press after its premiere, one month after her death. *Variety,* which had so cursorily dismissed her in *Supernatural,* would say:

Carole Lombard's last picture needs no benefit of tragic circumstances to leave its impress of fine screen artistry. It is characteristic of the roles which were most becoming to Miss Lombard, lively with laughter, lush with entertainment, appropriate as the valedictory of a persuasive actress and a glowing personality.

No one would forget . . .

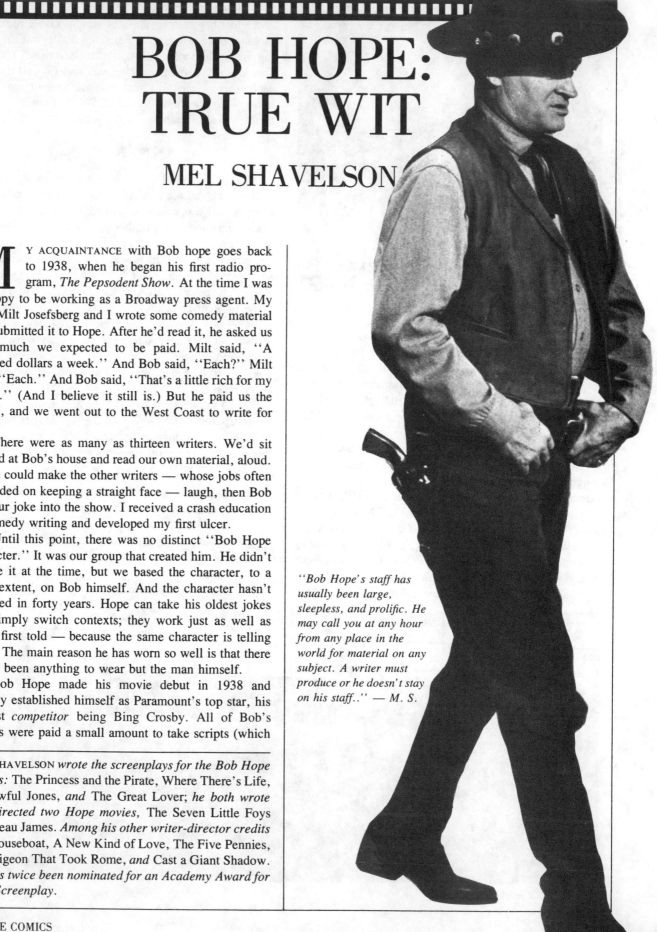

BOB HOPE: TRUE WIT

MEL SHAVELSON

MY ACQUAINTANCE with Bob hope goes back to 1938, when he began his first radio program, *The Pepsodent Show.* At the time I was unhappy to be working as a Broadway press agent. My boss Milt Josefsberg and I wrote some comedy material and submitted it to Hope. After he'd read it, he asked us how much we expected to be paid. Milt said, ''A hundred dollars a week.'' And Bob said, ''Each?'' Milt said, ''Each.'' And Bob said, ''That's a little rich for my blood.'' (And I believe it still is.) But he paid us the salary, and we went out to the West Coast to write for him.

There were as many as thirteen writers. We'd sit around at Bob's house and read our own material, aloud. If you could make the other writers — whose jobs often depended on keeping a straight face — laugh, then Bob let your joke into the show. I received a crash education in comedy writing and developed my first ulcer.

Until this point, there was no distinct ''Bob Hope character.'' It was our group that created him. He didn't realize it at the time, but we based the character, to a large extent, on Bob himself. And the character hasn't changed in forty years. Hope can take his oldest jokes and simply switch contexts; they work just as well as when first told — because the same character is telling them. The main reason he has worn so well is that there hasn't been anything to wear but the man himself.

Bob Hope made his movie debut in 1938 and quickly established himself as Paramount's top star, his nearest *competitor* being Bing Crosby. All of Bob's writers were paid a small amount to take scripts (which

''Bob Hope's staff has usually been large, sleepless, and prolific. He may call you at any hour from any place in the world for material on any subject. A writer must produce or he doesn't stay on his staff..'' — M. S.

MEL SHAVELSON *wrote the screenplays for the Bob Hope movies:* The Princess and the Pirate, Where There's Life, Sorrowful Jones, *and* The Great Lover; *he both wrote and directed two Hope movies,* The Seven Little Foys *and* Beau James. *Among his other writer-director credits are* Houseboat, A New Kind of Love, The Five Pennies, The Pigeon That Took Rome, *and* Cast a Giant Shadow. *He has twice been nominated for an Academy Award for Best Screenplay.*

somebody else had written) and punch jokes into them. Hope would present some of the jokes to his producer, who would usually throw them out, and we would slide the rest between the pages of the script so it would seem that Bob was ad-libbing in front of the camera. This created his reputation for having a quick wit on the set.

Between 1944 and 1957, I wrote seven scripts for Hope, two of which I directed. I was able to observe him very closely. He always follows his scripts because, well, he paid good money for them. The expression "He squeezes a nickel till the buffalo squeals" applies here; he pays for the best and uses what he gets — with little departure.

Hope liked to play down his dramatic ability. He seemed ashamed that he could act. When I directed him in *The Seven Little Foys* (1955), I was able to force him away from his standard one-dimensional character and make him attempt difficult acting. After successfully playing a dramatic scene, he would make some joke to try to cover up the fact that he had just been "acting." But he *can* act, and when he is forced into playing a complex character, such as Eddie Foy or Mayor Jimmy Walker, he obviously succeeds. I think he might have been more durable in motion pictures if he had continued to play complex roles such as the ones in *The Seven Little Foys, Beau James* (1957), and *The Facts of Life* (1960).

Working with Bob on a movie is like working in a three-ring circus. His real business, as far as he is con-

With Gable and Margaret O'Brien on Armed Forces Radio.

cerned, is as a stand-up comic, and all the time that a movie of his is in production he is usually preparing for a personal appearance or a golf date or, back then, his radio show. The movie is somewhat of a sideline, or at least he likes to pretend it is.

The Princess and the Pirate, *scripted by Mel Shavelson. With Victor McLaglen (L) and Walter Slezak.*

DANCING PARTNERS: HOPE AND CAGNEY

I WASN'T SURPRISED by Bob's dancing in *The Seven Little Foys*. I was more surprised by Cagney's. We asked Jimmy, who was at Parmount at the time, to reprise his George M. Cohan character (for which he'd won an Academy Award) in the Foy picture. He said, "I'll do it on one condition: that you don't pay me." It seems that Eddie Foy, in the old days on Broadway, when Jimmy Cagney was a starving chorus boy, would invite Jimmy to his home and feed him so that he'd get through the week. Jimmy never forgot a friend. But he never had a chance to repay Foy until that moment, and he did actually perform in *The Seven Little Foys* for no money at all.

When Cagney agreed to do it I said, "You know, Jimmy, we want you to dance; you may be willing to walk out on the set for a day for nothing, but it's going to take a little rehearsal." He said, "I happen to have my dancing shoes in the car." He went to the dance bungalows and started rehearsing. Hope noticed him there, three weeks before shooting was scheduled to start. Hope quickly got out his dancing shoes too.

Bob did a remarkable job, but I also think the camera did a remarkable job; there are many ways of increasing anyone's athletic ability with film. At any rate, Bob *was* a dancer — he had to be in the old days of vaudeville. He's gotten a little heavier on his feet, but I think that he can still do the dance in *The Seven Little Foys* as well as he did it then.

— M. S.

Film doesn't suit Bob as well as television. TV gives him the opportunity to do stand-up routines which he does best. I am not denigrating his movies, which have been for the most part funny and successful with audiences. The "Road" pictures, for instance, were a phenomenon of their time — and they hold up nicely. Hope and Crosby were brought together simply because they were both at Paramount. It was after the success of *Road to Singapore* (1940) that they became good friends. I don't know how much of their rivalry was put on, but I do know much of what was real. Bob was greatly affected by Bing's death, unapproachable for at least a week. (Bob, Bing, and I had a handshake deal to make *The Road to the Fountain of Youth;* now it might be done with Bob and George Burns, building the film somewhat as a tribute to Bing.)

There were other films that Bob and I planned that never got off the ground. The one project we were going to make, believe it or not, was a comedy about the Vietnam War. That was forsaken with the invasion of Cam-

Partners in comedic intrigue. Bob Hope and Dorothy Lamour — without Crosby to interfere — in My Favorite Brunette.

A quick venture into slapstick in Fancy Pants.

BOB HOPE'S FIRST TELEVISION EXPERIENCE

IN 1947, PARAMOUNT asked me to write the first television show ever made west of the Mississippi, for an all-star cast of performers. Bob Hope was to be the emcee.

When we did the show in front of television cameras and the studio audience, none of the jokes came off. Bob came to me between sketches and said, "What's wrong? These jokes must be pretty bad." I said, "They can't be bad. They're the same ones that you've always done. But you've got a script in your hand." He said, "We always do the show with a script." I said, "You do a radio show with a script, and the audience for a radio show accepts it. On television, they're watching you on a monitor and you're supposed to be out there just as you would be on a stage or on the screen." So he threw the script away, and what a mess it turned out to be. Nobody could remember a line. When it was all over, he came to me and said, "Television will never catch on. What actor will ever give up his golf to learn a script?"

Then along came Milton Berle, who learned an hour script every week, and most actors had to give up golf. Not Bob. As he started studying scripts, he built a golf course in his backyard.

— M. S.

bodia, which took place while the comedy was being prepared. I called Bob and said, "I think we'd better forget about this one." He agreed. Then he said something revealing to me — revealing because Bob never discussed the Vietnam War with anybody below the rank of five-star general. He said, "I was just leaving my hotel in Washington, putting my golf clubs in my car when some kids drove by. One of them leaned out and said, "Hey Bob, we're gonna bring them home to you this Christmas!' " I think that was the beginning of a change in him, from his extreme hawkish attitude to one that was a bit more in tune with where the rest of the country was at the time.

I don't think anybody has deep insight into the "real" Bob Hope. I do know that he was affected by his very tough childhood. I know he hasn't forgotten being pulled in by the police for having taken some items from a sporting goods store. Or the fact he came from poverty. Years later, when he had no reason to worry about money, he still did worry about it. That's part of his character that can't be changed. And he wouldn't be Hope if it could.

Today, Hope is such a public figure I couldn't guess what his concept of the world is. His life, I think, is full of laughter and those who like him — he seldom comes into contact with the other kind. Bob is insulated from a lot of reality and, at this point, maybe he deserves it.

The underrated comedy team of Bob Hope and Bing Crosby. This duo's humor was based on their well-known friendly rivalry.

ABBOTT AND COSTELLO: WACKY CAMARADERIE

CHARLES BARTON

ABBOTT AND COSTELLO were great stand-up comics, used to performing before burlesque and radio studio audiences. They had to adapt to working without audience reactions when they started making movies in 1940, but this was an obstacle easily overcome. They both had photographic memories, enabling them to look at a script only once and know it by heart; I discovered that the best way to direct them was to allow them moments in the script for spontaneity — their timing is what made them so great.

Although Lou Costello played a sweet little guy who made a lot of mistakes, and was the perfect patsy for Bud — or anyone else — in real life, Lou's was the stronger personality. Lou made the decisions for the team, including which routines would be used in a film. He was a good family man, but — like Bud — a poor businessman. Once when he was unhappy with a certain studio decision, instead of trying to work it out, he took a trip to Europe and invited thirty-two guests to go with him. It was like Lou to run away from problems in his professional life.

Lou was the first to admit that Bud was the greatest straight man ever. He was much less temperamental than Lou, and never let his personal problems interfere with work. If he was frustrated he would take it out in the dressing room. In public, Bud was always quiet and even-tempered.

Bud and Lou sometimes disagreed intensely, but a half hour later they had forgotten all about it. Bud's feelings were more fragile, and he would become hurt quite easily when Lou treated him roughly, yet he always

On film, Abbott (R) cared little about Costello's welfare.

managed to overlook what Lou did or said to him. They loved each other, and the hard times they had together, the fights they had, unified them even more.

There was one very bad period, however, that, I believe, did permanent damage to the team. Someone advised Lou that he should get more money for his pratfalls. So, characteristically, he threatened to quit. Of course, Universal went after their gold mine, but he held out for an increase in salary and asked for a larger amount than Bud. To resolve the situation, their manager Eddie Sherman asked Bud to go along with the idea. He

---

CHARLES BARTON *directed Abbott and Costello in* The Time of Their Lives, Buck Privates Come Home, The Wistful Widow of Wagon Gap, The Noose Hangs High, Abbott and Costello Meet Frankenstein, Mexican Hayride, Abbott and Costello Meet the Invisible Man, *and others. Among his other credits are* The Shaggy Dog *and* Toby Tyler. *This article was written with the help of* GREG LENBURG *and* JULIE BARTON.

did, but it broke his heart that Lou wanted him to take a pay cut.

What halted the success of Abbott and Costello, not once but twice in their career, was that the studio flooded the market with their films. At the same time a new film was released, an old one would be reissued. They became overexposed, and eventually, in the early fifties, stopped being box-office giants. But they were important to the forties and essential to the art of comedy. As the owner of Universal Studios once said, "Thank God for Abbott and Costello!"

On the set: Costello, Charles Barton, and Joe Besser.

PECCADILLOES AND POKER

DURING ALMOST EVERY PICTURE that I worked on with the team, props would disappear from the set. Once a grandfather clock was missing. Nobody knew where it went. It turned out that Lou had had a truck come to the studio, pick up the clock, and deliver it to his house! Another time, a canoe disappeared. It had become a planter in front of Lou's house. Despite these problems, Lou's childlike antics were excellent at relieving tension on the set.

What I did find annoying was the entourage of sidekicks Lou and Bud invited to the set for big-money poker games. Whenever either of them ran out of cash, the game stopped while one of their stooges would go to the bank and withdraw $10,000 or so. In the meantime, the boys wouldn't shoot a scene until their money arrived. When I was assigned to an Abbott and Costello movie, I didn't know whether to laugh or cry.

— C. B.

A SPECIAL BRAND
OF HUMOR

Pardon My Sarong,
one of the team's best films.

Promoting Abbott and Costello Meet Frankenstein, *the 1948 film that revived their career.*

Abbott and Costello Meet the Mummy, *a film in which the gentle prospector Costello refused to "strike the mother lode."*

COSTELLO PLAYED characters conspicuous for their lack of intelligence — at least on the surface. This coupled with his naiveté made him more of a playful child than an adult. We cannot help feeling sympathetic:

ABBOTT: Did you ever take a good look at yourself in the mirror?
COSTELLO: No. Why should I hurt my own feelings?

A visit from a loved one.

Though a fool, Costello is a conniving fool. On his own level, he has the shrewdness of a philosopher:

COSTELLO: If I get married, it'll be to a homely girl, 'cause a beautiful girl would just run off with someone else.
ABBOTT: But wouldn't a homely girl run off, too?
COSTELLO: Yeah, but who cares?

As it was with W. C. Fields, Costello was his funniest when he placed himself in direct contact with characters of an odd or obnoxious nature. In effect, he becomes the straight man:

COSTELLO: You're crazy.
MADMAN: My brother's crazy. I'm not crazy.
COSTELLO: Who told you?
MADMAN: My brother.

ROAD RUNNER AND WILE E. COYOTE: THE BIRD AND THE BUSHWHACKER

HARRY BROWN

THE POPULAR TEAM of Road Runner and Wile E. Coyote has yet to act in a picture that has lost money. Their films are profitable because (1) the scripts, with rare exceptions, call for only two characters, (2) they are a corporation and do their own producing, (3) every shot is an exterior filmed around Deep Canyon, Arizona — really nothing more than a post office — near where both stars have their year-round homes. Add to this the fact that they have a simple, surefire formula for their pictures: carnivore wants bird, carnivore chases bird, carnivore gets whopped.

I believe Wile E. is the "hero" of these films. I see him as too human, too fallible, and too accident-prone to be truly villainous. He's also too nervous, too flaky, to keep company with the likes of Bill Sykes, Jack the Ripper, and Professor Moriarty.

As for Road, I find in his screen character a certain androgynous quality that keeps him from being a true hero, let alone a spurious heroine. He's more tease than villain. I suppose he should have our sympathies, if only for his comparative size, but this has to be balanced against his overconfidence and general downright sneakiness. An unexpected "*Beep-beep!*" from Road, who has crept up behind him, will send Wile E. straight up twenty or thirty feet, like as not to conk his noggin on

HARRY BROWN *is a novelist and screenwriter, who won an Academy Award as co-writer of* A Place in the Sun *and received a nomination as solo writer of* Sands of Iwo Jima. *Among his other screen credits are* Arch of Triumph, Bugles in the Afternoon, All the Brothers Were Valiant, *and* Between Heaven and Hell. *He is the original author of* A Walk in the Sun *and* El Dorado.

a rocky overhang. He's aware that, no matter what Wile E. attempts in the way of bird-catching, the poor devil's going to blow it somehow and end up much the worse for wear. Wile E. knows it, too, but he's game enough to gamble, over and over again. Such blind persistence, in the face of such bitterly long odds, is courageous, praiseworthy, and admirable. He sets his idiot-cheerful incompetence against Road's unbelievable speed, aware of being foredoomed to failure, biting the dust in ten dozen different ways, only to rise again, like the Phoenix, to think up yet another lost-cause scheme.

Wile E. seems based, to a considerable extent, on Buster Keaton — except for the important difference that Keaton is a genius with machinery. Our hero, however, fascinated by technology, is so inept with machines that he can't — while in a tunnel, say — differentiate between a bird wearing a miner's hat and the headlight of an approaching locomotive.

The machines, incidentally, are fascinating; and even more fascinating is their source — a well-stocked mail-order house called Acme. This would appear to be, on an enormous scale, the present-day equivalent of Johnson Smith, a company whose inch-thick catalogues gave so much pleasure when I was a boy. But from Acme a boy, or Wile E. Coyote, can get anything his little destructive heart desires. From an Acme "war surplus" sale Wile E. once ordered, and received, a World War I biplane. It had survived four years of a world war, true, but piloted by Wile E. it lasted, as might be expected, all of twenty-eight seconds.

That none of these purchases achieve the end for which they were bought is less the fault of the merchandise than of Wile E.'s inevitable ineptness. In fact, there was a time when I was convinced that he actually *owned*

Acme, but after watching him, again and again, being splattered across the landscape by such vehicles as an Acme Garment Co. truck, I decided that, when the chips are down, Wile E. is just a well-to-do, incompetent all-thumbs guy.

His body, nevertheless, is anything but incompetent. Although he'd never be mistaken for Mr. America, our Wile E. is in tip-top shape. Seemingly scrawny, he is capable of extraordinary assaults and compressions. He can flatten himself into the filling in a rock sandwich or become a one-dimensional inhabitant of Flatland or, thanks to the pressure produced by a falling five-ton boulder, become either a stove lid or an accordion on legs.

These minor metamorphoses are all temporary and quite beyond the histrionic talents of Road, whose strength is in his speed. He's so fast that you get the Doppler effect even before the damned bird has reached you. He can always take the measure of Wile E. in a no-holds-barred race. Wile E., understandably, is sadly aware of this, hence all the paraphernalia shipped postpaid from Acme.

Mel Blanc, the first voice specialist to have his name included in a cartoon's credits, supplied the voices for such Warner Brothers stars as Bugs Bunny, Porky Pig, and Daffy Duck. For Road Runner, he provided ''Beep-beep!''

Picture, then, this lean and hungry Cassius of a flesh-eater, tense and ready next to one of his lethal Acme-sent toys: in this case a ballista, a great stone snuggled in its cup. *Wh-o-o-o-s-s-hhh!* The cloud of dust that is Road flashes by. Wile E. pulls the cord that will release the deadly stone. Nothing happens. Another pull. Again nothing. The dust is long gone, dissolved. Wile E. climbs up on the ballista, mounts the stone. Jumps on it. And then — *wham!* A few moments later Wile E. is in orbit over southeastern Nevada. And then the camera, panning down, reveals what our apogee'd hero failed to notice when he assembled this siege-engine: The ballista may have been ordered from Acme, but on its base a tiny plaque announces that it was BUILT BY THE ROAD RUNNER MFG. CO. Indeed, Road could very well be an Acme stockholder or, at the worst, a silent but potent partner in the firm. I wouldn't put it past him, the seed-pecking slyboots.

As to why these violent one-on-one confrontations should be received so rapturously by audiences, I don't find the answer especially difficult. What Wile E. and Road do is give us an opportunity to release our aggressions as *spectators,* rather than participants, somewhat in the way a pro football or hockey game does, but in a far less painful way. There is no blood in a Wile E.-Road film. Flesh is resilient, bones delightfully stretchable. The flesh and bones, it goes without saying, are always those of Wile E. Innumerable sticks of dynamite go off, but nobody (i.e., Wile E.) is hurt. Blackened around the edges, maybe, but still in one damn-the-torpedoes piece. Of such is the kingdom.

Canis Latrans.

A PAGE FROM THE ACME CATALOGUE

AMONG THE INTRIGUING ITEMS that the Acme mail-order company has sent to Wile E. are:

- a bounce-less trampoline
- a can of paint that renders any surface invisible
- a giant rubber band (for tripping roadrunners)
- a pair of hand-jets
- a package of dehydrated boulders
- a do-it-yourself tornado kit
- a set of drafting tools
- a coyote-size roadrunner suit (female version)
- a bottle of earthquake pills
- thirty miles of railway track

— H. B.

JUDY HOLLIDAY: DUMB BLOND WITH A DIFFERENCE

DOUGLAS MARSHALL

Holliday's women always tried to improve themselves, socially and intellectually.

HER FACE WAS RIGHT OUT OF RENOIR, her body from Rubens. Her voice was equal parts Baby Huey and Baby Snooks. Her hair (it varied from film to film — from ash to doxy white) was piled atop her head. Her eyes were round, brown, and tragic — even when she smiled. Her specialty was playing dumb blonds.

There had been other dumb blonds before her — so many that by the time her Billie Dawn sashayed onto the screen in *Born Yesterday* (1950), the type was a certified cliché: alluring, dense, predictable. Jean Harlow had started off playing gangsters' bonbons, but she quickly eclipsed the breed with her spunk and self-reliance. Marian Martin typified the tradition in the forties, but she lacked the interest and variety to keep from suffocating in her sables. Marie Wilson's Irma was certainly lovable — but you'd worry whenever she'd cross the street, and that took away the fun.

Then along came Judy Holliday, and the dumb blond was elevated and ennobled for all time. Others would carry on the tradition: Marilyn Monroe (and *her* imitators), Carol Channing, and Goldie Hawn. But Hol-

DOUGLAS MARSHALL *is a Los Angeles–based comedy writer and film critic, who has written extensively on Robert Redford and film composer David Raksin.*

liday set the standard by which they would all be judged.

Even at their daffiest, Holliday's actions carried pathos and vulnerability — a yearning quality that went right to your heart. Like all great comediennes, she was truly a great actress. Dumb blonds are, by definition, shallow; Judy gave them depth. She did it with right-on-the-money timing and attention to detail. She was a surpassingly intelligent woman (as was Monroe), and therein lies the clue: One has to be smart to play dumb. An ordinary starlet cast as a dumb blond would essentially play herself; a bright actress — like Judy or Marilyn — illuminates the character with her own sensibility.

After her success on the stage, Judy went to Hollywood, and at once became something of a pioneer: She was the first leading lady to be urban and ethnic. (Streisand would follow almost twenty years later.) Prior to her arrival, filmdom's leading actresses were WASP-ish, and ethnicity was relegated only to colorful supporting players. Holliday's looks and manner implied the very specific backgrounds of Billie Dawn, Doris Attinger (*Adam's Rib*, 1949), Florence Keefer (*The Marrying Kind,* 1952), and Gladys Glover (*It Should Happen to You,* 1954). All were young women who had grown up in Flatbush tenements during the Depression. When we see them in comic jousts, battling for upward mobility, we are not put off by their voraciousness. Rather, we are touched by their hunger for a better life. We love them for trying, and we wish them well.

Holliday's technique was clean and sure. Recall her virtuoso gin rummy game in *Born Yesterday*. It's a lengthy pantomime sequence — no dialogue, just two actors sitting across a card table. As Broderick Crawford puffs his stogie, Judy, in her best lounging pajamas, performs the card-cutting and dealing with ritualistic gravity and exactness. Her face reflects a concentration usually reserved for threading needles. There's a lull as Crawford contemplates his cards. Judy waits for him and hums — scats, actually — "I Can't Give You Anything But Love, Baby." Her rendition, delivered in piercing pitch, embraces not only the melody but the entire orchestration, complete with trumpet runs and rim shots. Her serenade takes its toll. He bellows at her to shut up. She looks back evenly. A beat. She pats her hair with hauteur, discards, takes a new card. As he is about to do likewise, she croaks "gin," and slams her cards down on the table. The game continues for two rounds. In dealing the cards, rummaging through her hand, her rhythms, attacks, and hesitations have the sharp control of a ballet. Ever in command as her opponent fumes (the cards just aren't on his side), she trounces him.

Perhaps her finest moments were in *The Marrying Kind*, the bittersweet saga of a blue-collar marriage. As an urban housewife, she hits highs and lows — from giddiness (the courtship, the honeymoon) to disconsolation (the death of her son and subsequent disintegration of her marriage). The film's harrowing and unforgettable

At her peak in The Marrying Kind. *With Aldo Ray.*

sequence is the Decoration Day picnic. Judy and her husband (Aldo Ray) are seated on a blanket in a park. Their little girl is with them and their son Joey has just gone off to the nearby pond to go swimming with friends. The family is blissful as they extol the pleasures of sunshine and open air.

While the husband naps, Holliday takes a ukulele from the picnic basket. After the obligatory "my dog has fleas" tune-up, she begins strumming and singing a winsomely inane song, "How I Love the Kisses of Delores." As the song continues we notice people in the background running past the family. Judy is oblivious. A little boy, terrified, gasping, runs up and cries: "Joey, he . . . he's . . . ." "Joey's swimming," Holliday replies. "He's drowning!" cries the boy. Holliday and Ray react with horror, then race down to the pond, where a crowd has gathered along the marsh. As Ray charges into the water to retrieve the dead child, we see Holliday on the shore, screaming the boy's name over the hubbub of the onlookers.

The scene dissolves to a judge's office (the picnic had been a flashback), where Holliday has just retold the incident to the judge. She's sobbing and beating her fists on the desk. Stunningly directed by George Cukor, her quicksilver shift from sunniness to hysteria is chilling.

The accuracy and conviction of her performances could make one assume that Holliday was just like the characters she played — that she was simply being herself. But she was nothing like her dizzy, raucous ladies. She was a quiet, introspective woman — and something of an egghead. She had an IQ of 172, and was addicted to double-crostics and intricate word games (her highest Scrabble score was a phenomenal 825!). Her knowledge of classical music was encyclopedic; volumes on psychology and philosophy were light reading to her. Her normal voice was soft and modulated, without a trace of her native New York. She loved refinishing antiques.

Despite the apparent ease and naturalness of her work, Holliday was a hard-driving technician, never satisfied, always questioning her mastery of a scene. Colleagues in the theater remember her as a merciless self-critic and perfectionist, given to retreating to her dressing room in sobs if she believed she'd not done her best. For two of her motion pictures, she viewed her completed screen footage, deemed her performance inadequate, her appearance unattractive, and tearfully vol-

unteered to buy her way out of the film and reimburse the studio for any expense. Both times the producer prevailed and she agreed to finish, but her insecurities remained unabated to the last.

We'll never be privileged to see her Amanda in *The Glass Menagerie*, her Juno in *Juno and the Paycock*, her *Mother Courage*, or any vehicles written just for her, like Florence in *The Marrying Kind*, that would utilize her beautiful gifts. We lost her far too soon.

New York theater people still speak of the crowds that would collect outside the stage door after her performance in *Bells Are Ringing*. Not your standard swarm of gawkers and palpitating celebrity freaks, but polite, patient, middle-class couples who stayed behind after the show, not for autographs, but simply to say goodnight.

A dumb blond smart enough to take on the big shots. In The Solid Gold Cadillac *she challenges Paul Douglas.*

JERRY LEWIS: ENERGETIC MADNESS

JANE STERN

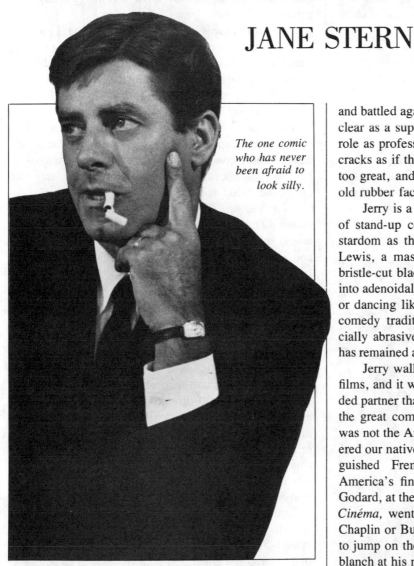

The one comic who has never been afraid to look silly.

FEW PEOPLE CAN REMAIN NEUTRAL about Jerry Lewis. You love him or you hate him, or you love him *and* you hate him. If you expect him to act like a juvenile retardate, he comes on sincere and intellectual. Expect him to be serious, and you get Jerry the clown. Lewis, like an adolescent, has rejoiced in the role of the mischievous goofball and alternately raged

and battled against it. He periodically comes on loud and clear as a super-man, in his annual telethon, and in his role as professor at U.S.C. Just as routinely, the image cracks as if the strain of holding this shining maturity is too great, and a grimace or whining shriek contorts the old rubber face into the familiar infantile mask.

Jerry is a mutant outgrowth of that breeding ground of stand-up comics, the Borscht Belt. He rocketed to stardom as the frantic half of the team of Martin and Lewis, a mass of energy from his white socks to his bristle-cut black hair. When he wasn't twisting his face into adenoidal frenzy, he was walking, talking, hopping, or dancing like a spastic child. He was, in the musical comedy tradition, a perpetual juvenile — of an especially abrasive sort. He was "the kid," a persona that has remained as part of his repertoire past the age of fifty.

Jerry walked knock-kneed through his early days in films, and it wasn't until Jerry Lewis shed his heavy-lidded partner that he was recognized, at least in Europe, as the great comic he always knew he was. Ironically, it was not the American critics but the French who discovered our native treasure. For instance, *Positif,* the distinguished French film publication, proclaimed him America's finest comedian since the silents. Jean-Luc Godard, at the time an editor of the influential *Cahiers du Cinéma,* went one better, rating him better than Charles Chaplin or Buster Keaton. But American critics refused to jump on the bandwagon, and today, they continue to blanch at his name on a marquee. Jerry Lewis has maintained his status as a major personality of the show biz world, despite the lack of support from the American press.

This complex man, candidate for sanctimonious sainthood, part innovative genius, is, for certain, a uniquely American phenomenon.

He was born Joseph Levitch in Newark, New Jersey, on March 16, 1926. He was the only child of show people. Sometimes the young child accompanied them on the road, often changing schools before the teacher learned his name. "Thirty times in two years," he reports. Usually he was left in the care of his grandmother.

JANE STERN *is the author of* Trucker: A Portrait of the Last American Cowboy *and is coauthor of* Amazing America *and* Roadfood.

She was his favorite, and Lewis states that it was after her traumatic death (he was eleven) that he started to "clown around to get attention." His formal education ended during the first year of high school, when he punched a teacher in the face for slinging an anti-Semitic remark his way.

At this time he made a meager living playing clubs. His act consisted of lip-synching to a phonograph playing an opera offstage, a *shtick* he carried with him throughout his career. It was at the Glass Hat Club in New York City that Martin and Lewis first met. It was the summer of 1946. Polar opposites, they excited audiences and rapidly became the most popular comedy team since Weber and Fields. "I was attracted to Dean almost immediately," Jerry said. "I thought of him as the big brother I never had. Where I was weak, he seemed to be strong. . . . I didn't feel alone and frightened when I was with him. So we teamed up."

Television — Las Vegas — Hollywood. Martin and Lewis could do no wrong. They made sixteen movies together, none of which captured the razor-edged tension that characterized their volatile act. Among the

You're Never Too Young. *With Dean Martin, he was always "the kid."*

best of these films, however, were those directed by Frank Tashlin. Both *Artists and Models* (1955) and *Hollywood or Bust* (1956) capitalize on the natural antagonism between the two stars, and in the latter film Tashlin allowed Lewis to rise above his stylized hollers and mugging. Lewis' work in this film moved one reviewer to call it "the myth of the man-child in a devouring plastic world." One of the elements of that world that threatened to devour Jerry was his worldly-wise partner.

The differences that made Martin and Lewis so popular were also the grounds for their inevitable, cataclysmic separation. Lewis remembers a vividly disturbing tableau from his youth, in which he was wandering the dark streets looking for his mother. He found her — working as a cocktail waitress in a seedy bar. "Ever since then," he confesses, "if I see a drunk, I want to throw up." Martin's famous boozing and laziness certainly contributed to the end of the relationship, but more significant was his reluctance to let Jerry step out of the "kid" role.

The kid finally became a teenager in his first solo picture, *The Delicate Delinquent* (1957). This was released two years after *Rebel Without a Cause* (1955), and it is worth noting that the development of Jerry Lewis' neurotic, misfit, insecure image during the 1950s runs parallel to straight and serious versions of essentially the same image — in James Dean and Paul Newman. It was a decade of insecurity; what James Dean was able to express in his adolescent slouch and tortured sneer, Jerry conveyed by falling flat on his face. With his methods radically different from the matinee idols, Jerry Lewis became the anti-hero of comedy.

It was in his self-directed films that he explored the enigma of his own paradoxical personality by giving himself complex roles that often revealed contradictory or negative aspects of the Jerry Lewis phenomenon. Characteristically, it was French film critics in particular who responded to his directorial artistry, to his self-analysis, and to his place in the classical American comic tradition.

He first directed himself in *The Bellboy* in 1960. What is fascinating about it is the appearance in the film of a character named Jerry Lewis — a great and successful movie star. This great man stands in marked contrast to Stanley the Bellboy (also played by Jerry Lewis). With this dual role, Jerry Lewis introduced the major theme of his own films, and the puzzle that would characterize the rest of his career: Which is the real Jerry Lewis?

His films are filled with multiple characters, all played by him. The sight gags and slapstick humor that one expects in screen comedies are incorporated into uncomfortable stories about split or fragmented personalities, all of which focus on the hero's deterioration, his inability to keep his mask on.

☞ Jerry's a mousey chemistry prof who invents the greatest new drink since Dracula discovered bloody marys.

PARAMOUNT PICTURES presents **JERRY LEWIS** as "THE **NUTTY** PROFESSOR" (A Jerry Lewis Production)

☞ ☞ **What does he become? What kind of monster?** ☞ ☞

TECHNICOLOR

CO-STARRING **STELLA STEVENS** · DEL MOORE · KATHLEEN FREEMAN · PRODUCED BY ERNEST D. GLUCKSMAN · WRITTEN BY JERRY LEWIS and BILL RICHMOND · DIRECTED BY JERRY LEWIS

A comic version of Jekyll and Hyde.

This schizophrenic dilemma reaches a zenith in Lewis' best film, *The Nutty Professor* (1963), in which Jerry plays the meek Professor Kelp, hopelessly in love with a beautiful student, Stella (Stella Stevens). He concocts a potion that transforms him into a suave and debonair swinger — the monstrously unctuous Buddy Love. Kelp's problem is that the potion wears off at awkward moments, allowing the professor's ridiculous personality to intrude, invariably at a seductive moment with Stevens. Addicted to his own formula, Kelp finally breaks down in a comic nightmare scene in which both personalities deteriorate and mesh. Lewis allows his audience to witness this brutal confession, in which Kelp/Love stands before a gymnasium filled with students and admits his deceit and humiliation.

It is easy to pin the Dean Martin label on all the slick, boozy alter egos Lewis assumes, but like everything else about this complex man, easy answers seldom explain him away! Even the most devoted Jerry Lewis followers can be repelled by his maudlin sentimentality, and even his staunchest foes find it hard to suppress a laugh when confronted by his mastery of comic timing and sight gags.

Jerry Lewis is best known today not so much for his films, but for the annual telethon that brings us all a twenty-four-hour dose of his sincerity each year. He is a

devoted person — to his cause, to his wife and six sons, who have miraculously survived the pressures of Hollywood. He is devoted to his class at U.S.C., and he is devoted to exploring the fascinating and perplexing phenomenon known as Jerry Lewis. He is devoted as well to bringing his latest film — his first "serious" effort — to the public. Hung up in legal battles for over two years, *The Day the Clown Cried* is the story of a clown who led the children in Nazi concentration camps into the gas chambers. Like all Jerry Lewis projects, it has the potential for greatness, for sentiment, for tastelessness. But one easy guess is that it will combine all these elements into something that is extraordinarily Jerry Lewis.

With Kathleen Freeman. It is important to Lewis that he is physically the weakest person in his films.

WOODY ALLEN: THE NEUROTIC PHILOSOPHER

TONY ROBERTS

Ready to face the world.

THE THING ABOUT WOODY ALLEN is that he always surprises you. Just when you've got him pegged as the guy who's got everything figured out, he ups and admits that he's totally baffled by problems that the rest of us have long ago accepted as part of our lot and given up worrying about. For instance, he says to me one afternoon in some obscure Chinese restaurant, "Max, how is it possible to conceive of a world in which nothing exists?"

"Pass the duck sauce."

"Not until you answer my question. How is it possible to think that at one time, way back in the beginning, there was nothing. It doesn't make sense. There's no such thing as nothing. Even God had to come from something, right?"

I am afraid to answer. If I agree with him he will find another idea that I can't understand. And if I disagree, he'll ask me to elaborate. Meanwhile, my spareribs are getting cold. "Max," I say to him "why don't you stop worrying about it? It's not going to do you any good to figure it out either way because it can't be figured out!" And I can see that I've ruined his appetite.

Woody Allen is a philosopher. As far as I know, no one has ever called him that before and it may be the only thing they haven't called him. It's not just that he reads Kierkegaard the way the rest of us pick up *New York* magazine, it's that he actually lives most of his life acutely aware of the basic facts and realities of his existence — and ours too, for that matter. Most of us find ways to avoid thinking about our inevitable end and skirt

TONY ROBERTS *starred in the stage versions of two Woody Allen plays,* Don't Drink the Water *and* Play It Again, Sam. *His movie credits include* Serpico *and two Woody Allen films,* Play It Again, Sam *and* Annie Hall. *He was the star of the television series* Rossetti and Ryan.

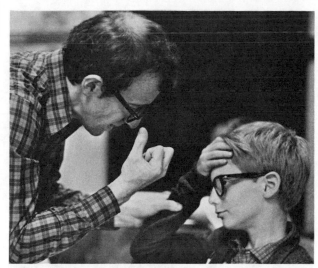

Allen always reminds viewers that they are watching a movie — and not real life. In Annie Hall, *during a flashback sequence, Alvie Singer interrupts the actor playing him as a boy to give instruction.*

the whole issue of death. We construct a framework for our lives which pretends to foreverness, permanence, immortality, worth, merit, value. We think it's morbid, or at least "uncivilized," to be reminded so often of our own fragile existence. But Woody uses his cognizance of man's finitude as a beginning: a jumping-off point from which to seize life and make the most of it. Relaxation, as most of us think of it, is cosmic waste to Woody, which accounts for his prolific output in all sorts of areas. It's not that he doesn't know how to stop, it's that he doesn't *want* to stop. To stop would mean to be less than what he can be, and that for him is the only great sin. It's experience itself that he respects, and his interests are as varied and as avidly pursued as any three people I have ever known. He will tell you the box scores of certain basketball games between two teams that only a handful of sports fans in New York could possibly care about. He will tell you anything that was ever printed in *Ring* magazine (a publication about boxing), who is currently hitting over .300 in each baseball league, what the best films to see will be before they're shown at the New York Film Festival, what plays and performances are worth watching on and off Broadway, which article was noteworthy in last Sunday's *Times,* which galleries along Madison Avenue to stay out of, where the best French provincial furniture is to be found, what makes an Oriental rug different from a Persian, who has the scoop on the real story behind closed doors in Washington and New York's city hall, and why Sibelius is more sublime than Shostakovich. All this he somehow makes seem peripheral to his major endeavors, i.e., the writing, directing, acting, journalizing, essaying, and performing of his own inventions.

Relaxing for Woody is drinking an Orange Julius in his dressing room between acts, or beating the luggage lines at airports by traveling with only carry-on luggage no matter where he's going or for how long. Relaxing is throwing a softball in Central Park, or shooting baskets in a schoolyard, as long as there aren't too many guys around who care who he is. It's practicing his clarinet, which he does faithfully every day for an hour or more. Sound busy? Perhaps. But if you're alive enough to know the frailty of things, there is no other way. The only limitations are those we set for ourselves. Woody Allen is an intellectual Auntie Mame. He has the same joy of discovery, of seeking out, of expanding his horizons. Just don't expect to get the duck sauce when he asks you about "cosmic nothingness."

In a park with Janet Margolin in Take the Money and Run. *Allen's characters always take the women they are courting for a walk in the park. How similar are Allen's characters to Woody Allen? An actress friend tells me that on the one afternoon she spent alone with Woody Allen, he took her for a stroll through Central Park. Several weeks later she ran into Allen and another woman as they were taking the same stroll through the park.*

— *Danny Peary*

While most stars' characters try to imitate Bogart, Allen's idolize him.

In The Nutty Professor, *a serum turned Jerry Lewis into a great lover. Allen's results with a serum were less impressive.*

THE MATURATION OF WOODY ALLEN

THE FIRST TIME I ever worked for Woody Allen was as an actor in the first play he wrote for Broadway, *Don't Drink the Water*. He never performed in the play himself, but at some point during the out-of-town tryout he made a brief attempt to take over the directing chores until a more experienced stager could be found for the job.

I remember that he demonstrated the most hilarious piece of business for me that I have ever seen, but that I could never manage to bring off properly. Over and over again he would lean casually on one arm of a sofa in an attempt to seem debonair for some alluring ingenue. Then he would lose his grip and disappear from sight as he fell to the floor behind the couch. Each time it was perfect. Each time I marveled at his grace, his timing, his talent. It never did work for me, and it is significant, I think, that he realized that and didn't try to force me into it. Neither did he fire me. On the contrary, two years later when he wrote *Play It Again, Sam*, he asked me to be in it.

He was adaptable, and that is one of the rarest gifts a playwright can possess. He knew what worked and what didn't. There are writers who refuse to edit, refuse to rewrite, refuse to cut — even when the audience tells them they're bored, restless, tired, and so forth. They seem to want to force something on those poor captive souls who have already emptied their wallets and subjected themselves to God knows what. But not Woody.

He once told me during the run of *Don't Drink the Water* that his sole ambition at that time was to reduce an entire theaterful of people to such an intense level of hysterical laughter that they would beg for the play to stop in order to catch their breaths. He was even sorry that there had to be straight lines, because that meant people would have to stop laughing for a moment in order to hear the next setup.

I think he has changed his aspirations somewhat since then, but his desire to dazzle, entertain, make contact is still just as real. Making people laugh is his way of making contact with them, and I think it's important to understand that as a prime motivating factor in any serious discussion of his work. He is never "on" in a room the way most comedians are driven to be. I'm not sure he ever really enjoyed performing his "act" all that much. But by cloaking himself behind his screen character (an invention of neurotic complexities often compared to Chaplin's little fellow with the cane) or, better still, as the author-director of a carefully controlled progression of images paraded before an audience without his actual presence even required, he is able to perform his real magic. His films work because they are the perfect expression of his need to reach out to people and tell them what's in his heart and mind. And more and more it is his heart that is speaking, which accounts for the sentiment in *Annie Hall*.

The point I'm trying to make is simply that as an artist he has grown from the days I first knew him, when his only message was to effect sidesplitting reactions, to the more complex and personal identification his films evoke in audiences today. As a natural resource he is invaluable because his need to share his thoughts and feelings with the world will never diminish. And as he continues to grow, audiences will continue to reap the benefits of that growth. How lucky for everyone!

— T. R.

WOODY'S WIT

SOMEONE ONCE SAID that wit was the ability to make a connection between two, or more, seemingly unrelated bits of information. Since everyone who has ever had a by-line has interviewed Woody Allen, and praised him for his wit, perhaps I can make a contribution to the abundance of material already written about him by relating a story of personal remembrance which demonstrates the way Mr. A.'s wit can sometimes work.

I had invited Woody and Diane Keaton to spend a weekend with me at a new house I was about to purchase in Ocean Beach, Fire Island. It was one of Woody's rare ventures out of New York City, and he tolerated the sun and sand for an entire day and a half before fleeing by seaplane back to his apartment in Manhattan. He arrived Friday evening with one large valise, almost impossible to lift off the ground and filled entirely with medicines of various sorts. Should some incident require it, he had remedies with him for everything from snakebite to malaria. He didn't like being caught off guard.

He did make a pilgrimage to the beach on Saturday afternoon after spending the better part of the day in bed (which happened to be the living room couch), reading the newspapers. His entrance into the Atlantic Ocean is superseded in my recollection only by the vivid memory of James Mason walking into the Pacific in *A Star Is Born*. Woody wore a white bathing cap for a disguise and disappeared into the foam, arms flailing, while the rest of us held our sides with laughter on the shore. He is a good sport.

On Sunday I left the house early for the mainland in order to sign the closing papers for my new house. Anyone who has ever bought a house knows that a certain ceremonial importance accompanies any "closing," and mine was no exception. My lawyer was a man named Arthur Silsdorf, and I mentioned this to Woody in passing and apologized for having to be absent for the better part of the afternoon. The name struck Woody funny, for some reason, and when I returned to the house I discovered that my guests had left a note on the door which read as follows: "Max — Urgent. Don't sign anything. Silsdorf is an imposter and has arranged everything as a trick to get your money. Love, Max."

I giggled to myself and enjoyed the gag, having just put my John Hancock on no less than twelve dotted lines.

A year later I had occasion to ask Woody for some advice. I was having marital problems and was seeking the name of a good psychiatrist. Woody, as always, could be very helpful in this area and suggested a Dr. Herman Kleindienst. I never actually made contact with Dr. Kleindienst, but a few days later I opened in a Broadway play and received the following wire: "Max — Stop Everything; Silsdorf is Kleindienst."

That's wit! — T. R.

The Academy Award-winning Annie Hall. *Woody Allen, Tony Roberts, and Diane Keaton.*

THE HOLLYWOOD CANTEEN

WOODY ALLEN'S CHARACTERS spend a lot of their time around food. In *Play It Again, Sam* (Top, L) he ran into wife Susan Anspach while grocery shopping; in the same film (Bottom, L) he demonstrated, for Diane Keaton (back to camera), Tony Roberts, and Jennifer Salt, the art of shoveling down Chinese food. In *What's New Pussycat?* (Top, R), Allen feasted in front of Peter Sellers. And in *Love and Death* (Bottom, R) the impoverished Allen and Diane Keaton had snow for dinner.

THE ENTERTAINERS

AL JOLSON: CROWD PLEASER

HENRY LEVIN

A L JOLSON WAS NEVER really an actor. He could play only one part: Al Jolson. But as an entertainer, ah, it is difficult to imagine anyone greater.

"Jolie" was born to sing. His father was a cantor, and his voice was his gift to his son. But the singing was not enough to young Jolson; he needed an audience: beaming faces, clapping hands, smiling eyes were everything to him. I'm certain that his divorced wife and his widow would both attest to that — Jolson demanded the adulation of an audience. His ego was such that when he heard applause for another star, he reacted as though he had been robbed. All the applause in the world belonged to him.

This feeling was probably responsible for his feelings about Larry Parks, who portrayed Jolson in *The Jolson Story* (1946) and also in *Jolson Sings Again* (1949). It wasn't that he didn't like Larry personally or admire him professionally, it was the fact that Larry was getting the attention up there on the screen portraying Jolson, who must have been frustrated that he wasn't up there playing himself.

During the filming of *The Jolson Story,* I witnessed a profoundly emotional scene. It was on the day the Winter Garden Theater scene was to be filmed in which Jolson (Larry Parks) was to bid farewell to a Broadway audience before leaving for the Coast by singing, at the end, "California, Here I Come." Jolson was there to

It was important for Warner Brothers to inaugurate sound films with a loud bang. Al Jolson in The Jazz Singer *was ideal.*

HENRY LEVIN *directed* Jolson Sings Again.

watch Parks perform the song Al had prerecorded. The set was enormous, duplicating the orchestra floor of the huge New York theater. Some eight or nine hundred extras were seated in the audience, many of whom had sat in real theaters watching Jolson shows over the years.

It took a long time to light the opening shot. Three cameras were being used, and it took the crew two hours to prepare the first long shot. It could have been a boring wait for that audience of extras. But Jolie took over. He came onto the stage and looked out at that captive audience. I'm certain, however, that none of them would have left even if they had been allowed to — not with Jolson up there in front of them. He started singing, and singing, and singing. Then he told stories and joked about the time it took to light the set. That audience laughed and cried and clapped their hands sore, enjoying every minute of Jolson's "turn," remembering with joy the hours they had listened to him.

A similar scene took place on the recording stage at Columbia Studios, during the sessions when we were preparing to start production on *Jolson Sings Again*. Jolson was prerecording the songs which would later be lip-synched by Larry Parks. During the intervals beween songs, when the sound engineers were involved in their technical procedures — repositioning microphones, reloading tape — the orchestra members did not leave the room as they would have done ordinarily. No, not with Jolson there, enthralling them with anecdotes drawn from years of entertaining. Again, an audience. Jolson could not resist one.

When the engineers were ready, another song was recorded, then played back. And after each playback, the orchestra applauded loudly — and sincerely, because Jolson was in great voice, possibly better than he had been in the twenties and thirties. This was in 1948, and Jolie was nearly sixty-five years old.

Jolson with Ruby Keeler in the 1935 film Go Into Your Dance. *They had married in 1928.*

NANCY CARROLL: FIRST STAR OF THE TALKIES

JOHN SPRINGER

Once the queen of the Hollywood musical.

S HE WAS THE FIRST star created in the new talking-picture medium.

She led the polls of the time as the most popular girl on the screen.

She was number one in the first wave of movie musicals.

She was nominated for an Academy Award for her first dramatic role.

She was washed up in the film industry within five years.

JOHN SPRINGER *is the publicist for such movie stars as Myrna Loy, Henry Fonda, Sylvia Sidney, Elizabeth Taylor, Sophia Loren, and Liv Ullmann. He was the coordinator of the historical guest-appearance series "Legendary Ladies of the Movies."*

Nancy Carroll's Hollywood discovery is classic. Anne Nichols, author of the long-running stage play *Abie's Irish Rose,* happened to be at the Paramount gate when she noticed an unmistakably Irish beauty, blowing her redheaded top because the guard refused to let her through. Nichols knew she had found her Rose for the movie version of her play. It was quite a break for Carroll, whose single movie credit till then had been as a supporting player.

Abie's Irish Rose (1928) was conceived as a silent film, but when they decided to make it a sound picture, a song-and-dance number was added, and Nancy Carroll became the first woman ever to sing into a movie microphone and tap-dance on a sound stage. Playing opposite the popular Buddy Rogers, her impact was immediate. Audiences loved her. Movie magazines featured her on their covers. Paramount, realizing she was a hot property, awarded her the title role in *The Shopworn Angel* (1929), teaming her with another rising young star, Gary Cooper. This is a bittersweet drama about the unlikely romance of a naive soldier and a hard-as-nails chorine. A high spot is a sequence in which Carroll — knowing her soldier has been killed — dances and sings, as she's blinded by tears, "A Precious Little Thing Called Love." Critic Walter Kerr still regards Carroll's performance in this movie as a model of film acting. It won her the important lead in *The Dance of Life* (1929).

Nancy Carroll was an accomplished dancer also capable of singing in a funny, cooing, but wholly charming voice. She was the natural choice to star in the "all talking, all singing, all dancing" movies that were the vogue of the late twenties. By the thirties, she had established herself as the most popular woman on the screen. Unlike most of the major female stars of the period, she was neither a holdover from the silent era (Janet Gaynor, Joan Crawford, Norma Shearer, Marion Davies, Greta Garbo), nor a former star of the stage

With Fredric March in Laughter, *her big success.*   *With Fredric March (R) and Alan Hale in* The Night Angel, *her big flop.*

(Claudette Colbert, Ruth Chatterton, and Ann Harding).

Carroll's only non-musical of this period was *Dangerous Paradise* (1930), a melodramatic version of Joseph Conrad's *Victory*. Then came her outstanding dramatic pictures.

The Devil's Holiday (1930) was originally planned for Jeanne Eagels. But after Eagels' death someone remembered Carroll's strong dramatic performances in *The Shopworn Angel* and *The Dance of Life.*

IRISH ROSE

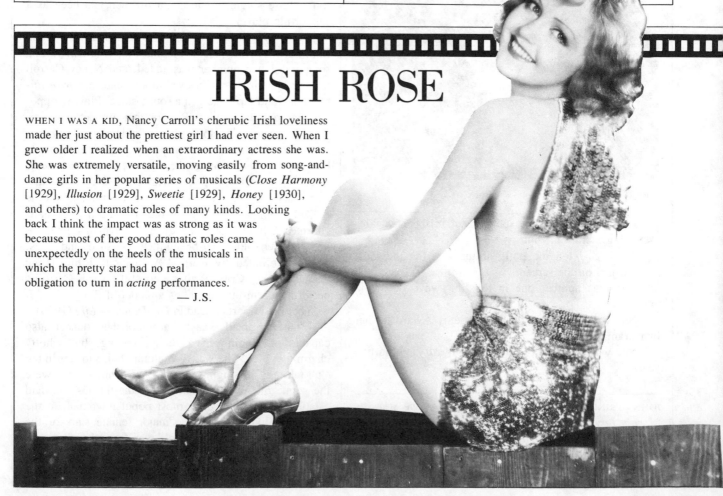

WHEN I WAS A KID, Nancy Carroll's cherubic Irish loveliness made her just about the prettiest girl I had ever seen. When I grew older I realized when an extraordinary actress she was. She was extremely versatile, moving easily from song-and-dance girls in her popular series of musicals (*Close Harmony* [1929], *Illusion* [1929], *Sweetie* [1929], *Honey* [1930], and others) to dramatic roles of many kinds. Looking back I think the impact was as strong as it was because most of her good dramatic roles came unexpectedly on the heels of the musicals in which the pretty star had no real obligation to turn in *acting* performances.

— J.S.

"America's Sweetie" (as Carroll was known) in a dramatic role meant for Eagels? Her performance was so vivid that she came out second to Norma Shearer in the Academy Award balloting for Best Actress. (Runners-up were announced back then.)

Even more memorable was Carroll's brilliant performance in Donald Ogden Stewart's *Laughter* (1930), one of the earliest of the sophisticated movie comedies. She was less triumphant, but still worthy, in George Abbott's *Stolen Heaven* (1931), a rather implausible but affecting drama about a street girl and a thief who use stolen money to finance an idyllic holiday.

Then everything went wrong, for a number of reasons: a bad case of temperament; unhappiness in private life; an unfriendly press and an incredibly bad picture called *The Night Angel* (1931). Without the last, the other causes might have been surmounted. But *The Night Angel* and the pictures that followed lowered Carroll's box-office appeal. And the other problems played havoc with what was left of her popularity.

The Irish temper that had attracted Anne Nichols helped put the seal on her career. It wasn't the calculated "queen-of-the-lot" temperament of a Gloria Swanson or Pola Negri, but the explosive kind — for which she usually apologized.

She insisted that her tantrums never hurt anyone, but

With Buddy Rogers, her co-star of many films.

they were widely publicized and hurt *her* badly. "I was going through some unhappy times," she said. Her seven-year marriage to playwright Jack Kirkland was breaking up, and after her 1931 divorce from Kirkland she would enter another unhappy marriage to magazine editor Bolton Mallory. (This ended in divorce in 1935.)

Carroll's unpopularity with the press was partially due to her refusal to cooperate with the studio publicity department. Among other things, she would not hide the fact that she had a small daughter named Patricia through her marriage to Kirkland. Stars — particularly youthful dream girls like Carroll — were supposed to keep children hidden. But Nancy was proud of her daughter and refused to play down her existence. (With Nancy's support, Patricia went on to become a successful Broadway and television actress in the fifties.)

And then there was *The Night Angel*. It had originally been planned for Dietrich, but because of the success of *Laughter,* Paramount decided to again team Carroll with Fredric March. She was atrociously miscast as a Magdalene of Prague, and the picture laid one of the biggest box-office eggs of its time.

And for Nancy Carroll, the years following were ones of mistakes, misfires, and missed opportunities. She would eventually leave Hollywood, only to return to make two films in the late thirties. She would have later success on stage and in television, but for Nancy Carroll and the movies, it was all over.

THE LATER YEARS

Nancy Carroll in 1965.

IN 1942, FRESH FROM COLLEGE and working as a fledgling newspaper and radio reporter, I had a chance to interview Nancy Carroll. She was every bit as pretty as I had expected, warm and friendly too, unlike some stars who would brush off a newspaperman of no particular distinction. I'd see her again over the next couple of years when, now in uniform, I did public relations for the Air Force show, "ATC Contact Caravan." Nancy Carroll made several appearances with the show along with Rita Hayworth, Madeleine Carroll, Marlene Dietrich, Danny Kaye, and others.

Back in New York, I'd see her often. She was usually a delightful, sparkling companion.

Over the years I shared her ups and downs, mourned with her when a hoped-for role fell through, was happy for a triumph. She talked much about her movie heyday and was unsparingly honest about the mistakes she'd made, never blaming anyone but herself. She was pleased when she read stories about Cary Grant and Gene Raymond, who both said how much they had learned from working with her. They praised her as an ultimate movie star.

★ ★ ★ ★ ★

In August, 1965, she phoned me in Los Angeles, where I was working on a film. She was doing *Never Too Late* in Nyack, New York, with Bert Lahr, and was enjoying it. She was also being considered by Hitchcock for an important role in his *Torn Curtain* (1966), and there was chance of a TV special with Lucille Ball. She couldn't have sounded more optimistic and cheerful.

We made a date for me to go to Nyack when I returned to New York the following Thursday. But the day proved sweltering, and the last thing I wanted to do was travel to Nyack. Besides, an urgent business matter had come up. I called, apologized, and promised to come Saturday night, the last night of the play's run. Nancy said that was fine — there would be a closing-night party and we'd celebrate after the performance.

Saturday morning I was awakened by friends. They told me Nancy Carroll was dead. She hadn't appeared for her Friday evening performance, and the management had notified her daughter. Patricia and her husband Don Bevan went to Nancy's East Side apartment and found her there, clad in a nightgown and slippers, kneeling before a flickering television set. The autopsy never really explained her death; "natural causes" was the official report.

The time of her death was Thursday night, shortly after Bert Lahr had dropped her off after the performance. Thursday night was the night I should have been with her.

It is still a wrenching memory.

— J. S.

BING CROSBY: CAREFREE CROONER

MARSHA HUNT

BING CROSBY was a constant in all our lives, a comfy, lighthearted presence steering a steady unruffled course through nearly five decades of shifting cultural fads. He was a cherished staple.

It was his talent that I loved. I knew him only slightly, but closely followed and appreciated his career. And when the news came that his life had ended my sense of loss, like millions of others, I suppose, was as sharp as for a family member.

There had been an earlier scare, in January 1974, when he was hospitalized in northern California. Obeying an impulse, I wrote to him (and received a charming, grateful reply). Rereading the carbon of my letter today, it seems appropriate to share it now, as merely one of uncounted recollections.

★ ★ ★ ★ ★

January 13, 1974

Dear Bing,

Possibly, no one has ever explained to you that "living legends" are not allowed to get sick. But since you are now, and are clearly in violation, you will please oblige all of us whose legend you are and shape up!

All the same, your indisposition has provided me with the excuse to indulge in something I've long wanted to do: Thank you for the large role you have played in my life.

It began for me, I guess, during the summer of 1931, when I was attending a girls' summer camp in the pine woods of Maine. Boyless until fall, we dreamed our dreams to the current love songs that poured forth from our portable phonographs. And it was your voice, singing your songs, that gave wings to my dreams. The next four years, while I was growing up and finishing school,

in New York, your singing became part of the fabric of my life.

We were a musical family, and during summers in Connecticut, my sister, young uncle, and I formed a vocal trio, performing Friday evenings over WICC, a

In Dixie.

MARSHA HUNT *is an actress whose career spans more than four decades. Her film credits include* Pride and Prejudice; Blossoms in the Dust; The Human Comedy; Raw Deal; Mary Ryan, Detective; *and* Johnny Got His Gun.

Famous W. C. Fields poker game in Mississippi. *This film was made in 1935 when Crosby's film career was beginning to take off.*

Bridgeport radio station. As trio song-scout, I'd hover over our radio, memorizing tunes and scribbling down lyrics for us to perform. Your songs: "Old Ox Road," "Just One More Chance," "It Must Be True," "My Silent Love," "I Surrender Dear," "Lazy Bones." To this day, I haven't forgotten a single lyric.

And suddenly I was seventeen, it was the summer of 1935, and there I was under contract to Paramount — your studio! Sometimes I would haunt your set, dis-

creetly, to watch you work. I saw a parade of pretty girls play opposite you, but alas, we never did work together. I was in one musical there, but it was one of the few Paramount made without you. Once I came close —

East Side of Heaven. *Crosby's movie popularity helped his record sales.*

Hope and Crosby were the two dominant box office actors of the forties, and they both worked at Paramount. Between 1940 and 1962, they would make the studio a fortune with their seven "Road" pictures.

As Father O'Malley in Going My Way. *With Barry Fitzgerald, Rise Stevens, and Frank McHugh.*

Rhythm on the Range [1936] — but Frances Farmer beat me out in a close finish. Still we did meet a few times, and you would greet me when we passed on the lot. Once I sang a charming cowboy lullaby for you, which a cowhand had written and asked me to show you. You were most kind about it, and even about my singing.

I heard nearly every Kraft Music Hall you ever did, delighting in the style of speaking you developed. It was a self-kidding form of articulation, which made use of a wider vocabulary than one usually heard in show business. You were thoroughly clever and sneaky about it. There was always an implied "Get *me*, would you!" as you unfurled some polysyllabic gambit, but all the while, you were bringing a welcome tone of savoir faire to your entertainment, and treating the public as if they might just be intelligent, too.

As to your much-touted and still-imitated casualness — hard-won, I happen to know — it always carried validity, from the "Road" romps through *Going My Way* [1944] and *The Country Girl* [1954]. You made us cry just as hard as Garbo did. And no one made us laugh more delightedly. Whatever you did, you accomplished it with your own particular style and grace. Even now, your occasional forays into television remind us what true professionalism really is. I guess it could all be summed up as "class."

But in my eyes, you were never classier than when, in 1960, I wrote asking you to take part in a documentary film I was making to salute the United Nations' World Refugee Year. It was my own project, I had no financing, production company, title, secretary, or even letterhead. So I wrote you merely about the need, and the film that I hoped would bring some public awareness and response to it. The next thing I knew, it was you on the phone saying simply, "Sounds pretty good — dark blue suit all right?" Not a query about auspices, or when and where the film would be shown, what other stars would be appearing — none of that. It was hard not to sniffle

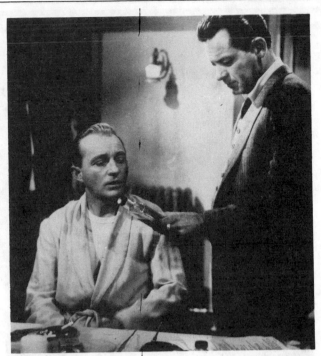

As an alcholic ex-star trying to make a comeback in The Country Girl *with William Holden.*

my gratitude over the phone, and not to hug you on sight when you came to do your spot. Perhaps I never told you, that program became the chief public informational and fund-raising device on behalf of refugees, and played on more then fifty channels throughout America. And yours was my favorite spot, by far the most moving.

For all of the above, I thank you. And since starting this, the news is that you're resting comfortably, and due for a short rest-up, before being fit as ever. That's the best news of 1974. And I'm glad to have unburdened this, while you're still a captive audience in a hospital.

Health, and long life, dear Bing.

Marsha Hunt Presnell

Crosby and Grace Kelly sang "True Love" in High Society.

GINGER ROGERS: UP FROM THE CHORUS

ALLAN SCOTT

A star — with or without Astaire.

I HAVE ALWAYS BEEN mystified by what makes a star. Lots of actresses were as versatile as Ginger Rogers, and could play as many different parts as she — flappers, nightclub entertainers, white-collar girls, even murderesses. Certainly others could act as well. And lots of actresses were as beautiful, too. But the camera had a love affair with Ginger.

ALLAN SCOTT *wrote many films that starred Ginger Rogers*: Top Hat, Roberta, In Person, Follow the Fleet, Swing Time, Shall We Dance, Carefree, Fifth Avenue Girl, *and* The Primrose Path.

I signed with RKO just as the older stars, such as Ann Harding and Constance Bennett, were in decline; Katharine Hepburn had just smashed through with "A Bill of Divorcement," and Ginger was emerging. They were in the middle of shooting *The Gay Divorcee* (1934) when I met her, a warm, friendly, vivacious girl, with a lissome figure and a Clara Bow mouth. I watched her grow to stardom.

Everybody knows that she began by winning a Charleston contest in Texas. Then, almost immediately, she played vaudeville, which led finally to Broadway, then to Hollywood.

She was always accompanied by her mother Leila Rogers. Leila (or "Lee-Lee," as Ginger called her) was not a run-of-the-mill stage mother. She'd been a professional herself and had written silent pictures. She was Ginger's counselor, traveling companion, and friend. In addition, she acted as Ginger's press agent and acting agent — and it was she who got Ginger jobs during her first years in Hollywood. Finally, after a very rough period, Ginger landed an ordinary player's contract at RKO. With her chameleon-like personality, she didn't know who she was. Was she going to continue playing flappers or wise-cracking blonds? She once told me she even thought of trying to be a Mae West type. Nevertheless, she remained dedicated to anything that allowed her to act and work.

Almost by accident (she replaced someone else) Ginger became Fred Astaire's partner in *Flying Down to Rio* (1933). The eventually famous duo were billed fifth behind Dolores Del Rio. The picture is a potpourri of gags and nonsense (at one point girls dance on the wing of a plane in flight), but toward the end of it, Fred and Ginger suddenly dance "The Carioca." That dance, although Ginger didn't realize it at the time, was her first big break. They caught on. Shrewdly, Pandro Berman, the executive producer at RKO, bought *The Gay Divorcee* for them, and their popularity was confirmed.

When I finished my draft of *Top Hat* (1935), the first of six Astaire-Rogers films I worked on (there were ten in all), Katharine Hepburn slipped into my office

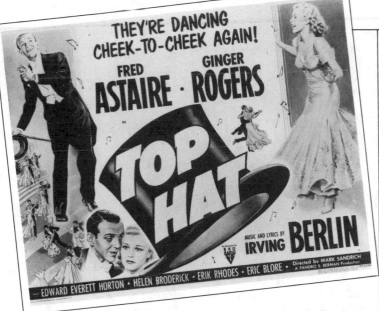

THEY'RE DANCING
CHEEK-TO-CHEEK AGAIN!

FRED   GINGER
ASTAIRE · ROGERS

IN

TOP
HAT

MUSIC AND LYRICS BY
IRVING BERLIN

EDWARD EVERETT HORTON · HELEN BRODERICK · ERIK RHODES · ERIC BLORE

Directed by MARK SANDRICH
A PANDRO S. BERMAN Production

"A modern fairy tale, far from the reality of the Great Depression." — A. S.

after reading the script and uttered the line, "She gives him sex, and he gives her class. They're doubly lucky in finding each other." It was not said in a bitchy way, but as an astute and accurate statement of the facts. Fred and Ginger made stars of each other, they needed each other. His Pierrot face played perfectly against her youth, good looks, and natural grace. With Ginger, Fred became a leading man in his own way, as attractive and sexy as Gable or Cary Grant — but *he* made love with his dancing. (People used to say she faked her dancing, that she used long gowns to cover her inability. Those are slanderous remarks. With her lithe body — her tennis game attests to that even today — she could have followed him to the ends of the earth.)

Yet as I got to know her better, I realized her all-embracing ambition was to play straight or dramatic roles. She was determined, and if there was occasionally no steel in her makeup, Leila provided her with it. Ginger was a bit annoyed that the roles she wanted were going to other actresses, even stars imported from other studios. So, one day she began to make her desires known in her own way. Two or three weeks after *Top Hat* had become a big hit, she came into my office carrying a tear sheet of a magazine story by Samuel Hopkins Adams (the author of *It Happened One Night*). It was an amusing story called "In Person," about a successful actress afflicted with agoraphobia who flees to a rural community, where she falls in love. I liked it well enough, I told her; so she said, "Let's go see Pan about it now." I objected to such a direct approach, but arm in arm we went to Berman's office.

Her excitement was infectious, so when Pan said, "I'll get a synopsis," Ginger stopped him. "No," she said, "let Allan tell it to you." So I did, as briefly as possible. Halfway through, Pandro threw up his arms and said, "Look, if you kids want to make this, go ahead." And we did. (We managed to get George Brent, and the picture was a mild success.) Perhaps it was this very dedication and determination that caused her many marriages to end in divorce; her career always came first.

The Gay Divorcee has the usual Astaire-Rogers courtship scene in which Astaire is brash and Rogers aloof.

Lucille Ball is between Rogers and Hepburn in Stage Door.

Very witty in Lucky Partners *with Ronald Colman.*

By this time, there was almost open warfare between Katharine Hepburn and Ginger. They were terribly jealous of each other. Nevertheless, after Ginger's first solo performance, Pandro (characteristically) decided to co-star Ginger with Katharine in *Stage Door* (1937), the play by George S. Kaufman and Edna Ferber, directed by Gregory La Cava. (The big joke among the writers was that only one line from the original play was used.) Unintimidated by Hepburn's presence, Ginger thrived.

In her later films, she made all her performances look as her dances with Freddie had — casual, easy, so natural that they seemed impromptu — an effect only a skilled technician can accomplish. In 1938, when she

Carefree

and Fred made *Carefree*, Ginger — not Fred, as always before — dominated the picture. She was poised, elegant, funny, and sure of herself. And thus, she began her climb to the top without Freddie.

She played opposite Jimmy Stewart in *Vivacious Lady* (1938). Then came *Having a Wonderful Time* (1938) with Doug Fairbanks, Jr., and *Bachelor Mother* (1939). Then, La Cava starred her in *Fifth Avenue Girl* (1939), an original of mine. Her next picture of consequence was *The Primrose Path* (1940), a play about a

Ginger Rogers won an Oscar as a working-class heroine in Kitty Foyle.

prostitute by Brudner and Hart. Several films after that, she did *The Major and the Minor* (1942) with Billy Wilder, impersonating a pig-tailed youngster. As Billy once pointed out, this picture anticipated *Lolita* by some twenty years.

The last time I was professionally involved with Ginger Rogers was on *Lucky Partners* (1940). Despite her own stature, Ginger was awed by her co-star, Ronald Colman — with his reputation and his vibrant, cultivated voice and manner — as any little girl from Missouri would have been. Ginger had her share of humility, but she worked like hell on the picture, and when it was

Rogers replaced Judy Garland on The Barkleys of Broadway.

Chorus girls Rogers and Joan Blondell in Gold Diggers of 1933.

over, Colman said to me, "That young woman has made me work harder, just to hold my own, than I've done in the last ten years."

This was followed by *Kitty Foyle* (1940), Christopher Morley's best-selling novel. It was one of her greatest successes and won her the Academy Award for Best Actress. By this time, she was recognized as one of the best comediennes in the business, and she also had achieved her ambition of becoming a dramatic actress. She had reached the apogee of her career.

She followed Kitty Foyle with a very successful picture called *Tom, Dick, and Harry* (1941) and *Tales of Manhattan* (1942). Then, at Paramount, she played the part of a neurotic magazine editor in *Lady in the Dark* (1944), which Gertrude Lawrence had played in New York. She was miscast, and the picture limped along miserably. From that point on, although Ginger did many more pictures, her popularity began to wane. It got a shot in the arm when Leland Hayward managed to reunite her with Freddie for *The Barkleys of Broadway* (1949), but that boost lasted only a short time. More unimportant pictures followed. She played summer theaters, did revivals of old musicals in St. Louis and Chicago, played one of the "Dollies" in New York and *Mame* in England — and even took *Bell, Book and Candle* on the road.

After Leila died (she was in her late eighties), Ginger once again hit the road with her own act — four dancers and Ginger. She played nightclubs, cabarets, and dinner theaters all over the country; occasionally Las Vegas, occasionally TV spots. She's still a professional, still slim, still exuberant, still funny . . . still Ginger, enchanting all her fans who remember the glory days, as I do, after thirty-five years.

FRED ASTAIRE:
A TOUCH OF CLASS

BUD YORKIN

I DO NOT USE the word "genius" lightly, but it is fitting when discussing Fred Astaire.

Although I had seen his classic movie musicals of the thirties, forties, and fifties, I did not meet the famous dancer until 1957, when I was fortunate enough to be assigned to write, produce, and direct his initial television special, "An Evening with Fred Astaire." At that time, Fred was around sixty, and I was amazed by his stamina and how quickly he got into perfect condition for his rigorous activities each day. Often I would come to the rehearsal hall at eight in the morning, only to find him already there limbering up, doing stretching exercises, preparing himself for the arrival of his back-up dancers. He was always in tip-top shape — despite the fact that he neither worked out in a gym nor jogged on a track.

I found it fascinating to work on the creation of a musical number with Fred, learning how he conceived those magnificent dances in his movies. It was similar to a group of writers sitting around a table trying to work out the beginning, middle, and end of a particular script. We would spend hours developing ideas for each number. Once Fred was thoroughly convinced that it was worth doing, he took over. Working intimately with his choreographer, Hermes Pan, he would ingeniously work out every step and nuance, changing movements and small bits of business much like a writer rewrites a script. When he announced that he was at last happy with a particular bit, there was no doubt in anyone's mind that it would be brilliant. He wouldn't be satisfied with less.

It goes without saying that Fred Astaire is a thorough musician. His sense of timing is probably as perfect as any metronome. Once he has set a tempo, you

The elegant Astaire, appropriately in top hat, white tie, and tails.

BUD YORKIN *is the director of such films as* Come Blow Your Horn; Divorce, American Style; Inspector Clouseau; Start the Revolution Without Me; *and* The Thief Who Came to Dinner. *He is the co-creator of the TV series* All in the Family, *and writer, producer, and director of two of Fred Astaire's television specials of the late fifties. He has won six Emmy Awards.*

know that tempo will never vary, no matter how long a dance sequence runs. Many times I would take out a stopwatch and time a given number after he had set the tempo. At the end Fred could accurately tell the pianist how many seconds slower or faster than planned it had been.

I can say that Astaire is the most meticulous performer with whom I have ever worked. Everything would come under his scrutiny, from music to his co-stars' wardrobe. I'll never forget the first shot of our live special. It was a close-up of Fred's feet. I had told the stage manager to give Fred a ten-second warning before we would be on the air, and he did so. With only about three or four seconds to go, Fred suddenly checked his shoelaces to make sure they were tied.

When making motion pictures, Fred often felt that his best takes were his first takes. Consequently he was thrilled to be using the live television technique which permitted him to shoot a number in fifteen minutes instead of the two or three weeks it took with film. Fred thoroughly enjoyed performing in front of a live audience, as he had done many years before on Broadway. I remember Fred kidding about the fact that he would not need "idiot cards" because he thought it would be a cardinal sin not to have memorized what he had to say or do. Fred's medley of songs lasted some thirteen minutes

and included portions of roughly twenty-four numbers. Not once did he forget a lyric or a movement.

During Astaire's movie career, he introduced many dancing partners, including Ginger Rogers, Leslie Caron, and Cyd Charisse. It would have been easy for him to have worked steadily with any one of these great partners, but Fred prefers to give young, new talent a chance to earn instant fame. That is why he selected Barrie Chase to be his partner for "An Evening."

As it turned out, Barrie was the ideal partner for Fred. Not only was she an excellent dancer, but she also had the patience and the temperament to strive for the perfection Astaire insisted upon. I could only marvel at Barrie and Fred as they rehearsed. They would stand in front of a mirror, working out precisely where their hands would fall on each step. Fred would constantly give her words of encouragement. When the red light went on for the show to begin, Barrie had the self-assurance of an old pro. This was due to Fred.

Fred does not live in the past. He is not interested in duplicating musical numbers from his old films. Furthermore, he likes to say that today's talent far exceeds that of his day. Of course, one would find it difficult to agree with his sentiments, but they do reveal to us the nature of his optimism.

With Rita Hayworth in You'll Never Get Rich *(L), and Ginger Rogers in* The Story of Vernon and Irene Castle.

ASTAIRE AND KELLY TAKING TURNS

CYD CHARISSE

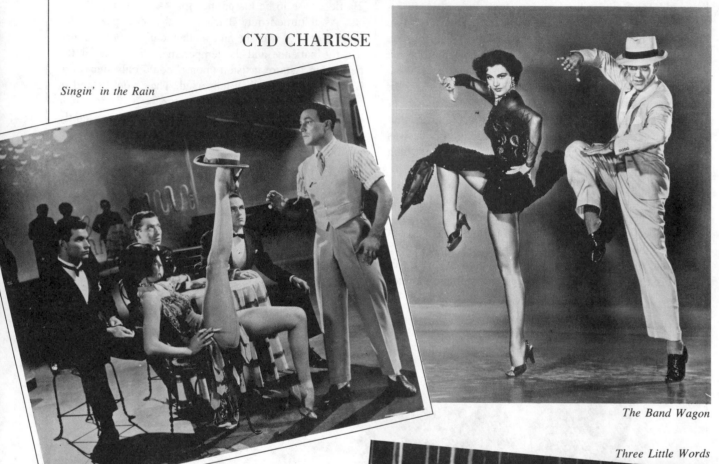

Singin' in the Rain

The Band Wagon

Three Little Words

VERA-ELLEN

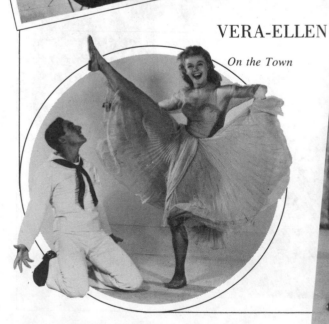

On the Town

JUDY GARLAND

Easter Parade

Summer Stock

TOGETHER

Daddy Long Legs

Ziegfeld Follies

LESLIE CARON

An American in Paris

GENE KELLY: DANCING ATHLETE

SAUL CHAPLIN

Gene Kelly did not enter movies until he was thirty.

IN 1943, MORRIS STOLOFF, the head of Columbia Pictures' music department, assigned me to write a comedy routine for Gene Kelly and Phil Silvers. They were then rehearsing *Cover Girl* (1944). So I walked over to the set, and there were Kelly, Silvers, and Rita Hayworth dancing and laughing uproariously. My first thought was that the gaiety was part of the number. I later learned that it was their general demeanor when the three of them rehearsed together.

SAUL CHAPLIN *is a song writer and producer who won Academy Awards for Best Scoring for a Musical for* An American in Paris, Seven Brides for Seven Brothers, *and* West Side Story. *Among his many compositions are* "Bei Mir Bist Du Schöen" *and* "The Anniversary Song."

I watched their rehearsal for about half an hour, until they finally took a break. Phil, for whom I had written musical material for several years, introduced me to Gene (I already knew Rita), saying I was King Gustave of Sweden, whom I vaguely resembled at the time. After about ten minutes of joking and small talk, I was able to get around to the reason for my visit. Suddenly the laughing ceased and everyone became serious. They each had many notions about the routine I was to write, Gene in particular. He discussed everything that he thought might affect the routine: the set, the other characters, the method of shooting, the plot of the film, and many other elements that I would have thought were irrelevant. As he spoke, I kept feeling more and more that he was going to be impossible to please. His parting words, however, allayed my fears and surprised me: "Make Phil as funny as you can, and don't worry about me — I'll take care of myself." I was to have a long association with Gene, and he would always maintain this attitude. And he always *would* be able to take care of himself.

★ ★ ★ ★ ★

It is difficult to imagine Gene Kelly *not* having become a big star. He has every prerequisite of a movie star. First and foremost, he is enormously talented. Physically, he's handsome, not in an "eight-by-ten glossy" way but more like the best-looking guy in the neighborhood. He is a naturally gifted athlete, and athletic prowess has been admired by moviegoers since the silent days of Douglas Fairbanks. His singing voice is pleasant, with a nice easy style. Audiences identify with its simplicity; that's how they sound in their showers, they think. His dances, usually more complex and intellectual than they seem, appear to be improvised and are great fun to watch. His ideas are always fresh and original, and his intent is always crystal clear. His costumes are usually plain, everyday clothes. (He describes himself as having come from the "sweat-shirt generation.") When you add to this his ingratiating Irish smile, an irresistible screen personality, superior intelligence, and a keen sense of showmanship — how could he miss?

Today Gene Kelly, as a dancer and a choreographer, is universally credited with having reshaped the motion picture musical. The "alter ego" dance in *Cover Girl,* the cartoon sequences in *Anchors Aweigh* (1945) and *Invitation to the Dance* (1956), several numbers from *On the Town* (1949), and others advanced the techniques by which dance is interpreted on film. As a former amateur violinist with a useful knowledge of music, Kelly has always exerted more than the usual influence on the sound and style of the music for his numbers. He always approaches musical numbers from a dramatic standpoint, and since he's such an accomplished actor and dancer, the results are often quite extraordinary — as demonstrated by the varying moods of the *An American in Paris* ballet and the "Slaughter on Tenth Avenue" number in *Words and Music* (1948) and, at the other end of the spectrum, the uninhibited joy of his roller-skating number in *It's Always Fair Weather* (1955) and, of course, almost everything in *Singin' in the Rain* (1952). In fact, if a song doesn't lend itself to dramatic treatment, Kelly isn't interested.

Because Kelly is such a marvelous song-and-dance man, his skill as an actor is often overlooked. He has played straight dramatic roles with excellent critical results in more than a dozen films. He was once asked what acting method he used. His reply was simply, "I pretend to be as much like the character called for in the script as I can."

Another of Gene's unsung talents is his ability to work with children. He can get them to do anything. He teaches them at their own level without ever being condescending. He has infinite patience. An easy answer for his success in this area could be that he taught dancing when he was younger at his parents' dancing school. He genuinely loves children. In the "I Got Rhythm" number in *An American in Paris* (1951), the children were all represented as being French. Actually, most of them were American, but under Gene's tutelage they all *became* French. He taught the French children English, and the American children English with a French accent. They all adored both the game and their teacher.

One more thing: Gene has a positive genius for

In An American in Paris *he sang and danced with children — a treat for Kelly.*

making non-dancers look like they've been dancing all their lives. One has only to look at Frank Sinatra dancing and jumping on beds in the ''I Begged Her'' number from *Anchors Aweigh,* or Phil Silvers in *Cover Girl,* or Jules Munshin in *On the Town* and *Take Me Out to the Ball Game* (1949), or Kay Kendall, in *Les Girls* (1957).

His stature as a long-standing superstar is unques-tioned. In point of fact, he is adding to his fans among the younger generation who are discovering Kelly for the first time through *That's Entertainment* (1974) and *That's Entertainment, Part II* (1976) and the revivals of his films. On TV, attired in a dinner jacket, he some-times appears to be a show business elder statesman, but when he starts to sing or dance the years fall away.

He could be mild-mannered as in It's a Big Country *(Top) when he courted Janet Leigh. But he could also be tough (and scar-faced) as in* Black Hand *as he dealt with the likes of J. Carroll Naish.*

With Jean Hagen in Singin' in the Rain, *a top fifties musical.*

With Walter Matthau on the set of Hello, Dolly!

HIS LEGENDARY PARTIES

OUT OF THE BLUE, on the first day I met Gene Kelly, he invited me and my wife to his home for a party. We arrived at the Kellys at about ten-thirty the following Saturday night. We were overwhelmed. It seemed that all Hollywood had gathered for a convention: Judy Garland, Mickey Rooney, Johnny Mercer, Hugh Martin, Ralph Blane, Vincente Minnelli, John Garfield, Kay Thompson, Phil Silvers, Lena Horne, Lennie Hayton, Frank Sinatra, and many others were there. I soon learned that the Kellys hosted these gatherings every Saturday night. The Kelly front door was always open, literally and figuratively, so you might meet anyone there.

These parties had a definite routine. First came charades, played by two competing teams. Gene and Betsy Kelly were the two captains. When we began playing, I immediately sensed that there was something a bit sinister about the atmosphere. Everybody was going at it extremely seriously, as though it were a matter of life and death. I soon figured out that it was a reflection of the attitude of the captains; both Gene and Betsy were quite competitive where games were concerned. They were for winning. Losing took all the fun out of playing.

Following the game came the most remarkable part of the evening, unplanned entertainment that I'm sure has never been equaled before or since. Everyone who could perform did — not reticently but happily. They performed singly and in combinations, so that after Judy Garland had sung a couple of songs, she might be joined by Frank Sinatra or Gene or both, and they would do several more. Then maybe Johnny Mercer would preview a new score he was writing. Material was sometimes created on the spot. In fact, Phil Silvers' nightclub act consisted mainly of material he had ad-libbed in the Kelly living room. Since part of the guest list changed almost every week, the "show" varied accordingly, but the high level of creativity and performance was staggering.

It usually continued until dawn. When it was light enough — about five A.M. — a volleyball game would start in the Kelly backyard. Again, it was played with the fierceness of a war. Gene — the superb athlete — dominated all. Despite the tension in the air, Kelly was fun to watch. He was incredible. He was a one-man team, making the most impossible shots from all over the court. They would play until seven or eight in the morning and then disperse. Very often I would drop by the Kelly household on Sunday afternoon at about one o'clock and a volleyball game would be in full swing again. Gene would be playing with entirely new teams. Had he slept at all? I never found out. — S. C.

DORIS DAY: NOT POLLYANNA

GEORGE MORRIS

Never a passive heroine.

THE MERE MENTION of Doris Day's name usually elicits a series of tired jokes about goody two-shoes, gauzy filters, and staunchly defended virginity. Like most preconditioned responses, however, this reaction is based more on hearsay and memories of movies watched long ago, than on perceptive, inquiring evaluations of the thirty-nine films in which Day appeared.

Doris Day starred in her first movie, *Romance on the High Seas,* in 1948 and remained a major personality until her last film (to date), *With Six You Get Egg Roll* (1968). In an industry in which the life span of women stars is notably shorter than that of their male counterparts, Day's twenty years of staying power are a phenomenon. There are better singers, better comediennes, and certainly better actresses. But could it be, as Molly Haskell suggests in her book *From Reverence to Rape,* that there is something in Doris Day's persona, unlike other female stars of her era (e.g., Marilyn Monroe, Elizabeth Taylor, Grace Kelly, and Audrey Hepburn), that reflects most accurately the self-image of the American woman?

This animated girl-next-door, with her ready smile and sanguine disposition, is determined and ambitious. And it is precisely her impulse to get ahead, rather than get a man, that makes her appeal to both female and male audiences. In her early musicals, Day is eager to abandon anonymity for stardom as a singer; while in the interchangeable comedies she later made with Rock Hudson, Cary Grant, James Garner, and Rod Taylor, she typically plays an independent woman with a terrific job. Day is unique among her contemporaries in that she does not seek to define herself as a mirror reflection of a man's

GEORGE MORRIS, *film critic for* Texas Monthly *contributes regularly to* Film Comment *and* Take One. *He is the author of books on Doris Day, John Garfield, and Errol Flynn.*

Storm Warnings smiling stars: (L–R) Ronald Reagan, Ginger Rogers, Day, and Steve Cochran. It was actually a serious film about the KKK.

fantasies or desires. Day exists for herself, evolving a-cross two decades of stardom a persona that renews and alters itself at various intervals, creating the truest approximation of an existential woman in the American cinema.

A direct honesty shines through Day's performances, an individuality and self-reliance that distinguishes her from the sex sirens of the fifties. Her no-nonsense approach to life may not be the stuff that sexual fantasies are made of, but she *is* sexy in an open, robust way. She gets out and works in the daytime, but one can believe that she finds time for nocturnal pleasures as well. Whether teaching in *Teacher's Pet* (1958), breeding lobsters in *It Happened to Jane* (1959), heading a labor grievance committee in *Pajama Game* (1957), or chasing potential advertising accounts in *Lover Come Back* (1961), Day never denies herself a love life when the opportunity arises.

The actress' career falls into three distinct periods. From 1948 to 1954, when she was under exclusive contract to Warner Brothers, Day starred primarily in musicals, most of them forgettable and innocuous. She played tomboys (*On Moonlight Bay,* 1951), devoted wives (*I'll See You in My Dreams,* 1951), ingenues (*Tea for Two,* 1950), and career-minded singers (*My Dream Is Yours,* 1949). Most of these films suffer from bad directors, worse scripts, and the vulgarizing influences of Warner Brothers' resident dance director, LeRoy Prinz, and orchestrator, Ray Heindorf.

Given these films' ineffectiveness, it is surprising how good Doris Day is in them. The fact that she is genuinely talented is often obscured by her enormous popularity and the petrification her public image suffered in the late sixties. Her mellow singing derives from her apprenticeship as a big-band vocalist with such orchestras as Les Brown's and Bob Crosby's. Day's apprecia-

Doris Day, seen here with James Cagney, scored a triumph as a dramatic actress in Love Me or Leave Me, *a biography of singer Ruth Etting. Reviewers pointed out that Day, in revealing dresses, was trying to establish a more daring image.*

tion for the contours of a melody, her sensitivity to the phrasing of a lyric, her sheer self-assurance, increased with each fifties film. By the time she made her best musicals (*Calamity Jane,* 1953; *Love Me or Leave Me,* 1955; *Pajama Game;* and *Billy Rose's Jumbo,* 1962), Day had developed into the best musical actress in films. Unfortunately, her growth coincided with the decline of the musical as a popular genre. To survive, she was forced to find alternate outlets for her talents.

In 1955, the actress changed directions radically, appearing as Ruth Etting in *Love Me or Leave Me,* a musical biography of the Ziegfeld star whose career was "sponsored" by a petty gangster (brilliantly played by James Cagney). It was the shrewdest move Day could have made; she embarked on a three-year period in which she gave the best three performances of her career. Anyone who thinks of Doris Day only as a smiling, eternal virgin should look again at *Love Me or Leave Me* and her subsequent films *The Man Who Knew Too Much* (1956) and *Pajama Game.*

In *Love Me or Leave Me,* Day's entire physical appearance is transformed — her necklines plunge, her skirts rise, her makeup becomes more stylized. Although she has lost none of her vulnerability, she is now tougher and more resilient. She is also extremely sexy, whether twitching to the music in a dime-a-dance lineup or belt-

ing a torchy ballad while wearing a clinging black sequined gown.

In *The Man Who Knew Too Much,* Day responds to Alfred Hitchcock's direction by giving her top performance. A master at exploring and undermining his stars' images, Hitchcock insinuates the actress' healthy facade into a multileveled portrait of a woman who resents

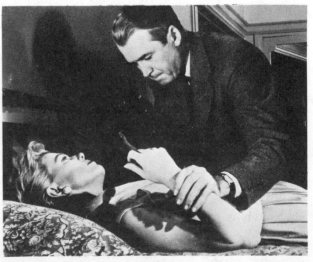

Calmed down by James Stewart in The Man Who Knew Too Much.

abandoning her career to rear a family. She overcompensates for this loss by neurotically mothering her son, and depends on pills to maintain her precarious emotional equilibrium. There are two scenes in this film that stand as Day's most brilliant. One is when she learns from her husband (James Stewart) that their child has been kidnapped, and the other is the virtuoso set piece at the Albert Hall concert, where Day must decide between the silence that will bring death to a stranger and a scream that will endanger the life of her son. The controlled hysteria she brings to these moments should erase any doubts one might have concerning Day's acting ability.

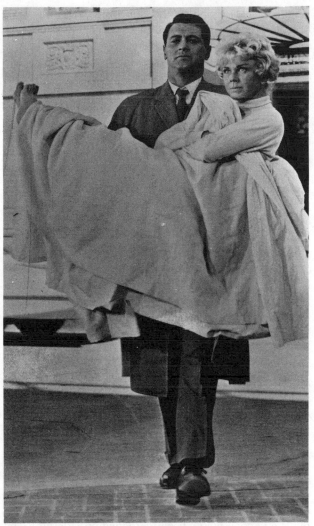

Hudson asserting himself, and Day not happy about it. Pillow Talk *started a wave of American bedroom comedies.*

Doris Day and John Raitt in George Abbott and Stanley Donen's top-notch musical Pajama Game.

Day's Babe Williams, in the ebullient adaptation of *Pajama Game,* is one of the great musical comedy performances in movie history. She's an apple-chewing seamstress in a Midwestern pajama factory, gutsy enough to head her union's grievance committee, yet vulnerable to the charms of the new superintendent (John Raitt), whose role in management represents everything she's fighting. Within *Pajama Game*'s musical comedy framework, her portrayal has remarkable range and depth. Her performance is strongly physical, her gestures and movements providing kinetic thrust to the film. Furthermore, in Richard Adler and Jerry Ross' score, she has some of the best songs of her career to sing, and she attacks every one of them with gusto. Her renditions of ''I'm Not at All in Love,'' ''Small Talk,'' and the reprise of ''Hey There'' provide excellent examples of how Day could both create character and define emotions through song.

The third and final phase of her movie career is the one with which Doris Day is most closely identified.

With musicals dying at the box office, Day found it necessary once again to shift her energies in a different direction. Producer Ross Hunter and writer Stanley Shapiro were waiting in the wings with *Pillow Talk* (1959), the phenomenally successful sex farce which served as a model for most of the actress' later movies.

When *Pillow Talk* first opened in 1959, its leering tone and pruient humor was cited as a sophisticated breakthrough in "adult" comedy. Today, that film and its mutants, such as *Lover Come Back* and *That Touch of Mink* (1962), look merely offensive, most of their purported humor deriving from aspersions cast on the sexual prowess of either Day or her leading man. One enduring assumption surrounding these movies is the delusion of Day's virginity. But the only film to which this might possibility apply is *That Touch of Mink*, the most execrable of the Hunter-Shapiro trilogy. In *Lover Come Back,* however, Day's refusal to bed down with Rock Hudson is motivated not by her wish to retain her virginity but by her disgust at the elaborate ruses he devises to seduce her. Paradoxically, by maintaining her own integrity, she salvages his as well.

What is at stake in these films, then, is *not* Day's virginity, but her probity, her sense of herself as an independent woman. It is this aspect of these indistinguishable farces that gives them their interest today, unified by the stabilizing influence of Day's persona. The virginity issue is both irrelevant and inapplicable in movies such as *Please Don't Eat the Daisies* (1960), *The Thrill of It All* (1963), and *Move Over, Darling* (1963) in which Day plays married women with children. In *Move Over, Darling,* a turgid reworking of the Enoch Arden tale, she plays a woman who's been marooned on a desert island for five years with Chuck Connors, and much of the ostensible comedy derives from husband James Garner's efforts to discover just exactly what she and Connors did to entertain themselves. Even in *Pillow Talk,* Day admits, to herself, that she's been with a lot of men in her time, which she feels gives her the experience necessary to decide that Rock Hudson's her jackpot.

During the years between 1959 and 1968, a nine-year period in which the star dominated those elusive barometers of public opinion known as "top-ten polls," there were notable exceptions to the Ross Hunter-Stanley Shapiro syndrome. Charles Walters' elegiac musical *Billy Rose's Jumbo* features one of the actress' loveliest, most subdued portrayals, and in the two films she made under master satirist Frank Tashlin's direction, *The Glass-Bottom Boat* (1966) and *Caprice* (1967), Day gamely complements his absurdist vision by delivering appropriately stylized performances.

Apart from these exceptions, the actress remained a formidable presence for the rest of her film career. Even when the Hunter-Shapiro formula congealed through repetition, and she lost some of the spontaneity and energy of her best comedy performances, Day continued to radiate a self-assurance rare among Hollywood actresses of the period. Free-willed, free-spirited, renouncing domesticity while questioning society's assumption of female subservience, Doris Day triumphantly embodied the most forward-looking heroine in American movies of the fifties and sixties.

For seven years she was Americs's top female movie star.

ELVIS PRESLEY: ROCK MUSIC PHENOMENON

ALLAN WEISS

A top film star for fifteen years.

W E HAD ALL SEEN HIM on television, the swiveling hips below the bottom of the screen, unseen. But it wasn't just sex; it was an indefinable energy that transcended that. The question was, would it show on film?

I had been called to the test stage at Paramount to play back ''Blue Suede Shoes'' for a screen test of Elvis Presley. There was no time to transfer the commercial disc to a synchronous one; Hal Wallis would listen to a less-than-perfect sound track.

The transformation was incredible. We knew instantly that we were in the presence of a phenomenon; electricity bounced off the walls of the sound stage. One felt it as an awesome thing — like an earthquake in progress, only without the implicit threat. Watching this insecure country boy, who apologized when he asked for a rehearsal as though he had done something wrong, turn into absolute dynamite when he stepped into the bright lights and started lip-synching the words of his familiar hit. He believed in it, and he made you believe it, no matter how ''sophisticated'' your musical tastes were.

I had not been a fan until that point, but to deny his talent would have been as foolish as it was impossible. He was a force, and to fail to recognize it would be the same as sticking a finger into a live socket and denying the existence of electricity.

The number was completed in two takes, and they moved in for close-ups. He protested mildly that he hadn't been ''dead on'' in a couple of places. It was explained that the closer shots would be intercut to cover it. I don't think he understood, but with characteristic

---

ALLAN WEISS *has written screenplays for such films as* The Sons of Katie Elder *and the Elvis Presley films* Blue Hawaii; Fun in Acapulco; Roustabout; Paradise — Hawaiian Style; Girls, Girls, Girls; *and* Easy Come, Easy Go.

trust, he did what he was told. No stand-in was provided, and he stood uncomplainingly while the lights were being adjusted — bathed in perspiration.

The musical number was completed and then he did a scene from *The Rainmaker,* which Wallis was then casting. Elvis played the rebellious younger brother, Jimmy Curry (the part done in the film by Earl Holliman), with amateurish conviction — like the lead in a high school play. His performance was believable, but lacked the polished subtleties of a professional.

In viewing the test, one thing was clear: It would be a mistake to try to force this strong personality into a preconceived role. His parts must be tailored for him, designed to exploit the thing he did best — sing. This proved to be correct. While he was more than competent in his early dramatic pictures such as *Love Me Tender* (1956) and *King Creole* (1958), he was much more comfortable and successful in lighter pictures that cast him as a singing personality.

One of his biggest hits:
Viva Las Vegas! *with Ann-Margret.*

An ad for one of Presley's most serious films, with a screenplay by Clifford Odets.

Blue Hawaii,
written by Allan Weiss.

84

Later, following a trip to Hawaii, I wrote a short story called "Beach Boy." It seemed to be the right kind of vehicle for Presley. I gave it to Wallis' associate, Paul Nathan, and they bought it. It became *Blue Hawaii* (1961), one of Presley's biggest grossers. I followed that with five more Presley films.

The screen character that we created was essentially a loner who appreciated women — preferably in quantity — but whose underlying attitude was audacious and arrogant, even a little contemptuous. Presley fit this characterization easily and well. Perhaps some element of it was close to the real person underneath.

I tried to integrate the musical numbers into the screenplay, so that each had a reason for existence, knowing that we could not simply have him pick up a guitar, take two paces forward, and start to sing. He liked the way some of these numbers worked, and he said so. If he didn't like something, he was too polite or fearful of offending to be direct. We learned to read signs. If he asked me to explain a joke in the script, I learned that it wasn't that he didn't understand it, but that he thought it was vague or not funny. At first, not knowing this, I would explain the joke and leave it in — to find that at the preview no one laughed. He knew his audience — and how they would respond — like few performers do.

We were on our third picture together before he agreed to call me "Allan" — and even then an occasional "Mr. Presley" was necessary to remind him of a lapse in this agreement. This was not formality, but painful politeness and genuine humility.

There were great inconsistencies. He was a musician avant-garde enough to have started a whole new direction in music; his personal morality was old-fashioned, almost puritanical. He rarely swore, and when he did he looked around the room to see if there were women present. He was rebellious, yet he had a great love and respect for his mother, with whom he spoke daily.

Barbara Stanwyck was strong co-star in Roustabout.

His dietary habits were deplorable by any standard. He was a junk food addict, hamburgers (with everything) probably being the only healthful thing he ate. No vegetables, lots of French fries and soda pop — all the things used to appease adolescent appetites. During the shooting of several pictures his lithe body swelled up to the point where an additional wardrobe of a larger size had to be matched, and in one or two shots made near the end of a picture seams that had been let out could be observed in the rushes.

His extravagances were few: expensive custom-made cars fitted with bars, refrigerators, television, and powerful tape systems; Cadillacs as gifts to friends; and his beloved Graceland, refuge from the world.

He never learned to read music, but he knew the sound he wanted, and he heard it all — even through his

With Richard Egan and Debra Paget in Love Me Tender, *Presley's first film. "He had much of the brash unencumbered quality of James Dean."* — A. W.

own singing. He would ask for more "*zziz*" after the break, or less "*thwump*" before the start of the chorus. The musicians always understood. They trusted his instinct, just as he did.

He had mixed feelings about his overwhelming success. He loved and respected his audience but resented his inability, because of his celebrity, to go out and enjoy himself like anyone else. Going out always protected by his bodyguards was the same as giving a performance. So, a lifestyle inevitably evolved. He surrounded himself with a group of his contemporaries who would provide insulation from the outside world, prevent loneliness, and supply some of his physical and psychological needs. He could relate to them, but even they had to learn to respect his ever-threatened privacy.

He was highly secretive about his relations with women, possibly out of old-fashioned chivalry, but more likely out of fear that his public might resent any impropriety. He was often concerned that a casual date might try to exploit him. While his generosity was frequently excessive, giving was not the same as being forced to give.

He admired other entertainers. The Beatles probably impressed him most. He spoke of how thrilling his first meeting with them was, and knew each of their songs, frequently note for note. He became excited and enthusiastic when we told him that we were trying to get Mae West to work with him in *Roustabout* (1964). Each admired the other greatly, but it couldn't be arranged.

Did he improve as an actor? Probably not very much. He had no interest in becoming an Olivier, but then why should he have? Olivier has no interest in becoming a rock star, either. Only Hollywood makes such

unreasonable demands. For Elvis, it was enough to be "one of the first white singers to sing like a black."

Every time I am interviewed about Elvis Presley the subject of drugs comes up. I never knew him to be on anything more powerful than an occasional prescription for sleeplessness. Toward the end I lost contact with him and therefore have no personal knowledge of his later habits, but I doubt that he was hitting on anything very hard.

Some say that his premature death was predictable, even inevitable. I have to think of it as an accident. The last time I saw him — after a smash opening in Las Vegas — he was so alive that it appeared it would take a nuclear bomb to do him in. I still don't believe that he is gone.

Having Fun in Acapulco.

BARBRA STREISAND: AN ORIGINAL

HERBERT ROSS

Barbra Streisand, the most popular movie star of the past ten years.

BARBRA STREISAND is a phenomenally gifted woman with extraordinary charisma. She could have been a tremendous success during any period of the twentieth century. She is certainly an

---

HERBERT ROSS *is the director of such films as* Goodbye, Mr. Chips; The Owl and the Pussycat; Play It Again, Sam; Funny Lady; The Seven-Percent Solution; The Turning Point; The Goodbye Girl; *and* California Suite.

---

important figure in film history, one of the few stars who was able to cross over from being a musical performer to being an actress. Moreover, she did this at at time when there were very few successful women in movies.

I knew Barbra before she went to Hollywood to launch her film career. In fact, I was present at her first audition for a Broadway show, *I Can Get It for You Wholesale*, and directed her in her show-stopping "Miss Marmelstein" number. That was her first really big success. Even then, I believed that she was gifted, not only as a singer, but also as an actress.

When she arrived in California to do *Funny Girl* (1968), the story of Fanny Brice, she went through a perfectly normal set of responses. She was nervous and frightened of being rejected by the public. We were all unsure whether Barbra would succeed with a film audience, because at the time her special qualities were relatively unfamiliar — and certainly no one in the history of movies ever had her particular combination of special beauty and special talents.

But once we saw her screen test, we knew she was able to project on film as well as she had projected on stage; if anything, the film medium was more flattering to her. Although it wasn't difficult for Barbra to think of herself as a ''leading lady'' of a major picture, we were more comfortable thinking of her as such after we had seen the test. None of us, of course, anticipated the popular success she would become with that one film.

Barbra was extremely lucky to make her film debut in *Funny Girl*. Having had the advantage of playing Fanny Brice for two years on Broadway, Barbra knew her part inside out. It was ideally suited to her range as an actress and a singer.

My relationship with Barbra, as choreographer and director, has always been enormously pleasant and

THE LOOK OF LOVE

healthy. We have each other's confidence and respect each other's talent. The first non-musical film for both of us was *The Owl and the Pussycat* (1970). I thought she was perfectly cast and, indeed, the project was conceived with her in mind. [I think this role — along with *Funny Girl* and parts of *The Way We Were* (1973) — captures the essence of Barbra Streisand.] When *Funny Lady* (1975) was being planned, it seemed to Barbra, producer Ray Stark, and myself that I was the logical choice to direct it.

All top actresses are different and work differently, but there are some important qualities that are essential to all. Like Diane Keaton, Shirley MacLaine, Jane Fonda, and Ann Bancroft and some of the other actresses with whom I have worked, Barbra has the ability to project pathos and vulnerability. This is a terribly important gift — it enables an actress to get an audience's sympathy and to make it empathize with the character's problems. Barbra's ability to accomplish this is a major reason for her box-office success.

Barbra is a canny actress who understands the essence of her humor and her talent. I don't think she has, in her own mind, what is often referred to as a "set image" — one which shouldn't be tampered with on film. She is anxious to become her part rather than to have it molded to fit the public's image of her — even if

THE ROMANTIC SCENES in Streisand's numerous films seem so similar that it is likely she helps in their direction. (L–R) With Omar Sharif in *Funny Girl;* with John Richardson in *On a Clear Day You Can See Forever;* with Robert Redford in *The Way We Were;* and with Kris Kristofferson in *A Star Is Born.*

After George Segal in The Owl and the Pussycat.

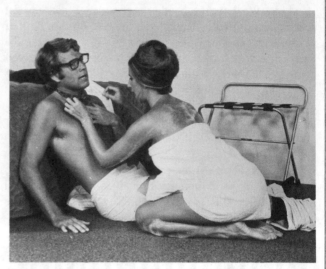

Seducing Ryan O' Neal in What's Up, Doc?

it involves altering her physical appearance to better characterize each role she plays.

In the late sixties, Barbra was totally original both physically and in terms of her attitudes, youth, drive, talent, and native intelligence. I think these attributes are what made her so attractive to audiences of the time. I thought Barbra would embark on a more adventurous career — one that would encompass more challenging material; however, she has chosen to do otherwise, and I don't believe she has reached her potential.

The reasons for her popularity have changed over the years. She has become an Establishment figure, which she certainly wasn't in the beginning. Of course, time does that to every rebel.

As Fanny Brice, for the second time, in Herbert Ross' Funny Lady, *with Omar Sharif.*

THE
GREAT
STAGE ACTORS

JOHN BARRYMORE: PROFILE OF A ROYAL PERFORMER

HERMAN WEINBERG

TOO MANY GODS have been propitiated in the name of entertainment, but the art of John Barrymore as an actor on both stage and screen was very great indeed, and is recognized as such in the highest places. Jean Mitry, for instance, founder and head of the Institut des Hautes Etudes Cinématographiques in Paris, correctly describes Barrymore as "one of the glories of the cinema since [its origins]," and chooses to remember him on the screen by citing *Dr. Jekyll and Mr. Hyde* (1920), *Beau Brummel* (1924), *Don Juan* (1926), *Moby Dick* (1930), *Grand Hotel* (1932), *Dinner at Eight* (1933), *Romeo and Juliet* (1936), and *Marie Antoinette* (1938). But even this "roll of honor" does not call attention to some of Barrymore's most impressive characterizations, not the least of which are his hell-scarred visage of Captain Ahab in *The Sea Beast* (1926); his evocation of François Villon in *The Beloved Rogue* (1927); his demon-haunted *Svengali* (1931); his boys' school teacher of *Topaze* (1933), whom he plays exquisitely with the most ineffable tenderness; his brash Hapsburg prince in *Reunion in Vienna* (1933); not to mention his excursion into the realms of self-mockery in the comedy classic *Twentieth Century* (1934), playing the half-satyr, half-David Belasco, half-Sadakichi Hartmann producer extraordinaire Oscar Jaffe, capable of encompassing three halves in anybody's lexicon.

And these were just the movies, well, not exactly "just" the movies, being far better than that, but they do not take into account his presence on the stage in such roles as *Peter Ibbetson, Richard III,* and, most notably, *Hamlet.* No one who saw and heard him on stage can

---

HERMAN WEINBERG *is the author of* Josef von Sternberg: A Critical Study; The Lubitsch Touch; Saint Cinema; The Complete "Greed"; The Complete "Wedding March"; *and* Stroheim: A Pictorial Record of His Nine Films.

Barrymore looking as if he is about to deliver a soliloquy from Hamlet, *but actually this is a scene from* Don Juan, *a silent film.*

forget the moment when he interrupted himself:

> *To die, . . . to sleep,*
> *To sleep! Perchance to dream:*

Then:

> *Ay, there's the rub . . .*

No one could forget the bitter smile and high inflection of voice with which he intoned that "Ay." All the contrariness of life is imbued there in the way he said it, and having heard it, it will be with you forever. That's what the actor was on his highest level. To be sure, Laurence Olivier was also a forceful Hamlet, on the screen (1948) as on the stage, but not in the same league with Barrymore. Olivier was sleek, his voice was like music, his anger a true *actor's*. It was a performance, in short, "of burnished gold." Barrymore was a suffering man, the wellsprings of his voice glinted the words he spoke, making of them drops of sorrow; every look, every gesture, but above all the hurt in his eyes that was reflected in his voice. I would have wished for one more film from him when he was at his peak — *Hamlet*.

In the history of the cinema there have been very few personalities who, it can be said, had a corrosive wit, who exhibited a true sense of irony. Most of these figures were writers and directors; Stroheim, Sternberg, Hecht, Lubitsch, Paul Bern, Joseph Mankiewicz, Marcel Pagnol, and Preston Sturges are the ones that readily come to mind. As for actors, who had we in the same class (as we used to call it) as John Barrymore, an actor, who, as Jean Mitry says "created a style of intellectual dandy which he carried off with a delicate refinement and not without a certain wry humor." Not even his brother Lionel, good "all around" actor that he was. Who then? Well, perhaps Noel Coward in *The Scoundrel* (1935) or Claude Rains in the mordant *Crime Without Passion*

Barrymore
gave his finest, wildest comedy performance opposite Carole Lombard in Howard Hawks' Twentieth Century.

(1934) or Lionel Stander in *Spectre of the Rose* (1946) or, of course, Marlene Dietrich in her Sternberg films. But only John Barrymore had the very *presence* that conveyed a true sense of irony to an audience. Barrymore, thus, was the possessor of one of the rarest of screen qualities; it is practically nonexistent today.

Grand Hotel.
The glorious faces
of Garbo and Barrymore.

94

JOHN CARRADINE ON JOHN BARRYMORE

JOHN BARRYMORE was a serious actor who did a great deal of research for all his parts, until, I guess, he was around fifty. Then he started drinking heavily. He told me: "I've done everything I've wanted to do. . . . I've played Hamlet in London; I've had every woman I ever wanted; I have a son to carry on my name. . . . I'm bored and I'm tired." He also told me that he was not a good enough Catholic to go to Mass, but too good a Catholic to kill himself. So he drank himself to death. It took him ten years.

Du Maurier's Svengali was a strange figure from the East who spoke French with a German accent and a Polish intonation. Barrymore spoke standard English . . . but with a flavor of German and French, and a Polish intonation. It was his most remarkable role.
— *J. C.*

But then, an actor like Barrymore would hardly find a place on the screens of today. Look over the list of his films and you will see that however picaresque the plots and excruciating his disguises, the roles relied on the dialogue with which the characters were delineated. In some the dialogue was of paramount importance, being even more important than the role — such as in Pagnol's *Topaze,* in the adaptation by Ben Hecht; in *Twentieth Century,* from the Hecht-Charles MacArthur screenplay; and, of course, beyond all else, Shakespeare's *Romeo and Juliet,* in which Barrymore played Mercutio. But today the accent is no longer on dialogue. Joseph Mankiewicz put it succinctly when he was asked why he no longer wrote and directed films like his brilliant *All About Eve* (1950) and *A Letter to Three Wives* (1949): "People no longer come to films to listen — they come to stare."

Maybe the creeping illnesses that finally did him in had for some time been silently but lethally affecting him as a personality in his work. Certainly from *The Great Profile,* 1940 (and that was two years before his death) onward, his acting eroded. Just look at *The Invisible Woman, World Premiere,* and *Playmates* (all 1941). Maybe the crackup of his four marriages took its toll — well, at least the dissolution of his marriage to Dolores Costello, whom he truly loved.

"They said that in his latter years," quoting the obituary in the New York *Herald Tribune,* "he had become a 'caricature' of a once magnificent figure. But none of this was news to Barrymore, nor did he allow it to disturb him unduly. To the end he faced the world with a charming impudence . . . saucy, cocky, Rabelaisian and, in his fashion, as gallant a gentleman as ever trod the boards." Others blamed it on his "hitting the bottle," clucking their pious tongues. But that's too easy. When you're bedeviled with hyperstatic pneumonia plus liver, kidney, and stomach ailments, resulting in a weakened heart, as his doctors diagnosed it, you don't need to come up with facile, all-too-facile, reasons. Still, he didn't give up. Gene Fowler visited him in the hospital just before the end.

"Come closer, Gene," said Barrymore, "and hold my hand while I sleep."

Almost reverently, Fowler took his hand.

"Lean over closer, Gene, I want to ask you something very important," he said.

"Gene," whispered Barrymore, "is it true that you are an illegitimate son of Buffalo Bill?"

The Great Profile, with Mary Beth Hughes. "Those who gave him those last pitiful roles cruelly exploited his crackup."
— *H. W.*

WILLIAM S. HART: FIRST AUTHENTIC WESTERN HERO

WALTER SELTZER

I T WAS PROBABLY INEVITABLE that William Surrey Hart would be a strong force in the development of motion pictures. Before moving to Hollywood, he was a star on Broadway and on the road throughout the United States.

Hart's first part as a western character was on the stage, Cash Hawkins in *The Squaw Man*. It was Broadway's first glimpse of an actor who really knew the West. Although born in Newburgh, New York, Hart's boyhood was spent among the Cheyenne and Sioux Indian tribes, and he was a master of Indian sign language. His authenticity was such that enthusiastic audiences packed the house for two full years. Hart had further theatrical successes: in *The Virginian*, *The Barrier,* and *The Trail of the Lonesome Pine*. At the end of his last long Broadway run he went on tour, and he became famous coast-to-coast. It was while on the road that he was exposed to the early "flickers." He was captivated by the potential of the new medium, although he considered the first crude westerns as burlesques of the West he knew so well.

He contacted his friend, Thomas Ince, who was then producing films in California. Ince, who honestly thought the market for westerns was dead, tried to discourage Hart's interest. But Hart persisted. He moved West and, when he saw Ince's "studio" — a makeshift camp of Indians, horses, gear, and jerry-built sets overlooking the Pacific Ocean at the mouth of Topanga Canyon — Hart bullied through a deal, the financial aspects of which later caused a rupture in the relationship, an oft-repeated occurrence between Hart and his business associates. He finally organized his own company.

WALTER SELTZER *is the producer of such films as* Shake Hands with the Devil, Paris Blues, The Naked Edge, Will Penny, The Omega Man, Skyjacked, *and* Soylent Green.

Hart researched his own movies, wrote the scripts, directed, produced, and starred in them. He sometimes wrote stories with early-American themes (one being based on the life of Patrick Henry), but westerns were his main interest, and he went to great lengths to ensure their authenticity. Whatever the cost in time and effort, Hart's

Formerly a Shakespearean actor, Hart made the first adult westerns. His "good-badman" hero was strong and silent.

search for realism paid off: audiences across the country filled the theaters, and his success made the western a motion picture staple.

In his film roles Hart set out to create a special hero — a character who would have been as much at home in New York City or Dubuque as he was in the Old West. Hart managed at once to be proud, strong, virile, virtuous, God-fearing, hard-drinking, honest, and law-abiding. His attitude toward women (with the possible exception of a dissolute harlot) was courteous and courtly. He might as easily have worn a cape as buckskins.

Though he frequently brandished his famous six-guns, he generally dealt with his adversaries on a one-to-one basis.

Bill Hart was dynamic. He was deeply emotional, having the uncanny ability to project his feelings to audiences. His impact on women, whether teenager or dowager, was powerful, even though his profile was something less than Greek and his expression about as warm as chiseled granite.

Bill always appreciated talented and beautiful women. His devoted long-term friends included Louise Dresser, Marjorie Rambeau, the Talmadge sisters — and Jane and Eva Novak. But he was closer to his sister Mary (Mamie) than any other person. She was his right hand — they collaborated on story ideas, she helped him with his innumerable juvenile adventure books (the "Injun and Whitey" series), and later his autobiography, *My Life East and West*. She also managed his sprawling household. His marriage to Winifred Westover, encouraged by Mamie, lasted only a few hectic months. It dissolved in great bitterness, though Hart's generosity to Winifred and to their son, born some months after the divorce, continued until Hart's death — he left her the largest inheritance then known in the film capital.

My most vivid memories of Bill Hart are placed at the large parties he gave at La Loma de los Vientos, his Spanish-style hacienda. These were notable events, planned by Mamie, crowded with famous names from both stage and screen. At one party, I recall, the guest list included Harold Lloyd, Will Rogers, W.C. Fields,

ALMOST AN IN-LAW

JANE NOVAK, my mother-in-law to be, appeared as Hart's leading lady in five films. They became engaged, but the romance eventually came apart at the proddings of Bill's sister, Mary, who managed to channel her brother's interest in the direction of a then-budding actress, Winifred Westover. Though their engagement was abruptly terminated, Jane and Bill's friendship weathered the Westover marriage and continued throughout the years until his death. Jane's daughter (my wife) still visits her mother's trundle bed at the William S. Hart Ranch-Museum in Newhall, California.

— W.S.

With Jane Novak.

Hart rarely indulged in technical gimmickry, but in this case he tried superimposing one shot on top of another so he could play two parts. Unfortunately the trick didn't work, and one hand all but disappeared.

Moran and Mack (the ''Two Black Crows'' of radio fame), Lew Cody, Clara Bow, and Rex Bell. Hart was a great fun lover and raconteur, a warm and wonderful host.

During World War I the federal government selected four motion picture stars to tour the country on behalf of the Third Liberty Loan Drive: Mary Pickford, Douglas Fairbanks, Charles Chaplin, and William S. Hart. Later, the same group repeated the junket for the Fourth Liberty Loan. Among them, they raised hundreds of millions of dollars for the war effort.

Bill Hart's last film was the great *Tumbleweeds* (1925), which was about the opening of the Cherokee Strip to settlers. It did well with audiences, but industry leaders pressed Hart to reconsider his contractual insis-

tence on producing, directing, and starring in his own productions. Movies were becoming big business, and the moguls wanted complete control. Hart refused to accept a new deal, and the upshot was that he became anathema to the studio heads. Hart charged that he was being blacklisted.

But the two-gun man didn't go down without a fight. Charging the distributors of his films with fraud, he fell into a series of litigations. But those who by then controlled the industry had become too powerful for one man to buck; it was the end of Hart's career. This not only was anguishing for Hart, but was certainly a loss to the industry — his magnificent voice and stage presence would have been a huge asset to the still-new talkie market.

CLAUDETTE COLBERT: BROADWAY BELLE

ALLAN SCOTT

One of the few actresses to have equal success in theater and film.

I FIRST SAW CLAUDETTE COLBERT in 1927 when she was appearing on Broadway opposite Walter Huston in *The Barker*. All I remember of the play, then and now, was an attractive young woman with a velvety voice and a flashing pair of silken legs in patent leather slippers. Later I saw her in several more plays — and in her movies. From afar, I had admired Claudette as a deft comedienne, with a sparkling personality and whiplash timing; her reading of comedy was always sharp and accurate, underlined by the husky, throaty charm of her voice, but I did not meet her until 1940, when she was Paramount's reigning actress. I was assigned by the studio to write the script for Samson Raphaelson's play *Skylark* (1941). I had often wished I could write for her but, alas, I hadn't liked the play. In the film, Claudette was to play the role Gertrude Lawrence had created on the Broadway stage.

Claudette was in director Mark Sandrich's office when I entered. She was smiling graciously and swiveling her marvelous, big brown eyes. Sandrich asked me what I thought of the project. Before I could stammer out my apprehensions, Claudette, sensing my uncertainty, said: "Look, Mr. Scott . . . May I call you Allan since we're in this together? . . . I don't like the play either, so let's tear it to pieces. We *have* to make it." And that's exactly what we did.

Claudette was very objective in her criticism, accurately pinpointing the script's flaws and analyzing the role from the actress' point of view. She never argued or debated a point and was willing to listen to the suggestions of others. By the time our first session together was over, I realized that I had experienced one of the most exhilarating and productive "story conferences" I ever had. I knew that I had been talking to someone who knew her business.

ALLAN SCOTT *has written many screenplays, including* Quality Street, In Name Only, A Woman Rebels, Notorious, The Paradine Case, Wait Till the Sun Shines Nellie, The Five Thousand Fingers of Dr. T, Imitation of Life, The Four Poster, *six Fred Astaire-Ginger Rogers musicals, and three films for Claudette Colbert.*

With Joel McCrea in Preston Sturges' The Palm Beach Story, *a film that made good use of her sophisticated comedy talents.*

Colbert was probably the best screen Cleopatra.

I wrote two more films for Claudette, *Remember the Day* (1941) and *So Proudly We Hail!* (1943). If she had trouble with the script, she would call me to her dressing room or home to discuss it. I would explain to her what I meant by what I had written. Sometimes she was content. Other times, when she was still bothered, she was quite clear as to why the scene wasn't working for her. She never said, ''I can't play this scene'' or ''There's something wrong with it'' or even ''It stinks.'' Her attitude was ''I think I'm missing something here,'' and I instinctively knew that there was probably something wrong. She never gave up on a scene or a line because

she knew they weren't easy to come by.

Claudette's professionalism was as evident on the set. She always knew where the key light was, and actually knew more about lighting than most of her directors. She had one eccentricity; she insisted that the set be built around her because the right side of her face was apple-cheeked, and the lights brought that out even more. When you had to shoot the right side of her face, she insisted it be done with long shots, *never* in close-up. She knew how she wanted to look and was powerful enough to gain that luxury. This also went for the way she dressed. She and Edith Head, Paramount's head

BRANDY AND SYMPATHY

WHEN MY WIFE of over thirty years died suddenly, I received a note from Claudette Colbert expressing her sympathy and asking me to visit her in Barbados. I refused. But in the desperate vacuum that followed, I made myself write a play. It was purchased, and when the producers asked me who should play in it, I said, ''Colbert.''

Within a few days Claudette called. ''Allan, why didn't you send me the play yourself? If you want me to do it, you must come down and visit me at once for an extended vacation, and if you don't, I'll never talk to you again.''

I flew to Barbados. For days, she wouldn't talk about the play. Instead, she made me escort her to all the

social functions of the island. Then, finally, one night over brandy, very softly as I remember, she said as she took my hand, ''Allan, I'm not going to do your play. And furthermore, you ought not let them do it. Sure, it's funny — you can always make people laugh, but you won't like it, as I don't. Your grief and bitterness show on every page, and even if it's a hit, you will be sorry.''

We were silent for a moment; I didn't know what to say. Then she said simply, ''My dear Allan, most of us don't know about happiness until it's over,'' and kissed me lightly.

When I got home, I called off the play and destroyed it.

— A. S.

So Proudly We Hail *was a tribute to army nurses on Bataan.*

costume designer, would talk endlessly and Edie would sketch endlessly until it suited them both.

As her star faded years later, she didn't wait for leads in less important pictures. She took herself to France, where she made several pictures, taking advantage of a tax loophole of the time. Claudette amassed another fortune and retired to Barbados.

After her husband's death, Claudette returned to Broadway, where she began. As the years went by, she still retained that youthful gaiety I remember so well, and looked half her age. She has enormous vitality, charm, technique, undeniable sex appeal — and, still, those legs.

Married to Fred MacMurray in the comedy hit The Egg and I.

COOKING UP A STORM

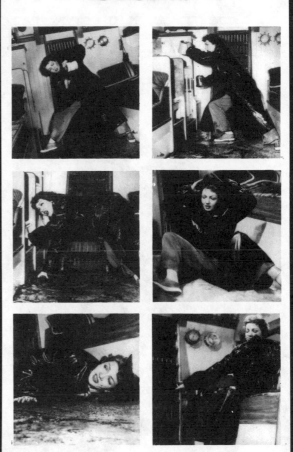

IN *Skylark* Claudette Colbert had a tightly blocked comedy routine. She had to prepare a meal aboard a yacht during a storm. It is one of the most hilarious scenes I have ever seen on the screen: As she tries to make a meal, the salad and salad oil fall on the floor and the food she is cooking slides off the stove, spattering. She slips and flounders all over the floor of the galley, trying to rescue some coffee beans she has spilled. She slides the length of the floor, falling against the refrigerator, which opens to a solemn, sad-eyed fish looking at her.

Then, mucky and disheveled, she scoops up some beans, gets back to the sink, grinds the beans into a cup, pours in some cold water, and, determined not to spill a drop (and she never did), makes her way gingerly up the stairs. When she triumphantly reaches the top, the boat suddenly lurches and she slides back down the stairs, across the galley floor once again, and ends up in a heap, weeping.

Claudette did it in one take, a marvelous piece of funny improvisation. As she passed us on the set, she merely said, ''Who the hell said I couldn't clown?'' I'll bet Claudette could have repeated it.

— A. S.

FREDRIC MARCH:
A MAN IN CHARACTER

DELBERT MANN

Hollywood noticed him when he played John Barrymore on stage.

F REDRIC MARCH was one of the first major actors to move from theater to films and back to theater again, achieving ever-growing and deepening work in both mediums. The man with the beautiful voice made the even more difficult transition from dashing,

DELBERT MANN *is the Academy Award-winning director of* Marty. *Among his other credits are* The Bachelor Party, Desire Under the Elms, Separate Tables, The Dark at the Top of the Stairs, Lover Come Back, *and* That Touch of Mink.

handsome, romantic leading man to mature character actor with never a pause in his career, as only a handful of actors have been able to do.

"He made that transition earlier than he had to," remembers Florence Eldridge, his wife for more than forty years and his favorite acting partner, both on stage and in films. "He had observed the awkwardness of other romantic male stars who, after years of wobbling around, suddenly found it time to be a character actor. So, by choice, Freddie started to play character parts in films and on stage."

She says that he was essentially a "character actor," always searching for the reality of the character he was playing. "For all his apparent gregariousness, for all his liking of people and liking to be liked by people, Freddie was a very private man. When he could hide behind another person in a role, he was more comfortable than when playing himself." As with many other great actors, Freddie would often find an external thing — a walk, a voice, some physical manifestation — and from that be stimulated into building the whole character. He discovered the outer part and from that found the inner.

Freddie's method of working was the same for theater, with its lengthy rehearsal period, as it was for film — which normally has no such rehearsal structure. He was, of course, aware of the differences in technique such as vocal and physical projection, but his search for the character — for the truth — was the same. In film, as in the theater, Freddie always did his homework. When he started a film he understood the entire role.

Character traits and mannerisms were thought out in great detail. He understood the character's background, his physical and emotional history, everything from the shoes on his character's feet to what he would have in his pockets. The margins of Freddie's scripts were filled with hundreds of notes. This was his method of deep analysis and study, of working from within himself, a personal system he had firmly established for himself long before "The Method" became popularized.

Often when he had a long or complicated speech to learn, Freddie would improvise first. Once he had the

With Olivia de Havilland in
Anthony Adverse.

the Night (1959), Willy Loman in *Death of a Salesman* (1951), Al Stephenson in *The Best Years of Our Lives* (1946), Norman Maine in *A Star Is Born* (1937), Vronsky in *Anna Karenina* (1935), Jean Valjean in *Les Misérables* (1935), Robert Browning in *The Barretts of Wimpole Street* (1934), Prince Sirki in *Death Takes a Holiday* (1934), *Dr. Jekyll and Mr. Hyde* (1932), and many more.

The list of his credits include seventy-one films, four live television dramas, eighteen Broadway plays, two Antoinette Perry (Tony) Awards (for *Years Ago* and *Long Day's Journey into Night*), two Academy Awards (for *Dr. Jekyll and Mr. Hyde* and *The Best Years of Our Lives*), plus three more Oscar nominations. He chose parts on the basis of the quality of the material as a whole. He never looked for a great role in poor plays. He always felt that he would grow more in handling rich material than just star vehicles. Of the Broadway plays he did, seven were among the season's Ten Best Plays and two were Pulitzer Prize-winners (*The Skin of Our Teeth* and *Long Day's Journey into Night*). His is one of the most truly distinguished careers in American film and theater.

complete thought and feeling expressed in his own words he would find a way to express it in the author's words and, having great respect for writers, he made himself letter perfect.

Freddie's skill at underplaying seems to be one of the reasons his performances have not dated. In performance after performance, Freddie's character moves across the screen, alive and real for today — Harry Hope in *The Iceman Cometh* (1973), Matthew Harrison Brady in *Inherit the Wind* (1960), Jerry Kingsley in *Middle of*

Freddie March combined talent, taste, skill and professionalism with an honesty and a warmth of personality. He never complained; his only demand was equal professional dedication from others. He emanated an enormous sense of security in his professionalism and a great sense of humor that made the difficult work easier. There was also an all-too-rare openness to direction, a free, respectful give-and-take-between-actor-and direc-tor-where a raised eyebrow or a half-articulated phrase or

In the Lubitsch comedy
Design for Living (L),
March courted the
wonderful Miriam
Hopkins. Earlier he had
treated her with much
less respect in Dr. Jekyll
and Mr. Hyde.

One of his best characters. The Adventures of Mark Twain.

simply a pause communicates everything. It is a relationship so special it generates a lasting love and friendship.

He did not find it easy working with rigid or dogmatic directors, the "now-at-this-moment-you-will-turn-and-cross-and-do-it-this-way" type. Florence Eldridge has said, "I have seen him give less than his best if a director tried to show him exactly how to do it. He could, however, always work within a director's framework. He could always accommodate himself to the overall plan."

Doing one's best was a family trait learned in childhood from a father he adored. March was competitive, ambitious, motivated, but friendly, well-rounded, and well-adjusted. It was not fear of defeat that drove him, but rather a challenge he accepted with courage and security. A fellow actor said, "Freddie on an opening night could come out and play over his head, with joy. While everybody else was throwing up and barely able to move, he would be having the romp of his life!"

Freddie was a professional who continued to grow throughout his creative life. Many believe that he did his best and richest work in his last ten years — it seemed to be a summing up of all he had learned and known. The last years were made difficult by deteriorating health, but his professionalism, his summoning of all his remaining

The Road to Glory, *directed by Howard Hawks and scripted by his friend William Faulkner. (L–R) Lionel Barrymore, Warner Baxter, June Lang, and Fredric March.*

A MASTER OF NUANCES

Kim Novak and Fredric March in Middle of the Night, *directed by Delbert Mann.*

IN THE FILM *Middle of the Night,* Fredric March plays Jerry Kingsley, a still-vital, active middle-aged New York garment manufacturer, caught in a struggle with well-meaning friends and relatives who wish him to conform. With the young Kim Novak, Freddie heartbreakingly conveyed the joy and pain of his character's situation. He was like a teenager going through the sweet anguish of a first love, but when necessary, Fred appeared defeated, tired, old before his time. Fred was able to do this so convincingly, because he was able to probe from within, to find; and to express clearly the deepest nuances and truths of the character so specifically conceived by Paddy Chayefsky.

— D. M.

strength, overcame the problems and resulted in his triumphant, heartbreaking performance in *The Iceman Cometh.* At tremendous cost to himself, it was, in essence, his final gift to his audience and his fellow performers. He continued to the end with pride in his craft, dedication to the nobility of his beloved profession.

As Jean LaFitte in lavish costume drama. At right in scene with Evelyn Keyes.

EDWARD G. ROBINSON: MIND OF AN ARTIST

LEONARD SPIGELGASS

IT WAS HARD AT FIRST to look at Eddie's picture on TV. I found myself trying not to cry, and not succeeding. I missed him — and the talks we had. Long talks, so diverse, so intelligent (on his side, surely), . . . so gone.

I tried not to let him go.

I completed his autobiography *All My Yesterdays*; I did the required TV and luncheon tours to promote it; I wrote pieces about him.

But he was not with me.

Not until six years have passed.

Not until now.

He's back. The hurt is over; the joy is back. I can think about him again, and write about him again —

even laugh about him again. What I *cannot* do is to tell you about what he'd think of current art or current performances.

He had the supreme, and in our time, infrequent, ability to change as the world changed. He embraced — after a "trial period" — new schools of art and even accepted an abstract theater. But he was basically unable to accept in theater what he accepted in art: that visual communication was superior to verbal communication.

He loved to talk. He loved to listen. He loved a theater in which actors talked to each other, and at each other, and maintained a relationship throughout the two and a half hours of a play. He never reconciled himself to the movies in which you did the last scene first, and in which you never had the opportunity to sustain a performance, but tried to create characters in fragmented bits.

Talk — conversation — was so desperately important to him, because he had come to it with such difficulty. Born in Rumania, Edward G. Robinson was a classic steerage immigrant to this country. When he arrived he was fluent in Rumanian, French, German, Russian, Yiddish, and Hebrew, but had no English whatever.

Surely, when he learned to speak it, the language of his adopted country, he would have an Eastern European accent. How, then, did he get that mid-Atlantic voice — deep, resonant, utterly unaccented? It was because, he told me, that by some quirk of fate he was not, in his first school in this country, assigned to a class with other immigrant children, but was placed with native-born Americans. They spoke English with a New York

The end of Rico in Little Caesar *was the beginning of a magnificent movie career for Edward G. Robinson.*

LEONARD SPIGELGASS *has written six plays, five books, and seventy-five screenplays, including* Gypsy, A Majority of One, I Was a Male War Bride, All Through the Night, *and* So Evil, My Love. *He received an Academy Award nomination in 1950 in the Best Original Story category for* Mystery Street. *He was Edward G. Robinson's friend for forty years.*

Little Giant, *another Warners gangster film.*

He was graduated from the Academy, after playing a lot of Ibsen. But Ibsen was not in vogue in the theater of the day, so he took a job with a stock company, mostly running to get cigarettes and booze for the stars, and was only occasionally permitted to appear on stage — maybe as a coolie or a slum kid. This was

accent, but even that, over the years, he winnowed out of his voice.

The second influence on the way he spoke was the theater. Almost from the beginning, he became one of the Gallery Gods, installed in the second balcony. From there he listened to the great Shakespearean actors — the tragedians, both male and female — and he copied them, impersonated them, made their way of speaking his. They were his elocution teachers. And soon his elocution was good enough for him to begin making public speeches on behalf of political candidates — William Randolph Hearst, for one, a gentleman whose views in later years were so radically different from his own.

The political stump gave him the courage to work in school plays, to enter amateur contests at Loew's theaters, to decide — when he was still a sophomore at C.C.N.Y. — to become an actor, and to go to school to learn his craft. He was accepted at the American Academy of the Dramatic Arts and worked on his voice, his stance, his walk, his dueling.

What he could not work on (then or ever) was his look, his height, his inability ever to be tall and blue-eyed and square-jawed — minimum essentials for true stardom in the theater in the second decade of this century.

And yet, dark and short — and, in a very real sense, homely — he prevailed.

How?

Because he had no choice. The urge in him, the need in him, was so great that he could not permit himself ever to be discouraged. (Years later, I would sit with him and he would discuss the future and his plans for it, theatrical plans — and there was no discouragement in him at the age of seventy-nine, even though he knew he was "under a death sentence.")

An immigrant himself, Robinson was perfectly cast in films such as Silver Dollar *(Top) with Aline MacMahon, but he did just as well in* Confessions of a Nazi Spy *where he exalted the American way of life.*

With Bogart in the comedy-gangster film Brother Orchid.

With Bette Davis in Kid Galahad.

hardly making his future career a gilt-edged security. Then came World War I and the Navy, and the ability to play skits for servicemen, and that gave him a sense of comedy and timing.

Then, the war over, a chance in a real play — only because he spoke French and German and was willing to play seven parts for one salary. He played them all beautifully — and I've got press cuttings to prove it. He was on his way to forty plays in the New York theater and stardom.

And then came the movies — and he certainly became a movie star — and I can now tell you what he was getting around to tell you in his book when he died: He never liked it.

He loved the money and the status, and while he frequently suggested he hated autograph hunters, he secretly adored them. But acting in the movies took so little of his talent, so little of his energy, so little of the real man inside the actor, that he turned to other loves.

With an eye rarely equaled in our time, he began to buy paintings and sculpture — some deep instinct guiding him — and eventually had not one but two art collections, the first sold after a divorce, and the second at his death, for millions. Today those pictures by Matisse and Picasso and every great French Impressionist, would be in the $50-million bracket. But take my solemn oath on it. It was not for their monetary worth that he bought them; it was because those works of art were so beautiful, so gentle, so caressing, so fulfilling to his spirit.

And the fourth side of his life (the first of course, was his marriage and child, his mother and brothers) was his passion for human justice, a passion that brought him into serious and thoroughly unjustified conflict with the House Un-American Activities Committee. He went through a bad time, indeed. And I suspect the only time he really loved the movies was then, when he was prevented from doing them.

But he came back, and watching him, as I'm able to now, at a poker table with Steve McQueen in *The Cincinnati Kid* (1965), or acting bewildered in *The Old Man*

Who Cried Wolf (TVM, 1970), you come to see how all the facets of his life were used to make him a consummate actor. (And you can see that he may be short, but he is tall indeed; and that his face is perhaps not Barrymore's or Redford's, but is somehow even more beautiful.)

Strange that he is gone now, but that he lives late at night. I turn on the TV set and watch him, and his warmth and his philosophy and his influence on the Dustin Hoffmans and the Sylvester Stallones and the Marlon Brandos is palpable.

Star he was — my friend he remains.

As a supporting player to Steve McQueen in The Cincinnati Kid.

LAURENCE OLIVIER: THE POWER AND THE GLORY

CHARLES BENNETT

I FIRST MET Laurence Olivier in 1927, (when he was still called Larry) at London's then-recently formed Arts Theatre Club. Although only around nineteen, he was already making his mark on the West End stage. But so were many others and I have wondered why it was Larry, my junior, who stuck in my mind. In no sense was he pushy or flamboyantly assertive. Instead, I'd describe the Larry of those days as shy, diffident, retiring, not easy to know. But neither was he easy to forget.

Years passed before Larry and I were to meet again, but when that occasion came, it couldn't have been at a more dramatic time: It was 1944. War. After nearly a decade in Hollywood, I was back in London, writing for the British Ministry of Information (the MOI), happy to do anything I could to upset Hitler's applecart. I was working for the MOI for expenses only and was not averse to earning some money on the side by writing a screenplay — at the invitation of Filippo Del Giudice — about seventeen-year-old Madeleine Smith, who was charged with (but not convicted of) murder, in 1857.

Olivier was to produce and direct the movie, with his wife Vivien Leigh playing the young Scottish suspect. So, again I met Larry . . . by this time a famous actor, director, and personality. In a way the reunion was a shock. The shy young man of 1927 had become an entirely self-possessed individual with a mind which, unlike most producers of my working acquaintance, could leap ahead of a writer's thought with gratifying

A serious posture in That Hamilton Woman.

swiftness. I soon found that talking with the matured Larry was an intellectual and creative delight. And yet behind Larry's not infrequent flashes of brilliance, I still sensed that same retiring diffidence. That barrier which had once seemed to be shyness might now be construed as aloofness. But it wasn't — and isn't — aloofness. Under Larry's exterior one finds a man who takes a quiet delight in friendship and in increasing the enjoyment of

CHARLES BENNETT *is an English playwright, novelist, and screenwriter, who wrote many of Alfred Hitchcock's early films, including* Sabotage, The Thirty-Nine Steps, The Man Who Knew Too Much, *and* Foreign Correspondent, *for which he received an Academy Award nomination. He wrote the script for Laurence Olivier's planned, but never filmed,* Madeleine Smith.

With Joan Fontaine in the home movie in Hitchcock's Rebecca.

other people. This soon became clear to me over the next few weeks.

In Britain in World War II, particularly during the Blitz, the question of morale was all-important. The job of artists such as Larry was to entertain and help keep up the national spirits.

So when I went to Glasgow on MOI business, coincidentally Larry was there too, playing, in effect, for the government at the King's Theater in a repertoire of plays. It was entertainment necessary to the aforesaid question of public morale. Since Glasgow was Madeleine Smith's city, we took advantage of the lucky coincidence while we both carried on with wartime chores. Larry performed in the evenings, but in the daytime he put in many usefully exploratory hours. Joined by novelist Compton ("Monty") MacKenzie, we delved

into the secrets of the still-standing Smith residence, from which, through a small sidewalk-level window, Madeleine had allegedly passed cups of hot cocoa — well-laced with arsenic — to her young lover, Emile l'Angelier. We explored the woods of Roweleyn above Gare Loch, where Madeleine first made love with the young Frenchman. We even made a trip to Edinburgh and visited the scene of the trial. We examined Madeleine's yellowed-with-age — and sizzling — letters to her lover. Finally, with Larry researching with all the thoroughness of Sherlock Holmes, we unearthed evidence, never known or produced at the trial, that would most certainly have sent the young lady to the gallows. Luckily for Madeleine our discoveries came nearly a hundred years too late.

And we took some time to be just tourists.

Somehow Larry learned that I had never seen Stirling Castle, so he rented a car and off we went. Larry, like a professional guide, showed me around the great fortress, paraded the magnificence of the battlements with all the pride of the king of the castle, obviously reveling in my appreciation.

In using the word "reveling," I should add that Larry's emotions, though genuine, always seem to be *underplayed*. Fortunately he can carry this trait into his art, be it in film or theater.

Theatrical history relates that in 1742, David Garrick astounded a Drury Lane Theater audience by speaking Shylock's lines naturally, as though he were actually *thinking* them. This was a violent change from the ranting form of delivery then acceptable. The audience was mystified, but before the evening was over it was enthralled by a new acting technique — underplaying.

With Geraldine Fitzgerald (when he should have been with Merle Oberon) in Wuthering Heights, *his first American film.*

THE BATTLE WON

LAURENCE OLIVIER has a bend-over-backward desire to give credit to others — a generosity sadly lacking in many stars, producers, directors, writers. Too many of us are happy to grab credit rather than give it. Not Larry.

Once, over a sparse, wartime-rationed lunch at the Garrick Club, Larry talked to me of his admiration and gratitude to Two Cities Films' Filippo Del Giudice. He told me Del had given him carte blanche to make the films and deliver the messages so necessary during those desperate war years. Take *Henry V*. Larry was star, director, and producer. Del was head of the production company, the studio, the *money*. But according to Larry, Del saved the film from what could have been a disaster.

For those who saw the film version, few can forget the charge of the French knights at the Battle of Agincourt. To me that scene surpasses the destruction of Atlanta in *Gone With the Wind*. The charge — that tremendous piece of visual drama — called for scores (possibly hundreds) of splendiferously costumed knights on horseback . . . the flower of French chivalry.

Larry Olivier planned and directed the brilliant British campaign, both visually and technically. Always creatively imaginative, Larry had a railroad track laid alongside the mile or so of the scene of battle, from which the camera, mounted on a traveling flatcar, could shoot the entire length of the famous charge of French knights, adjusting its speed and gathering momentum as the action advanced.

The knights started their steeds at a walk, which increased to a trot, becoming a canter, merging into a gallop . . . finally becoming the full, thundering charge. Masses of heavily armored assailants hurtled toward a meager army that seemed about to be overwhelmed. Then came director-Larry's magic moment. A direct cut to the long, thin line of waiting English longbowmen. *ZING!* Off went the arrows, arching, hitting the advancing horde. Down went the knights, horses screaming, dying . . . and, in effect, as history relates, the battle was won.

But not Larry's battle. When the negative was examined it was found to be badly scratched, all of it — hundreds of feet from one end to the other!

Naturally, director-star Larry was heartbroken — and terribly worried that the battle scene would be forever lost because of the tremendous costs involved in redoing it. Despite the money, Filippo Del Giudice said the magic word: ''Reshoot!''

Larry did as he was permitted, magnificently and gratefully. The result was one of the greatest and most morale-lifting movies ever made, with a tracking shot beyond anybody's dreams. The credit? According to Larry it went to Del for having put artistic endeavor (and an investment, which happily paid off) before that dreaded word ''cost.''

— C. B.

In our century, Sir Gerald du Maurier, who could ''throw away'' a line and yet have its force hit the back of the gallery, was recognized as the master of this art form. Sir Gerald is no longer with us, but Larry is, and his underplaying, when necessary, is the tops. Nothing could be more gentle, more quietly wistful than his ''Upon the King'' soliloquy in his film version of Shakespeare's *Henry V* (1944). I was lucky enough to be

Olivier co-starred with and directed Marilyn Monroe in The Prince and the Showgirl. *After her death, he said: ''Hollywood made her the complete victim of ballyhoo and sensation . . . she was exploited beyond anyone's dreams.''*

Olivier's film career was revived when he starred with Michael Caine in Joseph L. Mankiewicz's Sleuth *in 1972.*

present at the film's premiere at London's Carlton Theater. Larry's performance was so compelling that when a V-2 bomb fell less than a quarter mile away, seemingly tilting the theater upside down, Larry's quiet delivery had the shaken audience hushed and listening again for his whispered words even before the shock of the bomb had subsided.

But the same Larry who could hypnotize an audience with a whisper could also stir it into frenzy. In the same film young King Henry exhorts his troops before the walls of Harfleur: "Once more unto the breach, dear friends, once more, or close the wall up with our English dead." Larry's delivery carried his audience way beyond Harfleur, reminding the wartime world that even Hitler's "Fortress Europe" — his envelopment of a defeated continent — could still be "breached," given the guts to attempt it. Larry's ringing tones, Shakespeare's words, were sounding when the "wall" was breached on the beaches of Normandy.

A few of the great actors of the British stage and screen have achieved the royal honor of knighthood. Of course, Larry is one of them. But knighthood aside, our shy, diffident nineteen-year-old early member of the Arts Theater Club went on to achieve heights which no actor on earth has ever dreamed of attaining. I'm not talking about money — unlike fellow countryman Ronald Colman, Larry preferred to work away from Hollywood where he might have made a fortune — but the fact that

Larry is a living legend. He is an incomparable actor who creates mammoth characters through a critical analytic process; a director who doesn't just instruct but shapes his films; an artist, a creator who is only the fourth man in history honored by having a London theater named after him. This writer salutes the Baron (Lord) Olivier of Brighton. *Larry!*

As the evil Nazi dentist in Marathon Man.

OLIVIER AS DIRECTOR

FEW FILM DIRECTORS or actors want to risk failure in adaptations of famous plays or literature. Olivier, however, prefers to face such a challenge. Since Shakespeare is the most difficult playwright to transfer to film, Olivier has acted in and directed several of his plays. Besides *Henry V,* he has given us heralded productions of *Richard III* (Top left) with Claire Bloom; *Hamlet* (Top right); and *Othello* with Maggie Smith.

RUTH GORDON: LATE BLOOMER

GARSON KANIN

In her prime.

GARSON KANIN *coauthored three screenplays with his wife Ruth Gordon which were nominated for Academy Awards:* A Double Life, Adam's Rib, *and* Pat and Mike. *He also wrote screenplays (alone or with Gordon) for* The Marrying Kind, It Should Happen to You, The Rat Race, Where It's At, *and* Some Kind of a Nut *and was the original author of* Born Yesterday *and* High Time. *He has directed films that include* The Great Man Votes, Bachelor Mother, My Favorite Wife, They Knew What They Wanted, *and* Tom, Dick, and Harry. *He is the author of the best-selling biography* Tracy and Hepburn.

". . . AND THE WINNER IS . . . ," says Tony Curtis. He takes a little more time than he needs to open the easy-to-open envelope, removes the slip, and reads, "Ruth Gordon, for *Rosemary's Baby*!"

Applause. The diminutive, seventy-two-year-old dynamo, dressed to the nines, bounds up onto the runway and takes the stage.

She accepts the statuette and bestows the traditional kiss upon the donor. She looks at the Oscar, then at the audience, and says, fervently, "Well, I can't tell you how encouragin' a thing like this is!" The audience responds with laughter and further applause and delight. Ruth goes on. "The first money I ever earned was as an extra in 1915, and here it is 1969. I don't know what took me so long. Thank you, Roman. Thank you, Bob. Thank you, Mia. Thank you, Bill. And all of you who voted for me, thank you. And all of you who didn't, excuse me."

The next morning, among the messages and cables and wires — one that reads:

DEAR RUTH: WHAT DID TAKE YOU SO
LONG? CONGRATULATIONS AND LOVE.

MARY PICKFORD.

In the seventh decade of her life, Ruth Gordon became an authentic movie star and would soon solidify that position with *Where's Poppa?* as well as *Harold and Maude*.

Hope for us all.

When I was invited to write about her for this collection, I hesitated, wondering if I should, in view of the fact that she has been, for thirty-six years, my wife.

Gertrude Stein said, "Writing is telling what you know." I proceed, then, because if there is a single subject on which I qualify as an expert, it is the subject of Ruth Gordon.

I know how she lives. I know how she works.

She claims to be a taught actress rather than a born one. Hard to believe, but that is her story. She began, she insists, clumsily and negatively and almost always badly reviewed. Her dream at that time was to be included in the list of "Also in the Cast" instead of being singled out

Ruth Gordon joined the film ranks in 1940, playing opposite Raymond Massey in Abe Lincoln in Illinois.

for a slam. She learned from her husband, Gregory Kelly, a dazzlingly accomplished actor. Later, a long association with Jed Harris, the finest of directors, opened new vistas. She acknowledges many debts. Among them, to Arthur Hopkins, Alexander Woollcott, Max Gordon, and especially to Guthrie McClintic and Thornton Wilder.

"I think I can learn anything if someone will just take the trouble to teach me."

On the subject of women, Cornelius Hackl in *The Matchmaker* says, "Golly, they're different from men. And they're awfully mysterious, too. You never can be really sure what's going on in their heads. They have a kind of wall around them all the time — of pride and a sort of playacting. I bet you could know a woman a hundred years without ever being really sure whether she liked you or not."

For Cornelius Hackl read "Thornton Wilder" and for Thornton Wilder read "The Rest of Us," whose secret wonderings he taps with his poet's wand. I have known my wife, Ruth Gordon, for something less than a hundred years, and although I am reasonably certain that she likes me, she is indeed mysterious, and yes there is that wall and that pride. As for playacting, well, of course that is her occupation — rather, one of her occupations. She has several. Married to this versatile creature, I enjoy many of the advantages of polygamy without having to deal with its complexities.

There is the stage actress, dining at 5:30 P.M., then inaccessible until the curtain falls, and throughout the day preoccupied with considerations of the evening to come. What will the audience be like? Will she make it?

The screen actress rises at 6:00 A.M. and is seen no more until nightfall, when she begins to worry about how she could have — should have — done what is already done. The companion between roles is a cornucopian delight, ever surprising. Beginning a day, she may say, "Good morning," or "They never should have thrown away the double-decker buses!"

The housekeeper is impeccable; the critic, tough; the collaborator, impossible; the helpmate, indispensable. (At my side throughout rehearsals of *The Diary of Anne Frank,* she kept warning, "It's getting *dearie* again!" and kept me from falling into the trap of sentimentality, which would have been fatal to that work.)

The writer is fiercely disciplined, exhaustingly thorough, keep-out private, and maddeningly stubborn. I was divorced from this one in 1951, after writing four original screenplays with her: *A Double Life, Adam's Rib, Pat and Mike,* and *The Marrying Kind.* We quarreled on each of them with increasing intensity and decided to go our separate ways thereafter insofar as writing was concerned. Since that time, a return to Eden — for the most part.

I reflect that in thirty-six years of marriage, our only serious disagreements have been related to creative efforts. Our closest friend accuses us of taking our work more seriously than we take ourselves or each other. I wonder if this is so.

Ruth contends that imagination and endurance are what matter most in work and in life. She cultivates both assiduously.

To develop the former, she avoids the clutter of information, gossip, trivia, and — to a great extent

With Mia Farrow in Rosemary's Baby, *the horror-thriller that earned Gordon an Academy Award.*

while she is at work — other works of the imagination. She reads French theater memoirs, the diaries of John Adams, miles of Thoreau's journals, piles of biography and history. Even in the city of New York, even in the middle of the twentieth century, she finds ways of pursuing the contemplative life. She remains close to nature — a sphere I cannot enter with her — engrossed in weather, animals, flowers, and food.

As to endurance, she concerns herself with health and nutrition and exercise and optimism, making each day a time to begin. I talk about what one must do; she does it. Normally gregarious, she resists the big city's enervating temptations.

She is staunch in crisis, but weeps at the sight of a

With George Segal and Ron Leibman, her sons in Where's Poppa?

parade. She accepts criticism stoically, but cries at a compliment. And, during the war, when the time came for me to go overseas, she kissed me good-bye and smiled. The tears came when I returned two years later.

From her Broadway debut in *Peter Pan* with Maude Adams in 1915 to Hollywood stardom has been a long and rocky journey. Ruth has acted in over fifty plays — four of which she herself wrote. There have been ups and downs, seven fat and *several* seven lean, hits and flops.

She went to Hollywood in 1935 with an MGM contract but made no films until 1939, when she played Mary Todd in *Abe Lincoln in Illinois* (1940) at RKO and Mrs. Ehrlich in *Doctor Ehrlich's Magic Bullet* (1940) for Warner Brothers.

In 1942, she made two films at Warners: *Edge of Darkness* (in thirteen weeks) and *Action in the North Atlantic* (in two days!).

It was not until the 1960s that Ruth began to act steadily in films, making *Inside Daisy Clover* (1965), for which she received an Academy Award nomination, *Lord Love a Duck* (1966), *Rosemary's Baby* (1968), and *Whatever Happened to Aunt Alice?* (1969).

On December 21, 1965, Ruth celebrated her golden anniversary as an actress. She vetoed every suggestion for its celebration. "The thing is to have a job," she says. "My *part* is my party."

The seventies brought *Where's Poppa?* (1970), *Harold and Maude* (1971), and many television appearances.

She became a star of the major talk shows, discussing her career and her biographies *Myself Among Others* and *My Side*.

As I write this, Ruth has just completed *Every Which Way But Loose* with Clint Eastwood, has completed a new book, is planning a future one, and is preparing appearances at two Ruth Gordon film festivals, one in Baltimore, the other in San Francisco.

★ ★ ★ ★ ★

In my personal dictionary, the word "professional" is the highest praise, the least bestowed. I know thousands of practitioners, hundreds of talents, dozens of stars, and several geniuses — but only five professionals. Ruth is one of these. Once engaged, the performance of the job comes first. When she has a part in a play, she is in the habit of going over that part every day. She played *The Matchmaker* 1,078 times (without missing a single performance), and on the afternoon before the final performance, I was astonished to come upon her "doing her part."

She prepares her film roles in the same painstaking, imaginative way. Ruth plans her wardrobe, her accent, her slant on each part as if it were the *only* part. She has remained blissfully stagestruck, with the power to transfer the lovely madness to others. Ruth has not submitted to plastic surgery for the sake of rejuvenation, nor has she achieved her youthful appearance and spirit from pills or magic elixirs.

Among her closest and most intimate friends these days are the young people she has encountered in the course of her recent work. They are interested in her; she is interested in them and in their problems and careers and aspirations. Mia Farrow says, "I don't think I'm a hippie. My only hippie friend is Ruth Gordon."

Ruth says, "I'm in love with the past, but I'm having a love affair with the future."

Her convictions, based upon preparation and study and thought, are unshakable, even in the face of strong opposing evidence. Establishments, as such, no matter how august, do not faze her. She says, "It takes courage. It takes believing in it. It takes rising above it. It takes work. It takes you liking me and me liking you. It takes the dreaming soul of the human race that *wants* it to go right! Let's never stop dreaming.

"Think it over."

★ ★ ★ ★ ★

There comes a moment in life when you know that you have made it. Ruth's came not so long ago. She had spent the afternoon with her five-year-old grandson, Jack Harris. When she left, a playmate asked him, "Do you *like* your grandmother?"

"Of course," said Jack.

"Why?" persisted his little friend.

"Because," Jack replied with indignant logic, "she's a *movie star*!"

NOT YOUR STANDARD LOVE AFFAIR

Harold and Maude is scheduled for re-release in February 1979. The film has proved to be a nonesuch. Relatively unsuccessful at first, this story of a love affair involving an eighty-year-old woman and a twenty-year-old boy has developed into a cult film. In cities all over the world — especially those with large college-age populations — it has achieved runs of two to three years. It is constantly revived everywhere. The fan mail is voluminous. Hardly a day passes when Ruth is not approached on the street by someone who wants to tell her that they have seen the film six times or sixteen times or forty times. In almost every case, it is a young person, although many older people have reported a similar response.

This suggests to me that there is in the psyche of the community a deep, visceral desire for peace between the generations.

— G. K.

The seventies' favorite movie couple: Bud Cort and Ruth Gordon.

RICHARD BURTON: A TRUE PRINCE OF PLAYERS

PHILIP DUNNE

A perfect choice for Edwin Booth.

IN 1949 MY WIFE AND I, vacationing in London, went to see Christopher Fry's play *The Lady's Not for Burning*. John Gielgud was the star, but even his formidable presence failed to eclipse the performance of the young actor who played the juvenile lead.

His name was Richard Burton, and he brought far more than mere technical excellence to his performance. He played with a smoldering intensity and with a sense of poetry that more than did justice to Fry's deliberately archaic blank verse. In theater parlance, he "took" the stage and kept a firm grip on it during every one of his brief appearances.

When we returned to Hollywood — I was under contract as a writer-producer-director to Twentieth Century-Fox at the time — I sent a note about the young actor to the chief of production, Darryl F. Zanuck. Darryl replied that the studio was already interested; soon afterwards, Richard Burton was signed to a contract.

Three years later, Zanuck asked me to undertake the rewrite of *The Robe* (1953). When I asked rather glumly what I was supposed to do with it, he replied succinctly: "Put it in English." It was not my favorite assignment. I am not fond of what the motion picture industry calls "biblical epics," in particular the compounds of sex and sadism masquerading as religion-according-to-De Mille. My task, fortunately, was made easier by the knowledge

PHILIP DUNNE *received Academy Award nominations for Best Screenplay for* How Green Was My Valley, *1941's Oscar-winning picture, and* David and Bathsheba. *Among his other screenplays are* Stanley and Livingston, The Rains Came, Son of Fury, The Ghost and Mrs. Muir, The Late George Apley, Pinky, *and* The Robe. *He both directed and wrote such films as* Ten North Frederick, The View from Pompey's Head, Blue Denim, *and* Blindfold. *He holds the Writers Guild Laurel Award for lifetime achievement.*

that the two leads would be the talented Jean Simmons and Richard Burton, by this time a rising movie star. And in fact, their performances and the fine direction of Henry Koster lifted *The Robe* far beyond most biblical

Zanuck made The Robe *in Cinemascope. It was a sensation.*

epics; the picture, the first in the new Cinemascope process, was an enormous financial success.

Darryl Zanuck didn't encourage writers to visit sound stages, so I saw very little of Richard during the shooting of *The Robe.* A year or so later we were thrown into a situation of great professional intimacy when I directed him in Moss Hart's screenplay of *Prince of Players* (1955), the film biography of America's renowned nineteenth-century actor Edwin Booth.

No director can make a bad script into a good movie, but a good script can be destroyed by a failure of communication between director and actor. If one or the other is selfish, stubborn, egomaniacal, or simply inept, the inevitable result is chaos. I can say with certainty that only once, with Gary Cooper on *Ten North Frederick* (1958), did I experience as warm a rapport with an actor as I did with Richard Burton on *Prince of Players.*

I suppose that in part this was because there was nothing I could teach Richard about his craft. All I had to do was point the camera and let him alone. This was particularly true when we filmed the excerpts from Shakespeare which Moss Hart had included in his script. Richard had already done a superior *Hamlet* at the Old Vic in London; we transferred his performance intact to the film. We had more creative fun with excerpts from *Richard III* and *Romeo and Juliet,* neither of which he had played before. If Shakespeare — and before him the saintly Sir Thomas More — maligned the hapless Last of the Plantagenets, Richard made his royal namesake a frenetic leering monster but imbued him with the saving grace of humor.

Moss Hart had provided a delightful milieu for our rendition of the balcony scene from *Romeo and Juliet.* According to Moss' script, Booth meets the woman he is to marry while recruiting a cast in New Orleans. In studio lingo, they were to "meet cute." Maggie McNamara, as the amateur actress who is to play Juliet, goes to the theater for rehearsal and learns that her Romeo has disappeared. Determined not to lose her one opportunity to play opposite the great Edwin Booth, she goes in search of him, venturing into places where a lady of that period was never seen.

She finds him in a brothel. That is, she barges into a courtyard, above which is a balcony on which are seductively draped several ladies of the evening. Overhearing the commotion caused by the young woman's entrance, Booth staggers in dishabille from one of the cubicles, glares drunkenly down at her and asks: "Who the hell are you?"

"I'm your Juliet, Mr. Booth," she primly replies.

Burton then flings wide his arms and exclaims: "Oh speak again, bright angel!" And we are launched on the famous scene, but with Romeo on the balcony and Juliet below. Cute and double cute.

While the technicians were lighting the scene, Richard asked me how it would be if he had a couple of belts before he played it. They might, he thought, embelish his performance. We had often had a drink together at the end of the day, but this was ten in the morning. I asked how it might affect his memory of the lines, and he told me not to worry about that. Drunk or sober, he'd remember. I finally approved and we went to a nearby bar. Burton, in perfect sobriety, methodically measured out two stiff ones and tossed them down like medicine. The result was sheer magic. Out he came, red-eyed, just a touch unsteady on his pins, unshaven and unkempt, obviously a man who had spent the night

Burton and wife Elizabeth Taylor in The Taming of the Shrew.

As wife-killer Bluebeard. *With Raquel Welch, fifth victim.*

carousing. But the lines — the glorious lines — poured out in all their beauty and majesty, and in Richard's own matchless diction.

I suppose you could call it living the part. Later, he did something similar when, as a Booth going mad, he played a Hamlet also nearly mad in the duel scene with Laertes. In Burton's frenzy his sword almost decapitated the professional fencer playing Laertes, and in fact did slash through a lot of the stage set. I had heard of actors chewing up the scenery, but Richard was the first I had ever seen literally cut it to ribbons. This intensity, among his other virtues, has won him a place at the top of his profession. Yet I believe that he is more effective on the stage than on the screen. I am in no sense denigrating Richard Burton as an actor; I simply believe that the stage is the proper forum for his great talent.

There is a difference between acting for the stage and acting for the screen. A stage actor projects directly across the footlights to his audience. A screen actor, brought into contact with his audience, has little need to project; the great moments on film are those in which the actor *reacts* to a situation. (As a somewhat illiterate director I know once put it: "Movies are a reactionary art.")

Charles Chaplin, Gary Cooper, Spencer Tracy, and all the great screen actors have known this. After my first day's work with Cooper on *Ten North Frederick,* I was vaguely dissatisfied with what we had achieved. But when we ran the film, I saw that Coop had done wonderful things I hadn't even noticed from behind the camera. Producer Charles Brackett summed it up to perfection: "Coop writes his performance in invisible ink, directly on the film."

In *Prince of Players,* each of Richard's scenes was a masterpiece of projection on the sound stage, but there was no invisible ink on the film. It was not his fault, and I certainly had no cause for complaint. His was a great stage performance by a great stage actor, who simply lacked the cinematic experience of a Cooper or a Tracy. I must add, however, that I hope that the fates will permit me to work with Richard Burton again. No writer can hope for a better reading of his lines than Richard can give him; no director can hope for a better performance of his scenes.

We cannot know what a performance by Edwin Booth was really like, but through the magic of film, our children and grandchildren will see one of the great performers of our time as *we* saw him. I predict that the passing years will rob Richard Burton of none of his luster. He will *always* be one of the great ones.

Burton successfully transferred Equus *from theater to film and won an Academy Award nomination. With Peter Firth.*

THE
SEX SYMBOLS

THEDA BARA: SHE-DEMON

DOUGLAS HEYES

Theodosia Goodman of Cincinnati, Ohio, was the first publicity-made movie star.

I'M ONE OF THE FEW survivors of the Vampire's embrace: I was actually kissed by Theda Bara. I was too young a fool to enjoy or fear it, being short of seven months when the great Demolisher of Men, garbed in the shades of night, slid her sinuous white arms around my pink and pliant form, and planted on my lips the Maddening Curse of Her Kiss.

DOUGLAS HEYES *directed and wrote the screenplays for* Kitten with a Whip *and* Beau Geste *and the TV miniseries* Captain and Kings. *His other screenplays include* Drums of Tahiti *and* Ice Station Zebra.

Fate had decreed our meeting long before I was born — when my dad (Herbert Heyes) made his "movie" debut as Theda Bara's leading man. Dad was luckier than some others. In his first encounter with the Female Fiend Incarnate, she didn't drive him to drink, divorce, dishonor, death, or anything worse. In *Under Two Flags* (1916), though he was a true-blue Legionnaire and she was "Cigarette," she wasn't even harmful to his health. In fact, she gave her own life to save his!

Seems dad had struck a superior (but rotten) officer and was booked to be shot at sunrise, when — I have it here in dad's crumbling scrapbook, in a yellowed tradepaper review of Thursday, August 3, 1916:

". . . she arrives with the reprieve at the last moment, riding in with the papers in her hand just as the shot is fired. She is killed by the bullets intended for the man she loved and dies in his arms, while kissing the flag of France."

Such decency was rare for Miss Bara.

Theda Bara was the first feminine star to fatten her fame on sheer sensual gluttony, the first sex-bomb, the first "other woman" to be the Main Attraction, not second-slink to some simpering soubrette.

She was the *femme fatale,* the she-demon. She was deadlier than the male. She was lustful, lascivious, carnal. She had no heart; she had no soul.

Like the succubus of yore, she'd drain the manhood out of men. She'd cast them aside like empty peanut shells, and (just to be mean) she'd grind them under her high spiked heels. So she was a popular favorite with the ladies.

She cast her filthy spell over my father in films like *The Vixen* (1916), *The Tiger Woman* (1917), and *Salome* (1918). But he had the unique male privilege of lousing her up when she tried to be nice (again) in *The Darling of Paris* (1917). They named it that so there'd be no mistake about who Miss Bara was, as this movie was actually *The Hunchback of Notre Dame* — six years before Lon Chaney's version. She was the gypsy Esmeralda, whose hopeless love for dashing Captain Phoebus (my old man) got her all mixed up with an ardent but asymmetric and somewhat slobbery bell ringer (Glen White).

She would have been wasted in supporting roles.

Again, her feminist fans demanded she stick to sticking it to the men.

Yet she was, in fact, a man's invention.

William Fox, a failed-vaudevillian-turned-movie-exhibitor, had formed a company to make his own films — and then felt a gut need for some antidote to the saccharine formula for such Sweethearts of the Silver Screen, as (God's truth!) Blanche Sweet, Arline Pretty, Louise Lovely, and — of course — the fair-haired Mary Pickford.

But one fair-haired girl, daughter of a Jewish tailor, some years before had decided *not* to be the pretty blond she really was. She had dyed her hair jet black, to become a truly "dramatic" actress. She had painted her face to look "dramatic." She had put on funky-exotic-dramatic dresses and slunk around onstage in a career that was already going (dramatically) downhill.

Making the rounds, looking for work, she met a man who knew a lot about William Fox's plans for a new kind of star: Frank Powell. He was set to write and direct Fox's first major film: *A Fool There Was* (1915). It would be based on Kipling's misogynist poem "The Vampire." And "The Vampire" was to be the matrix for Fox's Freudian/Frankenstein-created-woman.

Powell thought she had The Look. So he stuck her in the background of a picture he was shooting for Pathé — far back, where she couldn't be recognized. She needed the money. And he wanted to see how she took direction.

O.K.: Powell went to Fox with the proposition that she be starred in the "Fool" thing. Fox didn't mind; he couldn't afford a real star. Also, he didn't want any prior (and possibly pleasant) impressions of his monster before he gave it the juice. So: what was the kid's name?

Well . . . on stage, Theodosia De Coppet. But in fact: Theodosia Goodman.

That could be fixed (or Foxed).

So she was signed and set to become the first made-to-order Instant Movie Star.

Neither Claudette Colbert nor Elizabeth Taylor were inspired by her Cleopartra.

In the beginning was The Word, and The Word was: THE VAMPIRE, in Fox's biggie, would be nothing short of The Real Thing — The True Personification Of Evil — *in the flesh* — THEDA — BARA!

Who?

"THEDA," it was soon revealed, was an anagram for "DEATH." And "BARA" was (what else?) "ARAB" spelled backwards. For this woman with "the wickedest face in the world" had been "born on the banks of the Nile," out of a forbidden (unsanctified) tryst between an Arab princess and a romantically mad Italian (or even French) artist. Theatrical background? *Ah, oui!* She was, of course, the dark star of the world's most infamous horror show: the Grand Guignol of Paris! In evidence thereof, Fox unleashed an avalanche of stills showing the beauty-that-drove-men-mad in bare-shouldered frolics with serpents (of the Nile), bats (vampire),

mummies (Egyptian), ravens (black), skulls and skeletons (human, male), and other things nice girls don't mess around with.

My mother told me of those early days when Theodosia stood at bay before a pack of reporters, all slavering for more meaty scraps out of her lurid past. One said: "Miss Bara, we all know you were born on the banks of the Nile. But *where?*" Theodosia fastened her great dark eyes upon the asker and answered gravely: "The Left Bank" (Fox's flacks pinned that one down: "In the shadow of the Sphinx").

No one really *wanted* to doubt that when this Theda Bara came unwrapped, she'd be the most devastating package of sin ever imported from depraved Paree.

Whether or not they were deceived, they were not disappointed. When she did flame out as "The Vampire" (in 1915), the word "vamp," both as noun and

One more "fool" enters her web.

verb, became a sudden necessity to the language. There wasn't anything in use quite to describe her character — or what it *was*, exactly, that she did.

"Vamping" was the new sensation. Theda Bara powdered and painted her face like a hussy: hussy cosmetics boomed. All over America women writhed and wriggled, snaked and snarled, batted their lashes, nibbled their pearls, and trampled on the groveling bodies of worshiping men — if only in the wishful shadows of a movie matinee. To this day, when they murmur "Kiss me, my fool" (while kissing their fools), they're flashing on Theda Bara's best-remembered line. It was spoken (in subtitle) while she laughingly scattered rose petals over the drained-dry and very dead body of her first victim.

She made every one of her 39 films for Fox in less than five years. In 1919 she dropped out, drained (like one of her fools), and was quickly trampled under by a stampede of substitute vampires. The post-World War I fans were less naive: Sex and sin were still in, but not All Bad. Six years passed before an independent would gamble on her in a comeback film. It was a flop, a joke. Next year she put an end to it all in a suicidal Mack Sennett comedy. She played a thickly made-up caricature of herself as the Vamp — and was shoved out of the spotlight by Sennett's slapstick comics.

She tried comebacks on the stage. The critics drove the stake through her heart.

The quality of badness doesn't age well. She was "available" for 29 years.

When she died (in 1955), she still hadn't found work in any kind of film.

In panning one of her last efforts on stage, critic Alexander Woollcott wrote: "She is pretty bad, but not bad enough to be remembered always."

He was wrong.

AT ODDS WITH AN IMAGE

THOSE I KNEW who knew her have all since followed her off the stage. But they loved her well and forgave her pretensions. Because she was, in truth, almost *too* nice, too straight, too stainless. Not that she was all soft beneath the paint. She had strong beliefs not shared by most: faith in the powers of spiritualism, faith in her own powers as an actress.

That's why she took the part of The Vampire, though her chaste heart cried out against playing a woman with no redeeming virtue. She had to tell herself it was just a step — only one necessary step — to establish her talent.

It was one step to a pinnacle of stardom she could never approach in any other part. She had poured her own breath and fire into Fox's creation and brought the thing to life. Though she forever struggled (with the studio) to dispel her evil image, she could never live it down — because she was an original when she lived it up. Soon there were clones vamping all around her. But she alone, of all who vamped, could not escape the vampire's clutch.

— D. H.

An intelligent, outspoken woman, she often complained about her poor treatment at Fox, and denounced the ways in which men exploit women, saying that if women responded by treating men as her vamp did, they deserved it. "I am a feministe!" she declared.

DOUGLAS FAIRBANKS: ROMANTIC ACROBAT

ROBERT PRESNELL, JR.

"Nearly all of us have found someone to help fashion us, someone to admire, someone to dream of being like. Douglas Fairbanks was mine."
— R. P.

FIFTY YEARS AGO, there was no one in the world more famous than Douglas Fairbanks. His insouciant grin, remarkable agility and grace, romantic, confident, free-spirited, youthful, and adventurous manner made him the American ideal. There may have been greater athletes, greater romantics, greater performers — but no one has ever looked as marvelous doing what he did.

I copied him. I grinned. I was gallant to the ladies. I entered rooms with a leap. Although I was only eleven, I was Robin Hood, the Thief of Baghdad, Zorro, the Gaucho, and especially D'Artagnan, with a small group of friends who weren't always as intrepid as I about leaping from trees, swinging on ropes across chasms, and dueling with wooden swords. Naturally, there were some injuries, but none to me. I was as invulnerable as Doug.

It came as a surprise to me one day when I was about fourteen that my father was going to see Doug to talk about a script — and that he was going to take me along!

Although by this time my fantasy of *being* Douglas Fairbanks was under control, he was still on my mind. When I participated in track meets I made sure that when I was high jumping, broad jumping, pole vaulting, and running the hurdles that I was displaying an insouciant grin to show spectators there was nothing to it.

We visited the great man at his Spanish hacienda, Rancho Zorro, in San Diego County. I was almost comatose when I saw that famous face smiling at me. And he sounded as if he were pleased to see *me* (my father had told him about my interest in athletics). I didn't even notice he was a little older, with thinning hair, and heavier, but it did surprise me that I was a little taller than Doug. I'd expected him to be at least seven feet. He

---

ROBERT PRESNELL. JR. *has written screenplays for such films as* Conspiracy of Hearts, Let No Man Write My Epitaph, Legend of the Lost, *and* The Third Day.

told me to go to his stable to get a horse and mooch around his estate while he and my father went off to confer.

In the late afternoon, Doug called me to the house. When I opened the door I was tapped on the top of my head, and I looked up and saw Doug grinning at me over the top of the door. He was perched on the doorknob on the other side of it, and he said something like, ''I hear you are able to do all my tricks — how about this one?'' Then he showed me how to do it. (I lived on that trick for years. In fact, for a while when anyone came to my room, I was always up on the doorknob peering over the top of the door, tapping them on the head.) I showed him how I could jump over a chair from a standing position — and he jumped to the top of a spinet piano the same way. Then we went all over the house, jumping chairs and coffee tables and seeing if we could go all around a room without touching the floor, just using furniture. We went outside and jumped fences and gates, playing follow the leader, and I swear he ran up a tree. Ran right up it, hung by his knees from a branch, swung and skinned the cat and landed on his feet without a

wobble, arms outflung. I gave up. And then I saw him on the roof of the house, jauntily reclining, one arm bent and lazily propping his head — grinning of course.

And then came the silly part.

I told him I'd heard he could run at an open car that was moving toward him, leap up and land in the back seat, facing front. And I said I'd done it. He looked at me with his eyes dancing, put his finger to his lips, looked around warily, and then walked me to the garage, saying

Looking dashing in The Private Life of Don Juan. *With Benita Hume.*

Mr. Robinson Crusoe. *Joan Gardner was added to the story to give Fairbanks a romantic interest.*

he'd always wanted to use it in a film but had never found a place for it. There was a black Phaeton in the garage. Doug got the stableman to drive, and we put the top down and folded the windshield down onto the hood (you could do that then) and drove out to a field. The stableman balked when he found out what we were going to do, but Doug said he'd fire him if he didn't drive. So that's what we did — the stableman drove at six miles an hour, about the pace of a walking horse, and I leaped up, absolutely believing that if I failed in any way, I'd shoot myself. I made it. Then Doug did it, soaring in the air as if in slow motion, turning and landing gracefully in the back seat. Then we did it together, landing in the back with our arms folded, grinning our insouciant grin. It was the nearest I'd ever been to heaven.

And I got hell from my father. He said, "What if he'd tripped? Do you know how many millions of dollars hang on that man?" I said there was nothing to be worried about, Doug could do anything. My father said, "Yes, *could* — but do you realize he's now forty-five years old, and he hasn't done these things for years?"

I hadn't. I hadn't thought about his having any age at all — and I didn't even imagine that maybe what we were doing was as important to him as it was to me. He'd be ninety-five if he were alive today — and I'll bet he could still do it all.

Fairbanks in Naples during the thirties.

RUDOLPH VALENTINO: LATIN LOVER

ANTHONY SLIDE

"**P**OOR RUDY," comments veteran cinematographer Paul Ivano, who had been Valentino's friend, confidant and one-time roommate. Those two words serve as an apologia for and a summation of the life and career of a man hailed in his time as the screen's greatest lover and certainly one of its greatest stars; a woman's man who never had any luck with his own women; an actor whose dramatic gestures on screen today provide more guffaws than gasps of admiration; a man (who, were he alive today, would be in his eighties) who could never have survived in the film industry with the coming of sound. All things consid-

ANTHONY SLIDE *is the author of seven books dealing with silent movies, including* Early American Cinema *and* The Films of D. W. Griffith *(with Edgar Wagenkneckt). He is a professional film historian on the staff of the Academy of Motion Picture Arts and Sciences Library.*

130

ered, the years have not been kind to Rudolph Valentino.

Without question, in the America of the seventies, it is hard to understand the appeal Rudolph Valentino once had. There are too many problems involved in trying to come to grips with his popularity. His acting ability lacked the naturalness of his only serious contemporary rival, Ramon Novarro. His on-screen lovemaking, for all its undercurrent of sensuality, leaves an impression of bulging eyes and rippling muscles.

On the other hand, much of the actor's appeal in the twenties was that he was different. Just as Douglas Fairbanks' characterizations were larger than life, so were Valentino's. He was not restrained and self-controlled. On the screen he was impetuous, a man of wild, forceful action. His appeal was to the unliberated women of the world, secretly yearning to escape from the conservative milieu of house and family, without having to experience any of the pain and anguish that such an escape might mean.

In some ways, Valentino's own life was an example of escape from a dreary existence. He was born Rodolpho Guglielmi di Valentina d'Antonguolla on May 6, 1895, in southern Italy, to middle-class parents. There was nothing out of the ordinary about his family background or his Italian upbringing, a matter Valentino later tried to remedy when *Photoplay*, in its February-March-April issues of 1923, published "My Life Story" under his by-line, an autobiography actually written by a publicist named Herb Howe. Of all his many biographers since, only Irving Shulman has made a concerted effort

Delighted Valentino proceeding with famous conquest of kidnapped Agnes Ayres in The Sheik.

to uncover the truth, dull as most of it is, concerning Valentino's youth in Italy and in America, where he arrived on December 23, 1913.

When and why Valentino first decided to try his luck in films is clouded in mystery. In all probability the cinema represented nothing more than another way to earn a few dollars; it was certainly no different or worse than other means he had tried from gardening to hustling. In his autobiography, *Two Reels and a Crank*, cinema pioneer Albert E. Smith claims that Valentino made his screen debut as an extra in a 1914 Vitagraph production titled *My Official Wife*. This film has not survived, and there is no way of knowing if Smith's story is true, but as Smith also claims that Leon Trotsky was in the production, his credibility is somewhat in doubt. There is no question, however, that Valentino did appear in East Coast-produced films while he was in New York; he is quite recognizable in the 1916 Irene Castle serial *Patria*, and in a still from *Seventeen*, a Jack Pickford-Louise Huff vehicle of the same year, he is very much in evidence grinning broadly over Pickford's shoulder in the wedding sequence.

As the teens progressed, so did Valentino's film career, without, it would appear, any conscious effort on his part. From 1918 onward, he was very active and was becoming typecast as the villain. Those of his films that survive from this period give absolutely no indication that a matinee idol was in the making. Playing opposite Clara Kimball Young in *Eyes of Youth* (1919), Valentino is the classic screen villain, exuding melodramatics at every opportunity. Here is an actor apparently unaware of any necessity for restraint, forcing Young to compromise her acting in order to adjust to his style. Only in *Stolen Moments* (1920), designed as a starring vehicle for opera singer-turned-would-be-film-star Marguerite Namara, does Valentino appear subdued and give hints of a gentler acting nature.

Valentino's life changed drastically in 1920 when Lewis Selznick released the prophetically titled *The Wonderful Chance*. Viewing the film today, it is hard to work up much enthusiasm for Valentino's characterization. Although his playing is a little less severe and slightly more jaunty, he is still basically the oily, slick-haired un-American (i.e., foreign-looking) villain. Critics at the time ignored Valentino's performance, but June Mathis, one of the most influential scenarists of the silent era and a powerful figure at Metro, was impressed. To her must go much of the credit for the creation of Valentino the sex symbol — the man who became an escape from reality for a generation of women. It was Mathis who scripted Valentino's first starring vehicles: *The Four Horsemen of the Apocalypse* (1921), *The Conquering Power* (1921), *Camille* (1921), *Blood and Sand* (1922), and *The Young Rajah* (1922). (It is ironic that when she died, only a year after Valentino's passing, she was taken to the same funeral parlor in New

Classic tango in The Four Horsemen of Apocalypse. *With Beatrice Dominguez.*

York in which her star's body had reposed, and today she lies beside him in the mausoleum of the Hollywood Memorial Cemetery.)

The Four Horsemen, the film that made Valentino a star, stands out as his best work. If June Mathis deserves credit for discovering Valentino, it is director Rex Ingram who should be credited for making Valentino an actor — not that Valentino was to give much evidence of any acting ability in the years to come. In Ingram's *Four Horsemen*, Valentino displayed a sensitivity lacking in his earlier work and most of his later films. As Julio Desnoyers, Valentino is the ideal screen hero — beautiful, delicately sensual, and in the celebrated tango sequence, exudes a sexual fire in every step. Here, for the first and last time, was Valentino, the Latin lover. Virtually every other film that followed made a mockery both of his sensuality and limited acting ability. For example, *The Conquering Power*, also directed by Ingram, required little from Valentino or his leading lady, Ingram's wife, Alice Terry.

With Vilma Banky in Son of the Shiek, *his last film.*

Valentino often went bare chested, as in Monsieur Beaucaire.

Before his starring role in *Horsemen*, Valentino had been what is probably best described by the dated expression "a gigolo" — a man who would dance with women for money, and perhaps do more if adequately compensated. Because of his reputation, no one wanted to be seen talking to him, but once Valentino became a star, everyone was a friend. Before co-starring in *Horsemen*, when they were both just bit players, Alice Terry would accompany Valentino to dances. "He was a very nice person, really," says Terry. "He said nothing, but you felt, 'God, he's charming'." As Valentino became a star, did his personality change? Terry believes not.

Valentino certainly had no illusions about his worth as an actor, and the adulation of his fans was frankly an embarrassment to him. Bebe Daniels, one of Valentino's leading ladies in *Monsieur Beaucaire* (1924), attests to his humility: "I have never met a more modest man in my life. He went to Italy and when he came back, I said, 'Rudy, what happened? They must have mobbed you.' He said, 'Nothing happened, because I look like every other Italian on the street.' He didn't know what conceit was."

If anyone or anything changed Valentino's personal life it was Natacha Rambova, a wealthy dilettante with visions of becoming a film director. By controlling Valentino on and off screen, she was able, to a certain extent, to attain her wish. It was Rambova who designed the sets for Nazimova's ludicrous 1921 production of *Camille*, in which Valentino played Armand Duval. The

With a female extra in The Conquering Power.

three became firm friends and, with Paul Ivano, moved into a small bungalow at 6612 Sunset Boulevard. In 1922, Valentino and Rambova were married. (The star's first marriage to Jean Acker in 1919, lasted less than one night. Its raison d'être, according to Ivano, was because Acker, a minor screen star, knew a lot of people who Valentino thought would help his career. Miss Acker, still alive, will not talk about the marriage.)

With his marriage to Rambova, it was as if Valentino took a masochistic pleasure in bowing to her demands and in allowing her to order his life. Doris Kenyon, another of Valentino's leading ladies in *Monsieur Beaucaire*, recalls Rambova sitting on the side of the set, indicating with hand movements how Valentino should play the scene. It is, of course, interesting that Rambova was deeply involved in productions such as *Monsieur Beaucaire*, in which Valentino is dandified and overly made up, giving an appearance of effeminacy and emasculation. (Valentino's two less-than-happy marriages and his preference for male company off-screen have led many to assume that he was a latent, if not a practicing, homosexual. This assumption is strongly denied by all who knew him.)

It was *without* Natacha's approval that Valentino signed to appear in the film for which he is best remembered, *The Sheik* (1921), a ludicrous romantic melodrama involving an Arab sheik (who for reasons of early-twentieth-century morality turns out to be the son of an English father and a Spanish mother) and an English lady (Agnes Ayres), played against a backdrop of the Sahara. *The Sheik* cost a mere $189,000 to produce but earned millions for its producer, Paramount. Valentino's sensual glances, which according to director Robert Florey were nothing more than squints brought on by nearsightedness, aroused passion in every female breast, as did his arrogant treatment of Miss Ayres. *The Sheik* apparently remained in Valentino's memory until the end, for its final subtitle, "The darkness has passed and now the sunshine," is almost identical to the final words supposedly uttered by the star on his deathbed.

The Sheik was released in 1921, but it was not until five years later that United Artists released a sequel, *Son of the Sheik* (1926), which was Valentino's last film. Vilma Banky played Yasmin, the dancer carried off by the Sheik's son, while Valentino portrayed both father and son in this delightful tongue-in-cheek extravaganza of sword fighting, rape, and sadistic whippings — the perfect formula for a box-office hit!

In the intervening years, Valentino had starred in eight features, some downright bad, while others such as *The Eagle* (1925), thanks largely to some nice interplaying between Valentino as a cossack lieutenant and Louise Dresser as the czarina, had moments to admire. One of Valentino's lesser-known works that is deserving of more attention is *Moran of the Lady Letty* (1921). As a wealthy San Francisco socialite shanghaied by vicious sea captain Walter Long, Valentino displays a healthy masculinity usually missing from most of his starring roles. His bared chest seems quite in keeping with the demands of the role — that the audience be aware that here is a virile male. In many other films his stripping down seems merely narcissistic.

Death came to Rudolph Valentino on August 23, 1926, the result of acute peritonitis. Robert Florey, a close friend of the actor, claimed that in the early twenties an amusement park palm reader had predicted — and Valentino had believed — that he would die young. With his death a legend was created, and despite the generally poor quality of his work there can be no question that his name at least will live on. His leading lady Alice Terry once made a comment to me that might just as well serve as his epitaph: "The biggest thing Valentino ever did was to die."

As a glory-hungry bullfighter in Blood and Sand.

JEAN HARLOW: BLOND BOMBSHELL

IRVING SHULMAN

The Good/Bad Goddess.

N UMEROUS THEOGONIES tell of gods and goddesses in their pantheons who walked our earth unrecognized by mortals until, for various reasons, they made their presences known. During the first three days of June 1930, such a revelation occurred in Hollywood, California.

Where in Hollywood? Why, at Grauman's Chinese Theater, which featured Howard Hughes' production of *Hell's Angels,* starring Ben Lyon and James Hall. *Daily Variety* judged the movie to be "the biggest air picture . . . and brim full of sex." Of the leading lady's performance — an unknown without credit on the film's original posters — the reviewer wrote of an actress who "wafts plenty of 'that' . . . It doesn't make much difference what degree of talent she possesses. . . . She'll probably have to play these kind of [sexy] roles, but nobody ever starved possessing what she's got."

The public and one of its scribes had recognized the screen's first blond good-bad goddess. *Variety* had acknowledged her by name, and subsequent one-sheets and lobby cards for *Hell's Angels* introduced the principals as:

JEAN HARLOW

BEN LYON & JAMES HALL

Jean Harlow differed markedly in physique from the Venus of Willendorf, a Stone Age sculpture of limestone worshiped some five thousand years ago by a fertility cult. That Venus has swollen hips, hefty thighs, steatopygian buttocks, bovine breasts, and a huge stomach. Our Venus, affectionately referred to as the Blond Bombshell, was a far different number: come-on hips, shapely thighs, callipygian rear, marvelous breasts,

---

IRVING SHULMAN *is the author of* Harlow: An Intimate Biography, The Amboy Dukes, The Big Brokers, *and other books. His screen-writing credits include* City Across the River, Baby Face Nelson, *and* Rebel Without a Cause.

and a little stomach. In the history of theophany, she was the hottest-looking dish ever to come down the pike.

Principally worshiped in darkened theaters heated by fantasies, movie screens displayed her to millions of sighers, slaverers, and lip-lickers who wanted nothing more from this unfair life than to know her once, then die gladly, because to know her was fortune enough for any man. Paradoxically, women resented the goddess, yet made every possible effort to emulate her through imitation of hair color and styling, shape of brows, posture, wiggles and jiggles, wisecracks, and the way she looked dressed and undressed.

The Harlow look was aped to the profit of grateful merchants who blessed the good-bad goddess for returning profits to capital ventures. With her every appearance, Harlow was worshiped fervently by boys and young men, husbands and fathers. They stared at Harlow

in features that never failed to deliver: *The Secret Six* (1931), *Goldie* (1931), *Public Enemy* (1931), *Platinum Blonde* (1931), *Three Wise Girls* (1932; a heretical error of testamental judgment because the good-bad goddess was cast as a good-good girl), *Beast of the City* (1932), *Hold Your Man* (1933), *Bombshell* (1933), *Reckless* (1935), *China Seas* (1935), and *Riffraff* (1936).

Row upon row of men dreamed the goddess would recognize them as really great guys, long down on their luck and in need of a big lift, which she proceeded to supply. The next morning, thinking on the day before with the goddess, they'd lick the world with bare hands.

Studio high priests (known respectfully as executive producers, presidents, and board chairmen) offered her rich creature comforts, praying that Harlow would continue to do as she had since 1930: remain, for decades to come, the box-office anodyne who kept Johnny Public

The tender side of Harlow was apparent in this scene in Hell's Angles, *her breakthrough film. With Ben Lyon.*

SHE CHANGED HISTORY

FROM THE TWELFTH-CENTURY romances of King Arthur's court, where Elaine, "the lily maid of Astolat," died for love of Lancelot, to the seventeenth-century fictions of Mrs. Aphra Behn, who wrote of fair-haired heroines and dark-complected wantons; from the eighteenth-century novels of Samuel Richardson, who endowed his women, light and dark, with psychological motives; through similar women of Sir Walter Scott, and those who peopled the novels of Charles Brockden Brown, Nathaniel Hawthorne, Herman Melville, William Dean Howells, Henry James, and Theodore Dreiser, readers were offered bland heroines ever virginal of spirit.

Movies carried on these moral traditions of light and dark women . . . until Harlow.

— I. S.

from joining forces with seditious types determined to destroy the American Way through unionization, sit-down strikes, and violent revolution against government and business. Bread and circuses kept the Roman populace quiescent during government and economic crises. Bread and movies featuring the sex goddess worked the same magic.

And who but Harlow could have altered, with her first appearance of consequence, in *Hell's Angels,* ossified sociocultural sexual myths that always presented dark-complected women as the most sensual? Who but she could have made it possible and permissible for blonds to have more fun?

Temptresses of yesteryear were invariably dark-haired, olive-skinned wantons who wore exotic, vaguely mysterious Eastern raiment, brass brassieres, and an overabundance of baubles. They lived in weblike Turkish corners with cushions and furs all about a swan-boat bed of a Jezebel, and lured men to their doom through the use of sinful postures. Of these, Theda Bara, Valeska Suratt, Nita Naldi, and Pola Negri are best remembered. (Myrna Loy breathed fire into this tradition. No man of blood will ever forget the little cloisonné pipe she puffed so wickedly in *The Mask of Fu Manchu* [1932].)

Cary Grant and Franchot Tone (shown here) shared her in Suzy.

Cagney treated her better than he did Mae Clarke in Public Enemy.

Before Harlow, all blond American women were hailed as virgins and brides, the best of wives, homemakers, mothers — even if they were "colder" and less satisfying than dark-haired women. The good blond women of the movies (Mary Pickford, Lillian Gish, Mae Murray, for instance) always, just before The End, rescued and then forgave innocent, gullible, and dopey heroes — also blond of heart and soul. All this was altered after a bit actress, a blond, replaced Greta Nissen when Howard Hughes decided to make a talkie of his silent feature about World War I aviators. (Too bad for Miss Nissen that she had a Norwegian accent.) Thereafter, her coloring, form, and throaty voice would identify every actress offered as her successor. (Of these, only Marilyn Monroe has achieved a cult of worshipers.)

Many have competed for Jean Harlow's pedestal. Some aspirants were better actresses and more beautiful; others had richer voices and larger equipment. None, though, achieved even a toehold on the elevation occupied by the good-bad goddess. Harlow anticipated the

seventies: sex before marriage wasn't sinful; women had the right to enjoy sex; sex after marriage could be fun, too; anyone, even actors and actresses who lived together without benefit of wedlock, should be accepted in society and at the box office.

She gave us more: The good-bad goddess looked and spoke like, and *was* the girl or woman next door. She gave style to expensive and casual dress, to a bath towel and tennis shoes. She presented a woman's body as healthy, thereby dealing a mortal blow to America's brown Victorianism. She presented us with the classless modern woman.

Harlow's stay on earth was short-lived — only twenty-six years. Some months after her demise, however, she returned briefly. A 1938 issue of *Modern Screen* included an article titled "A Year Without My Jean," by Jean Harlow's mother. The woman confided how, on a sunny Sunday when all was bright outside her windows, she had cried out: " 'Oh, Baby, Baby, Baby!' *And she came to me.* I do not mean as a vision . . . she walked into the room, her footsteps light and soft because she was wearing the little white rubber-soled sneakers she always wore around the house . . . white slacks . . . fuzzy sweater . . . and carried one of her large white silk handkerchiefs, polka-dotted in red."

Who among us dare say it did not happen exactly as told to *Modern Screen?* Or that anything is impossible for a good-bad sex goddess who set the style for blonds when she took *It* out of the closet, then placed *It* in the light of day, where *It* belongs?

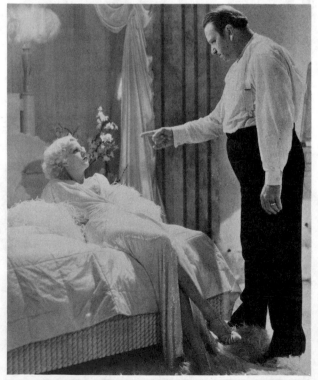

Very funny married to Wallace Beery in Dinner at Eight.

MARLENE DIETRICH: FROM DEVIL TO ANGEL... AND BACK

W. W. LEWIS

MY FIRST ENCOUNTER with Dietrich came through her films of the 1950s. At that time movies for me weren't fictions; they were reality. And Marlene, with her arrogant entrances, her imperious domination of the screen, was an outrage. How, I wondered, did this austere, formidable, somewhat elderly lady manage so easily and thoroughly to monopolize masculine attention? If only the younger and more approachable females would stick around to give her a run for her money, rather than keep to the background or vanish altogether from the screen whenever she arrived. . . . Since what happened around Marlene was unaccountable, my reality was abused and the movie spoiled. She was a cheat and a lie, and I steadfastly avoided her until I happened to see *The Scarlet Empress*.

Then I understood.

Marlene "worked" for me only in the films she made with Josef von Sternberg, at the beginning of her Hollywood career. Compared to these, her later performances were not as immediate or as credible. The original Marlene, the one who resulted from the combined efforts of Dietrich and Sternberg in the seven films they made together, was a true, consistent source of excitement. The Marlene we saw later was only a pale reflection.

It was clearly Sternberg who recognized her possibilities. He implanted Dietrich forever in the imagination of the world with *The Blue Angel* (1930). But "Marlene" — Sternberg's Marlene — was a continuum, extended and refined from film to film. Close inspection suggests that she was defined in the first four Dietrich-Sternberg films they made after he brought her to Hollywood. *Morocco* (1930), *Dishonored* (1931),

W. W. LEWIS *is a cinematographer working in Hollywood. He has contributed articles on film to numerous publications, including* Film Comment.

Shanghai Express (1932) and *Blonde Venus* (1932) all have a curious quality of seeming to face both ways, attack and defense. In *The Blue Angel*, in which Dietrich was cast for the role rather than the role made for her, she is a sadistic femme fatale with no humanly redeeming features. From *Morocco* on, her role inevitably involves prostitutions to some degree. But her exclusion from respectable society, and subsequent relegation to the demimonde, is borne with calm dignity, even pride. Marlene's degradation comes as a natural consequence of her uniqueness; it confirms her as a singular individual in a relentlessly plural, hostile world.

Marlene's response to this world is to conceal herself behind a provocative mask. She appears to be an indolent and hard-boiled calculator who worships self-interest. Yet her actions are contradictory: They show her to be loyal, honest and self-sacrificing, capable of the grand gesture. But she resists definition, preferring in-

Displaying her famous legs in Seven Sinners.

stead the freedom to be what she appears to be, an alluring ambiguity — she is, and she isn't, what she seems.

Examples abound in her films. In *Morocco,* she impulsively follows Gary Cooper into the desert (in high heels) instead of staying in the Rolls-Royce with Adolphe Menjou, which is at once both romantic nonsense and good sense. Most would admit only the first view, but Menjou is a subtle, sympathetic spirit who understands, loves, and respects Marlene. Since he approves of her unconditional allegiance to love, he does not interfere, makes no attempt to dissuade her. By choosing to be governed by her heart, not her head, she will suffer physically, but she will live emotionally. This all-for-love ethic continues to motivate the Marlene of *Dishon-*

Winning Mischa Auer's pants in Destry Rides Again.

ored, a woman who betrays her country and sacrifices her life rather than betray Victor McLaglen, her lover. It also motivates the woman in *Shanghai Express,* who jeopardizes Clive Brook's love by trading her body to save Brook's life. And it impels the woman in *Blonde Venus,* who stoically surrenders herself and all she values for her husband and child.

Marlene is a regretful prisoner of her looks. Men make her into an unwitting man-killer, but she is no demure virgin posing as a vamp. If her open enjoyment of men is a vice unredeemed by her virtue, so be it; the opinion of others is a matter of complete indifference.

This apparent contradiction may explain her appeal to both sexes: Women admire her boldness and self-sufficiency; men want what they can never have. Marlene may be ready for a liaison, but she will never grant any of the ancillary rights. Marlene promises neither fidelity nor permanence. She insists on her freedom. It remains for the man to change in order to accept her, not the other way around.

That she can be had, but not possessed, is a test for the male ego. Her attitudes deprive men of the excitement of the chase, as well as the triumph of conquest. The male sexual target may be led to feel that he is attacking, but too soon the real nature of the situation becomes clear: Marlene has selected *him.* How humiliating to have performed a love dance for such a cool spectator!

Through Sternberg, Dietrich saw something she had perhaps glimpsed before — the chance to become Marlene. It was in pursuit of that possibility that Dietrich

THE FEMININE PREROGATIVE

ALL THE CONJECTURE about supposed bisexuality in the Sternberg-Dietrich films has obscured the obvious: Marlene chooses to wear men's clothing just as she chooses to approach sexual satisfaction — with a freedom ordinarily considered a masculine prerogative. Most men in her life are bound by convention and behave predictably; they are so easily managed by Marlene that she can hardly be reproached for an occasional indulgence in man-tormenting.

— W. W. L.

She was most alluring in her Josef von Sternberg films. She was a man-killer in The Blue Angel (Top L), but she softened because of Gary Cooper and Adolphe Menjou in Morocco (Top R). She sacrificed everything for the love of Victor McLaglen in Dishonored (Bottom L), but was back as a man-killer, and part of Sternberg's decor — in their final film together, The Devil Is a Woman.

went to Hollywood — she had to be near the dreamer and his dream of her — and remained there through the vacant years before stardom brought her power and comfort. She understood that less is more, that into her enigmatic immobility could be read an infinitude of signs and significances. Since Dietrich and Sternberg had a common demon — ''Marlene'' — his perfectionism, so galling to others, only whetted an appetite which his perversity could not dull, nor his obsessive gift for glorifying her satisfy. For her patient endurance of Sternberg's direction Dietrich was rewarded: She became ''Marlene.''

Perhaps Sternberg, under the influence of his passion, mistook Dietrich's devotion to the Marlene ideal for devotion to him. Perhaps he spoke truer than he knew when he said, ''In my films Marlene is not herself. Remember that. Marlene is not Marlene: I am Marlene.'' The real nature of this triangular relationship can only be guessed at. While characterizing himself as a creator of memorable scenes, Sternberg has diminished the importance of actors. He compared them to paint used by an artist and referred to them as puppets — decor elements that move. Sternberg awoke from his dream of Marlene to find that this particular puppet had become more important than her master.

Sternberg's disenchantment with Dietrich is reflected in his last two films with her, *The Scarlet Empress* (1934) and *The Devil Is a Woman* (1935). In *The Scarlet Empress* Marlene progresses from innocence to experience, using the power of sex discovered along the way to secure her throne. Little of the passionate romantic survives. But all vestige of it is gone from the cruel Concha of *The Devil Is a Woman,* whose sole diversion is ruining men. Concha is just what she appears to be, and though she is as lovely as Marlene, the magic tension between seeming and being has vanished. The mysterious character in *The Devil Is a Woman* is Lionel Atwill, who supervises his own ruin with a dignity that approaches perverse delight.

Sternberg left Dietrich's screen character much as he found her: The only important difference is that Lola-Lola of *The Blue Angel* claims she can't help it, while Concha's power over men provides all her pleasure. The cycle of glorification and vilification is complete.

Despite the box-office failure of her last three films with Sternberg, Dietrich was able to negotiate a new contract with Paramount. Sternberg, the puppet-master who had relinquished control of his puppet, was let go. Lubitsch, now production head of the studio, felt he could produce a new Dietrich, make an ''angel'' of this devil (the title was his, imposed against Sternberg's wishes). But even his considerable skill could not undo what had been done: By now Dietrich was *Marlene,* for better or for worse. What no one realized was that she was undergoing the transformation from actress to legend.

SAM JAFFE ON DIETRICH AND STERNBERG

Jaffe wed Catherine the Great in The Scarlet Empress.

JOSEF VON STERNBERG wanted to impose himself on everyone to a point where anyone with any individuality could no longer tolerate it. Sternberg tried to absorb you.

When I met Theodore Dreiser he told me that he was suing Sternberg for what he did to *An American Tragedy* (1931). When I mentioned Dreiser to Sternberg, he said, ''That (so and so) was complaining about one line. And that was the only line I kept of his.'' That gives you a measure of Sternberg's ego.

I had a scene in *Empress* in which my sister, the queen, was laid out on a bier, and I was supposed to pour out my antipathy toward her. Sternberg made me do it about forty-nine times, and wanted me to do it again. When I told him I couldn't, he said, ''If you can't do it, come in and just spit.'' Well, I said, ''If I spit, it will be right in your face!'' So I took off my wig and was through. Of course, Sternberg couldn't have me walk out in front of everybody on the Paramount lot, so later when I calmed down, he came to me and offered me his hand. He then told me how great he was, bragging about the seventy million followers he claimed to have in Japan alone. I said, ''That's wonderful; Christ only had ten.'' He didn't like that. Our relationship was not very good.

On at least that one film, Marlene did listen to Sternberg. She would fight back a bit in the sense that she would balk at doing some things, but after a quiet conversation with him in German, she would continue. One thing I remember about his filming of Marlene: When she couldn't get the dialogue the way he wanted it, he'd have her raise her skirt a little. That was a kind of treatment she was subjected to. But she gave a very good performance.

A few years ago, I saw Marlene in her very fine one-woman show in New York. Afterwards, we sat together at Sardi's. She told me that Sternberg offered to preface her show with a biographical account. But she wouldn't have it. She wouldn't have him.

— Sam Jaffe, interviewed by
Danny Peary, December 1977

CLARK GABLE: MEMORIES OF HOLLYWOOD'S KING

MERVYN LeROY

H E WAS CALLED "The King" and he was a king. He was probably the greatest star ever.

When I was set to direct *Little Caesar* (1930) for Warner Brothers, I was searching for just the right actor to play a supporting character named Joe Massara. One evening in Los Angeles I went to the theater to see a prison drama called *The Last Mile*. One

Perhaps the most popular male star in movie history.

In Idiot's Delight, *the King and his court.*

MERVYN LeROY *was producer of* The Wizard of Oz, *and was either the director or director-producer of, among others,* Little Caesar, I Am a Fugitive from a Chain Gang, Gold Diggers of 1933, Waterloo Bridge, Random Harvest, Madame Curie, Mister Roberts, The Bad Seed, *and* Gypsy.

Romance between Gable and Norma Shearer dominated Strange Interlude.

actor caught my eye. He was very handsome, and all man — the type who never went unnoticed. He also had a certain magnetism — a quality that I never would be able to comprehend completely.

After the last curtain call, I went backstage, and asked about the actor who played Killer Mears. They told me his name was Clark Gable. When he walked through the stage door, I asked Clark if I could talk to him. He was very cordial and polite, and listened patiently. I asked him if he was interested in going into motion pictures. "I certainly am," he answered quickly. I knew I had found the one to play Joe Massara, but I told him I would have to make a screen test to show to Jack Warner and Darryl Zanuck, and we arranged a date.

I directed the test, and when I ran it for myself I was very impressed. I immediately called Warner and Zanuck and said I had a surprise for them. They came to the projection room, and I ran the twenty-minute film. When the lights came on, I cheerfully asked the two men what they thought of my new discovery. They both said, "His ears are too big." And — do you believe it — they turned him down! Of course, Gable went on to be the biggest star in the world while under contract to MGM, and remained "The King" of motion pictures for more than thirty years. Many times I would pester Jack Warner with the question: "How would you like to have him now, or just his ears?"

The earthquake was more interesting than the romance in San Francisco.

RUGGED AND GENTLE

Gable and Lombard out on the town.

CLARK'S LOVE of the outdoors — of hunting and fishing — is well known. He was a large man, with a rugged build, who looked as if he belonged in the wilderness. This is why he was so appropriate in all those adventure films he made, such as *Call of the Wild* (1935) and *Mutiny on the Bounty* (1935). But Clark, contrary to what has usually been said about him, didn't avoid the indoors. For one thing, he enjoyed spending time at home alone with Carole Lombard. I know that Clark loved Carole. When she was killed, he took it very bad, and I don't think he was quite the same until some time later when he met Kay. That marriage worked out very well. Unfortunately he did not live long enough to see his only son born.

— M. L.

A surprisingly fine comedy performance in It Happened One Night. *Both he and Claudette Colbert won Oscars.*

Eventually, Clark and I managed to make two pictures together: *Homecoming* (1948) and *Any Number Can Play* (1949). He was extremely easy to work with and to direct, which is not always true of great stars. He was a pro who was serious about acting and thought a great deal about how good he could make a part. And he was a fine actor — one who had his own style. He was proud of his ability, and it disappointed him when he thought he hadn't done his best.

Over the years, Clark and I became very close friends, and he would come to my home many times. I often showed movies; afterward we would sit and talk.

Vivien Leigh and Gable as the screen's most famous lovers in Gone With the Wind.

He had a good sense of humor and often told jokes, but mostly he took life and his craft seriously. In all the time we spent together, I never heard him say a mean thing about anyone.

I never knew anyone who didn't like Clark Gable. He was a great individual, a great citizen, and was admired by all who knew him. He will be remembered when most other stars are "gone with the wind."

A MUTUAL ADMIRATION

To Mervyn
Thank you for
giving me my first break
I appreciate it Sincerely
Clark Gable

BY THE TIME I had the opportunity to direct Gable in *Homecoming* [*Above, with Marshall Thompson*] and *Any Number Can Play* [R, with Alexis Smith], we had known each other for seventeen years. Although Clark did not get the part I tested him for in *Little Caesar,* he never forgot that I had tried to help his career. The note you see on this page means a lot to me. — M. L.

MAE WEST: AN ENDORSEMENT FOR SEX

KEVIN THOMAS

Popular because she dared to be outrageous; a sex symbol less for her looks than for her attitude.

MAE WEST is one of the twentieth century's great originals. Her impact on the sexual mores of her times has been incalculable and enduring. She is the ultimate bosomy blond, swathed in feathers, fur, and diamonds, with a hand on her hip, and a string of quips that have become part of the language. Her intense blue eyes framed by dark lashes, the flared nostrils, sensual mouth, and husky, purring Brooklyn-accented voice are familiar around the world. Mae West has been imitated for decades.

She's been painted by Salvador Dali, photographed by Richard Avedon and Francesco Scavullo, admired by George Bernard Shaw, praised by F. Scott Fitzgerald ("Mae West is the only type with an ironic edge, a comic spark, that takes on a more cosmopolitan case of life's enjoyments"), and damned by William Randolph Hearst at a time when she and he were the highest-salaried man and woman in America. Said Hearst: "Is it not time Congress did something about Mae West?" She's been jailed for staging a risqué play and credited with saving Paramount Studios and its seventeen hundred theaters during the Depression.

Mae West was one of the first to suggest to the American public that sex could be fun. She has done more than any other woman to destroy the double standard and to free us from Victorian prudery and hypocrisy, and she has done all this strictly as a popular entertainer.

There has never been a career like Mae West's, and it's not likely there will ever be again. In her 1959 autobiography she tells us that she was born on August 17, 1893. By the turn of the century she was singing at Elks Club shows in Brooklyn. She spent her adolescence in stock companies, playing children in melodramas like *East Lynne*. On September 22, 1911, she made her

---

KEVIN THOMAS *is a film critic for the Los Angeles* Times.

With George Raft in Night After Night, *West's first film.*

Broadway debut in a revue called *A la Broadway and Hello, Paris.* The New York *Evening World* remarked, prophetically: "She seems to be a sort of female George M. Cohan, with an amusingly impudent manner and an individual way of making her points."

For her vaudeville sketches, Mae had always written or reworked her own material. In 1926, at the urging of her mother, she tried her hand at writing a play for herself, which she dared to call *Sex* — and it was this production that landed her in jail for eight days. The charge: corrupting the morals of the young.

In 1928 she unveiled her most famous creation, *Diamond Lil,* an easygoing, man-loving, diamond-collecting Queen of the Gay '90s Bowery. Mae West has often said of Diamond Lil, "I'm her, and she's me," and by now the line between the woman and the image has become blurred beyond detection. In the largest sense, Mae West is indeed her own creation. The mythical, eternally enigmatic Mae rests on a foundation of granite, built over a lifetime of dedication to the promotion and perpetuation of her image. Mae West is a glorious egomaniac — and she's the first to admit it.

No one has established so sure a place in film history on the basis of so few films. After her first movie in 1932, Mae West made only a dozen pictures. The first nine were for Paramount in the 1930s, followed by *My Little Chickadee* (1940) with W. C. Fields and *The Heat's On* (1943), a minor effort she regrets. She did not make a film again for twenty-six years, when she was persuaded to return for the controversial *Myra Breckinridge* (1970). In 1977 she completed *Sexette,* adapted from one of her plays and patterned after her thirties' classics.

Although Miss West varied her ever-outrageous plots, she basically played the same sexy lady, which is to say, she played herself — with exaggerations, of course. She once said, "It's hard to be funny when you have to be clean," and there's no question that the screen censorship she helped bring about put a crimp in her own bawdy style. Yet the advent of the Hollywood Code did make for one of her most touching pictures, *Klondike Annie* (1936), in which she played a San Francisco shady lady forced to flee to Alaska and pretend to be an evangelist. She discovers there's something to be said for religion after all.

Miss West's personal favorite is *Every Day's a Holiday* (1938). She says the film's story — in which she plays a New York con woman who disguises herself as a brunette French chanteuse — came to her in a flash, a phenomenon she regards as her first experience with ESP.

Miss West's best film is probably *I'm No Angel* (1933), a wonderful work directed with easy wit by

Men stood in line but she never once tried to steal one from another woman.

Perhaps more than anyone, Mae West recognized the appeal Cary Grant would have for a movie audience. She cast the little known actor in two of her films, She Done Him Wrong *and* I'm No Angel *(shown here).*

Wesley Ruggles. Miss West plays Tira, a carny dancer and later a lion tamer who conquers Manhattan society and wins Cary Grant in the process. She remains, nevertheless, her earthy self throughout. This is the picture in which Mae shrugs off a momentary setback with the famous throwaway line, "Beulah, peel me a grape." (The inspiration for the line came from a grape-peeling monkey, one of many Miss West has kept as pets over the years.) This is also the film in which Miss West, having performed her suggestive "Sister Honky Tonk" number for an ecstatic sideshow crowd, mutters offstage, "Suckers!" So much for men and their frailties; Mae West has always played women who live by their own rules — and win.

The Heat's On *with Victor Moore.*

Meeting her match. With W. C. Fields in My Little Chickadee.

Miss West's Hollywood apartment has been her home since the William Morris Agency retained it for her when she arrived in Hollywood to make *Night After Night* (1932). Everything is white-on-white, with gilt-and-white Louis XIV and XV furniture. The living room is dominated by a grand piano with pastoral scenes painted on its sides, a gift from her longtime admirer, former heavyweight wrestling champion Vincent Lopez.

On the piano stands a nude marble statue of Miss West that was sculpted in 1935 — and also its plaster model, moved from her recently sold Santa Monica beach house. Over a couch hangs an oval painting of Miss West reclining, also in the nude. Of the statue she quips, "That's me, Venus with arms," and of the painting she says, "Gee, they musta painted that when I wasn't looking." (Of her famous mirror-ensconced bed she once remarked, "I like to see how I'm doin'.")

But the main attraction of the apartment is Mae West herself. Much has been made of her alabaster complexion and youthful hands. Reporters are forever being surprised to find her an easygoing, relaxed woman utterly free of self-pity, with none of the intense Norma Desmond aura legendary stars are expected to have. "I avoid unpleasantness if I can," Miss West says frequently. "And I don't hold bad thoughts about people because that doesn't do me any good."

Behind the legend of Mae West, then, there is a thoroughly remarkable woman determined to sustain the image of glamour she spent a lifetime creating. Somewhere along the line she made a deal with herself: Her career came first, and all would be sacrificed for it, including a family and children. Twenty years ago she wrote: "A real star never stops." She meant what she said.

Philip Reed was one of her suitors in Klondike Annie.

CHARLES BOYER: FRENCH CHARMER

CHARLES HIGHAM

He convinced Americans that foreigners are great lovers.

CHARLES BOYER was the only male star from France, aside from Maurice Chevalier, who succeeded in making the transition to the American film with no noticeable loss of quality. He has never been assessed in a book or even in a critical essay — a serious omission in view of his extraordinary talent and indi-

CHARLES HIGHAM *is the author of major biographies of* Charles Laughton, Marlene Dietrich, *and* Errol Flynn, *and several other movie books. He has written on film for numerous publications, including* The New York Times.

vidual style. It is possible that the "Continental lover" image that was created for him by the publicity machinery of Hollywood in the 1930s affected his career, making it impossible for critics to treat him with more than tacit respect. His most famous romantic film, *Algiers* (1938), was in fact his worst, a travesty of Duvivier's *Pépé Le Moko* (1937).

Boyer had little or no contact with the press during his long lifetime. When he returned briefly to Hollywood to appear as the High Lama in Ross Hunter's horrendous reworking of *Lost Horizon* (1973), he declined all interviews, even to *The New York Times*. During his great years, he remained equally isolated. He occupied an imitation French chateau in the Bel Air section of Los Angeles with his wife and son, was almost never seen at parties, and entertained rarely. He never tried to be "charming," and was never the object of gossip. When his only son committed suicide in 1965, he moved to the foothills of the Maritime Alps, where he lived until his wife's death and his own tragic suicide in 1978. His privacy and remoteness impaired his acceptance as a major figure.

His greatness lay in his capacity to enter into the character he was playing, observing with sensitivity changes of mood, delicate expressions, vibrations and shadings in the delivery of speech. Short in stature, tending toward stoutness, prematurely bald, he was the opposite of the person he appeared to be in pictures. Wigged, corseted, heavily made up, he was as completely transformed and was as formal and meticulous in his acting as a Kabuki actor. Not only was his physique changed by the arts of studio makeup and wardrobe departments, but his entire personality was altered by his own will. Instead of being recessive, he became romantic and considerate; instead of being shy, he became urbane and gregarious; instead of being isolated, he became part of the sophisticated world of white ties and tails, cocktails on the promenade deck. In order to achieve this magical transformation, he had to concentrate very hard indeed. He was as disciplined as a ballet dancer. He was capable of unselfishness on the set, yet he seemed to be occupying, like Garbo, a special island of his own.

His list of performances is impressive in its length and variety. He was at his best playing men who were secretly wounded, whose charm and grace concealed an intense inner anguish which was only disclosed at moments of dramatic crisis. Whether he was concealing a betrayal of noble station (*Mayerling,* 1936); the priesthood (*The Garden of Allah,* 1936); his wife (*Back Street,* 1941); his host (*Tales of Manhattan,* 1942); or his country (*The Battle,* 1934), he always made one aware of the moral torment he was undergoing. One had the impression of a man devoted to duty, honor, obedience — all of which were undermined by some personal flaw that he could not overcome. This rendered him identifiable and understandable to a middle-class audience which, in the 1930s and 1940s, was still paying lip service to old-fashioned moral principles.

He is particularly good in *All This and Heaven, Too* (1940). This is the story, based on fact, of the nineteenth-century murder of the Duchesse de Praslin by her husband in Paris. Bette Davis plays Mlle. Déluzy-

Desportes, a governess romantically involved with the duke, who is accused of being involved also with the duchess' murder. Rachel Field, the author of the novel on which the film was based, was actually related to the schoolteacher who had married the governess.

Boyer is ideally cast as the Duc de Praslin. With his pale oval face, heavy-lidded, liquid dark eyes, and aristocratic neck and shoulders, he conveys (despite his own modest origins) the correct high-born qualities. Subtly, intricately, he suggests a growing impatience with his wife, portrayed sullenly by Barbara O'Neil. When his children are involved, he combines a subdued fury with a degree of tenderness that is extraordinarily delicate and refined. Because he has deliberately underplayed the scenes up to this point, his murder of his wife is all the more horrifying. The shocked face of the duchess, bloody handprints on mirrors and walls, his eyes enlarged with rage, his hands fastidiously manicured, striking the death blows — here is a scene masterful in its orchestration by the director Anatole Litvak, and still more masterfully played. Boyer's subsequent suicide scene is equally skillful in its shadings. Dressed in a

As Pépé Le Moko in Algiers *the film that launched Hedy Lamarr's Hollywood career.*

153

striped silk robe, lying against white lace pillows, barely able to breathe because of the poison he has taken, he manages to convey guilt, affection, and fear in counterpoint without seeming to act at all. The somber furnishings of the room — the rich draperies, the suffocating clothes of the bed — frame him as perfectly as a passage in Dumas *Père*.

He is admirable also in another period film, *Gaslight* (1944). In this film he plays Gregory Anton, a ne'er-do-well who seduces opera star Alice Alquist and murders her in cold blood. Fascinated by the scene of the crime, he returns to the house in Thornton Square, London, to seek out the priceless jewels which Mlle. Alquist had hidden. In order to gain entrée to the house, he seduces and marries Alice's niece, the heiress to the property.

GASLIGHT

CINEMA TEACHER/CRITIC DIANE WALDMAN: *Gaslight* still elicits a powerful emotional response. I think this is because the plight of Paula, the plight of the ordinary housewife, twisted to grotesque proportions: a woman dominated by her husband, who keeps her a virtual prisoner in the house, denying her perceptions of external events, denying her contacts with the outside world. I explained this theory to my students, and one asked her mother about it. "Mother remembered being scared and angry," she reported. "but not for *those* reasons. It was because Ingrid Bergman was threatened by that horrible man."

Hold Back the Dawn. *Cad Boyer charms Olivia de Havilland.*

Using quiet, deadly strokes, Boyer limns a portrait of deceit and cruelty. He drives his wife, played by Ingrid Bergman, insane — at first by suggesting to her that she is hopelessly absentminded, and later that she is guilty of theft. Boyer is at his best in a scene at a musical soirée in which his wife discovers that a missing brooch is contained in her handbag. Boyer, of course, has secreted it himself, and his pretended anger at her is played with piercing precision. The finest moment in the movie occurs when Anton takes his wife on a tour of the jewel room of the Tower of London. Here, the writers convey Anton's greed for jewels in a clever symbolic episode. Anton looks at the royal gems and settles on a particular item. As he does so, his eyes gleam as though they have caught the reflection of the jewel itself. He says, "The Koh-in-Noor, or Lake of Light, is the largest diamond in the world." Boyer's soft, obsessed voice, his increasing pallor, the rigidity of his body and the slight, almost imperceptible clenching of his hands amount to a case study of grand-manner acting.

Still another fine performance occurs in *Tales of Manhattan*. This is an elaborate omnibus movie directed by Julien Duvivier from a potpourri of scripts including one by Ben Hecht. Boyer appeared in the first episode, which introduced the adventures of a tailcoat with its manufacture in a salon on Fifth Avenue, proceeding to its demise on a scarecrow in the Deep South. Boyer plays a matinee idol, who, following a triumphant opening on the New York stage, drives off to a rendezvous with a married woman (Rita Hayworth) in what presumably is Newport, Rhode Island. Her husband, a drunken big game hunter played by Thomas Mitchell (was he ever sober in pictures?), is jealous and shoots the matinee idol with a high-powered rifle at close range. Giving the performance of his life, the actor pretends that the shot went astray and manages to make a brilliant exit, reducing the treacherous wife and the would-be killer to pictures of embarrassment.

This trifling *conte* would have sunk most players, but Boyer gave it a richness and variety the writers did not deserve. Poised, cool, immaculate, he evokes a career of playing boulevard melodramas and comedies. Confronted with a foolish girl and a savage husband, he effortlessly suggests contempt and cynicism. He is always two steps ahead of them in everything: One wants him to make a grand exit, and he fakes it brilliantly; when he reaches the car and his valet, played by Eugene

Pallette, sees the blood on the starched shirtfront, he makes us bleed for him.

Most of Boyer's movies were set in upper-middle-class environments, but he was capable of slumming in

Together Again. *Irene Dunne, an American lady, and Boyer, a French gentleman, proved to be an effective film duo.*

Boyer as Napoleon and Garbo as his Polish mistress, Countess Valewska, in the romantic spectacle Conquest.

style. In Duvivier's *Flesh and Fantasy* (1943), he is a tightrope walker in a circus, pretending to do a drunk act while fifty feet above the ground. Distracted by the jangling, harp-shaped earrings worn by Barbara Stanwyck, he goes to pieces on the high wire. In *Confidential Agent* (1945) he earned the approval of Graham Greene as the defeated intellectual trapped in a seedy lodging house in London during the Spanish Civil War. His essential melancholy — to be found in all his performances — his introspection, his sense of human futility, ideally echoed Greene's private world. His tense confrontations with a ferocious Katina Paxinou are memorably acted; his sweetness to the frightened slavey (played by Wanda Hendrix), and his final discovery of sexual feeling with a haggard Lauren Bacall are equally fine. He manages to convey days of little food and nights with little sleep; damp raincoats worn in stuffy hallways; nervous political meetings held under the glare of street lamps in the fog. He brought to the artificial Hollywood-London a true rigor and moral sense, an incongruous touch of humanity.

It is instructive to see how much he makes of the runaway monk in *The Garden of Allah*, David O.

Selznick's romantic Technicolor bosh set in a Palm Springs desert standing in for North Africa. While Miss Dietrich poses and breathes heavily against tomato ketchup sunsets, Boyer contrives to give an authentic portrait of a man unused to speech — private, virginal. His face is as closed as the door of a Trappist cell. His eyes look inward, devoted and abstract. He carries with him a heavy burden of suffering. Against the beige sand, the chugging steam train, the papier-mâché nightclub, he expresses a harsh isolated unforgiveness.

He succeeds in out-acting Garbo in *Conquest* (1937); he provides sympathy and warmth for Margaret Sullavan in *Back Street;* he is convincingly musicianly in *The Constant Nymph* (1943); and he is witty and cunning in *Tovarich* (1937). In Europe, he is flawless in Max Ophuls' *Madame De . . .* (1953), a film noted for its buoyancy and romantic elegance of style; unfortunately, he sank to character roles, but he gave much to his portrait of world-weary intelligence in *Stavisky* (1974) by Alain Resnais, and he was excellent in *The Cobweb* (1955), Vincente Minnelli's study of life in an institution for the mentally disturbed.

Versatile, dedicated, Boyer never enjoyed his due.

ERROL FLYNN: GENTLEMANLY ROGUE

STEPHEN LONGSTREET

A swashbuckler in the tradition of Fairbanks.

HE CAME UP TO ME on the Warner Brothers lot sometime in 1940. As he held out his hand, he had that wry smile and charm from head to toe. "I say, John Barrymore tells me you paint. There's a Gauguin I've just bought, would you care to have a look at it?"

I had been writing radio material for John Barrymore; later it would strike me how much alike the two men were. Both were very intelligent (rare among even the best of actors — intellect having little to do with acting ability, as many have pointed out). Both were well read and mannerly (but could be raucous). They were both witty too, although John's wit was wildly obscene.

Errol, I discovered as he took me through his pleasant house in the hills, had a fine art collection. I remember a marvelous Whistler of skyrockets over the Thames, a really extraordinary Van Gogh, and, of course, the new Gauguin, a South Seas subject glowing with fruity greens and tawny pinks. (What has become of these museumworthy paintings is one of Hollywood's mysteries.)

As we became friendly it was clear that Errol Flynn saw himself as a victim. "Hell, it's inelegant, a life here in fast motion. You once liked the blissful mobility, but then you wonder, who's the *you*? And who's the chap on the screen?"

This was in the early 1940s. Later, when a bit full of drink, he would tell me, "It's unbearable, the sentimentality here, combined with the greasy hunt for the big dollar that makes this picture business a disembodied presence. You know I catch myself acting out my life like a goddamn script."

He was a man who believed his public image — even the "in-like-Flynn" myth. The macho stance was

---

STEPHEN LONGSTREET *is an artist, novelist, film critic, and playwright, who wrote the screenplays for* Uncle Harry, The Jolson Story, Stallion Road, Silver River, *and* The Helen Morgan Story. *He is the original author of* The Gay Sisters, Untamed Youth, *and* The Secret Door.

at first a pose, and later an obsession. Unlike Barrymore, who was a born hedonist and womanizer, Errol worked hard on his lascivious posture. But it was clear to many of us close to him that he was the victim, rather than the conqueror, of women. They bilked him, married him, preyed on him.

He was careless of his worth, and yet he was an amazingly good actor, though probably not a great actor. In such films as *Captain Blood* (1935), *The Adventures of Robin Hood* (1938), and *Gentleman Jim*, (1942) the fitting for Flynn was perfect. But when his character had to have a truer sense of history, in *The Private Lives of Elizabeth and Essex* (1939), for example, Bette Davis outranged him. Good acting consists of staying within boundaries. Flynn knew this. But the industry exploits personalities, not genius, and Errol's stance, grace, and charm seemed at first to be indestructible rather than expendable.

When I was working with director Michael Curtiz on *The Helen Morgan Story* (1957), he told me in his Hungarian English: "That son of a bitch Flynn, you never find on him some angle that does not photograph fine. I first use him in *Captain Blood*. A bit player with two pictures only, and yet I see this is a star. But now he bad boy, do not want to live long."

Errol liked to sit, drink, and talk philosophically about himself and his world — but only if he were sure you weren't going to run to some gossip columnist.

"I'm a colonial, old boy, you know. Tasmanian from down under, a bloody place that. My mother didn't like me. My father, well, he was some kind of a buggering big brain. So it was me cut free and the world out there. Oh, I've had times, yes, I've had lots of times. Good, and now, here and there, bad."

By 1947, Flynn had deteriorated. His drinking dominated, and I suspect drugs too. His debts grew; his wives, he'd say, were like shackles. And he was finding it hard to face a camera. The drinking had angered Warner Brothers, and he was about to be let go. That year I wrote the screenplay of *Silver River* (1948), to star him and Ann Sheridan. She too, as a director told me, was "lapping up the sauce."

Raoul Walsh, who was directing *Silver River*, came to me and said: "Kid, write it fast. They're not drinking, they promised Jack Warner that, but you never know."

While Clint Eastwood and Burt Reynolds use strength to defeat opponents, Flynn used his agility. He was appropriately a "scientific" boxer in Gentleman Jim *and a fair swordfighter in* The Adventures of Robin Hood, *with Basil Rathbone.*

Threatening Barton MacLaine in Silver River, *from a script by Stephen Longstreet. Tom D'Andrea looks on.*

At first the shooting of the picture went well. Work was good, as Walsh, experienced at handling actors, kept matters in control. But one morning I found Walsh tearing pages out of the script. I asked why and he said, "Removing the chicken shit. The dialogue. Too much yak-yak."

I knew then the picture was in trouble. Yes, the morning shooting was satisfactory as the stars sipped ice water. But by noon the lines were blurred, the action a bit wobbly.

I went over and tasted the ice water. It was pure ninety-proof vodka. No wonder the picture was running behind. Errol was amused when I told him I'd discovered his trick.

"Well, it's just all so inelegant, isn't it, this picture business? I can't make head or tail out of your story. I'm going to chuck it all — going to retire to amorous reveries. Life, you know, it's becoming inextricably complicated."

The stars' behavior resulted in delays, which led to cost overruns, which forced the studio heads to declare *Silver River* finished. It is the only major studio film I know of for which there is no ending; the picture ends in midair, but no one, as far as I know, ever bothered to ask why.

After one more picture, Warners let Flynn go. He drifted until 1958, when he played John Barrymore in *Too Much, Too Soon*. Like the character he was playing, the star was in ruins. It was in that year that I turned down an offer to help him with his autobiography, *My Wicked, Wicked Ways*. It would have been too painful to work with the bloated wreck, the haggard face, a countenance on which I already saw, as the Elizabethans put it, "the skull beneath the skin."

The last time I saw him was in London after the failure to finish *William Tell*, which he had been producing in Switzerland. He was desperate for money, his hopes lay shattered.

Audiences believed, from films like Desperate Journey (L) *that Flynn won World War II single-handedly.* Dawn Patrol (R) *showed that he had also won World War I.*

Dodge City, *one of many films with Flynn and Olivia de Havilland.*

"It's like, old boy, fading out like the Cheshire Cat," he said. "You know we begin as hunters and end, don't we, on our arse, as quarry. A little fun, a little booze, a bit of slap and tickle. I don't know, I just don't know. And all those years we were at Warners — we didn't know, did we, it was the good times? Well, I'll get the lolly and finish *Tell,* and then . . . [did] it ever strike you the enviable life always belonged to someone else?"

William Tell was never finished. But Errol was. He was dead at fifty in 1959.

It is strange how Flynn remains vivid in my mind. So many other actors I worked with in films are nebulous, vaporous — mere wisps. Perhaps they were greater stars than Flynn, better actors. Yet Flynn is locked in my memory. His poise, his stance, a man always ready for a congenial romp. It's all clear, the maniacal logic of his later years when he had no sense of his obligations.

I remember a New Year's card he once sent me. There were two lines from Shakespeare on it:

> *All the wealth I had*
> *Ran in my veins; I was a gentleman.*

And under this, in a shaky hand, he added:

> *And so is your old man.*
> *Errol.*

The Private Lives of Elizabeth and Essex *was history Warner Brothers style. Flynn managed to hold his own with Bette Davis.*

BETTY GRABLE: SOLDIERS' DELIGHT

JEANINE BASINGER

Between Alice Faye and Marilyn Monroe, she was Twentieth Century-Fox's reigning queen.

*"I want a girl,
Just like the girl,
That married Harry James."*
— American folk song (c. 1945)

T HE GIRL THAT MARRIED Harry James was Ruth Elizabeth Grable, better Known as Betty, Hollywood's most popular pinup girl of World War II. Today, more than thirty years later, Betty Grable is too often remembered only as that cute kid in a white bathing suit, who peeked coyly over her shoulder, flash-

ing a smile worth a million dollars. An ankle chain graces one of her famous legs, and not one hair is out of place in her slightly shellacked forties upsweep. She is wholesome enough to reassure mom and pop, sexy enough to satisfy the lonely G.I.s on the front lines. But that photograph of Betty Grable was incidental, and she

JEANINE BASINGER *is an Associate Professor on American film history at Wesleyan University. She has contributed articles on film to* The New York Times *and* American Film.

With George Montgomery in Coney Island. *"When a man tried to tell her what to do, or that she was wrong, she put up a fight. ('Just because I don't agree with you, doesn't make you right.') She didn't jump at opportunities for marriage. ('What can he give you? An apartment? You've already got one.') She*

was even cooler when it came to handling the men who chased her. Once when told to stop eating and pay attention to a prospective lover, she pointed out, 'My steak will get cold. He won't.'"

—J. B.

deserves better than to be *defined* by that one image. She had one of the most successful careers in movie history.

Betty Grable was the first woman to dominate the box office. Her ten consecutive years among the top ten draws have never been equaled by another female star. Her movies grossed over $100 million, and she personally earned more than $3 million in the days when stars didn't pull in high salaries or receive a share of the profits. At one point she was the highest-salaried female in America.

In the mid-forties, Betty Grable received a record average of ten thousand fan letters a week, with one peak month in 1944 bringing in ninety thousand adoring letters. Her face appeared on the covers of *Time* and *Life,* countless movie magazines, and more bombers, tanks, and PT boats than anyone bothered to count. Betty Grable accomplished all this without ever having been in a truly top-notch movie. She carried her films, they didn't carry her.

Betty Grable herself contributed to the myth that she was just an ordinary talent with extraordinary success.

She took every opportunity to point out her limitations. "As a dancer," she would say, "I can't compete with Ginger Rogers or Eleanor Powell. As a singer, I'm no Doris Day. As an actress, I don't take myself seriously. I have some looks, without being in the big beauty league."

The truth is that Betty Grable had more than a little of everything it took, and together it was more than enough. As a dancer she was skilled, well-trained, capable of executing difficult steps with lightness and precision. When she ripped through an athletic romp with Gwen Verdon in *Meet Me After the Show* (1951), Grable showed she could more than keep up.

As a singer, she had a pleasant — though admittedly small — voice, melodious and clear. But she knew how to sell a song. She was responsible for introducing many of the big hits of the forties. ("My Heart Tells Me," "Kokomo, Indiana," "You Do," "I Had the Craziest Dream," and "I'm Always Chasing Rainbows," to name a few.)

As for acting, Grable wasn't equipped to perform

serious drama. She knew this and wisely steered away from attempts to change her image. When Darryl Zanuck offered her the part of the dipsomaniac in *The Razor's Edge* (1946), which eventually won Anne Baxter an Oscar, Grable laughed in his face. ''Oh, come on,'' she told him. ''When Sophie drowns herself, my fans would expect me to surface two minutes later with lily pads in my hair, singing a love song.'' The audience believed in the roles Grable played. By musical comedy standards, she was an honest actress, always in character.

Although Grable considered herself an average-looking girl in a world of Hedy Lamarrs and Lana Turners, she was a standout in Technicolor. She glowed, and her platinum hair, red lips, and blue eyes made her an all-American dream girl. Other characters in her films always looked as if they had just wandered in from a black-and-white, low-budget movie.

Her most famous features were her shapely legs, insured by Lloyds of London for $1 million, preserved for eternity in cement at Grauman's Chinese Theater. Grable herself said Dietrich's were better, but the public didn't agree. As if to protect herself against accusations that she was a two-legged wonder, Grable often repeated lines from one of her movies, *Billy Rose's Diamond Horseshoe* (1945) ''I'm in show business for two good reasons, and I'm standing on both of them. Put me in a long dress and I'd starve to death.''

Grable's intense modesty throughout her career resulted partly from the fact that she never really *wanted* a career. It was Lillian Grable, her mother, who pushed her. ''I had the stage mother to end all stage mothers,'' Betty often said. ''I had every kind of lesson there was

Betty Grable did many more pinup photos than the over-the-shoulder shot for which she is best remembered.

except eccentric dancing. Tap dancing, toe dancing, ballet dancing, acrobatic dancing, twirling, ice skating, roller skating. I can even play the saxophone — and not bad either."

Bitten by the Hollywood bug, Lillian Grable had Betty dancing in a Fox chorus line for $60 a week in 1929. Betty was only thirteen and had to lie about her age (fifteen was the legal limit). Depite this early start and the hard work Betty Grable put into it, success did not come easily. She was twenty-five before she finally made it. She progressed slowly from chorus girl to front-line hoofer to specialty dancer to band singer, then on to modest acclaim as a Paramount starlet who played campus cheerleaders. It was a tough life for a young girl who didn't want any of it in the first place. The endless disappointments made her want to quit. But Mama always said no. "It was like a poker game in which you know you're holding four aces," Lillian Grable explained. "I knew Betty had what they wanted."

Few remember that Betty Grable's breakthrough in Hollywood came via Broadway. Her youthful marriage to former child star Jackie Coogan had blown up, and she either wanted to make it or get off the hook. She accepted a choice part in *DuBarry Was a Lady,* a hit show

with Bert Lahr and Ethel Merman. When Grable stole the show and walked off with rave reviews, Hollywood grabbed her back.

The key to Grable's box office success lay in the fact that she appealed to both sexes. She offered men everything. She was nice. She was cheerful and healthy. She was ordinary enough not to intimidate, special enough to make them proud. She seemed like a girl you could take home to Mother, but with that body and mouth, anything might be possible. Most of Grable's films exploited her overt sex appeal by including at least one low-down dance number. She would be costumed in hot pink and black lace — or in blackface and a tight slit skirt.

Grable's appeal to men seems obvious. Her appeal to women is more complex. Her personality was modern by forties standards. At a point in American history when women first began to flood the job markets, Betty Grable almost always played a woman who worked. She belonged out in the world, earning her own living. Even in films that stressed the role of wife and mother, as in *Mother Wore Tights* (1947), Grable returned to work and left the kids with Grandma.

Grable usually played a girl who couldn't be fooled by men. She knew a wolf when she saw one. "We'll

Footlight Serenade, *with Jane Wyman. Grable's characters were unusual in that they enjoyed both male and female companions.*

keep the table between us," she told her dates. When a handsome man tried to soft-soap her, she was more than ready. "Aw come on, baby," says young Tyrone Power in *A Yank in the R.A.F.* (1941), "nobody can hold a grudge for two years." "Well, I can," she snaps back. "But I haven't even looked at another girl in all that time," he whines, flashing his best profile. "Oh, yeah?" she responds, turning on her heel. "Well, I've looked at other men."

Grable played the kind of girl who, when she smelled another woman's perfume on her boyfriend, walked right out and slammed the door. If she was stood up, she never wept or sang a torch song as Alice Faye might have. She simply put on her mink and went out with one of the fellows waiting in the wings.

Sometimes the Grable character was a bit hard. A girl who had been around and wasn't going to be foolish about money versus love. But she basically portrayed girls who played fair, were good-natured and reliable. As in her own life, she had personal dignity, even when it came in a down-to-earth form. Her genuine warmth was apparent whenever she smiled. She could take care of herself but was willing to share.

In her private life, Grable exhibited the same openness associated with her film roles. In an era when stars were supposed to be little homemakers, Grable admitted that all she could cook was "toast and coffee, and I need a cookbook for the toast." She appeared to have no vanity, and was dubbed a "director's dream" by her coworkers. She was professional and loyal. When I asked her about an article I had read that suggested that Lauren Bacall had been jealous and catty toward Marilyn Monroe while filming *How to Marry a Millionaire* (1953), she reported, "How unfair! Lauren is the nicest person in the world, and she was nicer to Marilyn than anybody else. Whenever you read nonsense like that, don't believe it." About Alice Faye, she always said with a gorgeous smile, "I love Alice. Everybody loves Alice."

When Marilyn Monroe came along to take Grable's place as the number one blond at Fox, Grable cared not a whit. Moreover, she treated Monroe with warmth and sisterly affection, helping her to learn the ropes and build her confidence. When I asked her about Monroe, Grable said, "Oh, she was a good kid. She used to come over, and we'd have a steak."

Grable's fame lasted well into the fifties, up until her voluntary retirement. Her fans maintained their loyalty throughout her retirement, until her death from cancer in 1973, at the age of fifty-six. Her long-time husband, Harry James, said after her death, "People who had known her and hadn't seen her in over twenty years came to the funeral. All kinds of people. Grooms from the race track. Little people from the studios. They all wanted to pay their respects. And you know that it takes a very special person, a lady in the true sense, to inspire that."

At her peak in Tin Pan Alley.

RITA HAYWORTH: UNLIKELY DELILAH

THE GORDONS

"Some early critics called her a pussycat siren, but she fooled them all. She was a sex goddess for twenty years."
— The Gordons

ON CRETE there stands, proudly defying time, an ancient city of the Minoans, Knossos, some three thousand years old. As we prowled it, we stood in awe before a billboardlike fresco. And there gazing down on us was Rita Hayworth. At least that's how this ancient painting of a goddess struck us; it was obvious to us that the twentieth-century Rita Hayworth is a reincarnation. She is one of many reincarnations that have added a little zest to the dull pages of history.

They have been called by many names: love goddesses, sirens, vamps, Loreleis, Delilahs, and sex symbols. For the more serious-minded, they have presented excellent studies in the mores of many ages and peoples.

THE GORDONS *wrote the original novel and the screenplay for* Experiment in Terror. *Among their other credits are* Down Three Dark Streets *and* That Darn Cat.

Whether staid Victorians or "swingers" living in today's anything-goes society, we have felt a need to create them. Since man began, he has longed to worship a beautiful, exciting woman whose eyes and body promised heaven — but a glamorous heaven, never cheap, sordid, or even realistic.

Probably the most unlikely of all candidates for such adulation was Margarita Carmen Cansino, and she was destined to become the most durable. During the forties and fifties, she was adored by a cult of millions. As her career declined — as it must for all women whose beauty, youth, and sexuality have been bartered in the marketplace — a new generation discovered her on television's late movies. And a new cult came into being.

★ ★ ★ ★ ★

For us it all began a long time ago, in 1940. We walked on the set of *Blood and Sand* the first day of shooting. Rita Hayworth was wearing slacks, her legs wrapped around a director's chair. She was shy but friendly and ever so young. She was more than nervous. She was frightened, and this was strange, for she had been in many films during the previous five or six years. She had played Latins, Indians, and other dark-haired damsels as a $200-a-week stock actress. She had been in Charlie Chan, Nero Wolfe, and the Lone Wolf pictures. Then had come a role as Richard Barthelmess' wife in Howard Hawks' *Only Angels Have Wings* (1939) and critical acclaim in *Angels Over Broadway* (1940).

Now she was playing opposite Tyrone Power — next to Clark Gable, the foremost male star of the day — in a challenging role as the siren Doña Sol in the famous Vicente Blasco-Ibáñez story of love and death. She was being directed by an urbane intellectual, Rouben Mamoulian, certainly one of the greats in the theater and in films. She had climbed only recently out of roles that had attracted merely passing attention.

She unwrapped her legs and rose to greet us. She had been reading Homer. She tossed her red hair — dyed only one picture before — in that happy way that was to become a trademark and said, smiling, "I read all the best-sellers.'' We fell in love with her. But a sex goddess? Nervous about seducing Ty Power? Reading Homer? Was this the Helen of Troy expected to launch a thousand ships filled with gold for Twentieth Century-Fox?

Even then it was evident she possessed lasting talents and qualities. She appeared quiet, even languid, but she was intensely disciplined. At sixteen, she was dancing with her father, Eduardo Cansino, and was taught to do her homework. She never forgot her heritage.

She was prepared that first day on *Blood and Sand,* and each day thereafter. She stayed up nights studying. She and Bette Davis, at the opposite poles of the spectrum both in temperament and acting, became known as the hardest workers in the movie business. Fred Astaire, with whom Rita danced in two pictures, said she could master a choreographed scene within an hour or two. He would go over the steps in the morning, and when he returned after lunch she would have them down pat. She would skip lunch to think and work her way through the routines.

She was consistently easy to work with. She had no pretenses, no temperament. She could have arrived on *Blood and Sand* with the typical ego confidence of an established actress; instead, she honestly wanted help from Mamoulian, Ty Power, and Linda Darnell (Power's wife in the film). She had a smile for everyone, and soon she had eighty people working for her. From Mamoulian on down, they gave her that personal attention that can mean so much on the screen. Mamoulian would hold up scenes until he got them lighted exactly right. She never failed to thank people and to show her appreciation. In *Blood and Sand* she seduces Ty Power, but during the filming she seduced the entire set.

In *Blood and Sand,* Mamoulian was trying to match color with the emotions they stir up in most of us. He had studied the subject avidly, and he needed Rita's cooperation with costumes and makeup. She plunged into the

As the temptress Doña Sol who caused bullfighter Tyrone Power to stray from his wife (Linda Darnell) in Blood and Sand, *Hayworth was first true vamp since the silent era.*

subject with enthusiasm and tested for hours on end in one costume after another as he ranged from El Greco to the pageantry of the bullring. In *Blood and Sand* Mamoulian painted, with her help and Darnell's, one of the most artistic films of that generation.

Yet hard work and a cooperative spirit would never in themselves have won the hearts of the ninety million people who went to the movies in that era. There were other qualities, and foremost was her wholesomeness.

A wholesome siren? Who ever heard of such a thing?

Yet a sex symbol, to gain the adoration Rita Hayworth had, must appeal as much to women as to men. She was the seductress in film after film, but all the time you knew she had good intentions. You knew it not from the scripts but by the way she looked.

Newsweek once said, ". . . the principal thing one can complain about is Rita Hayworth's unquenchable wholesomeness . . . [she] has a hard time being as dirty and nasty as the part requires."

She tried, but a little of the real Rita Hayworth invariably came through. Probably she didn't know it, and we doubt if few producers or directors did, but this "goodness" set her apart and brought her the fantastic following of the war (and postwar) years.

Hayworth films were highlighted by her singing or dancing. In Salome (L), she did the "Dance of the Seven Veils." In Gilda (Above), she sang "Put the Blame on Mame."

Excellent as Astaire's partner in You'll Never Get Rich.

With Frank Sinatra in Pal Joey.

We remember two very trivial, but meaningful, incidents. One day we phoned her home when she was in the shower. We told her secretary we would call back. But no, the secretary said, she must inform Miss Hayworth first. Then came the soft voice, and we could envision her standing there dripping wet, ruining an expensive carpet.

Another time we awakened her and apologized. ''Call me anytime,'' she said. ''It's my business, the same as yours.''

A sex goddess talking like that? Ridiculous.

Without question, World War II was a factor in her durability. The armies, navies, and air forces of half a world needed desperately to idolize a beautiful gal who epitomized their dream woman. And so Rita Hayworth and Betty Grable, another ''girl you wouldn't be ashamed to take home to your mother,'' were their choices. Their likenesses were spread around the globe.

Still, with all of this, Rita Hayworth possessed one even more important ingredient. When she walked on, she lighted up the screen. There was some spark of personality — today we might call it charisma — that no scientist can ever pin down, no sociologist ever satisfactorily explain.

After *Blood and Sand* she was to make many pictures. As the 1950s rolled by, however, she was being punished by time. There was *Pal Joey* (1957) and some other fairly good films, but the dreary pictures began to out-number the exciting ones. Yet no matter how bad the film or poor the dialogue, when she was on screen you sat up and took notice. The spark was there. It never died. It still hasn't.

Partying with Errol Flynn, Nora Flynn, and husband Orson Welles in 1946.

JENNIFER JONES: TEMPTING FATE

BILL HORRIGAN

In the appropriately titled The Wild Heart.

WITHIN A TWENTY YEAR PERIOD — from the early 1940s to the early 1960s — Jennifer Jones' best films offer a remarkable succession of heroines unable or unwilling to see further than their own desires. Often headstrong to the point of neurosis, her characters attempt to define the world on their own terms, and, by force of their own energetic

BILL HORRIGAN *is the assistant editor of* Cinema Journal *and is a former co-editor of* The Film Reader.

example, to make others buy those terms as well. Obviously, such attempts rarely succeed. What happens instead is that their behavior comes to be regarded as deviant or inexplicable. Yet Jones' women persist in acting on the commands of their desires, which partly explains why her heroines so frequently find themselves oppressed, penalized, and headed for no good end.

At first glance there may seem to be an apparent split in Jones' work between her "genteel" impulses (principally seen in *The Song of Bernadette* [1943], *Since You Went Away* [1944], *Good Morning, Miss Dove* [1955], and *The Barretts of Wimpole Street* [1957]) and her more fully sensual, even florid, ones (in such films as *Ruby Gentry* [1952], *Duel in the Sun* [1946] and *Madame Bovary* [1949].) However, to leave it at that is really to seize on a most unpromising coincidence. Rather than opposing one another, the genteel and the sensual impulses at work in Jones' characters seem to be taking her down merely alternate routes leading to the same unhappy destination.

But more interesting to observe is how nearly every character she plays is guided by a force, by a voice, beyond her control, as though she is constantly tuning in to a mystical circuit entirely her own. Bernadette's celestial hookup then marks her as different in degree only from Singleton in *Love Letters* (1945), who is totally innocent of any knowledge of her own history, or Gwendolen Chelm in *Beat the Devil* (1954), a pathological liar sensitive mostly to her own versions of reality, or Dr. Han Suyin in *Love Is a Many Splendored Thing* (1955), in which she is all the time attentive to the dictates of her racially mixed heritage despite there being no family present to enforce such demands. In *Portrait of Jennie* (1948), she exists as a phantom and thus is subject to the rules of a netherworld; as the schizophrenic Nicole in *Tender Is the Night* (1962), she has other voices to heed.

Even in the more conventional romantic relationships of her films, Jones brings to them a degree of intensity satisfied by nothing other than the obliteration of everything outside the privileged orbit of the couple. In *Since You Went Away*, her portrayal of the supposedly

At twenty-four, a fourteen-year-old in The Song of Bernadette.

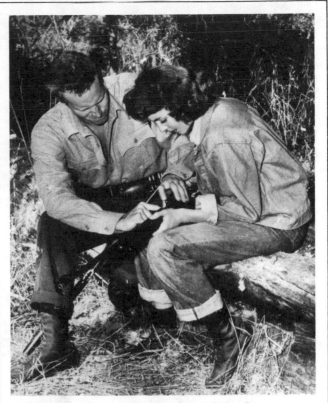

With Charlton Heston in the tumultuous Ruby Gentry.

typical teenage daughter in a supposedly typical wartime family is infected by the sense of true obsession and hysteria she conveys, most memorably in the scenes she shares with boyfriend Robert Walker (to whom she was then actually married).

In another fling at "typicality" — as an American housewife neo-realistically adventuring abroad — she spends virtually all of Vittorio De Sica's *Indiscretion of an American Wife* (1954) engaged in an intensely protracted farewell scene with her Italian lover (Montgomery Clift). A true curiosity, this film seems totally comprised of travelogue shots of Rome, radiant close-ups of the lovers, and elegantly composed long shots in a Rome railway station that are quite ahead of their time in the paranoid emptiness they spell. As such, it contrasts almost absolutely with King Vidor's deliriously decorative and Technicolored *Duel in the Sun*, in which Jones, as Pearl Chavez (another half-breed, and torn between the destinies decreed by her "good" blood and her "bad" blood), gives a performance of flamboyance probably not equaled by an actress since the days when Lillian Gish was being marooned on ice floes.

Comparably, *Ruby Gentry*, her other King Vidor collaboration, climaxes with an outrageous love-death shoot-out in the Everglades, but this film is less interested in such apocalyptic moments than it is in the observation of a kind of melancholy sadness, particularly in the epilogue in which the widowed Jones is viewed as being forever alone in a world left her by those who've died around her — those who've died "because" of her.

As in most of her films, what she's thinking remains mysteriously unspeakable, and her troubled close-ups, signaling the failure, the uselessness of speech, insist instead only on the fact of her presence on the knife edge of private crisis.

The film in which all the crucial tendencies of Jones' career find their most satisfying expression is undoubtedly Vincente Minnelli's version of *Madame Bovary*,

With Joseph Cotten. Duel in the Sun *had spectacle and sex.*

offering her a role that makes everything she did before seem like a rehearsal, and, shadowlike, it stalks all successive ones as a standard of performance. Often maligned for failing in the impossible (and, it might be said, unattempted) task of keeping faith with Flaubert's novel, the Minnelli-MGM-Jones film positions itself squarely in sympathy with the fantasy life of Emma Bovary, even as it insists at the same time that her fantasy and her reality cannot, can never, meet. What matters is that the quality of the passion invested in that dream is seen as in no way ignoble. Jones' Emma does see this, in her way, but the knowledge counts for nothing; she persists — obsessively, ferociously, poignantly — because she has no choice. She has no choice because her location in the present is unbearable, and that present won't change to provide what she needs.

In this film supremely — but as she moves through her other works as well — Jones is marked as an outcast as much in her own eyes as in the eyes of those who turn their backs on her in farewell as they're setting her adrift.

She remains an outcast — never anywhere at home — by virtue of having to pursue what her destiny denies she can possess. As with the work of some other stars (John Garfield and Ava Gardner come to mind), discussion of Jones' portrayals sometimes manages to resurrect a certain notion of fate or, rather, what passes for fate in Hollywood's book; the unhappy ending reserved, as we know, for the unhappy few. Jennifer Jones is among that lot, and so it is that fate to which she bears witness on the screen, on the screens of memory.

UNDER THE INFLUENCE

QUITE OFTEN analyses of Jennifer Jones' career are mistakenly framed in terms of the influence exerted on it by producer David O. Selznick (whom she married in 1949). These discussions hold that whatever successes she may have had were to his credit, as though his wife were little more than a photogenic mannequin around whom the proud husband could mount expensive productions. Selznick did undoubtedly play an enormously formative role in her career, dating from that day in 1942 when he decreed that Phyllis Isley Walker would henceforth be known as Jennifer Jones. He did, furthermore, produce a number of her films, select the roles she was to play, and, as his famous memos indicate, involve himself in virtually all aspects of productions besides his own with which she was associated. But surely it is a misconception of the most disreputable kind to judge the Selznick-Jones alliance from this perspective only. Certainly it is intriguing to speculate on the view Selznick must have held of his wife, that he should have recommended to her the roles that he did, and intriguing, too, to learn of Jones' personal and career misfortunes since his death in 1962. And from such speculation nothing honorable would result.

— B. H.

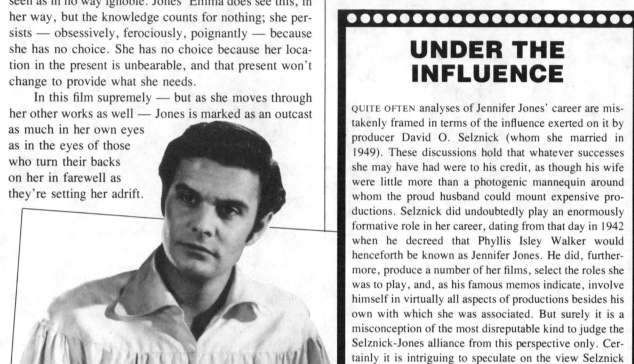

With Louis Jourdan. In Vincente Minnelli's Madame Bovary, *she sacrificed everything and everyone for love.*

AVA GARDNER: EARTH GODDESS

RICHARD ELMAN

ONCE, IN THE ELEVATOR of one of New York's better department stores, where I had gone to meet a young girlfriend, *she* stood almost at my side, briefly.

"Ah . . . Va . . . "

Her physical magnificence at that moment has not dimmed for me after nearly thirty years: the luster of her hair, her scent, the curve of one calf, a *pudeur* I could almost taste, refined, and piquant, and yet hearty, like the scent given off by certain southern trees.

Superb apparition — or goddess sent to earthbound New York City? It does not matter; at that moment, Ava surpassed even my expectations. My date was forgotten. In the first ripe effulgence of late adolescence I stayed on after she had left the elevator — and rode up and down, down and up, and down again. . . .

★ ★ ★ ★ ★

What effect do movie goddesses have on young people? Ava Gardner, so it seems, caused a lot of us to fall out of love with our mothers. Throughout my own adolescence these two grown women warred for my attentions; both southern ladies, but so very different. From our first exchanges of glances in the dark I felt myself being pulled toward Ava. She was no phony. Even when she had to act in what I then considered a silly folly such as *Pandora and the Flying Dutchman* (1951), she let us know she knew. Ava had a way of chewing at her lip. In the caramel-scented dusk of the cinema she would smile, or frown, seductively, and then, briefly, she was human and incredulous, her physical splendors, no longer quite passive or serene, were enhanced by some sort of lonely air of self-knowledge.

Separated from Ava by more than her wealth and glamour — by time and experience — I presumed she was not just another pretty face, and that was certainly presumptuous of me in that she was beautiful, but, you

A Spanish beauty in The Naked Maja.

must understand that young men like myself thought she should be our mistress, our instructress, our ticket into another, better world.

I thought I was certainly available to Ava in ways a lot of men she seemed to know were not. (I was certainly more appropriate than Mickey Rooney.) I felt in her world she was kept from being as devout and sincere as she probably needed to be. Under the circumstances she

---

RICHARD ELMAN *is a novelist-poet, whose latest book of poems is* Homage to Fats Navarro. *He is the author of the novelization of* Taxi Driver.

Publicity photos of the glamorous Ava Gardner emphasized her earthy, almost animalistic, sex appeal.

Pandora and the Flying Dutchman, *with Harold Warrender*.

A heated embrace with Burt Lancaster, making his cinema debut, in The Killers.

probably had to *seem* so hard and so guarded, I thought, so alone. She had need of a real friend.

Mom disagreed. She said Ava *was* fast, called her a *tramp*. When I had loved Paulette Goddard she had said the same things; now she was recommending Paulette Goddard as, at least, being from Brooklyn where we then lived.

It really doesn't matter what she says, I assured Ava in the darkness, *because I'll always love you.*

But I was guilty of one real act of disloyalty to this dark lady. In her movies I came to demand of Ava that she fall in love, hopelessly head over heels in love, as we used to say, because she always seemed so unhappy in love, on film, as well as what I knew of her real life, and that way she would need a "friendly fellow" like me all the more.

When Ava started to show she cared for Clark Gable in *The Hucksters* (1947), I was certainly glad for her. Compassion of that sort was the aftertaste of jealousy. Ava needed to be more in touch with her more tender feelings, I told myself, without fear of hurt. And Clark, I reasoned, was a decent-enough chap, with a sense of fair play. When they started doing all those Hemingway stories on film — *The Killers* (1946), *The Snows of Kilimanjaro* (1952), and *The Sun Also Rises* (1957) — I thought, *that's the wrong crowd for you, Ava, heartless and violent.* Appearing in such films seemed to be self-destructive for her. But how could I presume to help Lady Brett Ashley? She seemed to know what she was doing. She could take care of herself. She was, how shall I put it, *worldly* for her time. . . .

I always thought Ava knew she had a lot to learn about herself. Her films, however flossy, glossy, or trivializing of human beauty, suggest intensity and arouse curiosity. She had agreed to do business with the world through her physical self, a treacherous business, but that was her own ticket to what she had probably hoped might be less of an embarrassment than poverty, or small-town life. She did not marry to advance herself, but negotiated — now here, now there, tentatively — as a contingent being. She was passive at first and then more aggressive.

My first glimpse of Ava is still vivid: It is a *Life* magazine photo of a young woman, a little overweight, in a cotton dress, or wraparound, in the sun and dust of North Carolina, smiling, with a faint sweat mustache above her upper lip. There's the slightest suggestion of wind that day. . . . There's a gawkishness — a suggestion of intimate and physical life (her body is ample to the flimsy fabric), but certainly not glamour. There's a certain embarrassment, perhaps even bashfulness, to this pre-career snapshot, but you can see that she is brazening it out, and I thought to myself as time went on that I still saw her often that way though she was sleek and groomed for *others*.

The years in which she kept leaping ahead of me and going abroad a lot were years in which I grew into manhood. I'd never be able to catch up to her now. (Ah, if I could have just spoken to her during that elevator ride.) As Ava grew older, I thought better than to seek her out with assurances of undying devotion. She might only consider me condescending. Better to watch over her

Watching an intense moment between Charles Laughton and Robert Taylor in The Bribe.

from a certain distance, be critical as I inspect all the items in the gossip columns, attend to her efforts in new films.

Ava seemed to be withdrawing from the public view gradually — making films only every other year — and with some grace, as one draws the blinds to shut out the afternoon sun.

"If beauty be the mark of praise," wrote Ben Jonson; and she was beautiful to me. Where empathy and desire are validated only at the movies, the romance of life takes place in the dark. Ava and her Hollywood sisters must not be faulted too badly because they glittered while others starved. They illuminated dark lives, such as my own, with truths that overcame hostile ignorance and brute gracelessness, so that in coming to love them on film, we were finally willing to seek out their like in our own lives, *for our own lives*. That's the only good reason men — and young boys — worship goddesses.

The Barefoot Contessa, *her most famous role.*

On the set of The Night of the Iguana.

ROCK HUDSON: BETWEEN KNIGHT AND DAY

MICHAEL STERN

ROCK HUDSON has been as unshakable as his name suggests. After he was established as the immovable masculine presence of the American screen in the mid-1950s, he deviated little from this delineation. He was Hollywood's incarnation of the strong, good-looking, handsome, clean-shaven American male. While James Dean, Paul Newman, and Marlon Brando — then his peers at the top of the box office — expressed more vulnerable aspects of the male personality, Hudson came to represent the ideal. He had only to be himself to fulfill audience expectations.

Douglas Sirk was the first director to realize that there is more to Rock Hudson than meets the eye. In his *Has Anybody Seen My Gal?* (1952), Rock plays a soda jerk, the butt of a lot of jokes. He gets his gal in the end, of course, but only after she recognizes him for the straight and true fellow he is. In this film, Hudson's earnest, honest aspects — so important to his screen image — are clear.

However, Hudson's ascent to full stardom came with *Magnificent Obsession* (1954), a remake of the 1935 melodrama. It became such a big hit this time around that it made the careers of director Sirk and producer Ross Hunter and established Rock Hudson as a major leading man. Rock plays the part of a dissolute playboy who wants nothing more of life than to career around in his sports car and his speedboat, get drunk, and date floozies. In a series of fateful events, he finds himself responsible for the death of an eminent surgeon and for the subsequent blinding of the surgeon's widow (Jane Wyman). He eventually falls in love with her and spends the second half of the picture atoning for his sins. He becomes a great surgeon himself and, ultimately, per-

forms a miraculous operation that cures his beloved of her blindness.

The film — especially Hudson's role in it — still arouses controversy. Sirk treated the maudlin material as a fairy story, an unreal tale of fate, coincidence, illness, and tears. Hudson is the story's prince, his operation on

His dominant trait was not his looks but his gentleness.

MICHAEL STERN *is the co-author of* Amazing America *and* Roadfood. *He guest-edited* Bright Lights' *issue devoted to director Douglas Sirk.*

Wyman the kiss that literally opens her eyes. His performance required a delicate balance of qualities: strength, resolve, dynamism, as well as a kind of dreamy, implacable perfection. The change from dissolute playboy to magnificent surgeon is the stuff of myth — "quite impossible," Sirk said, "and therefore just right."

What is remarkable about Hudson's portrayal is his melding of sturdy masculinity with gentleness and compassion. Once he falls in love he becomes protective but not overbearing, supportive but not aggressive.

At the time, Rock Hudson's reserved dignity was not considered by critics to be "acting" at all, not in comparison to the method acting that marked the decade in such films as *Marty* or *East of Eden*. But audiences accepted *Magnificent Obsession* as "myth," and Rock Hudson as perfectly suited to playing the mythological hero.

To cash in on this success, a second Sirk-Hudson-Wyman project was rushed into production. It was *All That Heaven Allows* (1955), which I consider to be the quintessential Rock Hudson vehicle. Rock played a young gardener who falls for an older widow from a higher social class (Wyman). The picture takes place in New England, Thoreau's *Walden* being its leitmotiv. "He's never read it," one of the characters says about Rock. "He just lives it." The personification of independence, nature, and free will, Rock is set against all the negative qualities of small-town life. The widow's children and neighbors resent his untamed spirit and scorn him as merely "a handsome set of muscles." Rock does not fight back — but neither does he run. He simply waits patiently for Wyman to see the light.

Conformity was a major social issue during the 1950s, and this film is a parable about a man who refuses to "keep up with the Joneses." It further established Hudson as an ideal for the neatly-groomed young generation (as opposed to the James Dean's blue-jean crowd).

Hudson's unswerving nature is prominent again in *Written on the Wind* (1956), in which he stands in contrast to his volatile supporting players, Robert Stack and Dorothy Malone. His inner strength is monumental. Throughout the picture he is pursued by a beautiful sexy nymphomaniac (Malone, as Stack's sister). Hudson re-

Magnificent Obsession. *Hudson and Jane Wyman played the Robert Taylor and Irene Dunne roles in the 1935 version.*

He seemed comfortable acting with the quiet Jane Wyman in All That Heaven Allows.

Written on the Wind. *Staid Rock Hudson seemed overwhelmed by stormy Dorothy Malone.*

fuses to touch her. West German filmmaker R.W. Fassbinder has called Hudson's character "the most pig-headed bastard in the world. How can he possibly not feel something of the longing Dorothy Malone has for him?" She offers herself, goes after guys who look vaguely like him so as to make him understand. And all he can say is "I could never satisfy you." God knows he could. Perhaps he *could,* but the audience knows he never *would.* He is too decent to make it with his best friend's sister, and besides, he loves another (Lauren Bacall). Nothing could lead him astray.

Rock Hudson's last picture for Douglas Sirk was *The Tarnished Angels* (1957), a film version of William Faulkner's *Pylon.* In it, Hudson gives one of his best performances, though he himself never liked it. Playing

a derelict reporter, he was called on for once to throw away his stalwart image, to play a weak man, a sympathetic victim disillusioned by his own futile attempts to find love and meaning in Mardi Gras New Orleans. It is a tour de force, perhaps the only time in his career when one senses the actor's infusing a role with personal longings.

Hudson did successfully counter his image some years later, in Howard Hawks' *Man's Favorite Sport?* (1964). The film is a comic inversion of his (by then) legendary masculinity. Rock played a sheep in wolf's clothing, an alleged authority on rugged outdoorsmanship who, when put to the test by an athletic Paula Prentiss, turns out to be a flabby incompetent.

Man's Favorite Sport? was itself a reversal of what had become, by the mid-1960s, the typical Rock Hudson vehicle: the bedroom farce. His turn from serious melodrama to comedy came in *Pillow Talk* (1959). The plot calls for Doris Day to think that he is innocent and naive when, in fact, the audience knows he is a wolf. The demands of sexual comedy brought a whole new shading to Rock Hudson's image. He had once symbolized simplicity and earthy independence; now he was worldly-wise and manipulative. The gentleness that graced his rugged nature in *All That Heaven Allows* turned to quiet cunning and sexual diplomacy.

Rock's irresistible charm was pitted against Day's virginity once again in a follow-up film, *Lover, Come Back* (1961), by which time Rock Hudson's comic coolness had become his most salient trait.

The team of Hudson and Day was a misguided sixties-style version of the Tracy-Hepburn match. The verbal (and sometimes physical) sparring of that classic couple was replaced by a more deceitful relationship in the Hudson-Day films, and a far greater polarization

SIRK REMEMBERS

DOUGLAS SIRK wanted to make a series of films about American life. He found in Rock Hudson — at the time a little-known contract player at Universal — just what he was looking for in a leading man. In *Sirk on Sirk:*

I thought I saw something. So I arranged to meet him, and he seemed to be not too much to the eye, except very handsome. But the camera sees with its own eye . . . and ultimately you learn to trust your camera. I gave him an extensive screen test, and then I put him into Has Anybody Seen My Gal? *. . . Within a very few years he became a number one box-office star in America.*

— M. S.

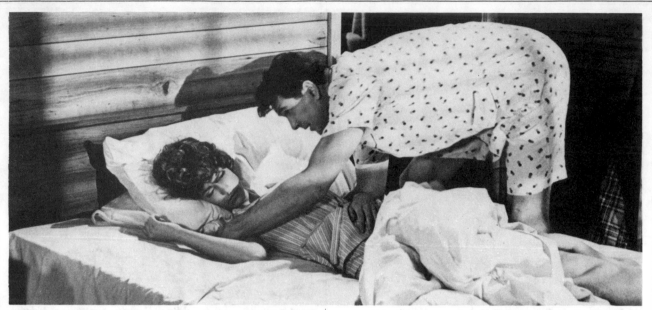

With Paula Prentiss in Howard Hawks' Man's Favorite Sport?

between masculine aggression and feminine resistance. There was a brittle, almost hateful, quality to their courtship shot with innuendo about frigidity and impotence. Hudson walked through these films with a wry smile on his face, as if detached from the machinations of the plot.

But whatever non-direction his career has taken, Rock Hudson did create a body of work that established him as the consummate symbol of the ideal American male — before the psychic and social upheavals of the late 1960s. The Rock has survived the alleged breakdown of the star system; his private life is very private, his public image still preeminently masculine; and one of the last Hollywood-fabricated stars still glows — even after Hollywood's disintegration.

Inspired casting brought opposites Hudson and James Dean together for Giant. *Elizabeth Taylor was drawn to both.*

KIM NOVAK:
HAUNTED BEAUTY

JOHN RUSSELL TAYLOR

In Of Human Bondage. *She said a studio head told her: "Never forget that all you are is a piece of meat, like in a butcher shop."*

CONSIDERING HOW SHE STARTED, it is amazing that Kim Novak ever got anywhere. There are, of course, those who would stoutly deny she ever did, but that does seem a bit unreasonable. How can one deny stardom, genuine stardom, to the Novak of *Vertigo* (1958) or of *Picnic* (1955)? And then there are the more esoteric delights of *Jeanne Eagels* (1957) and *The Legend of Lylah Clare* (1968).

JOHN RUSSELL TAYLOR *is the author of numerous books on film, including* Cinema Eye, Cinema Ear, The Hollywood Musical, *and* Hitchcock, *an authorized biography. He was the film critic for the London* Times.

Undoubtedly, Kim Novak had something. I think I first noticed it in *Pushover* (1954), a nice little film with Fred MacMurray that had heavy overtones of *Double Indemnity*. Though obviously unsure of herself, Kim Novak had a strange, haunting quality that made her memorable despite the fact that everyone knew she was Harry Cohn's puppet, an instant star he had invented to counter the queen of Columbia Pictures, Rita Hayworth.

In 1956, *Boxoffice* named Novak the top female star in the United States. Cohn's comment: "The success of Novak is due to great pictures. Any girl who gets six pictures like Novak got has got to be a star. We've got twelve to fifteen million dollars invested in her."

Tempting Fred MacMurray in Pushover.

Or, in other words, *I did it all — I could have done it with anyone I chose.* Cohn's attitude contains a contradiction: If he had really wanted to create an idol, and really thought he had done so, why did he feel the need to cut her down in the public's estimation, to destroy the mystique he had worked so hard to create?

The answer is that he knew his "invention" had gotten out of control, that she had a life of her own in spite of him. After all, we need only recall the sad story of Samuel Goldwyn and Anna Sten to see that all the promotion in the world cannot foist a pseudo-star on a public if it is unwilling or unable to respond. With *Picnic,* Novak's fifth appreciable role, the public started responding, and not because of the often idiotic promotion she had received. (There was all the nonsense about "the lavender blond" — how she refused to wear anything but shades of lavender.) Playing the pretty sister, just bright enough to know how small a brain she had, Kim seemed bovine, yes, but also touching. She looked out at a world she could not quite cope with through mistrustful eyes: There was something troubling, almost sly, about her. The quality is not entirely likable, but it was unmistakably there.

George Cukor liked to say of certain actresses, "She has a secret," meaning that there is more than meets the eye, a vital way in which she eludes our analysis. Kim Novak has that sort of secret. She never seems quite at ease with the world about her; she lives somewhere else, almost defying us to uncover her secret. There are some stars who have this constant subtext to their screen lives. Carroll Baker, so often cast as a sex-bomb, comes to life when she is playing the opposite; Lana Turner, so eager to be a lady, suddenly grows vivid when the long-suffering *Madame X* (1966) turns into a tramp. And Kim Novak "works" fully on screen only when she is required to be desperately insecure, to look out of her small corner like a wary child.

This appears to be the connecting link in all her best screen performances. (Let us not argue about whether she can, in any traditional sense, act — she works on screen, and that is the most important thing.) Think of the hopelessly confused Jeanne Eagels, following her star even to death. Think of the tortured mistress of a much older man in *Middle of the Night* (1959). Think of her unwillingly caught up in an extramarital affair in *Strangers When We Meet* (1960). Think of the mistrustful object of so much attention in *Kiss Me Stupid* (1964). All of them have a disturbing air, at odds with their environment, not completely at home in either the body or personality in which they find themselves.

Above all, think of the mysterious Madeleine and the shakily tarty Judy in *Vertigo*. It is perhaps appropriate that Novak's definitive performance would be under the direction of that wicked old puppetmaster, Alfred Hitchcock. What's even more appropriate is that she was the second choice, pitchforked into the role when Vera Miles had to withdraw because she was pregnant. Everything in *Vertigo* seems calculated to exploit Novak's uneasy air, and it indeed seems she was very uncomfortable in the role until Hitchcock countered her worries: "Kim, let's not go too deeply into these things. It's only a movie." This appears to have had its effect, putting her at her ease, giving her freer play to explore her screen nature. It is hard to imagine anyone better as the ethereal Madeleine in the movie's early scenes. Novak has never topped her work in that film.

She was her most beautiful during the period

With Dean Martin in the tasteless comedy Kiss Me Stupid.

With Lilli Palmer. The Amorous Adventures of Moll Flanders *tried to capture the flavor of* Tom Jones. *It missed.*

1956–58 when she made three films in succession for George Sidney, who first revealed her fully in *The Eddy Duchin Story* (1956). These were followed by the Hitchcock, on through *The Amorous Adventures of Moll Flanders* (1965). After that her films became infrequent, largely, it seems, by her own wish to remain a private person. But there remained one masterpiece, *The Legend of Lylah Clare,* in which, of course, she was given a role that left her own personality shifting and uncertain, under attack from all directions. The film was silly — but somehow she was not.

If Harry Cohn really thought he had invented her, and that he could have done the same with any reasonably good-looking girl, he was quite wrong. No one invented Kim Novak but Kim Novak, and it is doubtful she ever quite realized what she had created. For this is something that happens only between the shadow on the screen and the audience out there in the dark. With Kim Novak it happened often and intensely. It was no confidence trick — it was the true stuff of stardom.

AN ILL-FATED CAPER

I MUST CONFESS that Kim Novak was almost responsible for an attempted crime. For some years, when I was first living in Los Angeles, I was tormented by a shadowy presence in a health-food restaurant I occasionally visited. It was the portrait of Kim Novak from *The Legend of Lylah Clare.* She wears a white dress, holds a red rose. It's the painting under which she poses when she tells the world about her identification with the lost, lamented Lylah. Nobody at the restaurant seemed to know or care about the portrait, and it hung there in the gloom. I felt that the place didn't deserve it. But my best laid plans for a heist came to nothing when, without my noticing, the place turned into a bar and the painting vanished.

— J. R. T.

With Peter Finch in The Legend of Lylah Clare.

ELIZABETH TAYLOR: IN THE PUBLIC EYE

MAUREEN TURIM

ONE THINKS OF ELIZABETH TAYLOR'S screen image as having developed in stages: princess — queen — superstar. One also thinks of an offscreen evolution: from child-woman clinging to a horse named King Charles to a woman-child stumping behind her sixth husband, millionaire-politician John Warner — a Virginia horseowner. Five-and-dime irony. Undeniably, there are two stories, and it is unfortunate that the one about a gifted actress has been less interesting to journalists than the one of her publicity. Her public fame depicts a heroine/villain named Liz on a grand scale of wealth and seduction — ever-present bared shoulders, décolletage, and full-skirted evening gown overflowing with sensual promise. Like so many postwar stars, Elizabeth Taylor has become eclipsed by a media persona and an industry dependent upon marketing not talent but notoriety.

Only dimly remembered behind the headlines is the promising young actress a movie audience watched grow up. Could American men and women who shared adolescence with Elizabeth forget the first erotic image of her riding a horse in *National Velvet* (1944)? As Elizabeth grew from this child, who already possessed the beauty and charm of a woman, she acquired an expressive repertoire as an actress which includes intelligence, tenderness, strength, and anger. At her best Taylor is capable of nuanced portrayals of distinct social types; for a while her screen type was the rich, beautiful, and privileged debutante.

In her roles as the rebellious darling daughter in Vincente Minnelli's comedies *Father of the Bride* (1950) and *Father's Little Dividend* (1951), Taylor responds to the challenge of being paired with Spencer Tracy by matching his ease with her own expressive gesture and movement.

These two roles were a prelude to a more dramatic

As she matured on screen, she became more volatile.

version of the same type. In *A Place in the Sun* (1951) Taylor's perfect, polished features melt into the costumes and sets used to mark the class (''breeding'') of Angela Vickers. She becomes a desirable symbol of luxury and leisure, the sophisticate who is still pert and playful. As we watch her seduction of Montgomery Clift as George Eastman, each gesture and phrase delivers a sensuality legitimized by the wealth that surrounds it. Fingers curve knowingly around the boy's neck, eyes close, lips open. With this, something occurs that veers George Stevens' movie away from its Dreiser source, *An American Tragedy*. At once the film becomes a melodramatic love story; Taylor becomes as complex a

MAUREEN TURIM *has written on film for such publications as* Wide Angle, The Velvet Light Trap, *and the* Purdue Film Annual. *She is assistant professor of cinema at The State University of New York, Binghamton.*

In National Velvet, *she earned much press coverage.*

It was under Stevens' direction five years later in *Giant* (1956) that Taylor was again given a chance to act after a stint of mediocre roles in uninspiring films. Her interaction with James Dean has the same tension as it did with Clift, although here it is without the sexual proximity. Instead the encounter is channeled through a visit to Dean's as-yet-unproductive oil wells and concentrated on a tea ceremony that allows both Dean and Taylor to pull a thread of fascination between their wildly disparate characters. In her rebellion against husband Bick Benedict (Rock Hudson), Taylor voices a need for self-expression and fulfillment rare for a woman in films of the 1950s; she is convincing in that expression and in the strength of asserting herself.

Tennessee Williams created roles for women that were charged with the explosivity of blocked desire; Elizabeth Taylor performed two of these roles with an accuracy that leads one to imagine them written for her. In *Cat on a Hot Tin Roof* (1958), the frustration exudes as sarcasm and anger. Contemporary critics of the film remarked on a shift in Taylor's acting style—her newly revealed ability to project herself as cat-woman, incorporating a purring sensuality and claws tensed for both defense and attack.

Again Hollywood watered down its version of *Cat* as it had *A Place in the Sun*. Maggie (Taylor's role) is decidedly less a misogynist's fantasy than was her stage character; the ending is transformed so that her husband (Paul Newman) overcomes his impotence in their re-

character as Clift, instead of merely a factor in his imagination, social ascendancy, and decline.

In A Date with Judy, *neglected daughter receives needed attention from father, Leon Ames.*

A Place in the Sun *featured the ill-fated love affair between Taylor and Montgomery Clift.*

lationship and his guilt, which is also laundered of the homosexuality it carried in the play. Yet even with these changes the confrontation between male impotence (and homosexuality) on one hand and glamorous, sensual but neurotically demanding womanhood on the other is successful in the film. Taylor lends Maggie her erotic-goddess appearance but tinges her southern-accented articulations with a pain that arrises from her confined exis-

Screaming at Paul Newman in Cat on a Hot Tin Roof. *From the mid-fifties on she became tremendously emotional — as if that signaled she was an adult.*

TRUTH AND FICTION

IN 1963, *Cleopatra*, which was budgeted at $40 million, captured the public's imagination. There were three *Life* magazine spreads concerning the film between October 1961 and April 1963, including two covers, one of Liz in Egyptian costume, the other a portrait of Burton and Taylor.

An entire page was devoted to a mock photo album of all the children involved in the Reynolds-Fisher-Taylor-Burton couplings with a headline, "Please, Who's My Daddy Now?" As the innocents, Debbie, Eddie, and Sybil were delineated as having been undone by the ultimate pseudo-aristocratic partnership of Elizabeth and Richard. Director Joseph L. Mankiewicz claimed a vision of the film as a Shakespearean drama of the motivations of the powerful, but it was the glitter and scandal that sold the monstrosity, and real power was

asserted by Taylor. She commanded $1 million salary plus a percentage, and $50,000 a week overtime (for sleepwalking in a $6,500 dress of pure gold). The ancient triangle of Caesar, Cleopatra, and Antony was far less exciting to the public than observing Taylor, hailed as "the most beautiful woman in the world," discarding famous men off-screen.

When the married Taylor and Burton made *The Taming of the Shrew* (1967) years later, again *Life* became a forum for film publicity by running an interview with Burton in which he elaborated on Taylor as an offscreen shrew whom her husband could nonetheless tame. Thus Taylor's on- and offscreen personas were brought into alignment in an attempt to sell Shakespeare to the supermarket crowd.

— M. T.

Cleopatra.

The Taming of the Shrew.

tence, the emotional release she is denied.

A similar tension haunts Catherine, Taylor's role in *Suddenly, Last Summer* (1959). Catherine is caught in an intrigue generated by her cousin Sebastian's decision to use her as his bait for the young boys he needs to satisfy his closet homosexuality. At the film's opening, Sebastian's mother, played with aristocratic flourish by Katharine Hepburn, is trying to bribe a psychiatric hospital to lobotomize Catherine in order to conceal her dead son's sexual proclivities. Taylor's part develops in a series of psychiatric sessions with Dr. Cukrowicz, played by Montgomery Clift. As in *Cat*, we are presented with the essence of desirable feminine voluptuousness, again maimed by rejection, only this time it has grown into confusion and mental suffering. Catherine is suicidal, haunted; Taylor brings to this role a disturbed

gaze and frantic gestures that exactly capture the psychic trauma that must be released through the story's retelling. This happens at the end of the film, in monologue, as shots of Catherine are intercut with flashback visions. As in her role as Maggie, Taylor's ability to convey drama is highlighted as Catherine's memories are spoken with an anguish skillfully orchestrated to the climatic revelation.

Not until *Who's Afraid of Virginia Woolf?* (1966) does Taylor expand this talent for characterization in her evocation of Martha, the frustrated wife of university professor George, played by Richard Burton. Taylor broke the star's dictum, still strong in the mid-sixties, to remain as attractive as possible, by drastically aging her face and fattening her body for this role and appearing disheveled and slovenly in shocking contrast to her pre-

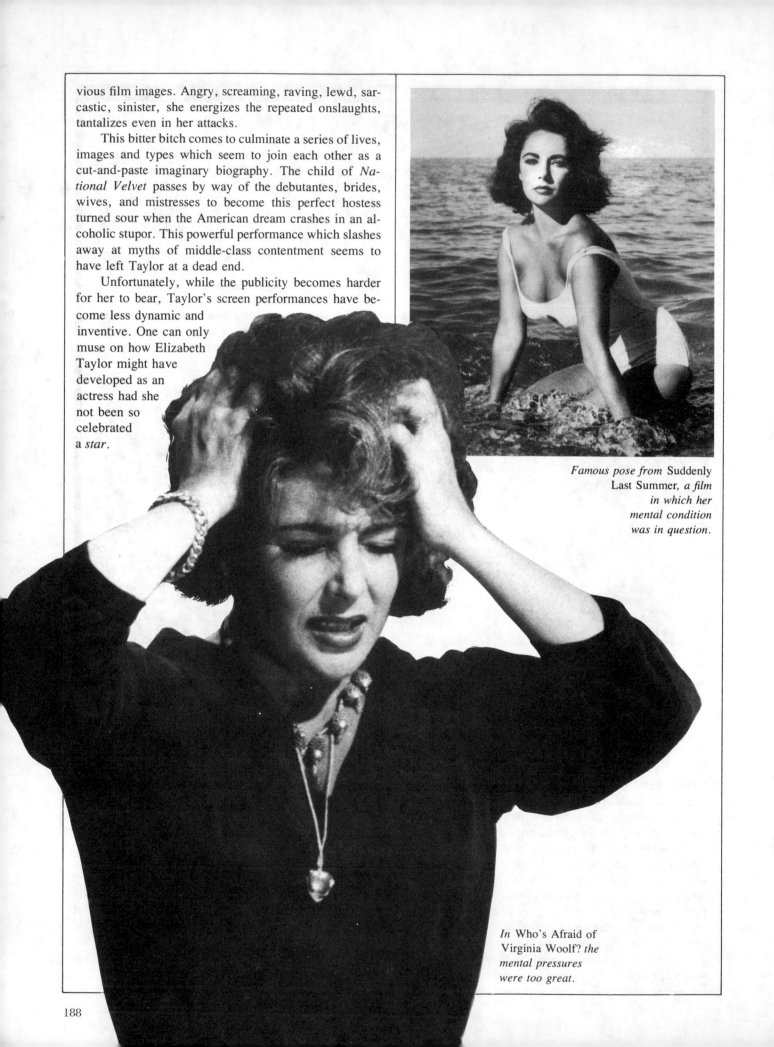

vious film images. Angry, screaming, raving, lewd, sarcastic, sinister, she energizes the repeated onslaughts, tantalizes even in her attacks.

This bitter bitch comes to culminate a series of lives, images and types which seem to join each other as a cut-and-paste imaginary biography. The child of *National Velvet* passes by way of the debutantes, brides, wives, and mistresses to become this perfect hostess turned sour when the American dream crashes in an alcoholic stupor. This powerful performance which slashes away at myths of middle-class contentment seems to have left Taylor at a dead end.

Unfortunately, while the publicity becomes harder for her to bear, Taylor's screen performances have become less dynamic and inventive. One can only muse on how Elizabeth Taylor might have developed as an actress had she not been so celebrated a *star*.

Famous pose from Suddenly Last Summer, *a film in which her mental condition was in question.*

In Who's Afraid of Virginia Woolf? *the mental pressures were too great.*

WARREN BEATTY: UNLUCKY SEDUCER

MICHAEL WILMINGTON

W HAT IS IT that Woody Allen once said? "If I come back in another life, I want to be Warren Beatty's fingertips." Thinking of Warren Beatty, one makes an immediate association — and it's always priapic. War/peace. Bread/butter. Warren Beatty/seduction.

While some actors capture our imagination almost solely by what they do on screen (Spencer Tracy, for example), Beatty's on-screen image (however formidable) seems but a pale reflection of how his life appears beyond the camera. It's a quicksilver image: evanescent, shifting, jet-set Casanova, serious student of society and the arts. The image is so various that it's no wonder Beatty professes to hate it. Yet, perhaps his frequent disavowals and his contempt for some journalists are another layer on the persona. Perhaps, underneath it all, he is secretly amused at the mammoth shock waves his image creates. Certainly, very few actors — even in film, the most narcissistic of all professions — project so much self-esteem or self-love. And it's precisely that self-love — that sense of delight and humorous exhilaration he takes in himself — that makes his on-screen character so fascinating.

What is that character? What's beyond the shrewd, intent, boyish stare; the phrases that seem to be softly muttered or escaping through a sunny, slightly crooked grin? Beyond the mixture of awkwardness and élan; the flaring explosions of temper; the hurt, spaniel bewilderment; the loose-limbed gallantry; the air of elegant sloppiness? What's behind the eyes like chilly almonds, and the casually athletic slouch? What are the subtle, symbiotic ties between Beatty and "Beatty"?

He himself has given one of the best definitions of the character: He calls him the "cocky schmuck." Beatty's schmuck is jaunty and cunning, but also naive.

MICHAEL WILMINGTON *is a film critic based in Madison, Wisconsin. He has written on film for numerous publications, including* Film Comment, The Velvet Light Trap, *and Boston's* The Real Paper. *He is the co-author of a book on director John Ford.*

As nightclub comic in Mickey One.

He was a sensation in his movie debut, Splendor in the Grass *(Above, with Natalie Wood, and R), a film considered daring at the time of its release in 1961. Today, director Eli Kazan considers Beatty the Actors Studio graduate whose later skills surprised him most.*

He's addicted to self-dramatization. He manipulates people but seems hurt or suspicious at being manipulated in turn. He's a romantic to the core — despite occasions when his ideas of romance seem derived from Zane Grey and the Saturday matinee. He tells crummy jokes. Women treat him like a child. He's fond of violent games, but real violence leaves him desolate, bewildered — and sometimes dead. He's a Golden Boy with a worm of decay gnawing at his guts. And, surprisingly, he has a persistent, somewhat prickly problem: Fate continually conspires to keep him from scoring.

Failure — sexual and otherwise — is the key to "Beatty." The man who boasts of such dazzling successes in his real life is preoccupied with his opposite number: a shadowy doppelgänger, a man who fails with women, fails to keep money, fails in society, makes mistakes, and often pays for his presumption with his life.

Is there, in all American film, a more painful, more agonizing visualization of romantic loss than that final scene in *Splendor in the Grass* (1961) where Deanie (Natalie Wood) walks among the bright, crackling stalks of corn (like the field where Clyde and Bonnie will later share a despairing embrace) and the baked autumnal fields of Bud Stamper's farm and sees her old lover imprisoned in domesticity and, relieved perhaps that the furnace of their desire is cooled, sees that his wife has a touch of the bovine and the slattern? The golden son of Icarus has seen the wax-smeared wings on his father's corpse and will fly no more; she is relieved that love is vain and passion a little heap of ashes in the stove as she smiles afterward and repeats, with maybe just a touch of hidden sadism, Wordsworth's sweet poetry of resignation.

The scene is annihilating. And it wouldn't have worked at all if Beatty, at the beginning, hadn't learned from director Elia Kazan how to effectively play William Inge's Kansas Adonis (like the homoerotic idealizations of Tennessee Williams or James Leo Herlihy — not all that easy to play) and if we didn't sense that the sap and blood of springtime, frozen after the Great Crash, couldn't once have poured through with a terrifying energy. Beatty was lucky enough (as he has often com-

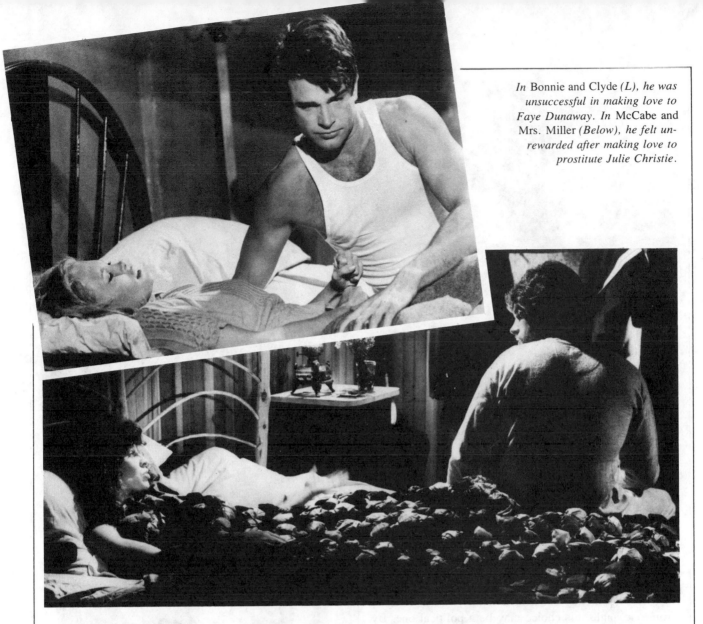

mented) to learn very early how to sense his own strengths, then play ruthlessly against them to create that magnetic turbulence, those seductive inner conflicts that made legends of Jimmy Dean and Marlon Brando.

Forgetting Berry-Berry in *All Fall Down* (1962) and the gigolo in *The Roman Spring of Mrs. Stone* (1961) — two roles that he believes, quite correctly, are not precisely in his groove — we next see him locked away from his love in *Lilith* (1964) and frustrated and pursued by an enigmatically hostile world in *Mickey One* (1965). He knows by now, knows absolutely, that he is most effective when he plays the closet failure.

And the catalogue of his failures becomes thick and rich. In *Splendor in the Grass*, he loses his father's wealth and house, and the love of the girl forbidden him by class; in *Lilith*, he nearly loses his entire world. In *Mickey One* (which has a rare, "positive" ending) he loses security, but also illusions and false comfort; in *Bonnie and Clyde* (1967), he loses, one by one, his "family" — and finally his life. In *The Only Game in Town* (1970), he loses his freedom; in *McCabe and Mrs. Miller* (1971), once again (it's becoming an idée fixe) his

love and then his life. In *The Fortune* (1975), it is his freedom and callow dreams. In *The Parallax View* (1974) he loses his life; in *Shampoo* (1975), again, his true love. Appropriately enough for an actor killed so frequently, *Heaven Can Wait* (1978), his first movie as director, is a romantic comedy about reincarnation.

With Gene Hackman in Bonnie and Clyde.

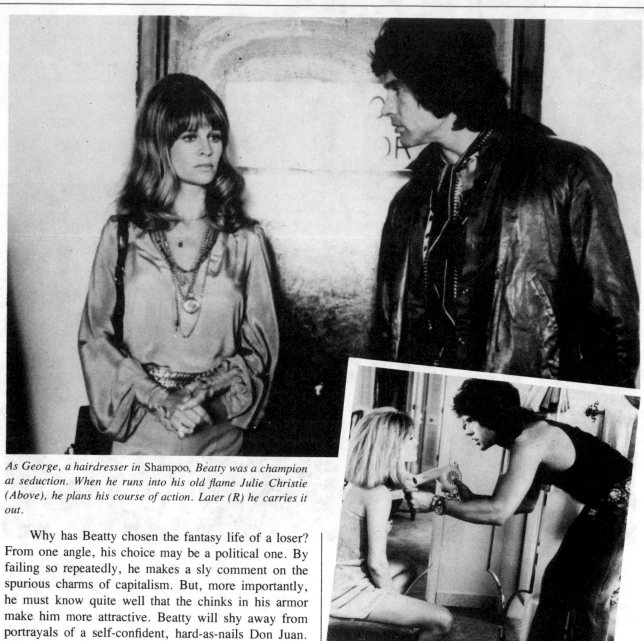

As George, a hairdresser in Shampoo, *Beatty was a champion at seduction. When he runs into his old flame Julie Christie (Above), he plans his course of action. Later (R) he carries it out.*

Why has Beatty chosen the fantasy life of a loser? From one angle, his choice may be a political one. By failing so repeatedly, he makes a sly comment on the spurious charms of capitalism. But, more importantly, he must know quite well that the chinks in his armor make him more attractive. Beatty will shy away from portrayals of a self-confident, hard-as-nails Don Juan. He prefers to show himself as a bluffer, a bit naive, confused, unsure of his power. He prefers to approach sexuality with a certain adolescent hesitance. When he does assay a macho type, he kills him off without tears (as seen in *The Parallax View*) or plunges the character into such obvious ridicule, as he does with the lady-killer in *The Fortune*, that he comes dangerously close to sabotaging his own performance. The last climax that Beatty and Robert Towne dreamed up for hairdresser George in *Shampoo* — with Julie Christie walking out — is probably the only one Beatty could imagine; to have him emerge unbruised and ebullient might have struck Beatty as repellent.

In *Shampoo* Beatty and Towne emphasize appealing helplessness in the face of George's southern California sensuality. In the entire movie, we never see George "hustling." Sexual conquests seem to drop into his arms like ripe fruit falling from a golden bough. Perhaps Beatty cheats a little, insisting on too much passivity in George; but perhaps he felt that sexual passivity, the way George drifts with the scenting of the womb and the hot winds of Hollywood and Vine, echoing the character's lack of politics or philosophy. Beatty superbly brings out two qualities in George: comic distractedness, as if the hectic pace of his life had suddenly sprung him loose from every mooring and swept him along on a mad wave; and a marvelous off-tempo quality to the sly responses and quick deceptions with which he greets every fresh crisis — as if he were just a beat late in every improvisation, and only blind luck were shielding him from eventual catastrophe. George is a gently hilarious character because his fantasies of control are such gossamer pipe dreams. The gun he carries, unlike Clyde Barrow's, is a harmless blower, with no ammunition and no deadly hair trigger.

But there's a darker side to failure, one that bursts bloodily into reality in *Bonnie and Clyde*. Failed sex explodes into murder by healthy, sunny, childlike folks who are pulled down inexorably, and all but unconsciously, into chaos. They are rebels, but their targets are dim and misty, beyond their vision, and, visually, their story is an orgasm of death. It rushes its audience along in a series of convulsive rhythms, until the climax — their own murder, the grand savage mock-copulation of the lovers, blood streaking their limbs like sweat, until they tumble in an embrace with the dirt. This is Beatty's finest film and performance, and the best answer to any charges of egoism or self-indulgence in his acting. He defers consistently to the brilliant cast he helped assemble, and that deference, that ability to listen and to respond to their best, becomes the most vital ingredient of his charm (along with the sinuous undercurrent of violence also present, which it counterpoints).

In the future, apparently, Beatty will carry his pursuit of the doppelgänger, the beautiful and deadly failure, to even grander and scarier limits. His two pet projects are film biographies of John Reed and Howard

With Jack Nicholson in The Fortune.

Hughes. John Reed was the Harvard playboy who became a revolutionary, a cohort of Lenin and Trotsky, the Homer of the "Ten Days." And Howard Hughes, the airborne stud from Texas, the manufacturer of planes and bras who became a billionaire recluse and a legendary oddball. One remembers, not without a twinge, that Reed died of typhus and Hughes of malnutrition.

Heaven Can Wait. *Beatty and Christie are the closest there is to a romantic team currently working in films.*

RAQUEL WELCH: STAR VS. ACTRESS

JAMES IVORY

ANYONE WOULD THINK that Raquel Welch has every right to be proud of her achievements. Here is a small-town, middle-class girl who has become, through her own efforts and energy as much as through her beauty and magnetism, an international celebrity, with fan clubs and a sophisticated cult following. Moreover, through her championing of various causes, she has access to a wider world than that of Hollywood. But somehow, in spite of all this, she does not appear satisfied with herself. It is as if she feels that the route she took to get there — by becoming a movie sex goddess, half Rita Hayworth, half Mae West — isn't dignified enough for her; so she must search for "serious" parts and for directors who will take her seriously, must go to acting school, must learn to sing and dance, all in an effort to realize whatever potential she may have. And this is done somewhat at the cost of her public image, which still feeds and supports her, and also feeds her ego when she is feeling low and isolated.

Nor does she take her appearance all that much for granted: One feels she has had to work at it more than many less beautiful women. Since she has come up the hard way, fighting agents, producers, directors, and critics whom she suspected of trying to keep her down, she is like certain self-made men who cannot really believe in lasting success: Everything may disappear in an instant. You feel this kind of desperation about her, and you cannot help sympathizing with her attempt to find better ways of expressing herself professionally.

It was in this mood that she accepted the role of Queenie in *The Wild Party* (1975), a film I directed and which was, as it turned out, an ill-fated vehicle for her. The part had everything she seemed to be craving. She was to be the glamorous mistress of a failing 1920s comedian — patient, loving, able to look at herself and her fate objectively and to talk about them articulately. Since

---

JAMES IVORY *has directed such films as* Shakespeare Wallah, Bombay Talkie, Savages, The Wild Party, *and* Roseland.

A top pinup in the late sixties.

She's come a long way since One Million Years B.C.

the film took place during a big party, and her role was that of an ex-Follies girl, she was given an opportunity to sing and dance in a star turn or two. In the last reel she was to die in her protector's arms.

As a director, I have the reputation of doing well by the women characters in my films; they have never been mere dumb things. So Raquel and I should have been able to work together on our joint conception of Queenie. But from nearly the first day we were at loggerheads, and no professional relationship, no *working* relationship, was ever established. She wanted to be an actress, not just a star, so I treated her as an actress, and not as a star. That was my fatal mistake.

When people ask me whether Raquel Welch has talent, I'm prompt to tell them that she has indeed, but that it is often eclipsed by her talent for being The Star. During *The Wild Party* Raquel the star fought the film every inch of the way. Her performance in it was good, sometimes very good. Most critics saw that at once and said so. But I always felt it could have been fifty percent better, for she depleted her energies in self-defeating battles in which both she and the picture were finally the

losers. She appeared intimidated by the arrival in Riverside (where we were filming) of a large contingent of East Coast and foreign technicians and executives, as well as by her co-star, James Coco, a gifted and skillful Broadway actor. Imagining perhaps some hint of disdain for Hollywood and for her on their part — some element of threat from what she saw as East Coast elitism — she began to fight with everyone about everything (except with the diplomatic Coco, of whom she was afraid). She fought over costumes and makeup, the interpretation of her part, the lighting, even over matters such as who would see rushes and who would not.

She used to come to work like the Victorian theatrical and operatic greats are supposed to have done, sending on an advance party of her retinue. It was always a little ominous, as the motorcycle outriders are in a presidential procession: The first to arrive would be her dresser, a young woman carrying perhaps a pair of shoes or a hat or gloves and a bag; then came the woman who did her hair, with her combs and sprays; then Charlene, her personal makeup artist, with her diminutive tins of color and her camel's-hair brushes; then Justin, her personal drama coach, wearing studded Levis and holding marked scripts against his chest like they were precious, holy books; then her boyfriend and costume designer,

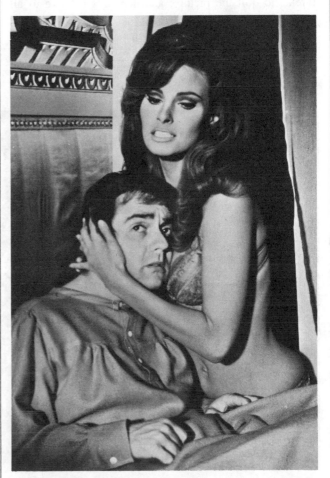

Small but memorable part with Dudley Moore in Bedazzled.

Ron Talsky, looking a bit wary. And in his wake, Raquel, in a black satin kimono, flashing looks when she was in a good mood, or staring sullenly down at the ground when she wasn't. The crew, extras, and other cast members would draw back as this procession passed on its way to where lights and camera had been set up, to where I stood with the cameraman, Walter Lassally.

I would then go over what I wanted her to do, and she would either do it or refuse to do it. If it was the latter, I would draw Jimmy Coco aside, and we would find some way in which my instructions to her would seem to originate with him. He was her only peer. Just before the first take Raquel would make Charlene look through the camera to check how she'd been lighted, and after the shot the embarrassed Justin's opinion would be sought to find out which was the best take to print. It was a very strange world, and I suppose I just accepted it after a time; stars are expected to indulge in such antics.

Sometimes when I looked into Raquel's eyes, nothing came back from them, I couldn't make contact. But at other times what I saw there was a look of real suffering, so that you wanted to do anything you could to help her. After a while, though, I came to recognize that this look was often the prelude to some tremendous onstage explosion, to be followed by flight, sobbing, threats to quit the picture, and demands to have us all fired.

The biggest of these blowups ended rather comically. On the morning of the day we were to do her big love scene with Perry King, I went very early to see Raquel to talk it over. She was about to apply her makeup. Her face was stripped and her mood was threatening. She painted away as Charlene handed her the brushes, and I cautiously put forward my idea of the scene. As I expected, she had her own conception ready, and as far as it went it wasn't bad, I must give her credit: Before being unfaithful to her long-time protector (Coco), she would divest herself ritually of the expensive trinkets he had given her. I said okay. What I didn't realize until the rehearsal later on, however, was that once she had done that, the scene was over as far as Raquel was concerned. She had no intention of letting King make love to her; she wouldn't even lie down on the bed with him. No sex! Everything was to be suggested by the deliberate (and lengthy) removal of her jewelry. And she was adamant about this, though technically she was in breach of contract. King was furious, and he told me that in the first take he planned to pin her down violently on the bed and hold her there until she threw him off; perhaps in this way we would get something simulating pent-up passion. I agreed and he did just that, but with such force the bed nearly collapsed. Raquel slithered out from under him, barked, "That's it, boys!" and jumped up.

Because the bed had almost fallen down, adding another note of the ridiculous to the scene, I said I wanted a second take. Raquel was fighting mad. What was the matter with the take we'd done, she demanded. Recklessly, I told her that I wasn't convinced of the couple's desire for each other. They should tear each other to pieces; as played, the scene was boring. "Boring?" she shouted. "Boring?" She rushed out, followed

Her prestige went up when she endured physical hardships as a roller derby star in Kansas City Bomber.

The Wild Party. *She becomes attracted to Perry King (Above) and disenchanted with James Coco (L).*

by her boyfriend, who turned to tell me I should not use such a word to describe a star of her magnitude.

A few minutes later the news came down that she had left the picture. With some relief I mentally wiped the three remaining scenes we still had to do with her from my vision of the finished film. But the financiers were not ready to do that. There was much telephoning to lawyers and agents before a solution was found: Raquel's public "humiliation" could only be paid for by a public apology from me before the assembled cast and crew. A financier edged up nervously to ask whether I could possibly bring myself to do this. I told him that I could and would. We all ate dinner.

Quite a few visitors had come to watch us that night. We were going to shoot a dance sequence Patricia Birch had been staging for days with Raquel and Perry. But also word had got around that something unusual was going to happen. The action was taking place in a garden, and when the lighting was complete the soundman rigged up a microphone so I would have a recording of this little scene — of this drama within a drama — a record intended as a form of protection in case our troubles escalated.

The moment had come. More than a hundred people were watching and a silence fell. Raquel stalked up to me in her black kimono, her heels tap-tapping over the garden's flagstones. The soundman angled his boom into position over our heads. She addressed me: "Mr. Ivory, I believe you have something to say to me?" I asked in a loud voice if everyone could hear. "Yes!" the crowd shouted back. I then apologized: "Raquel, if I've offended you, I'm sorry, but you know that whatever I did was only in the interest of the film." She thought this over, evidently decided that it would do, smiled a grim, wintry little smile, as I did, and turned away.

Despite the silliness of it all, I rather liked that tiny figure then, tap-tapping her way back to the safety of her ladies-in-waiting and the arms of her boyfriend. In this, her biggest scene, she had caught the grit and the pathos of Queenie perfectly.

BURT REYNOLDS: ALL IN THE GAME

PAT McGILLIGAN

Possibly the movies' best light comedian.

" A S AN ACTOR," Burt Reynolds says, "I don't get a chance to stretch at all. When you've been successful in a certain milieu, ninety-nine percent of the offers you get are within that framework. I get twenty-five scripts in the mail, and twenty-four

PAT MCGILLIGAN *is arts editor of Boston's* The Real Paper.

of them are about the same thing, and the other is not very good.

"I'm constantly accused of walking through films, although some people think I walk through them better than anybody else. I don't think anyone can catch me acting, as Spencer Tracy used to say. But it's time I took on something heavier, perhaps not serious drama, but subtle comedy, which I think I'm very good at."

It was June 1977, and I was talking with Reynolds at the Sam Goldwyn Studios in Hollywood. He had a stubbly beard and the low-key charm you might expect — if you are one of the people who take him seriously.

Trouble is, some people don't take Burt Reynolds seriously, and those who do have qualms. They think only of the *Cosmopolitan* centerfold, the gossip mill, and the long line of good-ole-boy movies. Like Pauline Kael, a closet admirer, they think of *The Tonight Show*. Kael once met secretly with Reynolds and pleaded with him to quit *The Tonight Show*. Too middlebrow, she hinted darkly. Bad for the image.

It probably is. As Reynolds himself says, people have the "wrong mental basis" of Burt Reynolds, because of a movie here or a talk show there. "I kinda perpetuate that, unfortunately, because talk shows are kinda cathartic for me. I can go on and get a lot off my mind. I find that a lot of heavyweight critics will never forgive me for that. They want me to go up on a mountain and make movies with mystery."

★ ★ ★ ★ ★

It's been a long haul. Born in Florida in 1936, Reynolds was an All-Florida running back at Florida State before a serious auto accident averted his dreams of a professional football career. He turned to acting, and in the 1960s graced a slew of forgettable pictures, interesting mainly for his development as a relaxed, virile leading man. Reynolds was particularly effective in action films that took advantage of his willingness to do his own stunts. As with the careers of Steve McQueen and Clint Eastwood, however, it was TV that provided the spark. Through his four series ventures — *Riverboat,*

Reynolds exaggerated his macho image as a rugged outdoorsman in Deliverance.

Gunsmoke, Hawk, and *Dan August* — Reynolds gained modest recognition, meanwhile carving his acting style and forging a bristling, authoritative screen presence.

It was likely that *Deliverance* (1972) marked the turning point. John Boorman's film, based on James Dickey's terrifying best-seller about a descent-into-hell wilderness excursion, was a thumping critical success, due largely to Reynolds' embattled performance. In fact, it is a Hollywood wisdom that Reynolds might have snagged the Oscar if it weren't for his *Cosmopolitan* flap, which occurred during the crucial voting period. After all, a pinup celebrity could hardly be deemed a *serious* actor by the Academy. (An example of Reynolds' prankish good humor and carefree down-to-earth sexuality, the *Cosmopolitan* episode inarguably backfired; even Reynolds rues the day.) Around this time, Reynolds began to dominate the chat columns and to cultivate his status as a sexy redneck superstar.

Not that it was a very cozy niche. Trapped in the gulf between image and ambition, Reynolds twisted and balked. Like other icon-stars before him — Cagney, for example, who was a thwarted song-and-dance man — Reynolds was cajoled into a second wave of movies unworthy of his expansive talents: *Fuzz* (1972), *White Lightning* (1973), and *The Man Who Loved Cat Dancing* (1973). Characteristically, too many of his post-*Deliverance* features were souped-up, watered-down, bare-chested, good-ole-boy movies. "Around Hollywood," Reynolds explained wryly, "I'm thought of as redneck heaven."

Often, to his continuing dismay, Reynolds' pictures are neglected outside the Deep South by distributors who still consider Reynolds to be a *regional* star. (Only *Deliverance* and *The Longest Yard* [1974], surprisingly, have been accorded wide European release.) His biggest

With Cybill Shepherd in the musical, At Long Last Love, *a tremendous flop.*

In love with Jill Clayburgh in Semi-Tough.

box-office smash, *Smokey and The Bandit* (1977), at last count edging near $100 million gross, has what they call "permanent legs" in the Deep South. It's a silly trifle, another one of those whiskey-and-women yarns Reynolds excels in, with a CB angle. Reynolds did it as a favor for the first-time director, his stunt man-roommate Hal Needham. He's always getting cajoled into one more good-ole-boy outing.

"Quite honestly, I'd go crazy sitting around, waiting for Francis Ford Coppola to call me on the telephone," he admitted bleakly. In fact, Reynolds would very much like to work with a director like Coppola,

Martin Scorsese, or Robert Altman. A while back, he was considerably buoyed when his name was floated in the trade papers as a possible star for Coppola's *Apocalypse Now* (1979). He was crushed when it became apparent that it was all a plot to raise money for "prestige" actors such as Harvey Keitel and Martin Sheen. "It was like being treated as a piece of meat," he said bitterly. "I resent that. If that's their attitude, I'll go off and make my own sand castle."

His first sand castle was *Gator* (1976), co-starring his friend Lauren Hutton. Like so many of Reynolds' pictures, it made a bundle south of the Mason-Dixon line. It was yet *another* good-ole-boy film, and Reynolds agreed to do it only if he could direct; unexpectedly the studio yielded. "It was like making chicken salad out of chicken shit," he says of *Gator*. And yet there are provocative twists in the movie, including three scenes hurriedly written by Reynolds, all deliberately unconventional and departures from the genre: (1) a challenging drugged-drunk scene, (2) an encounter with a child prostitute à la *Taxi Driver,* (3) an ending in which the heroine does not sink, contented, into the hero's arms. Reynolds directed with great vitality and humor, and *Gator* demonstrated that he not only understood above-the-line costs, but harbored a confident visual style — the high-speed swampwater chase is breathtaking.

"It's the difference between being a chess player and a chess pawn," says Reynolds about directing. "As an artist, it's so much more rewarding to direct. I've had pictures that I thought should have been cut differently or cast differently or sold with a different ad campaign. As an actor, it hurts. You bring your body there, do the work and then see it's been cut with an ax or comes out at the wrong time of the year. As a director, I can really fight against all that." He paused and added, "I *know* the camera. I care about learning and I really study. I do my homework."

With Sally Field in Hooper. *While actresses covered up in the seventies, Reynolds continued to unbutton his shirt.*

True, *Deliverance* and Robert Aldrich's *The Longest Yard* and *Hustle* (1975) are Reynolds' key pictures, but the actor has been overly harsh about his contributions to the rest. Among the movies he walks through effortlessly, and with delightful cavalier élan, are *W.W. and the Dixie Dancekings* (1975), with Reynolds as a roguish highwayman, and a gumshoe sleeper called *Shamus* (1972). He has bright moments in Mel Brooks' *Silent Movie* (1976) and shines (singing and dancing, credibly) in *At Long Last Love* (1975) and *Nickelodeon* (1976). Reynolds has a confessed soft spot for the latter two flops because at least director Peter Bogdanovich gave him a chance to explore his range.

Among Reynolds' most interesting recent films is *Semi-Tough* (1977), the football comedy based on Dan Jenkins' riotous novel. Reynolds' performance, which applies the devil-may-care attitude of his *Cosmopolitan* cameo with the split-second timing of his *Tonight Show* repartee, deserved an Oscar; it is that good. His role is tailor-made: he plays Billy Clyde Puckett, the wise-ass, womanizing running back who listens to Gene Autry records and gets "Pelfed" by Lotte Lenya. Finally, Reynolds is in his element, playing a bit of a rake, but evoking the trapped machismo of his own real life.

But the movie never really clicked; *Semi-Tough* was killed by the critics, and it died at the box office. Reynolds, whose performance was usually singled out as the film's redeeming feature, reportedly disagreed with director Michael Ritchie over the final cut of the picture.

This may account for why Reynolds wore a frown, when I next saw him, at the world premiere of *Semi-Tough* in New Orleans. There were other celebrities there, but Reynolds, whose entrance prompted a bank clerk to swoon in her husband's arms, was the center of attention. Journalists crowded the dapper star. Yet, at what ought to have been his triumphant moment, he seemed weary and nervous, anticipating what developed into a snide and ax-grinding reception among many members of the press.

At one table, as Reynolds passed, two aging Southern journalists loudly exchanged locker-room toupee jokes. One woman squeezed forward and asked Reynolds how Ritchie *ever* managed to coax such a terrific performance out of him. The inference was clear. Reynolds winced. Another woman inched forward, and asked Reynolds whether he, indeed, loved Sally Field. "Somebody's private life becomes more important than World War III," he said between clenched teeth, "and it becomes boring." It was all downhill from there.

It reminded me of my conversation with Reynolds earlier in the summer, when he had told me how it felt to be burned with a glance from Mike Nichols at a swank Hollywood party. Or how it felt to be put down, behind his back, by a director he genuinely admires. It's all part of that same trouble: the wrong mental basis. Thus Reynolds has seized the reins and turned, more and

On set of Smokey and the Bandit. *Director Hal Needham (R) looks on.*

more, to directing. "I have enormous faith in myself as a director," he said. "Quite honestly, it's what I do best, and what I want to do with my life. I could go on doing good-ole-boy pictures for the next twenty years. But I think I've got to roll the dice and take a chance."

The End (1978) was just such a gamble, an audacious undertaking and the movie Reynolds hopes will uncork his trapped image in Hollywood. Reynolds had been trying to purchase the script for years. "It's one of those situations that movies never touch," he asserted. "It's the story of a guy who's dying, and how he handles it, how badly and how well, all done with enormous humor. He has no hope to survive in *The End*. It points out how brave he is, and how important it is to have hope."

The choice to direct, alone, underscores Reynolds' intelligence as a film artist — and roles such as the doomed hero of *The End* confirm the imagination with which he views himself as an actor. It's heresy to praise an actor as accessible as Reynolds; better and safer, in critical circles, to laud technique and *angst*. Yet Reynolds is a natural, a star in the tradition of John Wayne, who exerts the sheer force of personality as his individual magic. His range is astonishing. *Deliverance* suggests the untapped depths and far horizons of his future. And Reynolds may already be the best light romantic comedian working in American pictures today. He isn't Cary Grant, but then, as Cary himself once said to a lady admirer, "Truly, madam, nobody is."

JACQUELINE BISSET: SIREN SPEAKS OUT

FRAN WEIL

Fantasy sequence in Le Magnifique.

A BEAUTIFUL FACE and curvaceous figure haunt the career of Jacqueline Bisset. The jade-eyed, British star insists she wants to be recognized as a serious actress who is pursuing a meaningful career in motion pictures. Yet she has consistently allowed herself to be exploited as a sex symbol — splashed on the covers of national news magazines as the girl in the wet T-shirt of *The Deep* (1977) or flaunted as that other Jackie in *The Greek Tycoon* (1978). She has risen from a starlet to star, but in terms of image, she has not really progressed since she played parts like the audaciously sexy Giovanna Goodthighs in the James Bond-esque film takeoff, *Casino Royale* (1967).

The thirty-four-year-old actress, intelligent and articulate off screen, has set her sights on becoming "respected." So far her good intentions have been thwarted by her own miscalculated role choices and the moviegoing public's reluctance to take Jackie at anything but face value. Think of Bisset, and images of the sensuous actress in *The Deep*'s wet T-shirt instantly emerge, as well as memories of the Hell's Angels rape victim, who loses her bikini top in the Malibu surf in the process, in *The Sweet Ride* (1968) and the every-man-wants-one lovemate of Steve McQueen in *Bullitt* (1968). Her strongest roles, as the fragile actress recuperating from a breakdown in François Truffaut's *Day for Night* (1973) and as the flashy countess in *Murder on the Orient Express* (1974), are mostly forgotten, buried under an avalanche of shallow parts in which the emphasis is on anatomy, not acting.

As Hollywood's reigning — if reluctant — screen siren, a rare actress with star power, Jackie is witnessing her film career take a steep upward climb, totally on the strength of her being packaged and sold as the slinky, sophisticated sex symbol who women would like to emulate and men possess. She's the Rita Hayworth of the 1970s, only more demure . . . a femme fatale with class.

FRAN WEIL *is an entertainment critic for the Boston* Herald-American.

For Bisset, the key to endurance in the movie industry depends on her selecting, and succeeding in, roles that depend on talent. But the roles she's offered, and accepts, for the most part, simply serve to showcase her cool, controlled but enticing sexuality.

"I have read a lot of scripts in which the parts I'm offered are wishy-washy characters that simply stand about. They're not bad parts, necessarily, but if your head's not in that area it's quite a step backward. And then it's a matter of repeating yourself. I find that very boring. I'm very critical of myself. Even repeating the way one looks physically is a bore.

"Ultimately, I suppose," Bisset says rather naively, I think, "if you work long enough you get some sort of physical image, and people think of you in that light. That upsets me. One of the things I always find hard to accept is people's judgment of you when they really don't know anything about you. They categorize you because you're an actress. And because I'm an actress who supposedly plays attractive women on a physical level, I get, well, a kind of jealous response from some people."

On the subject of her allowing herself to be exploited, Jackie has much to say: "Everything in movies is exploitation. For one thing directors exploit their actors constantly. They ask you for something extra

"I hoped the Giovanni Goodthighs role in Casino Royale, *would do for me what the name Pussy Galore did for Honor Blackman in* Goldfinger. *But good looks won't do it anymore." — Bisset to F. W. Yes, they will;* The Deep *made a fortune simply because it displayed Bisset's body.*

Being directed by François Truffaut in the award-winning Day for Night.

in each scene, hoping to capture some part of you. That's stealing. Directors try to steal emotion from you. The rest is up to you. I refuse to be exploited.'' At least Jackie believes she determines the when's and where's of the inevitable exploitation. ''If I feel someone is exploiting me, I think about it and consider whether I'm willing to go along with it. If it bothers me, I throw it out. If it's reasonable, I go with it. It's a matter of choices. It's like life. I think you are where you want to be, usually.''

Interestingly enough, Jacqueline Bisset stumbled into acting by way of modeling, a career noted for its exploitative aspects.

''Funny,'' she muses. ''I was thinking that I really wanted to do some acting. But I was a little ashamed at that thought. I suppose I didn't think it was a terribly dignified business. Of course, I didn't know anything about it at the time, but the way the press portrayed most actors in their lifestyles . . . it all seemed a bit tacky.

''I guess I was attracted to it on some clownish level. I figured if I could earn money I could take myself quietly off to an acting school and see what I could get out of the experience. I did the modeling to earn money. And through that I met people like Roman Polanski.

She appeared in Polanski's *Cul-de-Sac* (1966) and fell madly in love with moviemaking. ''It was all so totally absurd on the set. Nothing about the experience had any structure to it and I loved it. I decided it was the life for me.''

And so it began — her screen career rooted at the edge of respectability. In more than two dozen movies, Jacqueline Bisset has worked with top international di-

rectors like Polanski, Truffaut, John Huston, Philippe de Broca, and Stanley Donen. It's helped her career. Even though most of the roles were window-dressing parts, being in films directed by respected directors has given Bisset at least a small prestige tag. Of *Day for Night*, for instance, Jackie says, ''My involvement in the film classified me as being a good actress because a good director had chosen me. That movie had a special 'class' ticket on it. A lot of people think that was my best work. I don't know. I have never been satisfied with most of my films.

''I have always been doing this business a little bit with my head turned back over my shoulder. It's always been a case of my thinking that on the one hand there's my life, and on the other hand there's making movies. I always wanted to be very much half and half about the two so my career and private life wouldn't trespass on each other. But then, a couple of years ago, I said to myself, 'If you continue to do it this way, then you won't get total satisfaction on either side.' So I've decided to give myself a few years to concentrate on movies. And somehow, with that decision things in my life have concreted slightly.''

For now Jacqueline Bisset is saddled with a classy, sex goddess image. Despite her protestations, however, Jackie Bisset's rocky road to a meaningful acting career hasn't been all that unpleasant. ''It can be wonderful being an actress,'' she admits. ''You live all kinds of lives; experience all kinds of things. I don't know if I have been taking the right scripts yet. But I have been working. And as long as I am getting something out of the experience, I feel fine.''

JODIE FOSTER: YOUNG AND WILLING

BEN STARR

As a teenage prostitute in Taxi Driver. Some people saw the movie because of its artistic merits. Others saw it for its violence and sex.

BEN STARR, a writer for stage, screen, and television, is the past president of both the Radio Writers Guild and the Television Writers Guild. His screenplays include Our Man Flint, The Pad, Texas Across the River, The Spirit is Willing, and How to Commit Marriage.

WHY IS IT that just a handful of actresses manage to achieve true stardom, while all the many others, often more beautiful and intelligent, fail to make it to the celestial land? Is there a secret ingredient? Yes, there surely is, but don't look for it at your local cosmetic counter. It's called star quality, that unbuyable, unlearnable human component that makes viewers watch only one actress on the screen, no matter how many others are up there with her. When the top actresses were just learning their craft, they were stars waiting to happen. Ginger Rogers, for example, may have been used as an extra in the beginning, but she was still a "star." All she needed was for the camera to close in on her. She was just waiting to be noticed.

Which brings us to someone else who has it and who is going to be a star. Her name is Jodie Foster. She's just a kid right now but she's coming on fast. In Jodie's case the magic element is S-E-X, kid or no kid.

In My Sister Hank, a CBS-TV comedy situation pilot for which I wrote the script, Jodie portrayed a nine-year-old girl trying to break down male barriers and play baseball on a Little League team.

Now, there are endless pretty nine-year-old girls in this world. Every house in California has a garden where a stagestruck mother grows a pretty little girl whom she'll eventually dig up, wash and dress, and cart off to Hollywood. Why, then, with all this competition, was Jodie selected to play the part of Hank? Because she was the best actress? Not necessarily. Because she was the prettiest? Nope. She was selected because, in addition to being a competent actress, there was a Betty Bacall look in Jodie's eyes. And Jodie delivered her lines not like a precocious little nine-year-old but like a sophisticated young woman.

I don't know what Lauren Bacall, Lana Turner, or Rita Hayworth were like at age nine, but I wouldn't be surprised if they possessed the "Jodie Foster look." It's a look that says, "Hey, Mister, I bet you can't wait till I grow up, can you?"

What Jodie offers is the face of a cute little kid, but it's wrapped in a package that titillates. There is a suggestion of future wickedness.

In *Bugsy Malone* (1976), a delightful spoof in which children dress and act as grown-ups, a film in which whipped cream supplants bullets, Jodie was selected to star in the role of a ten-year-old blond moll. Who else? Jodie was perfect for the part, which called for a child who looks scrubbed but who also could sell sex. The send-up of the gangster film was a perfect cover for the sex bomb that is Jodie Foster waiting to explode. Made up as a Jean Harlow-type vamp, Little Jodie let it all hang out. Still, it was good clean fun.

Then came *Taxi Driver* (1976), the ineluctable next rung on the sex ladder for this talented young beauty. This time we see Jodie as the twelve-year-old prostitute who finally triggers Robert De Niro's one-man war against society. For this, the producers needed a child-woman and, once again, Jodie worked her magic. Without much difficulty, she convinced the audience that not only was she to be pitied, a victim of social and economic injustice, but that she was an accomplished young whore. Certainly the poor mistreated child didn't *like* being a prostitute. "Or did she?" viewers wondered.

How did Jodie get this way? She was born with "it," that's how. Liza Minnelli comes by "it" naturally. One moment those big eyes tear your heart out, but with the slightest adjustment, those same eyes let you know that a roll in the hay is just a wink away.

Except for rare exceptions, the most popular film stars somehow excite the glands. Jodie Foster knows the tricks and is using them. She's cool and laid-back. The kid can make films for tell-it-like-it-is directors like Martin Scorsese or for the Pollyannas who direct for Disney. In just a very few years, Jodie Foster will become a sex symbol. The kid's a future star. With a little hype she'll be a superstar.

Will it change her? Will all the selfishness that goes with being a superstar manifest itself? All the craziness? All the *me, me, me*?

You know it.

Almost all of Jodie Foster's roles have taken advantage of her natural precociousness. (Clockwise, from top left) In Tom Sawyer *she enjoys her first screen kiss. In* Bugsy Malone, *she plays an adult nightclub singer. In the spooky* The Little Girl Who Lived Down the Lane *she lives alone. In* Taxi Driver, *she works for pimp Harvey Keitel.*

THE
CULT FIGURES

LOUISE BROOKS: SMART AND SASSY

JOHN SPRINGER

In the late twenties, she adorned many magazine covers.

CERTAINLY SHE WAS A BEAUTY. Anyone with a memory going back to the 1920s knows that. They remember her as a *Scandals* and *Follies* girl who had not only beauty but individuality. They remember how her short, square, black patent-leather bob created a coiffure trend; they may remember that she had a reputation for devastating wit, and was considered an intellectual — a strange tag for someone with such a breezy, flapper personality.

JOHN SPRINGER *is an actor's publicist and film historian who has written on film for numerous publications. He is the author of* The Fondas; All Talking! All Singing! All Dancing! *and* They Had Faces Then.

She never took movies seriously. She didn't bother to watch rushes or go to the openings of her own films, and never went out of her way to ingratiate herself with the higher-ups. When, as in *Love 'em and Leave 'em* (1926) and *Beggars of Life* (1928) she had a role that called for more than mere prettiness or peppiness, she worked at it, but for the most part moviemaking was something to get through in the day so she could experience the life of a Hollywood star at night. This ex-chorus girl from Kansas was a darling of what today we'd call the jet set. Rich and powerful men courted her. The most publicized playboys sought her out. She was a particular favorite of Grand Duke Alexander of Russia. And she went blithely on her happy-go-lucky way.

But in Hollywood movies, Louise Brooks was always second-string. She made a series of nearly forgotten movies with Adolph Menjou, Richard Arlen, W. C. Fields, and other stars of the era. Only a few were notable. In *Love 'em and Leave 'em*, she was the gold-digging, conniving sister of star Evelyn Brent, and stole the picture from her and the distinguished Broadway star Osgood Perkins. In *Beggars of Life*, co-starring Richard Arlen and Wallace Beery, she played a down-on-her-luck girl masquerading as a boy. It was one of the few movie masquerades that you could believe.

And finally, she was cast in *The Canary Murder Case* (1929), the first of the popular series of mysteries with William Powell as Philo Vance. Talkies were coming to the screen about this time, and it was decided to release *Canary* as a talking picture. But Brooks, having finished her role, was off in Europe ignoring studio calls for her to return and dub her own voice. So her part was cut down and another actress, Margaret Livingston, recorded the Brooks dialogue. Although Hollywood was infuriated at Louise Brooks' defiance, she didn't care.

America didn't hear anything about Louise Brooks for a long time. Nobody knew that across the ocean she was at last discovering the rewards of real motion picture stardom.

G. W. Pabst, the German director, saw a vivid, exciting woman beyond the frantic flapper from Hollywood and persuaded her to make two films for him — films with raw, uncompromising, unconventional themes. These were *Diary of a Lost Girl* (1929) and *Pandora's Box* (1929), both filmed in Germany, both highly censorable for the American screen of the day. And then France's brilliant René Clair got her to star in *Prix de Beauté* (1930). All these films were heralded by critics on the Continent. They gave Brooks the kind of accolades reserved at that time for only such screen actresses as Gish and Garbo. But none of the pictures was an international triumph. They came at the end of the silent era, and there was little inclination to import German or French silent pictures to the U.S., when even domestically made silents were dying from the competition of the new talkies.

When Louise Brooks returned to Hollywood she was a has-been. There were no roles for her. After that, her name popped up infrequently. She did a couple parts in minor movies. Brooks, feeling there was nothing left

Impersonating a boy in Beggars of Life.

In wild costume for The Canary Murder Case.

for her in Hollywood except humiliation, exited the screen capital and entered into a long period of virtual obscurity. Occasionally, a report drifted back that she was working in a New York City publicity office or that she was a saleswoman at Saks Fifth Avenue. But Hollywood wasn't interested. The movie capital is quick to forget, and Louise Brooks was forgotten.

But there were those who remembered. Henri Langlois, of the Cinématheque Française, was one. In an exhibition of great films, in the late fifties, he included *Diary of a Lost Girl,* and wrote so extravagantly of Brooks' performance and her cinema magic that students of the screen flocked from all over the Continent to see her. There were others who came, too, one being James Card, curator of motion pictures at Eastman House in Rochester, New York. He, too, fell under the Brooks spell. Her other films were unearthed, rerun, studied. Film societies and archives in Great Britain, Italy, Denmark, Belgium, and other countries screened the Brooks movies. But the object of this adoration was completely unaware of it all.

Card, in the meantime, went on a search for her and, finally, discovered that she was living in New York City.

As Lulu (R) in Pandora's Box. *Alice Roberts played a lesbian countess.*

Card persuaded her to go to Rochester as a guest of Eastman House to see the films she had never cared enough to see when she had made them. She thought of them now in a different way: analytically, with appreciation and understanding of the cinema as an art. And she became, as Card puts it, "enraptured with motion pictures." She sat for hours a day, every day, watching scores of films. She became a brilliant and perceptive film critic.

With her new understanding of the film to supplement her firsthand knowledge of Hollywood during the twenties, she began to write an unusual study of women in motion pictures — women like Garbo, Clara Bow, Lillian Gish. She described her book as "a study of extraordinary, unique, beautiful women and the success with which they preserved their originality of face and personality against the vicious grinding of the producers who would reduce them to a commodity as uniform, as interchangeable, as expendable and cheap as canned peas."

Now in her early seventies, and living in Rochester, Louise Brooks works at her typewriter, leaving her room

DIXIE DUGAN

J. P. MCEVOY, the humorist, was an admirer of Louise Brooks and wrote a best-selling book, *Show Girl,* in which the principal character, Dixie Dugan, was recognizably modeled after her. Colonel Patterson, of the Chicago *News* syndicate, bought the rights to use the character of Dixie Dugan as a comic strip, hired John Strieble to draw it, and as Strieble tells it, he "pulled a still picture of Louise Brooks from a desk drawer and said, 'Draw her!' " Years later, Dixie, in the funny papers, was making lots of money but Brooks, who had fallen upon hard times, never received a penny for lending her looks and personality to the character.

She did, however, get an offer from Florenz Ziegfeld to play Dixie Dugan in the Ziegfeld musical based on *Show Girl.* The offer was cabled to her when she was with a party of friends on the S.S. *Majestic* en route to Europe. A man in her party intercepted the wire and, not wanting to lose the companionship of the dazzling and delightful Brooksie, destroyed the wire without showing her. The same gentleman also answered it: "Sorry, don't think you can afford me." And he signed her name. Ziegfeld, as Miss Brooks said, "had done wonderful things for me and he never forgave me. And I never had the opportunity to explain to him that it was this other gentleman's idea of a great joke." A chorus girl named Ruby Keeler took over the role, which started her on the way to fame.

— J. S.

seldom — only for a screening at Eastman House, a special movie at a Rochester theater, or an infrequent trip to New York or Europe as a guest of a cinema society.

But — years after her career as a pert screen beauty ended prematurely — she has achieved a respected position in the screen world that can, or will be, equaled by few other actresses. The little dancing girl is a movie immortal.

Louise Brooks today.

GRETA GARBO: ETERNAL MYSTERY

BOSLEY CROWTHER

Garbo. Imported from Sweden, she became America's top romantic star.

THE MYSTIQUE OF Greta Garbo is such that the mere mention of her name, even among those people who weren't alive when she was active in films, triggers a flood of luxuriant and anomalous images

---

BOSLEY CROWTHER *was the front-line movie critic for the* New York Times *from 1940 to 1967. He is the author of* Hollywood Rajah *and* The Lion's Share *and three volumes of critical reflections,* The Great Films, Vintage Films, *and* Reruns.

that put in the shade most of the legends of other great and near-great movie stars. There flash in the minds of old-timers odd and misty memories of indistinct silent films that formed a circling background for a clearly distinct and gorgeous face; or later images of a throaty artiste of incomparable poise and distant grace. Checkering these mental pictures are also likely to be some throwoffs from the long-ago gossip and exploitation mills that have attached themselves to the legend and given it a slightly lurid hue.

Famous exotic dance in Mata Hari.

So much has been written about Garbo and so many efforts have been made to fathom and analyze the mysteries of this metaphorical sphinx that a tangle of suppositional rhetoric is all an explorer is likely to find on the trail to a helpful understanding of the *persona* of the aging star. Right off, one tack is essential: A careful distinction must be made between her acting career and the very private life she has led. The two have no evident correlation, and any effort that is made today to match the romantic image that Garbo projected in her films and the cryptic, reclusive woman she was even in her Hollywood days is doomed to disappointment and defeat. Garbo was and is a vast enigma, a female Janus who presented one face — not always the same but generally semblable — in her twenty-four American films, made between 1925 and 1941, and who has hidden the other behind a darkly gossamer veil.

As for technique, her capacities were modest — at least insofar as one can tell from the limited demands on them that were generally made. What she usually projected was an aura of dignity and control that were appropriate to the moods of fated sorrows of the characters she portrayed. Since the essence of the natures of these characters was predominantly sexual — that is to say, they were usually women who had driving, shameless, passionate needs for men, not merely for sexual satisfaction but for the deeper fulfillment of the soul — what was required from her was a posture that would extrude this essence from the screen as a burning emanation. And that is what Garbo gave.

All of her lucky directors, especially her more respected and frequent ones such as Clarence Brown and George Cukor, have said that she seemed to have an intuition, an instinctive gift for playing a scene "just right," without any evident fret or study, defiance or argument. She seemed to know precisely what the director wanted — sometimes better than did he. To be sure, as I have said, the requirements were not too difficult or complex for an actress who had her endowment of manipulatable magic. And, except for a few rumored flare-ups and a famous walk-out on the studio, she was calm and collected at work, friendly but not chummy with her fellow actors, keeping her thoughts to herself.

Even on the sad occasion when the news reached her, on the set where she was making *Wild Orchids* (1928), that her early mentor and probable lover, Swedish director Mauritz Stiller, had died, she gave no perceptible indication of great emotion other than that she paled and stood stiffly for a few moments before excusing herself to go to her dressing room. There she remained alone for several minutes while all action was suspended on the set. She then returned and, without any further show of shock or grief, went on with the scene.

There were stories, of course, that she became difficult in later years, after her stardom was established; that she made demands upon MGM, her exclusive employer, especially for salary increases (undoubtedly deserved), under the guidance of Harry Edington, a talent agent John Gilbert got for her. Gilbert, as everyone knew, was not only her handsome and dashing vis-à-vis in several of her early pictures but was certainly the most

Love. *Garbo and John Gilbert were screen's top lovers.*

GRETA GARBO

Her first talkie opened new doors.

famous and ardent romantic suitor in her life. (The whole story of the Garbo-Gilbert romance is a Hollywood saga in itself, adorned with bizarre touches and heavy latherings of old-time ballyhoo.)

It is odd and altogether ironic that the major artistic achievements in Garbo's career could be numbered on the fingers of one hand — with the pinkie available as a spare. There was the title role in *Anna Christie* (1930), the Eugene O'Neill play. This was the incongruous vehicle in which she crossed the Rubicon of sound. Stark and devoid of her usual glamour, she made the role of the cynical dockside ex-prostitute a thing of poetic beauty, under the direction of Clarence Brown. There was her memorable performance under George Cukor in *Camille* (1936), a work of intense romantic drama and alabaster loveliness wherein her historic Marguerite Gautier was less a creature of reality than a vision of what the romantic, idealized heroine should be. And there was her complete about-face in Ernst Lubitsch's *Ninotchka* (1939), one of the liveliest satires ever made in Hollywood, in which she superbly demonstrated that she had the wit and flexibility to be a fine comedienne. There was also the fading ballerina she played in the all-star *Grand Hotel* (1932), a brief but effective character study from an actress who was then just twenty-six; and her *Queen Christina* (1933), in which she deftly romped in masculine costumes.

Theorists who like to make mountains out of the molehills of single striking scenes may wish to include a couple of her other sentimental films. They are entitled to their opinions. I wouldn't want to argue with them. But I can't go along with those enthusiasts who now are finding kind words to say about her grotesque performance in her last film, *Two-Faced Woman* (1941), which was a disaster of such proportions that it may have influenced her decision to withdraw.

CONTOURS AND COUNTENANCE

CONTRARY TO the generally held impression and the persistent dogma of the myth, Garbo was not a great actress as far as technical virtuosity was concerned. Nor were her films, with three or four exceptions, possessed of outstanding quality. She was, as is now apparent and was detected by keener critics in her day, the proprietor of extraordinary features and physical plasticity. Her face was a fascinating area that could be — and usually was — arranged by a platoon of makeup artists and experts with cameras and lights into a *chef d'oeuvre* of living sculpture that was charged with electricity. Set in this face of classic structure were large, sad, luminous eyes that expressed a limited but intense emotional range. From the whole there emanated a strange, almost tangible phosphorescent glow. The lips, too, were strong, wide, and sensitive, and the line from the chin down the neck to a generous expanse of bosom was as graceful as a Greek statue. It is notable that Garbo's beauty was exclusively revealed in black-and-white; she never made a color picture. One wonders how she would have looked if she had.

— B. C.

Strong, independent, majestic in the splendid Queen Christina.

As to her silent pictures, the foundations upon which her fame was based, they were largely florid and fustian as judged by the standards of today. That beautiful face and stately body were too often put to the cause of caricature — or, at best, to the cause of merchandising romantic balderdash. In an age when the popular taste in literary achievement was measured by the novels of Blasco-Ibañez, Michael Arlen, and Adele Rogers St. John, it is not surprising that the gifts of the youthful Garbo were employed in screenplays cut from such dross, or that the sum of her rococo period — a matter of ten films in her five silent years — should have included such now-faded relics as *The Torrent*, (1926), *The Temptress* (1926), *Flesh and the Devil* (1926), *A Woman of Affairs* (1928), and *The Kiss* (1929).

Today, the most prevailing and engrossing aspect of Garbo is her mystery. Why did this beautiful actress, this world-famous Hollywood star, decide to forgo acting, to

With new romantic idol Robert Taylor in the classic Camille.

give up a great career and casually drift into retirement? Many reasons have been mentioned: the occurrence of World War II, which blacked out the European market where Garbo's films had sold particularly well; her disgust with the silly haggling with the moralists who controlled the then-strict Production Code over the mild innuendos in *Two-Faced Woman* (which one critic brutally charged made the respected Garbo "a clown, a buffoon, a monkey on a stick"). Or perhaps it was sheer weariness and boredom with front-office pettifogging and the repetitiveness of working in Hollywood.

There is also the possibility that a circle of new friends — such worldlings as the writer Salka Viertel, Gaylord Hauser, and Leopold Stokowski (with whom she spent a flamboyantly publicized vacation at Ravello in Italy) — plus a sometimes quietly hinted transition in her sexual proclivities, might have proved distractions. She was already fabulously rich. And she grew, as many friends indicated, increasingly indolent.

Of course, she had numerous invitations to make a variety of films back in the 1940s and the 1950s. One she apparently wanted very much to do was a biography of the writer George Sand, to whom Garbo was often compared, but a succession of financial problems eventually finished that. She also was said to look with some favor upon a production of Balzac's *La Duchesse de Langeais*. There was even talk of her playing Shakespeare's *Hamlet*. But nothing came of them. Could it have been that Garbo intuitively feared she had outlived her kind of character and her day, that — as certainly happened with John Gilbert — the parade had passed her by?

Two-Faced Woman, *her unsatisfactory farewell to movies.*

Perhaps. But what is even more puzzling, why does this experienced woman have an apparent dread of people, of personal publicity, of being jostled in crowds and stared at? Why has she chosen to be remote from the environment that spawned her and from the mythology that she embraced?

The fact that she has not succumbed to the autobiographical urge, as have so many of her contemporaries, and has steadfastly refused to submit herself to interrogation by suppliant biographers is proof of the sincerity of her withdrawal. Although several biographers have done generally readable, informative, and thoughtful books about her, all have been without her help. She even broke her silence to deny publicly through lawyers and friends that she had assisted or endorsed a biography that a prominent publisher was reported to be holding for posthumous release.

And so we will probably continue to wonder and speculate about the thoughts and feelings of this famous star of the past. And she will continue to be of interest to the lion hunters in this hungry age. People and *paparazzi* will continue to spy on her walking in the streets or sitting with friends in a fashionable restaurant, and they will act as though they have discovered the footprints of the Abominable Snowman in the high Himalayas. She will remain a symbol of an obsolete romantic age, a cherished memory in the minds of dwindling elders, and finally she will pass and fade away into a footnote on a page in history.

Lubitsch's Ninotchka, *her most fondly remembered film.*

BUSTER CRABBE: SATURDAY AFTERNOON HERO

BUSTER CRABBE

M Y WHOLE LIFE was changed by one-tenth of a second — the time by which I beat the Frenchman in the four-hundred-meter swimming final in the 1932 Olympics. If I had finished second or third, Paramount wouldn't have given me another look. But they did. Paramount was interested in me because people knew who Buster Crabbe was, not because of my histrionic ability. They called me to test for *King of the Jungle* (1933), and my acting career was under way.

I must admit I don't like to dwell on my Tarzan pictures. Naturally, I had read many of the Tarzan books as a kid, and was interested in the early Tarzan films. My favorite Tarzan, of course, was the first — Elmo Lincoln. I was the seventh of fifteen Tarzans (to date), and I merely tried to make the character as believable as possible. It didn't always work; whereas I think *King of the Jungle* was an excellent picture, I think my Tarzan serial, *Tarzan the Fearless* (1933), was horrible.

Paramount then started to use me as a bit-part actor. After I had appeared in a couple of westerns — and got the feel of them — they cast me in several Randolph Scott westerns. Around 1935 Randy wanted to do a drawing-room comedy — and he was a big enough star to get his way. It was fine, as far as I was concerned, because when he stepped out of the Zane Grey westerns at Paramount, they put me in the leads.

LARRY ''BUSTER'' CRABBE *was known as the ''King of the Serials,'' appearing in such classics as* Flash Gordon, Flash Gordon's Trip to Mars, Flash Gordon Conquers the Universe, *and* Buck Rogers. *He also starred in numerous westerns during his lengthy career as well as the television series* Captain Gallant of the Foreign Legion. *An Olympic swimming champion in 1932, he has in the last few years completed his book* Energistics, *a physical fitness book for senior citizens.*

"I never got a shot at an A picture. Maybe that would have triggered something I never showed." — B. C.

It was Universal's idea to do *Flash Gordon* (1936). I had followed Alex Raymond's strip in the newspapers and thought it was fun, but I was horrified when I read in *Variety* that Universal was going to make it into a serial. I thought, what a crazy idea!

Out of curiosity and for no other reason, I decided to go to the casting office to see who was foolish enough to try out for the part. When I got there, fifteen or sixteen fellows were on the set. I recognized George Bergman, whom I had worked with, and thought, "Excellent. Absolutely excellent for the part of Flash Gordon." All they had to do was bleach his hair blond and he'd be perfect.

Somebody pointed me out to the producer Henry McRae, who came over and introduced himself to me and asked me why I was there. I told him that I had

Kaspa, the Lion Man, in King of the Jungle.

followed the comic strip and was curious. We chatted. Then he asked, "How would you like to do the part of Flash Gordon?" I thought to myself, no way. I said, "Well, I really don't know, Mr. McRae," He said, "You can have the part if you want it." And I thought, not a chance. Then he said, "I know that you are under contract to Paramount, but we'll borrow you." My automatic reply was, "I'll have to do what the bosses tell me." I bid the man good-bye, turned and started to walk away, thinking to myself, "I hope the studio tells him I'm not available."

You know the rest of the story. I was at Universal in October, 1936. Six weeks' shooting. Eighty-five setups a day. We finished *Flash Gordon* just before Christmas. I was glad to be be done with it, never thinking it would have a chance at the box office. It was released in 1937. By the end of the year, it was Universal's number two moneymaker. I made two more *Flash Gordon*'s in 1938 and 1940.

You must understand that we had to believe in what we were doing. If we had played it tongue in cheek, it would have been over the fence in the very first serial. *Flash Gordon* was the most expensive serial ever made. They spent $450,000 in the mid-thirties for a damn serial! Universal gambled on them and I must say that they made a lot on money for the studio.

The *Buck Rogers* serial (1939) was on the same order as *Flash Gordon,* with me playing a space hero once again. But by that time, maybe I was enamored with the part of Flash Gordon; Buck Rogers the do-gooder, didn't excite me.

I think I made more talking serials than anybody — nine in all. They called me the "King of Serials" at one time. There was the *Red Barry* (1938) series, in addition to *Flash Gordon* and *Buck Rogers*. Then much later, there was the *King of the Congo* (1952) serial, not to mention my quickie westerns and low budgets for television in the fifties. Serials were an important part of the industry, and they were always exciting to me.

All the things I've done were basically aimed at youngsters. And now these youngsters are not youngsters anymore. Some of them have children of their own, and some of them are grandparents. I didn't get nearly as much fan mail regarding Flash Gordon in

FLASH GORDON: THE GRANDDADDY OF SPACE ADVENTURES

Crabbe, Frank Shannon (Dr. Zarkov), and Jean Rogers (Dale Arden) meet the Clay King in Flash Gordon's Trip to Mars.

I'M AMAZED, just as a lot of other people, that Flash Gordon is still around. You name it: — *2001: A Space Odyssey, Star Wars, Close Encounters of the Third Kind* — all the current space pictures proliferating. For *Flash Gordon* they took parts of Alex Raymond's comic strip and duplicated it. Their special effects were good and new; they compare favorably to those in *Star Trek,* and even with some of the movies being produced today. Recently, I asked George Lucas where he got his ideas for *Star Wars.* He admitted that, as a youngster, he went to the Saturday matinees and watched the serials.

— B. C.

the old days as I do today, but I still get a fair amount of mail from the people who joined ''Buster's Buddies,'' a club I started on television in New York. At one time, there were thirty-five thousand members in the club, which was started at WOR and carried over to ABC. The fans are in all walks of life now. Some are well-known attorneys, some are doctors. It gives me a good feeling.

I celebrated my seventieth birthday in February 1978, and I weigh almost the same as I did when I competed in the Olympic Games in 1932. I hear that Italian producer Dino de Laurentiis has received permission from King Features to remake *Flash Gordon.* And, according to what I hear on the grapevine, I may be playing Flash's father. Isn't that a nice thought?

PHYLLIS BROOKS:
B MOVIE STANDOUT
WILLIAM SAROYAN

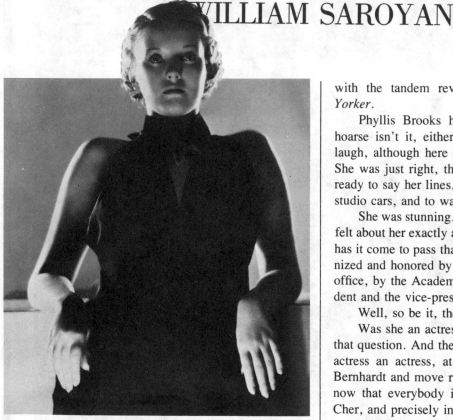

Beautiful, but never a household name.

I LIKED PHYLLIS BROOKS. She had an open-mouth simplicity that I found precisely right for the preposterous movies she appeared in for RKO and Twentieth Century-Fox. She smiled. She spoke words. She moved among the super-real, super-unreal people of surely two dozen movies as if she had been born in movies and, unlike outsiders, would never die. In movies, or anywhere else. I think this is true of many movie actresses, of many categories, but especially of Phyllis Brooks. And of course, we all know that she is not considered one of the great ones, at all. Indeed, she is in none of the erudite works about movies, beginning with the works of Gilbert Seldes and ending pretty much

WILLIAM SAROYAN *received a Pulitzer Prize for his play* The Time of Your Life *and an Academy Award for his novel* The Human Comedy, *which was voted the Best Original Story (made into a movie) in 1943.*

with the tandem reviewers of movies for the *New Yorker*.

Phyllis Brooks had a kind of hoarse voice, but hoarse isn't it, either. And she had a kind of hoarse laugh, although here again hoarse isn't nearly enough. She was just right, that's all. She was crisp, neat, and ready to say her lines, and get in and out of the various studio cars, and to walk.

She was stunning. I was sure everybody in the world felt about her exactly as I did. I still believe that, so how has it come to pass that Phyllis Brooks is still not recognized and honored by the trade, by *Variety,* by the box office, by the Academy, by the Congress, by the president and the vice-president?

Well, so be it, then, that's all.

Was she an actress at all? Perhaps we ought to ask that question. And then perhaps we ought to ask, is any actress an actress, at all, and let us start with Sarah Bernhardt and move right along to whomever it is right now that everybody is sure is great. I happen to like Cher, and precisely in the same manner that I liked and continue to like Phyllis Brooks. There is something irresistible in her insecurity, fear, nervousness, smile, and crackling voice. But Cher (as a TV star) is known to everybody, while Phyllis Brooks is still to be discovered.

She was the most real girl in the movies of the 1930s and on into the 1940s. Everybody saw her sooner or later, getting in and out of fine automobiles in every city of the country. Everybody heard her hoarse voice in talk and laughter. Everybody noticed the way she stood in her good, sensible clothing and how she moved. Her most memorable phrase was, "All right."

The neglect of this woman is not something to turn over to the American Civil Liberties Union, most likely, but what I want to know is how did it happen? I am sure that all of the young men of the 1930s fell in love with Phyllis Brooks — she was not as likely to appeal to women, perhaps, but I can only guess about that. But the young men had to love her, and partly because she was never suddenly thrust into the glaring limelight of mad stardom.

WANTED: A FESTIVAL FOR PHYLLIS

NOW, WE KNOW that there are Cecil B. De Mille Festivals, Ernst Lubitsch Festivals, and festivals for von Stroheim, von Sternberg, and the Keystone Kops. Well, I've seen some of the festivals, and whenever I am in New York I try to get to the movies at the Museum of Modern Art, but I am still waiting for a cavalcade of appearances, in all her films, of Phyllis Brooks. But what I'm really talking about is the inevitable discovery of not just Phyllis Brooks, with a festival both in Paris and Budapest, but the discovery of many other great movie girls and boys, men and women. So far there has not been even the beginning of a festival of "Snub" Pollard, who prevailed in the dark pipe-organ world of the Liberty Theater in Fresno from 1917 through 1919 in weird two-reel comedies, and then went on to become a director. And what about Arthur Edmund Carewe? Let's see about noticing him, too, if possible. Why? Well, he was an Armenian, for one thing. And for another, like Phyllis Brooks, he never became a star, and has been overlooked totally by the historians of the art of motion pictures, as L. B. Mayer learned from Irving Thalberg to put it.

— W. S.

I saw her last on the set of *The Shanghai Gesture* (1941), directed by Josef von Sternberg. Once his star had been Marlene Dietrich, quite famous, as we all know, but she did not have the special fame in which Phyllis Brooks lived and breathed, spoke and laughed. Phyllis Brooks had innocence. She didn't even suspect who she was. She didn't believe she *was* who she was. She just seemed to believe she played the comparatively unimportant parts that she was given for ten or more years — for wages.

Well, it's not so at all. She was, she is, the strange beautiful super-real girl of motion picture art itself, so to put it. Of America, of the happy days of Hollywood. Of the world, of the innocent days of universal desperation and boredom, before nuclear fission, as I believe it is put: She was the one — and the big big stars, good God Almighty, they were *not,* they were anything but the one. They were all frauds, and they fooled all of the people all of the time, while Phyllis Brooks couldn't be bothered and didn't fool anybody for one minute. Everybody knew perfectly well who she was every time she said her six crisp words in her easy hoarse voice, and then laughed, and like as not said, "All right."

Her starring roles in B *pictures like* City Girl. *A starlet at home (Inset). Later she'd marry a congressman.*

HUMPHREY BOGART: MORAL TOUGH GUY

JOAN MELLEN

Fred C. Dobbs *in* Treasure of the Sierra Madre.

T HE BOGART IMAGE that has been elevated to cult-approval status is not that of the tough guy of his thirties-gangster phase. Rather, it is the Bogie of the forties and fifties, fierce and unrelenting, but a man also capable of both love and unalloyed altruism. The man of feeling and the man of power and effectiveness are combined in one male figure. Physical strength need not preclude grace for Bogart at his best, nor need kindness suggest weakness or vulnerability.

Never succumbing to the temptation to explain his motives, Bogart's most attractive screen personality will always simply and silently do the "right thing" — and always by his own definition of "right." He is tough on the outside but, as the prefect of police observes in *Casablanca* (1942), a "sentimentalist" at heart.

In *The Maltese Falcon* (1941) this trait causes Bogart's Sam Spade to reject the woman he loves and choose loyalty to a dead partner for whom he had felt only contempt and indifference. For Sam Spade to betray his own sense of propriety would make him vulnerable to innumerable risks as a person without an anchor. This is something Bogart could never do.

The quintessential hero of the *film noir,* the Bogart character takes for granted that the world is corrupt and permeated with evildoers. He finds a code, however arbitrary, by which he can sustain at least a bit of integrity in defiance of prevailing disarray. His cynicism and world-weariness reflect the absence of all illusions — the Bogart hero entertains no expectations about his changing anything, he has no hope that he might impose his will or join with others to alter the world's myriad dishonesties. When Bogart and Bacall face each other, without touching yet in full communion, at the close of

JOAN MELLEN *is the author of* Big Bad Wolves: Masculinity in the American Film; The Waves of Genji's Door: Japan Through Its Cinema; Women and Their Sexuality in the New Film; Voices from the Japanese Cinema; Marilyn Monroe; *and* A Film Guide to the Battle of Algiers. *She is a professor of English at Temple University.*

The Big Sleep (1946), we sense that the pleasure they derive from each other is all the more precious because it must be wrested from a tawdry, heartless world full of sinister surprises and peopled by amoral lowlifes who betray one another automatically.

What has rendered Bogart so attractive to succeeding generations is his ability to maintain his balance in so menacing a world. He stakes the parameters of his tolerance with care. "I don't mind a parasite," he says in *Casablanca,* "I object to a cut-rate one." Physically he does not compete with such figures as the elegant Sean Connery or the austerely handsome Clint Eastwood. Yet he continues to surpass them in appeal. In his homely countenance was etched the proof that he had lived, a high-priority value for many in the 1960s who were seeking outlets to express their own awakened sense of justice. He taught the young that self-confidence was a moral, rather than a material, quality and need have no connection with physical perfection. In *The Big Sleep* Bogie joins in the joke about his shortness. "You're not very tall, are you?" taunts General Sternwood's younger daughter, trying to size him up. "I try to be," replies the self-possessed Philip Marlowe, undaunted by the culture's easy assessments of those presumed less than worthy. He moves on to her older sister, played by Lauren Bacall, who calls him "a mess." To this he replies, "I'm not very tall either," fully confident

With Leslie Howard and Bette Davis. *"The gangster he played so often in the thirties, and epitomized by Duke Mantee in* The Petrified Forest, *was mediated by a compelling combination of gentleness and unflinching rectitude."* —*J.M.*

that — masculine mystique aside — size finally counts for very little.

Like nearly every male star in the history of the American film, the Bogart character invariably assumes the superiority of men over women; Rick has no trouble with Ilsa's (Ingrid Bergman) request in *Casablanca* that he "do the thinking for all three of us (himself, her, and

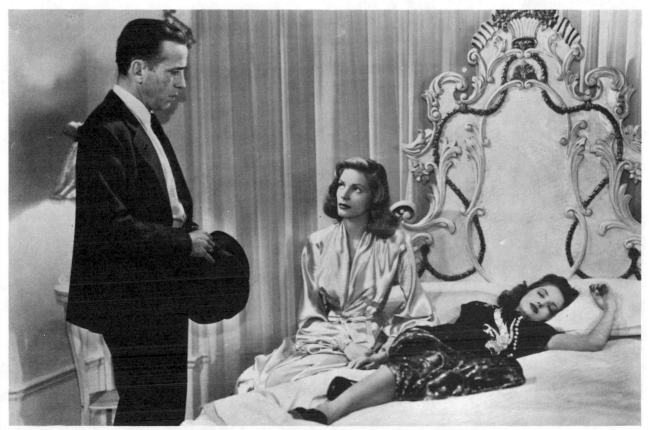

An erotic image from The Big Sleep: *Bogart, Bacall, and a helpless woman (Martha Vickers) on a bed.*

A FORMIDABLE DUO

WITH *The African Queen* (1952) Bogart became virtually the only major male star to succeed fully in a relationship with an independent, strong-willed woman who is his equal in every respect. Spencer Tracy, of course, frequently played opposite career woman Hepburn. But Tracy's image — stolid, paternal, sardonic — bespoke a comfortable, avuncular maleness and a sensibility devoid of sexual excitement. With Hepburn, Bogart integrated underlying erotic energy and a traditional male capacity for survival with an uncommon vulnerability, lack of pretentiousness, and an entirely unromantic physical facade.

Portraying an ordinary man who became extraordinary by virtue of his partnership with a woman who is his equal, he blinks incredulously at first as Hepburn outlines her vision of sailing down the rapids and bombing the German ship. Unthreatened by Hepburn's aggressive and unrelenting personality (she becomes softer as he becomes more self-aware, fueled with a sense of purpose provided by her), Bogart transcends his laziness and alcoholism to summon the resolve to forge a loving relationship with a strong, self-sufficient woman. Both are transformed — grubby Charlie Allnut and spinster Rose — as he becomes Antony and she Cleopatra sailing up the river on their barge, the *African Queen*. No matter that the removal of his shirt reveals a scrawny physique.

United after twenty years in movies.

In this performance (his single Academy Award-winning role) where he is deprived of the coolness of Sam Spade or Philip Marlowe, Bogart provides a far more compelling and desirable ideal than do later, more traditionally endowed physical specimens: the plastic James Bond and the often arrested-adolescent-male figures — from Charles Bronson to Clint Eastwood to Burt Reynolds — who would dominate the American screen in the seventies.

— J. M.

---

her husband [Paul Henreid]).'' Often Bogart remains aloof from women who pursue him, like the ever-available Bacall of *To Have and Have Not* (1944) who would demand the whistle that will call her to his side.

A gangster with emotions in High Sierra. *With Ida Lupino.*

But unlike the men played by Connery and Eastwood, the Bogart hero is capable of genuine respect and regard for women. He enjoys their companionship. He empathizes with their plight and appreciates the guile with which they must move through a world in which they are always at a disadvantage. The phrase ''You're good, you're very good'' became Bogart's classic declaration of esteem, not unlike Mae West's ''Come up and see me sometime.'' Using this line in film after film, with only slight variations, Bogart asserted that he preferred life with women to that all-male world of asexual buddies so peculiar to the American film. There is always the implication that he could walk out of a relationship any time, but as *Dark Passage* (1947) makes clear, being independent of women holds no particular fascination for him, nor would this freedom come as the relief it clearly does for many Hollywood male characters.

In his films with Bacall (*To Have and Have Not, The Big Sleep, Dark Passage,* and *Key Largo* [1948]), Bogart prefers a woman as spirited and independent-minded as himself. The traditional Bogart expression of appreciation, ''You look good, awful good. I didn't know they made them that way anymore,'' from *The Big Sleep,* could have been uttered by either Bogart or Bacall. His moral fiber does not allow him to become defensive no matter what corruption or perfidy is engineered by the world in which he is placed. He can prefer the confident, audacious woman whom he need not pamper or protect, who can provide him with as much comfort as he provides her.

The Bogart hero allowed men and women to accept themselves as they were. He usually seemed to suggest that we could carry on confidently despite recognition of our inevitable insufficiency. In the same spirit Bogart emerges from his first meeting with Sydney Greenstreet in *The Maltese Falcon* with his hand trembling. He looks down at this betraying hand, possessed of a veritable will of its own, and laughs — at himself, at our universal human frailty.

Of major importance in shaping the Bogart screen image was the implicit political role he played in films such as *Casablanca, Across the Pacific* (1942), *To Have and Have Not,* and *Key Largo.* In many wartime and early postwar films the male, however solitary his personal impulses, chooses commitment to battle as the only course worthy of his manhood. Bogart often played such a hero with his masculinity defined, as it is in the close of *Casablanca,* by his decision to come to the "aid of the democracies of Europe."

Key Largo carried the theme into postwar America, where the strong male is asked to transfer his commitment from fighting in the war to ridding the world of sinister elements. "I fight nobody's battles but my own," repeats the Bogart hero. "Me, die to rid the world of a Johnny Rocco? [gangster Edward G. Robinson]" Bogie is guided into the more manly course by Bacall: "If I thought your way, I'd rather be dead." The ending of this otherwise insignificant film is fine. Bogart's reward is that sense of peace which comes only to those large enough in moral stature to give up trying to define the world solely in terms of their own egos, a peace Bogart has in film after film. Bogart has transcended the sordidness of the *film noir,* a testament to his abiding goodness and integrity.

Casablanca,
*the most romantic
of his films.
With Dooley Wilson
and Ingrid Bergman.*

Thus, paradoxically, Bogart's appeal was realized through the *relinquishment* of his freedom in favor of the right goal. It is this dramatization of existential choice that is at the core of his romanticism and may be the most important reason for the enduring attractiveness of his screen image. The Bogart who describes himself in *To Have and Have Not* as a man with "no strings" winds up with both political and sexual involvements of a permanent nature. It is at once a victory for humanity and an erotic triumph. And reluctant masculinity won over has always seemed more desirable than the eager male who could be had without a struggle — those buffoons who are devoid of masculine dynamism.

Bogart, more than any other screen hero, played the male who has learned that standing for truth, justice, and compassion does not come cheap — physically or materially. At his most attractive, Bogart insisted that we can make such sacrifices, so necessary to our humanity, and yet survive. His image transcended its gangster phase and the narrow propagandistic purposes to which it was put during the war. Above all, the Bogart image was founded upon a truth now forgotten on the American screen. Mature masculinity, like mature femininity — in its only serious sense a passage toward self-discovery, self-acceptance, and commitment to matters larger than the self — comes only at great cost. It demands an experienced and seasoned, if partly cynical, person to perceive that integrity is impossible without sacrifice and yet to be prepared to pay that cost. That is the most fulfilling choice of all.

WHERE THERE'S SMOKE,
THERE'S FIRE

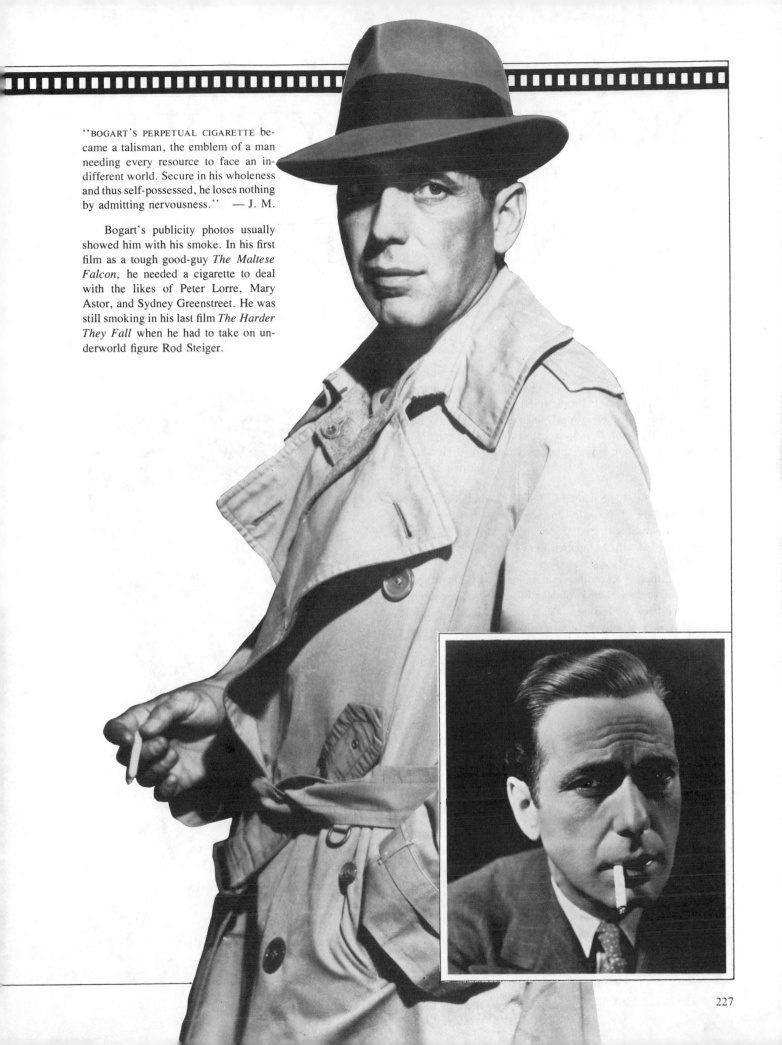

"BOGART'S PERPETUAL CIGARETTE became a talisman, the emblem of a man needing every resource to face an indifferent world. Secure in his wholeness and thus self-possessed, he loses nothing by admitting nervousness." — J. M.

Bogart's publicity photos usually showed him with his smoke. In his first film as a tough good-guy *The Maltese Falcon,* he needed a cigarette to deal with the likes of Peter Lorre, Mary Astor, and Sydney Greenstreet. He was still smoking in his last film *The Harder They Fall* when he had to take on underworld figure Rod Steiger.

227

MONTGOMERY CLIFT: FIRST OF THE NEW BREED

PATRICIA BOSWORTH

One of the most complex figures in film history.

IN 1949 WHEN I WAS FIFTEEN, I met Montgomery Clift by accident. I'd cut classes and arrived home early from school; I remember galumphing into the living room of our New York apartment, hoping to be alone with my *South Pacific* records, when I came upon a slender young man lying sprawled on the rug. He was talking so intently to my father he didn't notice me at first.

When he did, he leaped to his feet and stared at me with a mixture of curiosity and sympathy. His deep-set unblinking eyes glittered under thick dark brows; the pupils seemed almost opaque. I couldn't stop looking into them.

My father, who ordinarily remained in his law office except for special clients, hunched over the coffee table nursing a drink. "Darling," he said, "this is Montgomery Clift — you know the marvelous actor we saw in *Red River* [1948] and *The Search* [1948]."

Speechless, I bobbed a curtsy. Hooting with laughter, Montgomery Clift bobbed a curtsy back.

I couldn't say a word. I felt as if I was going down in a too-fast elevator.

I was — still am — a rabid movie fan. At that point in my life I had seen *Red River* six times. I had started keeping a scrapbook labeled "Monty Clift." The opening page was plastered with photographs of *Red River* and Monty as the cowboy Matt Garth who believes in justice, not violence, and who almost gets beaten to a bloody pulp by John Wayne as a result.

These photographs were followed by glossy stills from *The Search*, Fred Zinnemann's movie about the plight of European refugees. Monty's performance in that movie, as the laconic, gum-chewing soldier who

---

PATRICIA BOSWORTH *is the author of* Montgomery Clift, A Biography. *She is a former managing editor of* Harper's Bazaar, *and presently contributes regularly on the arts to* The New York Times.

rehabilitates a lost refugee child, had just won him his first Academy Award nomination.

However, on that afternoon so long ago I couldn't possibly have guessed that the Montgomery Clift, pacing around our living room talking rapidly about the terrors of the Hollywood blacklist, the Montgomery Clift who'd appeared on the cover of *Life* magazine as the most-in-demand new movie star, would turn out to be one of the definitive actors of the 1950s.

I only knew I had never met anybody who asked so many questions or smoked so much (as the afternoon wore on, the ashtray overflowed with his crushed Pall Malls). I remember he had an energy and an impatience as he spoke and he punctuated his conversation with bursts of almost maniacal laughter.

I saw Montgomery Clift a half dozen times after that. I found him to be a deeply private person, remote, disconcerting, hypertense. Aside from one brief chat with me in which he told of a group of admirers who had tried to tear off his clothes while he was in a Manhattan department store, he was usually locked in discussions with my father.

A top method actor, he was an instant movie sensation playing the gentle son of rugged John Wayne in Red River.

So I only saw Montgomery Clift in the movies. His appeal was such that when the camera zeroed in on him, something intangible happened — what appeared on screen was not just a splendid watchful face or a style, but a complex mysterious presence, full of depth, indisputably alive.

In his most romantic films — *The Big Lift* (1950), *Indiscretion of an American Wife* (1954), and certainly *A Place in the Sun* (1951; who can forget those erotic close-ups of Monty kissing Elizabeth Taylor?) — there was a sense of sexual ambiguity in his expression that was almost palpable.

But behind that beauty was a striving, a determination that kept him from succumbing completely to narcissism. That inner tension made Monty fascinating to watch.

In his great roles such as his nonviolent soldier Robert E. Lee Prewitt in *From Here to Eternity* (1953), Monty reflected the loneliness, the dislocation, the smoldering hostility, and the quicksilver charm that became characteristic of an entire generation of actors.

Clift and Elizabeth Taylor were one of the few romantic teams of the fifties able to produce an erotic intensity. (Top) A Place in the Sun. *(Bottom)* Raintree County.

As a pacifist in From Here to Eternity, *he is not Burt Lancaster's ideal soldier.*

His contemporaries Marlon Brando and James Dean watched and learned from him, and the eccentric-loser heroes who followed him — Al Pacino, Jack Nicholson, Dustin Hoffman, Robert De Niro — owe much of their film presence to him. Actor Bill Gunn put it this way: "Monty was the first movie star to seem obsessed — slightly nuts."

In the 1950s movie audiences were looking for new kinds of heroes — unconventional ones. Montgomery Clift fulfilled a need.

The loners, the stubborn idealists he played, the self-absorbed young men alienated from their culture, made Monty more than just a visual icon and fantasy figure. "You dreamt about him, but you related to him too," said a friend.

And the roles themselves, like the G.I. in *The Search* and the fortune hunter in William Wyler's *The Heiress* (1949), inspired him to create a new style of acting — internal, reasoned, oblique. But at the same time Monty appeared so natural that photographer Richard Avedon called his approach "documentary."

His nonchalance on screen, his insinuating glances were deceptive. He spent weeks, sometimes months, laboring over a script, working out every gesture, every inflection, every nuance of a character.

Trained on the Broadway stage (he'd appeared in twelve plays before he was twenty), taught by his mentor, the great Alfred Lunt, always to capture "the *essence* of a person," Monty believed that "the best acting is an accumulation of subtleties — like shaking the ash

from a cigarette when the character is supposed to be completely absorbed in a conversation."

Before he played the priest Father Logan in Alfred Hitchcock's *I Confess* (1953), he spent three weeks living in a monastery memorizing the Latin Mass, wearing a priest's robes. Later he decided to characterize Father Logan by his walk. François Truffaut says, "Montgomery Clift's walk in *I Confess* is a forward motion that shapes the whole film. It also concretizes the concept of his integrity."

Broncobuster in The Misfits.

Questioned by Maximilian Schell in Judgment at Nuremberg.

For a while after the near-fatal car accident in 1955 — during the making of *Raintree County* (1957) — that destroyed his beautiful face and drove him to liquor and drugs, Monty thought he was finished. His greatest fear was that, with his new twisted features, he would no longer be able to act.

But then he found a way. Although his left cheek was paralyzed and his lip deformed, his eyes still had their expressiveness, and he went about perfecting his

Candid shot from the late forties.

gift for stillness — his technique for projecting a power deep within himself. In every movie after the accident Monty cut his dialogue back to a bare minimum. In *The Young Lions* (1958), in which he played his favorite character, Noah — Noah the nonconformist, the proud young father who gets into absurd fights defending his manhood, his Jewishness — some of Monty's best scenes are done entirely in pantomime.

Strangely enough, in spite of four Academy Award nominations and sixteen movies in which he played a variety of characters who took risks — no one picture ever gave Montgomery Clift mythic status.

A Streetcar Named Desire (1951), for example, established Brando as the legendary T-shirted slob. But Brando's T-shirted slob was much easier for the public to take than Monty's cinematic series of feisty idealists, men committed to answering both society and self.

Brando solidified his image with his performance in *On the Waterfront* (1954), a movie Monty turned down. Instead he chose *Lonelyhearts* (1958), *Freud* (1962), and the peculiar, often tactless, government worker Chuck Glover in Elia Kazan's neglected classic *Wild River* (1960).

These choices were in keeping with the Clift screen persona — a man with ethical standards so high he judges himself as harshly as he judges his enemies.

What finally makes Montgomery Clift so singular in film history was his ability — his desire — to hide behind the warp and woof of a script. This is particularly true in *From Here to Eternity,* where Monty immersed himself so totally in the character of Prewitt that he seems to sink into the movie, while Frank Sinatra and Burt Lancaster bulge from the screen with their theatrics. But ultimately it is Clift's unsettling presence that dominates that film — most of his films, for that matter.

The last time I saw Montgomery Clift was in 1960 after a session at the Actors Studio. The place was jammed with Broadway and Hollywood stars because Marilyn Monroe had just performed her first "live" scene, acting with Maureen Stapleton in *Anna Christie.*

After the applause died down, I felt a hand on my shoulder. I turned and stared into a gaunt, ravaged face. "Hi, Patti," the face said. When I didn't respond, the face murmured, "It's Monty . . . Monty Clift."

He knew I hadn't recognized him but he chose to ignore that. Instead, with his hand still on my shoulder, he began telling me about the movie he hoped to make, Carson McCullers' *The Heart Is a Lonely Hunter,* in which he'd be playing a deaf mute. In preparation for the role, he'd been studying at the Gallaudet College for the Deaf in Washington, D.C. He thought it would be the supreme actor's challenge to play a character whose life and adventures are carried on in total silence.

We talked a bit more, and then he rose to go. But before he left, he bobbed me a jaunty curtsy. Then he was gone.

JAMES DEAN: YOUTH IN BOLD REBELLION

DAVID THOMSON

A symbol for misunderstood youth.

VIOLENCE ON FILM dates quickly: The shock goes and the spectacle remains. Glamour lasts much longer; seductive glances linger and their spell persists. This may explain why James Dean is less persuasive now as the intransigent rebel who drove headlong to the end of his night with the angry thrust of an adolescent yearning for eros or death. Dean was sometimes caught up in screen violence, and we cannot doubt his real-life capacity for brutality. He runs amok toward the end of *East of Eden* (1955) and drags his pious brother to face the shock of their "depraved" mother, Jo Van Fleet, withering from arthritis and solitude in the brothel that has made her rich.

In *Giant* (1956) he beats at Rock Hudson, who is being held back by the arms. In *Rebel Without a Cause* (1955) he briefly wields a knife and consents to the chicken-race ritual with a mocking, "That's all I ever do."

But he never nursed malice or gave off waves of aggression. It is glib hindsight that identifies him as the harbinger of youth-run-wild, drugs, reckless speed and moral abandon, rock 'n' roll, anarchy, and the anger that adopts outrage as a release.

In truth, James Dean was the last vulnerable romantic. And if his life and abrupt death substantiate the legend of willful rejection of control, that should not disguise his saturnine assurance and guile on the screen. Epitaphs say he was troubled and scattered, but he owned the screen and prowled about it with the moody shyness of Garbo, Cooper, or Bogart. In his pictures, he was in charge; he is the image of a star and master of that strange deceit that contrives to be intimate and revealing by pretending there is no camera. He does not show off or act out; he beckons us into his recessive self, with a

DAVID THOMSON *is a film critic for Boston's* The Real Paper *and is a regular contributor to* Sight and Sound. *He teaches film at Dartmouth College.*

Cal shows Aaron their mother — now a prostitute — in East of Eden. *With Richard Davalos and Jo Van Fleet.*

discreet flourish as sly as it is compelling. He was a kid who had studied actors, not people. That sense of artful hiding does not date. Dean's screen presence knows a turbulent secret and is contemplating sharing it (''You want to see your mother, Aaron?'' he teases his brother in *East of Eden*.) Possession of some awesome knowledge has a lasting power, for it matches our privileged status as watchers who will not be denounced as spies.

In *Rebel* and *Eden,* the two films that used Dean appropriately — in *Giant* he was mistakenly placed in a supporting role and deprived of his youth — there is a connecting passage between him and us, with enough darkness at the far end so that we are not sure whether we are touching Jim Stark or Cal Trask or Dean himself. Neither character is without flaw or mistake: An actor with less self-regard might have made these characterizations more objective, untidy, and suspect. But Dean brings these flaws to us with the earnest effort of desperate sincerity: Love me, he sighs to the viewer, just as he searches among the other characters for ''understanding'' and ''support.''

He is a loner in these films, in the spirit of adolescent retreat that reinterprets its isolation as a function of the world's defects. We allow the Dean character to possess a sense of humanity not dreamed of among the adults. His awkwardness is healed by this ability to see solitariness as a transfixing rebuke to foolishness and lack of feeling. Dean's romanticism is based upon a world-weary superiority, so much more graceful than a youth's everyday snarl of frustration; so much more romantic in that it reasserts a need for some kind of love that adults have denied him.

In *East of Eden,* Cal alone knows his mother lives in Salinas. He visits her, accepts her ravaged condition, and is not distressed, because he is simply curious about others and how they regard or serve him. (Dean's character searches for love, but coldly denies it to others.) He borrows money from his mother to become a farmer; his dream is one day to restore the funds his father (Raymond Massey) lost by attempting to ship refrigerated lettuce cross-country. Cal is a sharper businessman, a more perceptive dreamer, and altogether a more aware, robust person. The outcast from his brother's delicate trysts with Abra (Julie Harris), he sees there is more to her than his brother realizes and watches with a strength and longing that sometimes arrests her — as if she felt grave, understanding eyes fall on her. (The same thing will occur in *Rebel*, where Natalie Wood reacts with the startled wonder of someone caressed by Dean's wise attention. Julie Harris and Wood are brought into the films by Dean's scrutiny: he murmurs to us that they are worthy of him, and thus of all other light. His need gives them character and warmth, and early distance leads to enchanted idylls where these "rescued" young women become ointment to his hurts.)

East of Eden is a crucial youth film because it indulges the young person's unprincipled and shameless yearning to be the center of attention and affection. The brother is treated as a stooge rival; the girl is a docile mate who will come to appreciate the hidden Romeo she first thinks is a lout; and the father is a character denied any life or being except one that aggravates his tyrannical son. Emotion has grown to monstrous proportions in its introspective confines, and Dean is so brimming with feeling and reticence that he cannot be criticized or corrected. A hysterical thwarted sensibility prevails, and Elia Kazan's direction is unequivocally supportive of it. He had felt the sting of puritan moral judgments personally, and knew the misunderstood roamings of the lone wolf. I think he identified with Dean. The same thing would happen with Nicholas Ray on *Rebel* — and thus rooted the film in Dean's real brooding and dismay.

Kazan gilds Dean's apartness. He gives him scenes of splendid isolation and lets the furtive actor monopolize the CinemaScope frame: riding the train to Salinas; following his mother in the misty morning; venturing down the dark corridor to her office; spying on his brother and planning his overthrow; and, finally, being left in power and possession at the bedside of his stricken, mute father — the emotional vampire with his helpless victim. It is a "happy" ending that shows how demented and warping the search for satisfaction can be in American films.

With Julie Harris in East of Eden. *Females who felt unappreciated were attracted to Dean, who had the sensitivity all others lacked.*

The loveliest imaginable example of aloneness is when Dean dances across his bean field — he will find oil in *Giant* with the same uninhibited glee — and makes capitalist love to the earth (in the process, gazing into a ground-level camera, as if it were a rapturous accomplice). *Rebel Without a Cause* opens with a similar composition: Dean, drunk with self-pity on the city sidewalk, but clinging to an inarticulate humanity by caring for a forlorn teddy bear. Yet again, in *Rebel*, Dean overpowered an experienced director: Nicholas Ray would never find so eloquent or decisive a spokesman for his own fumbling sense of the nobility of the damaged outcast.

Rebel trembles with expressiveness, but it has much more to do with a derelict's romantic agony than with Californian juvenile turmoil in the age of Eisenhower. Dean's character is not delinquent, rather it is opposing social decadence and hollow lives. He is a philosopher who divines the hypocrisy of middle-class suburbia. (His authority is underlined by the oddity of a twenty-four-year-old playing a high school kid.) He wants order, peace, and a conventional, fruitful relationship; he is the soulful pilgrim in search of sincerity. He tells his raucous parents that he wants one day without confusion — and they are to take this request seriously. As a consort he elects a soda fountain Juliet, who will immediately help him form a new model family when he, Wood, and Sal Mineo go off to the deserted mansion. Their "rebellion" blithely reconstitutes the family pattern they loathe and suffer from at home. The film is not brave enough to admit Dean and Wood want to make love and discard one another.

Of course, Dean explores the role with glittering skill. The character is a little more honorable and less petulant than the wretched Cal in *Eden,* and Dean's improvisations brought moments of humor, recollections of

Sal Mineo with Dean and Natalie Wood, his surrogate parents in Rebel Without a Cause.

real teenage unease and the final, agonized denial of violence. ("*I*'ve got the bullets!" he cries to the police who've gunned down Sal Mineo.) It carries the pain of Kent State, even if it does not quite eclipse the sense that his cunning, his neglect, and his self-idealization have betrayed Plato (Sal Mineo), the true incipient madman, whose crazy mismatched socks earn parental amusement from the so-settled Jim and Judy (Wood).

Death tidied Dean's image and made him available for any Norman Mailer who wanted an existential phantom for half-grasped social diatribes. I think the truth is different and more alarming. Dean had a face loved by the camera, and a personality more than willing to be adored. His surliness was only his resentment at being so addicted to admiration. The vividness of his performances lies in the calculated mannerisms of an actor pretending to be ill at ease. The significance of his films is that they inaugurated the new young audience, and the way in which film, TV, and pop music would cater to its whining sorrowful immaturity in the name of sensitivity. Dean was not a rebel, but the first evidence that the young were ready to buy a dream and regard it as fulfillment. Like all great movie stars, Dean alleged that identity and spirit were covered by a dark look and an aloof manner. He sold the young to the dream merchants under cover of his refusal to compromise.

Rebel Without a Cause. *Frustrated from trying to communicate with father Jim Backus.*

BARBARA STEELE: HORROR QUEEN TALKS

JONATHAN DEMME and EVELYN PURCELL

As diabolical prison warden in Caged Heat, *directed by Jonathan Demme and produced by Evelyn Purcell.*

Q AS THE "QUEEN OF THE HORROR FILM" you are recognized throughout the world as either a full-fledged star or a cult figure. How did your movie career start?

A. I was doing repertory theater in Scotland in the mid-

JONATHAN DEMME *directed Barbara Steele in* Caged Heat. *He has also directed* Crazy Mama, A Small Town in Texas, Handle with Care, *and* The Last Embrace. EVELYN PURCELL *is a producer-director, who often works in collaboration with her husband, Jonathan Demme.*

1950s when a talent scout for the Rank Organization spotted me. I was offered a contract and was thrown into tons of movies during my first several months, having my confidence built.

In my first picture, I played a student, who had two words of dialogue. I had to say "Yes" and "No" in an extremely upper-class British accent. But I couldn't get it right, so they dubbed me.

After a year my contract was bought up by Twentieth Century-Fox for an enormous amount of money. We were bought and sold like football players in those days. I was with Fox for one year.

Q. Was it difficult being English and working outside of Great Britain?

A. It was extremely difficult for me in Hollywood. But it was not as bad in Italy or France — where one might assume it would be harder.

In Hollywood I was always self-conscious about trying to get work. I was terribly apprehensive and shy. When I first came to Hollywood, everyone wanted women with a specific sexy look. They changed the color of my hair from its natural black to blond and even asked me to go and meet the studio heads in a bikini. I couldn't do that.

Q. What films did you do for Fox?

A. Ironically, my first film under a Fox contract wasn't made in America or by Fox. There was a writers' strike in Hollywood, so Fox loaned me out to do Mario Bava's *Black Sunday* (1961), an Italian horror film that has become something of a classic. I didn't see any of the rushes, so I wasn't aware of how beautiful it was until I saw it recently.

Also, I made *The Pit and the Pendulum* (1961) for American International Pictures. That was one of several Edgar Allan Poe films Roger Corman made with Vincent Price.

Fox finally put me in a film and it turned out to be a memorable experience. It was an Elvis Presley western called *Flaming Star* (1960), in which I was to play a part that required a southern accent. In one scene I was to meet my star-crossed fiancé, Presley, after surviving the

In her most popular horror film, Black Sunday.

massacre of my family and riding one hundred and fifty miles across the desert. They had made these wonderful, very tight yellow jeans for me. It seemed totally improbable to me that after all I was supposed to have been through I would arrive looking like a professional virgin, so I rubbed sand and muddy water all over those beautiful jeans. The continuity department became hysterical and nasty because I had taken this initiative. I was under great duress, so I fled that night to New York, and never came back. Fox said, "You've got to come back. It's costing us ten thousand dollars a day." I was very young and didn't understand what I was doing — I was just petrified and humiliated. After a few days, I went to Europe. That ended the Fox contract.

Q. Where did you go?

A. Italy — because of my experience there on *Black Sunday*. I had no trouble finding work. I played a very small part in Fellini's *8½* (1963), and during the shooting, I made *The Horrible Secret of Dr. Hitchcock* (1962), directed by Ricardo Freda, in only eight days. It is an excellent color horror film — very different. *Black Sunday* has a haunting mystical air about it, but *Dr. Hitchcock* was more fun to make because it is more emotional and dramatic.

I also appeared in its sequel, *The Spectre* (1964). Later, I did a couple of horror films for Antonio Margheriti, one called *The Dance Macabre* (1963) and

With Vincent Price in The Pit and the Pendulum.

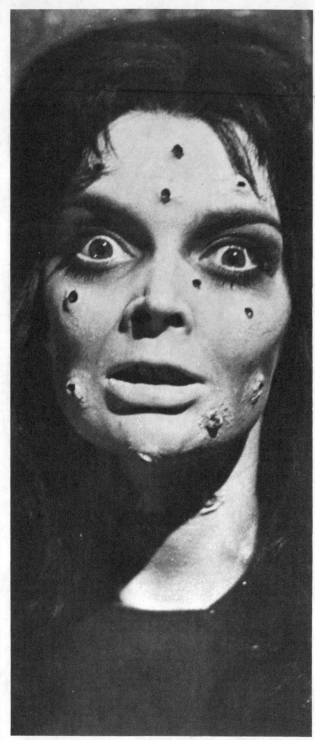

The arch-heroine of horror is a witch who returns to life in Black Sunday.

another called *The Long Hair of Death* (1964). We had an advantage because we filmed on location in extraordinary environments that helped a lot. We were in graveyards and decaying castles full of an extraordinary mood and feeling of the past. Italy is so sumptuous and rich and decadent — on a visual level, it's fantastic. You really felt these presences around you, going back generations and generations.

At some point, I began to wonder if it was a self-fulfilling prophecy, playing those strange parts. I had never been attracted to horror films because they deal in such a dark and negative area. You are dealing with archetypes, basically, and they are very Jungian. It really disturbed me, after doing so many, because I began to suspect that I was projecting all these intense, dark, and evil forces from within.

Q. You were alienated from your parts because of who you really were?

A. I wanted to play — I still want to play — a regular lady in a scruffy cardigan.

Q. Yet you were established as a film star in Rome by this point?

A. Yes. It's very odd, because the attention I received was way out of proportion to the work I was doing. Italy, you know, is full of gossip; I had this sort of street attention all the time, appearing on the covers of magazines. But at the same time I wasn't doing the kind of work I really wanted to do. In all, I did about twenty films in Italy, mostly inconsequential pictures. The last film I did in Europe, however, was a German film called *Young Torless* (1967). It was Volker Schlondorff's very first film project, a stunning movie.

Q. You left Europe around this time?

A. I left to have a love affair with James Poe, the screenwriter, and it ended in marriage.

Q. You returned to America?

A. Yes, but it was terribly difficult. I still had the bitter aftertaste of that whole starlet period. I had a very defen-

Evil in The Dance Macabre, *known in U.S. as* Castle of Blood.

sive attitude. I didn't work here for a long time, although I would occasionally go back to Italy or France and make a film because somebody asked me.

Q. I understand that James Poe wrote one of the parts in *They Shoot Horses, Don't They?* expressly for you.

A. Yes, but Susannah York ended up playing it when the studio decided to use a big-name cast. As Jim wrote it, it was a beautiful part. Charles Chaplin had once owned the movie rights to the book, and Jim had written to him when he was a very young man and tried to buy them from him. Years later, Jim finally had enough money. He wrote an absolutely glorious screenplay that was totally butchered by the time it was directed by Sydney Pollack. They made it very sentimental. It was a total tragedy that Jim wasn't allowed to make it himself. I could see, day by day, Jim losing a piece of it here, a piece of it there, a piece of his mind.

We went into hibernation. We lived in Mexico for a year, then went back to Europe for a while and traveled around. Then I came back to America, had a child and got divorced. Two days after I ended my marriage, you, Jonathan, asked me to do *Caged Heat* (1974), remember?

Q. Yes, I do, although I didn't know it was two days after all that.

A. I was walking along in the high pitch of a nervous breakdown, practically. I'll never forget you jumping out of a car with this big smile. I was thinking, "What in the world is this creature doing?"

Q. Ironically it was another instance of a writer writing a part with a particular actress in mind, never thinking that he would be able to get the actress. But fortune took a hand and you did *Caged Heat* for us. And now you're working fairly steadily. Have you attained a certain measure of fulfillment through your work?

A. Years ago, I read an article by Rip Torn on acting, and he said it was the one profession where he could truly express his emotions. That's basically what it's all about — to have this wonderful heightened capsule of time in which you can express your emotions. It's lovely and utterly gratifying. But there are also long drawn-out periods with little accomplishment, which are difficult and horrible. If you start to measure yourself by the amount of work you are doing, or the kind of work you are doing, you can go absolutely crazy. You get a boomeranging feeling about yourself; it all comes back to you and you say to yourself, "Am I the sum total of that?" Because you have to say to yourself, "There's this private part of me that really hasn't expressed itself."

At wedding of Brooke Shields to Keith Carradine in Louis Malle's controversial Pretty Baby.

BRUCE LEE: DEATH MACHINE

KENNETH TURAN

I T HAPPENED on July 30, 1973, in the Hong Kong apartment of actress Betty Ting Pei, where, so the official story goes, Bruce Lee had gone to discuss a forthcoming film. He complained of a headache, took a painkiller, and went into the bedroom to rest. Later, when he could not be wakened, he was rushed to a hospital where he died at 11:30 P.M. Just like that.

Since Bruce Lee's death, more than a dozen films have sought to trade on his notoriety, and almost as many biographies have spread confusion about his life. Was the name of his first film, made when he was a child actor in Hong Kong, *Birth of a Man,* *The Birth of Mankind,* or *The Beginning of a Boy?* Was his height five-feet-four, five-feet-seven, five-feet-eight, or, as the majority of observers claim, exactly five-feet-seven-and-a-half? And when he died, was he buried in the dark blue suit he wore in *The Chinese Connection* (1972) or the one he wore in *Enter The Dragon* (1973)?

Even his family got into the act, with his brother recording the lachrymose ''Ballad of Bruce Lee,'' and his wife, Linda Lee, writing a biography.

The reasons for the durability and breadth of Bruce Lee's posthumous celebrity are rooted deeper than

Prior to his death, Bruce Lee was possibly the world's most popular star.

KENNETH TURAN *is the film critic for* The Progressive *and is a general cultural critic for the* Washington Post. *He is the coauthor of* Sinema: American Pornographic Films and the People Who Make Them.

notoriety, starting in the man's curiously bifurcated personality, a juxtaposition of qualities his fans found uncontrollably attractive, a personality that by turns was and was not visible in his films. Lee's many biographers return again and again to the same sorry conclusions: He was immensely egotistical, a hothead. Even his wife sadly admits, ''Bruce was no plaster saint.''

Fanatical about success and perfection, Bruce Lee alienated as many people as he attracted. He pushed himself with an intensity that was awful: obsessively training in his specially equipped gym; doing endless thumb push-ups; even, one biographer says, having his sweat glands removed from under his armpits so he would look better. And toward the end, beset by an inquisitive press, studio lackeys, and money men who resisted giving him his due, he kept plugging away at his film projects, driven by a strange sense of mission.

Oddly enough, Lee's desperate qualities show to advantage in his films, in which he possesses an appealing life force. He truly seemed as one of his posters put it, ''Unstoppable! Unbelievable! Unbeatable!'' Sometimes he went a bit over the edge. ''The look on his face as he crushes Oharra's head,'' a fan magazine accurately noted of a scene from *Enter the Dragon*, ''is more animal then human.'' But, in general, Lee kept himself under control. Watching Bruce Lee on screen is the sheerest joy. His physical movements — the flying kicks, the leaps, the quicker-than-the-eye hands — managed to be death-dealing while they remained appealing, graceful, almost balletic. In presence and charisma, Bruce Lee was as good as they come.

In wonderful contrast to the harsher aspects of his image, Lee projects qualities on the screen that not everyone noticed in him as a person. He is refreshing, youthful, invigorating, with an ingratiating grin and a totally unexpected, totally winning boyish personality. It is this pixie quality, coupled with his boggling, deadly

physical abilities, that makes him, despite the amiable dross of low-grade exploitation films, irresistible.

In each of his films, Bruce Lee played the classic, mythic hero, the clean-living good guy who puts evil to rout. He would not have been out of place in a B western of the Monogram era. He does what he does, not for the glory, not for the girl — he usually gets her anyway — but because he must do it. He is bad but not evil, a killing machine with a heart of purest gold, a combination that translated easily into enormous popularity, both before and after his death.

Enter the Dragon, *his top-grossing film, features this climactic fight with a villain who has blades instead of fingers.*

With women, he was very mannerly.

It was in mid-1971 that Bruce Lee erupted on the scene. Bruce had returned to Hong Kong and, after turning down what he considered a degrading offer from Run Run Shaw, the Harry Cohn of Oriental cinema, he signed to do his first film. It was in the newly popular kung fu — or chop sockey — genre, produced by Raymond Chow of Golden Harvest Films. This movie, *The Big Boss/Fists of Fury* (1972), had a budget of under $100,000, including Lee's $7,500 salary. But it proved surprisingly popular at the Hong Kong box office, easily outgrossing the previous local champ, *The Sound of Music*. Three more films followed quickly, all completed within two years. The surge culminated in the ambitious *Enter the Dragon*, Lee's first and only glossy Hollywood production. It cost the enormous — for the genre — sum of three-quarters of a million dollars. His last media "appearance" was in an *Esquire* magazine article that came out the month he died, ironically subtitled, "Is Not Warner Bros. Ancient and Wise? Is Not Bruce Lee Young and Coming Up Fast?"

Lee's sudden death started endless rumors. Rumors that one emotional biography called, "the sordid speculation and intrigue surrounding Lee's last hours." It didn't seem possible, as his wife breathlessly put it, "that a man of Bruce's astonishing virility, vitality, energy, and sheer physical fitness should suddenly blank out like a snuffed candle." Had he died from his odd diet of raw beef, eggs, and milk, from his special high protein drink, or from his occasional habit of drinking beef blood? Did he have numerous mistresses, and keel over from massive sexual overexertion? And when his coffin arrived in Seattle slightly damaged by the trip from Hong Kong, it revived a Chinese belief that Bruce Lee's soul was not resting well, that perhaps he had met with foul play at the hands of mysterious folk who were upset at his popularizing secret doctrines. Mention was darkly made of secret herb poisons that resist detection, of something called "the vibrating hand" by which a practitioner could touch a man and cause him to die two years later. It was, all told, a totally inexplicable and untimely death. But, classically enough, it provided the perfect ending for Bruce Lee's life and times.

About to win a fight.

BOX OFFICE CHAMPIONS FROM 1932 TO 1977

Since 1932, film distributors have voted annually on the year's top ten box office stars for Quigley Publications. This section lists each year's most popular male and female stars and shows them in a film from their victorious year (or, occasionally, in a film released at the end of the previous year).

1932 **Charles Farrell** (L, with Janet Gaynor, *The First Year*). **Marie Dressler** (Above R, *Emma* with Myrna Loy).

1933 **Will Rogers** (Above, with Louise Dresser, *State Fair*). **Marie Dressler,** for the second time (with Wallace Beery, *Tugboat Annie*).

1934 **Will Rogers,** for the second time (with Stepin Fetchit, *Judge Priest*). **Janet Gaynor** (*Servant's Entrance*).

1936 **Clark Gable** (Above, with Jeanette Mac-Donald, (*San Francisco*). **Shirley Temple,** for the second time (*Dimples*).

1935 **Will Rogers,** for the third time (Below, R, *Steamboat 'Round the Bend*). **Shirley Temple** (with Adolphe Menjou, *Little Miss Marker*).

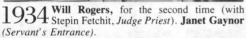
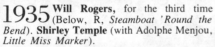

1937 **Clark Gable,** for the second time (Above, with Jean Harlow, *Saratoga*). **Shirley Temple,** for the third time *(Wee Willie Winkie).*

1938 **Clark Gable,** for the third time (with Spencer Tracy and Myrna Loy, *Test Pilot*). **Shirley Temple,** for the fourth time (with George Murphy, *Little Miss Broadway*).

1941 **Mickey Rooney,** for the third time (with Spencer Tracy, *Men of Boys Town*). **Bette Davis,** for the second time (with James Cagney, *The Bride Came C.O.D.*).

1942
Abbott and Costello *(Who Done It?).* **Betty Grable** *(Song of the Islands).*

1945 **Bing Crosby,** for the second time (with Henry Travers, *The Bells of St. Mary's*). **Greer Garson** *(The Valley of Decision).*

1946 **Bing Crosby,** for the third time (with Joan Caulfield and Fred Astaire, *Blue Skies*). **Ingrid Bergman** (with Cary Grant, *Notorious*).

1939 Mickey Rooney *(Out West with the Hardys)*. Shirley Temple, *for* the fifth time *(The Little Princess)*.

1940 Mickey Rooney, for the second time *(Young Tom Edison)*. Bette Davis (R, with Gale Sondergaard, *The Letter*).

1943 Bob Hope (Above, R, *Let's Face It* with Joe Sawyer). Betty Grable, for the second time *(Sweet Rosie O'Grady)*.

1944 Bing Crosby (Above, Center, with Frank McHugh, and Rise Stevens, *Going My Way*). Betty Grable, for the third time *(Pin-Up Girl)*.

1947 Bing Crosby, for the fourth time (with Joan Caulfield, *Welcome Stranger*). Betty Grable, for the fourth time *(Mother Wore Tights)*.

1948 Bing Crosby, for the fifth time (with Bob Hope, *The Road to Rio*). Betty Grable, for the fifth time (with Dan Dailey, *When My Baby Smiles at Me*).

1949 **Bob Hope,** for the second time (*The Paleface*). **Betty Grable,** for the sixth time (*The Beautiful Blonde from Bashful Bend*).

1950 **John Wayne** (*Sands of Iwo Jima*). **Betty Grable,** for the seventh time (with Victor Mature, *Wabash Avenue*).

1953 **Gary Cooper** (with Anthony Quinn, *Blowing Wild*). **Marilyn Monroe** (with Jane Russell, *Gentlemen Prefer Blondes*).

1954
John Wayne, for the third time (with, L–R, William Campbell, Wally Brown, and Robert Stack, *The High and the Mighty*). **Marilyn Monroe,** for the second time (with Robert Mitchum and Tommy Rettig, *River of No Return*).

1957
Rock Hudson (*Battle Hymn*). There was no actress in the top ten box office stars.

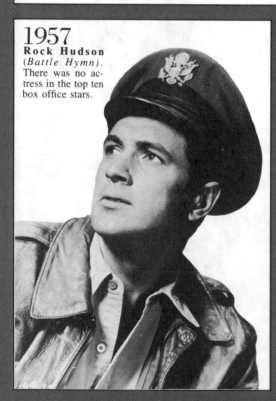

1958 **Glenn Ford** (*The Sheepman*). **Elizabeth Taylor** (*Cat on a Hot Tin Roof*).

1951 **John Wayne,** for the second time *(Flying Leathernecks)*. **Betty Grable,** for the eighth time (with Dan Dailey, *Call Me Mister*).

1952 **Dean Martin and Jerry Lewis** (with Don Defore and Robert Strauss, *Jumping Jacks*). **Doris Day** (with Ray Bolger, *April in Paris*).

1955 **James Stewart** *(The Far Country)*. **Grace Kelly** *(Green Fire)*.

1956 **William Holden** (L, with Kim Novak, *Picnic*). **Marilyn Monroe,** for the third time (with Don Murray, *Bus Stop*).

1959 **Rock Hudson,** for the second time (with Jean Simmons, *This Earth is Mine*). **Doris Day,** for the second time (with Jack Lemmon, L, and Steve Forrest, *It Happened to Jane*).

1960 **Rock Hudson** and **Doris Day,** both for the third time (with Tony Randall, Center, *Pillow Talk*).

1961

Rock Hudson, for the fourth time (with Gina Lollobrigida, *Come September*). **Elizabeth Taylor,** for the second time (with Laurence Harvey, *Butterfield 8*).

1962

Rock Hudson, for the fifth time (with Burl Ives, *The Spiral Road*). **Doris Day,** for the fourth time (with Ann B. Davis, *Lover Come Back*).

1965
Sean Connery (with Gert Frobe, *Goldfinger*). **Doris Day,** for the seventh time *(Do Not Disturb)*.

1966

Sean Connery, for the second time (with Adolfo Celi, *Thunderball*). **Julie Andrews** (with Max von Sydow, *Hawaii*).

1970

Paul Newman, for the second time *(WUSA)*. **Barbra Streisand** (with George Segal, *The Owl and the Pussycat*).

1969
Paul Newman (with Robert Redford, *Butch Cassidy and the Sundance Kid*). **Katharine Hepburn** *(The Madwoman of Chaillot)*.

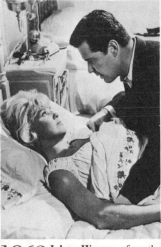

1963 John Wayne, for the fourth time (with Harry Morgan, *How the West Was Won*). **Doris Day,** for the fifth time (with James Garner, *The Thrill of It All*).

1964 Jack Lemmon (*Good Neighbor Sam*). **Doris Day,** for the sixth time (*Send Me No Flowers*).

1967 Lee Marvin (*Point Blank*). **Julie Andrews,** for the second time (with Mary Tyler Moore and Carol Channing, *Thoroughly Modern Millie*).

1968 Sidney Poitier (with Katharine Houghton and Spencer Tracy, *Guess Who's Coming to Dinner?*). **Julie Andrews,** for the third time (*Star!*).

1971 John Wayne, for the fifth time (with Maureen O'Hara and Patrick Wayne, *Big Jake*). **Ali McGraw** (*Love Story*).

1972 Clint Eastwood (*Joe Kidd*). **Barbra Streisand,** for the second time (with Ryan O'Neal, *What's Up, Doc?*).

Robert Redford (with Mia Farrow, *The Great Gatsby*). **Barbra Streisand,** for the fourth time (*For Pete's Sake*).

1973 **Clint Eastwood,** for the second time, (*High Plains Drifter*). **Barbra Streisand,** for the third time (*The Way We Were*).

1975 **Robert Redford,** for the second time (*The Great Waldo Pepper*). **Barbra Streisand,** for the fifth time (*Funny Lady*).

1977 **Sylvester Stallone** (*Rocky*). **Diane Keaton** (*Looking for Mr. Goodbar*).

1976 **Robert Redford,** for the third time (with Dustin Hoffman, *All the President's Men*). **Tatum O'Neal** (with Burt Reynolds, *Nickelodeon*).

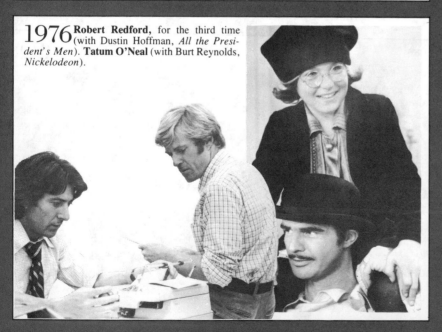

HOLLYWOOD
MISFITS

ORSON WELLES: MOVIE INNOVATOR

ALBERT ZUGSMITH

As Charles Foster Kane

ALBERT ZUGSMITH *is the producer of such films as* Touch of Evil, Man in the Shadow, Tarnished Angels, Written on the Wind, Slaughter on Tenth Avenue, High School Confidential, Invasion U.S.A., *and* The Incredible Shrinking Man. *He has directed such films as* College Confidential, Sex Kittens Go to College, Dondi, Confessions of an Opium Eater, *and* Movie Star, American Style, or, LSD, I Hate You!

ORSON WELLES the actor has never become a superstar or a box-office draw viewers swoon over. This is not because his acting ability is less than superb — it is unsurpassed — but, rather for another reason: he has chosen to sacrifice popularity for artistic commitment.

The young Welles of the 1940s was undeniably attractive; slim, handsome, and brilliant. But Welles was so absorbed in playing fascinating, often complex, roles in films such as *Citizen Kane* (1941), *Journey Into Fear* (1942), *The Stranger* (1946), and *The Third Man* (1949) that he did not try to project the romantic image he was capable of then, and which was necessary for male stardom in those days. By the time the mass mind began to accept actors who were not Errol Flynns or Clark Gables, Welles had already aged and put on so much weight that he had to settle for character parts (which he has done with the sensitivity and sense of dramatic import that only Orson Welles can project).

Orson Welles was not content being solely an actor. He felt compelled by the calling of his art to involve himself in every facet of a production: writing, direction, production, film editing, sound editing, musical scoring, and on and on. He was the first modern multi-talented threat to influence Hollywood — an influence that forced the motion picture industry to consider film as not just a means to make money, but also as a legitimate art form.

He dared to be different. And doing so, he challenged the ruling powers again and again.

Many feel that the young Orson delighted in his challenges to power and authority. They point out that Welles' *Citizen Kane,* a story of a ruthless newspaper magnate, is a but thinly disguised biography of the life of William Randolph Hearst, owner of the Hearst newspapers and a powerful figure in Hollywood. However, many, including myself, believe that Orson's primary concern has always been to tell dramatic and compelling tragedies, not to make waves. Unfortunately Welles' artistic triumphs, replete with his innovations and bearing the signature of his perfectionism, have never been the

Orson Welles and Ruth Warrick get married in Citizen Kane, *a film that revolutionized the industry.*

box-office successes studios prefer. Welles cared more about enlarging the scope of the film art than about commerciality; consequently, Orson too often has been denied the financing necessary to make his type of film.

I first met Orson Welles when he arrived at Universal Studios to be fitted for costuming for *Man in the Shadow* (1957), which I was producing. Welles, as so often is the case, plays the film's heavy. Immediately, he began making suggestions, valuable ones concerning wardrobe, makeup, and so forth. Soon he was deeply involved in the script, improving and deepening his role as well as those of the other actors. Knowing him only by his enormous reputation, I was pleasantly surprised that he would readily accept my rejections of his ideas or my changes in something he presented to me — *if* I could back up my decisions with sound dramatic reasons.

Since this was just after his return from his long European stay, a sort of self-imposed exile from Hollywood, I found Welles wanting to try his hand at taking one of Universal's story properties and making a film in the Orson Welles manner. Since my experience with Orson on our first film had turned out well, I kept an eye out for something suitable to his vast talents as a director, writer, and actor. Eventually the book *Badge of Evil* was assigned to me. A first-draft screenplay had already been written, so Orson took that and the book to read. When he developed a satisfactory approach to rewriting the script, I got Universal to give us the go-ahead.

What a joy it was to work with this incredible talent! We plunged into the script, then into casting and so on. Whenever his exuberant daring went over the edge, I was always able to reason with him. There were no arguments.

Once, when the script had to be shaped to a proper length, I suggested a scene be cut, although, Orson, as I told him, had done a very good job of writing it. Orson asked why I selected that particular scene for deletion. I answered that it might cause the leather-jacket crowd to get up and go out for popcorn. And the leather-jackets sometimes make the difference between a hit and a miss. At this point in his career, Orson evidently wanted a commercial success as much as an artistic one, perhaps to reestablish himself on the Hollywood scene. He agreed to cut the scene, without further discussion.

With Jeff Chandler in Man in the Shadow.

In *Touch of Evil* (1958), which was the new title, Orson was again the great actor, but he deliberately played his role in sloppy clothes, looking as unattractive as possible. He even had Marlene Dietrich, who, he made sure, looked magnificent, say to him, ''You're a mess.'' And, as a corrupt cop, Welles had cast himself as usual in a most unsympathetic role. He was content letting Charlton Heston be the romantic lead.

As a filmmaker, Welles' appeal always has been primarily to the most intellectual part of the motion picture audience; his preoccupation, for instance, with classical tragedy in its various forms has denied him some of the less literate segments of the audience. Although most of his critics have deep admiration for Welles, they often claim that his story lines are confusing, or that his dialogue sometimes takes indirect courses. But Welles knows what he's doing.

Welles is highly expert in every facet of movie production from editing to cinematography. In *Touch of Evil,* he had cameraman Russell Metty mount a camera on Charlton Heston's car and rigged it so that, while driving down the street, Heston could actually operate the camera focused on himself. Most directors would have been satisfied to have had an immobile car stationed in front of a process screen that had a (fake) background rolling by. And for the stunning eight-minute opening sequence, Welles had camera operator Phil Lathrop guide the camera into twenty-three camera positions, as walls were pulled back and forth and the actors performed uninterruptedly. Students of film continue to rave about this accomplishment.

Orson is a most complex personality, a genius who, everyone agrees, helped change the face of modern motion pictures. But the battles to achieve his successes have taken their toll. For instance, his later films have suffered, in the main, because he cannot obtain proper financing. And even the great Orson Welles cannot do it without money.

With Paul Scofield in A Man for All Seasons.

If there has been a lack of interest in Welles the actor over the last two decades, perhaps it is because producers have failed to offer him heroic parts through which he can get an audience's sympathy. Or perhaps it is Orson himself who, in his later years in particular, has no interest in arousing an audience's sympathy; if Orson has denied himself ''appealing'' romantic parts, it is because of his unwillingness to sacrifice his artistic integrity in order to become a crowd-pleaser.

Welles carefully selected his apparel for Touch of Evil.

With real-life wife Rita Hayworth in spectacular multiple-mirror sequence from the Welles-directed The Lady from Shanghai.

ROBERT MITCHUM: AGAINST THE GRAIN

ROGER EBERT

ROBERT MITCHUM inspires response. By "response," I don't mean recognition; there are probably dozens of celebrities the public recognizes more readily. But people respond to Mitchum: Taxi drivers hang out of their cab windows, people at lunch counters abandon their tuna sandwiches, and once in his Los Angeles office building, when Mitchum found himself in an elevator with a group of secretaries, there was such electricity in the air that he apparently felt the need to relieve it by saying, "I can't help noticing that you're all admiring my tie."

But the secretaries weren't reacting to his tie — they were reacting to the Mitchum aura of a totally self-assured man who, quite frankly, doesn't give a damn. People tend to be intrigued by someone who simultaneously attracts their attention and is not even the slightest bit concerned about it. Maybe audiences sense the same thing on the screen: Many actors do really *act*, reaching for a moment, for an effect. Mitchum, in the same scenes, will seem to do little more than exist. And yet audiences are looking at Mitchum.

He is, in fact, a consummate actor, no matter how unconcerned he may appear. He has what many of the great thirties' and forties' actors who are today's cult heroes had: a capacity to retain and even expand their dignity, their image, their self-possession, even in the midst of the worst possible material. As was the case with Humphrey Bogart, you see Mitchum in bad movies, but you can never spot him being bad, or ill at ease, or seeming to wonder how in the hell he got into the movie. His indifference to the situation (if that's what it is) allows him to stand aside from his inferior work, and to rise to the occasions of his best work.

Although you can't "see" Mitchum acting at many moments in any given film, the range of his various performances is astonishing. He can be tough, gentle, heroic, indifferent; Irish, English, Australian, Mexican; a big-city private eye, a two-bit hood. Each performance is done with such quiet assurance, with such an apparent knowledge on his part about why he's in the film and where his character stands, that the acting is invisible, just as John Ford said film editing should be.

"I've gotten grooved into making movies, and why not? It's too late for anything else."
— Mitchum to R. E.

ROGER EBERT *is the Pulitzer Prize-winning film critic of the Chicago* Sun-Times, *and has written often for numerous publications, including* US, The New York Times, *and* Esquire. *He wrote the screenplay for* Beyond the Valley of the Dolls.

More subdued than usual, with Jane Russell in Josef von Sternberg's Macao.

A couple of years ago, at Chicago's historic Biograph Theater, they were revving up for a summer of revivals, which would, of course, include a Bogart festival. Over a beer with the theater manager, I quietly demurred. The Bogart classics remain Bogart classics and always will, I said, but what about a Robert Mitchum film festival? The manager was at first astonished, then intrigued. He confessed he had always liked Mitchum . . . but was there an audience for a Mitchum festival? Did young people give a damn about him?

Apparently they did; the Robert Mitchum festival set a theater box-office record. The Mitchum films shown were some of his best, but my hunch is that the films themselves were not what the audiences were reacting to. Mitchum has made a lot of very good films, but he has not yet, in my opinion, made an absolute masterpiece.

He has not made his *Maltese Falcon*, even if *Farewell, My Lovely* (1975) contains a performance (as Philip Marlowe) as arresting, original, and haunting as anything Bogart ever did.

No, the audience wasn't there for the films (although they cheered *The Night of the Hunter* [1955] and seemed to know scenes from *Thunder Road* [1958] by heart). They were there for Mitchum — for the aura. For a big guy with sleepy eyes and a vast disdain for the ordinary. For an actor too intelligent to take the business seriously, someone who doesn't care enough to wait for the perfect film to come his way.

The people who've seen him in the movies somehow feel as if they know him. I felt that way the first time I met him. It was on the Dingle Peninsula in Ireland; he was in a pub, sitting in front of a fire, half-asleep, eyes at

With Jane Greer in The Big Steal.

half-mast, listening to a record of Marty Robbins' "El Paso." He was clearly not in the mood for an interview, and I hadn't yet learned the two basic rules about interviewing Mitchum. Rule One: Ask an interview-type question, and he'll grow terminally bored. Rule Two: Let Mitchum talk, and what comes out will be a wondrous tapestry of anecdote, insight, autobiography, fantasy, lies, and, principally, his own brand of truth.

I opened with an obvious question: How was he coming along with his Irish accent for *Ryan's Daughter* (1970)?

"I sit here weeping and practicing it," he said. "On *Secret Ceremony* [1968], they sat around discussing who they could get with the right accent. Finally Elizabeth Taylor suggested me, and Joseph Losey, the director, said fine, because they didn't want an Englishman, you know, whose English was so English it would bring Elizabeth into relief. So Losey called me in Mexico and asked if I could do an English accent. 'Sure. What do you want? North Country? Lancashire? Cockney?' 'Sort of an indifferent accent,' he said. Later I read a review asking what in hell Mitchum was trying to do if he thinks that's an English accent.

"They should write the director's directions alongside the film so you know who misled the poor dumb actor . . . but who gives a damn? I'm not concerned. I must be good at my job. They wouldn't haul me around the world at these prices if I weren't. . . . I remember when TV first came in, the movie stars were biting their fingernails and wailing, afraid it would diminish their value. In my case it didn't at all. The people watched my old films and saw that they displayed a versatility in my acting that each one individually did not."

With Kirk Douglas in Jacques Tourneur's Out of the Past, *a classic of the* film noir.

Susan Hayward holds her ground in The Lusty Men.

That's almost as close as he'll come to talking about his craft, but in a few words, it is very perceptive. David Thomson, in his invaluable book of essays, *A Biographical Dictionary of Film*, asks, "How can I offer this hunk as one of the best actors in the movies?" Because of, Thomson says in answering the question, "The ambiguity in Mitchum's work, the idea of a man thinking and feeling beneath a calm exterior so that there is no need to put 'acting' on the surface." And then Thomson makes this flat statement about Mitchum, which will be astonishing to some but was not to me: "Since the war, no one has made more first-class films, in so many different moods."

That will become more apparent, I believe, as Mitchum's best work is separated from his routine films and, indeed, from the vast disposable mass of most films of the last thirty years. The first Robert Mitchum film festival has not, so far as I know, been followed by another one anywhere, but it will be. The great film actors (whether you call them cult actors, or simply grand masters of the craft) do not always speak most directly to the audiences who saw them the first time around; it took the generation after Bogart died to properly set him apart from the stars who were his contemporaries and make him in his own right an object of respect, curiosity, and admiration. It's my belief that we are right on the edge of seeing that happen to Robert Mitchum.

As Philip Marlowe in Farewell, My Lovely.

MARLON BRANDO: METHOD AND MADNESS

BRUCE BERMAN

Asked if he showered or bathed, the young Brando replied, "I spit in the sky and run under it."

UNPREDICTABLE OR just an arrogant outsider? No one knows for sure. All we do know is that every few years at just about the time you're wondering where he's disappeared to — his Hollywood

BRUCE BERMAN *is a filmmaker and critic who has been published in* Millimeter, Take One, Film Comment, Film Library Quarterly, *and* The Columbia Journalism Review, *among others. He teaches film at C.C.N.Y. and Columbia University.*

mansion, his South Sea island retreat, an Indian reservation — he resurfaces to unnerve audiences with a ready mix of artistry and idiosyncrasy.

Even after a thirty-year/thirty-film career checkered by as many self-indulgences as hard-won kudos, he remains the "actor's actor." A successful mélange of myth, macho, and sheer talent, the guy has endured surprisingly well.

Schooled in the "method acting" of Lee Strasberg and Stella Adler, Brando made an explosive entrance

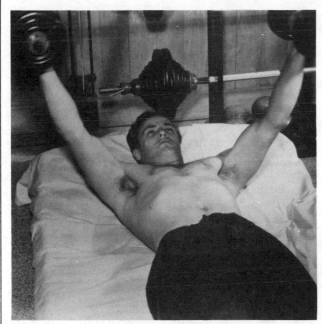

As a paraplegic in debut film, The Men.

onto the New York stage in the 1940s. In the fifties, he riveted moviegoers with his screen creations of Stanley Kowalski in *A Streetcar Named Desire* (1951), a role he had originated on Broadway in 1947 at age twenty-three, and of Terry Malloy, the punch-drunk union lackey in *On the Waterfront* (1954). But the seamy sixties brought unforetold obstacles.

Changes in the cultural climate, coupled with a series of puffed-up parts in mediocre films, rendered him something of an anachronism. Less out of step with the turbulent times than overwhelmed by them, Brando's infamous individuality was all but swallowed up by a maelstrom (or, perhaps, male-storm) of "new" nonconformity.

The heroic individualism that had been his personal watermark was overshadowed by the social complexities ignited by the Beatles, drugs, and Vietnam. The young Brando who "coulda been a contendah," the commanding figure of *The Wild One* (1953), which had been banned in England for fear it would incite gangs to riot, was supplanted by more "timely" outsiders. Newer rebels like Peter Fonda and Jack Nicholson were inspiring cults of their own and offering audiences something the enfant terrible of the fifties could no longer do.

Not even Charles Chaplin, who cast Brando as an American diplomat in his farce *A Countess from Hong Kong* (1967), could resurrect him. Brando, it was thought by many, was aging with something less than grace. But he defied the odds, and with *The Godfather* (1972) and *Last Tango in Paris* (1972), he established himself as the venerable star of the seventies.

From his first feature *The Men* (1950) — released two years after fellow method actor Montgomery Clift's screen debut — to *Apocalypse Now* (1979), in which he plays a deranged officer, Brando has orchestrated a career built on playing characters possessing conflicting characteristics. Magnetic even when unappealing as a rapist, a gang member, or a crime boss, Brando offers qualities which make his characters hard to reject.

Hard-riding Johnny of *The Wild One* and Don Corleone of *The Godfather* are familiar Brando characters. Both are members of organizations (outside traditional society's mainstream), yet both are so vehement in their individualism that they even differ from their own group of outsiders. Wild Johnny wants a "square chick," just as the Don, warlord that he is, refuses (ostensibly on "moral" grounds) to involve his people with "bad" crime (i.e., hard drugs). Both characters are vague reflections of each other.

Although script selection has had something to do with his success, only a screen artist with Brando's charm, tenderness, intelligence, and, above all, *potential* for violence can pull off the performances he does. Brando, along with Jack Nicholson, Robert De Niro, and maybe one or two others, has that rare gift which enables him to make the screen vibrate with danger. Strangely, it is not so much the Brando flare-ups that are so remarkable; it's those tense lulls before the inevitable eruptions.

With Kim Hunter in A Streetcar Named Desire.

JAZZED-UP "BEATS"
ON A BUST-UP BINGE!

MARLON
BRANDO
IS THE ONLY MAN
WHO CAN PLAY
The
WILD
ONE

"C'mon, baby,
let's have
a ball!"

HOT FEELINGS HIT
TERRIFYING HEIGHTS
IN A STORY THAT
REALLY BOILS OVER!

Brando's rebellious image was cultivated early.

A look at Brando's oeuvre reveals several tendencies, including a propensity for films in which he plays someone connected with but alienated from an established order: the disillusioned Nazi officer in *The Young Lions* (1958) and the homosexual major in *Reflections in a Golden Eye* (1967) are two examples. Oddly, Brando has played (reluctant) military or paramilitary figures on no fewer than two dozen occasions. Given a career that spans some thirty movies, this is no coincidence. Brando is also partial to actor-oriented directors such as Elia Kazan and Arthur Penn, an indulgence which frequently renders the films in which he appears only partially realized in lieu of his lone star performance.

Even Brando's most ardent supporters would not argue with the fact that he has squandered his skills on several occasions and has at times taken part in unredeemable pictures. Despite his skill and boldness as an actor, he tends to take refuge, every so often, in marginally inspired material handled by people with a modicum of vision. Still he's proved himself capable of elevating junk to respectable heights, namely, movies like *Julius Caesar* (1953), *Desirée* (1954) — where as one critic aptly put it, ''he takes on Napoleon less tack-

ling the role than avoiding ridicule'' — and, arguably, *Mutiny on the Bounty* (1962).

However, there have been a number of times when Brando has contributed with discretion to fully realized productions — although these tend to be his least recognized films. For instance, there is *One-Eyed Jacks* (1961), the western he directed as well as starred in, a perversely realized project. *The Chase* (1966) is another sleeper. Modulated but by no means overshadowed by the extraordinary cast (which includes Jane Fonda, Robert Redford, and Robert Duvall), Brando plays a contemporary sheriff who attempts to bring order to a lawless town. The finale, which finds a battered Brando knee-deep in water, protecting a young fugitive (Redford), is as brilliant as it is ironic.

Similarly, in *The Night of the Following Day* (1969) Brando delivers a tour de force performance as an androgynous chauffeur entangled in a kidnap plot of which he wants no part. Blond Brando in a black muscle T-shirt transforms decadence into poetry. Nowhere is his stuttering, twitching, and shouting as meaningful, yet nowhere is his method so mad.

Perhaps Brando's master performance is in the largely-unseen *Burn!* (1970), a brilliant depiction of imperialism in theory and practice directed by Gillo Pontecorvo of *The Battle of Algiers* fame. Brando is an intellectual political mercenary who leads an island's natives in a successful revolution against Portugal and then turns around and crushes the victorious rebels so England can assume control of the island (without having gone to war with Portugal). It is the most interesting character of Brando's career — a hero for half the film, a ruthless double-dealer in the second half — and Brando's commitment to his role and the political nature of the film is

With Eva Marie Saint in On the Waterfront.

As Don Corleone in The Godfather. *With Al Pacino (L) and James Caan.*

apparent. Unfortunately, *Burn!* was considered too radical, too pointed, to receive wide American distribution.

Brando has taken on a number of potentially deleterious roles — the despicable character in *Burn!*, the Don in *The Godfather*, the aging Romeo in *Last Tango in Paris*, to name just three, that many a Hollywood

As a very peculiar villain in The Missouri Breaks.

On the set of Burn!, *his most political film.*

WHILE BRANDO HAS often made expedient use of the media, there are occasions when the sincerity of his commitment to meaningful change cannot be challenged. Despite the superficial controversy, the Sacheen Littlefeather episode at the 1973 Oscar presentations probably did his enigmatic image more good than harm; it was not a meaningless gesture. Brando has been consistent in his political causes since early in his career.

In 1948 he quit his role (at $300 a week) in Shaw's *Candida* to work at one tenth the salary in *A Flag Is Born*, Ben Hecht's play about the founding of a Jewish homeland. Throughout the 1950s Brando was an advocate of civil rights reform and of the elimination of the death penalty and has lobbied personally for changes in these areas. In recent years he has devoted much time and money in working to right many of the wrongs committed by the American government at the expense of the Indian. Of a less controversial nature, Brando has reputedly donated millions of dollars to maintain the ecological integrity of his beloved Tahiti.

— B. B.

heavyweight would not touch with a ten-foot pole. No doubt such films have furthered his personal interests; they have entertained audiences while challenging "the system" or particular social conventions, despite their exotic contexts. His most meaningful characters of late are not heroes in the movie sense of the word; in fact they are scoundrels who meet their deserved fate. (The three characters mentioned above do not last to the ends of their movies.) But in playing such men, Brando successfully reveals to us a great deal about the dubious ideals to which many of us mistakenly aspire.

PAUL NEWMAN: BLUE-EYED MAVERICK

PAT McGILLIGAN

O F ALL THE STARS to emerge from the method school of acting — the rebel heroes Marlon Brando, James Dean, and, later, Warren Beatty — Paul Newman has had the most confounding and paradoxical career. He is a complicated figure, a loner, a maverick, an outspoken liberal who involved himself in politics as early as the 1956 Adlai Stevenson campaign. He abjures Hollywood, works independently whenever possible, and lives a quiet family life in Connecticut. His matinee-idol features (aqueous blue eyes and sensual mouth) are but a mask. Although an Adonis, he favors "character" roles (growing a beard, slinging an accent, applying nervous mannerisms) to playing classic leading men as he did so often in his early work. But his taste is not unassailable, and among his credits are an appalling number of mediocre — or at best insipid, uninspired — vehicles. It is a curious, puzzling list.

In roughly twenty-five years, Newman has acted in nearly forty movies, refining his image as the heel-hero, a golden boy with the devil's own grin. Although he was a surrogate for James Dean in *Somebody Up There Likes Me* (1956; before his fatal car crash, Dean was set to star) and Brando (Newman also did a spate of Tennessee Williams' plays on film), Newman's career lacks their adventure and cunning. He has made minor movies with major directors: Arthur Penn in his debut, *The Left-Handed Gun* (1958); Leo McCarey, in his dotage; Alfred Hitchcock, with whom he clashed over the "method" approach; John Huston; and Otto Preminger in his lavish *Exodus* (1960). And major movies with less audacious directors: Jack Smight, Richard Brooks, Martin Ritt, Stuart Rosenberg, and George Roy Hill. But there are no enduring masterworks — although a case can be made for *Hud* (1963), *The Hustler* (1961), or the Tennessee

Williams adaptations. The soft glamour of his celebrity has eclipsed the very "seriousness" of his work, and undermined his reputation.

A native of Shaker Heights, Ohio, Newman went on to Yale School of Drama and from there to TV and Broadway and study with Elia Kazan and Lee Strasberg. A featured role in William Inge's *Picnic* led to a fortuitous meeting with an understudy named Joanne Woodward (Newman had already been married once), and a seven-year Hollywood contract with Warner Brothers. His early movies are not especially auspicious: *The Silver Chalice* (1954), *The Helen Morgan Story* (1957), and *Until They Sail* (1957). Dissatisfied and restless, Newman occasionally retreated to the stage, and eventually bought out his contract with Warner to become a free agent.

But things never quite jelled — at least not in the way his deepest admirers had hoped. His sixties' titles

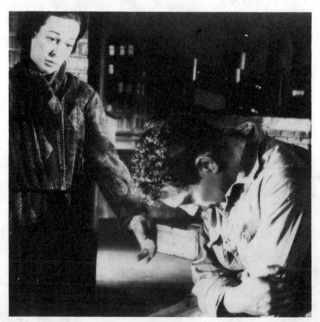

As Rocky Graziano, he was unafraid to show emotion in Somebody Up There Likes Me. *With Eileen Heckart.*

(Opposite) As Butch Cassidy.

PAT McGILLIGAN *is the author of books on James Cagney and Ginger Rogers, and has written on film for such magazines as* American Film, Film Comment, *and* The Velvet Light Trap. *He is currently writing an authorized biography of convicted antiwar bomber Karl Armstrong.*

With Elizabeth Taylor in Cat on a Hot Tin Roof.

comprise a modest grab bag. There were cameo appearances in Hemingway's *Adventures of a Young Man* (1962) and *What a Way to Go!* (1964); Irving Wallace and Romain Gary adaptations, and romantic vehicles opposite his wife, Joanne Woodward. There were also the four *H* pictures — *The Hustler, Hud, Harper* (1966), and *Hombre* (1967). They were among his most successful. (The *H* became a good luck omen. In fact, Newman reportedly asked for an *H* title for Ross MacDonald's *Moving Target*, and thus the detective, Lew Archer, became Harper.) Paul Newman's finest characterizations are as the pool hustler Eddie Felson and

Hud — two loners, two losers; the former obsessed by a victory over Minnesota Fats, the latter obsessed by women and himself. Released within two years of each other, directed by Robert Rossen and Martin Ritt respectively, *The Hustler* and *Hud* augured handsomely for Newman's future. Sadly, the rest of the 1960s was unexciting for the actor by comparison.

Yet Newman is resilient; he capped the sixties with his role as outlaw Butch Cassidy in George Roy Hill's *Butch Cassidy and the Sundance Kid* (1969) — one of his biggest hits. Ironically, the actor was teamed with another maverick-loner, Robert Redford, and together they launched a ''buddy-buddy'' wave in motion pictures that, practically overnight, swept the industry.

Butch Cassidy — a smart, comic melodrama — ushered in the movies of the seventies, in which Newman's pictures have gotten more off-beat, more iconoclastic. Mellowed, he has gravitated to roles as appealing bunko artists and has increasingly eschewed the harsher, disturbed image of his earlier work. Meanwhile, he has taken on the assurance of a leading man, appearing in an eccentric body of material: *WUSA* (1970), an anti-fascist parable about a right-wing New Orleans radio station; the flaky *The Life and Times of Judge Roy Bean* (1972) and the stark mystery *The Mackintosh Man* (1973), both directed by veteran John Huston; the broadly humorous *The Sting* (1973), in which Newman was reteamed with Redford and director Hill, resulting in one of the top-grossing films of all time; and the bewigged Buffalo Bill Cody of director Robert Altman's uneven *Buffalo Bill and the Indians* (1976). (The role of Buffalo Bill is kindred to Newman's portrayal of Billy the Kid in *The Left-Handed Gun*, and his most challenging, satisfying part in years. Newman himself had pursued the project since 1969 and, interestingly, George Roy Hill was initially set to direct.) This period of graceful aging has

A dramatic triumph, The Hustler.

Fighting with Patricia Neal in Hud.

One of Newman's most memorable roles of the sixties was as a rebellious prisoner in Cool Hand Luke.

In Robert Altman's Buffalo Bill and the Indians.

made for Newman's most imaginative sequence of pictures, marred only by stupid potboilers like *The Drowning Pool* (1975). His judgment, in such cases, can be disastrous.

AT THE CROSSROADS

ULTIMATELY, AND IRONICALLY, it may be Paul Newman's directing that proves the most creative, the most stable fascination of his life. Actually, the first thing he directed was a short in 1961, a twenty-eight-minute film called *On the Harmfulness of Tobacco*, based on the Chekhov playlet. In 1968, he was convinced by his wife to direct her in *Rachel, Rachel,* and it was a compelling success, attracting numerous awards. *Sometimes a Great Notion* (1971), if too ambivalent in its philosophy, at least confirmed Newman's visual flair and sensitive handling of actors. (Newman fired the original director and took over early in the shooting.) *The Effect of Gamma Rays on Man-in-the-Moon Marigolds* (1972) was gloomy but intelligent; like *Rachel, Rachel,* it starred Joanne Woodward. There has been nothing since then, which is unfortunate, because his development as a director has been encouraging, as well as a tonic and a therapy for Newman the actor. It puts the classic face behind the camera, unseen, but allows a greater vent for the expression of his personality.

— P. M.

Through it all, Newman has evolved into one of America's favorite movie stars, reputedly one of the most "bankable" people in Hollywood. He pops up in the celebrity columns; he is behind all the right causes. But beneath the merchandised image, the respectable home life, the earnest disciplined actor, is the melancholy drinker, the private doubter, the complicated actor whose own insecurities seem mirrored in the driven characters he is best known for portraying.

Like them, he sometimes seems like the perfect outsider, raging one instant and indifferent the next, alienated by the world and alienated by himself.

With Robert Redford in The Sting, *1977's Best Picture.*

SHIRLEY MacLAINE: EARLY REBEL

BILL CONDON

Pretty, funny, and tender in Irma La Douce.

SHE WAS FIRST KNOWN as the "kook." Hollywood has always been eager to label its misfits, to make them palatable, and the case of Shirley MacLaine is no exception. Since the beginning, she certainly has always been a misfit. She has lived apart, not only from the movie community, but also from her husband. She became, before long, the only female member-in-good-standing of the fast-living Rat Pack, with its peculiar mix of show business, politics, and underworld. (It is interesting to note that MacLaine, who was to become one of the leaders of the Hollywood political movement in the late sixties, witnessed the first post-McCarthy normalization of relations between Hollywood and Washington, which the Rat Pack, with its ties to the Kennedy White House, represented.) She would earn a reputation as being sexually daring (researching prostitution firsthand for her role of the prostitute in *Irma la Douce,* 1963), socially brazen (punching a columnist), and altogether rootless (always making some journey).

But the Hollywood community's only translation of MacLaine's personality was her incarnation as kook. Much of this was simply due to the way she looks. In repose, MacLaine might be considered beautiful, with her open, clean features, extravagantly curvilinear body, long and elegant limbs. But in motion, everything changes. When she walks, her arms seem to reach for the ground, aided in the attempt by a head that appears to find its most comfortable niche somewhere between her shoulder blades in a perpetual shrug. And her face is one of the plastic wonders of movie comedy: Who would suspect that such a delicate mouth could ever open so wide in surprise, that the otherwise sharp chin could disappear so quickly into a wrinkled mass of chagrin, that the once-clear eyes could suddenly twinkle so elusively?

This is the secret of MacLaine's comedy — beneath the beauty, there is chaos, always threatening to take

BILL CONDON *works for Avco Embassy Pictures in their marketing division.*

With Michael Caine (L) and Herbert Lom in Gambit.

over; she even seems to suggest that the beauty is dishonest, a social convention, a pose, and that genuine emotion is unwieldy, cumbersome, even unattractive. (The only film that took explicit advantage of this was *Gambit* [1966], in which MacLaine played a prostitute hired to pose as a beautiful Eurasian princess; the comedy of the situation sprang from her inability to remain as stone-faced as the princess was supposed to be.)

During the time (1958–1963) that MacLaine's film career was at its height, there were three basic variations on Shirley-as-kook. The first, and by far the least successful, offered up MacLaine as a "serious," realistic actress. Her kookiness in these films was shown in terms of actual sickness — suicidal lesbian in *The Children's Hour* (1962), repressed spinster in *Two Loves* (1961), eccentric waif in *Two for the Seesaw* (1962).

The second variation presented MacLaine as light comedienne, the gamine recently graduated from the chorus. It was in these films — most notably, *All in a Night's Work* (1961), *My Geisha* (1962), *Ask Any Girl* (1959) — that she was most purely a sex object.

But it was in the third variation that the MacLaine character took on full shape. Adding an undertone of pathos to her sexuality, she became the kindhearted tramp, the noble slob, the hooker with a heart of gold. Her relationship to men was altered: Although almost always a too-easy sexual mark, there was something in her "debasement" that made her comfortable, an equal, a buddy (most clearly in *Some Came Running* [1959] and *The Apartment* [1960]).

Onscreen, MacLaine repeated this performance often during the sixties; offscreen, her roles continued to

Fine partner to Jack Lemmon in The Apartment.

Big "Adam and Eve" production number in Can-Can.

vary. This kind of professional schizophrenia, common to many actors in that decade, would prove to be her temporary undoing. On the one hand, the flippancy of the early sixties was rejected — the Rat Pack, bereft of its political glow after the death of John Kennedy, was scuttled — as MacLaine moved on to more serious commitment, such as protesting Caryl Chessman's execution, marching for civil rights, speaking out against the Vietnam War. But in the movies, she was still a cartoon creation, a pop item that began to seem irrelevant, obsolete, even irresponsible. As it was for the nation as a whole, 1969 was a watershed year for Shirley MacLaine — the year of *Sweet Charity.*

Charity was meant to be the high point of Mac-

Sweet Charity. One of her many hookers with a heart of gold, with Ricardo Montalban.

Laine's career, the single role that would provide the clear iconographic identification she had lacked to that point. Once again, MacLaine plays a kook, but her hair is a brighter shade of red than ever before, and her skin is pasty white; the character is uneducated, aging, and alone, with a body that won't support her much longer. A very grim musical, but, true to its roots (Fellini's *Nights of Cabiria,* by way of Broadway), it wore a smile. Charity Hope Valentine was every bit as alienated as Ratso Rizzo in the year's *Midnight Cowboy,* but audiences wanted their misery straight up, and *Charity* almost put its studio, and its star, out of business. This is unfortunate, for in many ways it remains MacLaine's best performance.

MacLaine with *Charity* was able to close the book on the character with whom she had been so identified. Two years later came *Desperate Characters* (1971) — the very difference in titles speaks volumes — and soon after, *The Possession of Joel Delaney* (1972). These were properties that MacLaine developed herself, and her two roles are remarkably similar. In both films she plays upper-middle-class New Yorkers in their forties, who find themselves in a suddenly hostile environment. They have lost the values they might once have used to deal with the hostility. They are pampered, desensitized women who are responsible for their own alienation from society and men. At the conclusion neither woman has really learned anything — both face a life of continued victimization. (MacLaine brought a certain masochism to these parts.) There was much of interest to discover in her new incarnation. (For one thing, *Joel Delaney* was the first time in her entire career that she played a

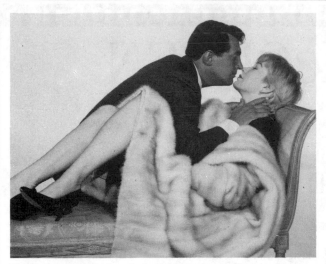

Dean Martin and short-haired MacLaine in Career.

Robert Mitchum and tall-haired MacLaine in What a Way to Go!

mother.) But these performances are marred by a familiar feature of star acting of the period: a relentless lack of kinship between actor and role. In MacLaine's case this resulted from an unwillingness on her part to invest these characters with any of the charm, humor, or general liveliness that had distinguished the best of her previous work. Yet it is understandable that she did not want to compromise her new found seriousness, and as it turned out, these films gave her the dramatic weight and presence she needed for *The Turning Point* (1977).

In *The Turning Point,* MacLaine once again played a character for whom she had little personal sympathy, a woman who had for twenty years quietly mourned the career she had given up for marriage. In fact, the character's original dilemma was so foreign to MacLaine — after all, MacLaine had both a marriage and a successful career — that she lobbied to have the script changed. But, having decided to play the part, she lost herself inside it, making palpable not only the bitter wife but also the loving, humorous mother.

A good example of her achievement is the scene in which she discovers that her daughter has lost her virginity. The conflicting emotions that MacLaine is able to convey, the combination of shock, envy, and delight with which she greets the news, the subtle comic timing that makes us smile through our sympathy for the character's confusion, all display a range as wide and developed as that of any actress working today. In many ways, *The Turning Point* presents the first happy combination of the early MacLaine character, winking and smiling through her tears, and the new, sober and reflective MacLaine.

The film that brought MacLaine her best critical notices.

Rehearsing with Anne Bancroft for The Turning Point.

STEVE McQUEEN: POWER DRIVE

HOWARD KOCH

EVEN BEFORE he'd actually achieved it, Steve McQueen saw himself as a superstar, bankable in his own right. His task was to convince the industry and the public that this is where he belonged. No doubt it would have happened anyway — given his ability and his offbeat, appealing personality — but Steve was anxious to hasten the process. It seemed to me that some of his more flamboyant actions were deliberately

Despite lack of good films, he rates with Redford at top of salary bracket.

designed to gain the kind of publicity that would help to build his star image.

My experience with Steve McQueen came at the time, in the early sixties, when his career was on the rise but had not yet fully blossomed. (He had made a name for himself in a successful television series, *Wanted: Dead or Alive,* but he had not yet starred in a major film.) McQueen was at his turning point; his career could go up or down.

Arthur Hornblow, a well-established producer, asked me to write a screenplay based on the popular John Hersey novel *The War Lover,* which is about American fliers stationed in England during World War II. The picture (released in 1963) was to be shot at British studios and locations, and Hornblow wanted McQueen for the lead. McQueen was interested; yet, in keeping with his not-yet-established-but-assumed star status, he made certain conditions. One was a demand (he was not lacking in self-confidence) that he meet and confer with me, the writer, before signing a contract.

At the time, McQueen was making *Hell Is for Heroes* (1962), a small-budget war film, on location in the Sacramento Valley in northern California. My son and his wife wanted to drive up with me to watch some of the shooting and, of course, to meet Steve McQueen. It was midsummer and the temperature was around 110. The actors, wearing heavy army clothes, were trying to act as though they were in cool Normandy, and the result was torture and flaring tempers.

We were Steve's guests at dinner that evening. He was the soul of charm. We talked in general terms about

HOWARD KOCH *received an Academy Award for his screenplay of* Casablanca *and was nominated for* Sergeant York. *Among his other credits are* The Sea Hawk, The Letter, Mission to Moscow, No Sad Songs for Me, Three Strangers, Letter from an Unknown Woman, Loss of Innocence, *and* The Fox. *He wrote radio plays for* Mercury Theatre on the Air, *including* "The War of the Worlds."

With Robert Wagner in The War Lover, *scripted by Howard Koch.*

The War Lover, but not in a serious enough way for me to justify the trip. At any rate Steve seemed satisfied and assured me he would sign the contract and do the picture.

The next day we watched the shooting out on the parched field. The actors did their best to cope with the trying conditions, but progress was slow in getting the scene the way the director — and Steve — wanted it. Suddenly three men appeared, studio employees sent by the executive producer of the company financing the picture. The production was going way over budget, a cardinal sin in the movie world, and these men had orders to seize the cameras. Whatever remained to be photographed would be done back at the studio — under the watchful eye of the producer.

It was then I saw the side of Steve's personality that brooks no interference with whatever he wants to do, whether it is to drive his car at high speed through city streets or start a fight. He walked over to where the three cameras were clustered twenty feet away. He picked up a stick and drew a circle in the sand around the cameras. Then he faced the three intruders, pointing toward his markings. "Anyone steps over that line gets the shit knocked out of him." The three men decided retreat was the better part of valor, and the company finished the shooting on location.

Later, I joined Arthur Hornblow in London with a first-draft screenplay. For Steve's arrival, his representatives arranged for reporters to meet him at the airport. The English barely knew who he was at this point, but not for long.

Steve was provided with a chauffeur-driven car for his stay in London; however, he quickly dismissed the chauffeur so he could drive himself, at his own speed — which was usually well above the legal limit. He and his family were put up at the Savoy, but before long, the hotel management let it be known to Hornblow that they preferred to have Steve sheltered elsewhere. Among their objections was his habit of driving full speed up to the hotel entrance, then slamming on the brakes, dousing other guests from puddles of London's abundant rainwater. (Arthur was able to move the McQueens to an elegant house in Knightsbridge, where

With the inimitable Tuesday Weld in The Cincinnati Kid.

McQueen has thrived in action films such as Nevada Smith, *in which he tracked down his parents' killers.*

most of our preproduction story conferences took place.)

The insurance policy Columbia took out on Steve to cover the course of shooting contained a provision restricting him from entering automobile races. Despite this restriction, Steve admitted to me that he had entered a race somewhere outside of London. I kept his secret but, of course, the news leaked to the press (as intended). He managed to come in second; no doubt deservedly

With Natalie Wood in Love with the Proper Stranger.

because he is actually an expert and experienced racing car driver. (What he didn't tell me was that a woman came in first.) By this time Steve had established himself, if not yet as a full-fledged star, at least as a celebrity.

From my point of view, I was aware that I would be dealing with an assertive and rebellious personality. One day, working in his apartment, we came into sharp conflict on a change he demanded in the screenplay. After much argument, we managed to work out an acceptable compromise, but I warned Steve that Arthur would have to approve the change. Steve summarily dismissed this reservation.

''To hell with whether he approves or not.''

''But, Steve, he's the producer.''

''So what? He needs me more than I need him.''

As brazen as that sounds, Steve was speaking truth. If a star quits a picture costing several million dollars, the financing is withdrawn and the preproduction money already spent is lost. Arthur and the director, Philip Leacock, took the ultimatum (and the change) with good grace. The film was made.

Despite our differences, I came to like Steve, and by the end of shooting, we were friends. As for *The War Lover* itself, I think it fails to live up to its potential. I hold myself at least partly accountable. Out of my respect for Hersey, I adhered too closely to the novel, which had more characters and situations than could be compressed satisfactorily into a two-hour film. Most of

Mitch Vogel (L), McQueen, and Rupert Crosse were mischievous trio in adaptation of Faulkner's The Reivers, *one of McQueen's better films.*

what interest it holds for audiences is Steve's personality as it is projected on the screen.

What is there about this personality that has lifted

With Dustin Hoffman in Devil's Island saga, Papillon.

McQueen into the superstar category? On a practical level, Steve has been shrewd in his choice of roles, making sure they are suitable for his particular qualities. From what I know of his background, his education came more from the streets of Greenwich Village than from any school. Early in his life he developed a toughness and a calculated determination, first perhaps for survival, later for his professional ambitions. He is not afraid to take risks, such as his car and motorcycle racing. He doesn't need a stunt man — he isn't afraid to do his own stunts. It appears that these "real" qualities in his makeup are sensed by audiences. And the arrogance which motivates some of his actions is mitigated by the charm of that quick half-smile which assures us that, at bottom, he is a "good guy."

NEW DIRECTIONS

RECENTLY I WAS SURPRISED and encouraged for Steve when he took on a project unlike anything he had done in the past — the role of Dr. Stockman in Ibsen's *Enemy of the People* (1978). I never would have thought of casting him as an intellectual idealist. And for this he deserves our respect — for taking on a difficult role, a man who, on behalf of human values, takes on the establishment.

—H. K.

PETER O'TOOLE:
STUDY IN SURVIVAL

TED GERSHUNY

In Otto Preminger's box office disaster Rosebud.

THE IMAGERY WAS UNFORGETTABLE: Peter O'Toole in a white caftan, his delirious followers chanting, *"Aw-rence! Aw-rence!"* At twenty-nine, with only three small parts to his credit, he was at the pinnacle. He had everything.

Today, there is a memory of lavish gifts squandered, a whiff of Barrymore and perdition, credits that read like a casualty list. The headline of a recent interview trumpets, THE WRECK OF PETER O'TOOLE. He bears the image of a ravaged deity.

What happened?

After David Lean's legendary production of *Law-*

TED GERSHUNY *is a director-screenwriter whose films include* Silent Night, Bloody Night. *He is the author of the nonfiction book* Soon To Be A Major Motion Picture.

---

rence of Arabia (1962), O'Toole's parts became a gallery of eccentrics, victims of delusions and obsessions, specialists in large losses: a king who slays his loyal adviser in *Becket* (1964); a general betrayed by twisted sexuality in *The Night of the Generals* (1966); another king, one who conspires against his progeny in *The Lion in Winter* (1968). Not one of these was a sympathetic part.

Throughout these roles, the actor maintained an aristocratic air, even when playing commoners. He was verbal, elegant, aloof. Finally, however, in *The Ruling Class* (1971), he seemed to react to his screen image, and laughed at the very notion of aristocracy. But the laughter was maniacal. Playing a loser, he was too imperious.

The rumors circulated: Drinking. Hell-raising. Failing health. Talent burnt out in a string of mediocre movies. Lawrence the idealist was reduced to an old, mad "gentleman," impotent, dreaming of impossible triumphs.

History was against him, too. In his class at the Royal Academy of Dramatic Arts were Albert Finney, Richard Harris, and Alan Bates. At one time the whole group might have been bankable. Not today. "British" films have disappeared, replaced by international productions in search of world markets. And action is more exportable than dialogue. Heroes outfight and out-cool their foes. But they don't wear costumes or write with feathers. In a world of speeding cars and bullets, O'Toole is displaced.

There is still danger in O'Toole's screen presence, a knife edge of challenge as sharp as Marlon Brando's or Dustin Hoffman's. But O'Toole is mostly dangerous to himself. He faces solitude in *Man Friday* (1975), cowardice in *Lord Jim* (1965), and compulsion in virtually everything.

To an age that worships self-confidence, O'Toole offers chasms of self-doubt, wry humor, mocking absurdity. In the public eye, which sees little beyond headlines, Peter O'Toole is a failure.

However, the man I met and watched for months was something else. I saw him create "Peter O'Toole,"

An instant star after Lawrence of Arabia. *With Anthony Quinn.*

a screen identity, which was partly the figure he wanted to be, partly what circumstances *made* him be — a graceful anachronism, a champion of reason and subtlety in an age of brass.

I was in Corsica in 1974, trailing the production of Otto Preminger's *Rosebud,* gathering material for a book on international filmmaking. Three days earlier, Robert Mitchum had walked off the set, bidding Preminger an angry ''Bon voyage'' and stranding the director with a full crew, sporadic phone service, and no star.

Preminger, fortunately knew Jules Buck, Peter O'Toole's partner. Through Jules, Preminger connected with his new star.

And thus it happened one night that O'Toole came to a town square that resembled a Fellini set. A breeze swayed the trees and blew scraps of paper across the empty plaza as he called to a soundman he knew, ''Robin, hel-*lo!*''

One discovered immediately, his ''otherness.'' American moviegoers cannot hear themselves in that voice. It is too rich, too theatrical, too dramatic. It makes you listen, and listening is work.

The splendor of his physical gifts mark him. Stepping into the light around our café table, he was louder, taller, thinner than the rest of us — a flayed, gangling root of a man, suspended like a puppet from wide, bony shoulders; narrow ankles sticking up from low boots; narrow wrists poking out of his jacket; a profile as sharp and scooped as a garden spade.

His entourage implied royalty. He arrived with his own makeup man, a stand-in/aide, and an English writer who would ''anglicize'' the dialogue of his role. Despite his pomp, he tried to make friends. He joked one morning with the crew about their drinking. Hearing that one

man had been up all night, O'Toole waxed melancholy: ''Ah, them was days, Joxer. Them was days.''

Yet the common touch was *work*. Sometimes you saw the effort. On the second day, O'Toole sagged against the hotel bar, spent, staring into his soft drink and listening politely to the chatter around him. Suddenly he eased off his stool, dead tired. ''It's all so *political,*'' he muttered. ''Keep the director happy. Keep the unit happy. Because in the end it's *you* up there on the screen.'' More and more, as work went on, the effort at sociability took its toll. He frequently lunched alone in his trailer.

Inevitably, his aloofness and superiority began to color his role — a CIA mercenary trying to rescue some hostages. O'Toole played the only rational character in a world of zealots, terrorists, partisans, and petrified victims.

At first, he felt his way through the part, looking overly made up and sounding overly snide. ''He's doing the Scarlet Pimpernel,'' said a grip. But he'd had the script two days before shooting; Preminger called it ''panic acting.''

Gradually, O'Toole started to focus the part. He wore his own raffish old suit (narrow lapels, stovepipe pants) with the lordly touch of a cigarette holder clamped in his mouth. He wore an Irish tweed hat in nearly every scene. ''It gives me comfort,'' said O'Toole with a smile. ''It's my whole performance.''

The character got clearer. As a mother broke down in tears, O'Toole lit up and smoked casually. As a hostage cried, he studied her clinically. He was a hero like a modern Sherlock Holmes — logical, lucid, ice cold, shorn of sentiment and false piety, a consummate ''agent.'' We wondered what was behind this composure. What did this agent feel? What did this *actor* feel?

With Richard Burton in Becket, *one of his many historical dramas.*

"I talked Kate out of retirement for The Lion in Winter. . . . *I knew it needed someone who could stand up and punch me back — and believe me, I can go a few rounds. So I sent it to her. She was in grief over Spencer. They'd both helped me when*

I was a boy. . . .and she called back and said, 'Let's do it before I die, pig.' What a tough dame she is. Always called me pig."
— *O'Toole to T. G.*

We found out in an apartment in Paris as he was handed an envelope addressed "TO THE ALLEGED IRISHMAN, PETER O'TOOLE." A note inside claimed that the movie insulted all national liberation movements, that O'Toole brought shame to the I.R.A., that a bomb would go off at noon.

"It's no joke," said a worried grip.

"Then let's fuck-off out of here!" yelled O'Toole.

Outside, in a swirl of police, fear and anger were reflected in the faces of the Irish crewmen. O'Toole was ashen.

Finally the true story emerged. The letter was left as a "joke" by the critic Kenneth Tynan. O'Toole disappeared with two crewmen.

"All right . . . all over," he later crooned. His knuckles were raw from the beating he and the others had given Tynan.

O'Toole's anger never showed on screen. All I know is that the fires were banked. Within an hour he'd resumed playing the civilized, rational hero.

In the last scene of the film (later cut) the agent tips his hat, turns from the whole bloody business, and shuffles into a convenient sunset — a thoughtful man who's had enough of lunacy.

To his public, which wanted to be swept away emotionally, O'Toole offered a man of reason. The screen image, perhaps, suggested the man he might want to be, an idealized vision of himself. With his emotions in check, he was opting for a better chance at survival.

With Charlotte Rampling in unreleased Foxtrot, *a new low.*

JANE FONDA: ACTRESS WITH A MESSAGE

JEFF COREY

IT HAS NOT BEEN Jane Fonda's wont to live in the insulated atmosphere of stardom, immersing herself in shop talk. Her high recognition factor notwithstanding, she rarely withdraws to the ivory tower. She has placed herself squarely where the action is, even in the most troubled and dangerous times. Although subject to wicked surveillances, frame-ups, cruel and arbitrary court action, she has held her ground like a winter soldier.

It seems evident that the firmness of her social outlook has shaped the actress she has become. Since her giddy bride in *Barefoot in the Park* (1967) through *They Shoot Horses, Don't They?* (1969), *Klute* (1971), *Julia* (1977), and *Coming Home* (1978), she has probed characters relative to the film's implicit social framework. Almost every role Jane Fonda has undertaken in the last ten years has been wrought in terms of the effect of environment on character, and character on environment.

Charles Laughton told Bertolt Brecht that the reason he wanted to act was because people knew so little about themselves, he wanted to show them. Fonda's acting has been marked by a similar wish to reveal and elucidate insights into human behavior — within specific physical, social, and psychological environments.

In *Klute,* for instance, Jane Fonda clearly understands the peculiar, sordid milieu of the hooker in midtown Manhattan — her creepy, pathetic clientele, the pathological fringe, the burgher-on-the-make, and the criminally violent. She understands, too, the multilayered cynicism of the call girl, the tricks, the maneuvering, the fee bargaining, the peril.

Fonda did not have to *live* that tackiness to under-

Dedicated to making politically responsible films.

stand it; it is not the emotion that an actor *has* that gives substance to a character but what the actor *knows* about that particular emotion. Fonda's portrayal in *Klute,* for which she won an Academy Award, is a consummate performance, thoughtfully designed and executed.

Her performance as Gloria in *They Shoot Horses, Don't They?* is equally impressive. She discussed that character with me, and came up with a strong and unifying device that serves throughout the entire performance. Gloria knows that in the Great Depression generally, and

---

JEFF COREY *is an actor-director who has appeared in such films as* Mickey One, The Cincinnati Kid, Seconds, In Cold Blood, True Grit, Little Big Man, *and* Paper Tiger.

A sex star in the late sixties, when directed by then-husband Roger Vadim, in a segment of Spirits of the Dead (L) *and* Barbarella, *with John Philip Law.*

example, what Fonda always seeks to reveal as an actress — the effect of environment on character.

In *Julia,* the most likable thing about both Fonda and Vanessa Redgrave in this film is that their credibility is earned. There are personal emanations, rooted in the real political struggles of both actresses, and it is that which makes their interplay remarkable.

In *Coming Home,* Fonda begins as a woman who insistently numbs herself to the world around her. She has been seeing things through her hawk Marine husband's eyes for so long that she has no political attitudes and no sense of her own potential. She decides to involve

the garish phenomenon called the marathon dance specifically, there is nothing within touch or view that can in any way help or alleviate her despair. Something far off might offer succor, but surely nothing in the immediate phantasmagoric dance hall.

Throughout her performance Fonda keeps looking far away, as though searching for some remote supportive source. Even when her scenes involve one-on-one exchanges, she looks at people but does not focus. She withholds her countenance. When she dances, she looks up beyond the ballroom skylight for some distant, evanescent presence. Audiences seem not to question, or to be distracted by this, because it has its own consistent logic and cohesion.

Several years earlier, in Neil Simon's *Barefoot in the Park,* she played a newlywed who has exuberant fantasies about never-ending nuptials. Her lawyer-husband, Robert Redford, in contrast, is determined to bring her around to the reality of the workaday world of homemaking and fiscal responsibility. She fanatically resists this inevitable middle-class incursion into her dreamworld. With whoops and hollers, she seduces and cajoles with great comedic effect and proves, by inverse

Her first interesting role was in Walk on the Wild Side *with Laurence Harvey.*

herself in the "real" world when she commits herself to working in a rehabilitation ward for Vietnam veterans. Of course, she has difficulty adjusting. She considers herself an intruder because she has no understanding of the war or what the men went through. It is when she takes a political stand against the other officers' wives and sides with her patients that she steps out of her isolation and develops a new awareness.

Fonda's adaptability and resilience as an actress is reflected in the range of her characters, beginning with her first film *Tall Story* (1960). She played a tough frontier hellion in *Cat Ballou* (1965), a stunning surreal doll in *Barbarella* (1968), Nora in *A Doll's House* (1974), an

Standout as prostitute in Klute, *psychological thriller.*

With Michael Sarrazin, marathon-dance partner in They Shoot Horses, Don't They?

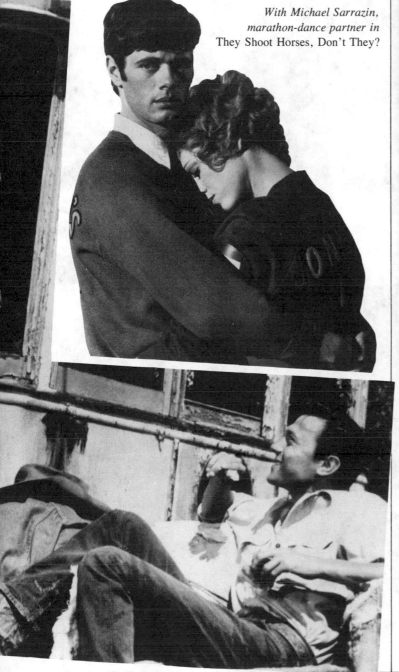

addlebrained stewardess in *Sunday in New York* (1963), and the abrasive whore-in-residence in *Any Wednesday* (1966). There have been several films in French too, including *Histoires Extraordinaires* (1967) and Schnitzler's *La Ronde* (1964). From time to time she returns to the stage, notably in the Actors Studio revival of Eugene O'Neill's *Strange Interlude* in the mid-sixties.

There seems to be no other bankable star today with such diverse capacities. It is even more remarkable that she has arrived at this status, in view of her intense political involvements and intermittent periods of virtual blacklisting.

Jane Fonda has not been content to wait for contrived, tailor-made vehicles made up of reshuffled ingredients from the latest commercial hit. She has, in fact, ventured forth with independent vigor, initiating film projects, bringing together writers, producers, and directors in fruitful collaboration.

If there is any validity to Stanislavsky's dictum, "The actor's prime function is to reveal the human spirit," Jane Fonda is an excellent example.

Her characters support, rather than compete with, other women, and have strong relationships with men as well. In Julia *(Top, L and R) she had time for both Vanessa Redgrave and Jason Robards. In* Coming Home *(Bottom, L and R) she was Jon Voight's lover and Penelope Milford's friend.*

ROBERT REDFORD: ALMOST PERFECT

DANNY PEARY

IN *This Property Is Condemned* (1966), Natalie Wood is about to blow out the candles on a birthday cake when she is first told to make a wish. At that instant, the camera switches to a shot of Robert Redford standing on top of the stairs. After her wish has been made, Wood sees Redford for the first time. It is understood that her wish — for a handsome prince who might rescue her from her dreary existence — has come true. In *The Way We Were* (1973), a film made seven years later, a romantically unfulfilled Barbra Streisand cannot believe her eyes when she discovers Redford (whom she had a crush on years earlier) asleep in a bar. When she later puts him to bed and makes love with him, she needs his confirmation that she is not dreaming. If, as critic Michael Stern contends, Rock Hudson was the handsome actor who represented a female wish come true in the 1950s, then Robert Redford certainly has had that distinction since the mid-sixties.

Since his less-than-dynamic beginnings, Redford has established himself as a very good, very likable film actor, who is adept in comic roles and convincing as rugged — yet vulnerable — action heroes. Redford has always been embarrassed by his handsomeness — perhaps he believes he was only allowed to develop his acting skills because his looks were enough to carry many of his early roles; however, he has had the good sense to choose parts that emphasize, rather than downplay, his good looks.

Time and again, Redford has played characters whose bad qualities or weaknesses are as glaring as they are because they seem to contradict what we'd expect from someone with such perfect features. Take his Gatsby, or his insensitive skier in *Downhill Racer* (1969), or his sheriff in relentless pursuit of Indian Robert Blake in *Tell Them Willie Boy Is Here*

Butch Cassidy and the Sundance Kid *hoisted Redford to superstar status.*

(1969) — all handsome men whose ugly actions throw us for a loop. We believe these men will live up to our expectations, but they don't. That is why we are so disappointed in McKay in *The Candidate* (1972) when we know that he is lying, and in Hubbell in *The Way We Were* at the moment he gives in to a movie producer and allows his novel to be commercialized for a film audience. In the former film, he plays a politician whose popularity, like Redford's, is based to a great extent, on the fact that he is handsome. When he sells out his good values and becomes morally corrupt, what we are actually witnessing is the genesis of a Dorian Gray, beautiful on the outside, deteriorating on the inside. In *The Way We Were* the irony is that the attractive, all-American

DANNY PEARY *has contributed on film to numerous publications, including the* Boston Globe, Boston's The Real Paper, The Velvet Light Trap, *and* Bijou, *and is the co-editor of* American Animated Cartoons: A Critical Anthology.

He prefers films with a historical context. In Jeremiah Johnson *he played a legendary nineteenth-century mountain man.*

W.A.S.P., Hubbell Gardiner, who seemingly has everything going for him, hasn't the courage to stand by what is morally correct, while the gawky, funny-looking Katie Morosky (Streisand) is willing to sacrifice everything, including her dream lover Hubbell, to follow her convictions.

For years now, Redford has had enough power to pick his own projects. During a time when studios have been reluctant to finance films that do not have contemporary settings, it is significant that Redford has had great success in films set in other eras. More than half his films take place in the past. Among his projects have been several westerns, including *Butch Cassidy and the Sundance Kid*, which in 1969 turned him into a bona fide box-office star, and *Jeremiah Johnson* (1972), actually a mountain picture which disproved the Hollywood axiom that movies with snow automatically flop. He has made war movies — *War Hunt* (1962), his first film, and *A Bridge Too Far* (1977) — that have had only minor impact, and several films set during the Depression that rank among his finest. Of these, *The Sting* (1973) made the best use of Redford's resourceful, understated acting

With Natalie Wood in This Property Is Condemned.

Receiving rough treatment from Robert Shaw in The Sting.

*Box-office dynamite:
Redford and Streisand in* The Way We Were.

style and tongue-in-cheek humor — which features an open-mouthed blank stare when he's trying to put someone on.

It is odd that, for someone with a reputation as a political maverick and a Hollywood misfit, his movies have been relatively tame in content. Considering that both he and Jane Fonda were dead-even at the time of *Barefoot in the Park* (1967), in that neither had yet mixed politics into their films, it is amazing how much further Fonda has ventured. True, Redford's films pretend to have some political viewpoint, but they all correspond to already acceptable liberal attitudes. *Tell Them Willie Boy Is Here*, which should have dealt with the potentially explosive issue of *how* American Indians have been treated, did nothing more than state what everyone believes, that Indians have been treated badly; likewise *The Candidate* said what few people dispute, that all politicians become corrupt. Scenes were cut from *The Way We Were,* toning down the harsher anti-House Un-American Activities Committee elements of the film; *Three Days of the Condor* (1975) and *All the President's Men* (1976) were both about the abuse of power in high government — a popular, no longer a daring, theme in the post-Watergate era. There is no denying that Redford, who could handle it, has avoided controversy in his choice of subjects. This is his major failing.

Woodward and Bernstein became Redford and Hoffman for the movie version of All the President's Men.

JEREMY LARNER ON THE CANDIDATE

REDFORD ASKED ME to write an original script about "a politician who sells out." He wanted to show the price we pay for winning. I said it doesn't usually happen by selling out. What happens, I think, is that the forces that play upon a public figure are much stronger than the person's own ideas of who he is and what he's doing. I said it's like what happens with movie stars. It's an old American story that every American thinks he's the sole exception to. There are many buyers for the fantasy of stardom, few who can handle the surreal impact of celebrity. It can hit like a tidal wave, swamping one's sense of self in a flood of other people's needs, symbols, and emotions.

That's what we tried to create for the character Bill McKay in "*The Candidate*" (1972). McKay's weakness is the other side of his appeal — a simple belief that he is and can remain a "natural man." Some of McKay's experience is drawn from what happened to politicians I've known; some is taken from what happens every day with Redford. In making the film we set up crowd scenes where we used reactions to Redford to show how the public came to confer star status on Bill McKay. The part was written so that Redford could create a character facing difficulties familiar to him but lacking in his own shrewdness and self-control. It was a challenging part if only because so much of McKay's changing, and slipping, has to be conveyed through his use of political rhetoric. As the movie unwinds we see McKay losing contact with his own words, spinning faster and faster in the pull of his "image." McKay senses his drift, makes valiant efforts to reach the shore or grab onto driftwood. But the current's too strong, he lacks the clarity to define himself against it, and at the end he's carried over the falls — to victory and stardom.

We're funny that way.

JEREMY LARNER won an Academy Award for his screenplay of The Candidate.

Corrupted idealist running for Senate in The Candidate.

JON VOIGHT: DEDICATED IDEALIST

JOHN BOORMAN

Jon Voight is one of the mysteries of the movie world. Every time he is on the verge of superstardom, he disappears from the scene to look for more fulfilling work than Hollywood can offer him. Coming Home (shown here) *was an exception.*

I STALKED HIM through the Hollywood jungle. He was an elusive quarry, hardly visible, nocturnal. He could seldom be found with the trumpeting elephants or arrogant lions. Occasionally one glimpsed him swinging dangerously from the highest branches. When I found him, he was huddled in a dark burrow, licking wounds inflicted by a bruising experience as a boxer in *The All-American Boy*. He was exhausted not only by the role but from protecting a first-time director. He took responsibility for everything, and it was burying

---

JOHN BOORMAN *is a British director, whose credits include* Deliverance, Leo the Last, Having a Wild Weekend, *and* Zardoz.

---

him. I dug him out of the burrow, inch by inch. He wanted to die with the movie. How else could he express the totality of his commitment? I insinuated myself, offering him *Deliverance* (1972). He resisted. He was too young, too tired. The role was outside his range. Perhaps.

It was the first of many encounters I was to have with his chronic self-doubts — and the beginning of an enriching friendship. Later in Clayton, Georgia, I was obliged to ban him from watching "dailies" because of the gloom he cast over crew and cast. Unable to bear banishment he begged to be allowed back into the fold. He promised not to grimace or groan. When the lights went up, his smile was painted on, convincing no one.

It was all over. We were doing post-production work in New York. Al Pacino dropped by and asked Voight about *Deliverance*. "I think my performance has probably ruined the movie. How's *The Godfather?*" Pacino shrugged morosely. "Worst acting I've ever done. I just hope the picture will slip out and not be seen by too many people. It's my only chance." They both sighed. Having exposed themselves, they now hoped for a miracle of anonymity.

This attitude, for all its agonies, is a useful antidote to the euphoric hyperbole of Hollywood and is based on an understanding of the treacherously shifting sands that provide the foundation on which movies are precariously built. In Voight it is an attempt to maintain a set of values, certain standards against which he perpetually measures himself. He avoids parties, lives modestly, buys no clothes — all attempts to avoid the pernicious influence of Hollywood, to maintain an independence of spirit and not succumb to stardom.

Burt Reynolds wants to be a movie star. He could not understand why Jon shied away from it. He admired Voight's skills as an actor — and Jon had been in a hit movie, while Burt had been trying and missing for years.

Burt watched Jon put his name in an autograph book with a pained reluctance that suggested he was signing his own death warrant. A bit later Burt raised the point, "Do you know what I like doing as much as anything in the whole wide world? Signing autographs. Writing my own name. Burt Reynolds. Over and over. Burt Reynolds. It's soothing. I feel like a mystic. It gives me power." Burt and Jon provoked each other like that all the time.

They were good for each other. Jon forced Burt to face issues in scenes that he would rather avoid, while Burt always understood how to connect an idea to the audience with a directness and simplicity that was hard for Jon to achieve. They became inseparable friends on the picture, Burt's ready wit bringing out Jon's marvelous manic humor, brilliant and wicked mimicry. Burt became more intense about his acting, Jon a little less so about his. One day they were feeling so pleased with each other, Burt wanted to express his affection. He said to Jon, "When they do my life story, I want you to play me." Burt, of course, is never without self-irony.

Voight's deep suspicion and skepticism extend to his own talents, which are truly prodigious. Acting, perhaps, comes too easily for him. His initial responses to a scene are often deadly accurate and full of magical revelation. Then he applies his intellect, which is also formidable. He sees the deep complexity implicit in any character and in the choices he must make in a scene. He challenges his instincts. Greatness can only emerge out of intellect applied to talent. Sometimes, in his case, the intellect overwhelms the instinct. He works very hard on any role and often is exhausted by staying up all night to grapple with a problem of interpretation. He has enor-

A real sleeper: Paul Williams' political comedy The Revolutionary.

In John Boorman's Deliverance.

Films such as Conrack, *that have a political slant, have attracted Voight.*

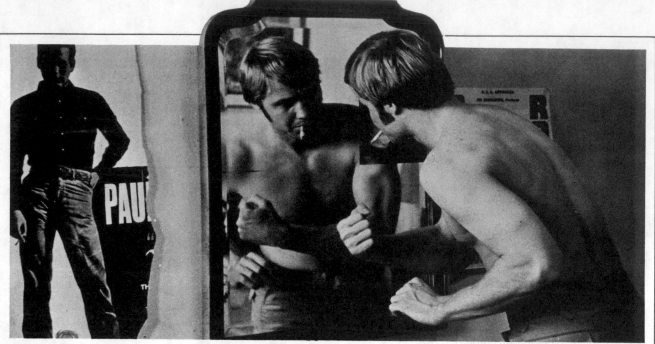

Voight burst upon the scene in 1969 with his stunning performance in John Schlesinger's Midnight Cowboy.

mous energy, yet he spends himself totally, as though only in this way can he prove himself worthy. I sometimes perceive this as a means of self-punishment. We both had a Catholic education, and I understand the deep wells of guilt that afflict him. This guilt directs his behavior in other ways. His frugal apartment is in an unfashionable part of Los Angeles. He gives away most of his money. He takes responsibility for a wide circle of family and friends. He helps and supports them with love, loyalty, and money.

Among these people he is full of grace, even radiant. His energy becomes directed into his humanity. He is powerfully "present" and infuses life into others. He laughs a lot, violent laughter that racks his body, and he makes laughter in others. It is not to do with humor, although it is that too, but rather like bathing in laughter, jumping in with others and splashing one another in laughter.

In this mood he is deeply sensitive to others. He is capable of insights into people that are sometimes uncannily accurate. I have seen him encounter a stranger who is suffering some distress and not only divine what is wrong but perceive an entire life, to *know* that person utterly and instantly even down to concrete facts. In this gift lies his real power as an actor, the power to become another, to possess a role. It is a disturbing and frightening ability. It makes him extremely vulnerable. It is partly responsible for the protective coloring, the suspicions and doubts.

Beneath the goodness, the sensitive humanity, the guilt, the intellect, the boyish charm, lies another darker level that he constantly grapples with. It is violent, self-destructive, predatory, power-seeking. It gives his acting a certain danger. The danger is real. The beast roars in him.

OFF ON RETREAT

WHILE BURT REYNOLDS went off to become a proper movie star, Jon wrestled with himself, a herculean contest that has gone many rounds, with many still to go. He immersed himself in *Hamlet,* performing it, typically, on a college campus. Hamlet, of course, had been waiting for him for years, perhaps hundreds of years. I am a collector of *Hamlets,* being a master of indecision myself. I saw it. The production was flawed, the acting uneven. Predictably, he elected to do the full version. It ran five hours. I reflected afterward that Hamlet should not be played that well. It is so rich. It is better played indifferently. Voight's Hamlet overwhelmed. It was blinding, scorching. An actor who is a vehicle for the poetry is all we need to experience the majesty of the play. Voight gave us more than we needed or bargained for. He had achieved a metamorphosis. He was swinging in the high branches. He was performing the act of becoming another. He ferreted out Shakespeare's mystery and put it up there on the stage for all to see.

His pacing fractured the poetic meter, for the meter will convey the meaning, left to itself. He would not allow that. Each line had to be renewed in Voight, and amazingly many were. He began with too much force and anguish, matching the lines rather than letting them do the work. One by one the characteristics I have described in Voight found themselves in Hamlet: the teasing of Polonius, the fellowship for Horatio, the doubts, the dark betraying intellect, the manic wit. It is a thunderous moment when an important actor finds his great role. The transference that night was eerily total. Voight became Hamlet, but more disturbing still, Hamlet became Voight.

— J. B.

HOLLYWOOD CASUALTIES

PAUL ROBESON: FREEDOM FIGHTER

WILLIAM TUNBERG

PAUL ROBESON was a memorable Othello because he had much in common with Shakespeare's great character. Both were black men in a white man's world. Both were men of ability, courage, and dignity. And both sustained rage against injustice. It is fitting that Othello gave Paul his popular identity, turning him into an international star before he had given serious thought to films.

Four years earlier — in 1924 — Eugene O'Neill had chosen the unknown Robeson to star in his new play *All God's Chillun Got Wings*, as well as a revival of *The Emperor Jones*. In rehearsals the playwright taught the young man how to evaluate a character. Forget yourself, Paul. Put yourself into it. *Become* the character!

Both plays were radical for their day; O'Neill was weary of the shuffling Sambos that passed for blacks on stage and screen. Jim Harris in *Chillun* was an intellectual who married a white prostitute. Brutus Jones in *Emperor* was a dishonest tyrant who abused power. However, it was only the white press that hailed Robeson's performance. Black critics declared he was perpetuating a stereotype. His Harris allowed himself to be destroyed by a chippie no white man wanted. His Jones was weak, cowardly, and superstitious to the point of idiocy. The "gentle giant," as Robeson was sometimes called (he was six feet three and weighed well over two hundred pounds), debated this with his peers. The O'Neill characters were, first of all, human beings. As for their shortcomings — what human is perfect?

Robeson's magnificent singing voice brought him his biggest popular success in the Jerome Kern–Oscar Hammerstein II musical, *Showboat*. He first played Joe the riverman in London in 1930 and again in New York in 1932. When he sang of the travail of the black dockwalloper beside the eternal and uncaring river, the audience forgot everything else in the somewhat superficial show. It was a moment of real-life drama related by

WILLIAM TUNBERG *is a screenwriter, whose credits include two Walt Disney films:* Old Yeller *and* Savage Sam. *He is the original author of* Garden of Evil.

a worker who knew it firsthand, and it brought the house down. Listening to the applause, he might have believed that New York City was his. And it was — as long as he didn't try to buy a meal in a first-class restaurant.

In his films Robeson sought to upgrade the image of the black man. Racism could be weakened if whites

On his tombstone are his words: The artist must elect to fight for freedom or slavery. I have made my choice. I had no alternative.

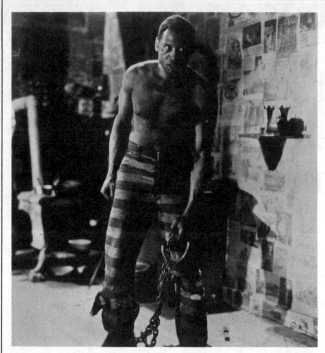

The Emperor Jones *was a major disappointment for Robeson because of the screenplay's stereotypical treatment of its characters.*

came to recognize the humanity they shared with blacks. And the more Robeson improved his skills as an artist, the more he could hasten the process. He worked hard at his singing. He gave concerts in America and in Europe. He researched the spirituals he sang, often tracing them to African origins, finding relationships with the folk music of other races. He learned French, German, Russian, and Swahili. And he worked hard at acting. A prime example is the thoroughness with which he prepared for the role of Othello. He read and studied all of Shakespeare, took up phonetics to better his diction, made his speech harmonize with the flow of Elizabethan language.

Hollywood did not offer Robeson a chance to perform in meaningful roles — he was disillusioned by what happened to his film *The Emperor Jones* (1933) — so he went back and forth between America and London in the mid-thirties. In London his status as a star lifted Robeson above racial discrimination. He was approached by director Zoltan Korda, with an offer of a major part in *Sanders of the River* (1935). He would play Bosambo, a chief who lived for the betterment of his tribe. A camera crew was shooting in Africa. There would be authentic footage of tribal dances, customs, everyday life. To Paul it seemed a rare opportunity to acquaint Europeans with real African culture. Instead, it turned out to be a glorification of British colonialism.

In 1936 Universal offered Paul his old part of Joe the riverman in a lavish film version of *Showboat*. After *Sanders* Paul was pessimistic about portraying a black

man honestly on the screen. However, he took the job, mainly for the money. And, of course, it brought him musical acclaim. "Ol' Man River" was as big a hit on film as it had been on the stage.

Back in England again, Paul starred in *Song of Freedom* (1936). The film, a foreshadowing of *Roots*, is an honest attempt to tell the story of a modern black who returns to the country of his forefathers to discover his kinfolk; once there, he is determined to bring the people an improved standard of living. But these themes were compromised by a bad script and clumsy direction. Robeson comes off as little more than a black Tarzan. *Song of Freedom* was offered to distributors, but there were no takers. Today it remains a curiosity in collectors' libraries.

Still thinking of Robeson as an African chief, Zoltan Korda offered Paul the role of Ombopas, "a splendid savage," in his production of *King Solomon's Mines* (1937). Again, Paul was wary. However, the budget was ample, the cast first-rate, and he figured Korda was not likely to trick him a second time. Paul accepted, provided he was permitted some editorial control over his role. While the picture and Paul's part came off quite well, most of Paul's ideas were lost in the rough-and-tumble of production.

In 1937 Paul made *Dark Sands of Jericho*, playing a black World War I doughboy who kills a bullying sergeant and flees to North Africa. There he falls in with a nomadic tribe, becomes their leader, and leads them in a trek across the Sahara. Whatever social significance Paul had seen in the character — a black American soldier hadn't been done seriously in films — is lost in an improbable, plotty story full of banal characters.

In 1939 producer Herbert Marshall cast Paul as an unemployed West Virginia coal miner who goes to sea as a ship's stoker. He ends up in Wales, where he gets a job with white coal miners, works beside them, eventually

ROBESON'S QUEST

IN THE MID-1930s, Paul Robeson went to the Soviet Union to discuss the making of a film about the Haitian liberator Toussaint L'Ouverture with the famous Russian director Sergei Eisenstein. The two artists became friends, but a conflict in commitments kept them from working together.

Russia itself amazed Paul. Here was a social system without racism, without unemployment, where every citizen enjoyed the fruits of his labors! He thought of Africa, where the colonialists were saying it would take a millennium before the African would be capable of self-government. What nonsense! Certainly Africans could do what the Russian peasants had done.

— W. T.

loses his life saving his fellows in a mine disaster. *The Proud Valley* (1940) received mixed reviews, but Paul felt it was the one film he could point to with pride.

Hitler had invaded Poland during its filming, and the struggle against Fascism had begun. Paul and his family left for America, where, he felt, they belonged in this time of world crisis.

Awaiting Paul was CBS producer Norman Corwin with *Ballad for Americans,* a cantata by John LaTouche and Earl Robinson. It was a lyrical argument for the brotherhood of man and Paul was delighted with it. Congressman J. Parnell Thomas, chairman of the House Un-American Activities Committee, snarled that it was Communist propaganda, but the public sided with Paul. *Ballad for Americans* was a smash. He sang it frequently on a concert tour across the continent, ending in Hollywood, where he agreed to do *Tales of Manhattan* (1942) as part of an all-star cast. It is a gimmicky six-episode odyssey about a dress suit that goes from owner to owner. In the final vignette, the jacket — stuffed with money — falls upon the skimpy farm worked by sharecropper Robeson and his wife, Ethel Waters. *Lawdy, Lawdy — forty-three thousand dollars! Right from Heaven! De good Lawd, He done took pity on us sinners!* Angry over the Uncle Tom implications but bound by his contract, all Paul could do was vow never again to act in a commercial film. He even joined protesters picketing a theater in which the film played.

In 1943, at the zenith of personal popularity, he appeared in *Othello* in New York, supported by Uta Hagen and José Ferrer. He had approached the role with humility: "I am not a great actor like José Ferrer. . . . I must make myself believe I am Othello. . . ." Once again he studied the character, analyzed his speeches carefully, tried to relate them more closely to current problems. The play ran for a record 296 performances.

Paul made many public appearances — not to enhance his stardom, but to urge true freedom for American blacks. Ultimately, he thought, the black man would have to ally himself with other workers and take control of the means of production. The goal was full citizenship and scientific socialism. Robeson also called for his people to support CIO unions, which, unlike the AFL, welcomed the membership of blacks.

As long as Roosevelt lived and as long as the United States and the U.S.S.R. remained allies, Robeson's political position was labeled as anti-Fascist. Then Roosevelt died, peace came, and the two superpowers were clenching fists over a prostrate Europe. Paul Robeson, whose favorable attitude toward the Soviet Union had not changed, was branded a Communist.

Under Harry Truman's Cold War administration, anti-Red politicians vied with Joe McCarthy in denouncing leftists. There was no equivocation about Paul; he was easy game for the witch-hunters. When he was invited to give a concert at Peekskill, New York, the bigots came at him in full cry. *Get the black Benedict Arnold! Stop the Commie songs!* With the connivance of officials, rioters were allowed to insult and attack people as they left the concert, and over one hundred and forty people required hospitalization.

Mass hysteria made it impossible for Paul to perform in America. There were offers from Europe, but the State Department decided it was not in the best interests of the nation for him to travel. His passport was summarily revoked.

Robeson fought the decision legally, appealing adverse lower court rulings to the Supreme Court. During the eight years he was blacklisted he sang where he could, including the Zion Methodist Episcopal Church in Harlem. Twice the International Union of Mine, Mill and Smelter Workers asked him to come to Canada for concerts, and twice he was stopped at the border by U.S. officials. Undaunted, he arranged to sing from the American side of the border to an audience on the Canadian side.

By 1958 the most rabid of the Red-baiters had been discredited. A more reasoned Supreme Court decided that Paul could again travel. At age sixty-one he went back to London and played *Othello* to rave reviews.

Paul Robeson made nine films. In each he tried to rise above stereotype casting. Even with his powerful personality and magnificent voice he succeeded only partially. Black characterizations in films of the thirties and forties were not far enough removed from minstrel routines, the cakewalk, and Al Jolson in black face.

Sadly, Paul Robeson the film star comes off a poor third to Robeson the stage star and concert singer. I am sad indeed when I think of what greater heights he might have achieved if he had been allowed to spend those eight blacklisted years before a camera.

Singing "Ol' Man River" in Show Boat.

INGRID BERGMAN: AN OUTCAST RETURNS

DIANE WALDMAN

IN AN INTERVIEW in 1968 in *Look* magazine, Ingrid Bergman spoke about her love-hate relationship with the American public.

> *Because of my face, which was washed with soap and nothing else, Americans never saw me as a Peer Gynt. They always saw me as a sister, a mother, even as a nun. My falling in love with Roberto [Rossellini] was too much of a betrayal for them. Don't forget it happened in 1948; now, it would be different. The new generation . . . reacts with astonishment when they hear the story of the hate that burst around me. They ask: "Why?" And when they are told, they smile, saying: "Is that all? So what?"*

Although a film star in her native Sweden in the 1930s, Bergman is best remembered and adored for her work in Hollywood in the 1940s: Ilsa in *Casablanca* (1942); Maria in *For Whom the Bell Tolls* (1943); Paula in *Gaslight* (1944), a role for which she won her first Academy Award for Best Actress; Sister Mary Benedict in *The Bells of St. Mary's* (1945), the role which was to have so many ironic reverberations in subsequent years; Alicia in *Notorious* (1946). Besides demonstrating her tremendous versatility, Bergman brought to each of these roles the quiet intelligence, shyness, innocence (even in spite of "experience," as in *Notorious*), vulnerability, inner strength, and unusual beauty (uncommonly tall, famous for her clear, rosy complexion, round face, and beautiful cheekbones) which were to constitute her special appeal to both men and women.

Within Hollywood parameters, her Swedish accent allowed her to function as a variety of ethnic types — she was French in *Adam Had Four Sons* (1941) and

Saratoga Trunk* (1945), Czech in *Casablanca*, German in *Notorious*, Spanish in *For Whom the Bell Tolls*, and Russian in *Anastasia* (1956); she simply came to connote "European-ness" to American viewers. At her best, she makes us believe in her as the passionate heroine of progressive causes, as the loyal wife of the Czech resistance fighter, the Loyalist in the Spanish Civil War, or the woman willing to sacrifice herself to atone for her Nazi father's sins.

Casablanca was the turning point in Ingrid Bergman's career, both as an actress and an economic

The "natural beauty" Selznick was looking for.

DIANE WALDMAN *has written on film for various publications, including* The Velvet Light Trap, Jump Cut, *and* New German Critique. *She has taught courses on women in film at the University of Wisconsin.*

With Gary Cooper in Saratoga Trunk.

At her most popular in Casablanca *with Bogart.*

property. By 1946, she was America's leading female star, and remained among the top ten actors and actresses in 1947 and 1948. Yet shortly afterward, she would become box-office "poison," not to make another financially successful film until *Anastasia* in 1956. The question of the unpopularity of her films during this period, is inextricable from the scandal surrounding her adulterous love affair with Italian movie director Roberto Rossellini and the birth of their child.

If one examines Bergman's pre-Rossellini films and pre-Rossellini writings about her, America's hysterical response becomes understandable, although no less repulsive. First, it was the very qualities that made her so popular — her innocence and vulnerability — that enabled the public to assume she had let them down. Secondly, as so often happens with Hollywood stars (but perhaps Bergman is the strongest example) there was a complete merging of her on- and off-screen image.

Prior to the scandal, magazine and newspaper articles stressed her natural, unaffected beauty and sincerity and attempted, as *Life* magazine did, to distinguish her from the typical Hollywood product: "Her natural good looks could compete successfully with filmdom's razzle-dazzle." A 1943 *Life* article reported: "Press agents and journalists groping for the precise metaphor have noted variously that she has "the scrubbed look of the countryside after a spring shower," "a freshly washed appearance after the manner of the soap advertisements," and "a quart-of-milk and apple-a-day wholesomeness."

Another leitmotiv running through this early hype was her happy home life with Dr. Petter Lindstrom and their daughter Pia, ironically drawing a distinction be-

tween her public and private life.

That this strategy ultimately backfired could clearly be seen after her fall from grace. David O. Selznick once told *Look's* Bill Davidson, "I'm afraid I'm responsible for the public's image of her as Saint Ingrid. I hired a press agent who was an expert at shielding stars from the press, and we released only stories that emphasized her sterling character. We deliberately built her up as the normal, healthy, non-neurotic career woman, devoid of scandal and with an idyllic home life." Or as Bergman herself told Davidson, "I was regarded as the wholesome, well-mannered girl, the actress without makeup, the Hollywood exception. People didn't expect me to have emotions like other women."

By the mid-fifties, after making five more films with Rossellini and two with Jean Renoir, there began to be

Bergman and David O. Selznick who brought her to America.

rumors of Bergman returning to Hollywood. Against the judgment of Spyros Skouras, president of Twentieth Century-Fox, who maintained that Americans had not forgiven Bergman, Darryl Zanuck and Fox offered her $200,000 to do *Anastasia*. One executive claimed, "It was a risk for us to use her in a big, expensive picture but we felt that if we could convince the public she was a courageous, long-suffering woman who had sacrificed all for love, the American people would accept her again."

Ed Sullivan flew to London and filmed Bergman on the set of *Anastasia*. This segment and a personal appearance by Bergman were to be telecast on his program. In an unusually outrageous and tasteless maneuver, Sullivan solicited viewer approval or disapproval for Bergman's appearance, reminding his audience that she already had done seven years' time for penance. Tasteless or not, this event seemed to turn the tide of public opinion in Bergman's favor. She won both the New York Film Critics Circle Award and the Academy Award that year for her performance in *Anastasia*, with the press falling all over itself to "welcome her back."

Now "forgiven," her divorce from Rossellini and marriage to Lars Schmidt barely ruffled a feather (perhaps because she was perceived as the "injured party" this time); Bergman continued to make films, stage appearances, and television dramas, winning an Emmy as the governess in the 1958 adaptation of *The Turn of the Screw* and a Supporting Actress Oscar for her portrayal of the neurotic missionary in *Murder on the Orient Express* in 1974. She has managed to age nobly and gracefully, falling prey to neither of Hollywood's usual solutions to the problem of the aging actress: the

Lewis Milestone directing her in Saint Joan, *in which she was miscast.*

older-woman-pretending-to-be-younger or the older-woman-as-monster à la *What Ever Happened to Baby Jane?* (1962). Unfortunately none of her new roles compared to those of the 1940s.

In another interview with *Life* in 1968, Bergman again alluded to the new generation "to whom the scandal means nothing." "They do know me in my old films," says Ingrid. "Thank God for the *Late Late Show*."

I agree.

As a psychiatrist in Hitchcock's Spellbound.

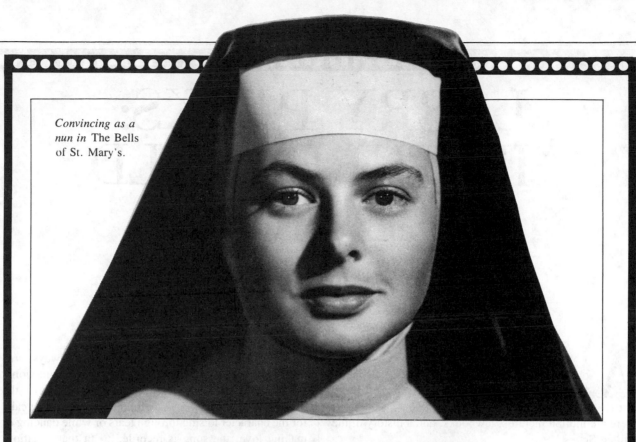

Convincing as a nun in The Bells of St. Mary's.

A NUN DOES NOT FALL IN LOVE WITH AN ITALIAN

IT ALL STARTED when Ingrid Bergman wrote this often-quoted and often misrepresented letter:

Dear Mr. Rossellini —
I saw your films, *Open City* and *Paisan,* and enjoyed them very much. If you need a Swedish actress who speaks English very well, who has not forgotten her German, who is not very understandable in French, and who in Italian knows only "ti amo," I am ready to come and make a film with you.

Best regards,
Ingrid Bergman

[The fact that "ti amo" was a line of dialogue she had spoken in *Arch of Triumph* (1948) was frequently omitted from the discussion of the "propriety" of this letter]. She went to Italy in 1949 to work on Rossellini's *Stromboli,* (1950) and her love affair with him (she was still officially married to Dr. Lindstrom) made her the subject of one of the most vicious scandal sheet campaigns in Hollywood history.

Louclla Parsons broke the story:

INGRID BERGMAN BABY DUE IN THREE MONTHS AT ROME

Life magazine later ran pictures of the expectant parents as part of a tactless special feature on their behalf: "Famous People Born Out of Wedlock." But that wasn't the end of it.

Newscasters, fan magazines, church and school groups all jumped on the bandwagon of condemnation; there was talk of boycotting, even banning, her pictures. Senator Edwin C. Johnson denounced her on the floor of the Senate as "a free-love cultist," "a common mistress," "a powerful influence for evil," and "Hollywood's apostle of degradation." He even asked that she be forever barred from the United States for "moral turpitude." In the period between 1949 and 1950 she received between thirty thousand and forty thousand letters — most of them from America — about what one writer termed her "so-called private life."

Not only did writers and photographers resort to outlandish schemes to gain entrance into Bergman's hospital room, the news media also printed stills from Bergman's films accompanied by captions that referred to events in her personal life. For example, a still from *Stromboli* showing Bergman in pajamas was labeled, "In the Villa Margherita Clinic, Ingrid is not smiling now." One newspaper even dredged up an old shot from *Notorious* showing her sick in bed from the poison administered by her Nazi husband and mother-in-law: "Ingrid at Rest" read the caption.

The Swedish press was equally harsh, calling her "a blot on the Swedish flag." One paper concluded that if the Swedish delegate in the UN General Assembly voted against Italy on a colonial question and sided with Haile Selassie, it would be all Roberto Rossellini's fault.

— D. W.

LARRY PARKS: HIS THREE-FOLD LEGACY

BETTY GARRETT-PARKS

A T MY HUSBAND Larry Parks' memorial service, our longtime friend and business manager, Louis Mandel, spoke of the memories Larry left the public: ''He will not be forgotten — as long as there are motion pictures, lawbooks, and a history of the United States.''

The Jolson Story (1946) is a landmark in motion pictures. It was among the first movies to gross millions of dollars. Larry's accomplishment in this picture was also a first. Biographies of famous people had been made before — but never using the actual voice of the celebrated subject. This fact makes Larry's accomplishment no less remarkable, and possibly more so.

''My bedroom windows look over the tops of trees that he planted. He loved trees, loved music, loved words, loved thoughts, loved children, loved his family.'' — B. G. -P.

Sound tracks on musical films are always *pre-recorded* by the actors playing the part or by professional singers. The circumstances and the placement of the song in the story are known beforehand; if the script calls for the character to sing through tears or while dancing or making love, the song is recorded to fit that situation. But Jolson, recording his own songs for *The Jolson Story*, ''sang every song at the top of his voice — as if there was no tomorrow,'' as Larry put it. Larry's job was to perform the numbers as recorded — and still make them fit the emotional context of the individual scenes.

Larry's synchronization in this film is a feat that has never been surpassed. For each musical number he practiced with a sound track recording until, on the day of shooting, his lip and tongue movements were in perfect sync with the sound track. Along with the choreographer and a playback man, Larry locked himself in a rehearsal hall for hours, with speakers set at a volume that could have filled Radio City Music Hall. There were full-length mirrors so Larry could be sure he was synchronizing perfectly. As a result of these long practice sessions, the cameras could come in so close that Larry's face often filled the screen. One critic pointed out that ''they seem to be shooting down his throat, and even his tonsils are synchronized.''

Contrary to publicity, Jolson was not cooperative with Larry's characterization. In their sessions together, he criticized Larry for ''moving about too much.'' Jolson then proceeded to demonstrate. As Larry would say,

BETTY GARRETT *starred in several of the top musicals of the forties and fifties* — Words and Music, Take Me Out to the Ball Game, On the Town — *and in* My Sister Eileen. *Her one-woman show,* Betty Garrett and Other Songs, *won a Los Angeles Drama Critics' Circle Award. She is currently appearing in the television series* Laverne and Shirley, *and is writing an autobiography:* An Album of Love.

"He did everything but hang from the chandeliers!"

To understand Jolson's attitude toward Larry, you have to understand the character of the man. I think it really bothered him that anyone but himself should portray his life. But as long as someone else was going to do it, he wanted it to be a big star. It was said that he favored Jimmy Cagney, who had won an Oscar for his portrayal of George M. Cohan. He must have felt that the casting of this young unknown, Larry What's-His-Name, was an insult to him. Not being a patient man — and with no encouragement to hang around — Jolson eventually took off for Florida and left everyone to finish the picture in peace.

★ ★ ★ ★ ★

Larry's place in law history is due to a suit that he brought against Columbia Pictures.

He had been under contract to Columbia for nearly four years and had made some forty pictures, for which he claimed the title "King of the *B*'s" — the reigning star of low-budget pictures. By the time *The Jolson Story* came up, he had graduated to feature roles in *A* films.

Larry made two screen tests for *The Jolson Story* — the first and the last. In between, there must have been fifty actors, known and unknown, who tested. None came up to Larry's remarkable rendition of "Toot-Toot-Tootsie, Good-bye."

Columbia's chief executive, Harry Cohn, broke the good news to Larry that he had been chosen. But, just incidentally, he would have to sign a new seven-year contract. Larry rebelled. There were three more years to run on his current contract, and he felt that after that he should be free to choose what he wanted to do next with his career.

Cohn was so incensed that he declared that not only would Larry lose the Jolson role, he would be given no other good parts for the remainder of his contract. Carrying out this threat, Cohn had Larry called to report to wardrobe to be fitted for a one-day bit in a low-budget picture. Larry, realizing that Cohn was really serious about his threat, capitulated. He signed as Cohn demanded, made *The Jolson Story*, then sued Columbia for release from his contract, on the grounds that they had used duress to get him to capitulate.

When the case came to court, Judge William Mathis ruled in favor of Columbia — on the grounds that Larry had enjoyed the fruits of the agreement. The judge said that Larry should have brought suit *before* he made *The Jolson Story*. Columbia was jubilant. However, Judge Mathis in a corollary went on to say that he believed Larry did indeed have a case and that the law was sympathetic. He said that he had spent some time studying the Screen Actor's Guild's standard seven-year contract, and considered it the most inequitable he had ever seen (with the possible exception of the baseball contract), and that if the agreement itself were ever challenged in a court of law, it would not stand up. Judge Mathis then went on to make a Solomonic decision. He took away Columbia's right of injunction. This removed the teeth from the exclusive clause in the contract. Columbia was no longer jubilant; they realized that, though they still

In The Jolson Story *(Above) and its sequel* Jolson Sings Again, *with Ludwig Donath. "I remember one of Larry's greater challenges in* Jolson Sings Again. *'Baby Face' was meant to be sung tenderly to Barbara Hale. But, Jolson belted it out when he prerecorded it. Larry made the decision to sing it to a large roomful of people, showing off in front of his girl and flirting with her across the room. That justified the volume and energy that came across on the sound track." — B. G. -P.*

had Larry Parks under contract, they could not stop him from working anywhere else.

Not long after that Columbia came to Larry with a considerable raise in salary to make a second Jolson picture, *Jolson Sings Again* (1949), and peace was made.

As it turned out, Columbia did not make use of the full seven years of Larry's contract. The infamous House Un-American Activities investigation intervened. It is a period that is hard for me to talk about; Larry would never talk about it publicly.

Larry's appearance before the committee brought him four-inch-high headlines on the front page of the New York *Daily News*. His prominence as an actor spotlighted him above other witnesses, and his stand was unexpected. It did not conform with those who advo-

With Elizabeth Taylor in Love Is Better Than Ever.

cated taking the Fifth Amendment, and I think it came as a complete surprise to the committee, who expected him to take the stand of the so-called "unfriendly witnesses." Instead he admitted that he had been a Communist Party member and defended his right to think as he chose. He hoped that his "sons, when they are grown, will think as they choose and not be like cows in a pasture." The committee and its supporters were not pleased with Larry's attitude, nor were the Fifth Amendment advocates. But Larry had made his choice, knowing that in the political climate of the times it was professional and economic suicide — in the film industry, at least.

That era and Larry's part in it are history. What I saw at home was a man who was greatly hurt but who had endless resources. With Louis Mandel, Larry started a building construction business. As was typical of Larry, this was not just an investment of money. He taught himself the business from the digging of the foundations to the final plastering.

And he was not totally inactive in his career. We formed a road company of a play called *Anonymous Lover*. We also put together a musical comedy act; we toured this country, we played the Palladium in London, and returned three more times to tour provincial variety houses all over England. Larry also toured the United States in *Teahouse of the August Moon* and, in another season, *Any Wednesday*. Together we took *Plaza Suite* on the road for nine months. He made only one more

The Swordsman, *a swashbuckler directed by Joseph H. Lewis.*

motion picture, *Freud* (1962). He received critical acclaim for his performance.

At home his love of gardening consumed a great deal of his spare time. In addition to the rose garden and the greenhouse, he planted every tree that could conceivably grow in southern California. He indulged his passion for reading — often a book a day, plus the newspapers and a dozen periodicals. And he took the singing and dancing lessons he had never had time for, and kept himself in great physical shape at the gym.

In his last years, his health began to give him trouble. A bout with hepatitis and the development of high blood pressure seemed to take a lot of the vigor from him. His death at sixty (just six months after our thirtieth wedding anniversary) came with shocking suddenness.

It is comforting to know that he will be remembered. The case against Columbia will be quoted in the lawbooks; his stand before the Un-American Activities Committee will be remembered as dignified and brave; his films will be shown and appreciated. I know Larry would have attached the most importance to the way his sons and I — and his friends and neighbors — now remember him.

THE GARDENER

SEVERAL YEARS before Larry died, I wrote a poem for him. It ended like this:

> He embraces his sons
> The way a man should embrace his sons,
> Fiercely protective against the world
> but gently —
> And they grow for him.
>
> He holds me
> With tenderness
> And respect
> And pride
> And love that I can feel.
> And like the flowers
> and like our sons,
> I too
> Grow for him.
>
> — B. G. P.

His last film was John Huston's Freud, *which starred Montgomery Clift (R).*

JOHN GARFIELD: BLACKLIST VICTIM

HOWARD GELMAN

T O THE House Un-American Activities Committee John Garfield seemed an ideal candidate for investigation. For one thing, his wife Roberta Garfield had been an active supporter of left-wing causes. Garfield himself had had political indoctrination with the Group Theater — and coming, as he did, from the slums of New York, he hardly needed pushing in the direction of Marxism. Later fame and wealth in Hollywood had produced enough guilt in him for having abandoned his roots that he kept jumping from cause to cause over the years.

Actors with points of view were considered deviants in the movie industry, and suspect as far as H.U.A.C. was concerned. The committee certainly didn't expect him to give startling testimony. The H.U.A.C. only wanted him to corroborate previous testimony, to give the same old names. They wanted an act of contrition from a famous movie star, and thought Garfield was their patsy. They were mistaken.

His appearance before the committee on April 23, 1951, was termed "friendly," but Garfield did not name anyone as a Communist. A contemporary who shared Garfield's experience with the blacklist commented that he "was not protecting himself, but old friends whose names had been mentioned dozens of times. He wasn't keeping a secret, just an idea of himself." His strategy was obvious — play dumb, and hope to be believed. Others tried, and some, such as Abe Burrows, succeeded. The committee did not believe Garfield.

It is a fact that Garfield never disavowed his past, or made a public confession or second appearance before the committee, despite extraordinary pressure. Even in his last hours, he was still resisting the final act of capitulation.

On May 20, 1952, John Garfield died at the age of thirty-nine of a heart attack. For thirteen years, he had been a major box office attraction, but his experience

with the H.U.A.C. and the pending F.B.I. investigations on perjury charges — he claimed to have *never* known a Communist — had effectively stopped his film career. He died angry. As his friend, screenwriter Abraham Polonsky (also a victim of blacklisting) so aptly summarized his life: "The Group trained him, the movies made him, the blacklist killed him."

In truth, Garfield, despite his exposure to Marxism, was really an innocent, psychologically incapable of political or intellectual involvement in more than a superficial way. That was not what made him tick. He was an actor.

"John Garfield was the best known and probably the most successful actor to be totally blacklisted in the industry — even though his name was never mentioned adversely in the testimony of any witness before the House Un-American Activities Committee; or was he ever connected officially with any subversive act, or was any incriminating evidence put forward against him."

— H. G.

HOWARD GELMAN *is a playwright, novelist, and author of the biographical study* The Films of John Garfield. *He is associate project director of* Earplay, *which produces original radio drama for Public Broadcasting.*

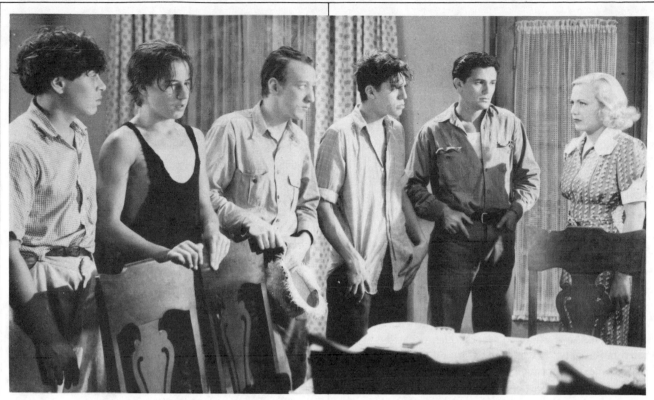

As a boxer on the run, he took refuge with Gloria Dickson and the Dead End Kids in They Made Me a Criminal.

"As an actor," Polonsky writes, "Garfield was the darling of romantic rebels — beautiful, enthusiastic, rich with the know-how of street intelligence. He had passion and a lyrical sadness that was the essence of the role he created as it was created for him . . . He didn't have the range of an Olivier, but then Garfield was a star who represented a social phenomenon of enormous importance for his times."

John Garfield was a symbol for a large segment of the American population, especially the immigrant urban poor — Jews, Italians, and Slavs from eastern and southern Europe. Like them he was an outsider searching for success in America. He was not handsome in the Hollywood sense; his features were dark and Semitic, his nose appeared broken, and his accent was heavy Bronx with Lower East Side shadings. No other actor who purported on film to be an American looked so alien. He presented a strong ethnic appearance, and in all of his roles he seemed to be living an exaggerated version of his own life — the struggle out of the ghetto, a fight for success, then disillusionment. Garfield understood his characters with an unconscious ease; it is there in his walk, his flippancy, and his immense energy. This sense of authenticity was an unusual quality in Hollywood. Quite simply, Garfield was capable of delivering the most realistic performance on the American screen of his time.

Between 1939 and 1946, Garfield waged an ongoing battle with his studio, Warner Brothers, for whom he had signed a seven-year contract, and was suspended more than a dozen times for refusing to work in what he considered to be inferior or repetitious films. It is true that Warners stereotyped Garfield, but it is also true that it was the ideal studio — considering its interest in making films about the middle and lower classes — for Garfield to work at. Warners made use of the screen image that Garfield presented best: the rebellious, cynical urban hero.

On the run with his best female lead, Priscilla Lane, his equal in every way in the underrated Dust Be My Destiny.

His first film was *Four Daughters* (1938). The story is sentimental, middle-class romanticism — except for Garfield, the outsider. As soon as Garfield enters the scene his presence brings an off-center tension to the movie. His rumpled clothes, cocked hat, frayed collar, and side-of-the-mouth delivery strike a note so out of tune with the tone of the film that it brings the story to life. His cynical dialogue — he is a born loser, a man who walks with a cloud over his head — is pitted against girlfriend Priscilla Lane's optimistic nature.

In one scene, Garfield plays a piano with great passion, thinking he is alone. Lane has seen him however, and she comments, "It's beautiful." He peeks at her from just under his eyelids, and spits out, "It stinks." In this film (and in many others) he is aware that he cannot fit into the world of the woman he loves. He does not want to take her down with him; at the end he drives off to die in a blizzard so Lane can marry the type of man she was meant for.

Four Daughters was directed by Michael Curtiz who would use Garfield on several other occasions as the rebel protagonist. It was under Curtiz that he gave some of his finest performances and developed a solid film acting technique. Garfield credited Curtiz with developing his persona: "I would normally have been a character actor, but he gave me the screen personality that carried me to stardom."

Unfortunately, Garfield often had to struggle with poor imitations of the Curtiz films by lesser directors. Appearing in hackneyed films usually brought out the worst in his acting style. He could be a terrible mugger and was often too aggressive and overbearing in his characterizations. In his worst films he would play with a

A lighter moment in the powerful Body and Soul, *with Joseph Pevney, Anne Revere, and Lilli Palmer (R).*

feverish intensity in which a simple sentence was packed with wasted emotion.

In 1947 Garfield left the studio to strike out on his own, hoping to display a maturity that was often lacking in many of the confining Warners films. His first film for his own production company, Enterprise, was *Body and Soul* (1947). He plays a boxer who fights his way out of the slums and gives up everything for fame and fortune. Although the story line is typical old-style Garfield, the film is made with a realism and understatement that make it work. The actor, playing his part with an odd, almost contradictory combination of cocky grace and humorlessness, earned his only Academy Award nomination as Best Actor.

That film was followed by a supporting part as a Jew in *Gentleman's Agreement* (1947), which he wanted to do strongly because it dealt with anti-Semitism. Then he appeared in *Force of Evil* (1948), written and directed by Abraham Polonsky (who had also written *Body and Soul*). Garfield gave a strong performance as the slum kid who makes good by choosing the easy road to a fast buck. The role is a variation on his earlier parts, but the character is handled differently. In *Body and Soul* and his Warners films he fought his way to success with his fists; here he uses his brains. The film has strong insight into the other, less heroic side of the success story of the ghetto achievers; here the actor's victims are the little people who in earlier films he had protected.

Garfield made only three more films. In his last, *He Ran All the Way* (1951) he plays a brutal murderer and was able to give the role sympathetic characteristics without making his actions heroic or pleasant — a difficult accomplishment.

Garfield's last performance hinted that he was truly developing as an actor with excellent range. But the film did not do well. It was released after the image-damaging appearance before the H.U.A.C., and consequently died at the box office. He could no longer find work in Hollywood. A year later, John Garfield was dead.

Blinded in battle in Pride of the Marines, *the story of real-life soldier Al Schmid.*

JUDY GARLAND: A FAREWELL

BUDD SCHULBERG

JUDY GARLAND was a little Mozart of song and dance. Of all the child stars who came out of the 1930s, a classic period for talented moppets, only Judy Garland somehow survived as a star of the first magnitude — a Lady Lazarus who kept rising from the dead, from countless suicide attempts and broken marriages and nervous breakdowns and neurotic battles with weight and sleep, to somehow pull her jangled nerves together, take command of the Palladium or the Palace or Carnegie Hall and bring down that audience one more time.

When she was good, meaning when she was there, she was so very, very special that we laughed with her and cried with her and begged for more in a marriage of requited love never before experienced in the theater. And when she was bad, which meant when she was ill, when she was atremble with indecision, when the steps wavered and the voice cracked in its die-hard reach for the high notes in the rainbow, then her love, the audience, turned on her in its righteous and wretched wrath and pelted her with rolls and bread and crumpled cigarette packs — as in that nightmare performance in her precious London not so long ago.

And so she took her final curtain call last week, as used as she was loved, as exploited as she was revered, sentenced to martyrdom and sainthood in a show-biz world that cries too easily but shies from the true cause of the tears that Judy has been crying from Andy Hardy days onward.

So much prose epitaph, adulation, and soul-searching flowed into print in the past week, from sob sisters and sentimentalists, from friends and hangers-on, seasoned observers and instant experts, that one hesitates to add to the cascade. This writer found himself thinking

BUDD SCHULBERG *received an Academy Award for his screenplay of* On the Waterfront *in 1954. Among his other screenplays are* A Face in the Crowd *and* Wind Across the Everglades. *He is the original author of* The Harder They Fall *and* What Makes Sammy Run?

Meet Me in St. Louis.

about Judy and her untimely, yet not unexpected, exit in terms of a rather cruel nursery rhyme that has baffled us since childhood. So we offer the following:

★ ★ ★ ★ ★

A VARIATION ON
'AN ELEGY ON THE DEATH AND BURIAL
OF COCK ROBIN'

Who killed Judy Garland?
"I," said the sparrow,
"With my golden arrow,
I killed Judy Garland."

"It was mama who wasted bundles of Judy's money on worthless ventures. And that was just the beginning. . . .''

Who saw her die?
"We all watched her try,
On the set and the sly,
We all saw her die."

"She must have tried it at least 20 times while we were married. . . . Someone had to be there every minute. We never dared to leave her alone. She's been on borrowed time all her life."

Who caught her blood?
"I," said the mother,
"She was mine to smother,
I caught her blood."

"Mother was a real-life witch. She was no good for anything except to create chaos and fear."

Who'll make her shroud?
"We," said the sisters,
"Since fame never kissed us,
We'll make her shroud."

"From the first time she toddled onstage, she wiped them out. Just when Judy was getting ready for the big-time at Metro, her father died, and her Cinderella sisters were already teenagers, and Judy always felt they were poisoning mama's mind against her."

Who dug her grave?
Said L.B. the Wizard,
"With our pills in her gizzard,
We dug her grave."

"They had us working days and nights on end. They'd give us pep pills to keep us on our feet long after we were exhausted. Then they'd take us to the studio hospital and knock us cold with sleeping pills — Mickey sprawled out on one bed and me on another. After four hours, they'd wake us up and give us pep pills again, so we could work another 72 hours. That's the way we worked, and that's the way we got thin. That's the way we got mixed up. And that's the way we lost control."

"No," said the M.D.s,
"We thought Secos and Benzies
Would alleviate frenzies,
But we dug her grave."

"Judy Garland had taken — perhaps in a state of confusion from previous doses — more barbiturates than her body could tolerate." ". . . prescribed on the Thursday before her death 25 tablets, the bottle found half-empty, and on Saturday, a bottle of 100 — found unopened."

"Who'll count the money?"
Said manager-agents,
"Are you being funny?
We took care of the money."

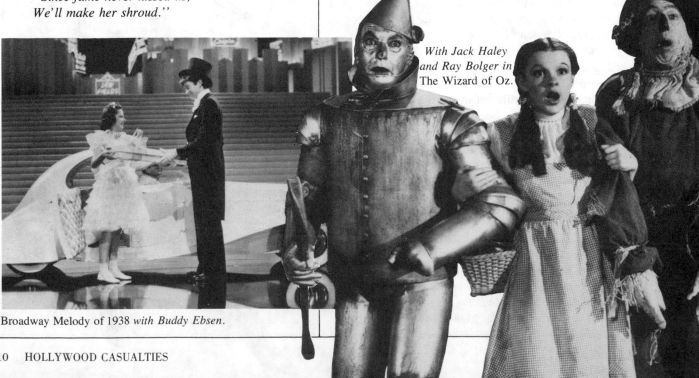

Broadway Melody of 1938 with Buddy Ebsen.

With Jack Haley and Ray Bolger in The Wizard of Oz.

"After the millions she made, Judy left debts of around a million, plus being in hock to Uncle Sam as big as Joe Louis, which means they can grab her house, record royalties, whatever she left. . . . "

Who'll herald the coffin?
"Us," cried the tabs,
"This show's up for grabs,
We'll herald the coffin."

"Judy Smash!"
"Judy Weds!"
"Judy Bombs!"
"Judy Flees!"

Who'll be chief mourner?
Poor Deans was the last one,
His marriage a fast one.
He'll be chief mourner.

"For the first time in my life and finally, I am completely loved. For the first time in my life I am really happy."

No, Liza's chief mourner,
She's out of the nest now.
She'll do what seems best now.
She'll be chief mourner.

"I think she was just tired, like a flower that blooms and gives joy and beauty to the world, and then wilts away. . . . I just want to send her off as she would have wanted to go . . . bright and lovely."

Dreaming of Gene Kelly in The Pirate.

Who'll carry the pall?
"Since we hired the hall
And we're press agents all,
We'll lay on a pall like there's
No tomorrow, we'll have an open casket, see,
And it'll be SRO just like Judy
Would've wanted and, get this touch,
We'll even fly in her favorite
Makeup man from Hollywood
To do the wax job.
I tell you, baby,
It's gonna be the biggest thing since
Valentino.
Come one, come all,
We'll carry the pall."

Babes on Broadway *showcased her range of talents.*

With Hedy Lamarr and Lana Turner in Ziegfeld Girl.

Who'll speak the word?
They cabled James Mason
From London to hasten.
He spoke the word.

"Her talent lightened the burdens of troubled people the world over at a time when poor little Judy was having things a little worse than they were. . . . She gave so richly and generously that there was no currency with which to reward her."

Who'll be the parson?
The parson who wed them
Came forward and led them,
"I'll be the parson."

"I shall never forget her tremendous strength through her frailty and her wonderful sense of humor even at the darkest times."

Who'll toll the bell?
Harburg? Arlen? The Cream —
"Since she was truly the songwriters' dream,
We'll toll the bell . . . "

"Clang Clang Clang . . . "

Farewell, Judy Garland, Farewell.

"Rockabye my baby . . . "

All the birds in the air
Fell to sighing and sobbing
When they heard the bell toll
For poor Judy Garland.

"If happy little bluebirds fly
Beyond the rainbow, why, oh why . . . ?"

Budd Schulberg for *Life.* Copyright © 1969 Times Inc. Reprinted by permission of the publisher.

An acting triumph in A Star is Born, *with James Mason.*

GROWING UP WITH JUDY AND MICKEY

I WON'T SAY that they were strict with Judy, Mickey, or me, but they were out to protect our image. They expected Judy (and me) to go out looking like young ladies, with her hair freshly shampooed and dressed to perfection. When Judy gave an interview, a studio person was always there to signal if she was saying the wrong things. I am amused today to remember that when they shot home layouts for publicity, they would never show the starlets in their kitchens doing what would be considered mundane things. But none of us resented the way we were handled, because we knew we were being protected.

The unfortunate part is that once their pictures became such gold mines, MGM cranked out more and more scripts for Judy and Mickey. The kids worked and worked and worked. It was twenty-four hours a day, and hurry right back. They were so enormously popular that between pictures they were sent all over the country on personal appearance tours. At the time they were young and seemed to thrive on it; looking back on it, I can see how much pressure they were under. Mickey would say to me, "Gee, Judy is awfully tired today. Maybe I can talk them out of doing that dance sequence." They cared and worried about each other.

But Judy and Mickey were thrilled by their successes. When we came out of a sneak preview, they would hurl themselves into each other's arms and hug each other gleefully because the audience had liked their picture.

— Ann Rutherford

They remained close until her death in 1969.

VIVIEN LEIGH: INTERNAL STRUGGLE

GAVIN LAMBERT

Often troubled, always dignified, she never failed to reach an audience on an emotional level.

THE SCRIPT OF *The Roman Spring of Mrs. Stone* (1961) was not written with Vivien Leigh in mind. While I was working on it, various people suggested actresses for the part, but none of them seemed

---

GAVIN LAMBERT *wrote the screenplays for* The Roman Spring of Mrs. Stone, Inside Daisy Clover, Vivien Leigh, *and two films for which he received Academy Award nominations:* Sons and Lovers *and* I Never Promised You a Rose Garden. *He is the author of several books, including* The Slide Area, The Goodbye People, On Cukor, *and* The Dangerous Edge, *and was, in the early fifties, the editor of the film magazine* Sight and Sound.

right to Tennessee Williams, to the director José Quintero, or to myself. Then, one day Tennessee said, "Vivien must play it." We immediately realized she was ideal. Why hadn't anyone thought of her before? At the time, 1960, she had not made a movie for five years (*The Deep Blue Sea*, 1955); the year before, she had collapsed during the first weeks of *Elephant Walk* (1954) and had been replaced by Elizabeth Taylor. She was separated from Laurence Olivier, a divorce was imminent, and those who claimed inside knowledge of her "condition" predicted another breakdown. She was a risk — a wonderful actress certainly, still beautiful, but a risk.

When first approached, Vivien did not want to play

With Maria Ouspenskaya (L) and Virginia Field in sentimental love story Waterloo Bridge.

the part. She had read the novel, and — alarmed, I think, by Tennessee's physical description of the character — found the portrait of an aging actress exploited by an Italian gigolo too "cruel" and too "grotesque" (her words). Then she read the script and changed her mind.

Our first discussion took place at the London flat she and Olivier had bought a few years before. She was indeed beautiful, also calm and smiling. The only sign of edginess was the number of cigarette packs scattered around the room — a new brand called Olivier.

With a hint of apology, she asked me to rewrite the opening scene. In order to establish that Karen Stone had begun to play roles in the theater for which she was too old, I had shown her as Viola in *Twelfth Night,* standing in the wings disguised as her twin brother Sebastian. The actor playing Sebastian, in an identical costume, came up to her, and as the camera moved closer it revealed how much older she looked than Sebastian. It wasn't the aging that Vivien objected to, only the way the point was made. She confessed, with a sudden scream of laughter, that after the movie she planned to play Viola in *Twelfth Night,* and why give the critics free ammunition? She was right, of course, and she was right about a few lines

she asked me to cut. "I don't have to say them," she explained. "I can *play* them."

Two weeks before shooting started, Vivien announced that she felt herself going "dry," and that she would take a shock treatment the next day. She mentioned this to Quintero and me with no more fuss than someone with a headache asking for an aspirin. Her lack of self-pity was touching and elegant.

The next afternoon at rehearsals she appeared eager and energetic. With her divorce case coming up and with reporters waiting at her door, she was under great strain. She'd go off for occasional further treatments, but there was no crack in her composure, personal or professional. Like her character, Mrs. Stone, she disciplined her terror. As so often happened in her career, life and art overlapped.

Twenty years earlier, after winning an Oscar for *Gone With the Wind* (1939), Vivien Leigh had been the most famous movie actress in the world. She was twenty-six then, and would go on to make only nine more movies. Few stars have had such an impact with so few appearances, but Vivien was never a conventional star. Under Olivier's influence, she devoted most of her time to the theater. While she achieved her greatest success in Hollywood, she continued to live in England. Her brilliant career was repeatedly halted by physical and mental illnesses.

She had her first breakdown after *Caesar and Cleopatra* (1946), and a year later medical tests revealed a tubercular patch on her lung. Not coincidentally, the Shaw movie was the last in which she played a character with direct Scarlett O'Hara affinities. She followed it with *Anna Karenina* (1948), a misfire that pointed to the tragic element underlying all her later work, from *A Streetcar Named Desire* (1951) to *Ship of Fools* (1965).

Of her early, mainly unremarkable British movies, only *The Sidewalks of London* (1940) — in Britain it was titled *St. Martin's Lane* (1938) — gave a hint of the actress who would grasp Scarlett so completely. She played a thief who joined a band of street entertainers and eventually became a musical comedy star. It was a warm-up for two of her greatest roles, Scarlett and Cleopatra. She was at once both light and ruthless, ambitious and romantic. In *Sidewalks* you could also sense her affinity for the camera. She had that essential, magical screen presence, definite and slightly mysterious. (It was never the same, by the way, in the theater. She lacked Olivier's classical range, and although she gave some remarkable performances, in *The Skin of our Teeth,* Anouilh's *Antigone,* and Chekhov's *Ivanov,* it seemed more of an effort for her to command the stage.) She glowed when she was in front of a camera, she was vital and confident. She knew how to grade her effects and, from long shot to close-up, how to communicate without words.

The pattern of her later screen career was set by her role in *Streetcar*. Drifting, vulnerable, it looked all the way forward to her last movie, *Ship of Fools,* in which she played another Southern lady on the skids. (Curious how the American South haunted an actress born of British parents in India, brought up in convent schools in England and Europe, and presented at court as a debutante.) Kazan's technique in *Streetcar* looks fairly dated now, and its effects overblown. Vivien and Brando play in different styles, yet her performance remains uncan-

She won two Oscars playing Southern women: the ambitious Scarlett in Gone With the Wind *and the defeated Blanche in* A Streetcar Named Desire, *with Marlon Brando.*

Doing the Charleston in Ship of Fools, *her last film.*

The studio contract system was at its most powerful when Vivien became a star, but she fought it from the first. Her contract with Selznick committed her to make one picture a year for seven years, but in fact they never worked together again after *GWTW*. He loaned her to MGM for the bland *Waterloo Bridge* (1940); refused to let her play Katherine in Olivier's film of *Henry V* (1944); then tried unsuccessfully to exercise his power of veto again for the stage production of *The Skin of Our Teeth*.

But even if her first commitment had been to movies, instead of to Olivier and the theater, one wonders how different the result would have been. Her great early success as Scarlett presented problems; a triumph of this magnitude becomes a kind of albatross. Perhaps she avoided it by making so few movies and leaving us to ask for more. Likewise, she fought to avoid the trap of her beauty. After *Anna Karenina*, which she made when she was thirty-two, she moved into "character" roles, deliberately ravaging herself for *Streetcar*, and in her mid-forties, rather than try to look younger, confronted middle age in *Mrs. Stone* and *Ship of Fools*.

With directness and grace, she communicated on the screen her early promise, then later her sense of loss. Her subtlety lay in the manner in which she related to both, hinting marvelously at the loss that would overtake Scarlett's promise, and the promise that lay behind Blanche's loss. You can "read" Vivien Leigh's screen performances chronologically as if she were a character in a time-spanning novel.

nily immediate in its deceitful frayed elegance, in its premonitions of defeat, and in its pathetic struggle for survival.

In *Streetcar,* she is Scarlett gone wrong. Almost 15 years later, as Mary Treadwell in *Ship of Fools,* she is Blanche continuing her struggle. As in Vivien's life, the odds against her are greater each time, and the effect increasingly poignant. Once, when a reporter asked her how she extended her range as an actress, she answered wryly: "Life." It was true, but not the whole truth, for some of her finest qualities as an actress were the intelligence, will, and humor that enabled her to keep, her own neuroses from the screen. In all her work there is nothing more precise and revealing than the moment in *Ship of Fools* when, alone in the ship's corridor, she breaks into a wild Charleston. It is disturbing yet funny, a comment on herself as a romantic, a woman who knows time is running out and refuses to complain. It seems like an echo of the moment in *Gone With the Wind* when Scarlett, a widow trying to be merry at the Atlanta ball, jiggles to the music all by herself.

The Roman Spring of Mrs. Stone, *scripted by Gavin Lambert.*

ROBERT WALKER: A WAYFARING STRANGER

DAVID NEWMAN

EVERYBODY IN OUR LINE of work is supposed to have had one movie that really got to them and made them suddenly realize that film was their destiny and not merely a Saturday afternoon diversion. . . . The movie that "got to me" like that was Hitchcock's *Strangers on a Train* when it first opened in 1951, and somehow Robert Walker's performance is all tied up with that new, unarticulated, barely *understood* realization I had that movies were really better than anything, even life, and that I wanted to be part of them.

On the simplest level, the revelation of Walker as Bruno, the sinister, charming, homicidal, Oedipal, psychotic maniac was that it was the quintessence of "casting against type." . . .

Until Hitchcock pulled that stunt, Robert Walker had always been this pleasant rather bland, slightly silly-faced MGM stock player, perfectly suited to the lightweight comedic demands of Private Hargrove and similarly moony, goony roles, though definitely pushed a few stops too high when somebody in the front office decided (mysteriously) that he had the right "sensibilities" to play all those composers (Jerome Kern, Robert Schumann, and were there any others?). It took Hitchcock to look deeper and cast him in a role that was a revelation for everybody concerned, not least Walker himself. And what a perfect performance for its (our) time. In a culture that was beginning to pride itself on neurotic self-awareness, here was our symbol — that edgy, psyched-out, psyched-up, fey, genuinely violent personality who appealed to old ladies. The homosexual thing — barely disguised, if at all — was the wild card there, and why hadn't we noticed it before, hey? It was a case of a director defining for the first time precisely that

DAVID NEWMAN *is a writer-director whose screenplays include* Bonnie and Clyde, What's Up, Doc?, Bad Company, *and* Superman. *He has often worked in collaboration with Robert Benton.*

Two unsuccessful marriages contributed to unhappiness in his short life. He died at thirty-three.

With Farley Granger in Strangers on a Train. *After playing light comedy roles throughout his career, in this film Walker found the part meant for him: murderer Bruno Anthony.*

unexpected quality in an actor which would determine his ''persona'' from that day forward.

Unfortunately, that was to be a short day. Choosing wrong and yet trying to maintain his new image, Walker went into *My Son John* (1952), Leo McCarey's scurrilous witch-hunting apologia, in which that same sinister, effete edge that Walker brought to *Strangers* was here to be equated with (and shorthand for) Communist sympathies. From Lavender to Pink in one easy move. Before the film was released, Walker was dead of a heart attack.

I remember going to see *My Son John* in sorrow, mad at Bruno for copping out, hating how ''they'' had botched what Hitchcock had just discovered, wondering whether it wouldn't be better just to go back and look at the Private Hargrove movies for black undertones. But finally I think Robert Walker lucked out. He had found the role of his lifetime — which he must have known — and before he had a chance to parody it and cheapen it — a process which had already begun with relentless haste — he was gone. But not forgotten.

Originally printed as ''People We Like: Robert Walker,'' by David Newman in *Film Comment,* May/June 1974. Copyright© 1974 by the Film Society of Lincoln Center. Reprinted by permission.

With Dean Jagger in My Son John.

With first wife Jennifer Jones in Since You Went Away.

MARILYN MONROE: SACRIFICIAL LAMB

ALVAH BESSIE

IN HER LAST PUBLISHED "INTERVIEW" (*Life,* August 3, 1962), which was acutally a very revealing piece of free-association, Marilyn Monroe quoted Goethe as saying, "Talent is developed in privacy."

Then she added, "And it's really true. . . . But everybody is always tugging at you. They'd all like sort of a chunk of you. They'd kind of like to take pieces out of you . . ."

"This industry," she said, "should behave [to its workers] like a mother whose child has just run out in front of a car. But instead of clasping the child to them, they start punishing the child."

On August 5, "the child," Marilyn Monroe was dead of an overdose of Nembutal. She was thirty-six years old.

No notes were left by the "sex symbol" of our time, but in the *Life* article she put her finger on her murderers. For "they" is the motion picture industry, and it is the motion picture industry that killed her. . . .

In a feature article in *Frontier* magazine (March, 1961) one of the Hollywood Ten wrote: "The bitch-goddesses hate her cordially and spare no pains to run her down, rip her up, castigate her for being late or 'uncooperative' or not properly 'grateful' to the industry. . . . But more important are other facts: She has not played the Hollywood game since her earliest days; she has not in years lent herself to the whole-cloth publicity which provides these parasites with their filet mignon and champagne; she does not call up Dear Hedda or Louella Dear to let them 'be the first to know. . . .'

"And still more important: She broke the Hollywood code, married a man held in contempt of Congress, stood by him while he was smeared all over the land and was finally vindicated by the higher courts. For there is no doubt that Miller's contempt is no small part of the contempt in which both she and America's leading dramatist are held by the movie columnists and gossips. . . ."

ALVAH BESSIE *is the author of* The Symbol, *which he based on the life of Marilyn Monroe.*

Lee Strasberg rated Monroe one of his two best pupils.

In the *Life* interview, Marilyn revealed a bit about what happened when Miller was on the rack: ". . . a certain corporation executive said either he named names and I got him to name names, or I was finished. I said, 'I'm proud of my husband's position and I stand behind him all the way'."

*With Arthur Miller,
Laurence Olivier, and
Vivien Leigh in 1957.*   *Belting it out in* There's No Business Like Show Business.   *One of her most sympathetic
directors was John Huston.*

Miller did not name names, and Monroe stood by him; she revealed in her *Life* interview some of her own contempt for the corporation executives who control the industry when she said: "After all, I'm not in a military school. This is supposed to be an art form, not just a manufacturing establishment."

Also — "I don't look at myself as a commodity, but I'm sure a lot of people have. Including, well, one corporation in particular, which shall remain nameless. . . ."

Also — "And I want to say that the people — if I am a star — the people made me a star — no studio, no person, but the people did. . . ."

Nor could she ever forget where she came from: the illegitimate child of a woman who had spent most of her life in a mental institution; farmed out to an orphanage and twelve foster homes; half-starved at times and kicked from pillar to post; "adopted" by religious fanatics and raped at the age of nine by "a friend of the family," she climbed from less than nothing to worldwide fame and financial affluence.

On top of this, she had suffered three marriage failures, one (or more) attempts at suicide, and two miscarriages and was tormented her entire life by the emotional instability almost inevitable to such a history. And the fact that this instability was one of the determinants of her death goes no distance at all to negate the fact that she was a victim of the industry's greed for profits and its

Newcomer stealing scene from veterans in All About Eve.   *The acclaimed comedy* Some Like It Hot, *with Jack Lemmon.*

PATRICIA ROSTEN ON MARILYN

SHE ALWAYS SEEMED to wear a plain, beige silk blouse, open at the neck; a straight, bone-colored skirt in perhaps a raw-textured fabric; flesh-colored nylons and the inevitable beige silk high stiletto heels. Her skin was pale, translucent almost, and sprinkled with freckles. I knew she was a famous movie star, but I wasn't overly interested in that. Her name was Marilyn Monroe. I was eight years old, and she was a new friend of the family.

Luckily, I am not burdened with inside information about the traumas of her love life, her other personal problems, or her professional conflicts. I have only a child's recollection of her. I don't even recall the first time I met her, although it must have been in our living room. Nor can I remember specific conversations we had, though we must have said a lot in passing over the seven years I knew her.

Mainly, I associate her with places: first, her apartment in New York and, then, rented summer houses on Long Island and, finally, the farm she and Arthur Miller bought in Connecticut.

For me, it was a treat to visit her apartment on Fifty-seventh Street in Manhattan. I remember that the apartment was spacious, but not huge, and that the living room was done in beiges. A fireplace was flanked by bookcases and two off-white love seats. There also was a large piano in the room, but I never saw anyone playing it. The dining alcove had a marvelous mirrored table that fascinated me because you could look at your reflection while you were eating.

Off to one side of the dining area was a small study; at the other side was the kitchen. (Marilyn was forever inviting guests to raid her refrigerator.) The guest bedroom and bathroom had lovely white porcelain doorknobs with flowers painted on them. They must have been at my eye level, for they remain so clear to me.

Marilyn's bedroom was kept quite dark and remains slightly mysterious to me, but there also, typically, everything was in beiges: the rugs, curtains, bedspread. She had a champagne-colored quilt on her bed; when I flopped on it, I felt like I was sinking into a pool.

One time I became bored with the adult conversation and began wandering through the empty rooms. When Marilyn discovered me, I was nose-deep in her enormous makeup box. She acted like it was the most natural thing in the world to find me there, and before I could even feel embarrassed, she had plunked me down at her vanity mirror and said that, since I was so intrigued by the art of makeup, she would show me how to do the job right. For the next twenty minutes I was in a dream as I watched her skillful hands transform my kid's face into something that even I might have called glamorous. She made my eyelids glimmer, my cheekbones appear accentuated, and my mouth rosy with color. Not content with just a partial make-over on her willing pupil, she also arranged my hair — lifting it off

my shoulders into an elegant French twist. Why, I thought, I could pass for seventeen. Then, proud of her handiwork, she happily took me by the hand back to the living room to show me off to the grown-ups.

★ ★ ★ ★ ★

Marilyn was fun to be with because she broke the rules — and children love being around grown-ups who can get away with that. She possessed a gaiety and an unstuffy quality that children find refreshing in adults. I remember, for example, that after Arthur and Marilyn had moved into their wonderful three-story farmhouse in Roxbury, Connecticut, she would not hesitate to allow her basset hound, Hugo, to come in rain-soaked and muddy from the garden to her newly decorated living room. She would let the front part of him in and carefully wipe off his front paws; then coaxing in the rest of him, she would carefully wipe off the back ones. All this in front of company. And when Hugo needed a soft bed, Marilyn gave him the best all-wool blanket in the house. No wonder Hugo adored her! (On the other hand, he was afraid of men and ran away from Arthur and my father.)

And then there was Cindy. While Marilyn and Arthur were spending a lot of time at the farm, a small, weak, half-frozen and half-starved beagle-type puppy had the luck to stagger out of the woods and into Marilyn's backyard. She immediately took in the foundling and, with the help of a local vet, nursed it back to health. The question remained: what to do with it? After working on my parents behind my back, she brought the dog to New York and gave her to me. Marilyn had real empathy for children and animals. And I later felt, as did others, that her life might have been happier if she had had a child of her own.

When Marilyn touched me or hugged me, I felt a warmth and softness (dare I use the word *maternal* in relation to her?) that was very reassuring. It was not unlike falling into that champagne-colored quilt that graced her bed. She, who was so much like a child herself, always had a sympathetic word or touch for "another" child, and it was this that endeared her to me.

PATRICIA ROSTEN *is a freelance writer, whose father Norman Rosten is the author of* Marilyn: An Untold Story. *She is a former editor for* McCall's *magazine.*

As Tom Ewell's sexy blond neighbor in The Seven Year Itch.

determination to make its "hot property" toe the line of total conformity.

How else explain the vendetta that pursued her ever since she quit Hollywood cold in the 1950s and went to New York to study at the Actors Studio? At that time she was at the crest of her career, and her films had made millions for her studio. But she wanted more: She wanted to become a fine actress, instead of cheesecake; she wanted better stories, better directors — and more money. And her studio capitulated.

But the vendetta persisted, and there was nothing this young woman did, whether it was expressing a desire to play Grushenka in *The Brothers Karamazov*, reading more books that were something more than superficial, or indicating that shee took herself seriously, that was not used to make her the butt of ridicule and calumny.

The film that Arthur Miller wrote for her (*The Misfits* [1961]) was under attack before director John Huston rolled his first camera. And when it was released, the avalanche of critical disdain for what was a progressive and superior story was overwhelming.

The sniping at Monroe, as a person, continued daily, and it came not only from Hopper but from Floribel Muir and Dorothy Kilgallen; from the sportswriter Charles McCabe; the gents' room journalists Walter Winchell, M. Miller, Herb Caen, and Simon Lee Garth of *Confidential*; from the "fan" and "movie" magazines; from San Francisco *Chronicle* writers Lucius Beebe, Donovan McClure, and Ron Fimrite; and even from such highbrow critics as Stanley Kauffman of *The New Republic*.

The death of Clark Gable, immediately after *The Misfits* was finished shooting, was openly rumored to be Monroe's "fault." The breakup of her marriage with Miller, simultaneously, was attributed to a romance with Yves Montand, who starred with her in *Let's Make Love* (1960).

Even her retreat to a psychiatric hospital in New York late in 1960 was made the occasion for snide comments by the harpies of the press. . . .

In 1956 Monroe told Pete Martin ("Will Acting Spoil Marilyn Monroe?"): " . . . I'm beginning to understand myself now. I can face myself more, you might say. I've spent most of my life running away from myself. . . ."

Sometime during the night hours of August 4–5, 1962, Norma Jean Baker finally came to understand herself, and the self-illuminating body burned out. . . .

She had never been permitted or helped to become the artist she wanted to become, and she finally understood herself and her situation in The Industry so well indeed that she ran away from herself forever.

From the San Francisco *People's World*, August 8, 1962. Reprinted by permission of the author.

CHARACTER
ACTOR
AS STAR

CHARLES LAUGHTON: MASTER INTERPRETER

RICHARD SCHICKEL

He created more memorable characters than anyone in film history.

RECENTLY I WAS ASKED by P.B.S. to cut down and slightly rearrange a rather pokey old B.B.C. documentary called "The Epic That Never Was," which included the surviving footage from the abandoned film project *I, Claudius,* which was to be adapted from Robert Graves' novel. Various survivors of that disaster speculated inclusively in the documentary

---

RICHARD SCHICKEL *is a film critic for* Time *magazine and was the film critic for* Life *magazine. He is author of* The Disney Version, His Picture in the Papers, The Men Who Made the Movies, *and the novel* Another I, Another You.

---

about why the production had suddenly shut down, and the narration shied away from blunt statement of the obvious implication of the testimony gathered here. Namely, that the canny producer Alexander Korda, sensing that the star, Charles Laughton, and the director, Josef von Sternberg, simply could not work together, used an auto accident that temporarily incapacitated actress Merle Oberon (whom Korda would marry, shortly after) as an excuse to close down the film and collect his insurance money.

It was too bad, for running the *I, Claudius* footage backward and forward in the Movieola, I came to the realization that what was in process of creation some forty years ago on those lavishly set sound stages in England was what surely would have been one of its era's most memorable screen performances — and the definitive statement of his art by a very great screen actor.

Since Charles Laughton's death in 1962, one has come more and more to appreciate his singular gifts. The voices of the nightclub impressionists ("Mr. Christian, come here") are stilled, the several bad, self-parodying roles of his later career are blessedly forgotten; we have come to know, as well, something about the hidden wound — his homosexuality — that was the source of both the pain that afflicted him when he played certain roles and the sympathetic understanding he brought to key performances in the course of his career.

This is not to say Laughton was underappreciated while alive. He had his Oscar for *The Private Life of Henry VIII* (1933) and the first New York Film Critics Prize for the same role, not to mention sundry other awards and nominations, and although his movie career flagged somewhat in the forties and fifties, there was the stage, where he prospered as a member of the First Drama Quartet (doing Shaw's *Don Juan in Hell* with Charles Boyer, Sir Cedric Hardwicke, and Agnes Moorehead) and with his own solo readings. Yet somehow I think we missed the point most of the time. He was fond of giving interviews, for example, in which he described himself as an incurable ham, and there were just

The rebellion of the animal people in H. G. Wells' Island of Lost Souls. *Laughton claimed he based his villainous Dr. Moreau on his dentist.*

enough performances in which he fell over the line that separates the bravura from the purely fustian that it became simpler to accept his own seemingly cheerful evaluation rather than to think seriously about him. Familiarity does breed that sort of critical laziness about performers — especially when it is accompanied by competence and softened by the sort of indulgent affection Laughton engendered in us over the years.

That's why it seems to me Laughton is ready for reevaluation. Looking through the clippings about him in preparation for this essay, I came across this comment by drama critic Eric Bentley about Laughton's performance in the title role of Bertolt Brecht's *Galileo,* which the actor adapted for a New York run in 1947: "Laughton . . . was able to seem an intellectual, and even a genius. The combination of physical grossness with intellectual finesse was theatrical in itself." It seems to me that Bentley isolated the main line of Laughton's work, indeed, that which made him so fascinating. There were exceptions to it, of course — his *Hunchback of Notre Dame* (1939) and his comically irascible bootshop owner of *Hobson's Choice* (1954), to name just two — since he was an actor who delighted in demonstrating his range. But consider some of the high points of his career: the brainy, bullying prosecutor in *Witness for the Prosecution* (1957); *Rembrandt* (1936); Doctor Moreau in *Island of Lost Souls* (1933), an intellectual, a scientist, corrupted by the power drive (of all the actors who played this sort of lunatic in the horror cycle of the thirties and forties, none was more chilling than Laughton); the English butler won in a poker game by a rude westerner in *Ruggles of Red Gap* (1935), a character with a delicate, intellectualized awareness of social distinctions

(his light, jabbing, counterpunching performance is a comic high point of the mid-thirties).

One might be hard-pressed to call Laughton's Henry VIII or his Captain Bligh intellectuals, but his Henry is not as purely lusty as one tends to remember him, nor is his Bligh as purely sadistic. Perhaps because he carried something of that air about his own offstage persona, each was tinged with the melancholy of the superior being — or at any rate the human being who conceives himself as superior, who is disappointed by circumstances, by the self-betrayals of the less desirable aspects of his own character. Neither of them is quite the man he thought he should have been, the gifts of the intellect undermined by defects of character and personality.

Such a man, too, at least by implication, is Sheb Cooley, the Southern senator of *Advise and Consent,* (1962), Laughton's last masterpiece. The film was un-

The Suspect, *perhaps his finest film. Rosalind Ivan is the nagging wife, not long for this world.*

I, Claudius, *the potentially great Laughton-Sternberg collaboration, was canceled in mid-production.*

dertaken when he was already ill with cancer and was released after his death. This man oozed fraudulent Southern charm to cover parliamentary guile, patriotic blather to disguise his shrewd political sense. One sensed that Cooley, too, was a disappointed intellect — someone who except for the accident of birth in a region denied national political power (until recently) and his unprepossessing appearance might have exercised his talents in a larger arena than the United States Senate's

inner circle. But with what amusement Sheb relishes his power therein, with what cheerful sadism does he play one force off against another as he slyly disguises how his pivotal vote will be cast in the balloting to confirm a dying president's choice of a new secretary of state. It's an absolutely delicious performance by Laughton — broad in outline, delicate in nuance, at once a believably realistic portrayal of a familiar political type but also a cleverly shaded parody of the type. It was a perfect valedictory for him, because for one last time he was playing, as he had in most of the roles we've been discussing here, a man testing the limits of power and discovering, in the process, the circumscriptions imposed on him by his own flaws or the world's rules.

This all brings me back to the point at which I started: Laughton's great "lost" performance as Claudius.

Claudius was a visibly flawed man; he had a limp and a stammer and he was also, at heart, something of a coward. He was, in short, a misfit in imperial Rome, content to let his peers think him a mental defective, while he tended his garden (actually a pig farm) and developed his brilliant intellect. Happily, a scene in which Laughton was able to establish this characterological base was shot, and as you can imagine, he was wonderful in it, for no one was better than he was at playing weakness — real or counterfeit. Also shot was the sequence in which he is summoned to Rome to confront the mad Caligula (Emlyn Williams) and forced to

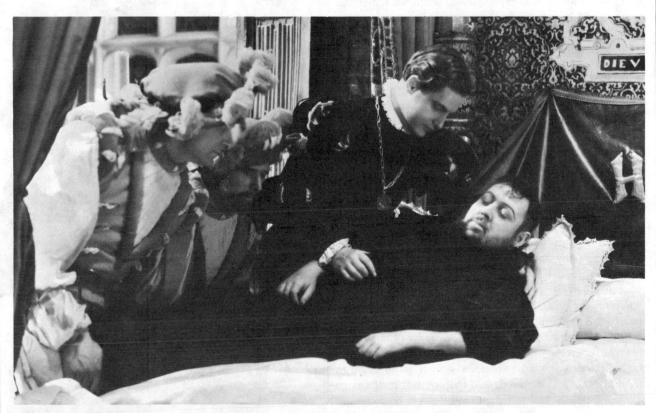

With Robert Donat in The Private Life of Henry VIII *for which Laughton won an Academy Award.*

Rembrandt *was very important to Laughton, an art connoisseur.*

abase himself in order that his life be spared. Finally, there is the scene where the senate hilariously offers the throne to this man they imagine to be a buffoon, and he arises to enumerate the terms on which he will accept it — first swallowing his stammer to level documented charges of corruption against his tormentors, then to movingly describe the rules under which he will reign, which can only be described as liberal and democratic. The abrupt juxtaposition of these fragments, unmediated by the transitional material that would have been present in the finished film, in a way represents the most powerful testimony we have regarding Laughton's gifts. Here, in microcosm, is his range — and it is awesome, no other word for it. It is especially so when we remember that he had been rendered desperately insecure by von Sternberg's coldness, that he was in a state close to panic on this picture, probably because he became aware as he studied the script just how close to him Claudius was, how much he would reveal of himself in placing this performance before the public.

Laughton did not stammer or limp. But he was apparently socially insecure in the company of the other actors with whom he trained, as a youth, at the Royal Academy of Dramatic Art. No more than the young Claudius did he think it prudent to expose his intellectual powers (in his case largely self-developed) to his peers. He did not begin to show that side of his character until late in life, when he began directing and writing his own material for his one-man shows. Buffoonery was his mask, as idiocy had been for Claudius.

Then, too, there was the matter of physical appearance to contend with. In the film, Claudius must joke about his looks, covering the pain his mirror caused him much as Laughton himself did, by seeming to snigger at himself before the strangers could, even by exaggerating his own defects. Beyond that, of course, there was homosexuality. Claudius is not visibly a homosexual in the film, but it is demonstrated that his self-image is so damaged that he had not slept, and thought he could not sleep, with women. How difficult it must have been for

Laughton, hiding within a convenient marriage and a publicly hearty manner, to enact those scenes.

And yet how bitterly one regrets that a director other than von Sternberg was not assigned to the picture, that Korda had not been so hard-pressed financially that he felt he could not risk going on with the film. For we have the evidence that, struggle though it was, Laughton was coping, was putting on film this truly self-revelatory performance. To see it now — even in bits and pieces — is to see, boldly stated, those qualities that were only hinted at, formed the subtexts, in his other roles. In *I, Claudius* he might have got to do what was always denied him elsewhere: show us strength and weakness struggling as equals within the same fascinating, ironic character. As it is, we must be content with suggestions, signals, interpretations. They are enough, to be sure, to secure our lasting affection for Charles Laughton, but it would have been grand if, just once, he could have played, with all the power and grandeur at his command — himself.

Captain Bligh in Mutiny on the Bounty.

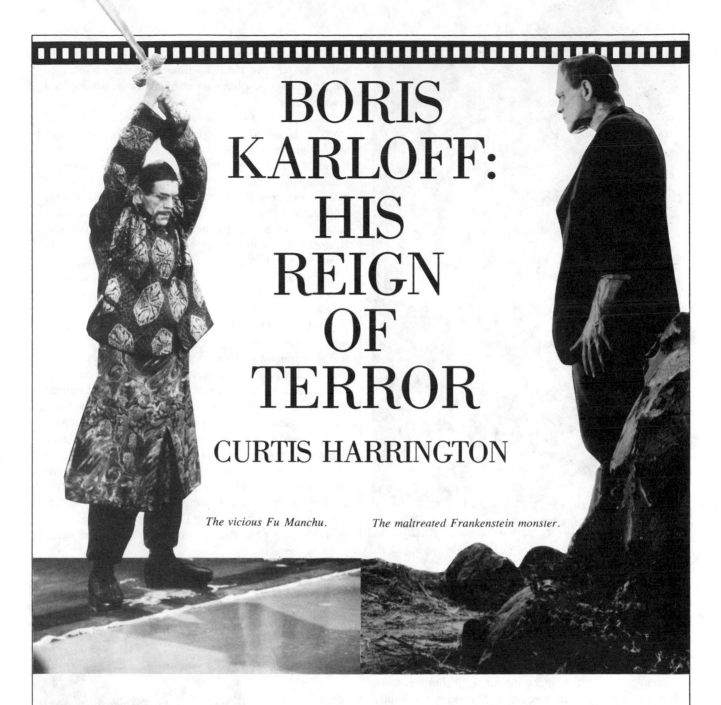

BORIS KARLOFF: HIS REIGN OF TERROR

CURTIS HARRINGTON

The vicious Fu Manchu.   *The maltreated Frankenstein monster.*

BORIS KARLOFF was to the sound horror film what Lon Chaney had been to the silent horror film. His very presence gave the most absurd stories dignity, intelligence, and the credibility necessary to make them "work" for an audience. For more than thirty-five years he provided the genre with a steady force that kept it interesting in the public's eye; looking back, one can see that it is because of Karloff more than any other figure that the horror movie has earned a re-

CURTIS HARRINGTON is a director who specializes in horror films. Among his credits are Queen of Blood, Games, What's the Matter with Helen?, *and* Who Slew Auntie Roo?

spected place in film history. Since he grew only more photogenic with age, it seemed for a while as if he would never die, and that the soft-spoken, slightly lisping English bogeyman would go on providing nightmares forever. It was a terrible, never-to-be-made-up-for loss when he died in 1969.

★ ★ ★ ★ ★

The image of Boris Karloff as the monster in James Whale's *Bride of Frankenstein* (1935) is one of my earliest cinema memories. I saw posters advertising the film and begged my parents to let me see it. They refused because it was, they felt, unsuitable fare for a child. Why I wanted to see it remains a mystery to me — why the image of Karloff affected me so strongly.

His most literate films, such as The Body Snatcher, *were produced by Val Lewton.*

The first really scary movie I finally was allowed to see also starred Karloff. After much coaxing, my mother took me to see *The Raven* (1935). I was fascinated, as I had expected to be, but also terrified. When Karloff awoke after the disfiguring facial operation (performed by Bela Lugosi) and began to shoot at the mirrors surrounding him in the operating room, I climbed down from my seat and hid beneath it. My mother promptly took me out of the theater, vowing never to let me see such a film again.

It must have been several years later, then, that I managed to get my father to take me to see a revival double bill of *Frankenstein* (1931) and *Dracula* (1931). By then my fascination was greater than my fear, and I enjoyed everything thoroughly. I could see what had so mysteriously attracted me from childhood.

Soon after that I managed to see a revival of *The Old Dark House* (1932), with Karloff in his stunning portrayal of the deaf-mute servant. As the years went by, I saw almost all of his films, even the more obscure and unrewarding, like *Mr. Wong, Detective* (1938). One that especially captured my imagination is the now largely forgotten *The Devil Commands* (1941), in which Karloff

devises a particularly sinister method of communicating with the spirits of the dead through the use of strange helmeted suits he places on corpses seated around in a séance circle.

In the late 1940s I met James Whale, who directed many of the greatest horror films of the early thirties, and who might be considered Karloff's discoverer. It was certainly Whale who turned the relatively obscure supporting player into a major star. The story has been told often about how Whale took over *Frankenstein* (1931) from Robert Florey, who had originally intended to put Lugosi in the role of the monster; and how Whale saw Karloff one day in the studio commissary and instantly knew Karloff had to play the part. Conceptually very different from what Florey had envisioned, Karloff was a fine actor who could express the anguish inherent in the monster.

Whale, whose films are as witty as they are scary, told me that when they were making *Frankenstein*, Karloff joked along with everyone else and seemed to find the task of playing the monster an amusing one. But later, according to the director, he began to take himself very seriously. One time Whale was asked by some junior assistant at Universal to visit the makeup department to see Karloff. He went, and was led with great ceremony into a room where a figure was seated, completely covered by a sheet. The assistant then removed the sheet, very much as if he were unveiling a statue. Karloff was revealed wearing the makeup Jack Pierce had created for *The Mummy* (1932). To Whale it looked as if everything but the kitchen sink had been plastered

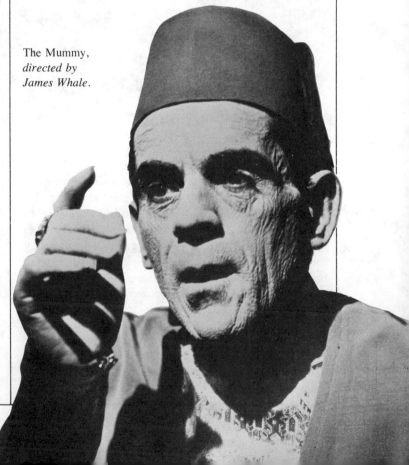

The Mummy, *directed by James Whale.*

Matching skills with George Arliss in The House of Rothschild. *He never realized how good an actor he was.*

on Karloff's face, but the actor solemnly announced: ''I think this is the most marvelous thing ever seen on the silver screen.''

★ ★ ★ ★ ★

In 1966, when I first went to work at Universal, I decided to see if I could locate and restore *The Old Dark House,* which by that time was regarded as a ''lost'' film. I persisted and the studio finally made a real search, and word eventually came from New York that both the original negative and the ''lavender'' protection print

THE MONSTER AND THE MOTHER

THROUGH THE YEARS some controversy seems to have arisen as to whether or not the original version of *Frankenstein* included a scene showing Karloff actually throwing the little girl with the daisies into the water. Although James Whale did not tell me at what point this was cut from the film (whether before its original release or later), he most certainly did film it. He told me with great humor that the child's mother, apparently the worst sort of aggressive ''movie mother,'' would yell after each take, ''Throw her in again!'' — C. H.

had been found. I also received a report that part of the negative had shrunk too much to go through the printer. Therefore, I began to search for someone to put up the money to make a new negative and print.

James Card of Eastman House, which rescues lost and damaged films, was on the phone to me the moment he received my letter, pledging the financing for restoration and preservation. A most important film, containing a fascinating portrayal by Karloff, was thus saved.

While I was under contract as a director at Universal, it was announced that Karloff would appear as the guest star in an episode of Universal's *The Name of the Game* television series. I was pleased, because I felt that I could manage to meet him; at the least, I would be able to watch him work.

I went on the set. Karloff was seated in a wheelchair on the sidelines, waiting to do his next scene. I had heard that he was crippled by arthritis, so I was not surprised to see him this way. What did surprise me was his amazing energy and agility when he got out of the wheelchair to do a scene. He seemed to have the ability that many performers have of increasing energy just for the time of performance.

I knew one of the other actors on the set and got him to introduce me to Karloff. What do you say when you first find yourself face to face with an idol of your youth, but who nevertheless seems as familiar to you as your closest friend? I heard the famous voice say, ''How do

With Anne Revere in The Devil Commands. *As usual he was a scientist who goes too far.*

you do?'' and he reached up and shook my hand. There was a gentle kindness in his eyes, and I wondered for a moment how he could be the same man who had so often terrified me from the screen. Then I remembered how he had, in *The Black Room* (1935), played good and evil twin brothers. The evil was the creative artistry of the actor, the good — himself.

I found myself telling him of my immense admiration for him, words that he must have heard thousands of times from fans. But then I had something special to tell him: the news about the rediscovery and preservation of *The Old Dark House*. He smiled and seemed truly pleased. ''Yes,'' he said, ''haven't seen it in years, but that *was* a good film. How nice. How good of you to tell me.''

Then his wife came by to wheel him to his dressing room. I said good-bye and expressed my pleasure at meeting him. As he went off, I could hear him saying to his wife, ''That young man told me they've saved *The Old Dark House . . .''

Never to be forgotten.

PETER LORRE: GENTLEST MURDERER

CHARLES BENNETT

Formerly a Brechtian actor, Peter Lorre became the movie's best scene-stealer.

I RONICALLY, I'VE OBSERVED, the meaner the actor's role on screen, the pleasanter the actor is in real life. Peter Lorre was the ultimate example of this, but with a twist. Peter carried his personal gentleness

---

CHARLES BENNET *wrote the screenplays for several films that starred Peter Lorre, including* Secret Agent, The Big Circus, Voyage to the Bottom of the Sea, *and* Five Weeks in a Balloon.

---

into his characterizations, and this was a great part of his magic. Peter Lorre, the "heavy," could kill — calculatedly, malevolently — and still remain amusingly lovable. This was practically a new art form. One wonders what Peter would have done with a vicious character such as Iago. Peter's "lovable-cum-whimsical" performance might have turned Shakespeare's *Othello* upside down.

My first meeting with the Hungarian-born actor was

As the insane Dr. Gogol, set on winning Frances Drake in the fascinating Mad Love, *a recently rediscovered gem.*

in London in 1933. After his hit in Fritz Lang's German-made *M* (1931), Gaumont-British brought him to England to play the heavy in the original version of *The Man Who Knew Too Much* (1934) for which I wrote the screenplay. Peter's English was about as good as my German, but somehow we managed to get along, and as the months passed into years, with Peter appearing in no

less than seven of my projects, we developed a warm relationship.

Professional contact with Peter came again with *Secret Agent* (1936), which I based on Somerset Maugham's Ashenden stories. Hitchcock directed and Peter played the "Hairless Mexican," once again a ruthless killer but this time on the British side. It was a superb performance; hateful but, as always, whimsically lovable. I remember one off-screen happening. Hitch had a secretary, Joan Harrison, down from Oxford and supposedly a French linguist. Peter's English hadn't improved vastly, but he could speak French. Once Hitch asked Joan to explain something to Peter in French. Peter listened attentively, then finally broke in, mystified frustration in his voice: "*Please* speak English!"

As time passed on, with Peter and me in Hollywood, our friendship continued. Still the heavy, but with that touch of sympathy, he played in Irwin Allen's production of *The Story of Mankind* (1957). Lorre portrayed Nero, fiddling while Rome burned. But since it was Peter who was fiddling, who gave a fig for Rome?

I remember Peter again, once more in an Irwin Allen production, our adaptation of Jules Verne's *Five Weeks in a Balloon* (1962). He played a whip-wielding East African slave dealer, lashing his lovelies into the presence of a sultan. From an actor's viewpoint, the dealer wasn't exactly an endearing character. Yet in spite of his

DOWN BUT NOT OUT

I HAD WRITTEN the first adaptation of a James Bond spy tale — *Casino Royale* for the Chrysler *Climax TV Hour*. It was a live production. Peter was the heavy, and with Bond inevitably winning out, he had to die at the end. James Bond indeed triumphed, and Peter expired as the camera sent the show across the nation live. But then, the director failed to push the right button, and instead of this scene jumping to the next, the cameras remained on "dead" Peter. Rightfully concluding that his job was done, he rose and quietly departed to his dressing room, smiling whimsically, to the utter bewilderment of possibly thirty million viewers.

— C.B.

With the notorious Evelyn Keyes in The Face Behind the Mask.

viciousness, Peter immediately established himself as "Mr. Adorable" and remained so until the movie's fade out. Looking back, I'm not sure that the screenplay intended it that way.

We all know the term "sympathetic villain." The audience recognizes an excuse for the character's villainy. I can't remember any movie of mine in which Peter's behavior was supposed to be excused, but audiences loved him just the same — perhaps because he killed with that alluring smile, or perhaps because his personal kindness came through.

Lorre, his frequent accomplice Sydney Greenstreet, and Geraldine Fitzgerald share a lottery ticket in Three Strangers.

LON CHANEY, JR.: A MAN LIVING IN A SHADOW

REGINALD LeBORG

LON CHANEY, SR. was called "The Man of a Thousand Faces." I believe Lon Chaney, Jr. could be called "The Man of a Thousand Contradictions." He was gentle and violent; sentimental and hard-boiled; liberal and conservative; a family man and a loner; an introvert and a show-off. He was capable of great love, yet one impassioned with hate. He was ambitious yet resigned — to the fact that he would never have the opportunity to prove himself as great an actor as his father, and to the realization that whatever stardom he achieved was due in part to his trading on his father's celebrated name. His was a career and, I believe, a personality that resulted directly from trying to embrace and, at the same time, disown the career and image of his late father.

That father and son were both fine artists, there is no doubt. Unfortunately their generation gap was greater than that of their actual years; it was marked by the added component of a technical achievement that changed the art of screen acting: sound.

Lon Chaney, Sr. was a unique talent; not only because of his superbly grotesque makeup, but also because even without extravagant disguises, and appearing as himself, he was innately a magnificent, sensitive actor. His emotional moments of wordless thought caught in prolonged close-ups are not likely ever to be surpassed. Had Lon Chaney, Sr. been active during the sound era, he would likely have been just as great an artist as he was in the silent days. His one sound picture, *The Unholy Three* (1930), shows this.

It is a moot poser to reflect whether, had Lon Chaney, Jr. been an actor during the silent era, he would

---

REGINALD LeBORG *was a director at Universal Studios, where in the forties he made four films with Lon Chaney, Jr. His other credits include* San Diego, I Love You; Sins of Jezebel; *and* Diary of a Madman.

have been as great an actor as his father. His physical bulk hampered a certain required agility, and I question whether he could have endured the agony that would result from distorting his body as his father did.

There are actors who can switch from one role to another as easily as changing a shirt. Still other actors live the part and become the character they started out merely to portray. I believe that Lon Chaney, Jr. became Lennie in *Of Mice and Men* (1939). He was perfect for the part, and because he was so good at it, he tried to feel it. Yet the softness and violence of Lenny were so indelibly transplanted in him, they invariably came to the surface in whatever role he played.

Lon Chaney, Sr. took great pains to create his characters. He would study the minutest traits and gestures and emotional shadings for his portrayals, innovating and engineering with exactitude the intricate makeup and training himself to be a different character each time — often wracking his body and face to a point bordering on masochism.

Lon Chaney, Jr. had a streak of violence in his personality. In roles that called for it, his rage could become almost uncontrollable. There is a scene in *The Mummy's Ghost* (1944) where the mummy is supposed to kill the professor, played by Frank Reicher. Chaney grasped him and squeezed his neck so forcefully, the poor fellow was almost strangled. Gasping for breath, Reicher sank to his knees. I called out, ''Cut!'' The scene had played beautifully, but was dangerously realistic. (Every time this scene played in theaters, audiences gasped.) Reicher, a short, slightly built actor cried out, ''He nearly strangled me!'' Chaney was most apologetic to the little man. However, at the end of that day, when I talked to Chaney and told him to be gentler in similar scenes, he did not take it too well.

In that same film, in the museum scene, there was to be a scuffle between the mummy and a guard. I had planned to have Chaney crash through the glass doors that led to the museum's Egyptian room. I asked that the plate glass be replaced with breakaway glass. But when I arrived on the set the day of shooting that scene, the breakaway glass had not been substituted. I didn't want to hold up production, so I told Chaney just to push the door open instead of crashing through. Chaney did as I

While he inherited the part of the mummy (L) from Boris Karloff, The Wolf Man *was his own creation — and how he is best remembered.*

He earned critical acclaim as the slow-witted Lennie in Of Mice and Men. *Burgess Meredith played George.*

suggested during the rehearsal, but when it came to the actual shooting of the scene, after the scuffle, he crashed right through the plate glass, slightly injuring one of his hands in the process. He wanted to show me he wasn't afraid to go through plate glass, and he smiled with gratification when I complimented his bravado. His father would have done it just like that, he asserted.

During our time together at Universal in the mid-forties, Lon Chaney, Jr. talked to me about how his father hadn't wanted him to be an actor, and subsequently of his early struggles in other jobs — even as a songwriter, a talent he was proud to have inherited from his mother, a singer. However, after his father's death in 1930, he immediately switched to acting, using his baptismal name Creighton Chaney in order to try to make it on his own. Although he was not happy when a studio

executive changed his name to Lon Chaney, Jr., by the time we met he was willing to take advantage of the crowd-pleasing image that went with the name Lon Chaney. (Yet, I think it is significant that he hated to be referred to by the "Junior" added to that name.) He mentioned to me the possibility that his father's movies would be remade with sound, and I could tell that he wanted his father's roles badly — although this would further entrap him in his father's shadow. I had heard that he had tried very hard to get the lead in *The Phantom of the Opera* (1943) and was terribly upset and angry when Claude Rains got the role. Lon was temperamental, but not one to hold a grudge for long, so he forgave and forgot — at least it seemed he did. It was obvious, however, that *something* was gnawing at him, because more and more he resorted to the solace of alcohol and

CONJECTURE

IF LON CHANEY, JR. had not had so famous a father, could he have achieved stardom? This is indeed an arbitrary thought, because stardom depends not only upon talent but also upon opportunity. Creighton was never given the opportunity on his own; it had to depend upon Lon Chaney, Sr.

A motion picture executive who knew exploitation figured correctly: i.e., Creighton Chaney could make it and be fairly successful as an actor. But as Lon Chaney, Jr. in a horror picture, he could achieve stardom. After all, as the old proverb says, "The fruit does not fall far from the tree."

— R. L.

sedatives. (Our producer on *The Mummy's Ghost* had warned me, "Be careful that you don't work too late with him, because in the afternoon he gets thirsty, and then he'll be difficult.")

Once Lon and I discussed those classic films of his father's, *The Hunchback of Notre Dame* (1923), *The Monster* (1925), *Mr. Wu* (1927), *The Unholy Three, The Road to Mandalay* (1926), *West of Zanzibar* (1928), and others. I expressed how much I admired his father and told him that he practically emulated him. "Emulate?" he questioned. "I want to top him!" I smiled and commented that in his own right he was tremendously talented, and demonstrated it unquestionably in his portrayal of Lennie in *Of Mice and Men* as well as his creation of *The Wolf Man* (1941). Lon's eyes glowed. Then and there I became his friend. His big hand pounded my shoulder. "We'll do something great together, Pappy," he smiled. I had strange emotions. I was but a few years older than Lon, but to him I had suddenly become a father figure.

Altogether Lon and I made four films together at Universal, *The Mummy's Ghost* and the first three "Inner Sanctum" films — *Calling Doctor Death* (1944), *Weird Woman* (1944), and *Dead Man's Eyes* (1944). He was particularly proud and excited about the times he was allowed to use his own concepts, such as on the mummy movie when he developed a gait that was quite different from the one Karloff had used in the original *The Mummy* (1932). I found him to be a very fine actor as long as he didn't fall into his Lennie characterization. In any case, all our films together were successful, and I was allowed by Universal to choose films more to my liking such as the comedy *San Diego, I Love You* (1944).

But Universal kept Lon Chaney, Jr. in the "Inner Sanctum" series, handing him to other contract directors. When I met him just prior to my departure for Paramount, he no longer considered me his friend. He poked his finger into my chest and said, "Traitor! We were supposed to do big things together."

"We will, Lon," I promised.

And I sincerely meant it.

"I've heard that story before," he said, and turned abruptly away from me.

It wasn't until twelve years later, when I was doing *The Black Sleep* (1956), that I met up again with Chaney. Chaney's role as a half-man, half-monster, fit him to a "T," and he played it admirably. But he still used that same shuffling gait he had invented for the mummy picture, with inarticulate grunts and facial expressions similar to those found in Lennie.

This film featured most of the horror character actors, Basil Rathbone, Akim Tamiroff, John Carradine, Bela Lugosi, and Chaney, and each of them tried to outdo the others. It was not easy to keep harmony within the cast and balance the performances.

A few times I noticed great antagonism between Chaney and Lugosi, which may have been a smoldering resentment carried over from their days at Universal when they had competed for the role of *Dracula* (1931). It struck me that here again, as it had been with *The Phantom of the Opera*, Chaney seemed bitter about what might have been.

The years had played havoc with his body. He'd gained considerable weight, and his face was puffed up, with his nose, jaw, and ears appearing more than normally prominent. While talking to him, I couldn't help but observe that he was coughing a great deal and his voice had become unusually hoarse. Later, I read that he had undergone several operations for throat cancer, the ailment that eventually contributed to his death in 1973. It was the same disease that had killed Lon Chaney, Sr.

Chaney, Jr. and Reginald LeBorg, in the mid-forties.

LON CHANEY:
A TOUGH ACT TO FOLLOW

LON CHANEY *was a master of macabre disguises. Among his most memorable were in (Clockwise, starting below)* The Phantom of the Opera; Laugh, Clown, Laugh; Mr. Wu; Out of the Fog; London After Midnight; The Unholy Three; *and* The Hunchback of Notre Dame.

341

CLAUDE RAINS: ASTUTE CRAFTSMAN

VINCENT SHERMAN

DURING THE SUMMER OF 1928, I was working as an extra in New York, in the Theater Guild's productions of O'Neill's *Marco's Millions* and *Volpone,* Stefan Zweig's version of the Ben Jonson play. The shows were alternating at the time, and the Guild was preparing to send them out on tour. I first met Claude Rains when he was engaged by the Guild to replace Dudley Diggs in the two plays.

Since we knew very little about him, other than that he was from the London theater, we all observed him with great curiosity. In the beginning, we thought he was painfully slow in his approach, deliberating over each line, questioning, considering every move and piece of business carefully.

Many of us wondered if he would ever achieve the necessary pace and vitality, the essential humor and irony. In rehearsals there was no sign of a real performance, just a slow, almost plodding progression. What was even more foreign to us was his extreme reserve, his aloofness. While he was polite enough, he was also distant and slightly imperious. We could not make up our minds whether it was his English reticence, shyness, or the fact that he was so completely absorbed in his work.

Little by little, however, we began to see his characterizations emerge. As he integrated dialogue, movement, and business, his pace picked up, and then his enormous vitality revealed itself. It was like watching a plant grow, develop, and finally flower. By the time the curtain rose he was giving a brilliant performance in both plays, with his special quality of humor and irony, sly looks and gestures. His voice was outstanding: deep, rich, and resonant with a mellow dignity.

We had come to realize that he was not a glib sight reader but a meticulous craftsman who knew exactly what he was doing. And I was soon to learn that he was

He brought class to every picture in which he appeared.

not a cold person. He was basically shy, but had a great capacity for warmth and laughter.

Although separated by age difference, we became good friends when the company went on tour. He was gracious and kind to me at a time when I needed it, when every young actor needs encouragement. After each performance, we would spend hours talking or playing chess. He rarely discussed any personal matters, although I did learn that he had been married two or three times in England, was unattached when he came to this

---

VINCENT SHERMAN *has directed such films as* All Through the Night, Old Acquaintance, Mr. Skeffington, Nora Prentiss, The Hasty Heart, The Adventures of Don Juan, Harriet Craig, The Naked Earth, The Young Philadelphians, *and* Ice Palace.

His face was never seen in his debut film, The Invisible Man.

sations, then and later, were about theater and films — he was a man of mystery otherwise, who guarded his privacy even in those early years.

A few seasons later, when the Guild produced *The Good Earth,* Claude was cast in the lead role of Wang opposite Alla Nazimova, who played his wife. I was given a small part in the play. Toward the end of the run, he was summoned to Hollywood to appear in *The Invisible Man* (1933), to be made at Universal Studios. I wished him well and said good-bye, not knowing whether I would ever see him again.

A few months later, however, I flew to Hollywood to appear in the film version of Elmer Rice's *Counsellor-at-Law* (1933). Immediately upon my arrival, I called Claude, and that night we had dinner together. He took me for a drive afterward and showed me the Pacific Ocean. *The Invisible Man* was a success, and after he made another film, *Crime Without Passion* (1934), which likewise was praised, he signed a contract with Warner Brothers and became a permanent resident of Hollywood.

In 1937, I was offered a three-way contract by Warners, to write, act, or direct, as the studio saw fit to use me. I accepted and found myself working on the same lot as Claude. By this time, we were both married and soon to be fathers. He seemed happier than I had ever seen him, had a lovely home in Bel Air, and his career was moving ahead steadily.

Then in 1940, after having written several scripts at Warners, they made me a director, and in my second film, *Saturday's Children* (1940), Claude was cast as the

country, and fell in love with a young woman in the company of Pearl S. Buck's *The Good Earth* (whom he later married — and divorced). Most of our conver-

George Bernard Shaw chose him to play opposite Vivien Leigh in Caesar and Cleopatra.

An intellectual villain in The Unsuspected, *with Audrey Totter.*

father of Anne Shirley. It was a gentle role, warm and sympathetic, similar to the role he had played in *Four Daughters* (1938). While we were friends and I felt he respected me, I was nevertheless worried about how he might react to my directing him. After all, he had been a star on Broadway when I was just a bit player, and he was now a well-known Hollywood figure, while this was only my second directorial effort. I had no cause for fear or doubts. On the first day of shooting, he was on the set on time and was letter-perfect in his lines. Early that morning, we rehearsed a long and substantial scene, and after I finished explaining what I hoped to accomplish to the cast, I glanced over at Claude. He was smiling and gave me an imperceptible — to all but me — nod of approval. I will always be grateful for that gesture. It gave me the courage and confidence I needed.

Saturday's Children was well received by the crit-ics, and Claude was happy for me. Later, we did our second film together, *Mr. Skeffington* (1944), starring Bette Davis. I had recently finished *Old Acquaintance* (1943) with Bette, and since we both knew Claude's work, we fought to have him in the picture. We were justified — his performance as Job Skeffington earned him an Academy Award nomination.

Directing him was only a matter of giving a slight suggestion here, a gentle nudge there. He was an immaculate actor, clean, precise, and exact in everything he did. There was no floundering about until he got the feel of a role, but a studied analysis with a design in the background that built bit by bit until the total architecture became visible. It was not consciously Stanislavsky, but he was doing precisely what Stanislavsky had formulated in connection with building a character. He knew what he wanted and why; Claude had great concentration, knew his attitude in each scene, played *with* his partner, and created an inner life for his character.

He was a professional in the best sense of the word. While he came on the set prepared, he always allowed room for the director to create with him. Having adapted to picture-making, he was aware that the film director must stage scenes with the camera in mind; he was always ready to make any adjustment in terms of movement and positions.

As I reflect upon his career, I am amazed at the variety of roles he played and his fantastic versatility. Gentle fathers, suave villains, sharp politicians, evil doctors, compassionate doctors, sophisticated artists — there was no end to the list.

Recently, I was glancing through a book written by John Gielgud and was astonished to learn that Claude had once taught him acting in London. Moreover, Laurence Olivier was also one of Claude's students. Claude had never mentioned this to me, like many other things in his past. They did not seem important to him. His life was his acting, the satisfaction of creating a memorable role.

Married to Bette Davis in Vincent Sherman's Mr. Skeffington. *Both stars won Academy Award nominations.*

LEE J. COBB: MY FATHER

JULIE COBB

RECENTLY I SAW *Anna and the King of Siam* (1946), which was made the year before I was born. It was fun, in a strange way, to see my father in his skimpy costume, bare-chested and in dark makeup, looking so strong and handsome. As I watched him I wondered what he was like then; what was his relationship to my mother and to my brother, who was then three years old?

When I was growing up, he was the biggest, strongest person in the world to me. I remember observing him in rooms full of people, and he was bigger than anyone there. His moods were bigger, his opinions bigger; he was more intense. There was a scary rightness about him. And when someone like that is in a bad mood or melancholy, they are unapproachable. That's the feeling I had. Cordelia has a line in *King Lear* about her father, "Was this a face to be opposed against the warring winds?" Well, no, my father's wasn't. His features were refined. His eyes were large and clear and soft. His mouth was sensitive, sensual. I think that the toughness that came through was due to an inner strength he had. Maybe because he had to fight his own way in his profession. Working and surviving in the movie industry imparts a kind of strength.

My father once said to me that his real life seemed less alive to him than his artistic life. And I believed him. He allowed himself certain leniencies in his work that he didn't allow in his life. When I look at his work today, I see parts of him I never knew: a beautiful, colorful range of human emotions. I also see parts of him I knew very well: his intelligence, his presence, his intensity. He was a serious man, a man who was nicknamed, as my mother tells me, in his Group Theater days, "Herr Moody," because of his black moods.

And I knew them well. He was extremely sensitive

"He was a spontaneous actor who approached each role differently; he was never miscast." — J. C.

to his environment, incapable of levity, although he was at times as capable as anyone of having a great time and enjoying something passionately. I would say he was trapped by his intellect; he saw things too clearly to be carefree. But despite his seriousness he was one of the funniest people I have ever known, an absolutely brilliant wit. One of the reasons I like *Come Blow Your Horn* (1963) so much is because it was one of the few opportunities he had to display his comedic side. Next to his voice, the thing I miss most about my father is his sense of humor.

The film industry limited him. Like so many actors, he felt the shackles of typecasting. With too few excep-

JULIE COBB *received the Los Angeles Drama Critics Circle Award in 1977 for her performance in* After the Fall. *She has done much work on television, including* Brave New World *and an episode of* Gunsmoke *in which another guest star was her father, Lee J. Cobb.*

BIRTH OF "SALESMAN"

DAD WAS UNDER CONTRACT to Twentieth Century-Fox and living in California when *Death of a Salesman* entered his life. Elia Kazan, his old colleague from the Group Theater, wanted him to play the part of Willy Loman. My parents were entertaining company when the script arrived at our home via messenger — a new play by Arthur Miller. My father excused himself and went into the study to read it. He emerged a few hours later, script in hand, and said to the guests, "You have to hear this! You have to hear this! It's the greatest play ever written." And he proceeded to sit down and read the play to them — all the parts — from cover to cover. At the end of the reading, they all knew it was the play of a lifetime and, for Father, the role of a lifetime. And, of course it was. I was just a baby when it first opened, but I did see him years later in the television production, and his performance was one of the most excruciatingly beautiful and painful I've ever witnessed.   — J. C.

Cobb's Death of a Salesman *for television. With Mildred Dunnock, also his co-star in the stage version.*

On set of The Three Faces of Eve, *with Joanne Woodward.*

He was never a superstar. He was, and I hate the expression, a character actor. Because of his maturity at an early age or because of his capacities as a man and as an artist, he took the more flavorful parts that many of the leading actors couldn't have played — parts that supported the star. Although he differed in every role, his own personality always stamped his work. His characters came through. You knew what their opinions were. You knew how they felt. Who they loved. Who they hated. Who they feared. That was perhaps his most dynamic point as an actor: the clarity of his convictions was always up front.

He was a father to a lot of people. This started with *Death of a Salesman*. I've been told that on the opening night of the original Broadway production, men and women in the audience wept and cried and sobbed, "That's my father! That's my father!" Of course, Arthur Miller's play was phenomenal, but it was my father who made Willy Loman breathe.

tions, producers saw him only as the stern, angry type—racketeers, labor leaders, megalomaniacs—tough men with their sleeves rolled up. When he did attempt offbeat (for him) characters, the results were as successful as they were refreshing. I wish he'd had more chances to show his tenderness and vulnerability, as he did in *Golden Boy* (1939) and *Anna* and *Green Mansions* (1959). And I love his low-key compassion and reassurance in *The Three Faces of Eve* (1957) and the lusty, guzzling, lecherous character he played in *The Brothers Karamazov* (1958). A number of people have spoken to me about his role in *The Exorcist* (1973) — the scene in which he asks Ellen Burstyn for her autograph. It's the only moment of charm in the whole film, and I treasure it.

Come Blow Your Horn, *with Frank Sinatra and Molly Picon.*

With Marlon Brando in On the Waterfront.

Charles Laughton came backstage one night and voiced what a lot of people had been saying: "You must play King Lear. You must!" From that point on, that was Dad's dream. During the next twenty years, there were often plans for productions of *King Lear* submitted to my father — plans that he would deem unsatisfactory or proposed productions that never quite panned out. He became so obsessed with the role that finally he *had* to play the part; I think he realized that he had to tackle it before he was too old. In 1968 his *Lear* opened in New York at Lincoln Center. Lear is an almost impossible part to play. It makes savage emotional demands on the actor and requires huge reserves of strength and stamina. Dad thrived on it! He was in superb shape while he was doing it. I don't remember ever seeing him so happy. The thing that struck me most about his Lear was his humanity. It was real. I remember being in the opening night audience and hearing audible sobs at the end of the play. I was almost unconscious with excitement and pride.

THE DARK PERIOD

WHEN *Death of a Salesman* was to be filmed in the early 1950s, my father was at the height of his controversy with the House Un-American Activities Committee. It was just before his so-called testimony, and he was bad news. The producers of the *Salesman* film knew that with Lee J. Cobb in the picture, they would all be subject to the government's scrutiny. He lost the part. This had to have broken his heart. In fact, in 1955 he had a massive coronary that almost killed him. When he recovered, he wasn't expected ever to work again.

I only spoke to my father about McCarthy once. It was during the 1960s when I was in college. I remember that my father and I were coming out of a restaurant, walking to our cars, when I brought it up. He looked away for a moment. And then he began — with difficulty at first, then the words began to tumble out with a gut-wrenching pain I had never seen in him. He said that he avoided testifying for over two years. He put the committee off until he was forced to testify. When he stood before the HUAC, he didn't take the Fifth Amendment. Father maintained that he didn't name new names — that he only corroborated names previously given to the committee. However, that was enough ammunition for his friends and colleagues to turn against him. "You have no idea, Julie," he said, "you have no idea what it means to have the United States government focus on you — what it's like when they decide they want something from *you*."

— J. C.

When he died, after my immediate reaction of personal loss, I experienced what I can only describe as a culture loss: the slamming reality that we could not have all the work that Lee J. Cobb had yet to do. This was a greater source of loss for me than my own personal grief. He was young, and he still had many roles to play.

The Brothers Karamazov, *with William Shatner.*

Twelve Angry Men, *with Henry Fonda.*

SYDNEY GREENSTREET: CIVILIZED VILLAIN

STEVEN GRANT

NTERING THE MOVIES at an age when most men consider retirement, Sydney Greenstreet adapted with amazing ease to the rigors of an unfamiliar medium. Drawing on his theatrical experience, he infused even his weakest roles with warmth and dignity. Though trapped throughout his career in supporting roles, he often outshined his leads; even Humphrey Bogart complained, albeit jokingly, about being upstaged by Greenstreet.

Greenstreet played many roles: black marketeer, saint, hopeless romantic, powerful publisher, and, most successfully, an outright villain. He usually portrayed complex, morally ambiguous gentlemen, notable for their polish — an effect aided by Greenstreet's direct, even voice and measured British accent. Many of his characters were opportunistic individuals operating under their own sets of peculiar values, genteel when possible, treacherous when necessary. As critic Bosley Crowther once observed, the typical Greenstreet role was "entirely an enigma — malefic yet dignified, urbane and full of enviable refinement, yet hard and unpredictable underneath."

Remarkably, Greenstreet did not make his first picture until the age of sixty-one. Long successful in the theater both in England and in America, he had been offered movie roles prior to that of Kasper Gutman in *The Maltese Falcon* (1941). But the villainous Gutman was the first character strong enough to appeal to him. It was Greenstreet's skill as a Shakespearean actor — altogether, he had appeared in over a hundred of the Bard's roles and could recite entire plays verbatim — that he brought to this sinister part. In Gutman we not only see "the very essence of blood-chilling menace, breathing corruption and evil," as one fan magazine of the day put it, but also an admirable precision and humor that makes the character even more sinister. Gutman, who was the prototype for *all* Greenstreet villains, is among the most interesting antagonists the movies have ever offered.

STEVEN GRANT *is a co-editor of the film magazine* The Velvet Light Trap.

Perhaps Greenstreet's most outstanding quality was his ability to control his expressions. The movement of a single facial muscle could alter his mood from unassuming politeness to cunning superiority or frantic despair. One magazine described him as "a ponderous fat man who can glare balefully out of puffy eyes, who can narrow his mouth evilly, who can paralyze victims with a bland glance."

Greenstreet often told stories about his weight, as when he plunged through a stage at an outdoor perfor-

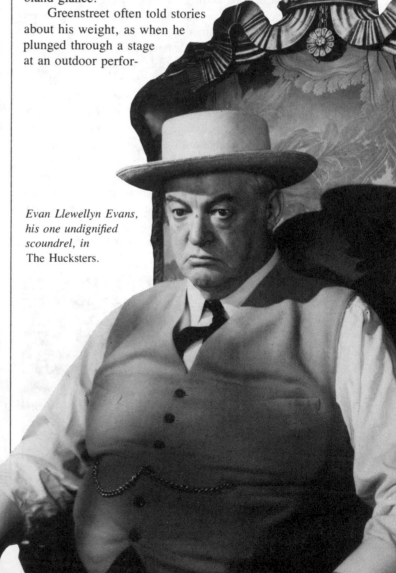

Evan Llewellyn Evans, his one undignified scoundrel, in The Hucksters.

With John Emery (L), Eleanor Parker, and Matthew Boulton in The Woman in White.

mance of *As You Like It,* or when he was trampled by a runaway horse in Central Park ("Didn't hurt me, but the horse had to be destroyed."). He accepted, or perhaps endorsed, the nickname "Tiny," but Greenstreet, who stood five-ten and weighed two hundred eighty pounds, was never quite at home in his own girth. He was irritated when moviegoers referred to him as "the Fat Man," a nickname left over from the Gutman role.

Contrary to popular belief, it was not merely his size that gave Greenstreet his screen presence, but rather the ease with which he moved that bulk. Having been active as a boy, Greenstreet continued to golf and bicycle, even when the rigors of going on the road forced him to inactivity. And his theatrical training gave Greenstreet great control over his body. Part of his sinister charm came from the sight of such a large man moving with such fluidity and speed.

Despite the fact that Greenstreet played several memorable non-evil roles — most notably General Winfield Scott in *They Died with Their Boots On* (1941) — Warner Brothers tried to relegate him to villainous parts. Greenstreet dreaded this typecasting. He once wrote, "An actor can play anything he looks. I daresay seventy-five percent of the roles I played on the stage were comedy. What I want, really, is any role which has color, philosophy, and the humane quality which makes a character warm and believable. I haven't minded villains so far; villains can be interesting people.

But a musician who can play Beethoven wants to play something besides Beethoven once in a while." Unlike

With George Raft in Background to Danger.

Peter Lorre, who had starred in films before signing with Warners and with whom he was often teamed, Greenstreet was unable to get a starring vehicle. A projected lead in an unproduced film called *The Fat Man* (a title used by William Castle for a 1951 film) never materialized, and Greenstreet's suggestions of a film about Benjamin Franklin as ambassador to France and a film version of *The Merchant of Venice,* in which he would play Shylock, went unheeded by Warners executives. The roles he craved were denied him, and Greenstreet was forced to play second bill to an assortment of actors and actresses. Unable to prove that he contributed to the financial success of a film, he was forced into increasingly mediocre parts.

Despite his treatment by Warner Brothers, Greenstreet remained in Hollywood. An aging man with a wife and son, he found that, after a life of touring, it was "pure heaven to have a front door to unlock, a garden to grow, and a teapot to put on the table at four in the afternoon." In addition to this, Greenstreet found himself enthralled by the medium of films, which, through changes of angles and distances, could manipulate audience attention. "Suddenly I am overwhelmingly conscious of a thousand little mannerisms I didn't even know I had. It is a startling discovery."

Although Greenstreet occasionally found a role at Warners that pleased him, such as the part of William Thackeray in the otherwise-syrupy *Devotion* (1946), he went free-lance in 1947, when his contract with Warners expired. His first non-Warners role was in MGM's *The Hucksters* (1947), one of the studio's biggest hits. It was, in many ways, a breakthrough for Greenstreet. The character Evan Llewellyn Evans, a soap tycoon (based on the real-life cigarette magnate George Washington Hill) was the archetypal Greenstreet character turned inside-out: dignity replaced by vulgarity, gaudiness substituted for subtle charm, English refinement lost to American bravura. Greenstreet successfully defined his character in a single, unforgettable scene, in which Evans spits on a table to make a point to Clark Gable: "Mr. Norman, you have just seen me do a disgusting thing. But you'll *always* remember it."

In one grand gesture, Greenstreet had answered both studio heads who felt that he could not help sell a picture and critics who accused him of being capable of only a single screen type.

The proof came too late. After six more films, including the decadent Sheriff Titus of *Flamingo Road* (1949), diabetes and Bright's disease forced Greenstreet into retirement — after less than ten years as a film actor. On January 19, 1954, he died. Sadly, the obituary in *Variety* contained little more than a description of him as "a character actor."

However, Sydney Greenstreet is remembered for his Gutman, for his Mr. Peters of *The Mask of Dimitrios* (1944), for his Nero Wolfe, the detective he played on radio, and for a score of other roles. A revival of interest in him is growing, and with that revival perhaps will come a recognition of Greenstreet as Hollywood's most captivating villain.

With Rosalind Ivan in The Verdict.

CLIFTON WEBB: WORRIED SICK

HENRY LEVIN

"Ask the average moviegoer if he remembers Clifton Webb and he'll probably answer 'Sure — he's that funny Englishman who poured oatmeal on the baby's head in Sitting Pretty.*' Wrong on two counts. He wasn't English; he was born in Indiana. It wasn't oatmeal; it was cream of wheat."* —H. L.

IT IS IRONIC THAT Clifton Webb, a tremendously gifted actor, dancer, singer, painter, composer, pianist, and raconteur, should have gained universal fame as a result of pouring gooey cereal on a baby's head in *Sitting Pretty* (1948). His success in playing an amusing English baby-sitter named Belvedere prompted Twentieth Century-Fox to produce two more "Mr. Belvedere" films, threatening to type the actor forever.

HENRY LEVIN *directed Clifton Webb in* Mister Scoutmaster, Holiday for Lovers, *and* The Remarkable Mr. Pennypacker. *He has also directed such films as* Belles on Their Toes, Journey to the Center of the Earth, The Wonderful World of the Brothers Grimm, Genghis Khan, *and* Murderer's Row.

In addition to these films, the studio added several comedies with children to Webb's schedule, proving once more that Hollywood executives prefer to repeat a success — until it fails — rather than try something fresh. In *Cheaper by the Dozen* (1950) he fathered twelve assorted offspring; in *Mister Scoutmaster* (1953), he had to tame a troop of disorderly Boy Scouts and one monster of a Cub Scout; and then in *The Remarkable Mr. Pennypacker* (1959), he made history by having two wives at the same time, in two cities, with seventeen children between them.

His career as a comedic baby-sitter-parent-bigamist has overshadowed his more serious work: the sinister Waldo Lydecker in *Laura* (1944); the greedy, villainous buyer of archaeological finds in *Boy on a Dolphin*

With Ginger Rogers in Dreamboat.

CLIFTON WEBB had a great deal to do with the success of *The Razor's Edge* (1946), aside from his superb performance. First of all, being a friend of Somerset Maugham, Clifton felt that he had contributed, if not to the writing of the book, at least to the screenplay. Certainly his role of Eliot Templeton was a composite of four odd characters Maugham and Webb had known in Paris.

He also believed that he had a lot to do with Darryl Zanuck's decision to buy the book for Twentieth Century-Fox. Most studio executives believed the story was "too intellectual" for movie audiences, and that belief infuriated Webb. He was angrily critical of the Hollywood proverb, "Make films for the twelve-year-old mind, not for the elite." The novel *The Razor's Edge* sold two million copies, as Clifton reminded us. "There aren't *that* many elite."

— H. L.

(1957); the cruelly witty socialite in *Titanic* (1953).

Clifton Webb was by no means a one-part actor. Even before his film successes he had amused audiences all over the United States in the national company of *The Man Who Came to Dinner* and enchanted both Broadway and the road in Noel Coward's *Blithe Spirit*. And before that, his dancing, singing, and mimicry had made him a Broadway star in *The First Little Show*, *As Thousands Cheer*, and *Three's a Crowd*, among other musicals. Add to that an early career in grand opera and one begins to appreciate the infinite variety of his talents.

He was more than a great interpreter of already-existing roles. Invariably, he brought something of himself into the part he was playing. As effective as his masterly delivery of lines was, it was his expressive face that really held his audience. The sinister gaze, the half-bored look of the experienced sophisticate, the raised eyebrow, the wonderful sudden flash of surprise that lit up his whole being, the subtle double take, the unsubtle comedic stare — they all played on the beholder with sure effect, making words superfluous.

The biting barbs and hilarious sarcasms rolled from his tongue with an air of spontaneity unmatched in these days of mumbling, tortured paroxysms of speech. And his debonair manner *never* deserted him, not even as a falling-down drunk in a scene in *Holiday for Lovers* (1959). There was a touch of elegance in his fall.

Watching Clifton Webb on the screen — graceful, elegant, precise in speech and manner — one believed that it all came easily to him. To the contrary, that spontaneity, that priceless timing was the result of long and careful preparation. Clifton would not begin a film until he had studied the completed script for many weeks. He always insisted that a dialogue director be placed at his exclusive disposal for at least three weeks before a pro-

duction's starting date so that the role could be thoroughly analyzed, rehearsed, and committed to memory by the time filming was to begin.

This meticulous method of preparation had its drawbacks, of course. An actor's lines are normally subject to a degree of change during the course of filming and it was torture for Clifton to alter a line — even a word — after he had engraved it on his tongue. And in spite of his exhaustive preparation, he suffered intensely while working. Each new scene gave him labor pains.

Whenever I directed Clifton, I made it a habit to stay up each night past my normal bedtime because more

Child-hater Webb becomes Mister Scoutmaster.

often than not he would telephone me at ten-thirty, or eleven, or eleven-thirty, usually on the verge of tears. "Henry," he'd moan, "this scene — tomorrow's work! Whatever are we going to do with it? I can't see myself saying those things somehow. It's all wrong, dear boy, don't you see?"

"Exactly what bothers you about it?" I would ask, throwing caution to the winds. (It is often fatal to ask an actor to be specific about his criticism of a scene. That question can cost a good hour of sleep.) At times Clifton would be vague. On the other hand there were times when he would spot a distinct flaw, a line out of character, or possibly just a word or two that threw the scene off. At any rate, for thirty minutes or more I'd humor him or soothe him or agree with him, assuring him that it would all be fixed in the morning.

Next day he'd arrive on the set carrying two large bags, one under each eye, looking not at all the dapper sophisticate he really was — both on and off the screen. He would move wearily to me, seize me by the arm and groan, "Oh-h-h, dear boy. What a night! *What a night!* At first I simply could *not* get to sleep worrying over this *dreadful* scene, and then when I finally dozed off, I was attacked — literally attacked — by this stabbing pain right here, like a rapier turning and twisting. *Well*, I finally *had* to telephone the doctor at two-thirty and he told me to take two of those *giant* tablets of mine and a hot soak. Finally I managed an hour or two of sleep, but oh-h-h, I feel dreadful. And this *scene*. How will we get through it?"

We would agonize through a few rehearsals, altering a word or a line or transposing a speech, perhaps. More often than not, it was basically the same scene it had been on paper, but after shooting the master scene a few times, finally printing a take or two, and after assuring Clifton enthusiastically that the scene was now perfect and that he had not only performed it exquisitely but that

Vain killer in Laura. *With Gene Tierney and Vincent Price.*

he had made it all possible by finding the problem — and the solution — then, and only then, would he relax. And when Clifton relaxed he was an absolute joy. He would tell delightful stories and expound on any one of a thousand subjects. His knowledge seemed limitless and his choice of words flawless. The cast and those of the crew who were not immediately involved in setting up the next shot would listen and be spellbound by him. His laughter and theirs would fill the stage. Each morning he would metamorphose from a soul withered by despair into a bubbling master of ceremonies glorying in the obvious admiration shining in the faces of his audience. The remainder of the day's shooting would be a lark; Webb's confidence and good feeling infected everyone else in the cast and crew.

Of course, fame came as no surprise to him. Legend has it (and it's probably true) that after the success of *Sitting Pretty* was assured with its first smash reviews and its opening financial reports, a friendly producer chided him, "Well, now that you're such a success, I suppose you won't talk to us."

"My dear boy," Clifton replied, "I have *always* been a success. One more [hit] will not unsettle me."

Sitting Pretty *began Webb's* Mr. Belvedere *series.*

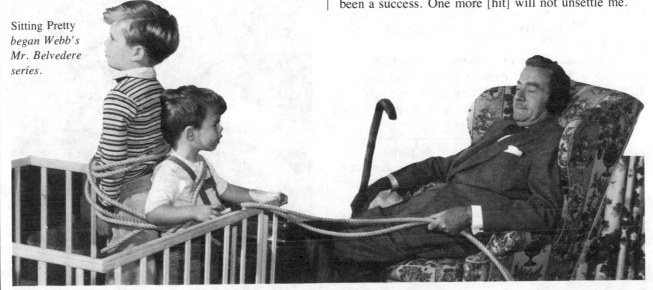

JACK LEMMON: NICE GUY WHO FINISHED FIRST

ALAN BROCK

WHEN I WAS an actor's agent in New York in the mid-1940s, many aspiring actors would visit our agency in hopes of being sent to audition for a movie or Broadway play. One of the unpleasant aspects of the job was the aggressiveness and insincerity of many of the actors — I often felt I was being conned. It was, therefore, a welcome relief to occasionally encounter a performer who did not try to make a false impression. In this category, Jack Lemmon stands out in my mind.

When we were called on to cast entire productions, our switchboard was never quiet and the office was hectic — uninterrupted activity. Contrary to the clammering of the others who jammed our agency, Jack Lemmon retained his usual calm. He needed work — everyone who contacted us did — but he never flaunted his needs. In the midst of chaos, he quietly went about making his visits to me and other agents. After interviewing scores of people, it was relaxing to talk with this unassuming young actor.

Jack would never try to convince me to send him out for a special role, nor would he attempt to change my decision regarding a part I believed was not right for him. He accepted my decisions, each time returning

Lemmon sang and danced in My Sister Eileen.

ALAN BROCK *has acted in television, in films, and on Broadway for George Abbott, Howard Lindsay, the Shuberts, Joshua Logan, and Elia Kazan. As a casting director and actor's agent, he represented such artists as Mrs. Patrick Campbell, Franchot Tone, Gypsy Rose Lee, Diana Barrymore, and Ramon Novarro. He has written on the theater and film for numerous publications, such as* Backstage, Playbill, Reader's Digest, Variety, *and* Classic Film Collector.

Mister Roberts. *With James Cagney, Henry Fonda, and William Powell, he won the Oscar for Best Supporting Actor.*

within a few days. Too many times I could sense the fury of a departing actor who felt rejected. But Jack was a rare case; he always left with a pleasant farewell. There was never any show of resentment, only appreciation. His manner generally paid off. I know, for instance, that he was sent by our office for motion picture auditions plus occasional commercial and documentary films. And I was always seeking him out when stage roles came up.

After Brando caused a sensation as Stanley Ko-

walski in *A Streetcar Named Desire* (1951), it became customary for juveniles to swagger into offices affecting

He was funniest being driven batty by fine comediennes, such as Shirley MacLaine (Above) and Judy Holliday.

His breakthrough as a serious actor: Days of Wine and Roses.

only social evening I spent with Jack was when I accepted his invitation to see his work at a successful nightspot called the Old Knick on Manhattan's East Side. Jack had gotten a job there as master of ceremonies. He had to sing, dance, crack jokes, and act in all the vaudeville skits as well as emcee the entire evening. He even played the piano.

It was a demanding assignment, but for the exceptionally talented Jack, it was a lucky setup. He could sing pleasantly, dance well enough, and be witty without being cheap. And it is important to point out that he performed his diverse tasks while retaining his own personal image. His clean-cut delivery gave the show a lift it would not otherwise have had. He showed his respect for his profession by refusing to stoop to the low comedy so often employed in nightclubs. Instead of using a sledgehammer to make a point, Jack artfully substituted a feather. He had — and has — great finesse.

Television broke the ice for Jack. It proved to be a great showcase for him. It brought calls for better roles. Among his early movie hits were *It Should Happen to*

rudeness, hair unkempt, wearing dungarees, sneakers, and T-shirts — totally opposite of the clean-cut look they had to have a few years earlier. Playwrights all wanted their actors to be exactly like the part they would be playing — yet Jack always had enough sense not to attempt to imitate any other type; he had the professional instinct to stick to his own attributes.

Whenever a play called for the typical American, in his early twenties, Jack Lemmon always came to mind. Whenever a part came up that called for a young man with style, who looked like a gentleman, I would think of Jack. I preferred to think of him for roles that needed a touch of class — high comedy was most appropriate — but knowing his need for work, I also called him when the part of a soda jerk came up. The odds were always against an unknown getting a part, but Jack was versatile, talented, and had salable good looks. There is an old truism on Broadway: ''You can put any actor into dungarees and he will be okay, but you cannot put any actor into a dinner jacket.'' Jack could wear either.

Curiously, we never met outside the office — never a lunch date, cocktails, or theater. Odd, since most ambitious actors know the value of these functions. The

You (1954) and *Phffft* (1954), two comedics in which he starred with Judy Holliday.

Lemmon's big break in movies came when he got to play Ensign Pulver, the typical American guy trying to make the grade in the Navy, in *Mister Roberts* (1955). While it was not a demanding role, dramatically speaking, it was more exacting than meets the eye. All of his scenes were with veteran stars — James Cagney, Henry Fonda, William Powell — and it was necessary for a special type of actor to be cast opposite them: one who would not be intimidated. Jack's solid stage training and deep sensitivity helped a great deal, and luckily the stars had faith in the ''newcomer'' and made him feel comfortable. Jack passed the test and, in the process, won an Academy Award for the year's Best Supporting Actor.

For the last twenty years, Jack Lemmon has been one of America's most successful actors, gaining a de-

When he ran out of suitable female partners, he found Walter Matthau in The Odd Couple.

On the verge of a breakdown in Save The Tiger.

served reputation as one of the most dependable comedic performers through a series of Billy Wilder–directed hits — *Some Like It Hot* (1959), *The Apartment* (1960), *Irma la Douce* (1963), *The Fortune Cookie* (1966), *Avanti* (1972), *The Front Page* (1974); slapstick parts in films such as *The Great Race* (1965); and roles in several Neil Simon movie adaptations, including *The Odd Couple* (1968), opposite his occasional co-star Walter Matthau. Ironically, Lemmon has received the most critical acclaim for dramatic roles; in fact he was nominated for Best Actor for *Days of Wine and Roses* (1962) and won an Oscar for *Save the Tiger* (1973).

To my knowledge, Jack does not adhere to any particular method of acting. He sets the pattern of his newest character from within. His acting is based on truth; the character grows from there. If Jack cannot believe what he is interpreting, he knows audiences will not either. Nothing phony is accepted, nor will he stoop to theatrical tricks. Jack's personal conception of his acting is solid.

The obvious reason I remember Jack so vividly, as he was when I first met him, is that he was, even then, in a class by himself. As success entered his life, he did not divert from his original honest purpose. The lasting appeal that Jack Lemmon has for movie audiences is this integrity. They too look for real people on the screen. Honesty touches everyone.

GEORGE C. SCOTT: ELECTRIC CURRENTS

ARTHUR HILLER

"His combination of traits produces in an audience an emotional response at the gut level." — A. H.

H E PROBABLY DOESN'T realize it, but I think if George C. Scott had his way, he'd like to be the world's greatest character actor and have nobody know him. It just doesn't work that way: He's close on the first count, but anonymity is something that a consummate actor can't have. It makes for a bit of inner turmoil.

If you asked me to describe Scott's acting in two words, I'd say gentle and volatile. If you asked me to describe his personality in two words, I'd say gentle and volatile. There are, of course, other words that fit: bril-

---

ARTHUR HILLER *is the director of such films as* Hospital, Man in the Glass Booth, The Americanization of Emily, Poppi, The Out-of-Towners, Plaza Suite, Man of La Mancha, Silver Streak, *and* Love Story, *for which he was nominated for an Academy Award.*

liant, creative, fearless, vital, original — and you can take it from there.

Scott's skill is his ability to produce an emotional response in you, his audience. He is not merely talented, he is bold, resourceful, and intensely serious, and you cannot help but come away with new emotions and new insights. Acting is his business, and does he know his business! He knows it in what we call a professional sense. When he arrives in the morning on the first day of shooting, he's totally prepared at that moment to film the entire picture without having to look at the script again. That's not to say he's rigid — his preparation lets him be flexible and responsive to direction, to feeling, or to changes that come from the other actors in a scene, or from the "environment" if he happens to be filming on location.

Now don't let me give you the impression he's perfect — sometimes he needs a second or third take during filming! For one sequence of *Hospital* (1971), we did six and a half pages of script — which usually would require turning the camera on and off about fifteen or twenty times — without stopping the camera. It was complicated: Scott came off an elevator in the hospital, crossed to a nurses' station, where he was told there was a problem in Room 806, walked around the nurses' desk, where he related to two crying people, headed down the lengthy corridor, was stopped to discuss the problem with a young doctor, entered Room 806, where he comforted a crying nurse and dealt with the problem (a dead doctor on a patient's bed), moved back out to the corridor, where he continued his discussion walking with the head nurse who had joined him, then stopped and turned away from a group of oncoming interns so they couldn't hear what he was saying, and proceeded to make decisions and give orders, before heading off to another elevator. Complicated? We had to do this one take seventeen times before I felt it was right. Not one of these repeats had to be remade because of George's flawed performance! On a few takes he was very good, and on all the others he was brilliant.

Those who saw *Hospital* will remember the scene in which he expresses his inadequacies, his feelings of im-

With Diana Rigg in Hospital, *directed by Arthur Hiller.*

potence, and his philosophical thoughts about life in general. It was a beautiful scene written to perfection by Paddy Chayefsky. I tried to stage it with the least number of cuts so that George would be able to build emotionally and not have to do it piecemeal. Three minutes into it there was a line in mid-speech where George was to say, "We have assembled the most enormous medical establishment and people are sicker than ever. . . ." As he approached the line with growing intensity, he said "We have established the most enormous — "then stopped for a fraction of a second as his mind obviously said to itself, "oh, oh . . . I just said 'established' instead of 'assembled,' so I can no longer say 'establishment' in this sentence — I'll have to think of another word." And he did: So the sentence came out, "We have established the most enormous medical entity. . . ." It's just remarkable that an actor could stay in character, and at the same time go through that outside thinking process and come up with not just another word, but a perfectly

suitable one. Not only that, but because of his searching, it felt even more as if he had pulled it up from his gut (which indeed he did). It gave one more dimension to the performance.

I don't mean to leave the impression that *Hospital* was Scott's only strong performance. I'm not about to forget his prosecuting attorney in *Anatomy of a Murder* (1959), his "user" in *The Hustler,* (1961), his marvelously quixotic general in *Dr. Strangelove* (1964), or his varied stage portrayals.

Maureen Stapleton told me of an incident that occurred on stage in the first act of Neil Simon's play *Plaza Suite.* The act tells of a fifty-year-old man (Scott) who wants to start life all over again. He and his wife (Stapleton) are discussing his fear of loss of virility and his insecurities "at this stage of life" and he says to his

A top supporting actor in The Hustler *(L, with Paul Newman) and* Dr. Strangelove.

As a doctor fascinated by the flighty Julie Christie in the neglected Petulia.

wife, "No matter what, Karen, in twenty-three years my feelings for you have never changed. You're my wife and I still love you." He then reveals he's having an affair with his secretary. Then he again proceeds to tell his wife how special she is and has been. The wife replies, "If I'm so special, what are you carrying on with secretaries for?" Now comes a moment in the play where he looks at her with compassion and for a moment can't decide whether to go to his mistress or stay with his wife. He finally decides to leave, and does.

One night instead of leaving, George came to Maureen and enfolded her, holding on for dear life. He had played the character so close to the line of indecision that he tipped the wrong way!!! Of course, he pulled himself

THE TROUBLE WITH OSCAR

THE ACADEMY AWARDS presentation of 1970 took place while George Scott and I were filming *Hospital* in New York. Scott had been nominated for *Patton* in the Best Actor category, and I had been nominated for Best Director (*Love Story*).

On Academy Award day, we began shooting at six in the morning so that I could leave on a flight that got me into Los Angeles at six-thirty that evening. My son met me at the airport with my tuxedo. I changed in the washroom and took a waiting limousine to the Awards. By ten-forty-five I, a loser, was on a plane returning to New York. I was back at work at seven-thirty next morning. I'd traveled six thousand miles and had nothing to show for it, while George C. Scott stayed in New York and won an Academy Award he didn't even want!

There was quite a stir because George let the Academy know that if he won the "Oscar" he would not

accept. It's not that he's against awards — he's against the competing with fellow actors for them. He really didn't mean to create a fuss; he was just trying to let the Academy know his feelings. The furor grew to such proportions that he told me that if there were a next time he would accept the Oscar. It was just too much trouble *not* to accept.

— A. H.

Conning his way through the South in The Flim Flam Man.

Scott's violent nature was apparent in Rage.

back, then left the room and the play continued. What excites me about that incident is that it illuminates his fearlessness in testing himself as an actor. He didn't play the safe two feet from the edge — he played right at the edge. Few actors have the courage or craftsmanship to do this, but it's this courage and skill that is the intangible that reaches right to the emotional gut of the viewer.

George is one of the few actors with whom I have worked who is also a fine director. An actor looks at the story and the relationships from the point of view of his character. That's what he is playing — a particular character in a particular situation that's the outgrowth of what has happened earlier in his life, *before* the film

story began. A director has to be able to figure out how the characters should relate to each other during one particular (film) story at one particular time. Most actors can't make that distinction. George can, and maybe that explains his uncanny ability to understand what emphasis or relationship the director is seeking with certain stagings and camera setups. He has an uncanny knack of being able to be totally in character and to look at his performance from the outside — as if he were directing. Each Scott performance lets us observe and feel the human condition in all its nakedness. It lets us feel it in a performance so full of fire and ice that it breaks through to some fourth dimension in acting.

ROBERT DUVALL: NO LIMITS

HORTON FOOTE

As Jackson Fentry in the critically lauded Tomorrow, *scripted by Horton Foote.*

I N OUR PRESENT DAY of glib journalism it is the fashion to put labels on actors, to limit them as to quality or type. It is argued that to win superstar status an actor must establish a definite personality or image. Therefore, Robert Duvall is puzzling to the journalistic mind because he cannot be so categorized. His range as a performer is extraordinary. When I go to see him in a role I have no idea how he will play it. His Boo Radley in *To Kill a Mockingbird* (1962), Jackson Fentry in *Tomorrow* (1972), and Edwin Stewart in *The Chase* (1966) were different in speech, mannerisms, and all visual detail — yet his work was never external, and these characters, through his talent, were each given a great degree of reality.

His best work is graced with a passion for exactness of the character he is creating. In talking with him about his approach to acting, one senses that he has an abiding interest in the human condition and is fascinated by the differences in people and in the most minute details of these differences. One feels that he never tires of observing people, analyzing how they talk, how they move, what motivates their behavior, and that this interest would continue whether he were acting or not.

He is never sentimental in what he shows us about human behavior, nor is he ever judgmental. He does not choose particular facets of his character to win an audience's sympathy or aspects that will show off his more appealing qualities as an actor. His choices have nothing at all to do with courting popularity or winning an audience's favor. He is after as much truth about the character, good or bad, as he can perceive and his talent reveal. He has a keen memory for details of performances he has admired by other actors, and he never seems to tire of discussing problems of his craft and his and other performers' solutions to them.

HORTON FOOTE *is a playwright and screenwriter who won an Academy Award in 1963 for his script of* To Kill a Mockingbird. *Among his other screen credits are* Storm Fear; Baby, the Rain Must Fall; Hurry Sundown; *and* Tomorrow. *He is the original author of* The Chase.

Capable of forcing great actors to perform at their peak, as in The Godfather *with Marlon Brando.*

I first saw him some twenty years ago. He was a very young actor performing in a play of mine, *The Midnight Caller,* at the Neighborhood Playhouse in New York. It was a difficult and complex part for so young an actor, but he performed with skill and great perception. Afterwards, in discussing his performance with friends who had seen the play with me, we talked as much about the details of the character he had created as we did of his talent as an actor.

I watched his work over a period of time on the character of Jackson Fentry in both the play and the film dramatization of *Tomorrow,* which I adapted from William Faulkner's short story. He first performed it for a limited run at the H-B Playhouse, a small studio theater in New York City, that seated not quite a hundred people. He brought to these rehearsals and twelve performances as much care and seriousness as if it were being seen by millions.

Jackson Fentry is an inarticulate Mississippi tenant farmer who goes to work in a sawmill and there meets and falls in love with a dying woman. Duvall brought to this man qualities of the rural South that were moving and original. Later, when plans were made to film the play on location in Mississippi, I wondered how the character he had created would stand up surrounded by the real South and its people. Nothing essential was changed in his performance, and the inarticulate, loving man was as believable surrounded by actual rural Mississippians as he had been in the small off-Broadway theater surrounded by a company of New York actors.

Over the years I have known him, his concern for his work has never diminished. He is as enthusiastic now about a part that really interests him as he was when he was a young actor. His work on a character he is to play is endless and all-absorbing. There are films of his I've seen that I wish he had not chosen to do, but we all have to work, and good parts in good films are increasingly difficult to come by.

He has directed one film, *We're Not the Jet Set* [a 1974 rodeo documentary] and has begun work on a second dealing with gypsy life in New York City. In discussing with him his work as a director, one finds the same fascination with the background details of his subject matter — in these instances, a group of people set aside by their racial or sectional differences — that he has when working on a character as an actor in a play or film. He has that special ability to enter another culture, to give himself to it and absorb it for creative use in his work. I find it most unusual in this day of unimaginative and lazy acting. I don't think we have seen his full potential as an actor; we shall only see that when writers and directors create roles in plays and films that will give him the opportunities to develop fully his particular gifts.

With Faye Dunaway and William Holden in Network.

GENE HACKMAN: HE CAN'T GET THE GIRL

MICHAEL RITCHIE

FROM ITS EARLIEST DAYS, Hollywood has had three distinct categories of male actors: "leading man," "younger leading man," and "character actor." The Motion Picture Academy of Arts and Sciences makes these distinctions official in their *Academy Players Directory,* the major casting tool of the industry.

But "character actor" in Hollywood has connoted "supporting player," or even "bit actor," and you find, through the years, everyone from John Carradine to Peter Lorre listed as "leading man."

In the popular imagination, the leading man is the one who gets the girl, most often the "leading woman" or perhaps the "younger leading woman." Physical appearance is not necessarily a factor. We wanted Spencer Tracy to get the girl, and he did. So did Jimmy Cagney. These days we root for Walter Matthau.

There is another category of stars who do *not* get the girl, and these are today's *star character actors*. Of these, Gene Hackman is the best. He may also be America's best actor, period. But his career, with all its ups and downs, can only be understood in terms of his frustration about not "getting the girl."

Working with Robert Redford in preparing *Downhill Racer* (1969), I kept mentioning Gene's name as a prototype for the ski coach. Finally, I said, "Why don't we stop saying someone *like* Gene Hackman? Let's get Hackman."

I met Gene for the first time and we talked about skiing, even though neither of us knew much about it at that point. We talked about planned rewrites and various crash programs to help him prepare for the role, and Gene was anxious to pick up any details about any real-life prototypes he could study.

We agreed to give Gene star billing, which in Hollywood is any billing above the title. I believe it was the first time for him. Yet Gene was frustrated and angered by the supporting nature of his role. Frequently during

shooting, he had to stand around, he felt, "like a high-priced extra." Some of his bitterness was over a recent loss of the starring role in John Frankenheimer's *I Walk the Line* (1970). I heard that Columbia had overruled

"The porkpie hat in The French Connection *is a classic, but Gene's choice of haircut was sublime. No actor in American films had a more real-looking head of hair. Who was his barber?"* — M. R.

MICHAEL RITCHIE *directed* Downhill Racer, Prime Cut, The Candidate, Smile, The Bad News Bears, *and* Semi-Tough.

Frankenheimer and insisted on Gregory Peck.

Whether on a ski slope or in a hotel lobby, Gene quickly breathed life into his character. He brought such strength and authority to the part that the only problems we had were over those scenes where Redford was supposed to leave Hackman bewildered and plowed under.

I think that Gene's finest scene is at the end of the picture, when Redford seemingly has won the big ski event and Gene tries to take the credit. But as news of another possible winner drifts through the crowd, Gene slowly, unconsciously moves away from his "student." Then the challenger falls, and like a victory machine unplugged and then replugged, Gene is again slapping Redford on the back, shouting, "I knew we could do it."

This kind of ambiguity and even outright duplicity is seldom found in parts for "leading men." After all, how could such double-dealers deserve the girl? But it's very human and it's at the core of Gene Hackman's greatest performances in *Bonnie and Clyde* (1967), *I Never Sang for My Father* (1970), *The French Connection* (1971), and *The Conversation* (1974). Gene was nominated for Best *Supporting* Actor for *I Never Sang for My Father,* although his part was the largest and most important in

With Robert Redford in Michael Ritchie's Downhill Racer.

the film. "I guess the academy is trying to tell me something," Gene sighed when I congratulated him on the supporting nomination.

I worked with Gene for a second time on *Prime Cut* (1972), a black-comedy, gangster opus of which neither of us is very proud. Gene had just finished principal photography on a New York street picture that hadn't

"*I Never Sang for My Father may be Hackman's best work to date. The character's emotional nerve ends were exposed as he was constantly held in check by his domineering father (Melvyn Douglas).*" — M. R.

With Angel Tompkins and Lee Marvin in Prime Cut, *a film in which he played a bad guy named Mary Ann.*

been titled and seemed destined for oblivion. So during those six weeks on *Prime Cut,* Gene seemed quite content with his character part, with all the professionalism and conscientiousness that the film industry has come to associate with its fine character players.

Six months later all bets were off. The New York street picture, called *The French Connection,* was a sensation, and Gene was suddenly a Big Bankable Star. When he accepted his Oscar for *Connection,* he modestly suggested that "maybe the award should really go to my car." He was referring, of course, to the incredible "demolition derby" chase with a subway train. But one sequence does not make a hit, and audiences were responding enthusiastically to Popeye Doyle, Hackman's rough, tough detective. His Popeye is a haunted man who has no private life, whose work is an obsession, who treats all "germs" equally, regardless of race or nationality. It's "up against the wall" for everybody. There is no sacred institution, not even Santa Claus.

Hackman's Popeye Doyle is not the common man. It is the common man's ideal of what he would like to be in a crowded, frustrating, unjust world. No leading man I can think of could have played that part as well.

The ultimate tribute that can be paid to both Hackman and director William Friedkin is this: Not only doesn't Popeye get the girl (there is no girl to get), he doesn't even get his man. Fernando Rey goes free and Popeye is left in existential limbo.

After his success in *The French Connection,* Gene went on to play the lead in *The Poseidon Adventure* (1972) that five years earlier would have gone to Gregory Peck. Then came a succession of eccentric roles and ups and downs. The ups are certainly Francis Ford Cappola's *The Conversation* and *French Connection II* (1975). The downs are *Zandy's Bride* (1974), *The Domino Principle* (1977), *Lucky Lady* (1975) *Bite the Bullet* (1975), and *Night Moves* (1975).

He did great work as a character actor *(Bonnie and Clyde, Lilith* [1964], and *I Never Sang for My Father),* before he became a big star. His best characters of his star period, Harry the wiretapper of *The Conversation* and Popeye Doyle, are not traditional heroes.

If Gene can find starring roles that continue in his character actor tradition, he may be acknowledged as America's best actor. But he also may have to give up any hopes of getting the girl.

In Arthur Penn's Night Moves.

ACADEMY AWARD WINNERS FROM 1927 TO 1977

This section reviews the Academy Award winners in the **Best Actor** and **Best Actress** categories since the ceremony's inception in 1927. A description of the role of each winner is included. In the first year of the awards, stars could be nominated for more than one film. Until 1934, Awards were given on a seasonal basis.

1927–28 **Janet Gaynor** was a farmer's wife in *Sunrise* (shown here with George O'Brien), a munitions worker in *Seventh Heaven*, and a poor artist's model in *Street Angel*. **Emil Jannings** was a czarist general turned movie extra in *The Last Command* (shown) and a bank cashier in *The Way of All Flesh*.

1928–29 **Mary Pickford** was a small-town flirt in *Coquette*. **Warner Baxter** (Below, L, with Dorothy Burgess and Edmund Lowe) brought to life O. Henry's highwayman the Cisco Kid in *In Old Arizona*.

1929–30 **Norma Shearer** (L) was more interested in romantic involvements than work in *The Divorcee*. **George Arliss** was British prime minister Benjamin Disraeli in the biography *Disraeli*.

1930–31 **Marie Dressler** (Above, R, with Dorothy Jordan and Wallace Beery) ran a waterfront hotel in *Min and Bill*. **Lionel Barrymore** (with Norma Shearer) played a criminal lawyer in *A Free Soul*.

1931–32 **Helen Hayes** found herself supporting her illegitimate son in many ways, including prostitution and working as a scrubwoman in *The Sin of Madelon Claudet*. **Wallace Beery** played an ex-boxing champion in *The Champ*. Co-winner **Fredric March** was a scientist cum monster in *Dr. Jekyll and Mr. Hyde*.

TIE

1932–33 **Katharine Hepburn** (with Douglas Fairbanks, Jr.) wanted to be an actress in *Morning Glory*. **Charles Laughton** (with Elsa Lanchester) was the king of England in *The Private Life of Henry VIII*.

1934 **Claudette Colbert** (Above, L) played a spoiled heiress in *It Happened One Night*. **Clark Gable** was a reporter in the same film.

1935 **Bette Davis** (with Franchot Tone) was a troubled ex-Broadway star in *Dangerous*. **Victor McLaglen** was an Irish revolutionary who sells out his best friend in *The Informer*.

1936 **Luise Rainer** (with William Powell) starred as ex-Follies beauty Anna Held in *The Great Ziegfeld*. **Paul Muni** was the famous scientist in *The Story of Louis Pasteur*.

1940 **Ginger Rogers** was a typist turned saleswoman in *Kitty Foyle*. **James Stewart** (with Cary Grant) played a reporter in *The Philadelphia Story*.

1939 **Vivien Leigh** played a flirtatious southern belle in *Gone With the Wind*. **Robert Donat** (with Greer Garson) played a kindly British schoolteacher in *Goodbye, Mr. Chips*.

1943 **Jennifer Jones** played St. Bernadette, the nineteenth century French peasant girl who claimed she saw a vision of the Virgin Mary, in *The Song of Bernadette*. **Paul Lukas** was a German engineer and a devoted revolutionary in *Watch on the Rhine*.

1944 **Ingrid Bergman** was a frightened newlywed in *Gaslight*. **Bing Crosby** (with Barry Fitzgerald) played Father O'Malley in *Going My Way*.

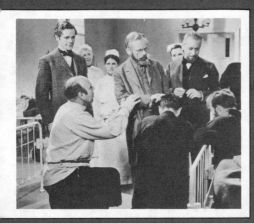

1937 **Luise Rainer** (with Paul Muni) was a poor Chinese farmer's wife in *The Good Earth*. **Spencer Tracy** (with Freddie Bartholomew) was a Portuguese fisherman in *Captains Courageous*.

1941 **Joan Fontaine** (with Cary Grant) was a frightened newlywed in *Suspicion*. **Gary Cooper** played Alvin York, the real-life pacifist soldier who became a World War I hero in *Sergeant York*.

1938 **Bette Davis** (between Spring Byington and George Brent) was a flirtatious southern belle in *Jezebel*. **Spencer Tracy** (with Mickey Rooney) played Father Flanagan, the founder of *Boys Town*.

1942 **Greer Garson** (with Walter Pidgeon) played a courageous English housewife during the Blitz in *Mrs. Miniver*. **James Cagney** (with Joan Leslie) was the great entertainer George M. Cohan in *Yankee Doodle Dandy*.

1945 **Joan Crawford** (with Zachary Scott and Jack Carson) began as a waitress and ended up owning a string of restaurants in *Mildred Pierce*. **Ray Milland** was a frustrated writer who became an alcoholic in *The Lost Weekend*.

1946 **Olivia de Havilland** (L, with Virginia Wells and John Lund) became the operator of a cosmetics firm to support her illegitimate son in *To Each His Own*. **Fredric March** (with Myrna Loy) returned from World War II to resume his banking career in *The Best Years of Our Lives*.

1947 **Loretta Young** (with Joseph Cotten) was a Swedish farm girl who became a maid and, ultimately, a congresswoman in *The Farmer's Daughter*. **Ronald Colman** played an actor who became too involved in his parts in *A Double Life*.

1948 **Jane Wyman** (Above, with Lew Ayres) was a deaf-mute farm girl in *Johnny Belinda*. **Laurence Olivier** (Below, seated) starred as Shakespeare's Danish prince in *Hamlet*.

1951 **Vivien Leigh** (L, with Karl Malden) was an unhappy English teacher visiting her sister in *A Streetcar Named Desire*. **Humphrey Bogart** (with Katharine Hepburn) played a drunken boat captain in *The African Queen*.

1953 **Audrey Hepburn** was a princess in *Roman Holiday*. **William Holden** was a prisoner-of-war in *Stalag 17*.

1952 **Shirley Booth** (with Burt Lancaster) was a housewife burdened with an alcoholic husband in *Come Back, Little Sheba*. **Gary Cooper** (with Grace Kelly) was a marshal in *High Noon*.

1954 **Grace Kelly** (with Bing Crosby) took care of her alcoholic husband in *The Country Girl*. **Marlon Brando** was a rebellious longshoreman in *On the Waterfront*.

1949 Olivia de Havilland (with Montgomery Clift) played a naive spinster in *The Heiress*. Broderick Crawford played a southern politician in *All the King's Men*.

1950 Judy Holliday (with William Holden) was a kept woman in *Born Yesterday*. Jose Ferrer re-created his stage role as the poetic swordsman with the long nose in *Cyrano de Bergerac*.

1956 Ingrid Bergman (with Yul Brynner) claimed to be the missing daughter of Czar Nicholas II in *Anastasia*. Yul Brynner played the king of Siam in *The King and I*.

1955 Anna Magnani played an Italian seamstress in *The Rose Tattoo*. Ernest Borgnine was a lonely butcher in *Marty*.

1957 Joanne Woodward (with Lee J. Cobb) played a woman with a multiple personality in *The Three Faces of Eve*. Alec Guinness was a British colonel held prisoner by the Japanese during World War II in *The Bridge on the River Kwai*.

1958 Susan Hayward starred in the true story of Barbara Graham, who was sentenced to death, in *I Want to Live!* David Niven pretended to be an ex-British officer in *Separate Tables*.

1959 **Simone Signoret** (with Laurence Harvey) played an unhappily married woman having an affair in *Room at the Top*. **Charlton Heston** was a Jew stripped of his wealth in *Ben-Hur*.

1960 **Elizabeth Taylor** was a prostitute in *Butterfield 8*. **Burt Lancaster** was a hypocritical revivalist preacher in *Elmer Gantry*.

1963 **Patricia Neal** played a housekeeper in *Hud*. **Sidney Poitier** was an ex-G.I. working as a handyman in *Lilies of the Field*.

1964 **Julie Andrews** (L, with Karen Dotrice, and Matthew Garber) played a nanny with special powers in *Mary Poppins*. **Rex Harrison** (with Audrey Hepburn) was a linguistics professor in *My Fair Lady*.

1967 **Katharine Hepburn** (with Katharine Houghton and Sidney Poitier) ran an art gallery in *Guess Who's Coming to Dinner?* **Rod Steiger** was a tough southern sheriff in *In the Heat of the Night*.

1968 **Barbra Streisand** played comedienne Fanny Brice in *Funny Girl*. Co-winner **Katharine Hepburn** (with Jane Merrow) was Eleanor of Aquitaine in *The Lion in Winter*. **Cliff Robertson** played a retarded bakery worker who becomes a human guinea pig in a scientific experiment in *Charly*.

TIE

1961 **Sophia Loren** (with Eleanora Brown) was a poor widowed Italian mother during World War II in *Two Women*. **Maximilian Schell** was a lawyer who defended Nazi war criminals in *Judgment at Nuremberg*.

1962 **Anne Bancroft** (with Patty Duke) re-created her stage role of Annie Sullivan, the teacher of Helen Keller, in *The Miracle Worker*. **Gregory Peck** played a southern lawyer in *To Kill a Mockingbird*.

1965 **Julie Christie** was an ambitious model in *Darling*. **Lee Marvin,** in a dual role, was an outlaw and an alcoholic ex-gunfighter in *Cat Ballou*.

1966 **Elizabeth Taylor** (with Richard Burton) was an unhappy wife in *Who's Afraid of Virginia Woolf?* **Paul Scofield** played Sir Thomas More, Henry VIII's Lord Chancellor, in *A Man for All Seasons*.

1970 **Glenda Jackson** (with Oliver Reed) wanted to be a sculptor in *Women in Love*. **George C. Scott** played General George Patton in the World War II biography *Patton*.

1969 **Maggie Smith** (with Robert Stephens) was a girls-school teacher in *The Prime of Miss Jean Brodie*. **John Wayne** played Sheriff Rooster Cogburn in *True Grit*.

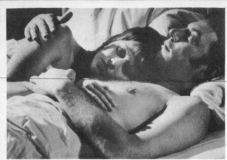

1971 **Jane Fonda** (with Donald Sutherland) was a high-class call girl in *Klute*. **Gene Hackman** (second from R) was real-life policeman "Popeye" Doyle in *The French Connection*.

1972 **Liza Minnelli** was a cabaret entertainer in Berlin prior to World War II in *Cabaret*. **Marlon Brando** played a crime boss in *The Godfather*.

1973 **Glenda Jackson** (with George Segal) was a fashion designer in *A Touch of Class*. **Jack Lemmon** was a disenchanted garment company executive in *Save the Tiger*.

1974 **Ellen Burstyn** starred as a widowed mother and waitress who aspired to be a singer in *Alice Doesn't Live Here Anymore*. **Art Carney** played a retired teacher traveling west in *Harry and Tonto*.

1975 **Louise Fletcher** was a nurse and **Jack Nicholson** a mental patient in *One Flew Over the Cuckoo's Nest*.

1976 **Faye Dunaway** played an ambitious television executive in *Network*. **Peter Finch** (Below, L, with Robert Duvall and Ned Beatty) as a TV newscaster in the same film.

1977 **Diane Keaton** (L, with Woody Allen) wanted to be an actress in *Annie Hall*. **Richard Dreyfuss** (with Marsha Mason) was an actor in *The Goodbye Girl*.

LADIES
AND
GENTLE MEN

RONALD COLMAN: ELEGANT ENGLISHMAN

JANE WYATT

RONALD COLMAN was one of the greatest romantic idols in screen annals, a heartthrob in motion pictures for four decades. Yet, many people who knew him well did not know that he traveled a long route to stardom.

Ronnie grew up in Richmond, a large suburb of London, on the river Thames. As a boy, he never had any desire to become an actor, but rather planned a barrister's career via Cambridge University. However, when the family fortunes collapsed with his father's death in 1907, he went to work instead.

He became interested in acting when a stranger happened to remark that he looked like an actor. In 1916, at the age of twenty-five, he got his first part in a British play. Three years later he was making his first film in England, and a year later he was given his first romantic role. After many successes, he came to the United States to try his luck: first small stage roles in New York, then national touring companies. He met William Powell, a fellow actor and they established a deep, lifelong friendship.

When he arrived in Hollywood, his agent sent his still pictures around to various producers. One sent them back with this comment: "This man will never photograph."

Fortunately, Henry King, the producer-director, was looking for a talented unknown to play opposite Lillian Gish in *The White Sister* (1923). This, Colman's first notable American film, was a hit. Others followed. The great Hollywood producer Samuel Goldwyn signed him to a contract and starred him in *Tarnish* (1924), *Romola* (1924), and *A Thief in Paradise* (1925), all big box-office hits. Then, with *The Dark Angel* (1925), Colman and Vilma Banky became Goldwyn's number-one romantic team.

JANE WYATT *is a star of stage, screen, and television. She won three Emmy Awards for Best Female Performer for "Father Knows Best," and appeared in such films as* Lost Horizon, None But the Lonely Heart, Gentleman's Agreement, *and* Task Force.

A Tale of Two Cities.

But Colman was not to be the ideal glamour boy of the fan magazines. He rarely gave interviews. He was basically a private person, never one to join in the Hollywood swim, preferring the company of a few friends. His closest were William Powell and Richard Barthelmess — "the three musketeers," as they were called. One studio executive urged Colman, then a bachelor, to swing with the social set. "Why should I go to dull parties and say dull things just because I wear greasepaint and make love to beautiful women on the screen?"

Deep inside he was a loner — far removed from some of the swashbuckling characters he played with

Even before he was able to use his marvelous voice, he established himself as a top romantic lead of the silent era. His best partner was Vilma Banky, but he was also attractive with Lili Damita (shown here) in The Rescue.

such enormous success. But those roles built his fantastic following.

Colman was handled by the greatest star-building teams in the world, under the leadership of Sam Goldwyn, Darryl Zanuck, and David O. Selznick. All the major studios had big stories written for him: *Stella Dallas* (1925, the top moneymaker of its time): *Bulldog Drummond* (1929), *Arrowsmith* (1931), *Cynara* (1932), *Clive of India* (1935), *A Tale of Two Cities* (1935), *Under Two Flags* (1936), *The Prisoner of Zenda* (1937), to name a few. Ronald Colman became a man of the highest professional stature in the business, and he became undisputed leader of the British film colony in Hollywood. With the coming of sound, he became even

more popular. His clipped British diction added to his romantic appeal.

I believe that *Lost Horizon* (1937) will be remembered long after all his other pictures because it came along at precisely the right moment for him. He had everything the part required. He was the right age and still had a lithe, athletic figure which made it seem possible for his character, Conway, to make the hazardous solo journey back to Shangri-La.

Above all, his intelligence and his sense of the spiritual were central to the part of Conway. It was wholly understandable that the High Lama would choose him from all others in the world to be brought to Shangri-La to take his place. Ronnie stamped the part with his

A RENDEZVOUS IN SHANGRI-LA

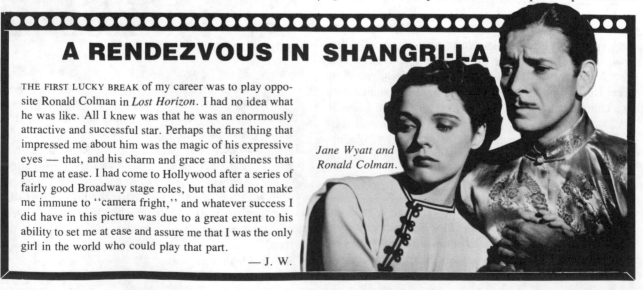

THE FIRST LUCKY BREAK of my career was to play opposite Ronald Colman in *Lost Horizon*. I had no idea what he was like. All I knew was that he was an enormously attractive and successful star. Perhaps the first thing that impressed me about him was the magic of his expressive eyes — that, and his charm and grace and kindness that put me at ease. I had come to Hollywood after a series of fairly good Broadway stage roles, but that did not make me immune to "camera fright," and whatever success I did have in this picture was due to a great extent to his ability to set me at ease and assure me that I was the only girl in the world who could play that part.

— J. W.

Jane Wyatt and Ronald Colman.

image and made it completely his own in the same way that Katharine Cornell did with Elizabeth Barrett, or Gary Cooper with Mr. Deeds, or William Powell with Nick Charles. Colman really was Conway. Like Conway, he was thoughtful and kind, and this came across to those watching the film and to those of us on the set.

The first day I worked on *Lost Horizon* I remember thinking that Ronnie must be underplaying Conway, and was surprised when director Frank Capra said "Cut and print." Later, at the rushes, I was amazed to see that the scene played beautifully; that Ronnie had done it with great subtlety and finesse. He had magnificent eyes, and I think fine eyes are the most important piece of equipment a *film* actor can have. On film the audience must be able to see the character think — to see the wheels go round. As the distinguished portrait photographer, John Engstead, has said, "I am not interested in photographing a face. I am interested in photographing a mind." Ronnie had the quality of being able to express every thought with his eyes. In this respect I cannot help compare him to Robert Young, my TV co-star of six years. Although they had vastly different personalities, they had much in common as actors, and they were both photogenic.

I think the secret of Ronald Colman's lasting success was that he was a complete Original, in personality, good looks, diversity and style. He added to this great self-discipline and an ability to be completely absorbed by a scene, to exclude all distractions while actually shooting, and to be able to relax between scenes. Last but not least, he was never, never late on the set.

On the set of
A Double Life,
*for which he won
an Academy Award.*

*He was an amnesiac
in* Random Harvest.
*Greer Garson played
the woman who tried
to recapture his love.*

IRENE DUNNE: NATIVE TREASURE

DeWITT BODEEN

She began as a singer, but her talents were unlimited.

HAVING WRITTEN the screenplay for *I Remember Mama* (1948), I was asked by director George Stevens to remain on set during its production; thus it was my good fortune to spend six days a week (we worked Saturdays then), from May to November of 1947, watching Irene Dunne bring *Mama* alive. She had eyed the project carefully when it was offered to her by producer Harriet Parsons. She knew that it would be an important departure for her, her previous heroines having been sophisticated, well-groomed ladies. Mama was a simple Norwegian, a carpenter's wife, and mother of four children who lived in San Francisco around 1910, and there was no chance for the leading lady to wear ravishing creations by top designers. Irene finally agreed to play the part if Miss Parsons would get one of five directors whose names she offered. George Stevens was one of them, and he agreed to do it; it was his first feature after returning home from World War II.

Irene went about preparing for her role. A Norwegian woman was engaged to help her with the accent; Irene decided on her coiffure — a blond, simply braided wig. Her wardrobe, which she gathered with Eddie Stevenson, consisted of "dresses which actually appear to be worn," as critic Bosley Crowther would remark. Mama had to be plumper than Irene, and padding was designed, over which Irene fastened corsets. Irene had learned to solve every problem before shooting started. As a result, she settled into interpreting her role with peace of mind.

Although Irene Dunne once said that she felt her best performance came on about the third take, every take was consistent in timing and action. If she paused slightly to pick up an object, she always paused at the same place, picking it up in the same way with the same hand. Her precision was remarkable. "If a director is lucky enough to work with Irene Dunne," George Ste-

---

DeWITT BODEEN *is a film historian and screenwriter, whose credits include* I Remember Mama, Cat People, Curse of the Cat People, The Enchanted Cottage, Mrs. Mike, *and* Billy Budd.

Filming Theodora Goes Wild, *with Melvyn Douglas.*

vens once said, "his worries disappear. Every scene she's in matches; she's the film editor's delight. I would say that she's just about as 'careless' as George Arliss." George Arliss, let me assure you, was not careless.

When the company went to San Francisco for ten days to shoot exteriors, Irene was in her element. San Franciscans adored her. Between takes, when we shot on the hillside streets, women invited her into their homes to rest. Irene sat, chatting amiably, drinking coffee while she waited for the crew to set up the next scene.

A FAVORITE OF THE FRENCH

IN PARIS, Irene Dunne's films were always treated with great adulation, and she could not understand why sophisticated Parisians received her so royally. However, she did figure out why one film, *Back Street* (1932), was being constantly revived in a little theater on the Champs-Elysées. Nearly every French person has known of a lady, like her character, who chose to live on some back street; the Parisians understood and cherished her sympathetic portrayal — she was one of them. (*Back Street* has been filmed three times, but the version with Irene Dunne remains the best, and the only one to be treasured by the French.)

— D. B.

Then there was the night George asked some of us to join him at dinner. I was waiting in the lobby of the Fairmont Hotel with Harriet, George, and his associate Ivan Moffat, when the elevator doors opened and Irene emerged. We were all accustomed to seeing her in Mama's aprons and worn gingham; now in our midst was a lady of style, wearing blue chiffon and a hat with a wisp of a veil. Mama Hanson disappeared for that night, and into her place stepped Irene Dunne, ready for an evening on the town.

With Allan Jones in Show Boat.

As the fiery teacher in Anna and the King of Siam, *with Rex Harrison.*

Irene Dunne went to RKO Radio Pictures in 1930, destined to rise quickly to stardom and to become one of Hollywood's most versatile actresses. She had already made a name for herself in the theater, as a charming singer in musicals, scoring a big hit as Magnolia in a Chicago production of *Show Boat*. RKO, noting that Bebe Daniels had put new life into a faltering career (and money in the studio coffers) by singing in *Rio Rita* (1929), decided they could use another singer on the lot and offered Irene Dunne a contract. By the time she arrived, however, the musical genre had fallen into disfavor, and the vehicle RKO purchased to introduce its new star was a Richard Rodgers-Lorenz Hart-Joseph Fields musical comedy, *Present Arms!* The picture was turned into *Leathernecking* (1930), an almost music-less comedy about a buck private and a society girl.

Miss Dunne was prepared for this turn of events. In fact, she had actually signed with RKO in hopes of playing the *dramatic* lead in the movie version of Edna Ferber's *Cimarron* (1931). But when her name was mentioned to director Wesley Ruggles, he replied that he was looking for an actress with more dramatic experience. As luck would have it, Fay Bainter, the actress favored for the role, lost favor with studio head William LeBaron. The coveted role was up for grabs, and Irene lost no time. She persuaded makeup artist Ernie Westmore and photographer Ernest Bracken to take a series of stills showing her as she aged from a pretty young girl to a successful gray-haired congresswoman,

as Sabra Cravat did in Ferber's novel. Monday morning the photographs and a note were on LeBaron's desk: "This is Irene Dunne, the girl who should play the lead in *Cimarron*." LeBaron ordered a screen test. Irene got the part. For this, only her second film, she received an Academy Award nomination as Best Actress of the Year.

From today's vantage, *Cimarron* is solely illuminated by Irene Dunne's portrayal of Sabra Cravat. She is the only one who underplays her role, the only one who seems to be thinking. Intelligent, intense, absolutely indomitable, the perfect lady, she established the image that was to define Irene Dunne throughout her career.

There were two facets to Irene Dunne's personality: one, the star; the other, the wife and mother who lived a private life away from the studio. From the beginning she was determined to prove that she could have an important career in films, and that she could also have a private life as the wife of a dentist, Francis J. Griffin.

A secret to the enduring success of Irene Dunne is that she knew what was important for her own career. Realizing that having the right director is essential, she always tried to have approval over the choice. She respected directors like John Cromwell, Gregory La Cava, John M. Stahl, James Whale, Leo McCarey, Clarence Brown, and George Stevens.

Irene Dunne's gallery of characters included heroines of modern marital dramas, sentimental soap operas, period pieces, film musicals, and comedy. One of her best comedic roles was in *Theodora Goes Wild*

(1936), a delightful, wacky situation comedy that brought her the second of her Best Actress nominations. Ironically, she tried everything in her power to get out of the movie, including sailing to Europe for six weeks in hopes that Harry Cohn, head of Columbia, would toss the part to some other actress rather than wait for her return. As she confessed later, ''My friends say, 'It's a good thing you did *Theodora Goes Wild;* Theodora's the one character that is really you!' ''

Her friends were not far wrong. In real life, there is an attractive vagueness to Irene Dunne. Her eyes twinkle in amusement just as Theodora's do, and she looks at you with a kind of open-eyed Gracie Allen bemusement. ''Being a little vague,'' she says, ''is a terribly good defense, a good place to hide.''

In Irene's second comedy for Columbia, *The Awful Truth* (1937), she co-starred with Cary Grant — for the first of three times. Director Leo McCarey, who has always been famous for allowing his actors to improvise, told me he played melodies on the piano to relax his stars. McCarey was aware that Irene and Cary liked each other, and sparkled as a team, so the director and his stars improvised, and *The Awful Truth* became the year's

With Barbara Bel Geddes in I Remember Mama.

most sparkling comedy. For Dunne it meant her third Academy Award nomination.

McCarey directed Irene again in *Love Affair* (1939), a dazzling comedy/love story. In this tale of shipboard lovers, Miss Dunne is properly beguiling opposite Charles Boyer. She even gets to sing again. This classic film won the actress a fourth Academy Award nomination.

She was nominated a fifth time for her performance in *I Remember Mama,* .her last important film. She made three others, but none was really worthy of her. When President Eisenhower appointed her as an alternate delegate to the United Nations, she and Dr. Griffin moved to New York, where they took up residence at the Hotel Pierre. Later, when her husband fell ill, she turned down roles to stay with him at their home in Los Angeles. Like Garbo, I don't think she intended to retire. But there were things to be done as Mrs. Francis Griffin, and when her husband died, she stayed on to run the businesses he had left her. Her life as a very private lady is maintained. As Leo McCarey said of her: ''You can really call Irene Dunne the first lady of Hollywood, because she's the first real *lady* Hollywood has ever seen.''

On set with director Leo McCarey (at piano) and Charles Boyer.

CARY GRANT: WORKING WITH A MAN OF QUALITY

IRENE DUNNE

I APPEARED WITH many leading men. But working with Cary Grant was different from working with other actors — he was much more fun! I think we were a successful team because we enjoyed working together tremendously, and that pleasure must have shown through onto the screen.

Cary and I were almost complete strangers when we met on the set of *The Awful Truth* (1937). I knew little about him except that he was one of the handsomest men in films. I was instantly impressed with his energy and enthusiasm. *The Awful Truth* was, I believe, his first major comedy role, and I could sense his reticence behind the bright spirits. Our director, Leo McCarey, bounded onto the set and blithely informed us that the script was nowhere near complete, but it didn't matter because we were going to improvise. *Improvise!* Cary was dubious and, frankly, so was I.

But as the filming progressed, Cary and I fell happily into step with Leo's breezy let's-try-anything style of filmmaking, and we grew to love and trust his wonderfully hilarious inventiveness. As I watched Cary working each day, I marveled at the excellence of his timing — the naturalness, the ease, the *charm*. Cary was wonderful in the film; it's my favorite comedy performance of his.

Our next film together was *My Favorite Wife* (1940), with Leo McCarey again set to direct. Just before filming commenced, Cary and I were heartsick to learn that Leo, who had been in a near-fatal automobile acci-

---

IRENE DUNNE *was a leading lady of the thirties and forties. Among her many films are* Cimarron, Back Street, Roberta, Magnificent Obsession, Show Boat, Theodora Goes Wild, Anna and the King of Siam, Life with Father, The Mudlark, *and three films with Cary Grant. She was nominated for an Academy Award as Best Actress five times.*

"I will always remember two compliments he paid me. He said I had perfect timing in comedy and that I was the sweetest-smelling actress he ever worked with." — I. D.

Irene Dunne and Cary Grant were a brilliant team, and it is regrettable they made only three films together; they are all classics: two comedies, The Awful Truth *(Above),* My Favorite Wife *(Above, R, with Randolph Scott), and a drama,* Penny Serenade.

FURIOUS...FABULOUS...FAR-FLUNG ADVENTURE!

...with three swaggering sons of battle! A picture with the seething, gusty excitement of a cyclone!

Gunga Din

starring

CARY GRANT · VICTOR McLAGLEN

and

DOUGLAS FAIRBANKS, JR.

co-starring

JOAN FONTAINE with **SAM JAFFE · EDUARDO CIANNELLI**

Produced and Directed by GEORGE STEVENS · Screenplay by JOEL SAYRE and FRED GUIOL · Story by BEN HECHT and CHARLES MacARTHUR
From RUDYARD KIPLING'S Poem "GUNGA DIN" · PANDRO S. BERMAN in charge of production

One of Grant's most popular movies was one of his few adventure films.

dent, was not sufficiently recuperated to work on the film (he was to become very much a part of *Wife,* however, as producer and guiding spirit). Our *new* director, Garson Kanin, proved a joy for both Cary and me.

Our third and, unhappily, our last film together was my personal favorite, *Penny Serenade* (1941). By the time we made this film Cary had become a far better actor than when we first worked together. Unlike our first

A rare bad role as Cole Porter in Night and Day.

With Rosalind Russell in Howard Hawks' His Girl Friday.

With Eva Marie Saint in North by Northwest.

two films, this one was serious — the story of a young publisher and his wife whose marriage is tested by domestic tragedy. Cary had few opportunities to display

his inimitable ebullience that had carried many of his films; instead he astounded everyone with the depth of his performance. I wish all aspiring actors could have witnessed Cary's concentration and preparedness during the production — an object lesson in professionalism. *Penny Serenade* earned him a much-deserved Academy Award nomination.

People usually react with skepticism when I say that Cary's intelligence and seriousness of approach were his strongest points as an actor, but this is true. Behind that carefree and sophisticated man on the screen, there's a painstaking worker and keen mind at work. When I acted with him he was too busy to really enjoy his stardom. He was a modest man who continually worked at his craft to show everyone that his popularity wasn't due to his looks — even when such proof was no longer necessary.

Personally, I would have hated for Cary to have played heavies. However, many people believe he was limited by his "nice guy" image, that it in fact frustrated him as an actor. I disagree. Early on, Cary realized that he had something going for him and that his most felicitous ploy would be to always "play himself." That is not as easy as it sounds; it requires a large degree of objectivity and self-discipline, and it certainly tested Cary's acting skills.

The last time I saw Cary he was looking forward to making a trip to Monaco to visit Princess Grace. He had the anticipation of a teenager. Cary is young for his years and still looks glorious. He still has that endearing enthusiasm. I don't know why he retired so early; he could still be a leading man.

With Stewart and Hepburn in The Philadelphia Story.

With Grace Kelly in To Catch a Thief.

GREER GARSON: BLUE-RIBBON WINNER

MALVIN WALD

ABOUT TWENTY YEARS AGO, I received a frantic phone call from an old friend, a record producer in New York. He was having contract difficulties with Greer Garson. Since I lived in California near Miss Garson, would I see her and try to straighten the matter out?

I had been a devoted fan of hers ever since her enchanting performance in *Goodbye, Mr. Chips* (1939). I had triumphed with her in *Madame Curie* (1943), and had acquired full faith in the British cause upon seeing her valiant wartime struggles in *Mrs. Miniver* (1942).

At last I met her in the Bel Air mansion she shared with her cattle- and oil-tycoon husband, Colonel E. E. "Buddy" Fogelson. Her greeting was frosty but polite. She was annoyed at my producer friend and assumed I was an attorney ready to sue her for possible breach of contract. I assured her I was not an attorney. I told her I was a screenwriter and simply a friend of the producer. Perhaps I could reason with her. She invited me in and we went into the library and discussed the problem; lo and behold, she was right and my friend was wrong! I acknowledged that and promised to relay the message.

Miss Garson, relieved at the ease at which we had settled our problem, graciously invited me to tea with her mother, Nina. We spoke about London, where a few years previously I had worked on a TV series. During that time I had met Lady Churchill, wife of the former prime minister, and Greer confessed that it was her secret ambition to portray that great lady on the screen.

Miss Garson invited me back again for future meetings about the record album. I always asked her questions about her career, which she seemed delighted to answer. She revealed to me that in all the years she worked at MGM, Louis B. Mayer never let her talk to the writers of her films. He kept her on a pedestal. When a new writer got an assignment, he was ordered to watch previous Garson pictures to get the touch that Mayer wanted — but never to meet her and learn her true feelings about the story. I was the first screenwriter with whom she ever had a chance to discuss these matters at great length. The talks always lasted until teatime, when her mother would join us. In 1959, her mother died, and somewhere in Greer's mind, I became one of her

Top dramatic actress during World War II.

MALVIN WALD *received an Academy Award nomination in 1948 for Best Original Story for* The Naked City, *which he adapted into a screenplay. Among his other scripts are* Outrage, Al Capone, *and* The Steel Claw. *He is the original author of* Ten Gentlemen From West Point, The Powers Girl, Not Wanted, *and* Man on Fire.

As scientist Madame Curie, *with Walter Pidgeon as husband.*

THE PART THAT GOT AWAY

ONE DAY Greer confided to me that she was tired of the image of the gracious selfless lady that Louis B. Mayer had so carefully created for her. As a skilled actress, she felt herself qualified to play earthier roles. The part she coveted was that of the army captain's adulterous wife in *From Here to Eternity* (1953). But the executives at Columbia Studios felt that the American public would never accept Greer Garson grappling on the beach with Burt Lancaster. As a result, Deborah Kerr, equally famous for her ladylike roles, got the part — and a new lease on her acting career.

— M. W.

mother's friends. In the years that followed we had many phone conversations, occasional notes of mutual congratulations on our respective careers.

According to newspaper accounts, Greer Garson was born in 1908, in County Down in Northern Ireland, of Scotch-Irish-Scandinavian heritage. Her mother, Nina Greer, was descended from the Scotch clan MacGregor. Greer's father, a descendant of the Vikings, was a native of the Orkney Islands. He died when Greer was very young.

She was educated at the University of London, from which she received a B.A. cum laude, and then attended the University of Grenoble in France for graduate work.

Garson's most memorable performance was as heroic Mrs. Miniver. *With her best partner, Walter Pidgeon.*

However, during Greer's childhood, Mrs. Garson had felt there was something very special about her little red-haired daughter. She encouraged Greer to compete for dramatic scholarships, and eventually the young girl attended professional classes and appeared in little-theater productions.

In 1932, an introduction led to an audition for the Birmingham Repertory Theater — a highly respected dramatic organization. Her debut was in the part of Shirley Kaplan in Elmer Rice's American play *Street Scene*, which dealt with life on New York's Lower East Side.

To fill the role of a young Jewish girl, Greer donned a black wig and studied the dialect of the New York slums. So convincing was she that it was a long time before she could convince people she was really Irish.

In 1935 she made her London stage debut in *Golden Arrow,* in which she co-starred with her director, Laurence Olivier. Noel Coward subsequently directed her in *Mademoiselle.* She also appeared in *Accent on Youth, Vintage Wine, Page from a Diary,* and *Old Music.* Before long Greer was one of London's leading theatrical stars.

Her performance in *Old Music* at St. James's Theater caught the eye of the famed Louis B. Mayer, head of Hollywood's MGM studios. He was entranced by her and envisioned her as a new Garbo. Promised immediate

As Eleanor Roosevelt in Sunrise at Campobello, *with Ralph Bellamy.*

stardom, she eagerly signed a long-term contract to go to Hollywood.

She arrived amid much publicity, but after a year found her career had come to a standstill. None of the producers on the lot had seen her work and they were reluctant to cast an unknown in their films.

Tired of waiting for a break, Greer was determined to return to the London stage. Then, suddenly, a British girl was needed to play Kathy, the young Mrs. Chipping in *Goodbye, Mr. Chips,* opposite Robert Donat, who had the title role. She was tested and won the part.

Her success in that role made her a movie star overnight. In the ensuing years she was to appear in a parade of memorable films, playing opposite such important stars as Robert Taylor, Clark Gable, Laurence Olivier, Gregory Peck, Robert Mitchum, and Errol Flynn.

Her teaming with Walter Pidgeon was a masterstroke. They were always at ease with each other, and there seemed to be great mutual respect as well as affection in the roles they played in *Blossoms in the Dust* (1941), *Madame Curie, Mrs. Parkington* (1944), *Julia Misbehaves* (1948), *That Forsyte Woman* (1949), *The Miniver Story* (1950), and *Scandal at Scourie* (1953).

For a while many people regarded her as the first lady of the screen, and she became a seven-time Academy Award nominee and winner of the Oscar for *Mrs. Miniver* in 1942. In 1960 she played Eleanor Roosevelt opposite Ralph Bellamy's F.D.R. in *Sunrise at Campobello.*

She was a four-time winner of the New York Film Critics' Circle Award and the *Film Daily* star-rating survey. In 1942 she appeared as the wife who nursed Ronald Colman, a wartime amnesia victim, back to health in *Random Harvest.* This movie broke records for the longest run at New York's Radio City Music Hall. Greer Garson's fame was truly international and she won popularity contests as the "most loved" or "best actress" in ten different countries.

What made her a star? First, I think, it was her incandescent beauty and patrician bearing. Her delicately featured face framed by red hair lit up the screen. Then there was her magnificent diction, cultured but natural. When she spoke, there was no doubt that she was a "lady." She projected the image of a warmhearted woman who was interested in something noble, something beyond the satisfaction of her own personal needs.

The one adjective ascribed to Greer's acting that she despised was "charming." "Satirical, ironic, and even menacing," was a better description she once told a journalist, "but never charming!"

Be that as it may, the image that will be remembered forever will be that of Greer Garson as gallant lady and steadfast wife in parts that have become cinema masterpieces: Mrs. Miniver, Madame Curie, Mrs. Chipping, Eleanor Roosevelt. As Louis B. Mayer would say, she is a lady with class.

GRACE KELLY: TRIBUTE TO A STORYBOOK PRINCESS

EDITH HEAD

I HAVE DRESSED thousands of actors, actresses, and animals (my first was an elephant that ate the outfit I made for it — a garland of leaves), but whenever I am asked which star is my personal favorite, I answer "Grace Kelly." She is a charming lady, a most gifted actress and, to me, a valued friend.

Grace Kelly was one of the most popular stars of the early 1950s. When she retired from films to marry Prince Rainier of Monaco she was at the peak of her movie career, the top female box-office star in the world. She had great appeal because she exhibited a rare combination of beauty, intelligence, and class that set her apart from other actresses of the period. Grace personified femininity, and audiences, particularly women, flocked to see her unparalleled beauty — *and* because she wore clothes so well. Men, I believe, were attracted to her because her characters were never vulgar or crude; on screen, Grace's language, manners, and movements suggested good breeding. When Grace Kelly married into royalty, no one thought that she would be out of her element.

I knew Grace Kelly had the "look" of a star the first time I saw her. She was immaculate, from her well-groomed hair to the fresh white gloves, which would become her trademark. She had a flawless figure, and with her modeling experience, she was the perfect subject for my designs. In the years that followed she provided me with some of the few moments in my career when I could say my sketches came to life.

My first picture with Grace was *Rear Window*

Critic Linda Gross: "Grace Kelly is blond, symmetrical, and classically perfect. She is fragile and perishable."

(1954), directed by Alfred Hitchcock. She was the editor of a great fashion magazine, which meant I would design the newest, smartest fashions possible. So I dressed Grace in fabulous clothes. There was one memorable risqué scene in which Grace visits the apartment of Jimmy Stewart. They are engaged to be married; he has had an accident, is confined to a wheelchair, and is un-

---

EDITH HEAD *has been nominated for an Academy Award for her costume designs on thirty-three occasions. She has won eight times. Her Oscars are for:* The Heiress, All About Eve, Samson and Delilah, A Place in the Sun, Roman Holiday, Sabrina, The Facts of Life, *and* The Sting.

HITCHCOCK'S HEROINE

KELLY'S CHARISMA was mythic, aloof, aristocratic, and webbed to the fifties obsession with covert sex. She is a male sex fantasy object whose icy exterior ambiguously suggests a fire within. In his famous interview by Truffaut, Alfred Hitchcock — who directed her in *Dial M for Murder, Rear Window* [R, Hitchock, Kelly, James Stewart, and Below, Kelly and Stewart], and *To Catch a Thief* — responding to a suggestion that Kelly's sex appeal was indirect, commented: ''You know why I favor sophisticated blonds in my films? We're after the drawing-room type, the real ladies, who become whores once they're in the bedroom.'' — Linda Gross

In an Edith Head gown in To Catch a Thief.

derstandably depressed about being immobilized. She drifts into the room in an exquisite pale rose-pink chiffon negligee and gown and murmurs, ''Preview of coming attractions,'' which immediately cheers him up.

Back then, Grace was living at a beautiful California hotel. With her deep sense of privacy, she did not want to swim there, so she would come nearly every day and swim in our hillside pool, then dine with us on the patio. It was the beginning of one of the most rewarding friendships I have ever known.

When we did *To Catch a Thief* (1955) together, Grace and I had to go to Paris. We shopped for a few items we couldn't get in America and, of course, ended up at the leather and specialty shop Hermes. As I mentioned, Grace is fond of wearing gloves, and it was not surprising that she fell in love with the store's enormous collection, the finest in the world. When they gave us a bill that totaled more than $600, I think even Grace was

in shock. She settled on quite a few, but not all she had wanted. Every time I see a beautifully groomed woman with fine gloves, I think of Grace Kelly and that shopping spree.

I have many recollections from my long career, but nothing was as pleasurable as filming *To Catch a Thief* in Cannes with Alfred Hitchcock, Cary Grant, and Grace Kelly. (I think I am prouder of the clothes in that film than those in any other picture on which I have worked.) Grace played a wealthy heiress, giving me the opportunity to provide her with a luxurious wardrobe. She was breathtaking.

It may be of interest to know that neither Mr. Hitchcock nor Grace Kelly ever discussed sex with me in relation to the clothes I made for them. As a matter of fact, Grace's clothes were glamorous, exotic, and alluring, but they were not meant to make Grace appear ''sexy,'' as this would have been inappropriate to the roles she played. Grace Kelly's sexual image was never a concern.

While few — if any — actresses have possessed Grace Kelly's elegance, I think it is important to point out that she was such a good actress that she could adapt herself to anything necessary for a particular role. For example, in *The Country Girl* (1954), she played a rather dowdy housewife, whom I dressed in very unattractive, ordinary clothes, and Grace was able to look the part.

The Swan.

 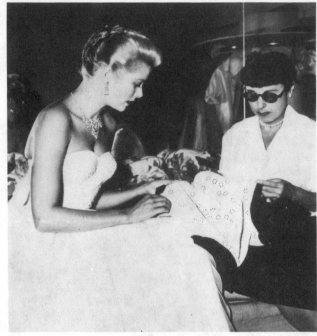

Conferences with Edith Head took place before shooting began (L) and between scenes on the set.

Playing opposite William Holden and Bing Crosby, she deservedly won an Academy Award for *acting*. It may have been great fun for me and other costume designers to dress Grace Kelly in our most extravagant creations, but even when she wore unattractive clothes, of course, her fine performances kept an audience's attention.

I always knew that Grace Kelly was talented, but I never thought she intended to give up her entire life to acting. And, of course, she didn't. Today we remain close friends and correspond regularly. Naturally, when she comes to California, she visits me; occasionally, I see her in Paris.

Stars come and go, but to me the superstar of all time is Her Serene Highness, Princess Grace of Monaco.

As bride of Gary Cooper in High Noon.

JULIE ANDREWS: A TALK WITH A FLICKERING STAR

LINDA GROSS

BETWEEN 1964 AND 1967, Jule Andrews was the screen's reigning female star. She became America's top box-office draw by making a series of lightweight, escapist musicals: *Mary Poppins* (1964), for which she won an Oscar; *The Sound of Music* (1965); and *Thoroughly Modern Millie* (1967).

By 1968, America was deeply marked with social and political unrest. And it was at this juncture of changing political sensibility that Andrews' film career began a dramatic decline. It seemed that this archetypal gracious lady, this Jane Austen-type heroine, was out-of-step. Julie Andrews represented safe and traditional values and remained popular only as long as the status quo was maintained in American politics.

The Andrews image is unique. Unlike Doris Day, the issue isn't virginity, and sex isn't really involved. Julie Andrews comes across as clean-cut, energetic, and refined. She has a nice body but she moves awkwardly — like a country gentlewoman with a trace of the tomboy. Even though she has appeared nude (in *Darling Lili* [1970]), crotchety (as Gertrude Lawrence in *Star!* [1968]), and promiscuous (in *The Americanization of Emily* [1964]), she holds an aura of sweetness and virtue.

Julie Andrews has never been able to shake this sugary image in a time when sugar is out of favor, its place taken by conflict and conscience, as personified by such actresses as Jane Fonda, Anne Bancroft, Liv Ullmann, Shirley MacLaine, and Diane Keaton.

With few exceptions, Andrews has played a series of nice, competent, average women who are courageous in private, sometimes banal, ways. They are old-fashioned and virtuous, the sort men used to take home to their mothers.

Julie Andrews' most sexual asset is her singing voice. She uses it, rather than her body, to tease. But her

She replaced Doris Day as top box-office star in early sixties.

LINDA GROSS *is a film critic for the Los Angeles* Times.

Surrounded by children, she had a hit: The Sound of Music. *Surrounded by adults, she flopped:* Darling Lili.

appeal is not sexual: It is that she is good-natured, reliable, and maternal — and men usually fantasize about women who need to be looked after, not those who nurture.

"I hope I am not as square as some people might think," Julie Andrews tells me. "I hope I have many facets."

Physically, she has hardly changed in twenty years. She wears the same efficient close-cropped haircut and her figure remains trim. She submits to an interview like a Victorian wife submits to sex: dutifully. She is polite, not spontaneous. Her manner is charming, but she appears ill at ease. An interview represents an invasion of privacy; she honors this demand of her profession, but it is clear she wants it over as soon as possible.

She is determined to play it casual. She orders and eats a takeout lunch while we talk. For much of the time, she sits near a public relations man who is a little too anxious to extol her professionalism and her commitment to family and career.

Julie Andrews *is* committed to motherhood — as fervently as Jane Fonda is committed to politics. Ironically, at an age when many women strike out on their own, she clings to her husband (writer-director Blake Edwards) and family. In fact, her life seems to be modeled on the role she played in *The Sound of Music.*

"When I am offered a project these days, it all depends on where Blake and the children will be. We try to never be apart for more than three weeks at a time. I am in the fortunate position to be able to work if and when I want, and I do work at some point every year. When I finish a job I come back to being a mom. Mostly, I've been Mrs. Blake Edwards."

Julie Andrews appears dependent on male support.

With Omar Sharif in The Tamarind Seed, *maybe her best film.*

When she was a child, her stepfather Harry Andrews guided her career and supervised her singing and dancing lessons. Now, she seems equally dependent on Edwards for career and emotional support. She sees herself through his eyes. When asked how she conceives of her own image, she replies self-consciously, "It's very hard because I am too close to me. I suggest asking Blake." (Characteristically, she would rather talk about her husband's career than her own.)

Julie Andrews realizes her career has suffered because she has been a victim of typecasting. When she tried to break out in films such as *Star!, Darling Lili,* and *The Tamarind Seed* (1974), the films failed.

"If you have a large success at something, you are inclined to get typed. I was allowed to get away with my character in *The Americanization of Emily* because it was so early in my career. I'm still looking for screenplays like *Emily* or *The Tamarind Seed,* but until recently the lack of good roles for women, and the bracketing, have made if difficult for me."

While it is true that her public image crystallized early, it also seems that Julie Andrews hasn't done much to change it. Even on television, where she has been relatively successful over the years, she isn't fluid and doesn't seem willing to try out new material. (The same can be said of her concert performances.) Watching her

With Paul Newman in Hitchcock's thriller Torn Curtain.

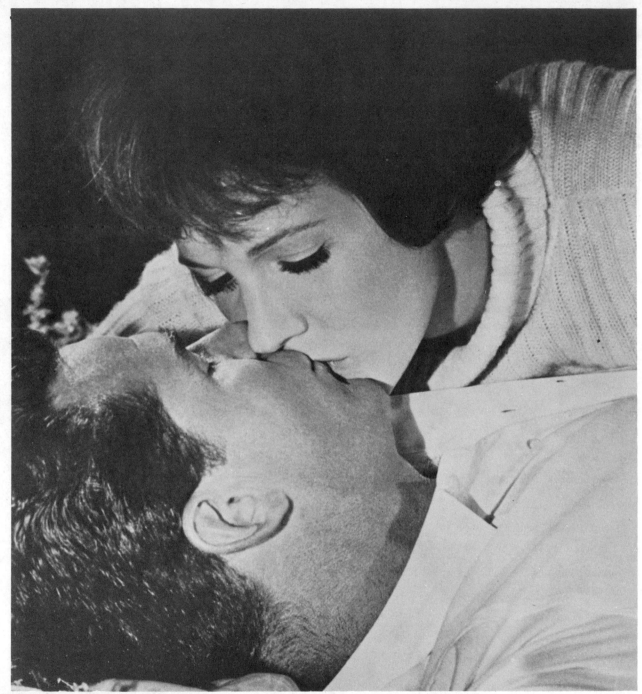

"She usually plays working women. Even when she makes love (as with James Garner in The Americanization of Emily), *it is part of her duty."* — L. G.

talk to some puppets on a recent TV special, one is amazed that she captured the public's fancy for as long as she did.

"I would love the chance to do more dramatic roles, comedies, and musicals. I'd like to be able to do them all without being typed. Children's films also interest me, although I don't want to do anything that will seem a pale copy of *Mary Poppins*. I don't think I'll mind particularly, however, if none of that comes about. I am very happy as I am."

It's difficult to tell if Julie Andrews' film career has stalled because of family priorities or a poor choice of roles. In any event, Julie Andrews is a better actress than she's generally given credit for, capable of convincingly playing a wide variety of roles. But it seems that the public isn't willing to accept her as a sexual woman, and the times may be out of joint for the Andrews brand of wholesomeness. But who knows, she may be rediscovered in the future. She could be smashing playing grandmothers.

THE VIOLENT MEN

KIRK DOUGLAS: LAST ANGRY MAN

MYRON MEISEL

K IRK DOUGLAS's hallmarks are easy to caricature: nostrils flaring, temples pulsating, robust humor, physicality, bombast, drive, and arduous sincerity. However histrionic, he is relaxed in the eye of the camera. He registers first, then builds his scene, using his core of energy to command the attention of the other players, the setting, and the audience.

Douglas excelled as the charismatic postwar anti-hero, creating his own special niche with his customary aggressiveness. His style was in marked contrast to the passivity of his contemporaries Mitchum, Peck, Holden, Heston, Hayden — or even Lancaster — and while always the hero, he was the most ferociously ambiguous of the lot. When Douglas held back, he restrained himself, like an oven that remains hot long after the knob is turned down. His highly involved, emotional approach to acting often brought him parlously close to hamminess. His temperament was emotional and expansive, unabashed, and unashamed. Douglas wasn't "cool," like the other stars; he routinely risked foolishness in the name of passionate intensity. It is fine with him that no one has ever accused him of being a natural actor: he seems to prepare for each scene by working himself into a lather *before* the camera goes on. Some of his finest early acting, in *Champion* (1949), *Ace in the Hole* (1951), *The Bad and the Beautiful* (1952), scored in part because of this impression, which seemed astutely calculated.

Before *Champion*, his playing had been cautious. His reserved manner worked well, if narrowly, in the offbeat-weakling roles in *The Strange Love of Martha Ivers* (1946), *Out of the Past* (1947), and *I Walk Alone* (1948). In *A Letter to Three Wives* (1948), he has the one role that suggested skills he would rarely evince again. This early trajectory pointed to journeyman stardom. But wisely he declined $50,000 for a second-string role in MGM's *The Great Sinner* for $15,000 and a

MYRON MEISEL *has been editor and publisher of* Focus!, *contributing editor for the* Chicago Reader, *a regular contributor to* The Boston Phoenix, *and has written on film for numerous magazines and books, including* King of the B's *and* Encyclopedia of American Filmmakers. *He worked on the crew of the stillborn* Touch-Me-Not *and wrote and co-produced the documentary* I'm a Stranger Here Myself: A Portrait of Nicholas Ray.

"When he is good, he can make us forget our bias for laid-back heroes and invite us into the emotional battlegrounds of his characters. And at his very best, he gives lie to all the sarcasms leveled at his overheated style." — M. M.

With Barbara Billingsley and Lana Turner in The Bad and the Beautiful.

profit share in a quickie, *Champion*. Douglas invested Ring Lardner's blackguard, Midge Kelly, with ameliorating touches typical of his compensatory approach. He seeks flaws in the hero, virtues in the heel, and humor in every character. Douglas magnetically attracted audience sympathy while confounding them with his unregenerate calumny: When Kelly slugs his crippled brother, Arthur Kennedy, we are shocked. Nevertheless, he has made us feel as if he socked a sanctimonious scrounge — even if that isn't the audience reaction producer Stanley Kramer had in mind.

Douglas became known for his voracious pursuit of plum parts. He reprised his driven-heel characterization with a bowdlerized Bix Beiderbecke in *Young Man with a Horn* (1950). He appeared in *The Glass Menagerie* (1950) and *Detective Story* (1951), and finally wiggled out of a constricting Warners contract. In Billy Wilder's *Ace in the Hole* (1951), he created the best of his classic bastards, a story-hungry reporter whose unredeemable working methods result in the death of a trapped miner. The reporter is such a master manipulator that he not only earns his comeuppance, he engineers it. What is exciting about Douglas's characterization is that he allows no shred of decency, while still suggesting a conscience. It could have been an easy, one-note role, but Douglas went at it the hard — and better — way.

He has always been an actor distinguished by his intelligence, which became even more evident once he began producing his own films in the mid-1950s. One of

the first stars to incorporate and manage his own production company, he asserted a marked artistic influence whenever he worked.

It is small wonder that many people associated the outspoken Douglas with the megalomaniacal characters he portrayed. Often his intelligence compensated for and shaded his own limitations of range, notably his relatively inexpressive voice, although at other times this intelligence overwhelmed the roles, as it did in *Detective Story* and *Lust for Life* (1956), two of his more acclaimed parts.

His best work in the fifties is divided between manic, grinning action heroes and low-key star roles in artistic productions. The one exception is his tortured producer in *The Bad and the Beautiful*, in which he successfully skirts self-parody by emphasizing the pragmatic side of his exploitation and charm. Yet he acquitted himself as well with his effortless (if strenuous) star turns in Disney's *20,000 Leagues Under the Sea* (1954), *The Indian Fighter* (1955), which he directed, and *The Vikings* (1958). Where necessary he would work to contribute to the design and effectiveness of the drama, as with *The Big Sky* (1952), *Man Without a Star* (1955), or his own *Paths of Glory* (1957). He does a stunning, gruesome *comedy* scene in *The Big Sky*, in which his finger is amputated and he drunkenly searches for it so he can go to heaven entire, if not whole. Douglas, who has a penchant for beatings, mutilations, and hideous deaths (after his grotesque eye in *The Vikings*, perhaps the only topper was his crucifixion in *Spartacus* [1960]), manages the scene with perfect broadness and a sense of the absurd.

By the sixties, he was beginning to change. Aside from forcing some over-anguished reactions in *Spartacus*, he strains to underplay the bombast, not always to good effect. But his anachronistic cowboy in *Lonely Are*

On guard for Bruce Dern in Posse, *which Douglas directed.*

With Faye Dunaway in The Arrangement. "*Above all he gave us the gift of Eddie Anderson, and for that I will always be grateful.*" — M. M.

ROOTS

LIKE MY GRANDPARENTS, Issur Danielovitch's parents emigrated to Amsterdam, New York, from the Pale around 1910. His father Herschel was an unsuccessful peddler; his mother Byrna, everyone agrees, was a "saint." His family was poor even by immigrant standards, and in the mid-1920s little Izzy Demsky worked at odd jobs. I've never been able to get it clear just why Izzy left my grandparents' employ as a delivery boy for Meisel's Kosher Meat and Poultry Products, but apparently it had something to do with his combative nature. "Did you ever see that movie, *Champion*?" my grandmother would later ask. "You should. That's the *real* Kirk Douglas."

Hollywood agreed. When Hedda Hopper asked him why stardom had gone to his head after *Champion*, Douglas set her straight: "I was an s.o.b. before *Champion*, but you never noticed it." — M. M.

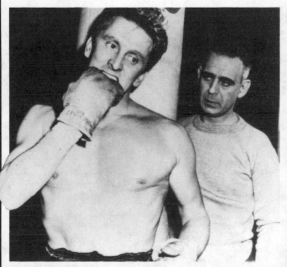

With Paul Stewart in Champion.

the Brave (1962) convincingly expressed the modesty of a man relaxed into his sense of self, and it marks a new subtlety and maturity in his acting. One need only contrast the melancholic Douglas in *Two Weeks in Another Town* (1962) with his characterization in its virtual predecessor *The Bad and the Beautiful* to note the growth. The earlier role was the better and was dynamically vanquished by Douglas, but the later one signaled that he had far more to give as an actor. Having worked on the edge of an emotional frontier, he was now calmer, working his way deeper, back inside himself.

Rejected by audience and critics, Elia Kazan's masterpiece *The Arrangement* (1969) showcases Douglas' one *great* performance. His scenes with Deborah Kerr and Faye Dunaway are purged of the cloying sensitivity of the love scenes in *Act of Love* (1953) or *Spartacus*; here, as Eddie Anderson, he achieves the difficult effect of establishing, in the mind of the audience, failures in Anderson's past while relating directly to both actresses. He makes the intractable side of Eddie Anderson's personality palpable. His behavior is erratic with wife and mistress. His obsessions are obscure, even to himself, and this inchoate drive gives the character a poignancy new for Douglas. Eddie expresses his feelings as an intelligent man out of control, and his inner conflict liberates Douglas as an actor. It's the same Kirk Douglas explosiveness, but here it is spiked with charm. It's the same body that moves, but it is subtle and supple with a stillness that suggests the unaccountable mysteries of the character. His flamboyant, finely honed performance gives coherence to fragmented narrative. Brando was to have played the part, but astoundingly, Kirk Douglas proves to have been the better choice.

Since *The Arrangement* he has been similarly restrained and effective. His scoundrel in *There Was a Crooked Man . . .* (1970) is assayed with genuine wit and guile, and he achieved the ultimate distinction of coming off as the most understated of all the players in *The Fury* (1978). His career has definitely downshifted, which is a pity, since he has more to offer now as an actor than ever, if only the parts can be found to tap the resources he has developed with age.

LEE MARVIN:
A DYING BREED

JOHN BOORMAN

Fighting for survival in John Boorman's Hell in the Pacific.

I HAD WATCHED HIM on the screen over the years, mesmerized by his unpredictable, explosive violence that was modified by an exhilarating eloquence, the saving grace of art. I met him in London when he was making *The Dirty Dozen* (1967). He was at the height of his powers, having just won an Oscar\for *Cat Ballou* (1965). I proposed *Point Blank* (1967) to him, and told him about the character he would play. He quickly understood that I was actually describing *him* — currents running deep in him. He agreed to do the film, to everyone's astonishment, for he knew nothing of my work. Not only that, when I arrived in Hollywood he arranged a meeting with the producers, the head of MGM, and his own agent.

Marvin asked: "I have script approval?" They agreed. "I have cast approval?" "Yes." "Approval of technicians?" "Yes." For the first time in his career he

had assumed the heady powers of superstar. Rising to leave, he lobbed the grenade into their midst. "I defer all these approvals to John."

Making my first picture in Hollywood, I was fortunate to have the gift of freedom. And he backed me all the way with a belief and loyalty that was inspiring. In addition, without ever intruding, he taught me a lot about film acting and filmmaking. He was endlessly inventive, constantly devising ways to externalize what we wanted to express. He taught me how actors must relate to other actors, objects, settings, compositions, movements. He has a dynamic relationship with the camera, a knowledge of its capacity to penetrate scenes and find their truth.

Together we made our exploration, and *Point Blank* managed to express some of Marvin's complex, paradoxical personality. A bruised sensibility is apparent, an acute awarenss that sees all too clearly the perfidy and cupidity of his fellow creatures. Because one also senses a yearning for heroic justice, one sympathizes with his need for cathartic violence. Implicit in this is the poignancy of his coming to realize that he is a doomed species, the last of a line, marooned.

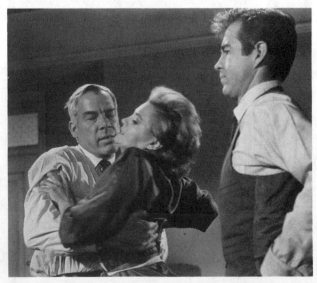

Point Blank, with Angie Dickinson and Clu Gulager.

JOHN BOORMAN *directed Lee Marvin in* Point Blank *and* Hell in the Pacific. *His other credits include* Having a Wild Weekend, Deliverance, *and* The Exorcist: Part II.

These days, a decade later, I make pilgrimages to his habitats. He can be found loping around his Arizona ranch among regiments of monstrous cacti, themselves evolutionary castaways, desert sentinels of an encroaching petrochemical suburbia. Or beached at Malibu, the skeptical green eyes scouring the bleached horizon for the romantic tidal wave that will surely drown L.A.

He picks through the midden of scripts, tossing them into the ashcan after a few pages. Only big-game fishing truly absorbs him today, but he reads on, waiting for the big one — the one that will redeem the rest, test him, draw out his powers in primal combat. He awaits the challenge, the call to heroic action. Part of him knows with a terrible clarity that such a test will not come, its time has passed. So it is with a cynical lilt of a smile that he greets the visitor: the icy green eyes that see everything, too much, his red face, the white hair, all conspire to strike fear into the hearts of the interloper. But it is more than fear, a profound unease, a sense that he has sprung out of our own darkest unconscious, this figure amongst the cacti. He casts the long shadow of Australopithecus, our mysterious animal ancestor that invented weapons and gave us our genetic compulsion for meting out death.

It is an easy jump across a convenient time-warp, and he reappears as the archetype of frontier America, genocidal, a brute force, angel of death, toting the poetic gun. His aspect reminds us how America was won. In many of his movies he gives us nightmarish reruns of the conquest. He has the awful clarity of the true artist. He does not flinch to show us how it was and how it is and (cynically) ever will be.

Just as we are chilled to the soul, behold, the magical transformation! Flip the coin! Discover another amazing Marvin! The laconic bitten-off lines become humorous diatribes; the strong face cracks into a thousand comic cuts; the taut body, a shambles of inchoate limbs; the lean, hard face sprouts whiskers; the mordant stoic becomes outrageously funny on a gargantuan scale. *Cat Ballou* was an apotheosis because he played the A side and the B side in the same movie, as he did in a more muted way in *Hell in the Pacific* (1968).

He suffers from being much bigger than the roles that are around, and that is our loss, perhaps our tragedy.

One morning some years back he found himself driving home after a long night in his beloved gin mills. He drove up to his home in Pacific Palisades, only to find the door opened by a stranger. He had changed houses two weeks before. The question was, where to? He cruised up to Sunset Boulevard, trying to remember. Suddenly, help was at hand. By the roadside was a sign reading MAPS TO THE STARS' HOMES. He bought one. He wasn't on it.

But we know where he lives. In the pantheon of true stars.

In Fritz Lang's classic The Big Heat, *Marvin scalded Gloria Grahame's face with hot coffee. She will return the favor.*

SEAN CONNERY: A PROPENSITY FOR STYLISH MAYHEM

MICHAEL CRICHTON

H E IS CHARACTERISTICALLY diffident about his career: "I never thought to be an actor. I was in London in the Mr. Universe contest, and looking for something else to do. I had an offer to try for the Manchester United football team, but I was twenty-two, and a bit old for that. Then someone told me they were looking for people to fill the chorus of *South Pacific*. So I found out where to go to audition, I got a job, and that was that."

For a man who had grown up in an Edinburgh slum, who had left school at fourteen and had in the next eight years worked as a milk delivery man, naval seaman, coal man, bricklayer, printer's devil, and lifeguard, a job as a chorus boy in a stage play must have seemed no more peculiar than any other. But he remained with the company for two years, and at the end of that time was determined to be an actor. Sean acted on British television for the next five years, first attracting attention playing the lead in Rod Serling's "Requiem for a Heavyweight" in 1956. A year later he became a contract player for Twentieth Century-Fox, and did ten films between 1957 and 1962.

In these early films, Connery exudes a rich, dark animal presence that is almost overpowering; his screen

MICHAEL CRICHTON *is the writer-director of* Coma, Westworld, *and* The Great Train Robbery. *Among his novels that have been adapted into movies are* The Andromeda Strain *and* The Terminal Man.

quality doesn't really work — in the way that the early Cary Grant films don't work, and for much the same reasons. Both men are physically so impressive that they benefited from the softening of age, and both men learned to use their considerable comic gifts to undercut and play against their sensuality.

This development can be seen over the course of the six James Bond films Connery did. Although almost no-

The sixties male sexual prototype: superspy James Bond.

Part of endless argument with wife Joanne Woodward in A Fine Madness.

body recognized it, James Bond is an impossible role in dramatic terms; it is in the nature of Ian Fleming's stories that while Bond is the hero, the villains have all the lines. In the books this is perfectly clear. Bond is chiefly characterized by his cream shirts, his gun-metal gray lighter, his specially made cigarettes, his martinis shaken not stirred. He is handy with a gun, lucky at cards and with women, but dull at the center — particularly in comparison to the baroque antagonists he confronts.

Fleming's dramatic structure is reflected in the first Bond film, *Dr. No* (1963). The most memorable performance belongs to Joseph Wiseman, in the title role. In the final confrontation, Dr. No announces: "You disappoint me, Mr. Bond. You are just a stupid policeman." Indeed Bond was — but not for long.

A year later, in *From Russia with Love* (1964), Connery was pitted against Robert Shaw and came out ahead, in part because Bond now had humor and had lost his self-importance. By the third film, *Goldfinger* (1964), the pattern was entirely changed. Gert Frobe's splendid Goldfinger never takes our attention away from James Bond, and if subsequent films developed into formulas, the public liked them all the better.

Eventually the advertisements proclaimed, "Sean Connery *is* James Bond." In fact Sean Connery invented James Bond, and he himself never confused the two. From the beginning of the Bond films he worked to separate his identity from that of the secret agent. He gave remarkable performances in such films as *Marnie*

Another Time, Another Place. *Early film with Lana Turner.*

Connery and Michael Caine were splendid duo in John Huston's magnificent The Man Who Would Be King.

(1964) and *The Hill* (1965), and if the public refused to see anything there but transmutations of Bond, that was their problem.

But now, of course, his career is clearer. He has provided a succession of varied performances in *The Molly Maguires* (1970), *The Red Tent* (1971), *The Anderson Tapes* (1971), *Zardoz* (1974), *Murder on the Orient Express* (1974), and *The Man Who Would be King* (1975). After so many years as an underrated actor, people are beginning to recall that before he did Ian Fleming, he did Shakespeare, Tolstoy, and Eugene O'Neill.

He is, in fact, quite remarkable to work with. Like all serious people, he prefers to laugh as much as possible; Connery is a light presence on the set. He is charming, easy, and generous; he's quick to help an actor who has trouble playing a scene, and I have heard him argue against cutting a scene from a script because it was another actor's best moment in the picture. At the same time, he is rigorously professional and has no tolerance for people who arrive late or hung-over or unprepared. He is quite capable of going into a towering (and entertaining) rage.

His sense of script is excellent, and he will fuss over scenes and lines of dialogue that aren't quite right. He is one of those actors who always attends rushes and seems to be able to view his own work objectively; he is perfectly prepared to be unsympathetic or foolish in a scene and has nothing but scorn for actors who back away from certain aspects of a part because they are afraid they will look bad. When it comes to doing stunts, he is physically self-assured and fearless.

Connery prefers not to talk about work when he is not working. He is a great raconteur and an accomplished mimic; sometimes we would block a scene alone, and he took great delight in playing everyone's part — men and women — as well as his own. He is absolutely direct, speaks his mind, refuses to engage in petty disputes.

In the course of making a film, a still photographer records daily work of the production. Looking at the stills, one can get a good sense of what is really happening on the set as well as on screen. The off-camera stills of *The Great Train Robbery* (1978) show Sean talking with members of the production unit. Most of the time, the photographs show people laughing, while Sean stands with a look of bemusement, as if he cannot understand what, exactly, they find so entertaining.

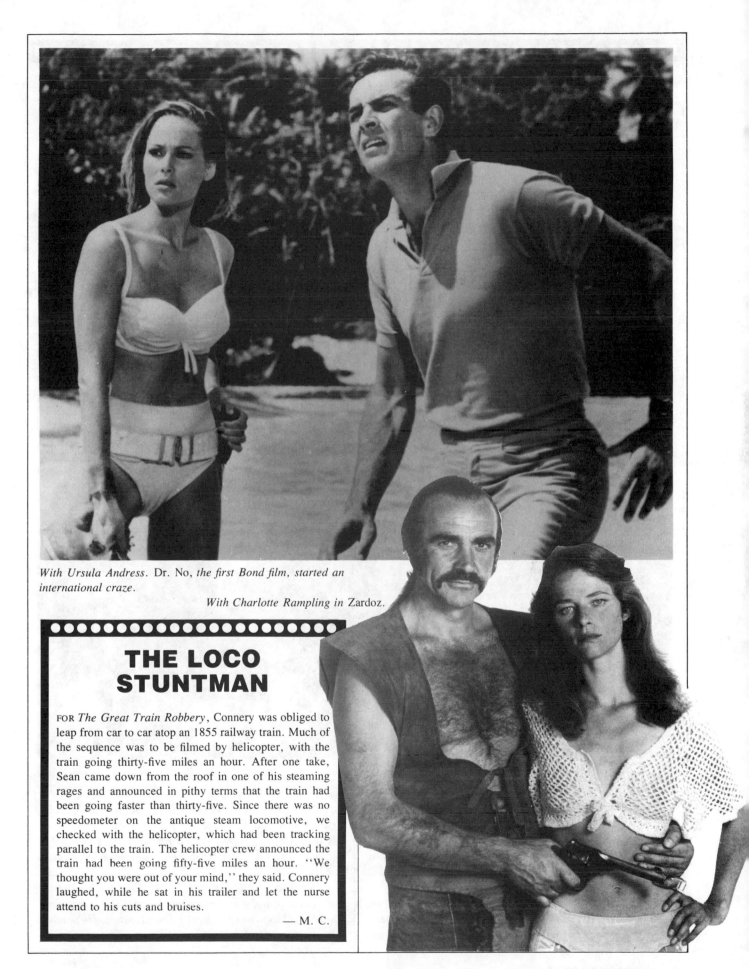

With Ursula Andress. Dr. No, *the first Bond film, started an international craze.*

With Charlotte Rampling in Zardoz.

THE LOCO STUNTMAN

FOR *The Great Train Robbery*, Connery was obliged to leap from car to car atop an 1855 railway train. Much of the sequence was to be filmed by helicopter, with the train going thirty-five miles an hour. After one take, Sean came down from the roof in one of his steaming rages and announced in pithy terms that the train had been going faster than thirty-five. Since there was no speedometer on the antique steam locomotive, we checked with the helicopter, which had been tracking parallel to the train. The helicopter crew announced the train had been going fifty-five miles an hour. ''We thought you were out of your mind,'' they said. Connery laughed, while he sat in his trailer and let the nurse attend to his cuts and bruises.

— M. C.

CLINT EASTWOOD: HE SPEAKS WITH BULLETS

STUART KAMINSKY

Eastwood has played detective Harry Callahan in three movies. Don Siegel's Dirty Harry *was the best, despite its right-wing bias.*

CLINT EASTWOOD — the actor and the character he portrays on the screen — did not suddenly spring forth in those celebrated Italian spaghetti westerns. The soft-spoken Eastwood cultivated his cool image throughout the late 1950s and early 1960s, developing his reserved acting style and creating his unmistakable persona: a hero who looks out for his own welfare, who is rarely taken in by emotion or women. The screen image of Clint Eastwood, antihero, was nur-

tured by Clint Eastwood the actor through years of television work and a number of little-known films before his breakthrough movie, *A Fistful of Dollars* (1964).

It really began in 1954 when Eastwood, then con-

STUART KAMINSKY *has written on film for numerous publications and has written books on Clint Eastwood, Don Siegel, and most recently, John Huston. He teaches film at Northwestern University.*

templating a career in business administration, was convinced by an ex-Army buddy to take a screen test at Universal Studios. When the test, actually a filmed interview, was shown to Universal executives, Eastwood was offered a contract guaranteeing him $75 a week for forty weeks. Eastwood quit school, and never returned.

For the next year and a half, he appeared, usually unbilled, in films that typically starred Rock Hudson and George Nader. Occasionally, he would get a line or two of dialogue, but generally he spent his spare time watching movies being made — and learning. "They shot a lot of cheapies in those days," he now recalls, "a lot of B pictures, and I'd always play the young lieutenant or the lab technician who came in and said, 'He went that way,' or 'Doctor, here are the X-rays,' and the doctor would say, 'Get lost, kid.' I'd go out, get lost, and that would be that."

When Universal refused to raise his salary to $125 a week, he decided to wait out the studio for six months. In six months, they dropped him completely. In 1957 and 1958, he made more money digging swimming pools than from acting, going without work for long periods of

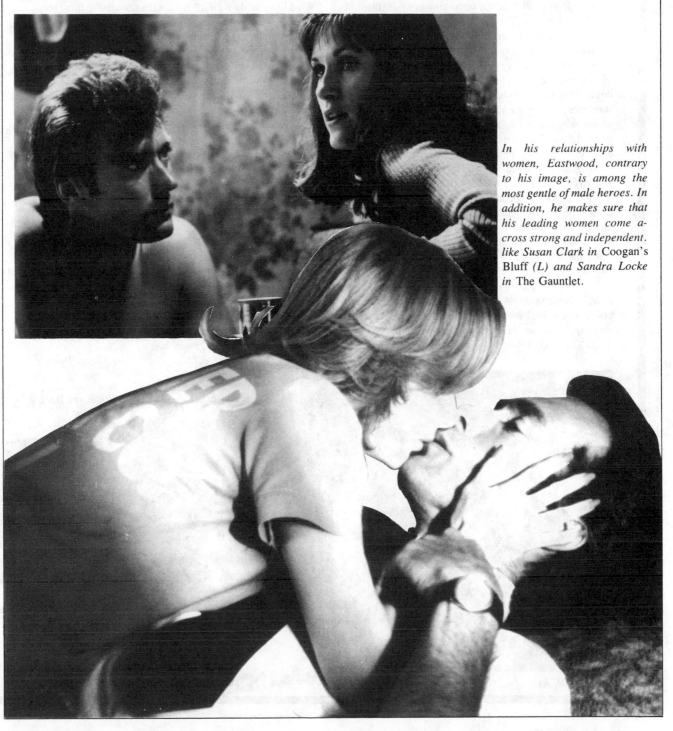

In his relationships with women, Eastwood, contrary to his image, is among the most gentle of male heroes. In addition, he makes sure that his leading women come across strong and independent. like Susan Clark in Coogan's Bluff *(L) and Sandra Locke in* The Gauntlet.

NEW WESTERN HERO

CRITICS HAD A HARD TIME coming to grips with the character Clint Eastwood played in the three Italian westerns that catapulted him into the superstar category. If they sensed that they had never seen a protagonist like him before, they were correct. Eastwood (and director Sergio Leone) unveiled the "new western hero."

Robert Warshow, in his 1954 essay, laid down what he considered to be the fundamentals of the Westerner. Almost without exception, western heroes in movies, before and after Warshow's important analysis, fitted his outline completely. The traditional Westerner, according to Warshow, is a loner. He would like to settle down, but there is *one* more thing that he must do first. There is a touch of melancholy in the Westerner that is usually caused by a sense of guilt; he realizes that what he has done in the past or must do in the future is, by society's standards, wrong; but moral, personal motives keep him on his wayward path. He wishes, but does not expect, that "the girl" will understand his point of view. At the end (of the movie), he must face his challenge — a villain — and try to win by fighting fairly. His battle with *himself* is then over, and he can: finally settle down with the girl who has begun to understand him, as Gary Cooper did in *High Noon*; leave town with the job done, as Alan Ladd did in *Shane;* or die as Gregory Peck did in *The Gunfighter*. At the end of each of these — especially the last — the Westerner has resolved something and his life has changed.

The Clint Eastwood character of Sergio Leone's Italian westerns breaks with almost all of Warshow's conventions. He is obviously a loner, but that is the only thing that is clear. In fact, you never find out *anything* about Eastwood's past or get any hints about his future.

You don't even find out his name. In *A Fistful of Dollars* he answers a woman's question about why he saved her life by saying succinctly, "Something happened once." You never find out what happened and you never expect to. From then on, there are no more questions, no more rescues, and no more women in Eastwood's life.

The plans of the "Man with No Name" are unpredictable. This bounty hunter rides away at the end of each film with large amounts of money in his possession. What does he do with it? With each successive film, we see that he has not settled down; he has remained a bounty hunter. There seems to be no regret, no guilt, and no touch of melancholy whatsoever.

These three films contain many showdowns. What is completely different here is that Eastwood not only initiates most of them, but also cheats to win. More than once he will shoot helpless, and surprised, enemies, as Jack Palance did as the unmatchable villain in *Shane*. There is no change in Eastwood's character at the end of a film; he has experienced no revelation. We have simply seen a typical incident in this man's life. The Man with No Name is still his same old rotten self.

Is this character a hero? In the situations he is placed, yes. It is apparent that all the scenes take place while the decent folks are out of town (they only come back for hangings). He is living the only type of existence that he can in order to survive in this evil world. It is lucky for him that he has such great potential for evil and is so impassive to his own cruelty. What makes him a hero is not that he is a wonderful person, but the fact that he kills so many wicked people. Gene Autry is as lenient as he should be in his world; Eastwood is as monstrous as he should be in his.

— Danny Peary

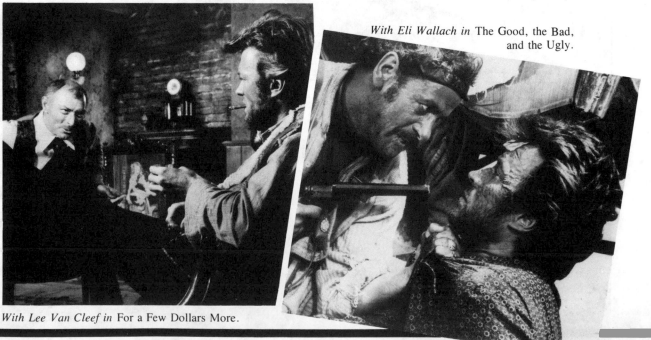

With Eli Wallach in The Good, the Bad, and the Ugly.

With Lee Van Cleef in For a Few Dollars More.

The Man with No Name, the most ruthless hero in motion picture history.

time. But the two films in which Eastwood did appear during this interim were noteworthy. First he played the second lead in a low-budget western, *Ambush at Cimarron Pass* (1958). And, in *Lafayette Escadrille* (1958), directed by veteran William Wellman, he played a pilot, the real-life flying ace George Moseley.

Eastwood managed to land a few television jobs — sometimes because he was willing to do stunts — including about a dozen shows in a syndicated series called *West Point*, playing the role of a cadet. "The trouble with that series," he remembers, "was that practically nothing ever happens to West Point cadets in real life. They march, go to classes, play football, study, and go to bed. We'd open an episode with some strong, dramatic line like, 'You stole my laundry!' Where do you go from there?"

Eastwood's first prolonged exposure came in the television series *Rawhide*. In almost two hundred fifty one-hour segments, Eastwood played Rowdy Yates, a brash, hot-headed gunfighter who was known for acting emotionally rather than rationally. While Yates was unlike the cool, clear-thinking, tight-lipped characters Eastwood would later play in all his films, he certainly formed the basis for Eastwood's manly "cowboy-bandit" (his words) image that would be refined in Italian westerns.

"The world's favorite movie star," in the words of *Life* magazine, he is a Hollywood maverick who prefers to work with directors and properties of his own selection. He insists on control of his films because he is wary of failure. Like other stars before him, Eastwood harbors the belief that his next film may be the last, that his fame might suddenly vanish. This fear is so unlike what one would expect from someone with his cool image.

In some ways, the real Eastwood is a living contrast to his screen character. His screen roles show him as an emotionally exhausted man who resorts to violence with little prompting. At home, however, he has been known to shoo a fly out the door rather than deal it a death blow.

In the past dozen years, he has moved from his role in *Rawhide* to stardom in Italian and American westerns to his situation today as actor, producer, director, businessman, and head of his own film company. The acting roles have included a Civil War soldier in *The Beguiled* (1971), a disc jockey in *Play Misty for Me* (1971), a soldier in *Kelly's Heroes* (1970) and *Where Eagles Dare* (1969), and a big-city cop in *Dirty Harry* (1971), *Magnum Force* (1973), *The Enforcer* (1976), and *The Gauntlet* (1977). He has moved away from his cowboy roles, but he contends that he has not done this to become a different type of actor: "I simply choose roles that interest me, that I know I can handle." As a director — *Play Misty for Me, High Plains Drifter* (1973), *Breezy* (1973), *The Eiger Sanction* (1975), and *The Gauntlet* — he is no less established, and has shown an exciting propensity to challenge himself as an actor

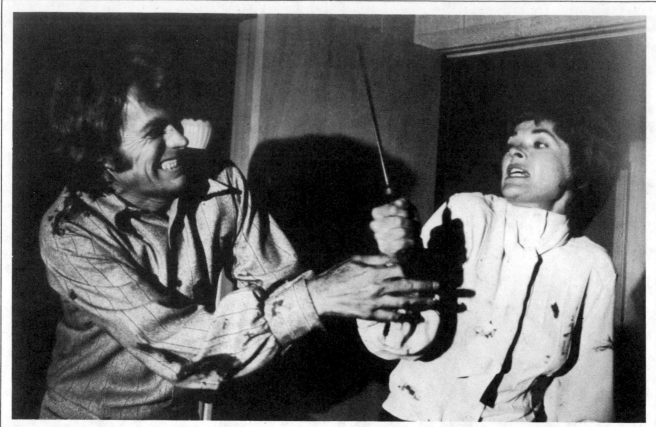

Jessica Walter was possessive and insane in Play Misty for Me, *his fine directorial debut.*

when directing himself.

Not that his acting ever shows — he has the remarkable ability to convince an audience that the actor and the character are the same, that what he is doing is not acting. In truth, it is difficult not to act, to appear natural, to make audiences believe that the character on the screen is you and that you are not merely an actor playing that character.

Laurence Olivier, George C. Scott, Rod Steiger, and Marlon Brando are actors whose performances are designed to flaunt their versatility and range, to win applause for their thespian skills. On the other hand, there are actors who mesh character and personality successfully, like Henry Fonda, John Wayne, or the actor to whom Eastwood is frequently compared, Gary Cooper. Fonda once told me that the secret of such style was "not to let the wheels show. This is the hardest kind of acting, and it works only if you look as if you are not acting at all."

Certainly, in Eastwood's case, his physical appearance is part of his appeal and his "non-acting" mystique. He is tall (six-foot-four), strong, and handsome, a man who plays characters who seldom smile unless it is private and cynical. His characters are perverse, worldly-wise loners. To earn even a thimbleful of their respect is a major assignment for the other characters. A cool image, in a word — but really the result of his ability to keep the wheels from showing.

Hang 'em High. *As is often the case he has been badly beaten up.*

CHARLES BRONSON: SILENCE UNDER THE FIST

JAMES DICKEY

CHARLES BRONSON, through the mysterious vectors of heredity, genes, and chance, emerges on the screen as a blend of authority and rugged authenticity, comfortable in the turmoil of violent action. But, as in *Death Wish* (1974) and *The Great Escape* (1963), there is always about him a silent and reflective personality hidden somewhere within or beneath a body redolent of the workingman — the coal miner, the factory worker, or the truck driver. He has had a very great variety of roles. In fact, the first time I saw him was in *Chato's Land* (1972), where he played the most *muscular* Indian I had ever seen on the screen — an Indian chief who had obviously been lifting weights. At the end of the film, as I recall, he was hanged, and the obvious consternation in the character he played, at what was being done to him for no reason he could ascertain, was portrayed with humor and resolution, and it was touching indeed.

The quality of authenticity and rough male ruggedness makes Bronson's performances much more *experienceable* by audiences than would those of a more conventionally handsome and delicate-featured man. This characteristic of believability and solid-hewn, aging, tough, essentially moral masculinity is Bronson's trademark.

It is ironic that Bronson's "star" status was determined by his enormous popularity in Europe in the late sixties, while he was regarded as no more than a competent bit player in America. Charles Bronson has since come back to this country and acted in a great number of films, most of them very bad, a few remarkably good. Yet always he has projected a figure full of virility and responsibility and, above all, of resourcefulness. He is

As professional assassin in The Mechanic.

JAMES DICKEY *is an award-winning poet who wrote the best-selling adventure novel* Deliverance *and its screenplay, which was made into a major motion picture.*

Eluding posse in Chato's Land.

the very epitome of what President Kennedy wrote about in his book *A Nation of Immigrants,* which held forth the conviction that people of all nations, given the opportunities that America afforded, would be able to bring from themselves remarkable sources of ingenuity, enterprise, and courage.

Even in his worst films, Bronson exemplifies these qualities. For example, in a piece of awful trash such as *The White Buffalo* (1977) he is, although certainly not anything like the Wild Bill Hickok he is supposed to portray, convincing as a human being, as a man in whom we are interested because he reaches and confirms positive virtues in us.

With Richard Attenborough in The Great Escape.

There is something archetypal about Bronson, no matter how bad his films are. He has never been in the masterpiece that I suspect him capable of carrying off. There are touches in his films, almost all of them, which lead me to believe that, given the right circumstances, his combination of forceful projection and an unexpected male tenderness might produce a truly haunting succession of images in the viewer's mind.

In *The Great Escape* — to take one of his better movies — he portrays an ex-coal miner terrified by claustrophobia. His key scene is not in a coal mine, but in a tunnel which he is digging as an escape route from a German prison camp during World War II. He is in a narrow tunnel, an almost surrealistic premature-burial setting. Here Bronson plays, with a stunning sense of reality, the situation of a very brave man caught, and quite literally buried, in the nightmarish version of his own worst fear, as the tunnel caves in.

The coal miner figure is a good one with which to identify Bronson: a first or second generation American of Polish or Central European extraction. The kind of character he generally plays (except for that weight-lifting Indian!) is very close to the popular notion of a strong, no-nonsense man whose appeal, say, to women, does not lie in his looks or in his money, but in his integrity and his great animal vitality.

A source of depth in Bronson's art lies in the fact that he can play off toughness and craggy intractability against a totally unsuspected affection and concern. At the beginning of *Death Wish*, for which to me is his best film, the scene with his wife on the vacation beach is extremely poignant. The viewer has the tendency to forget the actress who played his wife (Hope Lange), but is not likely to forget Bronson's projection of the kind of slightly embarrassed but protective tenderness that Bronson brings to the character. It is the remembrance of that scene during the awful events following it that helps to make the film as powerful as it is.

It is often said that works of art do not and cannot and should not influence the social structure in which they appear. I do not believe that to be true. I believe that *Death Wish*, truly understood, is capable of affecting change in the way we actually live. I believe that, thanks to Bronson, whose image was concreted through *Death Wish*, and the other people who made the film possible, the whole issue of law and order is brought into an unignorable focus. What Bronson's chilling performance indicates is that the average citizen — armed and ready — is more dangerous than any criminal that he is likely to encounter. The criminal wants only money, but the Bronson character wants the death of the culprit and will have nothing else. There are monsters among us, and Bronson's depiction of a man changed by implacable revenge — motivated into being a cold-marrowed, resourceful killer — could not, I believe, have been better played. But that is not all that the character projects. At the end of the film, he is not only avenging the cruel pointless death of his young wife, but has been cast by his actions into the role of a kind of universal avenger — a one-man force against what he considers universal evil. There is a strange, unresolvable ambiguity about the character Bronson portrays so well; the evils that he is so obsessed with eradicating are real enough evils, but Bronson plays the character as a man who has himself become the very thing that he wished to destroy. The criminals he kills are not the same human beings who perpetrated the crimes against his wife, but after several killings, that fact no longer matters to him. There is actually no possibility that he will ever find the real killers, although it is implied that he believes he will. Bronson is engaged in a mythical manhunt, and the film can therefore be seen as a *Moby Dick* of the city pavements. It is even possible that he is going insane, as Ahab did, with the intensity of his quest.

Bronson has created both by skill and intuition a veritable archetype of the beleaguered and fear-haunted, overcompensating person we all have become in the modern city of terror. He is the man who takes private arms against the nightmarish fear of our time: that of being set upon by malicious strangers.

The questions raised are ultimately philosophical ones. What happens when decency, in its own defense, turns killer? Is this a desired condition in society? Or is it something far worse than evil? Charles Bronson does not need to tell you about these issues. In *Death Wish* he acts them, so that you can draw your own conclusions. And that is his art.

Death Wish *was controversial because its hero, a common citizen, toured the streets killing criminals.*

JACK NICHOLSON: BADGE OF ALIENATION

ROBERT C. CUMBOW

The Passenger. *In films, as in public, he wears dark glasses, giving him a mysterious — almost sinister — aura.*

JACK NICHOLSON is a regular guy, subject — even prone — to failure; we expect little of him, therefore he becomes capable of anything. We feel *comfortable* with Jack Nicholson, and that comfort is the key to the popularity and versatility of the so-called "Nicholson type." He's one of us: lazy good humor; a laid-back style that makes even the most meticulously written dialogue sound improvised; cool, unpressured manner; never too up or too down.

The quintessential Nicholson role is still Robert Eroica Dupea in *Five Easy Pieces* (1970). ("I move around a lot. Not because I'm *looking* for anything, really; but 'cuz I'm getting away from things that get bad if I stay. Auspicious beginnings, y'know what I mean?")

That "know what I mean?" punctuates Nicholson's conversation a lot, in and out of character. There is never any doubt what John Wayne, for instance, means; but the "Nicholson type" is nothing if not misunderstood. Even when Wayne played a drifter or a man of serious failings, he focused his characterization on personal triumphs; while even in Nicholson's most plainly heroic roles, the

ROBERT C. CUMBOW *is a film critic for the* Olympia News *in Olympia, Washington, and writes regularly for the magazine* Movietone News. *He is writing a book on monster movies of the 1950s.*

Five Easy Pieces, *released in 1970. "Significantly, stardom came during a cooling-off period for beaten or compromised student radicals. A defeated idealist like Bobby Dupea, with nothing left to commit himself to except noncommitment, spoke volumes to those who had rejected the politics and aesthetics of John Wayne, and had nothing to fill the void." — R. C.*

emphasis is on failure and futility. Youthful but tired, righteous but defeated, Nicholson comes on like a man who has seen too much of life and has burnt out early — like Robert Mitchum's Philip Marlowe.

But it's with Bogart that Nicholson most readily compares; an actor who builds characterizations upon a consistent, familiar substratum of personal style; a star surrounded by an unmistakable, indefinable mystique. For both actors the mystique is principally vocal. Within the seemingly insurmountable limitations of his stiff-lipped half lisp and thick New York City accent, Bogart was capable of amazing versatility, while it softened his heroic roles engagingly. That voice just couldn't belong to a superior being. Neither can Nicholson's broad nasal twang, which tends to be comic where Bogey's toothy lisp was tough, but the genius of the actor extends the range. If Nicholson's voice seems best suited to overtly comic encounters like the restaurant scene in *Five Easy Pieces* ("Ya want me ta *hold* the chicken? I want ya to hold it between yer *knees*"), it can also lend a darkly comic ambiguity to moments of tooth-grinding serious-ness, like his deadly reckoning with Brando in *The Missouri Breaks* (1976) ("Know what woke ya up, Robert Lee? You've just had yer throat cut . . .").

Never much of a body actor (despite resonant mo-ments like his full-body snarl at a yapping dog in *Five Easy Pieces),* Nicholson fires with a battery of facial expressions: squint-eyed seriousness, hurt-puppy sad-ness, a cross-eyed, near-lunatic grin, and a toothy "killer smile" that can drop right out of existence without ever disturbing his face muscles, leaving behind earnest good looks, pale shock, or the stunning blankness of one who might do anything. But the glory of that face is still the voice that issues from it.

Nicholson constantly pushes his range of vocal feeling in new directions, creating moments of resonance

In Antonioni's The Passenger, *with Maria Schneider.*

A genuine heel in Mike Nichols' Carnal Knowledge, *with Candice Bergen.*

that belie the superficial hickishness of the voice: the quiet, slow build of Bobby's one-way conversation with his paralyzed father in *Five Easy Pieces;* the desperate futility in Jake Gittes' choked whisper at the end of *Chinatown* (1974); the gleeful, triumphant rage of a downtrodden Navy lifer with sudden power in *The Last Detail* (1973).

The generation that reveres Nicholson has also revived Bogart. Like Bogey, Nicholson rose through B films, playing more villains and victims than heroes. The experience prepared both men for the mock-heroic performances that characterized their stardom; the long climb from character parts to starring roles had a lot to do with the tiredness central to the styles of both actors. And the "taint" of what Nicholson has called "all these horror pictures" (he really made only three at American International) has considerable bearing on the credibility of the flawed anti-heroes of his maturity.

Bobby Dupea in *Five Easy Pieces* is really a modern Gothic hero — not the uniformed juvenile who saves the heroine in *The Terror* (1963), but the tormented Boris Karloff figure, from whom emanate both the horror and the anguish of that film. Bobby's aesthetic sense — developed in his upbringing — leaves him seeing only irony, the world as parody of what it could be — and makes his life "get bad." The only escape from that hopeless vision is his constant reshaping of his lifestyle. He climbs aboard the Alaska-bound semi without jacket, wallet, identity — a resonant archetypal image that Italian director Michelangelo Antonioni took advantage of in casting Nicholson as the identity-switching anti-hero of *The Passenger* (1975).

Alienation, then, is what the "Nicholson type" is finally about. If the flawed nature of his characters has an

equalizing, normalizing effect, lowering a potential hero to our own common level, the process often passes beyond the natural weaknesses of the dignified common man, creating an outcast *we* don't want to recognize. In *Carnal Knowledge* (1971), for instance, Nicholson makes us identify with — then draw back from — an image of what *we* could become. His Jonathan, reductio ad absurdum of the red-blooded American male, like

Nicholson's break came as oddball lawyer in trend-setting Easy Rider, *with Dennis Hopper (L) and Peter Fonda.*

Bobby Dupea, fears and resists being tied down, but buys his freedom at the price of total alienation. He suspends himself in an adolescent world of "getting it," his cynicism creating an increasing need for fantasy to offset encroaching impotence.

Though a considerable womanizer, the "Nicholson type" is never much of a lover. While many of his films have R-rated sexual content, none has a romantic focus. The closest is *The Missouri Breaks,* in which the Nicholson character actually falls in love and becomes a force for normalcy in a mad world. The film's lack of popularity may tell us something: He isn't *supposed* to be romantic or heroic. He's only supposed to fail; to embody the ordinary, fumbling guy — and to be utterly destroyed.

That, certainly, is the fate of *Chinatown*'s J. J. Gittes, a tired Nicholson anti-hero becomes a Polanskian hero-victim, unwittingly serving evil more than good. The Nicholson screen image is crucial to the characterization of Gittes — a man familiar with failure. Central to the film is the memory of his previous experience in Chinatown. ("I was trying to keep someone from being hurt. I ended up making sure that she *was* hurt.") If his earlier defeat in Chinatown was a loss of innocence, the new one demonstrates the ineffectuality of experience. "You never learn, do you, Jake?" says Lieutenant Escobar. Gittes, the would-be savior, is too human to do more than repeat the same cycle of cataclysmic failure.

The Last Detail. *Carol Kane is a prostitute.*

What better choice than Nicholson to play Randle Patrick MacMurphy in *One Flew Over the Cuckoo's Nest* (1975), a rebel so alienated and madcap that no one can tell he isn't really mad? MacMurphy's sad fate recalls the admonition of Kurt Vonnegut, Jr. in *Mother Night:* "We are what we pretend to be, so we must be careful about what we pretend to be." Nicholson's characters often become what they pretend to be, and are often destroyed by the consequences of pretense, like Jonathan and Jake.

But if Nicholson's horror film background sounds a resonance appropriate to these essentially neo-Gothic characterizations, his car and motorbike films of the sixties affected even more profoundly his development in the seventies. The aimless, unpredictable drifter was in his grain long before he played Bobby Dupea. And his performance in *The Last Detail* is a rhapsody on the theme. Badass Buddusky dances, rather than walks, on a wire stretched between two authority figures: a stern Navy NCO at the beginning, a threateningly colorless Marine lieutenant at the end. Himself a parody of an authority figure, escorting to prison a young sailor sentenced for an absurd crime, Buddusky celebrates "good times" as the sole meaningful experience in a world where human freedom is found only in transit.

The same existential vision, minus the fun, characterized Nicholson's screenplay and lead performance in *Ride in the Whirlwind* (1967). Three cowboys, caught in a crossfire between outlaws and a posse, are mistaken for the fleeing bandits and must keep running or hang for crimes they know nothing about. The film might easily be a motorcycle picture in a western setting.

Similarly, ten years later, *The Missouri Breaks* taps the motorbike background, pitting two former biker-rebels against each other: Brando's fifties sado-masochistic hardness versus Nicholson's sixties flower-child eccentricity. Nicholson's Tom Logan is enough like us to stand against the baroque fetishism of Brando's

With John Huston in Chinatown.

Robert Lee Clayton. If the alliance of rancher Brazton and bounty-killer Clayton recalls the all-powerful collusion of Noah Cross (John Huston) and the Los Angeles Police Department in *Chinatown,* Logan at least is sufficiently unorthodox to beat them at their own game — Gittes never even learns what game they're playing. Both Gittes and Logan are ultimately Nicholson rebels turned, however oddly, to the service of good — a far cry from the essential anarchism of both the heroic and the villainous Nicholson roles in the bike films.

The motorcycle connection was, of course, what first brought Nicholson to fame. Cast as the small-town lawyer, George Hanson, in *Easy Rider* (1969), he became, in a handful of scenes, the conscience of the film for a generation of young adults rebellious enough to cheer his insights into the power of true freedom, yet not so fed up to identify with the aimless, self-destructive anti-heroes of the film.

Hanson's drinking, his letter sweater, and his football helmet (ersatz biker headgear) ally him with the conservative, traditional side of American culture; but his openness to the long-haired dropouts makes him a middleman who might just reunite a polarized society. He wears the helmet like a badge of his alienation from both worlds: too straight to be a real dropout, too unselfconsciously zany to belong to "society."

Most of Nicholson's characters bear such marks of Cain: the gap-toothed grin of masochistic Wilbur Force (*The Little Shop of Horrors,* 1960), who visits the dentist for pleasure; the bandaged nose of J. J. Gittes; the lobotomy scar of R. P. MacMurphy. The Nicholson character wears his badge proudly. He never recognizes — as his creator surely does — that he is doomed, a modern scapegoat, both one of us and alien, prodded toward the altar with the unspoken charge: "Get in there and fail for us!"

His defeat comforts, reassures — and just maybe redeems us all.

A confrontation with villainous Marlon Brando in The Missouri Breaks.

DAVID CARRADINE: AMERICAN PRIMITIVE

PAUL BARTEL

AT ABOUT NINE-THIRTY, the doorbell rings. It is David Carradine looking worn and tired, but happy. There is much hugging and kissing. He is a warm, affectionate person. He seems as glad to see me as I am to see him.

As we talk, I study his amazing face — a plain, honest, American face. Howard Hawks had a theory that the only way an actor could be any good was if the camera "liked" him. The camera likes David Carradine and takes kindly to his craggy, sunken cheeks and his great, sincere eyes. David likes to see himself in a loincloth, flailing away with a sword and doing kung fu kicks. But I see him as the new Gary Cooper, a low-key, rock-hard man of honesty and ideals. Surely it is this homespun American persona that made him so touching and effective in *Bound for Glory* (1976). I believe that it was this same image, disguised under the sci-fi paraphernalia, that made his performance in *Death Race 2000* (1975) so resonant.

Death Race 2000 was the first of two films in which I directed David Carradine for Roger Corman, *Cannonball* (1976) being the second. Of the two filming experiences, *Death Race* was by far the more difficult and interesting.

Death Race 2000 was to be released in the summer of 1975, but prolonged problems with the script brought us well into the late fall of 1974 with no star lead and no starting date. Suddenly David, who was just winding up his popular TV series *Kung Fu*, agreed to play the lead. Until then tradition had it that TV stars were not likely to draw at the box office. Nevertheless, everyone agreed that Carradine's image from *Kung Fu* would be perfect for our bizarre horror-action comedy about the "national sport of the future": coast-to-coast auto racing in which points are scored by running down pedestrians.

The leading role in *Death Race,* a legendary race

champion named Frankenstein, might have been written for Carradine. The fact that it was played by Carradine, an actor the audience was predisposed to like, permitted us to treat the character ambiguously for the first half hour of the film. For nearly a whole reel I teased the audience by withholding David's face. I showed fleeting

An action hero of the seventies.

PAUL BARTEL *has directed* Private Parts, Death Race 2000, *and* Cannonball, *and has appeared in such films as* Hollywood Boulevard *and* Piranha.

With father John Carradine, top screen villain of the thirties.

glimpses of his long arms and legs swathed in black leather, and relied mainly on Carradine's deep, resonant voice to convey his fearsome character.

A few scenes later when Frankenstein meets "the girl" who is to be his companion in the death race, I shot David from the front for the first time. His face is partly covered by a black mask, but enough can be seen to anticipate that what is underneath is truly hideous. Before long, he and the girl are out on the road running people over.

To keep the audience from losing sympathy for David, the victims are carefully set up as "worthy" of being run over. The audience cheers and laughs when Frankenstein mows down a group of doctors and nurses who have pushed their geriatric patients out into the street as sacrificial offerings. A fascist device, perhaps, but an effective one.

The ambiguity in his character greatly appealed to Carradine. Toward the end of the run of his TV show, David had gotten a lot of bad publicity. Rumors circulated around Hollywood that he was into drugs and given to outrageous behavior. David felt that, for the public, he had actually become a sort of monster and he wanted to change that image. He believed that when, a half hour or so into the film, Frankenstein's mask is removed, revealing just a regular guy (who goes on to become president of the United States), it would suggest to the public that Carradine, like Frankenstein, was really a regular guy underneath the bad publicity. Perhaps, in some odd way, the film did function in this way for David. He has been kind enough to say that *Death Race 2000* saved his screen career.

The film was shot in four weeks on a budget of $480,000. The preproduction phase was particularly troublesome, and David was making things difficult too. He didn't like the fabric of his costume (although he had okayed a swatch of it), so he simply ripped the costume

up. He didn't like the shape of the helmet that had been specially designed and molded to his head, so it had to be redone in a hurry at tremendous cost.

It was, of course, a difficult period for him. He was just coming off a TV series that had made him a big star. But the basis of that stardom was now defunct and, in a

A DANCE LEGACY

DAVID CARRADINE could be wonderful in a dancing role. He claims to do a sort of "character dance" in all his films anyway, a subtle choreography of the character's movement which helps delineate the role — a legacy, perhaps, from Kwai Chang Cain. I remember with pleasure the strange, sweet little fox trot he does with Simone Griffith in the bedroom scene in *Death Race 2000*.

Doing a dance film interests him. Nothing like *Saturday Night Fever,* but something in the manner of the classic Fred Astaire films, perhaps co-starring his fifteen-year-old daughter, Calista, who is a regular dancing fool. (David and Calista are currently collaborating on a film of the life of Mata Hari which they expect will take years to complete. It's being filmed in bits and pieces around the world; last year eighty minutes were shot in India; this year they worked in the Netherlands.)

— P. B.

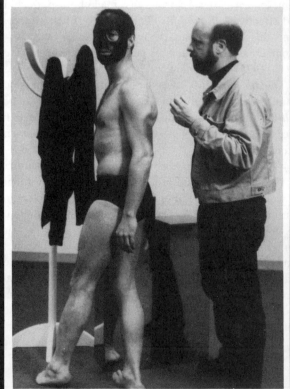

With Paul Bartel prior to fox trot in Death Race 2000.

sense, *Death Race* represented a step down for him. The working conditions on a low-budget film are far more spartan than those prevailing on a Warner Brothers TV series. It just isn't possible to give the star the "star treatment," and there isn't much room for temperament. I was becoming more and more irritated at David's behavior, but tried to remain diplomatic. Besides, it was the costume designer who was getting the brunt of his outbursts.

Finally David and I had a direct confrontation. It was over some boots that were part of the leading lady's costume. The leading lady was David's real-life girlfriend at that time and quite a gifted actresss. But in David's company she became as difficult and intransigent as he. Suddenly she could not remember having selected the boots she was to wear. If David said they were horrible, they *were* horrible. She wouldn't wear them. It was a trivial matter, but David and I got into an argument about it, and I saw in it the seeds of an impossible working relationship. I ended up putting my directorial authority on the line, and David, the star, laughed in my face.

I reported the incident to Corman, and asked him to replace David. Corman agreed and called Carradine's manager to tell him David was out. The costume designer and I both breathed sighs of relief.

A few days later, however, I received a telegram:

DEAR PAUL: I KNOW HOW YOU ARE FEELING. IT IS TRUE THAT I HAVE BEEN ARROGANT AND NASTY. I HUMBLY BEG YOUR FORGIVENESS. PLEASE DON'T KICK ME OUT OF THIS MOVIE. I WILL DO ANYTHING YOU SAY. YOU HAVE ALL THE POWER. I WANT NONE OF IT. ONLY TO PLAY THIS PART. PLEASE LET US GO AHEAD TOGETHER. YOUR FRANKENSTEIN MONSTER, DAVID.

I was touched. It seemed so abject. I felt like a louse. The next day there was a meeting among Corman, his attorney, the repentant Carradine, and his conciliatory manager. Corman relented, and David was reinstated. I still had some lingering fears, but Corman decided to go with David.

The highlight of his career, as folk singer Woody Guthrie in Bound for Glory.

Although in many ways, several problems got worse as *Death Race* moved into production, I must say that David Carradine was not one of them. He gave a strong and imaginative performance, all the while remaining patient and cooperative in the face of the myriad frustrations that are part and parcel of low-budget film production.

Moreover, he was an enormous source of moral support in my occasional conflicts with Corman. It was David who constantly encouraged me to have the courage of my convictions. In addition I learned a great deal from Carradine about the art and craft of acting. David has spent a lot of time unlearning many of the things his actor father had taught him, such as "how to speak" and how to "be a gentleman." His television experience has been very important to him, and there are traces of Kwai Chang Cain (his *Kung Fu* character) in many of the roles David has subsequently played in movies.

If *Kung Fu* changed David's world view, it may also have taught him some bad habits. When we first began to shoot *Death Race 2000,* I noticed that he had a peculiar way of breaking his sentences up with short . . . pauses in odd . . . places. These pauses gave his speech a peculiar rhythm that eventually became a part of his characterization (less appropriate for Frankenstein than it had been for Kwai Chang Cain). David, however, has an interesting explanation for these pauses: "I do it whenever I don't believe the next moment that's coming. I wait until I find one I believe because I don't want to get caught on film in an unbelievable moment. If the cutter doesn't like the pause, he has to solve the problem by cutting away or something. The point is, [in the edited film] the camera's never pointing at me when I'm doing it wrong."

"*I felt* The Serpent's Egg (*with Liv Ullmann*) *was a stretch I'd make for the sake of art. But after the incident with the horse being killed, I reexamined my attitudes. Bending my values to be in a Bergman movie is obviously a dangerous thing to do.*" — Carradine to P. B.

Boxcar Bertha, *with ex-wife Barbara Hershey.*

While I think David comes off quite well in the two films we made together, I have a sense of having failed in one major respect: the building of a compelling relationship between David and his leading ladies. Even when David has played opposite such heavyweight actresses as Liv Ullmann and Melinda Dillon, there somehow seemed to be few sparks struck. David is a loner — in life as well as on the screen. He certainly makes every effort to get close to the women he works with and in life has gotten very close indeed to a number of them. But somehow he remains curiously isolated on the screen.

Although David has a personal edict against performing in films which contain "gratuitous violence" or "macho bullshit," a certain combativeness is undeniably part of his image. While his characters never pick fights, they are always ready to hold their own. David likes to think of his character as Everyman. He will not play heavies; the roles he plays must be heroic. He will not accept scripts with unhappy endings or ones that glorify negative aspects of society, nor will he appear in horror films. (He bent this last rule when he appeared in Ingmar Bergman's *The Serpent's Egg* [1978], and now looks at his participation in that as a mistake on his part.)

Despite having made several expensive, "prestigious" films during the last few years, David keeps coming back to work for Roger Corman. David says, "Doing pictures for him is certainly, on my part, as large an experience as making *Bound for Glory.* And with him I do get to play characters antithetical to the ones filled with meekness, kindness, and Okie-ness that I usually play. People are always trying to tell me how terrible Corman's movies are, but all those that I've seen have stressed some homely virtue of something. And you know, what more can you ask?"

An actor of his caliber can and must demand more than homely virtues from the projects he undertakes.

THE
PROFESSIONALS

JEAN ARTHUR: PASSIONATE PRIMROSE

STEPHEN HARVEY

Wide-eyed and enthusiastic, she was one of the most likable movie heroines of the Roosevelt era.

WHEN DECLINING AUDIENCES and rising tempers of the nation's moralists inflicted the Production Code on the film industry in 1933, Hollywood reacted by substituting the cheery quip for the sultry double entendre. Hence a new sort of movie heroine was called for, and a fresh breed of performer was drafted for the task. The results were immediately apparent: before, Claudette Colbert was just another chic, hardworking dramatic actress; Carole Lombard, a platinum-blond second-stringer; and Myrna Loy, the prototypical Other Woman, irrespective of race, creed, or color. *It Happened One Night, Twentieth Century,* and *The Thin Man* changed all that, and by the mid-thirties, while paroxysms of tears still tended to win Oscars, it was clear that the tongue-in-cheek drollery of Hollywood's premier comediennes was the screen's most treasurable asset.

One of the more deserving beneficiaries of this new order was the irresistible Jean Arthur, whose career was an object lesson proving that — while talent and looks are all very well — as far as stardom is concerned, timing is everything. While waiting for her own style and the mass mood to catch up with one another, Arthur had to endure one of the longest apprenticeships in the business. In silents she languished as the obligatory cowboy's sweetheart in every third D-grade western; when sound came in, she tussled with Mary Brian for the pallid ingenue roles that Paramount deemed too inconspicuous for the likes of Nancy Carroll. After understandably deserting the movies for a brief sojourn on Broadway, Arthur's return to Hollywood seemed less than auspicious — as a contract leading lady at Columbia, then a déclassé haven for has-beens and never-would-bes. Yet as things turned out, she arrived at Harry Cohn's shabby

STEPHEN HARVEY *is the author of several film biographies, including one of Joan Crawford. He works with the film division of the Museum of Modern Art.*

fiefdom at precisely the right moment; now that *It Happened One Night* had given the studio a prestige boost, Columbia needed to bolster a paltry star roster in order to challenge the other studios. Jean Arthur's special sparkle soon proved the studio's most valued resource, second only to Frank Capra. Until the advent of Rita Hayworth during World War II, Arthur ruled the lot unchallenged, having asserted herself as the first performer developed at Columbia since Barbara Stanwyck — whose services were in demand at the grander studios as well.

Although bona fide stardom was still a year away, Arthur's image was set once and for all in 1935 when she strode blithely through *The Whole Town's Talking,* an otherwise minor footnote in director John Ford's career. Playing the first in her series of buoyant white-collar girls, from her opening scene she revealed that the key element of the Jean Arthur character was fearlessness — nothing, not Babbitty bosses, tommy-gun-wielding gangsters, or even a national economic crisis was going to faze her.

She exuded those qualities that Depression-era moviegoers liked to think of as typically American. Energetic and optimistic, she was guileless enough to utter phrases like "Gee whiz!" and mean it; yet emphatically, she was nobody's fool either. Physically, too, Arthur embodied the widely held feminine ideal of the prewar era; her streamlined blond good looks were fresh and appealing without being anything so intimidating as outright sexy. Best of all was that unmistakable voice — a sandy chirp rivaled only by Margaret Sullavan's husky quaver as the most distinctive sound in the movies.

Those supposedly homespun qualities of hers were probably what first attracted the notice of Frank Capra, then well on his way to becoming the movies' chief purveyor of timely jingoism. According to his autobiography, it was he who insisted on casting Arthur in *Mr. Deeds Goes to Town* (1936) over the objections of Harry Cohn. Whatever its genesis, their collaboration was an inspired idea, her astringency providing a welcome antidote to Capra's patriotic treacle. As the heroine of both *Mr. Deeds* and the subsequent *Mr. Smith Goes to Washington* (1939), her chemistry opposite Gary Cooper and James Stewart was sparked by a contrast in style and temperament — Arthur's worldly common sense smoothing away the rough edges of their hayseed gaucheness, their idealism awakening her finer instincts. With her impassioned monologues against Establishment injustice at the climax of each of these films, Arthur instantly became the movies' female champion of upbeat integrity — a kind of photogenic Eleanor Roosevelt. A decade later she made it to Congress herself in *A Foreign Affair* (1948), and it's no surprise that when the playwriting team of Jerome Lawrence and Robert E. Lee recently wrote a comedy about the first woman Supreme Court Justice, Arthur was their first choice for the part.

Thanks to her success in the two Capra movies, Arthur thereafter often found herself instructing wayward members of the opposite sex — teaching Charles Coburn the joys of unionism and Coney Island in *The*

*With Gary Cooper
in Frank Capra's*
Mr. Deeds Goes to Town.

Arizona, *with Porter Hall. She was fine in westerns because she could convincingly portray brave women.*

Devil and Miss Jones (1941), or offering Cary Grant a lesson in civics and giving Ronald Colman a few tips in simple humanity during *The Talk of the Town* (1942).

Her fierce air of independence (not to mention those long early years in the saddle) made her one of the few women stars of the time suited to play in westerns. Accordingly, in *Arizona* (1940) she stakes out a homestead practically singlehandedly, while in De Mille's *The Plainsman* (1936) she unfurls a broad prairie drawl and a wicked bullwhip as Calamity Jane opposite Gary Cooper's Wild Bill Hickok.

But the most engaging Arthur vehicles of the time found her typed as the feckless female plunked down in an alien milieu, relishing the challenge and nonchalantly learning to cope with a new set of ground rules if she couldn't bend them to suit her own requirements. The most antic of these was Mitchell Leisen's *Easy Living* (1937), with a particularly freewheeling script by Preston Sturges. Here she played a workaday wage slave to whom strange things keep happening: a kolinsky coat hits her from the heavens while she's innocently riding a

Fifth Avenue bus; she only needs to walk into the Automat and a food riot ensues; one careless word unleashes the biggest stock market panic since Black Friday. Naturally, while her romp through Manhattan might be compared to Sherman's walk through Georgia, she

With John Wayne in A Lady Takes a Chance.

remains unscathed throughout, even landing a nice young millionaire for herself by the final fade-out.

Even more memorable was Howard Hawks' comic melodrama *Only Angels Have Wings* (1939), with Arthur as a chorine stranded amid the sound-stage fronds of an imaginary banana republic; reluctantly befriended by a group of wildcat aviators, she learns to shed her "feminine" sentimentality to become one of the boys, only better. In this Hawksean ode to male camaraderie and professionalism, it's still Arthur's performance that lends conviction to this conceit.

With all her skill at breezy repartee, what really made her so disarming was that she seemed to take even the most trifling situation seriously. When something as momentous as love entered her life, however, the usually sensible Arthur was rendered totally nonplussed. Other actresses might wax lyrical in creamy close-ups, but this was practically the only emotion that could arrest the flow of Arthur aphorisms. Suddenly wide-eyed and inarticulate, fumbling her syllables and muddling her grammar, Arthur each time managed to make even the most perfunctory romantic-comedy love scenes seem spontaneous and human.

Equipped as she was with her artillery of comic mannerisms, she also knew when to discard the dismayed pout and cracked inflections when they didn't suit the occasion at hand. As the least certifiably demented member of the Sycamore family in Capra's adaptation of Kaufman and Hart's *You Can't Take It With You* (1938), she downplayed her almost patented ditheriness to give a poignant center to the movie's aggressively playful spirit. Similarly, Arthur was an unlikely choice for the high-flown romantic kitsch of Frank Borzage's *History Is Made at Night* (1937); yet the steady warmth generated between her and Charles Boyer in that film remains one of the highlights of romanticism in the 1930s.

The forties brought a gradual shift in her screen personality, her self-reliance and resolve betraying a new edge of sexual skittishness. As a wartime civil servant in *The More the Merrier* (1943) and an eastern dude vacationing on the range in *A Lady Takes a Chance* (1943), she expends inordinate energy to resist the no-nonsense virility of Joel McCrea and John Wayne, as if she were afraid to uncover the feelings hidden behind her brisk air of practicality. By *A Foreign Affair*, she's become positively puritanical, wrinkling her nose at the amorality of postwar Berlin, unwilling to realize that the codes of behavior which serve the Corn Belt don't necessarily apply in the Occupied Zone. Her screen appearances had become increasingly sporadic by this time, partially because the roles in which she had specialized were now in rather short supply — even had she remained at an age when she could still play them convincingly.

After a five-year absence from the movies, she returned briefly in 1953 to star in George Stevens' classic western *Shane*, acquitting herself ably in a role that could easily have been filled by a multitude of other actresses. Leading a secluded retirement far from Hollywood, Arthur occasionally surfaced for a television appearance or another try at the stage, but apart from a successful Broadway run as Peter Pan in 1950, her comebacks proved abortive. Ironically enough, despite the carefree resilience she emanated on screen, Arthur's personal insecurities made it impossible to sustain her career once its momentum faltered. We'll never know what she might have done with the role of Billie Dawn in *Born Yesterday*, which she played during its out-of-town tryout before Judy Holliday replaced her at the last minute, or whether Arthur was up to her long-held aspiration to play Shaw's *St. Joan*, which folded ignominiously in Chicago during the mid-fifties after a squabble between Arthur and the production's director, Harold Clurman.

Nevertheless, while one can easily lament what might have been, in Jean Arthur's prime — and Hollywood's — hers was one of the most invigorating presences the movies have ever known.

With Alan Ladd in Shane, *Arthur's last film.*

MYRNA LOY: LIBERATED WIFE

KARYN KAY

An ideal match for strong male leads, such as William Powell, Clark Gable, and Cary Grant because Loy's characters also demanded audience respect.

THE FACT THAT MYRNA LOY began her career not as the quintessential homemaker — Hollywood's renowned "perfect wife" — but as a devious home-*wrecker*, is often forgotten. In Loy's early films she played the vamp seductress, more in league with Theda Bara's spider woman than akin to a young, sophisticated Ma Joad. Loy's initial screen character was that of a sexual tormentress, breaking foolish men's hearts purely for the fun of it. In *The Squall* (1929), she pits son against father in their crazed love for her, the

KARYN KAY *is the author of* Myrna Loy, *the co-editor of* Women and the Cinema: A Critical Anthology, *and assistant editor of* Close-Ups.

wild gypsy Nubi. She abandons Robert Ames in *Rebound* (1931), reappearing now and then almost to decimate his marriage to wisecracking Ina Claire. Likewise she ditches Pat O'Brien, who finds his *Consolation Marriage* (1931) with sweet Irene Dunne.

Perhaps it was her dark, dark hair, the arch of her cheekbones, or the sensuously poetic ring of her name (Myrna Williams was renamed Myrna Loy by her poet friend Peter Rurick) that caused Loy to be typecast as a Third World mystagogue — a siren of generally unknown, but definitely exotic, origin. In John Ford's *The Black Watch* (1929), she is Yasmini of India, tempestuous leader of a guerrilla band who dies for love of British Army commander Victor McLaglen. In *The Mask of Fu*

Pointing something out to Dolores Costello in Noah's Ark, *her last silent film.*

Manchu (1932), she plays — in her own words — "a sadistic nymphomaniac," daughter of the evil tyrant. In *Thirteen Women* (1932), she is a devilish Javanese occultist seeking revenge against racism by murdering her former sorority sisters. Even in one of her earliest films, *Ben Hur* (1925), Loy plays (as a subtitle reads) "a Hedonist" — mistress to a Roman senator.

In 1933, however, with the filming of *Penthouse,* William S. Van Dyke accomplished Loy's metamorphosis. In the film she starts out as a ghetto strumpet; at the end she is a Park Avenue matron. In the beginning he made creative use of Loy's known sexual image, casting her as Gertie, the exemplary "whore-with-a-heart-of-gold," but he rewards her with marriage — and a new image. Upward mobility for Loy's characters meant marriage, but a marriage of fun and surprising spirit.

A year later Van Dyke cast Loy as Nora Charles, Nick's wife in *The Thin Man* (1934). In keeping with Dashiell Hammett's novel, Nora is rich, and idler Nick (William Powell) seems content to lie back and live luxuriously off his wife's inheritance. But bored Nora encourages Nick to introduce her to his low-life, underworld pals — the gangsters, gamblers, boxers, and brawlers he knew from his gumshoe days on the streets of New York. Nora also pushes Nick to involve himself in dangerous murder mysteries, with the intent of becoming equally involved herself.

Nick and Nora fought and fussed as if they were in a Howard Hawks screwball comedy, competing in mock battles with comic barbs. Whoever won the arguments only proved himself — or usually herself — the better wit. (Not surprisingly, Frank Capra tried to get Loy for the role of zany heiress Ellie Andrews in *It Happened One Night*.) Within the context of a proper upper-class marriage, the Charleses shared a lifestyle usually limited to singles in the movies. They were constant partygoers and steady imbibers, but Nick and Nora partied together, drank together, and went home together. Loy and Powell

managed the seemingly impossible — making marriage exciting and enticing.

On film, Loy and Powell enjoyed a lusciously sensuous but definitely monogamous relationship that extended to their non-*Thin Man* endeavors. Except for an occasional flirtation with infidelity, as in *Evelyn Prentice* (1934) and *Love Crazy* (1941), the Loy/Powell duo was one of stability. They were a sophisticated, intelligent couple who enjoyed themselves as man and wife. (And to round out the setting of complete familial content, they had children — a son in the *Thin Man* series, a daughter in *Evelyn Prentice*.)

Loy had made seventy-seven films by the time she played Nora Charles, but as she has described her work in *The Thin Man,* "the picture made me . . . from that time on I was typed as the perfect wife."

Loy and Powell were a couple in thirteen films, which includes Loy's cameo appearance as Powell's wife in *The Senator Was Indiscreet* (1947). Yet, when Loy was crowned Queen of the Movies in a 1936 Ed Sullivan popularity poll, her elected king was Clark Gable, a not-surprising public association since they had made several films together. While still maintaining that perfect-wife image with Gable, Loy emerged as something less than the "good sport" companion. Loy and Gable never maintained the perfect harmony of the Loy/Powell team. When Loy and Gable fought *they* wanted to transform one another. In *Men in White* (1934), Gable tries to reform Loy's spoiled heiress. In *Manhattan Melodrama* (1934), Loy challenges Gable's gangster Gallagher: Give up the rackets or she'll give up the gangster. In *Wife vs. Secretary* (1936) she is jealous of his secretary, whereas in *Test Pilot* (1938) she is jealous of his airplane.

Loy was also paired several times with Cary Grant, once as professional flying companion in *Wings in the Dark* (1935) and another time as the judge who sentences Grant to "time" with her teenaged sister in *The Bachelor and the Bobby-Soxer* (1947). But with Grant, Loy's perfect-wife character emerged in full in *Mr. Blandings Builds His Dream House* (1948). In that picture, a family of four goes mad in their typically minuscule Manhattan apartment and decides to buy a dream

The End. With Burt Reynolds and Pat O'Brien.

Vamp falling for Charles Starrett in The Mask of Fu Manchu.

She made six Thin Man *films with William Powell.*

house in Connecticut — which turns out to be a mansion no sturdier than a bird's nest in winter. In true perfect-wife fashion, Loy, as Muriel Blandings, shares the hardships of their first suburban winter. Together Loy and Grant freeze in their $15,000 purchase that is without heat, electricity, floorboards, or windows.

One of Loy's most significant perfect-wife roles was Milly in *The Best Years of Our Lives* (1946). Like Loy's Nora or Muriel, her Milly conveys a woman of total tolerance and sensitivity as she helps Al, her husband (Fredric March), through his postwar adjustment. On Al's first night home, she goes out with him to celebrate and tolerantly lets him drink more than he can handle.

With Clifton Webb in Cheaper by the Dozen.

Then she takes him home and rolls him into bed as if she has spent a life tucking in drunk spouses. It is a gesture of love, understanding, and patience — at once reminiscent of Nora while anticipating her Lillian Gilbreth in *Cheaper by the Dozen* (1950). In that picture she plays a mother and her husband's partner — the stalwart voice of reason standing between the chaotic demands of her dozen children and the childish obstinacy of their father, Clifton Webb.

In *Belles on Their Toes* (1952), the sequel to *Cheaper by the Dozen,* Loy's Lillian is widowed and has taken over her husband's business and lecture tours, as well as teaching and single-handedly raising the ebullient offspring. In a gesture of martyred widowhood, the still-perfect wife refuses a proposal of marriage. This film conveys the definitive Loy image: a totally modern woman — indeed a feminist sympathizer — who, ironically, remains an old-fashioned perfect wife. So much so, in fact, that she remains loyal to her husband long after his death.

With Jeanne Crain in Belles on Their Toes.

JOEL McCREA:
A QUICK GLANCE BACK

JOEL McCREA

Foreign Correspondent *publicity shot. During the thirties and forties, he was the leading man in more good films than anyone, but he never received due recognition.*

I WAS RAISED in Hollywood. As a kid I went to a lot of movies, and particularly liked seeing William S. Hart, William Farnum, and Gloria Swanson. When I was a newsboy, I delivered papers to directors and stars; one of those on my route was William S. Hart. What impressed me about Hart was that he made sure his westerns were filmed with authenticity in mind.

JOEL McCREA *was a leading man in movies for over thirty years. Among his credits are* Bird of Paradise *(1932 version),* Barbary Coast, These Three, Dead End, Wells Fargo, Sullivan's Travels, Foreign Correspondent, The Palm Beach Story, Buffalo Bill, The More the Merrier, *and* Ride the High Country.

I went to the University of Southern California, where I majored in drama and public speaking. The best break I ever got in my life was when Sam Wood, the director, picked me and about a dozen U.S.C. guys to be college boys in MGM's *The Fair Co-ed* (1927), starring Marion Davies. After it was completed Miss Davies chose me to play a bit in her film *The Five O'clock Girl*. We made it, but it was never released — William Randolph Hearst didn't like it.

So I was an extra in the late 1920s, when sound was coming in. I don't know why, but I was a very unsuccessful extra — only four or five days' work a month. I knew that I didn't want to stay in movies if I had to remain an extra, a bit, or even a supporting actor.

I was finally satisfied with the way my career was going when I got the leading role in RKO's *The Silver Horde* (1930), made in Ketchikan, Alaska. After that, I was in Henry King's big film *Lightnin'* (1930) with the one and only Will Rogers. I hoped my career in films would be lengthy, but I was not sure it would be until I had been working and in demand for roles for two years. David Selznick, who was then the head of RKO, helped me a great deal. He told me that he was going to make me into a "star." And he did his best, by casting me in *Bird of Paradise* (1932), which was a very big picture and important to my career.

In 1935 I began a four-year stint with Samuel Goldwyn, and he cast me in a lot of interesting pictures. One of the most successful I did for him was *These Three* (1936), which co-starred Merle Oberon and Miriam Hopkins. There was a great deal of controversy surrounding that film because of the lesbian relationship in the play on which the film was based, *The Children's Hour*. In those days the Motion Picture Code would not allow that kind of thing — and I think they were right. William Wyler directed it a second time years later as *The Children's Hour* (1962). There was no longer any code, so they put the lesbianism back, but it flopped — in spite of the fact they had bigger stars (Audrey Hepburn, Shirley MacLaine, and James Garner) than we did. Our "censored" version made more money.

Bird of Paradise, *with Dolores Del Rio.*

With Veronica Lake — pretending to be a hobo — in Preston Sturges' Sullivan's Travels.

After I had been in films for about ten years, people started coming to me with scripts. I turned down as many roles that I thought were beyond my abilities as I did ones I thought weren't good enough. I never realized that I had much talent until I worked with outstanding directors such as Gregory La Cava, George Stevens, and Preston Sturges. And even then I believed that whatever I did right was due, for the most part, to their talents. Before the big directors started giving me confidence, it was the women stars who tried to boost me and recommended me for parts.

I made films with many great actresses. The easiest for me to work with were Dolores Del Rio, with whom I made *Bird of Paradise,* and Ginger Rogers, who co-starred with me in *The Primrose Path* (1940). The best actress I ever worked with was Barbara Stanwyck. I made six films with her: *Gambling Lady* (1934); *Banjo on My Knee* (1936); *Internes Can't Take Money* (1937);

Colorado Territory *with Virginia Mayo, a remake of Bogart-Lupino gangster film* High Sierra.

Union Pacific (1939); *The Great Man's Lady* (1942); and *Trooper Hook* (1957). She is great. She never wants to quit acting; there is no becoming a housewife in her dreams. Barbara Stanwyck and Gary Cooper are both in the Cowboy Hall of Fame with me.

Other than Cooper, my best friends in the business were Frank Lloyd, La Cava, and King Vidor. I watched each of these directors and learned from them all — what to do, and at times, what not to do. The directors who impressed me most were La Cava, Lloyd, Wyler, Stevens, and Preston Sturges.

Preston Sturges was the most charming, humorous, talented, gifted man I ever met. He wrote the best dialogue. We made three films together and it was a joy each time. Sturges once said that I was one of the most underrated actors in Hollywood, and that has always meant a lot to me.

My peak moments in the movie industry were in the forties. It was then that I made such films as *Foreign Correspondent* (1940) with Alfred Hitchcock; *Sullivan's Travels* (1941) and *The Palm Beach Story* (1942) with Sturges; *The More the Merrier* (1943) with Stevens; and

Buffalo Bill, *McCrea's most famous western role. "I like the West and everything it stands for."*
— *J. M.*

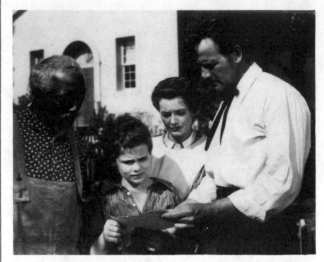

Stars in My Crown. *The boy is Dean Stockwell.*

Buffalo Bill (1944) with William Wellman. As I said, I like authenticity in westerns, but I wasn't unhappy with the way *Buffalo Bill* turned out. It was colorful and entertaining and helped the image of the American Indian.

No one had to tell me to be careful of my own image. I got the idea watching stars I admired: William S. Hart in the beginning, and Gary Cooper later on. Harry Warner — the smart brother — told me that I should never play a heavy or an antihero. I agreed and I never played a bad guy. I did play Wes McQueen in *Colorado Territory* (1949), a western in which both Virginia Mayo and I are killed, but Wes wasn't so much a bad person as he was a victim of circumstances. I liked that picture — and working with Raoul Walsh. I liked making westerns more than other types of films, and I think I was well fitted for them and did my best work in them.

Ride the High Country (1962), which I did with Sam Peckinpah, was a fine picture. In fact, I have been told that it is considered one of the top westerns of the sixties; I think people enjoyed seeing Randolph Scott and me in parts suited to us. That was a great film for both Randy and me to go out on.

I still watch my old films when I get the chance. They bring back great memories. The film I am most proud of today is *Stars in My Crown* (1950), in which I played a nineteenth-century parson who wore six-guns. It was directed by Jacques Tourneur, with whom I also worked on *Stranger on Horseback* (1955) and *Wichita* (1955), in which I played Wyatt Earp. Jacques Tourneur and I went to high school together. He passed on early this year.

My early ambitions to own a cattle ranch were never altered. But they were delayed until I made enough money in films to buy one. I've owned two or more ranches ever since.

So I have no regrets, except perhaps one: I should have tried harder to be a better actor.

BARBARA STANWYCK: A FIERY DEVOTION

JOSEPH H. LEWIS

BARBARA STANWYCK has always been a down-to-earth, gutsy type of gal. It dates back to her childhood, from what I understand. She admired the pioneers who traveled west (which may explain why she made so many westerns during her career). She was likewise enamored of Pearl White, the silent movie actress best known as the star of the serial *The Perils of Pauline,* and was determined to perform like her idol. As a youngster, Barbara loved to dance to the music of a hurdy-gurdy on the streets of New York while bystanders gathered around. From that seed a theatrical career was born, or at least the ambition to perform in front of others and be appreciated for her talent.

JOSEPH H. LEWIS *is the director of such films as* My Name is Julia Ross; The Undercover Man; Gun Crazy; Lady Without a Passport; Retreat, Hell!, *and* Terror in a Texas Town. *He has also directed for television, including episodes of* The Big Valley, *which starred Barbara Stanwyck, and* The Rifleman.

The former Ruby Stevens, just breaking into films.

Publicity pose for Ball of Fire.

When she was about fifteen or so, there was a Broadway show called *The Noose,* which had four chorus girls in the cast. In this play, there is a character who's condemned to a death by hanging, and his life is saved by one of the chorines, who simply, as a matter of humanity, pleads his case before the governor. The producer wanted somebody from the lower class for this part, and he picked Barbara. From then on, there was no stopping her.

Barbara Stanwyck went on to become one of the great stars in motion picture history. The thing that made her so special, and so valuable to directors, was that she could play any type of character with equal effectiveness. Her range was extraordinary. She could play roles suited for such diverse talents as Jean Arthur or Joan

A CONSISTENT TALENT

BARBARA NEVER CHANGED from the moment she started out. She always had that kind of dignity that's only affordable to those who have great talent, and you immediately recognize it. — J. L.

Impressing Preston Foster (Middle) with sharpshooting talents in Annie Oakley.

Many actresses refused to do westerns. Barbara perferred them. The Maverick Queen (R).

Banjo on My Knee (L). *Joel McCrea: "She is the best actress I worked with."*

Double Indemnity, *with Fred MacMurray.*

The Lady Eve, *with Henry Fonda.*

Crawford. She could be gentle and supportive and she could be hard-boiled and destructive. In comedies, she was at her best as a cynical woman who accepted her own bad reputation but is changed for the better by the innocent young man she tries to double-cross, as in *Ball of Fire* (1941) and *The Lady Eve* (1941). In melodrama she could be outright dangerous, as she was in *Double Indemnity* (1944), a film in which she tore everything in her path out by its roots. Even when Barbara played unlikable characters, audiences loved her because her integrity as an actress always came through.

Unlike most big stars, Stanwyck didn't fight her directors or make pretenses. She not only gave her best, but she had consideration for all the people she worked with. She earned the reputation as the most professional actress in the business.

Take the first day of shooting on a Stanwyck picture. The call is for 8:00 A.M. At 7:45 A.M., completely in

GOLDEN GIRL

BARBARA DID MAKE an appearance at this year's (1978) Academy Awards, and Bob Hope, as master of ceremonies, introduced her and fellow presenter William Holden this way: "A lot of gold's being given out tonight, but Hollywood will never run out of it as long as we have treasures like our next two stars. He made his sensational screen debut as *Golden Boy* [1939], and we'll never forget his leading lady, whose performances are never less than twenty-four-karat. . . . The Golden Boy and his Golden Girl are together again tonight — William Holden and Barbara Stanwyck."

After the two stars took the stage, William Holden looked out at the audience for a moment, and then summed it all up: "Before Barbara and I present this next award, I'd like to say something. Thirty-nine years ago this month, we were working in a film together called *Golden Boy*. It wasn't going well, and I was going to be replaced. But due to this lovely human being, and her interest and understanding and her professional integrity, and her encouragement, and above all her generosity, I'm here tonight."

As one of her directors, I was so moved by this genuinely beautiful outburst, which was held so long — thirty-nine years, to be exact — for the proper moment of expression, that I wept with an emotional joy rarely expressed by a guy who's supposed to be so strong and unmoved.

— J. H. L.

Golden Boy, *William Holden's film debut.*

costume, fully made up and ready for work, in walks the star. As is her habit, she exchanges a cheery "Good morning" with every member of the crew. There is an aura about her from the outset. This great talent then awaits the rest of the cast.

It isn't like this on the second morning, for promptly at 7:45, the entire cast walks in, made up and ready to go to work. It's caught on, this "Stanwyck magic."

Barbara had great respect for her director, cameraman, and crew. After all, she knew they knew their craft the same as she knew hers. Barbara just concentrated on her job and left it up to the people she worked with to determine the best angle or the best light or whatever. She trusted them and, having great inner confidence, trusted herself to do a good job. It was a pleasure working with Barbara. She is a real treasure.

Today, Barbara is just enjoying life. I'm sure she has offers every other week to do something. She recognizes that she has carved a niche for herself in the entertainment world, and that she will always be admired. But rather than taking on any new parts, she can just rest on her laurels.

TAYLOR-MADE COUPLE

I WAS VERY GOOD FRIENDS with Robert Taylor — I used to go hunting and fishing with him — but I didn't come to know Barbara until later in her career. Of course, Barbara was married to Taylor, and had also made several films with him. They were both down-to-earth. They were both superstars, and yet they were the kind of people you could talk to. There was no affectation. And in my humble opinion, they belonged with each other. They were both out of the same mold. When I worked with Bob, for example, he would arrive on the set fifteen minutes earlier than necessary, the same as she, fully made up and ready to go to work. They were just two pros. Why it didn't work out between them is none of my business, but I guess that's life.

— J. H. L.

Capra's The Bitter Tea of General Yen, *with Nils Asther*.

Lady of Burlesque. *"She's like the unpredictable sea."* — *J. L.*

SYLVIA SIDNEY: CHAT WITH A SAD-EYED LADY

KARYN KAY

During interview with Karyn Kay, spring 1978.

Q WHEN YOU CAME OUT TO HOLLYWOOD from Broadway in 1930, did you know what kinds of parts you were going to play?
A. Earlier I had made a film for Fox, and I had been unhappy with that experience. So I insisted that my Paramount contract state very clearly what the first picture would be. I didn't want to be considered just one more ex-Broadway actress in Hollywood with everyone asking, "What will we do with her?" My contract said

KARYN KAY *teaches film at Columbia University and Livingston College.*

that I would play Roberta in *An American Tragedy* [1931].

Q. But you did that later. Your first film with Paramount turned out to be *City Streets* [1931].
A. Right. Clara Bow was supposed to do it, but when she collapsed, they called me in the middle of the night to say, "Be at the studio tomorrow morning."

Q. Didn't you object?
A. I knew it had to be a good part because Rouben Mamoulian, a teacher with the Theatre Guild, had been brought from New York to direct it. I was lucky to have

him as the director. He taught me, took care of me, and never let me make a fool of myself on the screen or set. He gave me good training adjusting to a camera. He would say that it wasn't necessary for me to root myself to an object, because ''. . . the shot includes that.''

Q. Throughout the thirties, you played sad-eyed women who were characterized as being sweet and fragile. This completely contrasted with the reputation you earned while working — and fighting against studio policies — at Paramount.

A. Mr. Adolph Zukor, who was the president of Paramount, never considered me sweet and fragile, but he kept casting me in roles of that type. Since I was a good crier, and one of the youngest of the good criers, that was the mold I was put into. It never occurred to me that it was in the nature of an image.

Q. You have been compared to Lillian Gish in that you often played ''victimized'' women. In film after film, the man you loved either dumped you or was killed. Didn't you want your films to have more upbeat endings?

A. I didn't mind playing unhappy characters; every young actress thinks she's a tragedian — the more tragic the roles, the more you cry, the more you suffer, the better an actress you are. But, when I got a little older, a little more mature, I wanted to get out of my image of ''the victimized kid.'' I began to say, ''Wait a minute. There's a thing called comedy that takes an even rougher intelligence and more technique and knowledge of the craft.''

''I remember the rash I got from Spencer Tracy's beard during Fury.'' *— S. S.*

The title reflected Sidney's image: Good Dame

Q. One of your earliest comedic roles was in Dorothy Arzner's *Merrily We Go to Hell* [1932], a wonderful film.

A. That was the first film that helped me get out of my mold, but even that ends in melodrama — my baby is born dead and my husband Fredric March is off getting drunk.

Q. Your part is very striking because you start out as a sad-eyed woman, but at the end of the film she. . . .

A. . . . has balls! Excuse me. In a sense it was a kind of avant-garde picture. It was the story of a very protected gal who always lived in great luxury and didn't know what it was to be hurt. The problem is that this protected lifestyle made her lonely. So she meets this nut who exposes her to a lot. Finally she ends up a *woman* — for the thirties, anyway.

Q. How much say did you have in choosing your assignments at Paramount?

A. I had no say. On some films that were good, I just got lucky. But some others were real bombs, like *Confessions of a Co-ed* [1931] and another little thing meant to please Mr. Zukor called *The Miracle Man* [1932]. That film had originally been a great silent movie starring Betty Compson and Lon Chaney. Mr. Zukor once said that the only thing that made him like me was that he thought that I looked like Betty Compson. He didn't think I was ''Sylvia Sidney'' at all.

Q. After you were a hit in both *City Streets* and *An American Tragedy* and your name was becoming known in Hollywood, Paramount loaned you to Goldwyn for *Street Scene* [1931]. Many stars hated being loaned out to other studios.

A. That was the system then. You were under contract, you did not make choices. I wanted more freedom. When my contract was up at Paramount, they offered me all kinds of things to sign another contract. I sat there while they bargained with me, and I looked out at that damn fountain on the lot, and thought of all those dressing rooms, and said to myself, ''I don't think I could ever be happy here.''

Q. After you turned down Paramount, you signed a

A rare happy moment in You Only Live Once, *with Henry Fonda.*

contract with Walter Wanger, the independent producer. I know this worked out better for you.

A. Wanger produced *Mary Burns, Fugitive* [1935], the last picture on my contract with Paramount. He was more my style than Adolph Zukor. While we were shooting *Mary Burns* one day, Wanger came out on the set and said, "Paramount called me today and said, 'She is the most difficult kid. She's impossible. What does she want?'" I told Wanger I wanted a lot less money than Paramount was offering, but the right to do films when I wanted — limiting it to two or three pictures a year instead of five — and the right to go back into the theater. I also said that I wouldn't expect to get paid when I wasn't working. I was a great buy for Wanger, so *he* signed me to a contract. And it worked out marvelously. He was a true cosmopolitan gentleman.

Q. And you made *Trail of the Lonesome Pine* [1936], one of your classic sad-eyed-woman films, shortly after this?

A. Right afterward. That was the first color film shot outdoors with no phony lighting, no dyeing or fooling around with prints. It was a difficult film to make. It was the only on-location picture I had done, and I had no idea of the discomfort involved. It was so *cold*. When I showered, my legs would turn blue.

Q. I'm curious about how you worked with Alfred Hitchcock on *Sabotage* [1937], considering there were two strong personalities at work.

A. The scene in which I murdered Oscar Homolka was hard for me. I came in early in the morning expecting to shoot the whole scene. But I saw the marks for the staging and where the camera was set up. I asked Hitchcock, "What are you doing?" He said, "Oh! We're doing a close-up of you, darling. He's just dropped dead, and I want the shock on your face." Since I had never really killed off Homolka, I was confused: "How do we do the end of the scene before we've even rehearsed?" Finally he sat me down and said, "What is the point of going through all the earlier parts of the scene and doing the close-up at the end of the day when you'll be tired and emotionally drained. What I need is you *now*, wide awake." *Sabotage* is not a great movie — in a way, it's kind of dumb — but watch the technique carefully, because Hitchcock is a brilliant, brilliant man.

To answer your question: Yes, he can be very tough to work with — but once you learn his methods it's very easy. Then you begin to say to yourself, "My wishes are not that important. Give him what he needs." I could not have worked with Hitchcock if my attitude had been any different. Or Fritz Lang, for that matter. I was the only one to survive three pictures with Lang — *Fury* [1936], *You Only Live Once* [1937], and *You and Me* [1938].

Q. Your films with Fritz Lang are particularly interesting today in that they were social dramas that didn't hide the Depression as most films of the times were doing. *You Only Live Once,* in which you and Henry Fonda are love-struck desperadoes gunned down by the police, has become a cult classic. It anticipated *Bonnie and Clyde* by many years.

A. I am a great admirer of director Arthur Penn, but I much prefer the Lang film, although, between you and me, I thought it was too sentimental. Of the three films I made with Lang, I liked *Fury* best. When you consider the limitations of making a strong social statement in a Hollywood film, particularly back then, I think it was the best picture he made in this country. It was taken from the true story of an innocent black man who was hanged

City Streets, *with Gary Cooper, her first Paramount film.*

With Billy Halop, in Dead End, *then considered a hard-hitting depiction of life in New York slums.*

by a mob in southern California. It was later discovered to be a case of mistaken identity. In those days, no black actor ever played the lead in a Hollywood film, so the only way Norman Krasna and Joseph L. Mankiewicz could write the film was to make the lead a white man — Spencer Tracy — and to make it a love story, which is where I fitted in. Still, I think it made its point about mob justice.

Q. Another important, socially relevant Depression-era film you made was *Dead End* [1937]. Did you like having the opportunity to work with William Wyler?

A. No. I hated every minute of it. Mr. Wyler was, at that time, probably one of the most sadistic directors in motion pictures. Bette Davis to the contrary, I think most of his actresses will bear me out. But since he was a top director in Samuel Goldwyn's stable, he was granted every indulgence. Perhaps they originally wanted another actress to play my part — I don't know — but

he simply didn't like me or anything I did on the picture.

Q. Finally, in the forties, you retired — temporarily, it turned out — from films and went back to New York and the theater. Did you have trouble readjusting?

A. I discovered that I had forgotten how to act. I'd been coddled a great deal in Hollywood and had been catered to. It was difficult for me to simply stand on a stage, swoon, whatever. You don't have to do that in movies because they can stop a scene at any time and move into a close-up or pull back. But I also realized that I had benefited from my film experience. I had learned how to handle myself. Before making movies, I never knew what my body looked like. It was from filmmaking that I learned total body movement.

Q. Did you ever want to direct the films you were in?

A. I don't think I possibly could have. I can't see the picture as a whole. I only see it from where I am as a character — the writer's character. You don't watch *me* when you watch a film. You're supposed to know what I did under various instructions. It has nothing to do with me. The minute I start getting into other people's heads I do the character a disservice.

Q. Can you talk about how you work to create your characters for your films?

A. The audience creates my character. They decide if the character is in love with the man or not; if she hates him or doesn't hate him. The relationships come out of the story and how the audience looks at it, what they take from it. Realism is very simple; it doesn't take very much for an actress to be real. You play the simple areas. An audience will take it from there.

Q. You're being elusive.

A. Stanislavsky said that if you find something that works, don't tell anybody, because the minute you express too much of it intellectually, it will never work. When I was very young and working in the theater, they said I had true stage belief. When I was supposed to cry, for instance, it never occurred to me to tell myself some sad story in order to make myself cry. I *believed* that whatever was supposed to be happening on the stage that would cause my character to cry *was* really happening. Although we never express it — we don't have to — actors trigger a lot of different emotions for each other. An actor is a giving and receiving thing.

Film after film took advantage of the saddest eyes in Hollywood.

![film strip decoration]

DICK POWELL: STAR WHO LIVED TWICE

JUDITH M. KASS

E WAS THE *Broadway Gondolier* (1935), *The Singing Marine* (1937), and *The Cowboy from Brooklyn* (1938), the chirpy tenor with a face like an eager chipmunk who wooed Ruby Keeler on *Flirtation Walk* (1934) and *Forty-Second Street* (1933). In one picture after another he sang songs — usually dressed in a soldier, sailor, or Marine outfit. "I was so insipid I wanted to throw up," Powell complained when that era was over. "It took me five years of fighting to get out of those roles."

And when he did get out, Richard Ewing Powell was Philip Marlowe, Raymond Chandler's cynical, unshaven private eye, a new hard-boiled image for the baby-faced crooner. No star has ever been as successful as Powell at changing from one popular, set image to a second, entirely different — and equally popular — image. Powell was accepted as the rosy-cheeked American boy, singing and smiling through the thirties to help the country forget its Depression blues, and he stayed on top in the forties because his modern tough guy persuasively reflected postwar malaise.

"I started out with two assets," Powell said by way of explaining his success, "a voice that didn't drive audiences into the streets and a determination to make money."

Powell would demonstrate this resolve to make money repeatedly throughout his career. He would take time out — first from band singing and later his movie career — to sell real estate. He would branch out into radio, first as a singer-host on programs like *Hollywood Hotel* and then as a detective. He would direct in the theater and in movies. He moved into television as a

The early Powell of The Singing Marine *(Top, with Doris Weston) wore rouge and played a guitar, while the later Powell of* Murder, My Sweet *(with Ralf Harolde) needed a shave and carried a gun. Other differences included clothing, lighting, setting, companion, and his disposition.*

JUDITH M. KASS *is the author of books on Ava Gardner, Olivia de Havilland, and directors Don Siegel and Robert Altman. She is currently working on a book on the films of Montgomery Clift.*

director/producer and sometime actor, amassing a fortune as the financial wizard behind Four Star Productions. To understand Powell's commitment to changing his image to make it fit the times, one must realize that he was fully aware of the fact that the more versatile he was, the more money he would make.

★ ★ ★ ★ ★

Dick Powell debuted in films as a crooner in *Blessed Event* (1932), a *Front Page*-style newspaper comedy. "I don't know why," Powell said, "but *Blessed Event* was a hit, and *I* was a hit, and the next thing I knew I was signed to a long-term Warner Brothers contract." He progressed rapidly to leading roles in musicals, playing

With co-stars of Gold Diggers of 1933, *Ruby Keeler (L) and his second wife Joan Blondell. (He would later marry June Allyson.)*

happy-go-lucky, smart-aleck, singing juveniles with stereotypical names like Jimmy Higgins, Billy Lawler, and Scotty Blair. The lavish, show-stopping numbers in these otherwise trite musicals were often directed by Busby Berkeley. *Footlight Parade* (1933) was typical, with Powell warbling "By a Waterfall" to Keeler, then disappearing as hundreds of chorines become a human fountain.

Warner both acknowledged and made cinematic capital from the Depression. The Powell/ Keeler/Berkeley musicals were conceived of as a cheerful antidote to the country's economic and social ills. "When Mervyn LeRoy was my director on *Gold Diggers of 1933*, complained Powell, "he'd never use anything in which I wasn't smiling." A few of Powell's loan-out movies have a bit more substance than those he made at Warners. In *Thanks a Million* (1935), for instance, Powell is an aspiring singer who runs for governor so he can get on the radio, and here his manner at times presages his tough-guy image of the forties.

Powell knew that it was his Warners films and not the loan-outs that had established him as a "top ten" box-office star by 1935, but he also realized that typecasting would eventually shorten his career. With this in mind he was, as he said, "always fighting to get out of one thing and into something better." After refusing *Garden of the Moon* (1938), another Berkeley musical, the disenchanted Powell, accompanied by Joan Blondell, his wife of two years, left the studio.

Powell next signed with Paramount with the guarantee that his roles, although still in musicals and comedies, would stress character more than in his previous films. If Powell struck no new and exciting sparks, he was at least noticed under his new aegis. *The New York Times* called Powell and Ellen Drew, his co-star in his first Paramount movie, Preston Sturges' *Christmas in July* (1940), "a couple of nimble and captivating babes

in a madcap wood;" James Agee in *Time* referred to Powell's "graceful sportiness" in René Clair's fantasy about a reporter who predicts tomorrow's news, *It Happened Tomorrow* (1944); and *The New York Times* reviewer declared Powell "an altogether personable and capable actor" in *Model Wife* (1941), a comedy he made with Joan Blondell. But since Paramount was reluctant to let Powell play the dramatic roles he craved, such as the one that went to Fred MacMurray in *Double Indemnity* (1944), he asked to be let out of his contract.

RKO had just bought Raymond Chandler's *Farewell, My Lovely,* and despite the fact that director Edward Dmytryk, noting Powell's sagging appeal at the box office, objected to his playing Marlowe, the star pleaded so convincingly that Dmytryk took a chance. The film was renamed *Murder, My Sweet* (1944) so audiences wouldn't expect another Powell musical. "Golly!" turned into a wryly skeptical "Oh, yeah?" and Powell was Philip Marlowe, his first strong dramatic role. "I figured it would be my best or my last picture," Powell declared. "It turned out to be my best."

Murder, My Sweet owes as much of its enduring success to Powell's realistic, sweaty, and exciting performance as it does to Dmytryk's crisp direction and Harry Wild's moody *film noir* cinematography. John Paxton's hyperbolic script — "My mind felt like a

A Busby Berkeley extravaganza: Powell, Keeler, and chorus girls in Flirtation Walk.

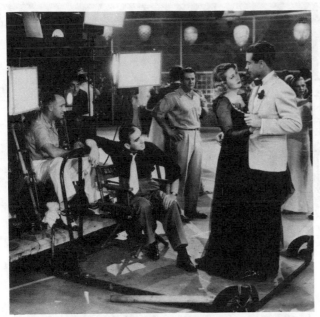

With Berkeley and Blondell on The Broadway Gondolier.

plumber's handkerchief'' — includes such bits as Marlowe striking a match on a cement cupid's derrière, but remarkably, after a dozen years of playing male ingenues, Powell does not seem miscast. *The New York Times* correctly noted that ''. . . while he may lack the steely coldness of a Humphrey Bogart, Mr. Powell need not offer any apologies.''

With this one film, Powell regained much of his box-office appeal. More importantly, *Murder, My Sweet* succeeded in changing his image. It altered it so strongly, in fact, that it threatened to type him as the snarling nihilist as firmly as he had been the inane youngster.

The innocent crooner Powell worships his girls chastely; the hard-boiled Powell admires a woman's sexuality and suspects her motives. The former Dick Powell sees success as the means to money; the tough egg knows it is the stuff by which men — and women — measure his worth. The singer shaves regularly and presses his suits; the post-Marlowe incarnations are often bleary-eyed, punch-drunk, and perspiring.

Powell's ''second'' screen persona is best illuminated in contrast to that of another latter-day Philip Marlowe, Robert Mitchum. Both actors' characters are interested in money and dames, but Mitchum has never hesitated to cross back and forth between out-and-out villainy and tarnished good guys. On the other hand, Powell, innately conservative, always took the surefire box-office route. He never played an outright villain because he didn't want to take a chance on damaging his image. The closest he ever came was in *Cornered* (1945), in which he searches for the World War II collaborator who killed his wife and, menaces an also-sweaty Walter Slezak as well as much of the population of Buenos Aires.

In the forties, with *film noir* the prevalent style of the American cinema, Dick Powell was one of a new breed of movie tough guys who went *To the Ends of the Earth* (1948), as one Powell title had it, to stamp out malefactors and prove their own mettle. His portrayals were so successful that never again would he have to convince anyone that he could be a strong dramatic actor with box-office appeal. He would be a dependable dramatic actor for the remainder of his movie career.

Before his unofficial retirement as a movie actor in 1954, Powell made one particularly noteworthy appearance — in *The Bad and the Beautiful* (1952), a classic commentary on the Hollywood success story. This, his most important film of the period, showcased one of his best performances — that of a novelist whose private life collapses as his career soars. The dry-humored sarcasm of Powell's writer perfectly complements Kirk Douglas' ruthless producer.

If early in his career, Powell seemed to be the movie father of Little Miss Sunshine, Shirley Temple, he later became someone much more significant: an engaging comedian, a persuasive tough guy, a not unskilled director, and finally, a businessman par excellence. Powell was realistic about his abilities and ambitions and adapted to the times to stay both marketable and popular. Powell's professional attitude was best summed up by Joan Blondell: ''He hated to sing and didn't like acting either. He wanted to be a producer. He was a businessman.''

Dick Powell provided his own epitaph, saying, ''What counts most in this profession is survival. There were lots of stars bigger than I, but I saw them come and go. Somehow, I've managed to survive, and that's what I'm proud of.''

To the Ends of the Earth, with Signe Hasso.

MICKEY ROONEY: THE BIGGEST MAN IN TOWN

ANN RUTHERFORD

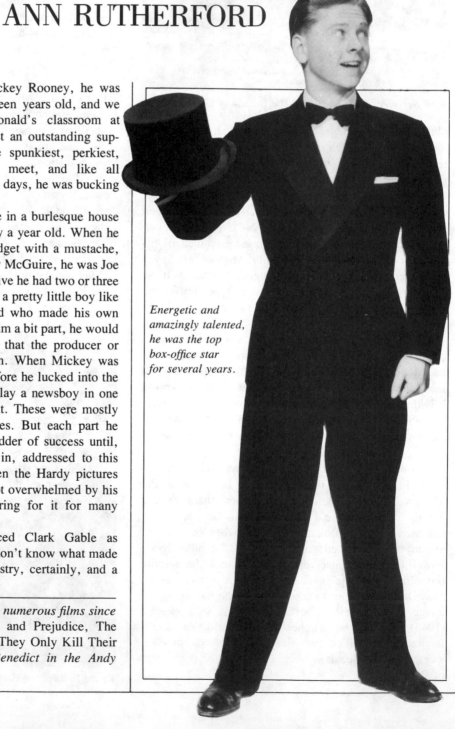

Energetic and amazingly talented, he was the top box-office star for several years.

WHEN I FIRST MET Mickey Rooney, he was about thirteen or fourteen years old, and we were in Mary McDonald's classroom at MGM. He wasn't a big star, just an outstanding supporting player. Mickey was the spunkiest, perkiest, cutest kid you'd ever want to meet, and like all youngsters in the business in those days, he was bucking to get ahead.

As a child he toddled onstage in a burlesque house with his parents when he was only a year old. When he could walk, he was playing a midget with a mustache, puffing on a cigar. He was Mickey McGuire, he was Joe Yule, Jr., and by the time he was five he had two or three other stage names. Mickey wasn't a pretty little boy like Jackie Coogan, but rather a child who made his own opportunities. If somebody gave him a bit part, he would somehow make it so memorable that the producer or director would think of him again. When Mickey was under stock contract to MGM, before he lucked into the Andy Hardy pictures, he would play a newsboy in one picture, a street urchin in the next. These were mostly fillers or, at best, supporting roles. But each part he played took him higher on the ladder of success until, finally, fan mail started coming in, addressed to this funny little snub-nosed boy. When the Hardy pictures caught on in a big way, he was not overwhelmed by his popularity — he had been preparing for it for many years.

It was Mickey who replaced Clark Gable as America's top box-office draw. I don't know what made him so magnetic. It was a chemistry, certainly, and a

ANN RUTHERFORD *has appeared in numerous films since the late thirties, including* Pride and Prejudice, The Secret Life of Walter Mitty, *and* They Only Kill Their Masters. *She starred as Polly Benedict in the Andy Hardy movie series.*

School at MGM between rehearsals. Mickey studies in blackface.

marvelous sense of abandonment. He was the embodiment of every darling, hateful, mischievous boy in America — the perennial Huck Finn and Tom Sawyer rolled into one. He appealed to people in all walks of life: black or white, rich or poor.

To watch him work was an absolutely incredible experience. He had a knack for coming up with little bits of business that were instinctive. And he had another knack — of knowing when he had created enough in a particular scene. If he started to go overboard, he would just say, "Cut! I gotta leave that part out. It's too much." He has a sense of fitness and a sense of right-

ness. George Seitz, the director of the Hardy movies, knew that Mickey was his own best director.

Mickey could act, sing, compose, dance, and play any instrument in an orchestra. You name the instrument, and he could get music out of it. He never had lessons and he couldn't read music. He just had talent. He was also marvelously coordinated. Very few people know, for instance, that, in 1939 or 1940, Mickey Rooney, with the scant amount of personal time that he had, attained the West Coast table tennis championship. His versatile talents were absolutely endless; they used to boggle my mind.

When I was first cast as Polly Benedict in the Andy Hardy pictures, I was meant to play opposite Frankie Thomas, Jr. Then it came to someone's attention that Frankie Thomas had grown since we had been signed. MGM looked among its stock players and found Mickey Rooney, who by this time had already acquitted himself admirably. Mickey was cast in the picture because the front office thought having a short Andy would be a little more amusing and more touching. That's how it happened, and that's how Mickey and I wound up working together. We had a warm friendship and a good working relationship.

Mickey was a pro from the bottom up. He was never

Rooney and Garland in Girl Crazy, *directed by Norman Taurog, with a score by George Gershwin.*

With Wallace Beery in the sentimental Stablemates.

Betty Garrett offers encouragement in Words and Music.

paranoid about his height and thought it kind of funny being cast opposite a taller girl. In fact, I used to rib him and tell him he was giving me a permanent curvature of the spine because, whenever it was time to kiss him or lean on his shoulder, I found myself slumping down or bending one knee. At no time did Mickey ever offer to wear lifts; nor did he ever demean himself by asking the prop man to provide a box to stand on. It was left to me to crook one knee or bend to bring myself down to the

proper level. But in my book Mickey stood on his talent: he was taller than Clark Gable, taller than almost anyone.

As Andy Hardy, I think Mickey represented to filmgoers an idealized version of what every young man should be like. He was everybody's favorite kid brother, first boyfriend, chum. And Mickey liked everything about Andy. Perhaps, subconsciously, Mickey had been viewing the Andy Hardys of this world all his life and

THE COMPOSER

ONE MORNING, I said to Mickey Rooney, ''You must be getting a big head or something. How come you never lunch with us anymore?'' His cocky little head perked to one side and he said, ''Well, because I'm composing an orchestral suite.'' Of course, I didn't believe him and he said, ''If you don't believe me, come with me.''

So he marched me down to our old original red schoolhouse, where there was a beat-up piano and a rather strange-looking young man, whom Mickey introduced to me as ''Eugene.'' He was Czechoslovakian or something. Mickey told me, with a rather haughty air, ''Eugene is my musical secretary.''

Eugene sat down and made beautiful music. I was impressed and said, ''Who wrote that?'' Eugene replied, ''Mickey Rooney wrote it.'' Mickey said, ''I'm ready for the next movement.'' Then Mickey sat at that piano and my hair practically curled. I could not believe what I was hearing. I asked, ''Mickey, what is this called?'' He said, ''Well the one you just heard was an autumnal suite. This is my scherzo.'' I said, ''Mickey, do you know what a scherzo is?'' He looked rather uneasy and he kind of nudged around a little bit before saying, ''Well no, but this sounds like it should be a scherzo.''

And I said, ''Mickey, you *have* written a scherzo.'' Because it *was* a scherzo.

Mickey did not know how to put the notes down on paper, so this is how the routine went: Mickey would sit down at the piano and play by ear, absolutely the most unorthodox piano performance you could ever witness, Eugene would listen to it, nod sagely, grab his pencil and paper and start filling in the notes.
— A. R.

Rooney and Rutherford.

CRYING ON CUE

MOST OF THE ADULT ACTORS in the days Mickey Rooney and I were making movies didn't have the abandon to cry. So they would have to suffer the indignity of having the makeup man blow through a menthol pencil at their eyes or having the prop man peel onions under their nose; and of course, there was always darling George Cukor's trick of twisting an actor's foot out of the camera's range. But Mickey had no problem crying on cue. Neither did Judy Garland or any of us. We'd have crying contests. Mickey and I used to laugh and talk about it, and he'd say, "Now where do you want the tears to stop flowing? Here or here?" And he'd put one finger beside his nose and the other on his chin. And he could cry exactly as much as he wanted.

— A. R.

soaking them up, ready to portray them; he just managed to pull the mantle of a normal, all-American boy over his head.

When World War II came along, Mickey went into the service, and when he came back he had not matured physically to fulfill the promise he had as an attractive young teenager; he had hit a very awkward stage. For the next few years, roles for him were very limited until his whole appearance changed. Only then could he begin playing character roles. So it was very difficult for Mickey to reestablish himself, but he did not just sit on his laurels. He took to the road. He did plays, he wrote, he did all sorts of army shows.

Many years later he called and told me he had sold a property to MGM for a picture called *Andy Hardy Comes Home* (1958). Mickey was going to reassemble the Hardy cast for at least this one picture. Of course, Lewis Stone had long since passed away, but Fay Holden (who played the aunt) and Sara Haden were still alive, and he wanted me to come back and play Polly. I turned him down. He was going to play Judge Andy Hardy. I said, "Mickey, in the first place, very few people grow up and marry their childhood sweethearts, so that gets rid of me right away. In the second place, you should not come back as Judge Hardy. You should come back as Andy Hardy; Andy Hardy would not grow up to be a judge. Andy Hardy would grow up to be Bob Hope or Red Skelton or a great radio performer." The film was not successful and I was sorry for Mickey's sake. I felt his judgment was not the best. That's about the only time I ever truly had a difference of opinion with Mickey. He was the most deeply talented person I've ever had the privilege of working with, and the most entertaining. I love him dearly. And who knows? Someday I may crawl out of retirement and do another picture with him.

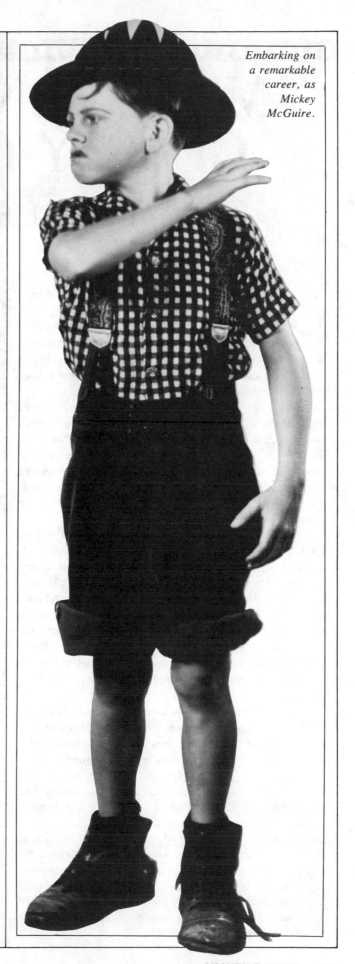

Embarking on a remarkable career, as Mickey McGuire.

MAUREEN O'HARA: CLASSY COLLEEN

GEORGE SHERMAN

ONE OF THE SEQUENCES in *Against All Flags* (1952) has Maureen O'Hara challenging Errol Flynn to a duel. On paper it was ineffective. Flynn, who had a marvelous sense of humor about his screen heroics, said to me: "Do you think this is going to work? You know I'm supposed to be the bravest guy on the screen. How could I fight a woman?"

I told him that I had worked with O'Hara before, and that she was quite capable of holding her own with a sword, a gun, or her fists, if need be — and I cautioned him, "You'd better be in shape." And when we shot the scene, Maureen, of course, handled herself with the grace and ability of an experienced sword fighter. Needless to say, Flynn's attitude about fighting with a woman changed radically.

John Wayne is another actor who has great respect for Maureen. She made many pictures with Duke — always at his insistence. He was wise enough to realize that with Maureen playing opposite him he would have added strength during a movie's usual conflicts and confrontations, the scenes would "stand up." Moreover, he appreciated her rare ability to "ride with the scene" — i.e., if he suddenly did something different from what had been rehearsed, she'd be quick enough to grasp the change without losing a beat. You just couldn't rattle her.

Even when she co-starred with such imposing figures as Flynn or Wayne, Maureen's presence was solid. Most of the women stars of today assume a masculine attitude in scenes played with strong males. Maureen had the ability, strength, and determination to control any scene — without sacrificing femininity. She could clash swords with Flynn or slug it out with Wayne,

---

GEORGE SHERMAN *directed Maureen O'Hara in* Against All Flags, Comanche, Big Jake, *and* War Arrow. *He also directed such pictures as* The Lady and the Monster, River Lady, Johnny Dark, Chief Crazy Horse, Count Three and Pray, The Enemy General, *and* The Bandit of Sherwood Forest, *and the made-for-television movies* Little Mo, Man O'War, *and* Trudy.

In George Sherman's Against All Flags.

but one need only take a look at *The Red Pony* (TVM 1972) with Henry Fonda or *Miracle on 34th Street* (1947), to see her approach is as effective when soft and warm.

She was an ideal "leading lady," blessed with talent and genuine beauty. (Photographers and cameramen said that they could "shoot" her from any angle and not be able to come up with a bad shot.) I was lucky enough to direct her in four films, and each time she made my job as director a lot easier. She was never late (which the punctual Wayne particularly appreciated), and ever prepared. Her suggestions were never intended to enhance her own role in the film, for she was sensitive to the story line of a movie, even when it meant taking a scene away from her.

But perhaps most of all, Maureen O'Hara embodies professionalism. I remember when we were getting ready to leave for Durango, Mexico, to film *Big Jake* (1971), and her agent was having difficulty reaching her because the phones were not working in the Virgin Islands, where she lives. We were concerned that she

With Charles Laughton on set of The Hunchback of Notre Dame.

could not get to L.A. in time for costuming. When she finally arrived, on the day we were leaving, I told her we did not have time to make any of her costumes. She told me not to worry, positive that there were costumes from former films which, mended and cleaned, would work fine. The offer was exemplary; few stars would have made it.

In Forbidden Street. *With red hair and green eyes, O'Hara was considered one of cinema's true beauties.*

John Ford considered Maureen his favorite actress and as close to him as were his own children. Whenever I'd shoot with her, he'd phone several times a week to check up on his redhead. She was equally devoted to him. She told me that she helped him when he was preparing and writing *The Quiet Man* (1952); in fact it was she who typed the final script. (Not only could she sword-fight, she could type ninety words per minute.) When Ford was seriously ill in Los Angeles while we were filming in Mexico, Maureen phoned his hospital every day. Making a call from Durango to L.A. isn't the easiest thing; but she did it without fail. This is typical of Maureen.

Showing athletic prowess in McLintock!

SUSAN HAYWARD: SUPREME EFFORT

ROBERT WISE

WHEN I WAS LOOKING for someone to play the lead in *I Want to Live!* (1958), the story of convicted murderess Barbara Graham, I knew. it was necessary to find someone who was more than just a good actress. Whoever played Graham had to be able to convey to an audience a poor background — a bad environment, a difficult childhood. And at the same time, I wanted this actress to express qualities that normally wouldn't be found in a person coming from this upbringing. I felt Susan Hayward was ideal for this difficult role.

Major stars usually don't make a commitment to do a film unless there is a finished script to read. But Susan Hayward had such great empathy and feeling for the character of Barbara Graham that she accepted the part on the basis of having read the outline Walter Wanger, the producer, had written and sent her.

ROBERT WISE *won two Academy Awards as Best Director for* West Side Story *and* The Sound of Music. *He also directed such films as* The Day the Earth Stood Still, Two for the Seesaw, The Sand Pebbles, The Hindenburg, The Andromeda Strain, *and the movie of* Star Trek.

I think that one of the main reasons Susan felt so deeply about Barbara Graham was that they both had had great trouble with the fourth estate. Susan had a history of bad press dating back to the beginning of her career; Barbara Graham's bad public image was a direct result of a slanderous media campaign that had unnecessarily revealed things from her past. Of course, Barbara Graham had no way to fight back, and this is what I think attracted Susan. She thought she understood what Graham had had to contend with.

I would learn that Susan Hayward was one of the most cooperative actresses in the business, but we did have a major disagreement before shooting began. It was not over how she should play the role, however, but over who the cameraman on *I Want to Live!* would be.

Susan was always concerned about how she looked photographically, so through her agents she had requested a certain man to film the picture. I sent back word that I wanted "Curly" Linden, who, I felt, could give the film an authentic look. Linden had photographed Susan a time or two, but she was nevertheless insistent on her choice. Finally her agents told her to talk to me

Strong performance as single mother in My Foolish Heart.

With Gregory Peck in David and Bathsheba.

With Victor Mature in Demetrius and the Gladiators.

personally. Susan came to my office, and we both made our points, defending our own candidates. We left the matter up in the air, although I was determined to get my man, and I gathered that her agents convinced her to give in on this point, because a few days later I got the message from them to use Linden. And that was the only real problem I had with her on the picture.

Once we agreed on the story and the Graham character, Susan came in day after day, rehearsed the scenes, then performed them beautifully. I don't mean to make it sound easy, it's just that she had a professional viewpoint about how things should run, and how one should do a job. Once in a while she would ask if she could change a word or phrase that seemed uncomfortable to her. Usually I would agree if I didn't change the character or the plot. Rarely did she want to move away from what was indicated in the script. In my mind she was one of the most professional actresses with whom I have worked, willing to explore her capabilities in order to give the best performance she could, and responsive to me and to the other actors.

Susan was not an easy person to know; she kept pretty much to herself when she wasn't rehearsing or shooting. Like many stars, she had her own group on the set — a makeup man or a hairdresser, and a wardrobe woman — and between setups they would stay in the dressing room chatting or playing cards.

I recall one time when Susan didn't appear on the set for shooting — a most unusual occurence. Unfortunately, this happened on a day when I had about two hundred and fifty extras ready for a big scene in the courtroom. Time passed and no one could find her; she wasn't home, her agents couldn't reach her. I managed to shoot a few scenes, but I couldn't fill the whole afternoon without Susan. Finally, I sent everyone home. It wasn't until that evening that Walter Wanger discovered what the problem had been. Walter told me that Susan had a sister who periodically caused problems of a family nature. Every so often, there would be a crisis that the actress would have to deal with. Sometime before Susan

Early publicity shot.

In Robert Wise's I Want to Live!, *Hayward's Barbara Graham, a tough party girl in man's world, continued to show fortitude in a woman's prison.*

was going to leave for the set that morning, she had gotten a call concerning her sister; she simply had to take care of the problem immediately — there was no alternative.

The next day, Susan arrived on time, in makeup. She didn't apologize or give any explanation for not appearing. She never said anything about it, and, of course, I respected her for her reluctance to talk about a personal problem, and I never pressed her on it. I just considered that it was something she couldn't help, that it was a situation that might happen to all of us, and we went on and did our day's work.

All in all, working with Susan Hayward was a satisfying, stimulating experience. Her characterization and performance were beyond any of our expectations. That she accomplished this with professionalism and lack of phony temperament is a tribute to the actress and the woman.

ALAN LADD: STRONG IMPRESSIONS

RICHARD MAIBAUM

THREE WEEKS after the release of *This Gun for Hire* (1942), Paramount had received three thousand fan letters for the previously unknown Alan Ladd. A month later there were five thousand letters a week. Even in an industry accustomed to runaway success, the response was phenomenal, all the more unusual since Ladd played the role of a professional killer in the film.

Paramount had forced Ladd to dye his blond hair black for his role in *This Gun for Hire*. But after his stunning impact, his wife and agent, Sue Carol Ladd, insisted he appear in the future as a blond — despite the then-prevailing casting cliché that romantic leading men should be dark (Valentino, Gilbert, Novarro, Colman, Gable, et al.). The instinct was sound. As a performer and personality, Ladd's appeal was essentially low-key,

He would have been miscast in comedies, but he ranked with the best in melodramas.

and black hair would have been too vivid for his quiet modulated voice and restrained expressions. Like Gary Cooper and Henry Fonda, Alan Ladd was a born underplayer.

He was unique among his contemporaries in being unusually athletic. Once a West Coast diving champion, with a slim, perfectly proportioned body, he was undoubtedly the most graceful American actor since Douglas Fairbanks. He didn't so much walk as glide. In *O.S.S.* (1946), the first of five films we did together, my script called for him to run at top speed across several fields, jumping over fences and stone walls in a hopeless attempt to rescue Geraldine Fitzgerald from the Gestapo. Without losing the impression of agonized desperation, he was able to project a beauty of leap and stride that was breathtaking. In this film and others, I was impressed by his fluidity of motion. I never saw him make an awkward or clumsy gesture — or one that wasn't manly.

He was underrated as an actor. Like Spencer Tracy, William Powell, and Gary Cooper, he was incapable of exaggeration. All of these actors were photogenic in the best cinematic sense. They had the perfect motion picture mask. Even their eyes were slightly veiled. Alan's restrained projection of emotion was not so much controlled by conscious thought as it was limited by physiognomy. He had precisely the right degree of facial muscular play.

His stardom was no accident. He knew what he was doing and what was right for the scope of his personality and what he could do on the screen. In *O.S.S.* the director asked him to cry when he discovered his girl had been captured and probably executed. Ladd thought about it, then quietly decided to play the scene dry-eyed. "It

RICHARD MAIBAUM *is a writer-producer. Included in his forty screenplays are five Alan Ladd films and the James Bond films:* Dr. No, From Russia with Love, Goldfinger, Thunderball, On Her Majesty's Secret Service, Diamonds Are Forever, *and* The Spy Who Loved Me. *Some of the films he produced are* O.S.S., The Big Clock, *and* The Great Gatsby.

wouldn't be me,'' he said. On film, his mute grief conveyed deeper emotion than would have been achieved by his actually weeping.

All actors have tricks. Tracy and Powell gazed steadily, then blinked. Barrymore had his raised eyebrow. Cagney used a variety of scowls. Ladd would keep his head down, his eyes slightly hooded. At the right moment he would look up slowly, widening his eyes a little. He also allowed an enigmatic, half-smile to flicker momentarily across his lips. The effect was a deepening of mood and interest.

Alan meticulously choreographed his action sequences. Time and again I watched him take a director's suggestion and improve it with cleaner, more playable movement. Invariably he'd add excitement and interest. Ladd performed his own stuntwork and particularly enjoyed this aspect of filmmaking. The stunt men working for other actors were his special pals. (He used to play cards with them and would invariably lose — deliberately, I think.)

Alan was affable on a set. He chatted with grips and gaffers. (And he loved John Seitz, the great cameraman, who made him look rugged.) Ladd seldom joined in the usual male banter about the physical endowments of starlets, although he once confided in me that he dreamt about melons while working opposite Sophia Loren in *Boy on a Dolphin* (1957).

Alan's most successful role was in *Shane* (1953). His scenes with Brandon de Wilde conveyed his deep love for his own children, who in turn adored him. His long farewell with Jean Arthur — in which they face

Ladd's best partner was tough but tender Veronica Lake. Adaptations of Graham Greene's This Gun for Hire *(Above) and Raymond Chandler's* The Blue Dahlia *were their two top films together.*

each other silently before he leaves to shoot it out with Jack Palance — is one of the most moving in the history of westerns. Talking about it, Alan, with his customary modesty, said, "I thought he'd never say cut." But director George Stevens knew the effectiveness of Alan's visual presence, especially in a scene with an actress like Arthur, and kept it going to the last possible frame. Alan as Shane was a triumph of typecasting, a perfect blend of role and actor.

Ladd had many other successful performances, including *The Glass Key* (1942), *The Blue Dahlia* (1946), *The Proud Rebel* (1958), and *O.S.S.* In *Paratrooper* (1954) he plays a man reluctant to assume command, another instance of the fortuity of typecasting. In *The Carpetbaggers* (1964), in an excellent and moving performance as an aging, tough, loyal henchman of a tycoon, he indicates what his future career might have been. The Oscars that eluded him as a leading man might have been his in strong supporting roles.

My personal favorite was Ladd's title role in *The Great Gatsby* (1949). Warner Baxter had preceded him as Jay Gatsby, and Robert Redford was to follow.

F. Scott Fitzgerald was literally out of print when I suggested to Alan and Sue that we ask Paramount, who owned the novel, to let us make it. I felt after *O.S.S.* that Alan could project the qualities uniquely suited to this role: strength, authority, grace, good looks, and, most of all, an enigmatic combination of naiveté and ruthlessness. Robert Redford is a fine actor, but at no time did I feel Gatsby had actually been a gangster, someone who had started out as a gunman. It may surprise some that Alan spent many hours discussing Gatsby. He instinctively understood Gatsby because, in a way, he was a Gatsby himself. Alluding to his Hollywood success, Alan once remarked, "Not bad for an Okie kid."

We had an excellent cast for *Gatsby,* including Barry Sullivan, who played Tom, Daisy's unfaithful millionaire husband. Barry is almost six-three, but when Tom and Gatsby are cheek by jowl in the famous confrontation scene at the Plaza, no one questions Gatsby's innately more dangerous physical menace. I think it has something to do with Alan's terse delivery, his authority, a catlike quality which suggests he would strike swiftly and surely. When shooting on *Gatsby* was over, for the

Betty Field as Daisy in the 1949 version of The Great Gatsby.

THE QUESTION OF HEIGHT

ALAN LADD wasn't physically large as leading men go but still managed to convey strength and authority. I personally think it was a mistake for the studio to try to conceal Alan's actual height. James Cagney, Humphrey Bogart, Edward G. Robinson, John Garfield, and others proved that modest size does not necessarily limit appeal. In Ladd's case, the deception — the use of lifts, platforms, specially designed sets — was unfortunate. I think this contributed to his skepticism about his own worth as an actor. Many popular actors dislike being seen in public, but Alan was unusually averse to it. I once helped Sue Ladd convince her husband to accept an invitation to a Royal Command Performance in London. After he finally agreed, he said to me, "They'll all see how short I am."

— R. M.

Brandon de Wilde's idol as Shane.

first time Alan commented on the height disparity between Barry and himself. "Please, Dick," he told me ruefully, "don't ever do that again. It's just too rough."

What made Alan Ladd a star? The answers are simple. Women in the audience loved him. Shopgirls, showgirls, college girls, housewives — they wrote him personal letters, sensing his devotion and protectiveness. There was more to him than his good looks. Men responded as well, vicariously sharing his heroic exploits. No fan letter went unanswered. Sue saw to that.

Sue had been right about the color of his hair — and a lot of other things as well. She once half-seriously said to me. "All I want in a script for Alan is for him to be in every scene." Excessive? No. A good script for Ladd was one in which the camera saw everything through his eyes.

Able to play heroic parts such as Jim Bowie in The Iron Mistress.

With wife Sue Carol, a former actress.

LAUREN BACALL:
A LOOK AND A VOICE

DAVID THOMSON

Howard Hawks found her on the cover of Harper's Bazaar.

SHE MADE MOVIES LOOK EASY, if only in two of her films, but that's one more than history requires if the ease is natural. And why not? For her brief moment of cinematic glory she was attended by the best gang of experienced but honorable guys a girl could ever meet. Her first movie, *To Have and Have Not* (1944), was loosely based on Hemingway's novel, even if he forgot to include her part. She had Howard Hawks as director, Jules Furthman and William Faulkner as writers, Sid Hickox as cameraman, and Andy Williams to sing for her while she shuffled her lean body to the lazy beat. On screen, for buddies she had Marcel Dalio, Walter Brennan, Hoagy Carmichael, and Humphrey Bogart. When they made that movie, Lauren Bacall was nineteen.

DAVID THOMSON *is the author of* A Biographical Dictionary of Film; America in the Dark: Hollywood and the Gift of Reality, *and two novels*.

Warners wanted another *Casablanca* (1942), and they kept throwing the Hemingway novel up in the air until it came down "American loner who is drawn into the war effort — against the background of a raffish café, all lowered blinds, hard liquor and soft touches." In *Casablanca*, Bogart does the right thing out of a sense of decency. The Hawks movie shrugs off that piety: Bogart helps the Free French, or whoever they are, because he's broke.

But the war in *To Have and Have Not* is a bore that no one allows to get in the way of the love story. It works against its own grain from the moment a tall, slender girl appears asking for a light, her long chin tucked into her shoulder and the almond eyes staring out of a sleek face. "We are going to try an interesting thing," said Hawks to the forty-three-year-old Bogart. "You are about the most insolent man on the screen, and I'm going to make a girl a little more insolent than you are."

Bogart may have sneered or fought back at first, but he fell in love with the girl in front of the cameras. It was maybe the most romantic thing that has ever happened to two movie stars, and they took it with good grace. They seem protected by their own feelings, and the picture looks like a home movie. "You do know how to whistle?" she wonders of him after a fulsome and not-too-mocking account of how he only has to whistle if he wants her. She gets up from his lap so her dress won't crease, makes her way to the door and turns in time, remembering her duty to poetic double entendre: "You just put your lips together and blow." It is the epitome of wholesome sophistication, a distinct peak of American culture — hard-boiled, but running over. And the girl was nineteen — going on fifty-five.

The voice was as deep as any woman has ever had on film, with a marinade of authority and experience that was more erotic even than the sleepy eyes and the thigh-shaped drop of hair that framed a brow like a new pillow. But Hawks had seen a face: his wife, Slim, showed him a magazine that had the young know-it-all face on the cover. (One can imagine Hawks running his finger across the glossy paper to see if the makeup smeared.) She had

She received bad notices for Confidential Agent, *with Charles Boyer.*

acted a little and modeled more. Hawks signed her up when he heard her nearly sinister delivery. She spoke so beguilingly it was a day or so before you — or Bogey — knew she'd tweaked your nose, or whatever else she could reach. She photographed a treat, and if she was sometimes timid about moving, why, shyness is becoming in someone so young. She just slouched or waited for people to come back to her. Put her in silk or fur, or the vivid dog-tooth suit she wears in *To Have and Have Not*, and her clothes seem to drift across the screen with sultry intentions. She was a young sexpot, a wife for Bogart, and a fashion sensation: Warners bought her from Hawks and called her The Look.

When Marlene Dietrich saw the film, she recognized the heiress to her aloof goddess of the 1930s. But Bacall was warmer. Youth at least shows in her merriment; there are moments when a girl's grin transforms her face. Bogart calls her Slim in that picture, in honor of Mrs. Hawks. She bats him back as Steve, though his name is Harry. They are embraced in a pact: When Bogey has to carry a pretty girl who has fainted, Bacall shimmies past him with the leering jab: "Trying to guess her weight?" At the end, they go off arm-in-arm to a jaunty tune. The romance was wholly fanciful, but it sustained the girl and an actor who had been truculent and desperate in earlier marriages. He was twenty-five years older, yet she was wise enough to handle him.

Betty Perske had become Lauren Bacall. It was an inspired name, as wavy as the hair that fell on her shoulders, as glamorous as a screen image and maybe too brazen for a woman who stayed Betty at home and never fell for the myth-making industry. Two years later, she and Bogart were back at Warners, with Hawks, Hickox, Furthman, and Faulkner for *The Big Sleep* (1946). Again, a familiar genre dissolves into the banter of a loving couple. They look married, but they drop sweetness for mock battle and sweltering innuendo. Bogart's Philip Marlowe finds her first in her boudoir, in pajamas. He's sweating and she's cool. They tease one another with the relish of butchers looking at prime meat. He makes a final thrust, and, like a good wife, she parries:

"You go too far, Marlowe."

The first two films Bogart and Bacall made together, To Have and Have Not *(R) and* The Big Sleep *(Above) had a constant sexual tension unequaled in any of the stars' other films.*

After a three-year respite, she co-starred with Marilyn Monroe (and Betty Grable) in the 1953 comedy hit How to Marry a Millionaire.

"Those are harsh words," Bogart/Marlowe replies, "especially when a man's leaving your bedroom."

The first time *The Big Sleep* came my way, I saw it three times in a day, unable to digest its intimacy. They have scenes together fresher and more daring than anything onscreen today: their duet for phone; their discussion of horse racing; and Bacall in a car, her face surrounded by hair and fur. It is a salutary lesson that in 1946 there was a commercial movie in which a man and a woman made love without touching, while the plot went to sleep and nobody bothered.

Those are the two films. Bacall made another in between them, *Confidential Agent* (1945), in which she had to be an upper-class Englishwoman who helps a forlorn Charles Boyer. It was too much for her, and she looked like a strained actress. (Being with Bogart had freed her from the need to act.) She was never anywhere near as good again, not even with Bogart in *Key Largo* (1948) or *Dark Passage* (1947). The best of their love was that it found itself in dry humor, and yet no one had the wit to put them in comedy. As Nick and Nora Charles they might have run riot and destroyed the drab cause of censorship for ever.

Bacall fought Warners, disliking the parts they gave her. She often took a studio suspension and happily stayed home instead. As the years went by, her leanness turned stringy, and she had a weakness: she did not photograph well in color. Her eyes grew too narrow and her complexion could look livid. The luster of nineteen moved on, and by the time she was thirty she merely looked older. She was good in *Designing Woman* (1957), and she always spoke pungent lines well. But she was not a dutiful lady to men of action, or at least not until *The Shootist* (1976), when her grim landlady watches John Wayne with understanding and respect. In *Written on the Wind* (1956), she looks pale and bitter, unable to prevent the movie being gobbled up by Dorothy Malone, who had been just a tasty side dish in *The Big Sleep*.

She is around still, and the smoke lingers in her eyes and her voice. She is now a distinguished, amusing lady. Perhaps she is as far from the startling girl as any of us. Never mind, Slim survives — the virginal whore who found and redeemed her dark angel on the very screen where we all longed to be.

An elegant murderess in Murder on the Orient Express.

GREGORY PECK: THINKING MAN

CASEY ROBINSON

I T WAS 1942, and after ten years as a writer at Warner Brothers I had decided to become independent and produce my own films. I had a project (*Days of Glory* [1944]) and an actress (Tamara Toumanova, the internationally famous ballerina), and now I needed a leading man. With what actor would I begin my new career? The important performers were tied into contracts with major studios and were jealously guarded. I was not satisfied to use *B* players.

Then on a winter's night in New York, Hal B. Wallis, chief of Warner Brothers Productions, and I went to the opening of Emlyn Williams' *Morning Star* and saw Gregory Peck in a supporting role, his first part on his first night on Broadway. My memories of this minor English war play have dimmed, but my first impression of this young actor have not. He was over six feet tall and darkly handsome, with a physical presence suggestive of a young Abe Lincoln. He had a deep, resonant, and quietly compelling voice. Here was an actor with charisma — that elusive star quality. Gregory Peck, I knew, was my man.

When I met with Greg, I didn't give him the usual sign-a-contract-with-me-and-I'll-make-you-a-star line. I told him that in my judgment he *was* a star and that it was inevitable he would become a very *important* star. I offered him the principal role in *Days of Glory,* and a contract with options that left him free of the bondage of an exclusive actor-producer arrangement.

One would suppose that a young and impoverished actor would leap at the chance, but Greg, while appreciative and friendly, was•reserved. The stage was his chosen career, and to go to Hollywood and perhaps own a swimming pool and the other tinsel-town accoutrements was no great ambition for him. However, he knew

CASEY ROBINSON *was the screenwriter or screenwriter-producer of many films, including* Captain Blood, Dark Victory, All This and Heaven Too, King's Row, Passage to Marseilles, The Corn Is Green, Two Flags West, The Snows of Kilimanjaro, The Egyptian, *and* This Earth Is Mine.

One of Hollywood's most noble figures in I Walk the Line.

that I was working on the screenplay of *The Corn Is Green* for Bette Davis, the last commitment of my studio contract, and the juvenile lead interested him. I told him I couldn't recommend him for the part — he was too big and too mature to sit at the feet of schoolmarm Davis. Although somewhat disappointed, he accepted my judgment and said that he would like to think the matter over.

The next time we talked I knew he was considering my offer when he asked when I would like him to make a

Peck's debut in Days of Glory *with Tamara Toumanova.*

With Greer Garson in The Valley of Decision.

screen test. I answered that I saw no need for a test, which greatly surprised him. He then told me that a year previously none other than David O. Selznick had tested and flatly rejected him, which surprised *me* but made no difference in my opinion of him. This clinched the matter and we shook hands on an agreement. If Gregory Peck

The Yearling *with Jane Wyman and Claude Jarman, Jr.*

decided to come to Hollywood, he would come for me. Which he did, soon after.

Days of Glory was financed by RKO. Made on a modest budget, it was not calculated to make the critics throw their hats in the air, although it did turn out to be a modest success. More important, it accomplished what I had predicted: Even before he had finished filming, the major studios came scurrying for Greg like cats for a bowl of cream. (Oddly, there was lack of enthusiasm only from Charles Koerner, production boss at RKO, who turned over his commitments to make films with Peck to David Selznick, of all people, who then claimed through his publicity people that Peck was his discovery!)

Twentieth Century-Fox used Greg first, in *The Keys of the Kingdom* (1944). It was not a box-office success, but Peck did give a fine performance. Then Louis B. Mayer asked to co-star him with Greer Garson in *The Valley of Decision* (1945) as the first of four films he wanted Peck to do for MGM. Although I had a commitment for Greg's services, I recognized that it would benefit his career to play opposite an important star like Greer Garson. Even more helpful to Peck's career was Selznick's *Spellbound* (1945) with Ingrid Bergman. Under Alfred Hitchcock's direction, Peck's performance earned him a Picturegoers Gold Medal. So, in two short years, the inevitable had come to pass: He had become a very important star.

But to become a star and to maintain that status over many years are two different things; and to appraise his assets that have made the latter possible is to take a look at the man himself. Solid, kindly, dignified, likable, and somewhat self-effacing, he is at his best in roles that match these qualities. When miscast, he has gone down

The controversial Gentleman's Agreement, *with John Garfield. It was the first film to deal with anti-Semitism in America.*

With Millard Mitchell. In Twelve O'Clock High, *he was forced to send men on suicide missions.*

with a dull thud; for example, in Selznick's flamboyant *Duel in the Sun* (1946) he was lost, playing a lecher. On the other hand, he was simply splendid in *Roman Holiday* (1953). In this love story, with Audrey Hepburn, he was a worthy match for a true princess.

During the first rehearsals of *Days of Glory,* I noted a flaw, which I talked over with him. He was still the drama student, I told him. I could see the wheels turning around in his head; and I warned him that the merciless camera photographs everything — especially thought. It was a fault he was to conquer quickly, in a remarkable way, by making the very act of thinking compelling and fascinating.

It is as the thoughtful man that he has always been matchless. Consider *Twelve O'Clock High* (1949), for instance (the first of a handful of Peck movies directed by his close friend and best director, Henry King), in which Peck plays a troubled Air Force officer obliged to order his men to undertake desperate World War II bombing

missions. His performance earned him a New York Film Critics citation as the year's Best Actor. Or an equally superb performance in *The Gunfighter* (1950), also King-directed, as a western gunman with a problem. Or in my own production, *The Macomber Affair* (1947), based on an Ernest Hemingway short story, as a thoughtful but cynical white hunter. Or *Gentleman's Agreement* (1947), Elia Kazan-directed, as a crusading journalist. Or the superb *To Kill a Mockingbird* (1962), which won him an overdue Academy Award as Best Actor. Or the recent *The Omen* (1976), in which as a

The Gunfighter, *in which he played man with shady past, one of his few offbeat roles.*

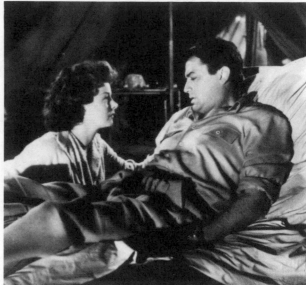

Casey Robinson wrote and produced two Hemingway adaptations which starred Peck: The Macomber Affair *(L), with Joan Bennett and* The Snows of Kilimanjaro, *with Susan Hayward.*

diplomat he exhibited personal qualities that could certainly have carried Gregory Peck to a distinguished position in politics if he had chosen that field rather than acting. These are just a few of the peaks in a marvelous, important career.

Our last professional contact was on *The Snows of Kilimanjaro* (1952), with Ava Gardner, Susan Hayward, and Hildegarde Neff, based on a Hemingway short story and directed by Henry King. Oddly, both Greg and I had qualms about the project. Greg's role dealt with a writer who suffered from too-easy popular success, and I had put words in his mouth that properly should have rattled off "trippingly on the tongue." I was worried that Peck's propensity to think words through would, in this case, make them seem false. And he was in great doubt about my screenplay, which used a stream of consciousness method with many flashbacks, new to the screen. There was no time pattern. I guess we both were a bit wrong, for it turned out to be one of Peck's best-liked films, and it amassed a box-office record, up to that time, for Twentieth Century-Fox.

Peck won his Academy Award as the southern lawyer in To Kill a Mockingbird. *Mary Badham played his daughter in the adaptation of Harper Lee's novel.*

JOANNE WOODWARD: TALENT TO SPARE

JOE PHILLIPS

In dressing rooms during filming of The Stripper *(L) and* The Three Faces of Eve *(Above). Woodward played characters unable to control their destinies in both films.*

No Down Payment, *one of her many soap operas.*

JOANNE WOODWARD is one of America's finest actresses, perhaps its most likable star; yet in twenty years she has appeared in but a handful of good movies, and probably none that is really worthy of her talent. Oddly, Woodward has been by-passed for parts by the more interesting ''cinematic'' directors and has found herself, time and again, in dreary dialogue pieces — conspicuous for their lack of energy and humor — that seem more fitting for theater than film. While her performances stand the test of time, the films in which they appear do not. Today, even her once highly regarded *The Three Faces of Eve* (1955) is dated, rather than classic. It is, in fact, tame in our age of *Sybil*.

She has specialized in playing southern women, warm of heart, maternal, vulnerable, and victimized. Their universal appeal is that they all make fools of themselves. They can be dumped on by supposed lovers as in *A Kiss Before Dying* (1956) or *Rachel, Rachel* (1968); or they can just look out of place, as does Eve

JOE PHILLIPS *specializes in writing brief essays on movie stars.*

A publicity shot from the fifties.

THOSE WHO WORK TOGETHER...

CONSIDERING THEIR TALENTS, Joanne Woodward and Paul Newman would seem likely to have been the most successful of all husband-wife teams to appear on the screen. However, this has not been the case. While most critics have lauded the two Woodward films Newman directed but did not appear in, *Rachel, Rachel* (Below, on set) and *The Effect of Gamma Rays on Man-in-the-zMoon Marigolds*, reception has been cool to their acting collaborations, such as (Clockwise, beginning top right, opposite page): *From the Terrace; Paris Blues*, probably their most underrated film, *The Drowning Pool* (on set); *A New Kind of Love;* and *Rally 'Round the Flag, Boys!*

— J. P.

Black in *The Three Faces of Eve* or the mother at her daughter's graduation in *The Effect of Gamma Rays on Man-in-the-Moon Marigolds* (1972). They are women whose undergarments show, who stumble on the stairs, who talk too loudly and naively, who spill things — when everyone is looking.

In her offscreen life, Woodward is educated, self-assured, and has a variety of interests ranging from the arts to politics. Surprisingly, few of her characters have reflected any of this.

Woodward's career cannot be entirely separated from that of her husband, Paul Newman. They both began in movies in the 1950s, playing emotional characters, often in hot, turbulent settings. They have appeared in numerous films together, and he has directed her twice. But, while interest in Newman's acting style has waned considerably since his exciting beginnings, Woodward has gained added respect through the years.

ANNE BANCROFT: SHE PAID HER DUES

KAREN ARTHUR

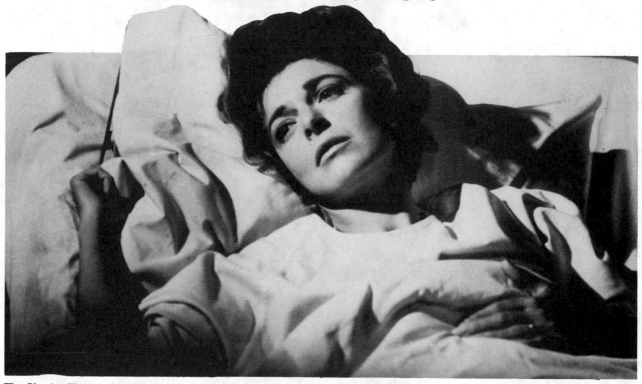

The Slender Thread. *Since the early sixties, she has been an ideal choice to play mature leading ladies.*

ANNE BANCROFT became a full-fledged movie star in 1962 with her Oscar-winning performance in *The Miracle Worker,* but her career in the performing arts had begun years before that. She began with television in New York; then, discovered by Hollywood, she spent six years as a starlet in some fifteen mediocre films. Seen in chronological order, her performances show that she was learning. Next came Broadway, where in 1958 she starred in *Two for the Seesaw,* for which she won her first Tony Award. A story told to many young actors is how Anne, during her audition, "became" in manner, attitude, dress, speech and actions, the character of Gittel. For some time everyone who saw it thought

Anne *was* Gittel; she had them convinced. A true actress had emerged.

She feels that this breakthrough period (the late fifties/early sixties) was one of the most important of her life. Psychoanalysis taught her a thinking process that helped her understand herself better. This not only aided Anne in dealing with her personal life, but it also overflowed into her acting; she now had the basis on which to build a strong craft. In her Hollywood starlet period she had conveyed raw unchecked emotion, but by this time she was learning to manipulate and control her emotional flow. Through personal growth, she was becoming more connected with her acting gifts and beginning to use them consciously.

Constant stage work was coupled with serious and dedicated study at the Actors Studio. Arthur Penn, her director on the play *Two for the Seesaw* and for both the stage and film versions of *The Miracle Worker* suggested that studying with Strasberg was a way for her

---

KAREN ARTHUR *is a former dancer and actress turned director-producer. She has directed two features:* Legacy, *which won the International Film Critics Award and Best Film Award at the Locarno Film Festival; and* The Mafu Cage. *She is now working on* Lady Beware.

During her starlet period, she was in Gorilla at Large *(for which this is a publicity shot), which did little for her career.*

to keep those new explorations and understandings alive. Her period with him solidified the technique that is so much a part of her current work.

Her choice of characters and material since *The Miracle Worker* reflects her exquisite taste. All the women she has played have inherent dignity, an inner strength. They are almost all outsiders, complex individualists fighting for their own space on their own terms — survivors. They are never degrading; rather, they push to expand and explore the female potential. One senses their wisdom through the intellect Anne naturally brings them. Most important is her deep human warmth which holds together even the most brittle moments of *The Turning Point* (1977) and which allowed us considerable compassion for her Golda Meier in *Golda* on Broadway.

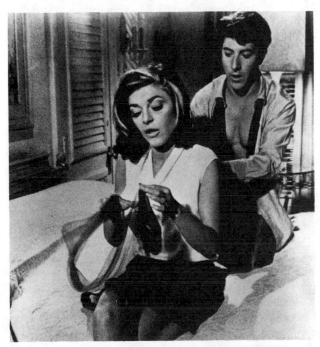

As Mrs. Robinson in The Graduate, *with Dustin Hoffman.*

The Pumpkin Eater *(with Peter Finch) is my favorite Bancroft film.* — *K. A.*

Hollered at by Jack Lemmon in The Prisoner of Second Avenue.

Fighting with Shirley MacLaine in The Turning Point.

Her women are passionate. They exude sensuality. They are also *physical:* witness the brutal fight scene between Anne and Patty Duke in *The Miracle Worker,* which is famous for its total conviction; and the rigorous ballet workouts we sensed her undergoing, despite their being offscreen, throughout *The Turning Point.*

She is one of the few American actresses whose characters work equally well on film and on stage. The subtle shadings of her portrayal of Annie Sullivan in *The Miracle Worker* on stage blended perfectly into the more introspective Annie she played on screen. Even when her part is weakly written and poorly directed, such as the lawyer in *Lipstick* (1976), she has the tensile strength to rise above the material. Often small bits of scenes are the most revealing of her strength as an actress, particularly those in which her character seems to go through a quick transformation, such as in *The Graduate* (1967) when she changes from seductress to rain-drenched shrew; or in *The Pumpkin Eater* (1964) at the moment she offers the sly smile of acceptance of her own madness. This is clearly some of her finest work.

Anne's characters, from Gittel onward, have spontaneous warmth and infectious humor which is predictable, for Anne Bancroft is funny. Her quick mind and attentive energy make use of every possible opening for a smile or joke. She can instantly switch tragedy to comedy, often combining the laugh with the pain, as was so beautifully shown in *The Prisoner of Second Avenue* (1974).

It is impossible to think of Anne Bancroft without recognizing her as the professional she is. At one period during the run of *The Devils,* a coactor was having personal difficulties and was at times walking through his part. Anne never gave less than she always did. Her quiet, steady attitude prevailed, and by the play's end both actors were performing at capacity, a very exciting thing to see. To be aware of and embrace a fellow artist's inertia is a part of the legacy of the professional.

With her multiple abilities and high peer respect, Anne constantly receives offers of work. It takes courage and daring to wait for a character that will be a challenge. Roles that are diverse enough to capture her imagination and energy are few. But as she has said: "Suddenly a role comes along, and I just have to show you this woman!"

NEW DIRECTIONS

ANNE BANCROFT AND I spent time together as part of the American Film Institute's Woman's Directing Workshop. The workshop provided us with a place to stretch creatively among other professional women, to share our feelings of vulnerability in approaching a new medium. One of the sessions began with Anne admitting to nervousness following a screening of her first directorial effort *The August,* a 45-minute short. And then she listened to the other women, to their observations, suggestions, critiques, and applause. She was expectant, wanting to discover and to learn from the other women.

Then Anne spoke candidly of her own frustrations while making the picture, how her experience and knowledge as an actress restricted her at times from thinking as a director in relation to her actors, as when she wanted them to play it as she would have, rather than helping them find their own way. And she said that making the film had confirmed acting as her first love.

After seeing *The August,* I believe she has the drive and stamina to plunge into a major directing project, and the cleverness and wit to accomplish it. As a director (and an actress) her choices are bold, definite, and abundant. Surely we will be moved emotionally and dazzled technically by this next step in her career, as we have been time and again by her acting.
— K. A.

THE
INSTITUTIONS

MARY PICKFORD: WORLD'S SWEETHEART

BUDDY ROGERS

Also, Mary was loyal to her public, and that is why she dressed as she did, wore those long blond curls, even trimmed her fingernails. It is also why she continued to play children even after she had greatly tired of the masquerade. Asked by *Photoplay* to choose roles for the adult Mary, fans selected such parts as Heidi and Cinderella. I think it is ironic that Mary's fans insisted that she play children over and over again.

But I do not want to give the impression that Mary was satisfied just playing children. In fact, she often resented that her most popular films were those in which

"Little Mary" was with Griffith and Zukor before she helped form United Artists in 1919.

P EOPLE HAVE ALWAYS ASKED Mary Pickford why she played so many children in the movies. For several years she *enjoyed* pretending to be a child. You must understand that Mary grew up in a poor environment and missed out on what one might think of as a normal childhood. So she was happy to have the opportunity to live again the life of a child — even if only on film and when she was an adult.

CHARLES "BUDDY" ROGERS *was a leading man in the motion pictures during the twenties and thirties. Among his credits are* Fascinating Youth, Wings, Abie's Irish Rose, *and* My Best Girl, *which co-starred his future wife, Mary Pickford.*

The end of Rebecca's circus career

MARY PICKFORD IN **REBECCA OF SUNNYBROOK FARM**

FROM THE PLAY BY KATE DOUGLAS WIGGIN AND CHARLOTTE THOMPSON
FRANCIS MARION DIRECTED BY MARSHALL NEILAN

ARTCRAFT PICTURES CORPORATION

One of her many roles that Shirley Temple would later attempt.

she was a youngster. In her autobiography, *Sunshine and Shadow,* Mary wrote:

> Every now and then, as the years went by and I continued to play children's roles, it would worry me that I was becoming a personality instead of an actress. I would suddenly resent the fact that I had allowed myself to be hypnotized by the public into remaining a little girl. A wild impulse would seize me to reach for the nearest shears and remove that blond chain around my neck.

If you look back at Mary's career today, you find it difficult to define Mary as simply an actress who played children. Film historian Edgar Wagenknecht astutely points out that "the composite Pickford character was considerably less simple than she is generally supposed to have been . . . she was 'America's Sweetheart,' America's darling child, America's problem child, and at times the Madonna. . . ." Mary Pickford did have many facets in the roles she played. It is true that many times she was a half-child/half-woman, but she also played mature women. She won her Academy Award for Best Actress playing a grown woman in *Coquette* (1929). No matter who she played, however, her character had to have sincerity of purpose.

Mary won fame by playing each part with what became the "Mary Pickford touch." She could say more with one small gesture than other stars could with a great effort. She was far ahead of her time in technique, and could switch from playing a comedic scene to a dramatic scene so easily that it would amaze those on the set. I particularly liked her performance in *My Best Girl* (1927), but maybe that's because I had the opportunity to

work with her in that picture. I learned so much from watching her and playing opposite her that I had to conclude that, as an actress, Mary was a genius.

Mary also liked *My Best Girl* and rates it with *Sparrows* (1926) and *Secrets* (1933) as among her personal favorites. But I tend to think she liked best whatever film she was currently working on at the time. (I do know,

Coquette. *An adult role won her the Academy Award.*

Long before marriage, Rogers and Pickford in My Best Girl.

Her only film with first husband Douglas Fairbanks was The Taming of the Shrew.

however, that she didn't care for *Rosita* [1923], *The Taming of the Shrew* [1929], or *Pollyanna* [1920].) Mary likes to give credit for many of her best films to her friend Frances Marion, who wrote many of her scripts. Mary felt that Frances understood women's roles as well as anyone and thoroughly enjoyed working with her.

After Mary retired from acting (but not from producing) in 1933, she continued to look through many scripts. But by that time she found living at Pickfair and producing films more appealing than continuing an acting career that had already spanned more than twenty years.

I don't know much about her fan mail in the early days, but I do know that now she receives many letters every day. Men write that they have always been in love with her or that their fathers were in love with her. Women write how they remember her and how they curled their hair the way she did and had it bobbed when she did and cut it short when she eventually got the urge to. Young girls write that they want to be a great actress like she was, and to ask if she has any suggestions for them.

Mary's career has been very satisfying. The fact that she is remembered and loved by her original fans, and has won over each new generation the world over, is very thrilling to her, indeed.

Charles Chaplin, Mary Pickford, and Douglas Fairbanks, three of the founders of United Artists. D.W. Griffith was the fourth.

LILLIAN GISH: STAYING POWER

DANNY PEARY

"... for young men to dream about forever." — Joseph Hergesheimer.

T HE EARLY MOVIE AUDIENCE, who wanted their stories kept simple and familiar, didn't demand talent in the performers — just appealing looks. At a time when overhead studio lighting caused harsh shadows and highlighted every wrinkle and line, it was necessary to find fair, smooth-skinned actors and actresses — when the movies were young, so were the players.

No filmmaker was more on the lookout for young faces than D. W. Griffith. It was quite common for him to snare some unsuspecting young individual who was

DANNY PEARY is the editor of *Close-Ups*.

simply visiting the Biograph lot, and to thrust that untried person in front of his camera. That is exactly what happened, in 1912, to Lillian and Dorothy Gish.

Lillian's thin, fragile, wraithlike appearance was in complete contrast to Dorothy's well-fed, healthy look, but it was Lillian who better fitted Griffith's criteria for leading ladies. All Griffith's heroines — Mary Pickford, Blanche Sweet, Lillian Gish, Mae Marsh — were of the same mold: Each had long, flowing, curly blond hair, delicate hands and feet, huge sensitive eyes, soft noses, bee-stung lips, and the overall look of a doll. In Griffith's eyes, these slim-bodied teenagers personified the helpless heroines of Victorian poetry.

The roles that Griffith dangled in front of his actresses suited them all (which is why there was so much rivalry among the women). Griffith was known to replace one actress with another on a film without altering the role in the slightest. This confirms that there was essentially only one (ideal) female image that Griffith wanted his actresses to convey.

Most important, they had to look pure and innocent. He often dressed them in rags (to depict their primitive qualities) or in white (to express their virginity). He had them all bouncing happily on the balls of their bare feet, playing with rabbits, squirrels, and mice or singing with birds; they picked flowers (an important image to Griffith, made clearer with the title *Broken Blossoms* [1919]) or attended church services. In her book *Screen Acting*, which was published in 1921, Mae Marsh described what she called "a regular Mae Marsh part": "I was the little heroine [who conquered] against great odds — usually after much suffering and not a few beatings." This could certainly be said for the other Griffith heroines, as well. In fact, Lillian Gish — who is considered the quintessential Griffith heroine because of the length of time (almost ten years) she worked with the director, and because his peak years coincided with her years in his employ — made her reputation as a heroine marked by passivity and suffering.

The world into which Griffith placed Gish consisted of beatings (by her father in *Broken Blossoms,* by German soldiers in *Hearts of the World* [1918]), insults, rejections, poverty, and dying babies. As critic Arthur Lenning wrote of *Broken Blossoms'* Lucy Barrows, the definitive Gish character, Lillian represented ''the innocent waif sacrificed in the moral and emotional slaughterhouse of the world.'' Griffith treated the Gish character with the kindness of De Sade when he sent Justine through her paces (although in Griffith, virtue is rewarded in the end). Like Justine, Gish never leaves her path of righteousness, never loses her faith or thinks an evil or vengeful thought. Although Gish suffers greatly throughout her films, her honor remains intact — she does not become the fallen woman who became the vogue in non-Griffith films beginning with the outbreak of World War I. To Griffith, a woman's worth could only be measured in terms of how much she could endure, and apparently the director carried this measure beyond the way his women appeared on the screen. How else does one explain why, for *Way Down East* (1920), he required Gish to do twenty-two takes of a scene in which she had to lie on an ice floe with her hand in freezing water?

Way Down East, which showcases a remarkably stirring Gish performance, is the one film that contains all the ideal elements of a Gish scenario. She plays a naive, trusting young woman who is duped into a phony marriage. The man leaves her pregnant and, as such — considering she isn't wedded — an outcast. She has the child, but it dies soon thereafter. When she falls for a farmer's son (Richard Barthelmess), the farmer, knowing about the illegitimate baby, forces her out of his house — during a blizzard. Wearing nothing but a skimpy dress, Lillian's death seems assured, but Barthelmess rescues her just as all seems lost.

On an ice floe in Way Down East.

With her sister Dorothy (L) in Orphans of the Storm.

Lillian was often presented as a Madonna, and there is no better visual example than the moment in *Way Down East* when she clutches her dead baby to her breast. Even in films when she has no offspring, her motherly instincts are at work. In *Birth of a Nation* (1915), it is these instincts that tell her to go to the army hospital to comfort and care for the injured soldiers.

When she does have a baby, as is often the case — and usually out of wedlock — Gish is at her best. The baby, however, is not long for this world; it must die before it can crawl. It does so for two reasons: Gish, having suffered the death of her child, is redeemed (according to movie morality) for having given birth illegitimately; Gish, as Griffith desired, can become a martyr and milk an audience's sympathy.

Just as Griffith's technical wizardry and genius for directing his stars cannot be denied, the treatment he afforded his women characters cannot be defended. It is sufficient to say he had an ''Image of Woman'' he never altered, and, perhaps justifiably, his failure to update that image led him to ruin in the profession.

Likewise, Gish's enormous talent is not in question. She had tremendous range as both a dramatic actress — her histrionics made the real-life father of the baby in *Way Down East* faint and a bystander watching the death scene in *Broken Blossoms* throw up — and a light comedienne (in Griffith's pastoral films, in particular). But what must be pointed out is that she not only accepted the roles Griffith put her in, she encouraged it. It was Lillian who asked that her musical motif in *The Birth of a Nation* be ''The Sweetest Bunch of Lilacs.'' It was she who worked with her cameramen to create her ethereal, ghostlike close-ups. As for her brutal treatment while filming the climax of *Way Down East,* Lillian's objection was not to the twenty-two takes — which she talks about with great pride to this day — but to the fact that she didn't think her dress looked soiled enough in the take that was finally used.

Characteristically, once Gish was independent of Griffith in the early twenties and could choose her own subjects, she continued to play virtuous, victimized women. It was her convincing acting — and only that — in these outmoded roles that kept her (and Mary Pickford) top box office during the femme fatale and flapper eras, long after her many imitators and Griffith's other heroines had fallen by the wayside. Audiences believed she was the woman she played, so Gish, even when under enormous pressure from MGM during the late twenties, would not waver from her carefully nurtured (and financially promoted) image.

The irony is, of course, that Gish off screen was never like the character she played on the screen. Virtuous? Yes. Innocent? Questionable. In her autobiography *Star,* Colleen Moore, the queen of the flappers, pointed out that while she herself and Theda Bara stayed home alone at night, it was Lillian Gish who was out on the town, often with one of her many admirers' from the intelligentsia. And Lillian was never one to be passive; Griffith (or ''Mr. Griffith,'' as she still carefully refers to him in public), MGM's Louis B. Mayer, and Mayer's entire work force often were challenged by this powerful

With adopted children in The Night of the Hunter.

woman. In fact, it was Gish's unwillingness to compromise herself to Mayer's way of directing her career that led to her temporary retirement in the early thirties.

When Gish returned to the cinema in the forties, to play character parts, she was as she always should have been: independent, complex, aggressive, stubborn, and, for the first time on film, actually *wise*. Now, here was a woman — perhaps the only one in Hollywood — who could not only take on the evil Robert Mitchum in *The Night of the Hunter* (1955) but could emerge victorious.

With John Gilbert in La Bohème, *her first film at MGM.*

PHOTO BY: CORI WELLS BRAUN.

Photo taken in 1978.

GLORIA SWANSON: INDESTRUCTIBLE ME

GLORIA SWANSON

W HEN THE EPIC MOVIES were playing at the Chicago Opera House, fourteen-year-old Gloria May Josephine Swanson used to go to Lincoln Park to hear Amelita Galli-Curci sing. I was not grown up enough to attend the opera (or the nickelodeons) but I used to watch the fashionable Chicago society ladies glide by in their quiet electric automobiles, lighted from the inside until they looked like grown-up dolls in decorated candy boxes.

My big dream was to be an opera star like the glamorous international femme fatale Ganna Walska — who was Polish like my one grandfather. I couldn't have dreamed of becoming a movie star because there was no such animal. Girls who appeared in early motion pictures were as anonymous as early porno players. Stars of the theater scorned celluloid show people. As usual it was audiences that changed things; they made stars out of motion picture players despite everything early producers could do to prevent it.

The ultimate impossible dream is exactly what happened. After audiences had made me a movie star, I finally got to play a make-believe prima donna — three times. The first time it was in the very first picture I produced myself after I left Paramount to join Doug Fairbanks, Mary Pickford, Charlie Chaplin, and D.W. Griffith in the formation of United Artists. The movie was called *The Loves of Sunya* (1927) and was the first attraction at the magnificent new Roxy Theater in New York. Later I played another opera star in the film version of the play *Tonight or Never* (1931). But in that one I never got to sing. That didn't happen until I played another singer in the Jerome Kern-Oscar Hammerstein operetta *Music in the Air* (1934). Preparing for that role, I got around to seriously studying singing with Caruso's throat doctor, Dr. Marifioti. He thought I had what it

---

GLORIA SWANSON *has been starring in movies since 1915. Among her films are* Male and Female, The Affairs of Anatol, Sadie Thompson, *and* Airport '75. *She received an Academy Award nomination as Best Actress of 1950 for* Sunset Boulevard.

"Nobody ever called me a 'silent film star' until 1929 when I made The Trespasser, *my first talking and singing picture. It was as if all of us who made movies before* The Jazz Singer *were mutes."* — G. S.

took to be a real opera singer if I would give up movies and study for a few years in Italy. It wasn't too late, but at the time I thought it was.

But the image of the opera star was something that must have had a great impact on me, consciously or not. Those were the ladies I admired. Grace Moore, Rosa Ponselle, Gladys Swarthout, and Lily Pons were my friends. (To those of us who knew both ladies, the film *Citizen Kane* [1941] had more to do with Ganna Walska than Marion Davies.) They were truly international — like the first film stars — as well known in Vienna as they were in America. They had dignity, style, ele-

EARLY SCREENINGS

FROM THE VERY BEGINNING, films were international because immigrant youngsters — who didn't know English, who didn't have enough money for vaudeville — made up the bulk of the audience. I happened to be Swedish, so the first pictures I saw as a child were films imported from Sweden — with a Polar Bear logo.

Early movies were called many names but never "silent films." American cinema began with makeshift terminology and wretched settings. Edison had grandly christened his system as Life Motion'd Pictures. This was speedily corrupted to "motion pictures." It certainly dates me, but that's what I still call them.

It was the customers with their nickels who first talked about "taking your girlie to the movies" or "the picture show."

From the first, movies had to live down unsavory associations — hastily converted storefronts like the early porno houses, then dark corridors that became nicolets, nickelettes, and then nickel-odeons — a word wedding of the buffalo nickel (admission) with the Odéon, the national theater of France.

By 1913, Italian filmmakers were sending colossal spectacles to this country. Makeshift hole-in-the-wall storefronts seemed totally inadequate to present imposing triumphs of Roman legions and mighty epics of the seas. Big movies required giant theaters. I remember they rented the Chicago Opera House to show epics like *Quo Vadis* (1913). Instead of the rinky-dink nickelodeon piano, they hired the seventy-piece Chicago Philharmonic Orchestra. So overnight, by association with upper-crust opera, working-class movies became more successful and respectable.

With new thousands to spend, film people — mostly immigrants themselves — sought to outdo the splendors of the opera houses they had been renting. Imported marble columns; massive, imposing furniture; ornate chandeliers from the palaces of Europe; and oil paintings and sculpture came to be standard fixtures for temples of the cinema.

As early as 1919, after I had left Mr. De Mille to star on my own, George Eastman, inventor of the Kodak camera and film, was one of the first prominent Americans to declare his faith in the future of the screen. He considered it a "medium appealing to the eye with artistic photography and to the soul with symphonic or organ music." The Eastman School of Music, which he endowed, very nearly became the first national academy of motion pictures. "There seems to be a natural alliance between music and pictures," Eastman felt. "I am going to build in Rochester [New York] a motion picture house with a view to using music and pictures in alliance." With the opening of the Eastman Theater in Rochester in 1922, Eastman realized that goal. His example led to the construction of colossal movie palaces across the country. First-run movies were shown twice each evening with full orchestral accompaniment. Each matinee was made more exciting by the throbbing of a "mighty Wurlitzer" pipe organ.

Not long ago I saw my last "silent" picture, *Queen Kelly* (1929), at an old-fashioned movie palace that survives in New York. That peerless theater organist Lee Erwin played his original musical score for the film on the mighty Wurlitzer. For an audience of young people, it was a revelation to see how it used to be.

— G. S.

gance — exactly the qualities Hollywood usually found in short supply.

I never considered myself part of the Hollywood crowd. I made my first pictures in Chicago at the Essanay Studios with Francis X. Bushman and Beverly Bayne and Charlie Chaplin — who hired me and fired me. Then I went to Hollywood. Keystone. Triangle. De Mille. Valentino. But in the early twenties, I escaped. I made some of my best pictures on Long Island, New York at the old Astoria Studios, with Ben Lyon, Ricardo Cortez, Rod La Rocque, Frank Morgan, Larry Grey, and H. B. Warner. In 1925 I made *Madame Sans-Gêne* in Paris with a French director and actors from the Comédie Française. I also made my first appearance in Technicolor in that year — the opening dream sequence in Allan Dwan's *Stage Struck*. I didn't make another film in color until 1952. But nobody ever called me a black-and-white film star. Colorless, either.

In 1932 I produced *Perfect Understanding* in London, choosing the then unknown Laurence Olivier to be my leading man.

★ ★ ★ ★ ★

With Rudolph Valentino in Beyond the Rocks.

Brilliant as ex-silent movie queen Norma Desmond in Billy Wilder's Sunset Boulevard. *With William Holden.*

I left California forever in 1938 and since that time I've lived in New York or Europe. But no matter where I turn up these days, I'm asked about that mythical kingdom called Hollywood. When I explain that I don't live there, *never* lived there when I could help it, and I've had an apartment in New York since 1938, the next question is: How is Garbo? Since I don't live in the smoggy suburbs of Forest Lawn, they picture me in some East Side Manhattan pantheon somewhere playing backgammon with Garbo.

It's even hard for me to believe I'm still around. When I saw one of Garbo's old films on TV where she was billed as John Gilbert's leading lady, the date was 1926. By that time I'd already been a star for almost a decade.

When I appeared in the play *Butterflies Are Free* in Milwaukee a few years ago, a couple friends got all gussied up to catch the opening night. As they were about to leave the hotel, they couldn't resist dropping my name. They announced in the lobby they were off to see their *friend* Gloria Swanson in *Butterflies*. The house detective looked at them as if they were out of their minds, driving all that distance. "Don't you *know?*" he said. "That's not *her*. They just dug up someone that looks like she used to."

There's no live television anymore so it's become difficult to prove you're not dead. So many of us are.

Sadie Thompson.

JOAN CRAWFORD: FROM RAGS TO RICHES

JEANINE BASINGER

"The definition of the word 'star'."
— J. B.

JOAN CRAWFORD, the star, was not born. She was built. A big-eyed, uneducated Texas girl named Lucille Le Sueur created her out of some glad rags, a set of beautiful bones, a hank of fiery red hair — and a whole lot of nerve. "Joan Crawford" was an image designed along classic lines. No matter what the current fashions she always looked sleek, fleet, available, and utterly modern. She was built to last.

Crawford's face and spirit seemed made for the camera. She cut a wide path through the worst of films, her huge eyes sparkling, her slash of a mouth firmly set.

JEANINE BASINGER *is the author of books on Shirley Temple, Lana Turner, and director Anthony Mann, and is a regular contributor to numerous film publications. She taught a course on Joan Crawford at Wesleyan University.*

In the beginning, as Pauline Kael has said, she looked "sexed to the gills." She was vibrant and intense, yet perfect as the ordinary shop girl. She starts out working in the box factory, or behind the counter in a department store, or in the kitchen of a mansion. But she ends up in a penthouse, drinking champagne, swathed in enough ermine to pay two years' rent for five or six families in the audience. Crawford knew exactly how to play the million-dollar baby from the five-and-ten-cent store. After all, it was the story of her life.

The story of Joan Crawford, movie star, is practically a household tale. In the days when fan magazines invented respectable biographies for Hollywood's chosen, Crawford openly revealed her miserable past. She frankly admitted to a lousy life. She talked about flunking out of school, near-rape by a lecherous stepfather, and countless cold and hungry days in which she scrubbed toilets for a living. With this honesty, she laid the foundation of her popularity with the masses. "I won't kid you. I was from the absolute bottom," she seemed to be saying. "If you work as hard, you can be me, too."

When Lucille Le Sueur first arrived in Hollywood, she had nothing but the standard short-term contract. No money, no experience, no education, no social grace, no contacts. She did have good health and gorgeous looks, but there was plenty of both those commodities in Hollywood back then. What Lucille Le Sueur had that the others lacked was an ironclad, almost pathological determination to succeed. She embarked on a self-improvement campaign that left the film capital breathless.

She capped her teeth, dieted, spent endless hours in a gym. She took elocution lessons, as well as voice, dance, and acrobatic instruction. She lingered around sets where top stars performed, then aped their mannerisms, tried on their costumes, memorized their lines. She read books on how to dress, how to walk, how to talk, how to use the right fork, and how to handle the headwaiter. She played every part to the absolute hilt, and willingly spent hours posing for studio photographers. She answered all fan letters in her own handwriting, always with the question, "How do you think I might do better?" Accordingly, she even abandoned her own name and took one that was suggested in a fan contest. She shucked off Lucille Le Sueur like the old skin it was, and stepped out — newly born — as Joan Crawford.

Fans loved her. "She brings happiness to us who are simple and poor," wrote one, and "Gee, she must be swell," mused another. "Before I saw Joan on the screen," a Crawford stalwart wrote in *Photoplay* magazine, "I had no ambitions, no talent, no hopes. But then I saw Joan. She blossomed in my heart, filling it with new hopes. She left me dreaming of a grand future like hers."

Joan Crawford lasted for fifty years as a reigning movie queen because she was the very first American star to truly understand the idea of "image." She could step outside it, study it critically, and shape it to the needs and desires of the moviegoing audience. She was shrewd enough to realize that people wanted her to *be* Joan Crawford.

Crawford played the role of The Star as she felt her public conceived it, mixing her on- and off-screen life in flamboyant style, and fulfilling everyone's notion of glamour — including her own. As a matter of course, she dressed the way she dressed on film whenever she appeared at a premiere or a gathering. Louella Parsons once wrote (for *Photoplay*) about a typical Crawford entrance to a Hollywood party: Crawford walked in deliberately late, so everyone would notice her arrival. She wore an enormous black picture hat trimmed with gigantic plumes, and her dress was Adrian-designed and stark black with dramatic lines. On one-well-padded shoulder she had pinned her famous star sapphires and diamonds. While other Hollywood beauties at the party faded into the woodwork, Crawford slowly, majestically, all eyes upon her, removed one long black glove to reveal a

With Douglas Fairbanks Jr. in Our Modern Maidens.

gigantic star sapphire ring, companion to the shoulder jewels.

Crawford felt she had arrived when she won the Oscar for her excellent portrayal in *Mildred Pierce* (1945). Crawford's Mildred, damp and desperate on a foggy night, is the perfect portrait of a woman trapped. Crawford understood that Mildred could never really get out of the kitchen, even if it were in the expensive restaurant she now owned. It is as Mildred Pierce that Joan Crawford is best remembered, although she represented

Her first husband was star-actor Douglas Fairbanks, Jr.

Her third husband was bit actor Philip Terry (R, at Armed Forces dinner thrown by Jack Warner, Middle).

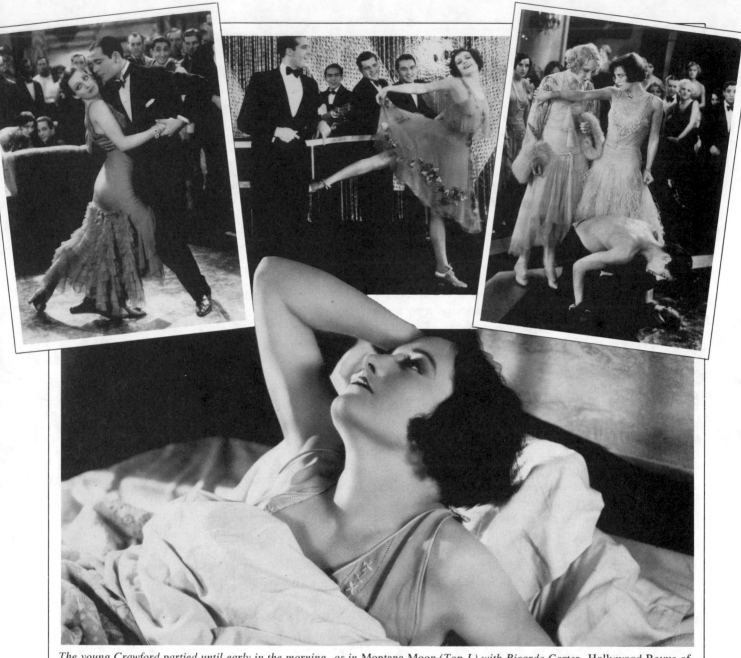

The young Crawford partied until early in the morning, as in Montana Moon *(Top L) with Ricardo Cortez,* Hollywood Revue of 1929 *(Top, center) and* Untamed *(Top, R, with Gwen Lee and Robert Montgomery) and woke up early in the afternoon, as in* Taxi Driver *(Bottom).*

the American woman for more than four decades. Through the years, she was the model for them all: flapper; shopgirl; sophisticated comedienne; career woman; older woman victimized by men after her money or power. Crawford even played with her own persona on film, as in *What Ever Happened to Baby Jane?* (1962).

Her appeal was mostly to women, as she seemed to embody their secret sufferings. She was clearly strong, intelligent, capable. To see her saddled by a weak man, or stuck in the small-town rut, made women feel better about their own fates. Crawford acted out for women their secret wishes; she defied the society that had bound them, and took society's punishment on their be-

half. Women who suffered, and waited, identified with the masklike determination that froze on Crawford's face as the years went by. It was an expression of sisterhood.

Crawford married four times, and, in retrospect, her husbands appear to be a part of her betterment program. Douglas Fairbanks, Jr., represented the grace, elegance, and patrician background to which she aspired. He was the royal prince of Hollywood, and she longed to be its princess. Ironically, long after he was forgotten in films, Crawford was Hollywood's queen.

Franchot Tone, her second husband, brought culture to her life. He was a self-avowed intellectual who completed her education and rubbed off the last of her rough edges.

Her third and least-known husband was Philip Terry, a small-time actor who filled the interim period of Crawford's life when she was between MGM and Warner Brothers. She cooked and kept house for him, but, as she herself put it, ''I owed him an apology from the first.''

Crawford's last husband was Alfred Steele, chairman of the board of Pepsi-Cola. With him Crawford found happiness and a new role as a public relations representative for the company. She shared his work and his life until his untimely death, and remained an active member of Pepsi's board until two years before her own death.

Contrary to popular opinion, Crawford did not always play the grande dame during those last years. She maintained a rigorous schedule, but at home she usually dressed simply, wore no makeup, and wore her hair tied simply in a knot on top of her head. She did much of her own cooking and directed the cleaning and running of her household, working closely with her staff. She had a marvelous sense of humor, which she could train upon herself. She was adept at mimicking others, and told funny stories with flair and drama. When I once expressed surprise at how funny she could be, she wryly pointed out, ''If I hadn't had a sense of humor, how could I have survived everything I obviously survived?''

But Crawford never forgot her image. When it was time to go out in public, she would excuse herself from our conversation, enter her bedroom, and emerge less than an hour later in fur and satin; the highest of show-girl heels, with the ever-present straps tightly in place; a glamorous light-blond wig; diamonds glittering at her throat, on her fingers, in her ears. I never had the impression that she was a bit confused about which of her two identities was which.

Some of Joan Crawford's accomplishments went unnoticed. She provided numerous scholarships for young people and supported a variety of charities. She pioneered single-parent adoptions and was instrumental in starting the first day care nursery in Los Angeles. In opening this establishment, she said, ''There are those who clamor that woman's place is in the home, that a mother of small children shouldn't be working. But who is to say who should work and who shouldn't. . . . Besides, the question is largely academic. Women *are* working. Let's face the future.''

She could be tough in business. When Carole Lombard was killed on a war bond-selling tour at the start of World War II, Crawford volunteered to take her place in a minor Metro film, *They All Kissed the Bride* (1942). She donated her entire salary — in Lombard's name — to war relief, and when her agent tried to take his usual ten percent, she fired him outright. As a friend, she was doggedly loyal and loving, generous and open.

Stephen Harvey, in an excellent obituary tribute, correctly analyzed her last years. ''In truth, Joan Crawford was trapped by none other than 'Joan Crawford.' Unfortunate as this might have been, it constituted a curious kind of integrity. A half century of practice had taught Joan Crawford that, above all else, it was the image that counted.''

Immediately following her death, her detractors spread rumors of alcohol, sex scandals, cruelty to her children (''Spare the rod and spoil the child is an adage I follow strictly in my home''), and possible suicide. It was a tribute to her strength of character that no one dared suggest such things while she lived.

As ''queen bee'' in Harriet Craig, *with Wendell Corey.*

Filming Mildred Pierce. *Zachary Scott was unworthy lover.*

"I DON'T BELONG TO ANY MAN"

"I don't belong to any man"

Two kinds of men...two kinds of love...in her life...and when she chooses it must be forever!

JOAN CRAWFORD
DANA ANDREWS
HENRY FONDA in

Daisy Kenyon

with
RUTH WARRICK
MARTHA STEWART
PEGGY ANN GARNER
CONNIE MARSHALL
NICHOLAS JOY · ART BAKER

Produced and Directed by OTTO PREMINGER · Screen Play by

A 20th CENTURY-FOX ROMANTIC HIT!

ALTHOUGH ALMOST ALL of Crawford's films through the years were centered around her attempts to find, entice, win, trap, control, marry, and/or hold on to a man, this ad for *Daisy Kenyon* (L), in which Crawford expressed her independence, was entirely believable and consistent with the public's image of Crawford. It is true that Crawford's characters thought that they needed men, but the public was always aware that Crawford's women were stronger, and far more interesting, intelligent, and worthwhile than the men she often fell for. The public knew that Crawford's women could make it on their own quite easily—and be better off. The fact that she usually *stayed* with these men and suffered is what women all over the country (in similar situations) related to.—J.B.

In her first film *Pretty Ladies* (Below), the only time she was credited as Lucille Le Sueur, Joan Crawford played a chorus girl with a drink in one hand and Tom Moore in the other. In *Paris,* Crawford found the first of her many unworthy love interests, an Apache dancer played by Douglas Gilmore. Joan Crawford typically represented the ''modern woman'' throughout her long career. She looked misplaced, and misused, when cast in period pieces such as *Winner of the Wilderness*. Tim McCoy, destined for stardom as a western hero, was also uncomfortable in this romantic tale set during the French and Indian War. Crawford became even more popular with the coming of sound. The flapper had become a shopgirl, but her interests remained the same. In *Our Blushing Brides*, Crawford was matched with handsome Robert Montgomery, a romantic lead whom M-G-M used to make its heroines look nicer. By 1956, when *Autumn Leaves* was released, Joan Crawford was firmly established as the Queen of Hollywood's suffering women. Psychotic Cliff Robertson was only one of the many destructive men who made Crawford's characters miserable.

GARY COOPER: NATURAL TALENT

JEFF COREY

He stands for basic American ideals.

THERE IS A CONTINUING THEME in early American drama that underscores the fledgling republic's distaste for snobbism. It is exemplified in Royall Tyler's *The Contrast,* which delineated, in 1787, the superficiality of the British as compared to square-dealing American colonists. The most popular play in the first half on the nineteenth century was Anna Cora Mowatt's *Fashion; or Life in New York,* which lauded American simplicity and honesty over the self-conscious foppishness of European aristocrats. The leading character was called Adam Trueman — an obvious play on a *damn true man*.

Gary Cooper, in most of his films, represented the mythic *damn true man*. He embodied all our folk heros: Davy Crockett, Johnny Appleseed, Uncle Sam, Old Hickory, Honest Abe, Wild Bill, and Dan'l Boone. He was endowed with a handsome, virile aspect, a lean body, a rustic grace that with enough rough edges made him appealing to men as well as women. There was no "pretty boy" in his nature.

He stumbled into the motion picture industry at one of its clumsiest junctures: the transition from silents to talkies. Standards appropriate to the new technology had not been fixed, and it appeared to be a felicitous time for this untrained young man who, until then, had made only a modest impression in silent pictures.

If there is a classification of "primitives" among actors, Cooper would be among them (along with Wallace Beery, Walter Brennan, and John Wayne). A primitive, in art, lacks professional and/or traditional training and has a capacity for intuitive and hitherto unlearned devices, improvising as he goes along. Cooper was a brilliant actor of this kind.

His ineptitude was often his appeal. People would watch him tolerantly — like doting parents at a school play. Among professionals there was grudging apprecia-

---

JEFF COREY *is an actor-stage director who has appeared in such films as* The Killers, Brute Force, Home of the Brave, Bright Leaf, The Next Voice You Hear, *and* Only the Valiant.

Worldly Barbara Stanwyck and duped, naive Cooper in Capra's Meet John Doe.

tion, tinged with the disclaimer "He really can't act." Yet many an actor, consciously or unconsciously, emulated Cooper.

It seems to me that in much of his work there is an unfinished quality that is often distracting. He came to the environment of the film but did not always *enter* it. He *approximates* Robert Jordan in *For Whom the Bell Tolls* (1943) and the deserter-hero in *A Farewell to Arms* (1932). It was because of Cooper's personal aura that audiences ascribed more credence to his characters than he himself could actually inject.

There were mishaps such as *The Adventures of Marco Polo* (1938), in which he awkwardly plays the Venetian explorer, and a series of drawing room comedies directed by the urbane Ernst Lubitsch in which Cooper, uncomfortably decked out in white tie and tails, goes through the motions.

There is a complaint about certain actors that "they always play themselves." It is a valid complaint when the actor's "self" is limited to a few highly recognizable and predictable mannerisms. There is another kind of actor whose range of self is so extensive that one cannot seem to get enough, such as some of Cooper's contemporaries, Paul Muni, Walter Huston, Claude Rains, and Edward G. Robinson. Others had wide scope for

characterization: Cary Grant, Robert Montgomery, James Stewart, Spencer Tracy, and James Cagney. But Cooper was unique: He got more mileage from his limited repertoire of devices than most others. When the amalgam of writer, director, and Cooper fused, the actor was remarkable. Very few players have amassed credits

With Marion Davies in Operator 13.

as distinguished: *Mr. Deeds Goes to Town* (1936); *The Westerner* (1940); *Sergeant York* (1941), for which Cooper received his first Oscar; *Pride of the Yankees* (1942); *Friendly Persuasion* (1956); and *High Noon* (1952), for which he received his second Oscar.

I did a screen test with Cooper in 1950. It was for *Bright Leaf* (1950), and I was competing along with eight or nine young actors. I was trying very hard and had some concrete ideas about how to play my role. Happily, director Michael Curtiz was pleased with my approach, and Cooper also indicated that he liked what I was doing. Then, in self-effacing manner, Cooper explained that he had not been before a camera for about a year (he had been on a safari with Ernest Hemingway) and apologized for his stiffness in the scene we had rehearsed.

I, in turn, overwhelmed that he was even doing a test with me, found myself assuring him that he was very good indeed, and that he needn't worry about it. Coop felt compelled to reply, "I only have two or three tricks at best, and that's not enough is it?"

We were called to the set, and in the course of filming he did, in fact, resort to highly recognizable Cooperisms. But I responded to them eagerly, and I'm sure they helped me get the role.

I talked a great deal with Coop during the making of *Bright Leaf*. He was a man of wide range and interests. I spent so much time with him that Curtiz referred to me as "Gary Cooper's student." I accepted the reference as an accolade.

One day Coop and I were discussing the theater. I had just finished a ten-week run in the Actor's Lab production of *Abe Lincoln in Illinois,* playing the title role. I discussed at some length my approach to Lincoln's character.

With Cecil B. De Mille on set of The Story of Dr. Wassell.

He was at his best with old-time character actors such as Vladimir Sokoloff in For Whom the Bell Tolls *(Above) and Walter Brennan in* The Westerner.

He won Oscar for High Noon *(Top, with Lon Chaney, Jr., Thomas Mitchell, Harry Morgan, Otto Kruger, and Grace Kelly), twelve years after he won for* Sergeant York *(L, with George Tobias and Joe Sawyer).*

Cooper offered some astonishing information. He not only knew a great deal about the play, but told me with some reluctance that Robert E. Sherwood had written it for him. (In fact, a portrait of Cooper as he might have looked as Lincoln had appeared in a 1936 issue of *Stage* magazine.) When the finished play was submitted to him, he admired it enormously but felt he didn't have the experience to cope with so massive a role. It had tortured him to refuse it, he said. But he may have been right to turn it down. His effectiveness on film may not have translated to the stage.

He knew theater people and all of them took to him. Clifford Odets, who wrote Coop's film *The General Died at Dawn* (1936), made a reference to him in Joe

Bonaparte's dialogue in his play *Golden Boy*. In the park scene Joe sees an expensive sports car go by and remarks, "Gary Cooper's got the kind I want."

When the Stage Society of Los Angeles was formed in 1951, Cooper attended Michael Chekov's acting classes. Along with Patricia Neal, Arthur Kennedy, and his friend Akim Tamiroff, he participated in some of Chekov's improvisations based on the play-within-a-play in *Hamlet*. It was evident that this modest superstar still held a deep interest in the acting process.

When I taught my first acting classes, Coop asked me if he could sit in on some of the sessions. I told him I would be very proud. And he sat along with the others, absorbed and attentive. I urged him to make comments along the way but, true to his taciturn nature, he rarely participated. Throughout his long career — thirty-four years and over a hundred and twenty feature films — there *was* that reticence, a visible reluctance to commit himself fully. His voice sounded tentative and unequivocal at the same time. He maintained a brave but modest posture, worried when assailed but damned capable in a pinch. His was a paradoxical presence, heroic and uncertain, able to hold his own in the most awesome confrontations — but who always seemed vulnerable.

MICKEY MOUSE: DISNEY'S STAND-IN

LAWRENCE EDWARD WATKIN

The Sorcerer and his apprentice in Fantasia.

©WALT DISNEY PRODUCTIONS

A S WALT DISNEY used to tell me: Animation was tough, but at least a producer didn't have to worry about temperamental actors. His animated stars never blew their lines; they behaved exactly as he wished them to behave. Mickey Mouse, Disney's most famous creation, behaved so admirably, in fact, that he enjoyed — indeed, continues to enjoy — a popular success and international appeal far exceeding that of any actor who ever lived. Furthermore, though he has undergone several changes in the course of his long life, he has remained basically the same likable little fellow — and the end is not yet in sight. Folklorists, digging through the rubble of our civilization a millennium or two hence, may conclude that the Egyptians worshiped a cat and Americans worshiped a mouse.

Before Mickey, Disney had had some success with a cartoon series that starred Oswald the Lucky Rabbit. He lost Oswald when his New York distributor exercised his option as owner of the character in an attempt to freeze Disney out.

LAWRENCE EDWARD WATKIN *is a screenwriter who had a long association with Walt Disney. Among his credits are* Darby O'Gill and the Little People, The Light and the Forest, Treasure Island, The Story of Robin Hood, The Sword and the Rose, *and* Rob Roy. *He is the original author of* The Great Locomotive Chase.

Instead of being defeated, Walt created Mickey Mouse. Alone and lonely in his garret studio in Kansas City, Walt had watched the antics of the mice who frequented his wastebasket. Legend has it that he gave the name Mortimer to the brightest little mouse. Somebody, probably Walt's wife Lillian, thought Mortimer too pompous. Mickey Mouse sounded less pretentious, and it stuck.

In many ways, Mickey's physical appearance was not so different from Oswald's: his head, body, ears, his big shoes at the end of his pipestem legs (a kid dressing up in his father's shoes), his plumlike nose, the two big pearl buttons fore and aft to hold up his pants. As with Oswald, no animal hair was showing. His hands, gloved

The first sound cartoon, Steamboat Willie.

to remove any unpleasant possibility of claws, had only four fingers, keeping them proportionately small and easier to animate. Like Oswald, he wore a black shirt and red pants, but unlike Oswald he became a character endowed with a distinct personality.

To understand the affection the public showered on Mickey Mouse, one must know his personality. Mickey is enterprising, adventurous, never satisfied with the same old humdrum — if safe — existence. Often life slaps him down, but he takes the lesson to heart and tries to do better. He is never defeated, suicidal, or filled with hate, jealousy, or vengefulness. His faith in himself never falters. His outstanding characteristics are his cheerfulness and his optimism. And he is mischievous. Not mean — mischievous. He shared almost all these traits with Walt Disney.

Mickey might have played out his limited role as just another cartoon character, but Walt, who hated repeating himself, wanted Mickey to be identified with something no cartoonist had ever tried: sound. With the help of a small staff (Ub Iwerks, Wilifred Jackson, and Les Clark figured most prominently), Walt designed a new sound cartoon for Mickey called *Steamboat Willie* (1928). It took time, money and a lot of salesmanship for Walt to get a New York studio to record a sound track, replete with music and sound effects. *Steamboat Willie* was a sensation. Booked at the Roxy, it was to the movie short what *The Jazz Singer* (1927) was to the feature picture.

In *Steamboat Willie* (and in Mickey's subsequent

sound films) it was the virtuoso combination of action and sound that made audiences cheer. The high point of the film is a rendition of "Turkey in the Straw." Mickey and Minnie, who was introduced in this film, play out the barnyard classic by turning domestic animals into musical instruments — a sow's udder is a bagpipe, a goat who swallows some sheet music is a barrel organ, a cat's tail a violin, a cow's teeth a xylophone — while the cook's pots and pans hanging on a bulkhead were an enticement to the characters. The short was so fast and merry it hit the unsuspecting audiences with a bang.

In subsequent shorts Mickey was always rescuing Minnie, either from lustful villains like "Pegleg" Pete or from burning buildings or runaway trains. In these roles, it is a boy in the body of a mouse who is performing these heroic deeds, an incongruity made acceptable by the casual and adroit manner of his derring-do. Mickey never essayed the grand manner of an Errol Flynn; rather his antics resembled the resourcefulness and comic style of two of Walt's heroes, Douglas Fairbanks and Chaplin's Little Tramp. (Walt admired Chaplin so much that he made his artists study his routines.)

After Mickey had played every imaginable adventure role, Walt might have changed his personality so that new stories could have been developed around him. Instead, he introduced a "gang" — Donald Duck, Pluto, and Goofy, who had the low buffoonery that Walt would not allow Mickey. The Mouse, as Walt always called him, remained lovable for his inherent goodness.

Many critics have praised and an equal number lam-

With Donald Duck in The Band Concert.

basted Mickey's unwavering decency. The scoffers insist that, for economic reasons, Walt was purposely toadying to the puritanical strain in the bourgeois American middle class. That was simply not so. Walt truly loved innocence. Hollywood moguls, envious of Walt's financial success, were aware that people who never patronized other types of films would go to a Disney movie. Although these producers tried to imitate Walt's decency, they never quite got the hang of it. The public knew the difference.

This strength of Mickey's character paid off in the first color cartoon, *The Band Concert* (1935). Both the public and the captious critics got a full measure of entertainment in this sparkling classic. Mickey, as the bandleader in the village park, is so earnest as he conducts that the viewer has to take him seriously, even though the long sleeve of his bandmaster's coat keeps falling down to hide his baton. You snigger but with a certain respect. Mickey, conducting the "William Tell Overture," is first tormented by a pesky bee. Every sideswipe of the baton is answered by the bandsmen. Mickey grimly regains his composure and is sailing along smoothly when a glowering Donald Duck waddles in as a spectator. The Duck can't abide the highfalutin music, sneaks a flute out of his clothes, and counters with "Turkey in the Straw," seducing the orchestra to play the diversionary tune. As fast as Mickey destroys the flutes, Donald produces another one, till finally Donald is apparently frisked clean. Now Mickey regains control and leads the band into a spirited storm passage that engenders a tornado. Musicians, their instruments, park benches, everything is whirled aloft by the power of the twister, but so forceful is Mickey's leadership that through it all no player ever misses a single note. Not a word is spoken but the film is magnificent. Toscanini saw it six times.

Like *The Band Concert,* the "Sorcerer's Apprentice" segment in *Fantasia* (1940) has no dialogue. The magician leaves his cave briefly, ordering his apprentice, Mickey, to fill a big vat with water. Mickey, averse to the drudgery of carrying so many bucketfuls of water from the well, can't resist putting on his master's tall hat and peeking into his book of magic. There he finds the charm that will turn a broom into a robot to fetch the water for him. Now Mickey is free to sit back and daydream. He dreams of conducting not an orchestra, a favorite theme in the cartoons, but the planets. His small baton keeps the sparkling, swirling gems in their orbits.

Standing on a promontory of rock, the tiny figure is silhouetted against a luminous heavenly background as he directs the white baubles clustered around his head. He directs an ocean wave to crash against the rock on which he is perched and is suddenly brought out of his reverie by real water splashing over him. The broomstick has filled the vat to overflowing, but Mickey can't find the charm to stop it. Attacking the automaton with an ax, Mickey smashes it to bits, but every splinter becomes another robot broomstick with its own bucket. They relentlessly bring in tons of water. Mickey, swept away in the maelstrom, clings to the book of magic, trying to turn the pages to find a reverse incantation. At the last moment the sorcerer returns and restores order. Crestfallen, Mickey resumes his humble apprenticeship, yet he had his moment of glory. Walt does not belabor the moral, but in this great tribute to Mickey, the Mouse attains a dignity far beyond the scope of any of his other cartoons.

In 1978, Mickey Mouse celebrated his fiftieth birthday. You can find him at Disney World, in Florida, where, as a live actor, he is the official greeter. I'm sure Walt would have wanted it to be Mickey to have this position, since he can no longer be there himself.

The late Walt Disney. His mouse lives on.

JOHN WAYNE: STRAIGHT FROM THE HIP

MOLLY HASKELL

The most durable star of the talking picture.

WAYNE REPRESENTS to me those true conservative values — personal humor and integrity, commitment, and responsibility . . . He represents the West as an imaginary land, a place of hope, compromised by death but undiluted by vulgarity. Monument Valley is our inverted Olympus, a place which sprung forth the gods and goddesses appropriate to our mental landscape. His West, encompassing home-grown fantasies, gave us myths built out of contradictory urges — the urge to settle down and the urge to move on; the need to be alone and the need to save; the love of woman and the love of man; strength and vulnerability. And it is Wayne who stands on all borders, at the crossroads of our mythic universe, reconciling, in a dozen glorious performances, the warring ambitions of which his political persona is a crude distortion.

It would be a mistake to take as sum of the man this stereotype drawn from Wayne's politics and, to the extent that it is based on his films at all, the war pictures rather than the great Ford and Hawks films which many have not seen at all. Consider the xenophobic, violently anti-Indian Ethan Edwards of *The Searchers* (1956), the arrogant and obtuse cattle driver of *Red River* (1948), the prudish male chauvinist of *The Quiet Man* (1952), the fanatic naval commander, "Spig" Wead in *The Wings of Eagles* (1957). These subtle and complex Wayne performances in no way correspond to the image of the neanderthal he-man, territorially and sexually on the make, with which his name has become synonymous.

Wayne was not a lusty sort in the oh-ho-ho fanny-pinching tradition, not one to carouse with the boys or leer at women. There was none of the compulsive

MOLLY HASKELL *is a former film critic for the* Village Voice, Viva, *and* New York *magazine. She has contributed to numerous publications on film and is the author of* From Reverence to Rape.

womanizing of the male chauvinist or, on a subtler level, the sexual indifference that is as much a part of the macho pose as swagger. Wayne had his own mission, his own promises to keep — to a woman, to a battalion, to a dead friend. The fact that it was a private sort of mission, one he wouldn't blab about, means that he would not fit in with the current notion — supposedly a by-product of the Woman's Movement — that men should drop the stoical pose and open up their souls and tear ducts.

Wayne didn't wear his heart on his sleeve (and frankly, does any woman really want a crybaby?), but he was as deeply emotional as his voice and his eyes would so eloquently convey. He was secure enough in his masculine identity to listen to women, and in his roles as character lead he could often respond to them with less vanity and more humanity than could a romantic lead. His relationships with women were shy, but giving. If he thought he was better off on his own, it was not from the narcissism of the compulsive loner, but because he hadn't yet come to understand what he generally would come to understand: that men and women could be not only lovers but friends. One of the nicest aspects of *The Shootist* (1976) is the December-December relationship with Bacall, a friendship that never feels compelled to blossom into romance.

Once a top star of serials.

Wayne has had more than one adult love affair on film — with Katharine Hepburn in *Rooster Cogburn* (1975), with Angie Dickinson in *Rio Bravo* (1959), with Colleen Dewhurst in *McQ* (1974), and perhaps most

COURTSHIP

gloriously with Patricia Neal in *In Harm's Way* (1965). How many other maturing male stars have allowed themselves to be paired with women who were roughly their contemporaries, instead of dropping back one generation, then another?

He might, from the vantage point of his own Puritanism, look askance at the woman of the world (Angie Dickinson in *Rio Bravo*) or the proud Irishwoman (Maureen O'Hara in *The Quiet Man*), but he would eventually learn the lesson of moral relativity at their instruction, and accept the self-defining woman on her own terms.

In his older roles, the aging gunfighters of *El Dorado* (1967) and *Rio Lobo* (1970), he has become quite frankly a father figure, leaning on his fictional offspring, acknowledging his limitations.

Perhaps the consummate image was in John Ford's great *The Searchers*, when Wayne finally comes upon the niece (Natalie Wood), now grown and living among the Indians, who has formed the object of his search and every waking thought for twelve years. Every reflex in this wracked and obsessive man points to casting her out, but Wayne leans down and picks her up, and embraces her. It is a reconciliation not only of uncle (or father) and

Not a bad film, but criticized for its anti-Indian sentiment.

daughter, but of polar emotions: Love dissolves hatred, mercy dissolves authoritarianism, maternal and paternal instincts unite in a single, all-encompassing parent figure.

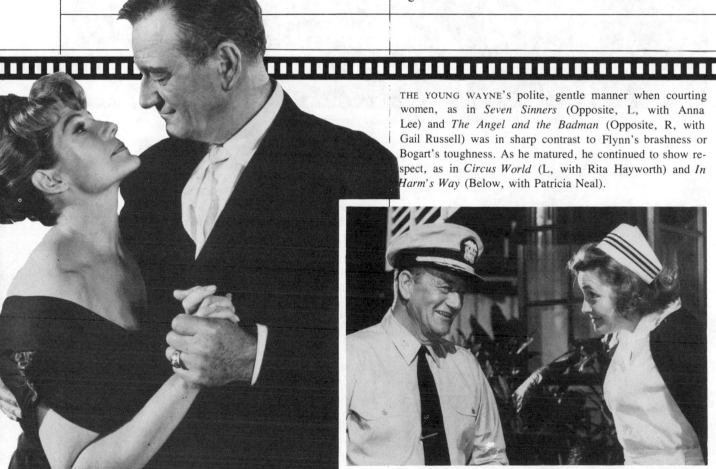

THE YOUNG WAYNE'S polite, gentle manner when courting women, as in *Seven Sinners* (Opposite, L, with Anna Lee) and *The Angel and the Badman* (Opposite, R, with Gail Russell) was in sharp contrast to Flynn's brashness or Bogart's toughness. As he matured, he continued to show respect, as in *Circus World* (L, with Rita Hayworth) and *In Harm's Way* (Below, with Patricia Neal).

In John Ford's She Wore a Yellow Ribbon. *With John Agar (L) and Harry Carey, Jr.*

As Davy Crockett in The Alamo, *which he directed.*

Women unblinded by the prejudice of fashion have always responded to the authentic, non-tough-guy Wayne — witness Joan Didion's lovely tribute to him in the *Saturday Evening Post* some years ago. It is men who seem to be made uncomfortable by him, by his politics, and increasingly, by his age — by his toupee, his "trying to keep up." Movie heroes, like movie heroines, are supposed to vanish with their first gray hair, so as not to remind us of our own mortality.

John Wayne keeps working. He turns down scripts that are too dirty (like *Dirty Harry* [1971]), or cleans them up. For instance, *The Shootist* was, he felt, too graphic in its description of the cancer, too heavy, too downbeat in its ending. In the original, before Wayne had it altered, the Ron Howard character is a thoroughgoing punk, who not only is unredeemed at the end but performs the final rip-off of the dead gunfighter. Wayne had it cleaned up morally and made funnier.

His conversation is full of four-letter words, and his

real-life behavior hardly conforms to his more idealized screen behavior, but as the characters he played in Ford's films understood, the legend must be preserved. The irony is that he has become the legend he once served. In *Fort Apache* (1948) and *The Man Who Shot Liberty Valance* (1962), it was he who did the gritty work for which others claimed the glory. Now it is he who controls, and others who sustain, his image. He will allow himself to look old, he will allow himself to be killed, but he will not go down in disgrace and without purpose.

As images go, it's not chic, but a man could do worse.

Wayne and James Stewart, who had very different screen personalities, appeared together in Ford's The Man Who Shot Liberty Valance *(Below) and in Don Siegel's* The Shootist.

JAMES CAGNEY: MAN OF PRINCIPLE

ABEN KANDEL

Present-day stars Redford and Eastwood rate him "the best."

O VER A SPAN of more than half a century, I have met and worked with stars of vaudeville, the legitimate theater, and films. I can say, emphatically, that the most dedicated of these, the most absolutely professional was James Cagney. And these qualities paid off; Cagney, in a long career of performances, produced imperishable gems, too numerous to catalogue.

I had the pleasure of knowing him when he was preparing to play the role of Joey, a prize-fighter in the film version of my novel *City for Conquest* (1940). In the book Joey fought as a lightweight, 135-pound limit. At that time Cagney weighed about 180. Of medium height, he had a powerful, stocky build. He moved with enviable speed and grace.

ABEN KANDEL *is a novelist and screenwriter whose book* City for Conquest *was adapted into a film that starred James Cagney. Among his screen credits are* The Iron Major, Singing in the Dark, Timetable, *and* Berserk!.

But because of the weight discrepancy, it was suggested that Joey could be made a middleweight of 160 pounds, or even a light-heavyweight, 175 pounds. Cagney shook his head.

"You wrote about a tenement kid from Forsythe Street, the lower East Side. Where would he get the grub to put that much heft and muscle on his bones? What did you weigh when you were living there? What did I weigh in Yorkville? Joey stays a lightweight."

This decision, in a single sentence, meant for Cagney a period of relentless, disciplined, agonized training. I know something about fighters and I doubt any title contender ever trained harder than Cagney did for that

On set of A Midsummer Night's Dream.

Gangster in The Roaring Twenties, *with Frank McHugh and Humphrey Bogart.*

film role. In addition to his gym togs, he wore a rubber suit to help him sweat off surplus weight. He worked the pulleys, the rowing machine, all the equipment. He jogged, skipped rope, shadowboxed, then sparred a few rounds. It was grueling work, day in, day out. I could think of no other star who would have made such sacrifices for a role. In the end, Cagney shed forty-five pounds. He entered the film ring as a legitimate lightweight.

For his opponent in the film, Warners cast a former professional boxer, who had not only been cautioned but scrupulously taught how to pull his punches. In one take, he lost his head and stupidly landed a haymaker on Cagney's chin. The enraged star, a veteran of a hundred street fights, retaliated with a punch that still rattles in my memory. The ex-pro's knees buckled, and as he sank to the canvas, ready for a long count, the director shouted, "Cut and print."

One memorable evening Jimmy invited me to have dinner at Chasen's restaurant with his brother Bill, who functioned as his producer, financial adviser, and inseparable pal. (In fact, all the Cagneys were close; the family was a model of love and unity.)

In the course of a marvelous talkfest that lasted through the night, Bill and I guzzled a couple of bottles of Jack Daniels, a carafe or two of wine, a decanter of Remy-Martin, and devoured a mountain of food. All through this orgy at this elegant restaurant, Jimmy sipped Perrier water and for dinner consumed a few lettuce leaves with lemon juice dressing. I marveled at his willpower. I also wondered about the secret of his Samsonlike strength. How could he survive the ordeal of his role, how could he portray a prizefighter so beautifully,

so naturally, with the enormous expenditure of energy the part demanded? The secret was within. He was born with a vast reservoir of strength and drive, remarkable dedication and discipline. His mind was organized and he had absolute control and mastery of his superbly trained body.

Talk was the nourishment Jimmy craved. That night at Chasen's we traded tales and reminiscences about the gutters of New York City in which we had been raised.

LOST ON THE CUTTING ROOM FLOOR

IN HIS AUTOBIOGRAPHY, Cagney recalled:

I worked like a dog on *City for Conquest*. There were some excellent passages in Kandel's novel, passages with genuinely poetic flavor, and all of us doing the picture realized that retaining them (as we were doing) would give *City for Conquest* distinction. Then I saw the final cut of the picture, and this was quite a surprise. The studio had edited out the best scenes in the picture, excellent stuff, leaving only the novel's skeleton. What remained was a trite melodrama. When I realized what they had done, I said to hell with it, and that cured me of seeing my pictures thenceforth. I even wrote a letter of apology to the author.
— A. K.

As boxer who loses sight in City for Conquest.

Mine was Forsythe Street, his was East Seventy-ninth Street in Yorkville. In terms of class and marginal prosperity, Cagney's street had the edge on mine. Some of the tenements on Forsythe Street still had toilets in the yard. Uptown, they were in the hall — one for every two families. But the poverty, the chronic unemployment, fear of eviction, and constant street fighting were similar.

We talked of the incessant need to work; at one point in his youth, Jimmy held down three jobs — and always the pay envelopes were delivered intact to his mother. One of his minor jobs was that of Shabbas *goy*. For one cent, he would light the gas stove in the house of an Orthodox Jewish family. This experience helped him cultivate his amazing fluency in Yiddish.

We both had electrifying memories of Election Day fires. In that period, more than sixty years ago, Election

CAGNEY WRITES ABOUT MAE CLARKE

MAE CLARKE was a very professional actress who knew what was required of her and did her job excellently. The [film] business being the uncertain quantity that it is, there is no explanation for the ascendancy of some and the lack of that for some. Mae worked for years in the business after our films together without receiving any great return.

— From a letter to Danny Peary, January 31, 1978

He treated Mae Clarke roughly in famous grapefruit scene from Public Enemy *(Top) and in* Lady Killer.

With Virginia Mayo and Edmond O'Brien in Raoul Walsh's White Heat, *one of his best gangster films.*

Day — for the gutter-ites — was very special because they enjoyed almost total freedom. With the police away at the polling places making sure foreigners and other riffraff voted for the correct Tammany candidates, the young hooligans used to build huge bonfires in the street. Jimmy and I recalled how we would start collecting wood in late August for the November fires, and how

many heads were broken in raids on the secret caches of this stored firewood. For hours the flames would consume stolen chairs, tables, mattresses, beds, sometimes whole pushcarts. The flames rose as high as the fifth floor, windows crackling like gunshots, tenants screaming in terror.

Well, if one had to reminisce about life in New York slums, the ideal place for it was Chasen's.

The Mayor of Hell, *with Madge Evans.*

Talking to James Stewart and Orson Welles.

SPENCER TRACY: HE COULD WITHER YOU WITH A GLANCE

STANLEY KRAMER

I CAN'T EXPLAIN why I was never able to say to him what I wanted to say: that he was a great actor. Everyone else said it a thousand times over, but I never managed it. Once I told him I loved him. That came quite easily, and he believed me and was emotional about it. But I was afraid to say, "Spencer, you're a great actor." He'd only say: "Now what the hell kind of thing is that to come out with?" He wanted to know it; he needed to know it. But he didn't want you to *say* it — just *think* it. And maybe that was one of the reasons he was a great actor. He thought and listened better than anyone in the history of motion pictures. A silent close-up reaction of Spencer Tracy said it all.

Those who know say that nobody — but nobody — could drink or fight or cause more trouble than Tracy in his early days in Hollywood. He came to California out of a smash success on Broadway as Killer Mears in *The Last Mile* and started a one-man rebellion. The studio publicity departments kept a lot more out of the papers than they put in. But he did *Captains Courageous* (1937) and *Boys Town* (1938) and a lot of other great things. And he looked and behaved like Everyman. Clark Gable was taller and more handsome and more of a sex symbol, but in *Test Pilot* (1938) all the men and half the women in the audience wanted Tracy to get Myrna Loy.

He was full of surprises. He never stopped rebelling, but he did stop drinking. And who could have forecast that the red hair would turn pure white? Or that he would

The Old Man and the Sea. *Tracy is probably the most natural cinema actor.*

STANLEY KRAMER *directed Spencer Tracy in* Inherit the Wind; Judgment at Nuremberg; It's a Mad, Mad, Mad, Mad World; *and* Guess Who's Coming to Dinner? *He has been nominated for an Academy Award as Best Director four times, and received a special Oscar for "his great achievements in the art of the motion picture." His latest film is* The Runner Stumbles.

rent a house on a hillside and, instead of going out every night, never go out at all? His intimate friends came to him, a few people at a time, on the hillside where he held court and exchanged gossip and news and conversation: Chester Erskine from *The Last Mile;* the Kanins, Hepburn, Cukor, and the Jean Negulescos from the full years; Abe Lastfogel, his agent. I brought up the rear like a chapter titled "The Last Decade." No matter what play or performance or book might be discussed, nothing could match his insatiable desire for plain gossip. What went on at the Daisy Club was really a fascination. He announced and savored as a choice tidbit each new pairing off of the jet set. I never understood his sources — most of the time I thought he made it all up — but usually he was right.

Spencer Tracy retired from films fourteen times in his last ten years. Before each film he announced his retirement — and then again upon its completion. Somehow I thought these last years were a great put-on. I mean he put us all on because he had become so impatient. Katharine Hepburn said many times that he was much too impatient for the time and place in which he found himself. He was impatient with agents and lawyers and publicity men and reporters and photographers and directors and the whole damned system. He knew he was irritable so he put everybody on to cover it. He was ill — on and off — and that didn't help. So he stood under the hot lights and perspired through the extra takes and the technical nuisances. The cameraman would ask for another take, and Tracy would just stare back disgustedly. He *was* disgusted, but he fixed that look so that you knew he would do it again anyhow. He would work now only in modern dress with no makeup. That meant he could breeze in ready for work with no "nonsense," as he called it. If a makeup man tried to powder-puff his forehead, Tracy would push him away and give him a look as though he were somebody he had just thrown up. The crew came to know those interchanges were really what Tracy enjoyed.

We would always start the film with a "closed set." Tracy didn't want a bunch of idiots clambering all over the place. One week later it was like Las Vegas. Everybody was there to see him: bookies, ballplayers, fighters, and press, along with a million actors just there to watch. He loved to get hold of a small press group and disagree with everything asked or said. He'd finally get himself into an indefensible position and then act his way out as though *they* were in the wrong.

Still photographers drove him crazy. He always said he hated stills, and he pretended that he didn't care by looking down at the ground or turning half away from the camera. Then he'd argue that that was the way people stood or looked naturally. He posed for a hundred thousand stills in his time and claimed none of them ever appeared — "except in the B'nai B'rith *Messenger.*"

On the first day of the first picture on which we were

With Loretta Young in A Man's Castle.

associated *(Inherit the Wind* [1960]), I asked him to do an additional take on a scene in which he had mumbled the lines. He looked at me for a full minute with the glance that withers. And I mean a full minute — not fifty-five seconds. He was just giving the crew and assorted spectators a chance to quiet down, and then he said: "Mr. . . . Kramer . . . [it took eight seconds just to say the 'Mr. Kramer'] . . . It . . . has . . . taken . . . me . . . 30 . . . years . . . to . . . learn . . . how . . . to . . . speak . . . lines. . . . If . . . you . . . or . . . a . . . theater . . . arts . . . major . . . from . . . UCLA . . . want . . . to . . . do . . . this . . . speech . . . I . . . am . . . quite . . . willing . . . to . . . step . . . aside." Then he picked me up, shook me a little, dusted me off and said: "All right, we ought to try it again." His speech had nothing to do with this particular scene. He was merely indicating that he couldn't stand still for a lot of takes.

During the filming of *Inherit the Wind,* we had Tracy and Fredric March nose to nose for long courtroom battles in dialogue and assorted histrionics. The stage was filled with people from every office and company on the lot. And how those two luxuriated in the applause of the audience! Every take brought down the house, and their escapades were something to see. March would fan himself vigorously with a large straw fan each time Tracy launched into an oration. Tracy had no props, but he got even. He sat behind March and picked his nose during a three-and-one-half-minute summation.

I think the role of the American judge in the film *Judgment at Nuremberg* (1961) was one of Tracy's favorites. He was nominated for an Academy Award and

With Hedy Lamarr and John Garfield in an adaptation of Steinbeck's Tortilla Flat.

told everyone within hearing that he was voting for Maximilian Schell, the defense attorney in the same film. Tracy would say facetiously, "I just sat there listening and these other fellows did the work." Maybe so, but when he read the last speech in court: "This is what we stand for . . . justice . . . truth . . . and the value of a single human being . . ." I *believed* that was what we stood for, and I won't soon forget how he said it.

Of course, it was impossible to outguess Tracy's attitude or concentration. At one moment he threatened to murder a fellow actor who was nibbling on a pastrami sandwich between takes in one of the courtroom scenes. And he meant it. The following day he played an intensely dramatic scene with Burt Lancaster in a jail cell, and as he turned to exit, he muttered under his breath to Al Horwitz, the publicist: "Nothing to it, Al. A cinch!"

Montgomery Clift was in *Nuremberg*. He was ill — very ill — and it was Tracy who pulled him through. Monty couldn't remember the lines — he was literally going to pieces. Tracy just grabbed his shoulders and told him he was the greatest young actor of his time and to look deep into his eyes and play to him and the hell with the lines. He did, and that saved Monty's life for a little longer because he got an Academy nomination, and he was proud of it.

Spencer Tracy liked Frank Sinatra. I guess it takes one impatient to know another. He would tell with great glee how Sinatra walked off one picture and flew to Rome. Or how he made a company rebuild all its sets in California because he didn't want to go to Madrid. I didn't think it half so amusing as Tracy did, because it had also happened to me. Tracy would complain that he had to play his over-shoulder close-ups in *The Devil at 4 O'Clock* (1961) with a coat hanger because Sinatra wasn't there. Then he would twinkle and say Sinatra had called him and told him he wanted him for his next picture. I don't think this ever happened, but I do think Spencer Tracy knew that he was Spencer Tracy and could afford the anecdote. He told it once too often, because during *It's a Mad, Mad, Mad, Mad World* (1963), Phil Silvers must have mentioned to Tracy a hundred times in front of a thousand people that he would ask for him in his next picture.

During the filming of *Mad World* with all the comedians, I think Spencer Tracy was in poorer health than I could remember: he had bad color and no stamina whatever. But then, even though this lack of energy showed, I think he had his best time ever during the making of a film. The comedians worshiped him. Never before or since has a king had the court full of jesters who strove

Tracy and Fredric March debated the theory of evolution in Stanley Kramer's Inherit the Wind.

only to entertain him so that his majesty might say, "That was funny," or just laugh or smile. Milton Berle, Jonathan Winters, Buddy Hackett, Phil Silvers, Mickey Rooney — even the silent Caesar — crowded about him and vied for his affection. They had it. And he talked about them to the very last; he loved them all.

Spencer Tracy was one of the most sensitive men I've known. He could be hurt easily by commission and omission. Once, after having finished *Ship of Fools,* I told a British newspaperman that I thought Oskar Werner was as fine an actor as I had known. Tracy covered up with what seemed to be a joke. He mailed the piece to me in London with a big red-crayon question mark on it. That was funny, but he actually felt hurt. I got out of it with the truth. I told him that I just didn't think of him in the same category with anyone else.

Tracy was bugged by one recurring question from the press. What advice did he have for young actors? Everyone was waiting for something profound, so he always said: "Learn your lines."

He had no patience with the antics of the young actors whose school technique showed. Many times I heard him say, when a young actor or actress would demand motivation for coming in a door, "You come in the goddamn door because there's no other way to come in the goddamn room."

He had a grand acting reunion on *Guess Who's Coming to Dinner?* (1967) with Katharine Hepburn. She is creative and hard-working and indefatigable. She has the genius to examine the material constantly for that little piece of something that will bring it alive or make it funnier or more poignant. But even Miss Hepburn had better not do this to Tracy too often. He could look at her until her eyes were drawn to his, almost sensing the

sharp edge of his stiletto: "Why don't you just mind your own goddamn business, read the lines, do what he says, and let's get on with it?" She'd make a funny face at him, but we got on with it.

Guess Who's Coming to Dinner? was his last film. He had the energy and the verve and the desire — and not an awful lot of stamina. He was frightened for all of us that he might not get through with the picture. But he did, magnificently, as ever before. Four days before we finished, he put his arm around me and said, "You know, I read the script again last night, and if I were to die on the way home tonight, you can still release the picture with what you've got."

Almost without fail, each time Spencer Tracy did an important scene, feeling the reaction of his fellow actors and the crew and the bystanders, he would call out to the cameraman, "Did you get any of it, Sam?"

Not to hear that again is a desperate thing.

Stanley Kramer for *Life.* Copyright © 1967 Time Inc. Reprinted by permission of the publisher.

With Marlene Dietrich in Judgment at Nuremberg.

A SPECIAL BOND

KATHARINE HEPBURN and Spencer Tracy built their relationship on an affection and concern for each other that shines through all their films together. Through all the battles that are a feature of their films, this affection remains evident. From the arguments over roles of men and women in *Adam's Rib* (1949) to the feminist-versus-family arguments in *Woman of the Year* (1942), to the more conventional family situation of *Guess Who's Coming to Dinner?* (1967), it is another feature of their films together, that each of them is allowed to appear very foolish at one time or another. Being a fool is possible only if there is a great deal of trust in your partner. A trust that is borne out, for in their films their relationship remains such that judgments are not made, reproach is never used, and the ultimate resolution never seems to involve ''winning,'' but rather agreement based on mutual respect. Even their early films are quite ''modern'' in this way.

— Edwin Owens

Desk Set

Without Love

Pat and Mike

Without Love

Woman of the Year

Keeper of the Flame

Guess Who's Coming to Dinner?

KATHARINE HEPBURN: YANKEE INCANDESCENCE

EDWIN OWENS

The cinema's most admired actress.

S HE'S A DIFFERENT KIND of lady. Certainly unconventional, Hollywood has called her an outsider, a loner. Garson Kanin has said she has "the smile of the world." Most people who have worked with her call her "a pro." Katharine Hepburn is a lady of strength and independence; moreover, she is a lady who cares.

In one of her early films, *Sylvia Scarlett* (1935), in which she masquerades for a while as a boy, a proposition is put to young Kate and Edmund Gwenn by Cary Grant: "In this world there is 'awks and pigeons — and those as are 'awks is always over the pigeons."

"I'll be a 'awk," says Edmund Gwenn.

EDWIN OWENS *has appeared on Broadway in* That Championship Season, *in the television series* The Waltons, *and in the latest film version of* King Kong.

"Sure an' so will I," says Kate.

But later in the movie, when she finds that being "an 'awk" involves " . . . doin' honest and workin' people out of their money, and poor servant girls out of their jobs," she wants no part of it. Her nature is to be different, certainly, but it is not her nature to be cruel.

In her first film, *A Bill of Divorcement* (1932), with John Barrymore, Miss Kate's character is called upon "to renounce the world" to take care of her insane father, and because she thinks she may be carrying the seed of madness within herself she accepts her fate with grace, giving up her hopes of love or conventional happiness. The audience can believe this rather outlandish circumstance because it is able to see, through her, that this action is not sacrifice, but simply the necessary and right thing to do — because of her genuine concern both for her father and for the world at large.

It is a truth that film stars and their films exist in a dialectic. The personality of the star illuminates the role, and the role illuminates the star. Throughout her career, Katharine Hepburn's roles are nearly always strong and independent characters. But her strength is that of a concerned person of principle — a strength that does not need or use intimidation. If she is independent, it is the independence of adherence to that principle.

As an actress, Katharine Hepburn is a pro. I say this in the sense that she is an artist who is totally committed to what she does. Her roles are always invested with elegance and style; her wide range of characters varies through careful choices and meticulous attention to detail. As the young sophisticate in *Bringing Up Baby* (1938), she moves with ease and assurance, her speech rapid-fire; and some years later, as a shy spinster in *The African Queen* (1951), she moves slowly and speaks haltingly, diffidently (if resolutely) as she deals with a world totally foreign to her.

Several years ago, a friend of mine was trying to produce a new play. It was a "modern classic," a quite

Disguised as boy in Sylvia Scarlett *with Brian Aherne.*

As small-town girl in Alice Adams. *With Fred MacMurray.*

beautiful and difficult contemporary retelling of the Agamemnon legend done in blank verse. Such plays are at best difficult, and this one was to be no exception. The roles included Agamemnon, Cassandra, and, most important, the central and towering role of Clytemnestra. With the hope that the interest of a star name in doing this Clytemnestra would pique investor interest in the play, scripts were dispatched to a number of "big ladies." Among them, quite naturally, was Katharine Hepburn.

The replies to this approach from an unknown producer to do a classical-style play in blank verse by an unknown playwright were almost identical brief notes from agents or attorneys: either "Miss_____ thanks you for your recent submission. However . . ." or "As agents for Miss_____, we do not feel . . ."

Howard Hawks' screwball-comedy classic Bringing Up Baby, *one of several films Hepburn made with Cary Grant.*

With James Stewart, John Howard, and Mary Nash in The Philadelphia Story.

Song of Love *with Robert Walker (Middle) and Paul Henreid.*

After three or four weeks, my friend thought all replies had been received. Then, at three o'clock one morning, he was awakened by the telephone ringing, and upon answering, there was that unmistakable voice and accent saying, "Hello, Mr._____? Katharine Hepburn here." It was, of course, only midnight in California, and literally unaware that both the hour of the morning and her own distinctive voice might have caused some stir at the other end of the line, Miss Hepburn plunged ahead, asking numerous questions about the play, the playwright, the proposed production, and ended by saying, ". . . well, I just wanted to thank you personally for sending the play to me. I think it is beautiful, and you

must do it immediately. I'm sorry I can't do it. I can't leave Spence, he's just too ill."

An actress friend of mine worked with Katharine Hepburn in a stage production of *Antony and Cleopatra* several years ago. My friend was playing Charmian, Cleopatra's servant and confidante, who is with her throughout the play and assists her in her death. Charmian has several lines of lamentation over the corpse of Cleopatra. One night, as she was saying these lines, she happened to glance down. There was Miss Hepburn, Cleopatra, lying flat on her back on the stage floor with her left (downstage) eye tightly closed, her right (upstage) eye wide open.

"What are you doing?" whispered Charmian to the dead Cleopatra.

"I'm watching you to be sure you do it right," whispered Miss Kate — out of the *upstage* side of her mouth.

As I said, the lady cares.

Dorothy Arzner's Christopher Strong, *with Colin Clive, is a favorite of feminist critics. Hepburn played an aviatrix.*

BETTE DAVIS:
A LIFELONG
LOVE AFFAIR

ALVAH BESSIE

"At our first luncheon, she told me why she was so good at playing neurotic women: 'It's because I'm one of the only non-neurotic women in Hollywood.'" — *A. B.*

IN 1934 I SAT WITH MY FIRST WIFE in a small movie house in New York City, watching *Of Human Bondage* (1934). When Bette Davis appeared on the screen, I took leave — spiritually and emotionally, if not physically — from my wife's side and silently vowed: (1) that I would meet Miss Davis; (2) that I would write a film for her; (3) that I would marry her.

It was therefore inevitable that I found myself in Hollywood, in 1943, at Warner Brothers, staring at Miss Bette Davis calmly writing letters at her luncheon table. A contract writer at the time, I introduced myself one week later and gave her two of my books. Vow number one had been realized.

I was certain nothing Bette Davis could do (aside from marrying somebody else) would ever disappoint me. But she disappointed me three times within the first

ALVAH BESSIE *is a novelist, political historian, and screenwriter. He fought with the International Brigade in the Spanish Civil War and was subsequently, as a member of the Hollywood Ten, imprisoned and blacklisted for refusing to testify before H.U.A.C. in 1947. His credits include* Northern Pursuit, The Very Thought of You, Hotel Berlin, *and* Objective, Burma!, *which was nominated for an Academy Award as Best Original Story of 1945.*

Memorable in Of Human Bondage, *with Leslie Howard.*

As designer in Fashions of 1934, *with William Powell.*

three years after we met.

The first time was at our first luncheon date, when she said that if I changed the ending of the novel I had given her she would get Jack Warner to buy it for her. I tried vainly to explain that the male protagonist's entire life *had* to lead to his electrocution. She was adamant that he could not get the chair. That *was* a blow because I had fondly believed that she was far above such base commercial considerations as upbeat versus downbeat, even in those days.

The second disappointment was not her fault. She had the task of reading the nominees for the 1946 Academy Award in the Original Story category. She emphasized my name beautifully (I was up for *Objective, Burma!* [1945]) — then announced that the Oscar went to somebody else.

But she was clearly at fault the time Vincent Sherman, her director on *Mr. Skeffington* (1944), and I called on her with a petition protesting the fact that Governor Thomas Dewey of New York had so rigged that state's election laws that servicemen who were out of the state at election time lost their vote. Everyone in Hollywood was signing it; there was nothing controversial, nothing radical. Davis was made up for *The Corn Is Green* (1945) as the teacher, Miss Moffat, and was sitting before her dressing-table mirror. She said, "I don't sign petitions."

We argued; we pointed out the un-American, unconstitutional and genuinely subversive nature of the governor's action.

"I'm on your side," she said. "I think it's perfectly scandalous. . . . I once signed a petition to every member of Congress. I've never heard the end of it."

Bette Davis can be simultaneously a magnificent, regal woman and a staggering disappointment — without turning a single blond hair.

★ ★ ★ ★ ★

The years after *Objective, Burma!* brought me a term of exile from Hollywood, thanks to the work of the House Un-American Activities Committee. Miss Davis continued to perform all over the landscape, as I went to prison, then worked five years as a publicity man and editor for Harry Bridges' union, then more than seven years as lightman/stage manager/disembodied offstage voice announcing the acts at the "Hungry i" nightclub in San Francisco. It was there, one night in 1960, that our star comedienne, Kaye Ballard, rushed over to me and gasped, "Guess who's on the same floor with me at the St. Francis Hotel? Bette . . . *Davis!*"

LIGHTMAN: You *want* her to see your show?

BALLARD: You know her?!

LIGHTMAN: Of course. I'll give you a note to leave at the desk.

Every subsequent night Ballard asked, "Has she answered?"

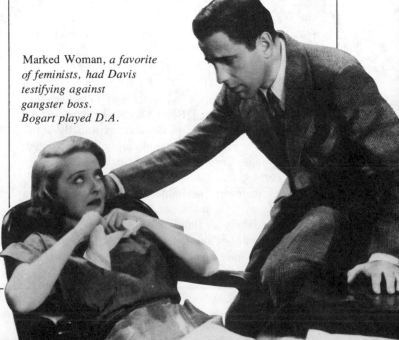

Marked Woman, *a favorite of feminists, had Davis testifying against gangster boss. Bogart played D.A.*

Jezebel, *with Henry Fonda and Margaret Lindsay.*

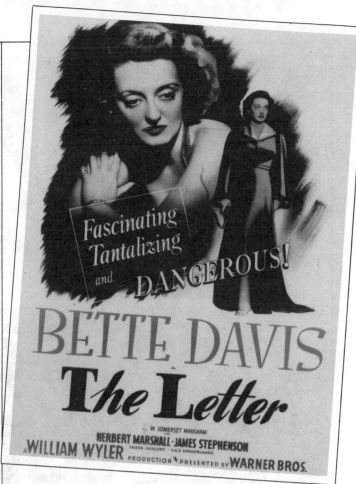

Fascinating
Tantalizing
and
DANGEROUS!

BETTE DAVIS
The Letter

W. SOMERSET MAUGHAM
HERBERT MARSHALL · JAMES STEPHENSON
WILLIAM WYLER   FRIEDA INESCORT · GALE SONDERGAARD
PRODUCTION ★ PRESENTED BY WARNER BROS.

One of her least sympathetic roles, as a murderess.

"No." I wondered what I had said wrong. Or, if she remembered me. After all, it was thirteen years since I had been slid out of Hollywood on my flat ass. I was a pariah, and she, though no longer the Queen of Hollywood, was still a star of the first magnitude.

She was in town to recite Carl Sandburg's poetry with her fourth husband, Gary Merrill.

At eleven one morning when I was sound asleep, my phone rang.

The Voice said, "*Ahl*vah?"

I said, "Huh? Who's this?"

"Betteh! . . . Betteh *Davis!*"

I was awake. I stammered. "How n-nice of you-you to c-call . . ."

"How nice of *you* to invite me to your show. Gary and I will be there Monday night . . ."

Kaye Ballard came on stage that Monday shaking from head to foot. She said in a teeny-tiny voice, "I don't know if I can do . . . do . . . my act . . . *She* . . . is . . . here!"

Bette Davis had already been spotted. People were scurrying back and forth with pens and paper napkins.

Ballard then said, "I want to do a bit about a movie star, but I want to assure Miss Davis that it is *not* about *her.*"

From the darkness came the voice of Margo Channing in *All About Eve* (1950): "*Do* the bit and we'll discuss it later."

Ballard was brilliant. Davis came backstage. I sat on my high stool in front of the switchboard, and after introducing Gary Merrill, she said, "What the hell're you doing *here, Ahl*vah?"

"Making a living," I said. "Sort of."

"Good for *you,*" she said. Then addressing both Ballard and me: "There will be tickets for *our* show, any time you want to come."

Not married at the time, I took my French fiancée. When I asked for our tickets at the box office, the lady looked at me and said dubiously, "You must be a Very Important Person. Miss Davis said you were to have the best seats in the house." I hoped this properly impressed Sylviane. But if that didn't impress her, Davis and Merrill did. They were not reciting Sandburg at all — they were acting him.

Bette Davis possesses not only insuperable acting intelligence but the ability to discern, instantly, the spine of the character she is playing, she can become that character immediately. In movies, she did it in *Jezebel* (1938), *Now, Voyager* (1942), *The Catered Affair* (1956), and *Dark Victory* (1939) — all very different women, all totally unlike the characters she created for *The Petrified Forest* (1936), *Watch on the Rhine* (1943), or *The Scapegoat* (1959). Though her face may not be as protean as it should, *she* is protean.

She became an instant hag, sitting silently in the Tower, in *The Private Lives of Elizabeth and Essex* (1939) after she sent her Essex to his death. With no change in costume or makeup. And in close-up.

In *What Ever Happened to Baby Jane?* (1962) she changed from an insane old bag to a small child in the final scene, with no change in makeup or costume.

And that night in San Francisco she became anything she wished to be, instantly, totally, and with such authority that, when she was supposed to be six feet tall, her four-feet-two became six. She wore an evening gown

Bette Davis characters were rarely friendly with other women. They were too intent on furthering their own ambitions in love and career to let friendship stand in the way. Among women she battled, resented, competed with, were Ann Sheridan in The Man Who Came to Dinner *(Top, L), Miriam Hopkins in* Old Acquaintance *(Top, R), Mary Astor in* The Great Lie *(Bottom, L), and Olivia de Havilland, her sister in* In This Our Life.

that was totally out of character with anything she was doing, but with a cheap shawl over her shoulders and with no change in makeup, she *became* a black woman pleading for the return of her baby. The woman is a theatrical genius.

I took my blue-eyed, rounded but *dark*-haired fiancée backstage to meet the lady. When she offered her hand, Sylviane, who is five feet six, looked down on Davis and said, with total sincerity and considerable awe, "When I was a little girl and saw you on the screen, I never *dreamed* I would someday meet you."

Davis withdrew her hand, turned to me and said, "*Ahl*vah, what're you doing these days aside from working in that sewer?" Another disappointment.

Bette Davis invited me to lunch with her and Gary. She did not invite Sylviane. "She may not like it," Sylviane said, "but the fact is, when I was fourteen she was twenty-six. Please go."

I went. The atmosphere was tense. Conversation was made — mostly by me. I asked the lady when she

was going to make another film. She waved her scotch-and-soda the way she waved her cigarette in *many* films, and said, "I'm a dead duck. In Hollywood they think I'm an old bag. Finished. Why else would we be on the road in this Sandburg thing?"

"Why don't you go to Europe? Even in the Soviet Union they think you're the *only* artist on the American screen."

"Yeah," Merrill growled into his drink, "w'y *don'* you go t'Yurrup an' make a film?"

Davis fixed him with the basilisk eye of Regina Giddens of *The Little Foxes* (1941), and said slowly and firmly, "We have discussed this before . . . (pause, putting down glass) . . . I am not going to Europe to make some shitty, little picture . . . (pause, pointing at ceiling) . . . I am a *star*. I will return to Hollywood when I have a story that pleases me. I will make it on my *own* terms and in my *own* . . . *good* . . . *time* . . . and, I, do, not, want, to, hear, another, word, about, it. . . ."

I was outraged; How *dare* this woman cut her husband down in the presence of another man they scarcely knew. I decided to cut *her* down to size by reminding her, in front of Merrill, of her foolish attitude during her meeting with Vincent Sherman and me. I asked her if she remembered the petition we had presented to her.

"No," she said, "but I'm sure I didn't sign it."

So I told her about it, and she remembered. She also remembered the one petition she *did* sign to every member of Congress. Her reason for signing *that* petition is forever engraved on the tablets of memory: "I am the president of the Tailwaggers' Society of America, and I'm opposed to vivisection."

I repeated this to Miss Davis and Merrill, including how Sherman and I did marvelous acting jobs concealing our desire to laugh. We had allowed that, yes, that *was* a controversial issue, but ours was not something she could get in trouble over. "I'm in no position," she had told us, "to sign petitions." We assured her she was the one person in "the industry" who was in the perfect position to sign it: She was the Queen. She had the respect of the entire population of the country; her example would . . .

Bette Davis had risen from her dressing table, appareled and made up as Miss Moffat, and had said with

all the authority of another person: "Gentleman . . . the audience is at an end."

My story over, Merrill stifled a laugh and stared at his new drink.

She recovered her place as Hollywood's premier actress in 1950, winning an Oscar nomination as Margo Channing in All About Eve, *with Gary Merrill (L) and Gregory Ratoff.*

Davis said quite firmly, ''I never said such a thing.''

I said, ''I'm sorry, Miss Davis. I am sometimes afflicted by total recall and I have told this story seven hundred and twenty-two times since you spoke those words. I have never failed to get the sort of reaction you would yourself expect.''

She sat very quietly, contemplating something invisible. Then she looked up and spoke: ''Perhaps I did say it. It sometimes happens that when I cannot win an argument, I become Queen Elizabeth.''

This sort of insight is typical of Miss Davis.

She came to San Francisco again, in the fall of 1969, for the San Francisco Film Festival. I wrote to say I would see her at her retrospective.

I was at the auditorium from 10:00 A.M. until 4:00 P.M., when the program director announced that she was delayed. I rose and went home to Sylviane. Early that evening the phone rang, and the Voice said, ''*Ahl*vah, where were *you?*''

We had lunch. Out of some spirit of contrition she gave me a witch's broom painted bright red — it had been given to her the night before at a Halloween party. She cackled like Apple Annie in *A Pocketful of Miracles* (1961). ''It's the most perfect present I've ever received.''

The conversation was desultory. She told me the name of the one man in her life she loved and wanted — a man who threatened to dominate her and from whom she ran like mad. She expressed regret that my latest novel, *The Symbol,* published two years earlier, had not sold despite the endorsement she had written and my publisher had refused to use. After all, would you use a plug that said, ''Alvah Bessie has written a

As Queen Elizabeth, a role she played several times.

The Old Maid *with Miriam Hopkins.*

fascinating book about Hollywood. Wanda Oliver is sensational but not typical''?

Let it be said in hushed tones that Miss Bette Davis is a passionate defender of the monstrosity called ''the industry,'' and while she had known and played in a film with and felt sorry for the alleged original of Wanda Oliver, she refused to believe she had been destroyed by Hollywood. *Nobody,* Bette Davis believes, can be destroyed — except by his or her self. And she should know.

The conversation picked up when I asked, ''If you could put on screen any woman whom you have not already played, who would she be?''

''Mary Lincoln,'' she said without a second's hesitation.

With pounding heart I said I would enjoy developing a screen treatment of Mary Lincoln's story, and she showed genuine enthusiasm. (Part two of my vow might still be achieved!) I marched from her hotel room, holding on high the bright red broom.

True to her word, Miss Davis sent me a rare book on Mary Lincoln and an unpublished play that she had had written for her on Mary. I started work on an outline, wondering if it were true, as she had assured me, that despite her age she could play the role: ''Makeup, my dear; medium shots and soft-focus in the close-ups.''

I wrote telling her of my progress and problems, notably the touchy question of how to prevent *Mister* Lincoln from running away with the film.

Her replies were discouraging; she had talked to producers of film and television on both coasts and finally suggested that she did not want me to spend too much time or energy. ''Nobody seems to *want* a film about Mary Lincoln . . . or maybe it is Bette Davis they do not want.''

So our love affair ended not with a bang but with a whimper.

SHIRLEY TEMPLE: SUGAR AND SPICE

RICHARD HARMETZ

I T IS IMPROBABLE that the truth of Shirley Temple's beginnings as a movie star will ever be satisfactorily sifted from the rivers of studio publicity that flowed and swirled around Temple's career. Although the young star's mother gave dozens of interviews, the interviews were always unfailingly sunny, relentlessly optimistic, and tinged with false notes.

What is certain is that without her dimples, curly blond hair, and strutting self-confidence, Shirley Temple would never have taken control of a movie screen. Without her mother's indefatigable zeal, she would never have got before a camera at all. What can never be clarified are the proportions of the contributions each made to Shirley's career.

Before Shirley turned four, Mrs. Temple had overridden her husband's objections and enrolled their daughter in a dancing school on what was then "film row," the area of studio exchanges and exhibitors' offices in Los Angeles. Gertrude Temple was aware that talent scouts visited dancing schools. Because of the success of Jackie Coogan, Jackie Cooper, and the Hal Roach *Our Gang* comedies, Hollywood was accustomed to sending its talent scouts out to look for child actors. A scout did visit Shirley's dancing school, and Shirley was one of the twenty-five children selected to appear in the low-budget *Baby Burlesk* series.

The *Baby Burlesks* were spoofs of popular movies. Children played all the parts. From the waist up, they wore elaborate adult costumes. Their bottoms were covered with diapers pinned together with gigantic safety pins. In the *Burlesks,* Shirley played parodies of Marlene Dietrich, Mae West, a beauty contest winner, a nightclub

RICHARD HARMETZ *is on the executive board of the International Center of Films for Children and Young People and is vice-president of the American Center of Films for Children. He teaches children's entertainment classes at the University of Southern California and Los Angeles Trade Technical College, and he was on the UNESCO jury of Spain's International Children's Film Festival.*

The most popular child star in the history of movies.

With two other stars of the Baby Burlesk *series.*

entertainer, and a big game huntress saved from a cannibal stew by a child Tarzan.

The *Baby Burlesks* thrived on what amounts to a carnival trick, the transformation of a child into a miniature adult. Later, when Temple left the world of the quickie short to become Fox's number-one star, the temptation to transform her into a miniature adult was rarely resisted. In *Dimples* (1936), with baton in hand, she leads an urchin band of harmonica players all older than herself. In *Rebecca of Sunnybrook Farm* (1938), she conducts an all-girl adult choir. In *The Little Colonel* (1935), she wears a soldier's uniform, is named an honorary Kentucky colonel, and shouts orders to soldiers. Even in *Heidi* (1937) — much less a formula Temple picture than most of her films — Fox succumbed to the girl-cum-adult formula, and in an unnecessary (to the film's story line) dream sequence, Shirley dances a minuet dressed in all the finery of a French aristocrat.

Her first important role for Fox was in *Stand Up and Cheer* (1934). The film is little more than a series of vaudeville acts. But it is important because Shirley, despite a small part, dominates the film. In *Stand Up and Cheer,* her star potential is clear, and she displays the qualities that would make up the character she would play in all her subsequent Fox films.

Much of her appeal in *Stand Up and Cheer* stems from her ability to do things that a tiny child is not supposed to be able to do. She could sing, dance, and act. If her singing voice was not strong, her acting exaggerated and cute, her dancing a bit cumbersome, so what? Most people didn't notice, and besides, one couldn't apply the same standards to a child that one applied to an adult. The key thing was that Shirley Temple was a marvelously engaging little girl, with a charisma and a power to make the screen her own that were shared only by the most popular adult stars. With her strut, her curly hair and infectiously happy singing voice, Shirley captivated her audience with her singing of "Baby Takes a Bow," and won a long-term contract from Fox.

She had, also — in this virtually plotless picture — established the main theme of nearly every film she was to make at Fox. She would be a little girl whose optimism, determination, and good sense would help older people conquer adversity and triumph over evil. In *Little Miss Marker* (1934), Shirley successfully reforms a bookie (Adolphe Menjou). In *The Little Colonel,* she reunites her irascible grandfather (Lionel Barrymore) with his daughter and helps her own father recoup his lost money. In *Captain January* (1936) she gives new life to a lighthouse keeper (Guy Kibbee). In *Dimples,* she saves her pickpocket grandfather (Frank Morgan) from jail; and in *Heidi,* she saves her grandfather (Jean Hersholt) from his own reclusiveness and misanthropy.

Not all of Shirley's leading men were grandfathers or grandfatherly types, but enough were to cause the then-film critic Graham Greene, in a legendary but now-suppressed review, to accuse Fox of using Shirley to appeal to the prurient interests of dirty old men. Both Fox and the Temple family sued and won.

Among Temple's later critics is Bill Cosby, who in the nationally televised "Black History: Lost or Stolen?" showed a succession of film clips of black servants, handymen, maids, and older children being

Box-office champs Temple and Will Rogers on the set.

Teamed with the great Bill "Bojangles" Robinson.

bossed around by the little white girl. Discussing Shirley's treatment of blacks in her films, Cosby remarked, "She was good to them, and they were good to her, a sort of master-and-pet relationship."

There is no getting away from the truth of Cosby's attack, but if it makes any difference, color made no difference to the Shirley Temple character. She bossed everybody, white and black. Indeed, part of her success in the thirties and on television reruns today has to be because she is not at all the sweet, innocent thing that people are determined to remember her as.

She makes a strong appeal to maternal and paternal instincts. She is that self-reliant, healthy, sure-of-herself person who all parents ostensibly want their children to be. She is a winner, and at the same time sufficiently dependent on the favors of the adult world to keep parents from feeling unneeded.

For children, her appeal goes beyond the obvious fact that she is a child. A major reason for her popularity with children is that, unlike other children, Shirley was

With Jane Withers in Bright Eyes.

able in her films not only to cope with the adult world, but to achieve every child's wish to dominate that world.

Eventually, though, Shirley Temple succumbed to the usual fate of the child star. She grew up.

WORLDWIDE FAN CLUB

Our Little Girl.

BY THE TIME SHE WAS SIX, Shirley Temple was the world's most photographed person; soon after, she was the world's number-one box office star. Sheet music of her songs outsold Bing Crosby's ("Polly Wolly Doodle" and "On the Good Ship Lollipop" each sold over four hundred thousand copies). Her worldwide fan club had four million members. George Bernard Shaw bid for her services as the child Cleopatra for his *Caesar and Cleopatra*. J. Edgar Hoover named her an honorary G-man, and she gave audiences at Fox to, among others, Noel Coward, Henry Morgenthau, Eleanor Roosevelt, General Pershing, and Thomas Mann. FDR called himself "her willing slave." He also claimed that Shirley's optimistic, spunky personality lifted America's spirits during the Depression.

At one point, she was the seventh-highest-paid salaried person in America. (In Hollywood, only Louis B. Mayer received a higher salary.) Her success was the main reason Twentieth Century-Fox became a major studio.

— R. H.

HENRY FONDA: WAY BACK THEN

TED SHERDEMAN

"He's a natural actor whose presence, in even the worst projects, is compelling."
— *T. S.*

I DON'T REMEMBER how I met Henry Fonda, but it was about 1924 in the Dundee section of Omaha, Nebraska, where we both lived. Maybe it was when I became a member of the club called the Buffaloes. We Buffaloes had a special call that identified us — a yell followed by whistling through one's teeth. (Years later in Hollywood, I was so ecstatic about seeing him in *Mr. Roberts* that I let loose with the old yell-whistle and Hank nearly fell off the stage, so quick was his recognition.)

In those days, I called him ''Heel'' — as did all his friends — a term used to describe a polite, gentle soul. The language may change, but Fonda remains a polite, gentle soul.

I recall one winter night when he was eating dinner at our house when we were having chili. My mother

made spicy-hot chili, but this night she overdid herself; after his first bite Henry ran out of the house, flopped down in the snow, clapped his hands like flippers and barked like a seal. As an audience, we ran the gamut from alarm to chuckles of appreciation, and he came back to the house and finished his dinner. Henry always had fine comedic qualities. I wish Hollywood had used them more.

The first Omaha Community Playhouse was on Dodge Street. When Henry wasn't acting in a play there, he was busy building and painting sets for their next production. The playhouse was originally a dance studio, but in the summer, with no dancing classes or drama activities, the building fell on hard times. So Henry thought up the idea of a nightclub. I was part of a five-piece band (of sorts) and Henry paid us about $3 each. I doubled in the floor show — a *divertissement* (a word that was explained to me by Henry). The place was nice, with card tables surrounding the dance area, each with a little candle lamp and a plate of finger-sized cucumber sandwiches on it. I don't know where the customers came from, but Henry managed to fill most of the tables. He also booked the acts for the *divertissement,* bringing over whoever was at the Orpheum, a local vaudeville house.

But successful as he was in the nightclub business, Henry never lost his interest in the theater. He acted at the Community Playhouse and trod the boards of the newer Omaha Community Theater who knows how many times. And when you work in a community theater, it's for free.

Henry left Omaha to work in vaudeville. I saw him once perform Abraham Lincoln in a skit at the old Orpheum. He would play him beautifully years later in John Ford's *Young Mister Lincoln* (1939), but already his Lincoln was perfect.

I lost track of Henry until we met again in New York. He was making the rounds of producers' offices, and I was forever auditioning for announcing jobs on radio.

In those days, there were double-deck buses in New

TED SHERDEMAN *has written screenplays for such films as* Lust for Gold, Them, The McConnell Story, Toy Tiger, A Dog of Flanders, Hell to Eternity, *and* Island of the Blue Dolphins. *Among the films he has produced are* Riding Shotgun *and* The Big Show.

York, and I remember Henry once deliberately taking a fall from the upper deck into the street. It startled me, the driver, and the conductor nearly to death, but Henry smiled, got up, dusted himself off, and then got back on the bus. He explained he was practicing falls for a role in a play that called for a character to tumble off a high pole. I told him to please practice when I wasn't around. (Incidentally, he didn't get the part.)

Henry would sometimes practice his acting in the New York subways. He would furtively look about, then pretend to take a firecracker from inside his coat, light "it," throw "it" under the feet of some poor passenger sitting across from him, then hold his ears and make a terrible face. I never saw it fail. The poor passenger would hustle to the other end of the car and wait for the explosion, terrified. When it didn't come, Henry would make a gesture of frustration. If anyone complained to a conductor, Henry and I would promptly get off at the next station.

With Margaret Sullavan in The Moon's Our Home.

Henry received his first New York notices for *New Faces* on Broadway. Then came *Farmer Takes a Wife,* and he was off and running. The next thing I knew, he was in Hollywood under contract to Twentieth Century-Fox. Henry never gave a damn about being a star. That it happened is nice, but it's of no importance to him. Only having the chance to perform matters to him. He has certainly earned the right to retire, but it's the furthest thing from his mind.

As a meek professor who tries to prove manliness to wife Olivia de Havilland in The Male Animal.

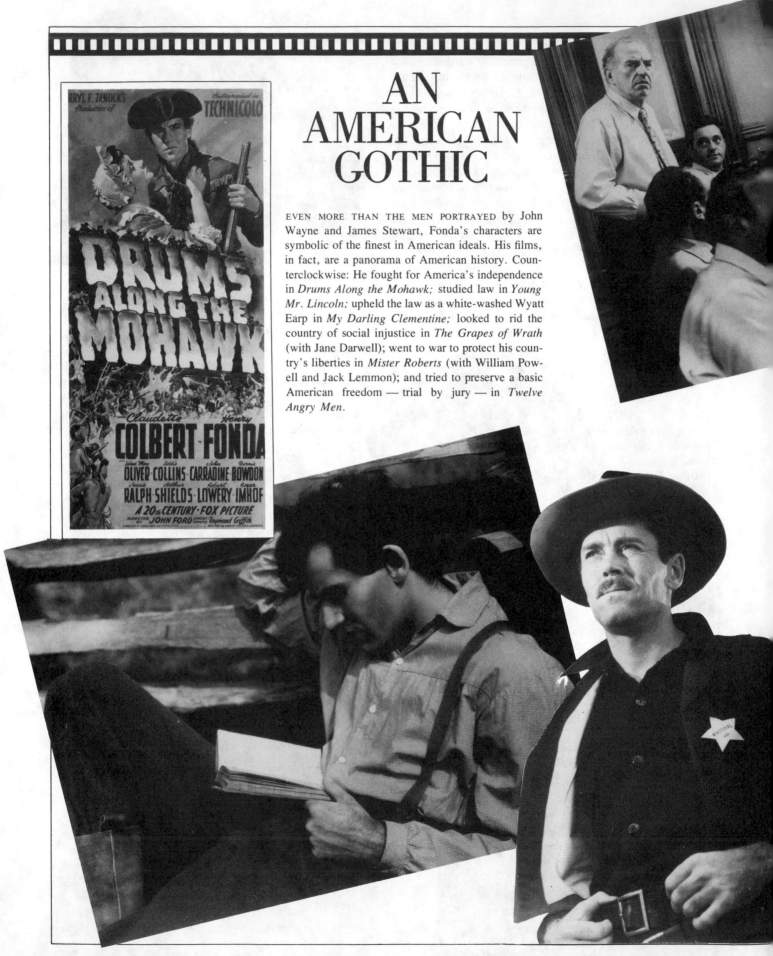

AN AMERICAN GOTHIC

EVEN MORE THAN THE MEN PORTRAYED by John Wayne and James Stewart, Fonda's characters are symbolic of the finest in American ideals. His films, in fact, are a panorama of American history. Counterclockwise: He fought for America's independence in *Drums Along the Mohawk;* studied law in *Young Mr. Lincoln;* upheld the law as a white-washed Wyatt Earp in *My Darling Clementine;* looked to rid the country of social injustice in *The Grapes of Wrath* (with Jane Darwell); went to war to protect his country's liberties in *Mister Roberts* (with William Powell and Jack Lemmon); and tried to preserve a basic American freedom — trial by jury — in *Twelve Angry Men*.

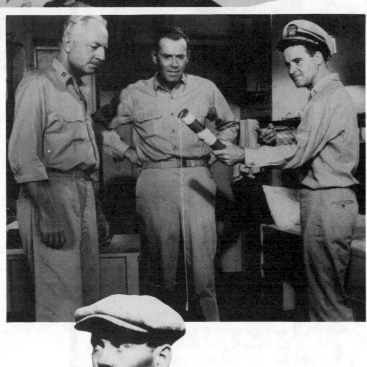

SERGIO LEONE REMEMBERS

I HAVE ALWAYS ADMIRED Henry Fonda. In the vast Hollywood panorama of good-looking leadingmen and tough guys of the Hollywood world, he stands out because he really has something more true and more human to offer: the parts he plays become more Hank than the invented character. Fonda "gets so much into his character" that he mingles with it, until he understands it in relation to himself, and makes it crystal clear to us. His gifts are great and probably have not even been completely revealed. Perhaps he has lacked someone who would write especially for him, who would know how to characterize a person of his dimensions and sensitivities.

Fonda's calm and measured acting style is the key to his believability; without straining, Fonda manages to polarize attention (even with a big-guns cast), to give a touch of scoffing, penetrating realism in settings as distant as that of the "western" or of our own times. I could mention dozens of films, recent and less recent, where his personality puts a stamp of prestige on the whole story.

In the spring of 1963, I sent him the script of *A Fistful of Dollars*, but his agent didn't bother to show it to him. Five years later I sent the script of *Once Upon a Time in The West* (1969) directly to Henry. After having read it, Hank didn't answer — neither yes nor no. He wanted to see my earlier films; so early one morning, in a private projection room in Hollywood, with the patience of a saint he saw without interruption: *A Fistful of Dollars; For a Few Dollars More; The Good, the Bad and the Ugly*. When he came out, it was already late afternoon. "Where's the contract?" is the first thing he said. Thus was born our collaboration, which has been for me an unmatchable experience, through which I came to understand so many things and to know one of the greatest actors of the American stage and screen. But a profound understanding of Henry came only when I saw his paintings.

When he came to Rome to meet with me, he had a neatly trimmed mustache and beard; he was dressed as the "bad guy" — according to the script. I didn't say anything; I didn't tell him that I wanted him clean-shaven, "real," as people had seen him for so long. I didn't tell him that I really wanted *the* Henry Fonda with such a human face. I didn't tell him anything, because I knew he'd come to understand.

"Now I understand!" he said to me, when he saw the test of the scene which would introduce him. After the opening massacre at the farm, the camera would reveal him slowly, circling around to fix him, the leader of the massacre, in an extreme close-up. The audience would be struck in an instant by this profound contrast between the pitiless character Fonda is playing and

Continued on next page

Fonda's face, a face which for so many years had symbolized justice and goodness.

Even among my closest and most gifted collaborators, I have never found a person like Henry, capable of foreseeing my intentions with such precision and immediacy — to the point of predicting my very words. His eyes always mirrored how his scene went. If he looked pleased, it meant it had gone well. I could count on that. The greatest difficulty I encountered with him was that of dressing him. No matter what I put on him — even the most worn-out old rags — he always seemed a prince, with his "noble" walk and his "aristocratic" bearing. I'd say that his best gifts are brought out most of all in extreme close-ups and in long shots. In close-ups because he can show his expressive capacity; in long shots because that's the only way the viewer can enjoy his incredible way of walking. It's true that a good actor can also limp; but I don't think I exaggerate if I say that his way of placing one foot before the other has an unequaled esthetic effect.

I have never known an actor with such craft, with such professional seriousness; such a pleasant man, full of humor, so reserved and so keenly quick-witted. But as work went ahead, an ever-stronger doubt began to gnaw at me, a fear. Hank seemed uneasy, uprooted in this unaccustomed role, as if he were embarrassed at finding himself in this different kind of part, and it seemed to me that he was reacting, with a performance which was monotonous and undeveloped. Then finally I saw the "rushes," and it was my turn to say, "Now I understand!" He had created such a mosaic of subtleties in his expressions; he had designed a character so real and human that he ran the risk of having his personality overwhelm the other actors around him. I thought then

that I understood Henry Fonda, but true understanding came only when I saw his paintings.

I'd already been told he was an excellent painter, but I'd always nourished the suspicion that his fame derived more from his name than from any painterly talent; I was quite mistaken. It is difficult to find pictures so minutely realistic yet so dense and alive in atmosphere. They remind me a little of the Italian "magic realist" painters, but I'd say that Fonda also has the capacity to visualize details apparently of the slightest importance, but which "open up" the realism and personalize it. This is how I really came to understand Hank; I understand that his gifts as an actor are his gifts as a person; what I knew of him as a man of the stage I found likewise in his pictures: a kind of silent creativity without indecision. Craft, experience, and seriousness are only the accessories of a spontaneous artistic sensibility.

Normally, I need few rehearsals for a take—four or five—to be sure the scene is good. With Fonda I could have done with less, but I always ended up taking a dozen. I never tired of it; yet it wasn't false adulation. I risked exhausting him and tiring myself as well, but the temptation and the pleasure of working with him were so great, it really seemed worthwhile. I had the feeling of going backward in time, that I was no longer the director of a film but was reliving certain long-ago moments when I was a boy of fourteen or fifteen, in dark and dirty movie houses in the Trastevere quarter of Rome, where I would go with my friends to see his films. I never imagined in my wildest flights of fancy that one day I'd be working with Henry Fonda, with the actor who was the idol of my youth.

SERGIO LEONE *is the director of* A Fistful of Dollars; For a Few Dollars More; The Good, the Bad, and the Ugly; Once Upon a Time in the West; *and* Duck, You Sucker.

JAMES STEWART: HOMEGROWN

JOHN BELTON

S CRITIC DAVID THOMPSON correctly points out, James Stewart, in his best roles, plays against his popular image. He is not, as often as one might imagine, the good-natured, charmingly awkward boy next door who lives with his mother (or writes her every day), falls for the girl next door, has a couple of kids, and lives happily ever after. Stewart is not that easy to type.

Just as he cannot easily be typed as a romantic lead, a wry comedian, or a folksy western hero, he eludes association with a particular studio or genre, or the vision of any single director. His major work was accomplished under four very different directors: Frank Capra, Anthony Mann, Alfred Hitchcock, and John Ford. They were each successful in their handling of Stewart because they individually recognized that his persona is a complex of fascinating paradoxes and contradictions.

His roles for Capra alternate between idealistic, Jeffersonian, agrarian reformers and bitter, disillusioned cynics; for Mann, between members of families or groups and lonely outsiders; for Hitchcock, between a conventional sightseer and a neurotic voyeur; for Ford, between comically corrupt, mercenary marshals and earnest, crusading young lawyers.

Capra's *Mr. Smith Goes to Washington* (1939) reveals Stewart's roundness of character. Stewart is introduced as the stereotype, Jefferson Smith, a naive, wide-eyed idealist duped by the corrupt political machine. But then Capra forces this boy to grow up, to become a multidimensional character. It is this more complex aspect of his roles that audiences tend to overlook. As Smith, he acknowledges, comes to terms with, then battles the corruption in the world around him, exchanging

his former idealism for a more realistic, though morally questionable, pragmatism. Smith's speeches reveal a transformation: his nervous, adolescently cracked-voiced proposal of his national boys' camp bill gives way to a highly emotional, demagogic filibuster. At the outset he is ill at ease with words; later he learns to manipulate them to achieve his own goals.

In shaping Stewart into a figure of populist mythology alongside men like Jefferson (Jefferson Smith's namesake), Jackson, Lincoln, and Bryan, Capra, unlike his predecessors, exploits Stewart's idiosyncratic fea-

*When he speaks,
his honesty shines through.*

JOHN BELTON *is the author of* "The Hollywood Professionals" *volume on directors Howard Hawks, Frank Borzage, and Edgar G. Ulmer, and has written on film for* The Village Voice, Rolling Stone, Movie, *and* The Velvet Light Trap. *He has taught film at the New School in New York City, Harvard, and Brooklyn College.*

tures — his twangy western drawl, his gangling Abe Lincolnesque frame, his boyish innocence, and his physical awkwardness. Yet Capra also demythologizes his character, playing upon Stewart's physical frailty and psychological vulnerability, as Mann and Hitchcock would later do. Jeff's initial energy and enthusiasms are soon gone; he begins to lose his voice near the end of his filibuster and finally collapses from physical exhaustion. Capra's final shot of Stewart shows him lying unconscious on the floor of the Senate.

During his World War II years in the Air Force, Stewart apparently rethought his prewar screen image of a small-town, boy-next-door, Norman Rockwell caricature. When he returned to Hollywood after the war, he opted for parts that were more mature, more obsessively tenacious, and more psychologically complex. As George Bailey in *It's a Wonderful Life* (1946), Stewart's prewar optimism has soured.

Stewart's momentary self-doubt in *Mr. Smith* becomes extended throughout *Wonderful Life* and intensified into a suicidal self-hatred. Though Bailey knows what he wants to do — travel, build bridges, have quixotic adventures — his failure to achieve his goals (which in themselves are extremely egotistical and antisocial) drives him first to question, then to hate, the populist qualities in himself such as self-sufficiency, good neighborliness, disregard for wealth, love of family, and faith in plain people that gave him inner strength in *Mr. Smith*. The postwar *Wonderful Life* presents a nightmarish inversion of Capra's populist mythology of the thirties, especially in the fantasy sequence in which Bailey wanders, like the amnesiac somnambulist of so many *films noirs* of the period, through Pottersville as it would have become had he never been born, hopelessly searching for family and friends.

Stewart's desperation in *Mr. Smith* — the result of the unwillingness of the senators to listen to or believe in him — is magnified in *Wonderful Life* to the point of paranoia and becomes, in subsequent films like *Harvey* (1950) and *Rear Window* (1954), an integral part of his screen personality.

Stewart's physical characteristics make him an ideal actor for westerns, a genre to which he repeatedly turned in the fifties. However, unlike Gary Cooper, whose laconic strength and solid physical presence correspond to the stereotypical image of the western hero, Stewart

Happy, tearful ending of Frank Capra's It's a Wonderful Life, *when George finds he is appreciated by family and friends. Donna Reed is his wife, Thomas Mitchell his Uncle Billy, and Beulah Bondi (R) his mother.*

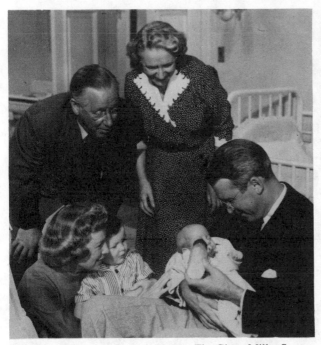

With June Allyson in Anthony Mann's The Glenn Miller Story.

Again with Allyson in Mann's The Stratton Story.

emerges as one of the genre's first *vulnerable* heroes, revealing himself to be physically, psychologically, and morally fallible. Mann's psychological westerns explore Stewart's weaknesses, subjecting him to excruciating physical pain: in *The Man From Laramie* (1955) Stewart is ambushed, his gun hand stigmatized in a nightmarish sequence, and in *The Naked Spur* (1953) he is wounded in the leg, topples from his horse down a ravine, and is forced to scale the sheer face of a rocky cliff.

Mann presents Stewart as a neurotic loner, always traumatized by some past event — the murder of his parent by his brother in *Winchester 73* (1950), his loss of a brother in *The Man From Laramie*, or his betrayal by a woman in *The Naked Spur*. In his primitive quest for revenge, Stewart pursues a doppelgänger across the rugged western landscape, confronts his double who is his brother *(Winchester 73)* or a man like himself *(Naked Spur, Bend of the River* [1952]) and either kills him or becomes indirectly responsible for his death. Though the conclusions of Mann's westerns are less then cathartic, Stewart does partially purge himself of his obsessive hatred, but he does so at a cost to himself; in killing his psychological double he destroys part of himself. Mann's westerns match the paranoia, self-hatred and self-doubt of *Wonderful Life* and even go beyond that film, making the psychologically unstable Stewart distrustful, mercenary, callous, brutal, quick-tempered, violent, and masochistic. Driven by furies within, Stewart, in films like *The Naked Spur*, stubbornly refuses to reconsider or swerve from his goals, even though he is aware of their questionable morality. This self-destructive tenaciousness serves as the cornerstone on which Alfred Hitchcock builds his films with Stewart.

Stewart's L. B. Jeffries in *Rear Window* (1954) bears a partial resemblance to Capra's George Bailey. Recuperating from a broken leg in his two-room Greenwich Village apartment, Jeffries anxiously awaits the day he will get out of his "plaster cocoon" and resume his adventurous career as a globe-trotting magazine photographer. Voyeurism provides Jeffries with a means

With Margaret Sullavan in The Shopworn Angel.

Ignoring Grace Kelly to spy on neighborhood dramas in Rear Window.

of escape, yet his vicarious involvement in his neighbors' lives and his discovery of a murder become less of an escape than a self-examination of his own contradictory feelings regarding Lisa (Grace Kelly).

Like Mann, Hitchcock employs the doppelgänger to deal with the schizophrenic aspects of the Stewart persona, using the murderous Thorwald (Raymond Burr) to act out Jeffries' suppressed desires and then punishes Jeffries for having these desires by forcing him to watch helplessly as Thorwald nearly kills Lisa when he catches her snooping in his apartment. Again like Mann, Hitchcock's use of the "double" forces Stewart to confront and deal with his own feelings. Thus the final struggle between Thorwald and Jeffries becomes a self-confrontation. Hitchcock's direction of Stewart in *Rear Window* draws upon the actor's charm and his nastiness, his sense of moral superiority and his physical vulnerability, his confidence and his self-doubt, constructing a morally ambiguous character out of these qualities.

In *Vertigo* (1958), after quitting his job as a San Francisco detective because of his acrophobia, Scottie Ferguson (Stewart) falls victim to an illusion created by a wife-murderer and his mistress. That illusion is

Comforted by Barbara Bel Geddes in Vertigo.

"Madeleine" (Kim Novak). Stewart's psychological instability, initially suggested in his obsessive fascination with Madeleine, only emerges fully after her (supposed) death, for which he feels responsible. His nervous breakdown, characterized by vertiginous nightmares, is followed by catatonic schizophrenia, then by despondency that, in turn, gives way to an obsessive, reconstruction of "Madeleine," using Judy Barton (also Novak) as his real-life mannequin.

Hitchcock's use of saturated, dreamworld colors, settings associated with the past, and hypnotically magnetic point-of-view tracking shots, is answered in the film's second half by Stewart's own neurotic attempt to reconstruct that dreamworld, to reenact Madeleine's death and thus to exorcise the guilt that haunts him. Yet the last image of the film is far from cathartic: torn between contradictory feelings within himself, a re-traumatized, off-balanced Stewart stands precariously near the edge of the bell tower from which Judy has just plunged to her death. Though cured of his acrophobia, Stewart has been driven, "one step at a time," closer and closer to an emotional paralysis. It seems unlikely that he will ever recover.

Stewart's performances for John Ford range from low comedy to high drama and, along the way, once

Endangered in Anthony Mann's The Man from Laramie.

again reveal a dual personality. He casts off his image as amusing buffoon and mercenary opportunist in *Two Rode Together* (1961) to become a knightly champion of

Stewart as an eastern lawyer is a curious figure to westerners in The Man Who Shot Liberty Valance.

With Betty Hutton in De Mille's The Greatest Show on Earth.

has a remarkable verbal facility. His energetic articulation of abstract ideas or of specific plans contrasts with Wayne's taciturn concealment of his feelings and gives Stewart an important edge in his relationship with Hallie (Vera Miles). Yet Stewart's careful phrasing and rhetorical posing as Senator Stoddard suggest the wary politician's gap between language and feeling: his words have lost much of their meaning. Wayne's eloquent performance serves as a foil for Stewart, calling attention to Stewart's physical awkwardness, his naive idealism, his lack of strength and self-confidence, his occasional insensitivity to the unspoken feelings of those around him. Stewart's fascination with abstract ideas causes him to ignore more immediate feelings and concerns, complicating his sensitivity to historically crucial issues and making him insensitive to more personal questions.

Stewart remains one of the American cinema's most intriguing personalities. As idealist and cynic, representative of the people and social outcast, determined reformer and frustrated cripple, a success and a failure, and healthy young man and neurotic, he embodies all the contradictions of American culture and its ideals. His gallery of performances for Capra, Mann, Hitchcock, and Ford reveals different facets of this truly complex actor.

With Astrid Allwyn in Frank Capra's Mr. Smith Goes to Washington.

Elena, angrily denouncing the hypocrisy of the people who treat her as a social outcast. And in *The Man Who Shot Liberty Valance* (1962), he not only plays the mature, glib, legendary politician Senator Ransom Stoddard and the idealistic, young tenderfoot lawyer Ranse (whom John Wayne aptly dubs ''pilgrim''), but he also unsuccessfully attempts to shed his identity as ''the man who shot Liberty Valance.''

Stewart's ''pilgrim'' recalls his role as Jeff Smith in *Mr. Smith*. Ranse is an easterner bringing law and order to the untamed West; Smith, a westerner restoring populist values to the East. Stewart conveys, in his schoolroom evocations of Washington and Lincoln, the same idealism and, in taking up a gun to fight the outlaw Valance (Lee Marvin), makes similar pragmatic concessions in order to achieve his goals.

Cast alongside of John Wayne's more traditional western hero in the film, Stewart appears weak and indecisive. It requires Wayne's intervention to save him from being killed by Valance and later to force him to accept his senatorial nomination. Stewart, again unlike Wayne,

STARS OF
THE SEVENTIES

FAYE DUNAWAY: BREAKING THE ICE

MASON WILEY

ARTHUR PENN, who directed *Bonnie and Clyde* (1967), explained why he cast Warren Beatty and newcomer Faye Dunaway as the legendary bankrobbers of the 1930s: "I wanted to portray them as they would have liked to have been remembered, not as they were." As Penn's romanticized Bonnie Parker, Dunaway brought to her character the glamour and style of a thirties movie star, one whom Bonnie herself would have admired. Dunaway gave Parker an unsettling combination of drive — ambitious on the outside, suicidal on the inside — and despair, thus establishing for herself the personality that would serve her best during her career. Better than any other actress, Dunaway has been able to present outwardly cool women whose interesting feature is their anxiety beneath the surface.

It is ironic that *Bonnie and Clyde*, Dunaway's breakthrough film, ushered in the downbeat-theme film era that would prove her temporary undoing. While Dunaway, in interviews, criticized the glossy, escapist films of the past in comparison to the emerging message films, it was apparent from the outset that she projected the type of glamour that fitted better into a bygone era than into her own. Even her kind of beauty differed from the healthy, unkempt look that was popular in the late sixties. Her high cheekbones, intense eyes, her sharp well-defined features evoked memories of Grace Kelly and Deborah Kerr. It was only her inner turmoil that made her different from them — and her contemporaries.

Dunaway's quick decline as a box-office attraction after *Bonnie and Clyde* is understandable when one looks at her vehicles. Her subsequent roles in the late sixties and early seventies all properly exploited her beauty, but failed to explore her tension. Elia Kazan tried to make her the symbol of liberating youth that frees middle-aged Kirk Douglas from his bourgeois prison in *The Arrangement* (1969). Jerry Schatzberg turned her into an

As ambitious programming executive in Network.

empty high-fashion model named Lou Andreas Sand in *Puzzle of a Downfall Child* (1970). This should have been an ideal showcase for Dunaway to display her talent for portraying women with hidden instability, considering that it dealt with someone having a breakdown, but the emphasis of the film was placed on camera technique, not on character. Even the most standard of genres, the western, was no refuge during this period, as directors chose to cynically invert its myths. In *Little Big Man* (1970), Arthur Penn forced Dunaway to play an affected nymphomaniac; in *Doc* (1971), Frank Perry cast her as a defiled Katie Elder. The only film of this time that wisely utilized the dichotomy between Dunaway's facade and her feelings was *The Thomas Crown Affair* (1968), a throwback to the glossy, escapist (caper) films of the past, and her one hit in the lot.

The Faye Dunaway renaissance came in the mid-seventies, when the waning alienation-for-alienation's-

MASON WILEY *is a former reporter with the* Nashville Graphic *in Nashville, North Carolina. He is currently film critic for* Hilife *magazine.*

A small part in Little Big Man, *with Dustin Hoffman.*

Very mysterious in Chinatown, *with Jack Nicholson.*

sake movie cycle gave way to the trend for big-budget entertainments spiced with old-Hollywood glamour and a post-Watergate paranoia. Dunaway blossomed in *Chinatown* (1974), a revamped private-eye melodrama

that paired her with Jack Nicholson. Director Roman Polanski established the persona that would define Dunaway for most of the decade: a 1970s Mary Astor — beautiful, but remote, chilly, and not to be trusted. As Polanski returned her to goddess status, he also revealed her masochistic tendencies, especially in the vivid Dunaway-talking-Nicholson-hitting scene: "She's my sister" — *slap* — "My daughter" — *slap* — "My sister" — *slap*.

Dunaway's self-protecting romantic invulnerability prevents her from falling for a guy. She has to be tormented a bit to help her make up her mind. In *The Towering Inferno* (1974), it isn't until she is trapped on the top floor of the world's tallest building that she decides to accept Paul Newman's offer to live with him in the woods. She doesn't become enamored of Robert Redford in *Three Days of the Condor* (1975) until he ties her to her commode. It takes psychic visions of murder to allow her to admit her love for Tommy Lee Jones in *Eyes of Laura Mars* (1978). Only when Dunaway fears physical danger does she let her emotional defenses down.

Yet, even when Dunaway is threatened by both external and inner peril, she is never totally sympathetic, however intriguing and alluring she remains. Her efforts to mask her emotions, her vulnerability, with a cool, unruffled facade always make her suspicious. This icy demeanor enables her to be a perfect villainess, if necessary, as Richard Lester proved with *The Three Musketeers* (1974) and *The Four Musketeers* (1975). In the sequel, Lester included a flashback showing that Dunaway's character, the scheming Lady de Winter, had years before been publicly branded as a harlot. By revealing this detail Lester makes her nature double-edged: she is a sympathetic femme fatale, a woman every man wants to help but doesn't dare.

Directors like Lester and Polanski added the glamour of danger and mystery to Dunaway's already

As the evil Lady de Winter in The Four Musketeers.

With Robert Redford in Three Days of the Condor.

Tommy Lee Jones teaches Dunaway how to protect herself in Eyes of Laura Mars.

enticing presence. Less charitable were director Sidney Lumet and screenwriter Paddy Chayefsky, who, with *Network* (1976), presented Dunaway as a hysterical projection of how they saw the young, determined career woman of the seventies. Certainly, Dunaway was a good sport and parodied her own zeal and nervous mannerisms, but it says something about the misogyny of Hollywood that this is the role which won her the Oscar.

During the present decade, in which American actresses like Jane Fonda and Ellen Burstyn began championing the modern, practical woman, Faye Dunaway has emerged as a contemporary version of the misbegotten romantic heroine. She may be brash and ambitious but she doesn't have the confidence to match her desires. Despite her efforts to be cool and distant, she often becomes a prisoner of her own feelings. A Dunaway movie — even *Eyes of Laura Mars* — centers on whether she can overcome her own neurotic obstacles and find love. Dunaway is the glorified neurotic, the self-doubting vamp, the nervous goddess. Dunaway is the seventies heroine who has to be rescued, not from dragons or tyrants, but from her own insecure self.

Bonnie and Clyde *was one of few films to emphasize her* wild, *sensual qualities.*

GENEVIEVE BUJOLD: IN TRANSITION

PAUL ALMOND

IT WAS 1965 and I was looking for the female lead for my adaptation of Jean Anouilh's *Romeo and Jeannette* for the Canadian Broadcasting Company. Eva Langbord, CBC's casting director, had someone in mind:

"Well, there's this young French-Canadian actress you could meet — everyone's talking about her in Quebec right now. Just back from playing with the Rideau Vert Theatre Company in Russia and Paris — before that, she never stopped working on television and radio, between plays. Won Best Actress at the Gala des

"I hope that in the Hollywood jungle, she won't become all teeth and claws and lose her most crucial quality — true vulnerability."
— P. A.

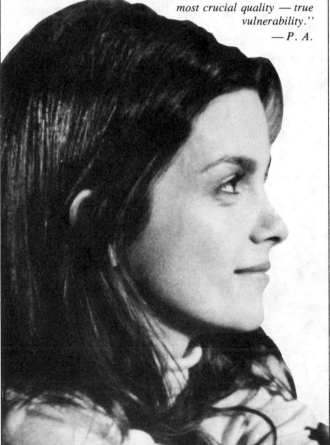

Artistes two years running, and she's only twenty-three. But she might not be free. . . ."

Genevieve Bujold was free, as it turned out, and on St. Jean Baptiste Day, June 24, she flew up to meet me. I was happy to cast her as Jeannette, and after that was over she stayed on. Among the other things we did were *Crime and Punishment* (in which she played the scrawny and shy Sonia, a complete contrast to the savage, explosive Jeannette) and Ibsen's *A Doll's House*. She was well suited to Nora, the child-woman who grows into accepting responsibility for herself.

Most of the preparation for our television projects took place in her moments of relaxation. I remember her taking the script of *A Doll's House* to bed one evening (once the contract was signed) and reading it slowly from beginning to end. She never picked it up again, and was always word perfect in rehearsals. It was the same with every script; one solid read, no more. She would read books about the period of the play and do other research, and often, at unexpected times, would bring up a certain moment in a scene, or a prop or costume or a phrase, and discuss it thoughtfully. Occasionally when we were filming, she would read over a scene during the morning makeup, but she never had trouble with lines or continuity, knowing precisely what went before each scene and what followed, always aware ahead of time of her hand props, always strictly overseeing her costumes with a view to how they would handle and look in a particular set or with other performers. She was extremely practical and knowledgeable.

But, nonetheless, television was never really Genevieve's medium — she preferred the sudden spontaneity that is (sometimes) possible on film.

In 1967, we began the first of the three films that later became known as a trilogy: *Isabel* (1968), *Act of the Heart* (1970), and *Journey* (1972). I wrote, produced, and directed them, and she played the central part

PAUL ALMOND *is a Canadian director-producer-screen-writer. He made three films with his ex-wife Genevieve Bujold:* Isabel, Act of the Heart, *and* Journey.

In Paul Almond's Act of the Heart, *a film that ends with Bujold's self-immolation.*

in each, that of a young girl. They were dissimilar characters but connected in a loose narrative way; all three films have interlocking themes and imagery.

We were married during the preparation of *Isabel. Journey* marked the end of a seven-year period during which we worked and lived together.

Although I wrote all three scripts for her, she never knew what was in any of them until they were completed and we never discussed them while they were being written. We had a pact that if she didn't like the part or script, I was free to cast elsewhere. After three or four months of writing, you can imagine what an exciting day it was for both of us when she read the draft script for the first time.

She added very little in terms of story or characters — that was up to me. Where she gave me great support and encouragement was in the setting up of the films, though she never became actively involved in that aspect of the business.

We shot mainly on locations we were both closely involved in. For us, of course, filmmaking was not a job, it was a way of life. She shared with me the theory that what goes on around the set will find its way somehow onto the screen; she was thus always aware of everything, always a great help in making the "chemistry" of the set just right, or cooperating if I would suddenly spring a scene on the cast, feeling the time was right to shoot it.

During our time together, Genevieve also worked with the major French directors of the day: Alain Resnais, with whom she made *La Guerre est Finie* (1966); Philippe De Broca, with whom she made the classic *King of Hearts* (1967); and Louis Malle, with whom she made

With Richard Burton in Anne of the Thousand Days.

Very self-sufficient in Swashbuckler.

Le Voleur (1967). And in London, while I was editing *Act of the Heart,* she made *Anne of the Thousand Days* (1969), for which she won an Academy Award nomination.

It was a great period, full of promise.

While she came to know a good deal about the vagaries of film financing and production, she never would take a part just for the reason that her participation might help the film get financing or because a big studio was behind it. It was the part itself that mattered.

Once Genevieve agreed to do a part, she put the director first, and then, a close second, the cameraman. Her leading man always came third. With him, it was as if she felt responsible, as if she alone needed to wring a performance out of him. But it was with the camera itself that she had her really powerful attraction: It was a relationship I could only observe, never fully understand. Even though I might be crouching right next to the lens during a take, I confess I never really knew just what was going on between her and that camera. Sometimes I would call for a retake, which she would do happily, as long as I printed the take she wanted. But the next day, in rushes, magnified many times on the big screen, we all could see exactly what she was about.

She is a special actress because there is a curious internal process going on in her that begins the moment she signs to do a picture. At the first ''Action!'' she has become the character, and it never leaves her until long after the last ''Cut!''

Audiences everywhere have the capacity to look past beauty and to discover real talent. Genevieve still has the body of a young girl, but modern international audiences can sense in this slight creature the great power, the dedication, and the total giving of herself to the camera, to the audience.

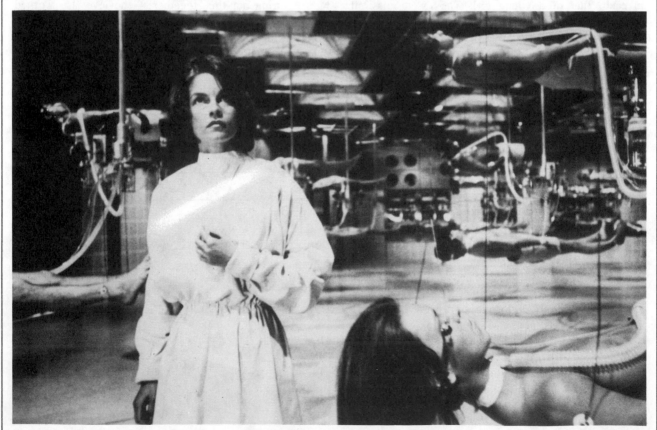
As a doctor investigating mysterious hospital deaths in Michael Crichton's thriller Coma.

ROBERT DE NIRO/ MICHAEL MORIARTY: OBEDIENCE TO SELF

MARK HARRIS

I HAD A LITTLE GLIMPSE not long ago into the characters of two film actors. One was Obedience and the other was Self, and I began to think that those might be the broad options of the worker in the arts.

The actors were at that time unknown to everyone

MARK HARRIS is a novelist, playwright, and essayist, who is the author of both the novel and the screenplay of Bang the Drum Slowly, *which co-starred Robert De Niro and Michael Moriarty.*

but a few colleagues, a few friends, and a producing company which had engaged them at a lucky moment when their talents were much more highly developed than their wages. One of the actors was Robert De Niro, who has become a ''star,'' and the other was Michael Moriarty, who has thus far been noticed less.

We were filming a baseball story. The day's work was done. I was standing at dinnertime at the window of my hotel room, looking down several floors into the outdoor swimming pool. Nobody swam at that hour but

Bang the Drum Slowly, *a lauded baseball film scripted by Mark Harris. Moriarty (L), not De Niro (R), seemed to be the one who would go on to superstardom.*

Moriarty was second male lead in Who'll Stop the Rain?

De Niro, and he swam alone, cutting through the water in a businesslike manner — in, across, up, out.

His was a small body. Most people will be surprised to learn that De Niro is a little fellow, not so much a sturdy hero as a growing boy. Yet he will soon play the part of a middleweight boxer as convincingly as he played the part of a big-league catcher. In life little, on the screen big, his passionate obedience enables him to become someone he is not. He loses himself. He gives himself away to become that ''star'' he means to be. His art is illusion.

I suppose his swift little swim refreshed him, relaxed him, by which I mean to say he had not swum for fun but for use. He had not come to frolic but to work. From the pool he went to his room and stayed there, studying the script for tomorrow, I am sure. I would not see him again before morning.

For his role De Niro learned to bat a baseball, catch it, throw it, and run the bases. Since he had never played baseball this was dangerous work, and he went about it with a dangerous directness. He did not teach himself to play baseball in some general gradual manner, as you and I would have done, by teaming up with other slow fellows and looping baseballs back and forth to get the old feel of it. No, De Niro strapped on the catcher's gear

Report to the Commissioner, *with Susan Blakely. Moriarty's performance was better than the film.*

and squatted behind the batter and came into instant relationship with baseballs thrown at him from the time-honored distance of sixty-feet-six-inches at a speed of a hundred miles an hour. He learned to catch thrown balls. He couldn't have caught a pop foul — but then he wouldn't have wanted to: The script didn't call for that. He learned only as much baseball as he needed for his role. I doubt that he ever cared to touch a baseball again.

In the same way, I understand, he has since learned to play the saxophone. He needs what he needs when he needs it. I saw him one day on the set plunge his fingers down his throat to bring tears to his eyes by gagging himself, and this he did not once but forty times to accomplish every "take," every trial shot. Try gagging yourself forty times of a summer day.

Where was Michael Moriarty when De Niro was swimming alone at the dinner hour? Moriarty was taking dinner with friends in the cast and company, sitting with them afterward in the hotel tavern until a late hour. Moriarty lived in the world in ways De Niro didn't. During the evening, when rushes were shown, Moriarty was there to see himself on film, and I think he enjoyed the critical talk which followed, the praise, the theorizing, the second-guessing, and the inevitable tendency of people in a nervous profession to settle upon people to blame things on.

Moriarty was never aloof from discussion on any topic. Beside the pool at swim-time, glass in hand at happy hour, tensely across a table in the tavern at night, he was inquiring, accessible, and open. If De Niro was small, dark, solitary, Mediterranean, Moriarty was tall, handsome, and fair. He drew a crowd to his table, he was at the center of hubbub, and because he was reachable, touchable, he was popular. People thought well of his friendliness. People in a nervous profession like to be mixed with.

De Niro as the young Don Corleone in The Godfather, Part II.

De Niro rehearsing Taxi Driver, with Cybill Shepherd and director Martin Scorsese.

From De Niro's point of view, a roomful of tense people watching rushes was the gateway to hell. He cared nothing for all that jabbering, all that speculation. Such a scene was pointless, like chasing pop fouls. Superfluous. Whether De Niro had sufficient confidence to ignore the rushes or too little to risk exposure to torrents of talk, I could not decide. For whatever reason, he remained in his room studying. If not studying, alone. If not alone, fabulously discreet.

De Niro's career advanced. The baseball catcher became the taxi driver became the Godfather became the last tycoon became the saxophonist. His talent is obedience. From the producer's point of view, it is a money-saving obedience. De Niro is no "troublemaker." He seems to believe in the system. He seems to play the game. When he receives *his* Academy Award, he will not send an Indian woman to make a speech on rights and abuses. Someone has quoted someone in print as saying De Niro as actor is "pliant," and someone else has called him a "robot."

But art is labor, talent, luck, origins, and De Niro has combined them into a self-denying discipline. Perhaps he learned from his painter-father that an artist

With Liza Minnelli in New York, New York. *De Niro studied the saxophone just for this part.*

pours all the energy of ego into the service of his daily work. Ignore the vulgar producer. Respect the director. Defer gratification. At least *appear* pliant. In that strategy De Niro has been masterful.

Moriarty may yet become so. After the baseball film Moriarty played for several months with distinction on Broadway, and opposite Katharine Hepburn in *The Glass Menagerie* on television. But in a letter to me three years after our brief acquaintance he felt compelled to express his skepticism by enclosing the word ''success'' in quotation marks — ''these past 'successful' years,'' he wrote.

He mistrusted acclaim, the sudden rush of admiration from people who seemed to confuse Michael Moriarty in the flesh with Michael Moriarty's image on the screen. He cared to be loved not for his reputation but for himself. The world he hoped to enter as a ''star'' now presented itself to him as vulgar in ways he could not ignore. This was not the game he meant to play. The end of so much talking, so much mingling, was a realization of Self which estranged him from Obedience.

He seemed to drop from sight. For a while he was a waiter in a restaurant. He was unable to play roles representing people he was not, at least until he discovered who he was. Time passed. Two years after his letter I saw a headline . . . MORIARTY RECOVERING FROM FAME, BITTERNESS. I hoped so. Obedience was coming into balance with Self, and that was good for him and all of us.

JEFF BRIDGES: POPULAR NON-ACTOR

BARRY BROWN

W E HAD NICKNAMES for each other. He was "Jeff Fury" and I was "Baron." But that wasn't until *Bad Company* (1972), two years after we'd first worked together on a film called *Halls of Anger* (1970). That was about the busing of a group of white students to a predominantly black high school, and my role was minor. By the time the picture began shooting my part had become even more obscure — in fact, one of my best scenes was rewritten and given to Jeff Bridges, son of Lloyd. I resented the fellow from the beginning. My small part, on which I had so painfully labored so that I could steal the picture, was whisked away, delivered on a platter to the unseasoned brat son of a veteran actor!

In the meantime, at least Mr. Jeff was guilt-ridden at the idea he had received the part due to his father's connections. After all, as hundreds of young actors his age suffered and struggled to obtain even a two-bit agent, Bridges had been able to walk off as a treasured client of one of the most prestigious agents in Hollywood, simply by virtue of strings pulled and favors met. But at least he seemed humble about it. If I didn't approve of the awkward performance I thought he was giving, at least I wasn't jaded enough to overlook that he wasn't a stuck-up, deluded phony.

So it was with this attitude that I accepted his friendly overtures and allowed myself to get to know Jeff Bridges. He was completely opposite of the prudish young man I considered myself to be, but somehow we clicked. He would suggest wild escapades, and I would tag along.

I saw him next in 1972 at Paramount Pictures. Stanley Jaffe, Robert Benton, and David Newman had decided to cast us as leads in *Bad Company*. When we arrived in Emporia, Kansas, where the picture was to be shot, I began to learn just how much Bridges had to teach

me about a subject on which I considered myself his superior: acting.

It became clear that our styles were contrasting, the classic matching of Mask versus Face. I was the former, he the latter. In Bridges' approach to a role, he thinks little about its final effect on the screen; his confidence is sturdy, but he evinces little pride in his accomplishments. In the late-night talks we had with each other about life and acting in general, Jeff would speak disjointedly about why he didn't think he had "control"

Quick fame from
The Last Picture Show.

BARRY BROWN *(1951–1978) co-starred with Cybill Shepherd in* Daisy Miller *and with Jeff Bridges in* Bad Company. *He also appeared in the television mini-series* Testimony of Two Men.

over his characters, or the right to judge the feelings of whomever he was playing, about how he just "let it happen." From there he lapsed into musings on the meaning of life, while I tried to rebut his inarticulate — though charming — mumbo jumbo. After all, he'd had little or no stage experience, and his powers of characterization were limited largely to how well he could mold his character's personality to fit his own. It was the antithesis of my approach, and we soon would change the subject — usually to women.

Each night over drinks, we would rehearse the next day's scenes with the director. I became increasingly intrigued by how little real difference there was in our work. Despite Jeff's inability to define his "non-

He was a writer of westerns in Hearts of the West.

method" of performing, it became clear that he understood his craft intuitively — the sort of gift that makes for the rare hybrid called good actor—movie star. It wasn't clear to me at the time, but I've learned to understand it since: Jeff is perceived by the average viewer as a non-actor. His flamboyance is not theatrical, nor does it intimidate. His characters invite sustained interest for their raw vitality. He is the boy next door — or the friendly rapscallion. He embodies no untouchable ideal of humanity: a comfort to the male viewer who doesn't want to have to live up to the image of a Clint Eastwood or a Burt Reynolds; a balm to the women who see in him the boyish frailities of their men. Bridges' present persona is that of a sensitive man who on the surface seems quite uncomplicated until the moment of unveiling (for instance, the moment when he breaks the beer bottle and stabs his best friend Timothy Bottoms in *The Last Picture Show* [1971]; the wistful gaze at the picture of Drew's mother in *Bad Company*). His men are generally optimistic, but vulnerable to depressions. They muddle through with bumptious, though sometimes erring, courage.

It is not an image he consciously cultivates, nor do I think he is particularly fond of it. Ironically, after viewing *Bad Company,* Jeff and I both mentioned the same thing to our then-mutual agent. He wished he were the actor I was, and I wished I were more like him. I don't know what he admired about me, but I know I saw life and natural energy in his performance, and a static deliberateness in mine. Jeff doesn't have the conceit of the "driven" actor-martyr who frets and suffers at the ignominy of his fate; as some grasping egos demand attention, Jeff humbly gathers and accepts it. He would like his audience to enjoy him, but if it doesn't — well, fair enough.

MY FAVORITE RECOLLECTION

IN THE FINAL DAYS of filming *Bad Company,* we'd gone back to Kansas for pickup shots several months after the completion of principal photography. On the way back to the motel, Jeff and I rode on the top of the company station wagon as it bumped along a dirt road, gazing at the sky as it reddened, our arms crossed behind our heads. As we had so often before, we talked about life and the women we'd lost. Of course, Jeff Bridges wasn't Jake Ramsey; nor was he Duane Jackson in *The Last Picture Show,* Ernie in *Fat City* (1972) or Lightfoot in *Thunderbolt and Lightfoot* (1974). But who could tell the difference? He was the sort of partner you could talk to, and the sort of actor who doesn't seem to be an actor at all.

— B. B.

With the late Barry Brown (L) in Bad Company.

DIANE KEATON: TRIPPING OVER HURDLES

DEBRA WEINER

THERE ARE PRESENT-DAY ACTRESSES who have captured larger followings than Diane Keaton. But most of these stars are untouchable — they exude too much confidence, too much glamour, too much ambition. On the other hand, Keaton, the gangly, bumbling soul-searcher, invites an intimacy, a sympathy, an interest. Like a rare handful of actors and actresses before her, she has the gift of being herself in front of the camera. And by a happy circumstance, she is able to reflect the wrinkles and aspirations of a great segment of today's movie audience. Diane Keaton is the heroine of the "it's-okay-to-be-neurotic" seventies.

Her southern California childhood — she's the oldest of several children in an Air Force family — reads like a Keaton scenario of adolescent anxiety. She worried about not being popular. She didn't make the cheerleading squad and didn't date handsome school athletes. At one time Keaton even suffered from a slight weight problem. But she had heady ambitions. Still a shy, insecure teenager, she found her way to New York City, where she eventually landed a role in the Broadway production of *Hair*, gaining renown as the only cast member who refused to disrobe in the climactic "nude-in." Later came the stage production of *Play It Again, Sam* and, with it, her friendship with Woody Allen.

That the Oscar-winning *Annie Hall* (1977) is a semiautobiographical story about Keaton and Allen's own romantic interlude is common knowledge. According to published interviews with each of them, they are still best friends, as well as each other's most frequent and most successful working partner. Keaton has appeared in Allen's one drama, *Interiors* (1978), and has co-starred with him in several of his comedies, *Play It Again, Sam* (1972), *Sleeper* (1974), *Love and Death*

In Woody Allen's Sleeper.

DEBRA WEINER *is a journalist who writes regularly for* New Times *and New York City's* Soho Weekly News.

Having an affair with Woody Allen in Play It Again, Sam.

Al Pacino's second wife in The Godfather.

(1975), and, of course, *Annie Hall*. (At this writing, the new Allen-Keaton comedy is untitled.) It wasn't until *Annie Hall*, however, that Keaton was permitted to become a pivotal character in an Allen film. In the previous collaborations, Keaton was Allen's sidekick, or his "straight man." Keaton has said of her work in the two Francis Ford Coppola-directed *Godfather* films: "I was background music." The same can be said of Keaton in the early Allen projects.

Allen tends to write similar female characters for all his films. They are addled, slightly phobic women (Allen's quintessential "blind date") — projections of his personal problems in relating to women. He depends on improvisation to create the necessarily muddleheaded ambiance. In her early Allen films such as *Sleeper*, Keaton looked uncomfortable improvising and trying to make herself fit Allen's image of a female. By the time she made *Annie Hall*, however, she had adapted to his method and characterization; obviously she was helped by the fact that Allen began to think — and write — of women in terms of Keaton instead of women he had known before her.

Although a distinction must be made between the Keaton dramas and Keaton comedies, she plays essentially the same character in both types of film. She is a woman of unrealized potential, stifled by her lack of confidence and the fear of being all wrong, all clumsy, all alone in a world she thinks is more together than she is. She is the exemplary representative of the single woman. She has come to the hard city from any small-town-U.S.A., and is alone and uncertain, sexually and professionally, in her new urban environment.

Keaton's women express a vulnerability that seeks companionship with equally insecure men. That is why she is attracted to Allen's characters, men who share all her phobias. In *Play It Again, Sam*, Keaton rebels against her stable husband (Tony Roberts) by having an affair with the romantically fragile Allen, a relationship seemingly made possible by their mutual need to take tranquilizers before making love. In *Annie Hall*, the audience knows (before Keaton and Allen do) why they are attracted to each other. They make smart conversation after their tennis match, but the audience sees their real thoughts written on the screen. Both feel inadequate; they share sexual fantasies and anticipate rejection.

In both her dramas and comedies, Keaton has scenes in which she screams at men who she feels are treating her poorly. Her repressed anger (perhaps stemming from

I Will, I Will . . . For Now. *With Elliott Gould.*

With Michael Caine in Harry and Walter Go to New York.

a strict upbringing, as in *Looking for Mr. Goodbar* [1977]) bursts forth in flailing arms and uncertain looks to the side and to the sky, as if some offscreen voice could assure her the right to such emotion. The results of her assertiveness depend upon the mode of the production and usually lead to a denial of strength, total isolation, or destruction of the character. In *Annie Hall* Keaton makes up with Allen by calling him in the middle of the night to have him kill a spider in her apartment; her reversion to little-girl behavior makes reconciliation with her lover possible. In the drama *The Godfather, Part II* (1974), however, expressed anger leads to exclusion from the "family" and separation from her children. Her angry self-assertion in Richard Brooks' nightmarish *Goodbar* leads to her own horrific murder.

Annie Hall is not far removed from Theresa Dunn, the twenty-eight-year-old schoolteacher of *Goodbar*. They are both women who need male confirmation of their worth, but Annie Hall's self-doubt has transformed itself into Theresa Dunn's self-hatred. Cruising singles' bars and picking up men becomes Dunn's means of expression — vulnerability and insecurity turned inward toward self-destruction.

Theresa Dunn reminds one of the obsessive screen characters of the past who relentlessly moved forward

Frequenting singles bars in Looking for Mr. Goodbar.

toward their own annihilation. However, there is an important difference. When Joan Crawford or Bette Davis played women of disturbed bearing, they were unapproachable, as if their inner lives were highly contagious. Keaton projects such vulnerability that audiences want to reach out to embrace and protect her. Never before have neurotic qualities been regarded as endearing. Diane Keaton gives unhappiness a whitewash and makes insecurity seem almost romantic.

She received raves for Goodbar, *but the year's Oscar for* Annie Hall *(shown, with Woody Allen).*

SISSY SPACEK:
WAVE OF THE FUTURE

ROGER GREENSPUN

She first received praise as a killer's girlfriend in Badlands.

S HE MUST HAVE COME ALIVE for most people, as she did for me, in the opening images of Terrence Malick's *Badlands* (1973). With her raw-boned teenage blankness, twirling her baton down some tree-lined Middle American street, with her hips, her shapely legs and her character all too bland for insolence but not for a self-conscious sexiness. That she should turn such elements, and such appeal, into a performance of major proportions (she is among the few beauties of the American screen who becomes more interesting the

ROGER GREENSPUN *is the film critic for* Penthouse *magazine and writes on film for numerous other publications. He teaches film criticism at Rutgers University and serves on the selection committee of the New York Film Festival.*

minute she opens her mouth) doesn't seem so surprising in retrospect. But Sissy Spacek was almost an unknown quantity in 1973, and to a special degree she seemed a function of the uninflected roles she played. Luckily for her and for us, in *Badlands* her Holly indulged in a voice-over commentary, a brilliant series of decidedly inappropriate reflections on the romantic adventure she saw her boyfriend's killing spree to be. That commentary, and her delivery of it, gave her a personality above and beyond her physical presence. Perhaps as much as anything, it established her as a very special type for American film in the 1970s. There's no forgetting what she looks like or how she sounds or who she is.

Years after *Badlands,* sitting near her at a New York Film Critics Awards party, I had a chance to compare the image with the reality. The reality that night was especially glamorous, like a sophisticated version of the happiest visions in *Carrie* (1976), and rather more beautiful in person than anything I had seen of her on the screen. But the screen image remained — strong, and utterly identifiable. You might contrast it to the Farrah Fawcett-Majors look that swept the country in the mid-1970s. The Farrah look only required regular features, enough teeth, and probably a couple of hours with the right hairdresser. And it worked. There was a time when any reasonably popular singles spot in New York City might boast ten imitation Farrah Fawcett-Majors at once flashing smiles in its sidewalk café. But no imitation Sissy Spaceks, not unless you were born that way. The image is too personal, too complete, and maybe too ambiguous.

It's no accident that her major roles — *Badlands, Carrie, 3 Women* (1977) — have her as an awkward innocent who is also a potential monster. *Carrie* takes the casting to spectacular extremes, but the contradiction exists in *Badlands,* and its investigation becomes the central dramatic turn in Robert Altman's *3 Women.* It's not the best thing about *3 Women,* the rebirth of timid Pinky Ross as the freckle-faced vamp of the Purple Sage Apartments, but I suspect it may owe as much to Altman's understanding of his actress as to the requirements of what you might call the plot. There are passages in *3 Women,* in the first days' friendship between Pinky and her new roommate Millie Lammoreaux (Shelley Duvall), that seem as sensitive, funny, gentle as anything in recent movies, and as beautifully observed as anything in Altman's career. Typically, the feelings generated by those passages are not to last, and the loss of innocence, which has been Sissy Spacek's major theme to date, proceeds as always from within her. Altman makes this all very fancy, loading his movie with images of amniotic fluid and ending with an interchange of roles among his actresses that becomes less and less interesting the harder you think about it. But he surely recognizes the unnerving potentials of the girl-woman who excites us to uneasy measures of pity and desire.

Brian De Palma has recognized those potentials best, and his *Carrie* succeeds like no other horror movie of the 1970s — not only in its shocks, but also in its ability to humanize those shocks, to give them both an intimate form and a place in the larger scheme of things by which we think ourselves to live. Even more than *Badlands, Carrie* works by means of nostalgia, by reminding us of the movies we grew up with and of the sweet pains of being young — in a way that even the young can respond to. Its terror is a continuation of that nostalgia. And the two aspects of Sissy Spacek — shy but radiant prom queen and blood-spattered, bug-eyed demon — manage to tie together both parts of one ambivalent fantasy, the fantasy of the forces inherent in an emerging sexuality. Like any good monster, Carrie is precisely what we make of her. And Sissy Spacek has, to an unusual degree, a talent for inviting us to dream.

Even at their worst — *Prime Cut* (1972), *Welcome to L.A.* (1977) — her films have been interesting projects. I can't believe that's just accident, or simply good career management. You hear a lot about fine actors in terrible movies, and given the ratio of actors to movies, that comes as no surprise. But the consistency with which Sissy Spacek appears in excellent movies begins to look like a function of her own awareness and capacity for self-appraisal. She is by no means a universal actress, and she does not automatically triumph over poor parts or poor direction, or perhaps no direction at all. Even in *3 Women* it was Shelley Duvall's presence that received most of the (well-deserved) attention. And in a TV movie, *Verna the USO Girl,* which seems to have been designed to exploit some kind of special Sissy Spacek poignancy, Sally Kellerman's older woman, a world-weary, sad-eyed torch singer, proved not only more authoritative but also more poignant than Spacek's innocence in the face of daily disillusionment.

But movies aren't contests, and Spacek happens to be quite a good ensemble performer. She actually gains from her matching with Shelley Duvall in *3 Women.* And if she loses next to Sally Kellerman — well, it's hard to make ambition and youthful shallowness seem more ap-

In the horror chiller Carrie, *she was named school prom queen. Her evening was ruined by a bucket of blood. She got her revenge.*

As the odd stranger who baffles Shelley Duvall in Robert Altman's 3 Women. She will take over Duvall's apartment and identity.

Spacek played a drugged teenage prostitute in Prime Cut, *her first film.*

pealing than depth, warmth, and sexual maturity. What's going to happen to her now, say in the next ten years, which will see her into her late thirties, depends as much on the future of American movies as it does on anything one bright actress can do. Her very individuality poses problems, and some unlooked-for advantages as well. The actress Altman chose for an important but relatively minor role, the bride, in *A Wedding* (1978) — Amy Stryker — is, at least in looks, already a recognizable Sissy Spacek type.

Just before writing this I taught a university film-criticism seminar featuring some legendary performances by actresses in the past: Jean Arthur in *Only Angels Have Wings,* Lauren Bacall in *To Have and Have Not,* Joan Fontaine in *Letter from an Unknown Woman.* I'm not uncomfortable thinking of Sissy Spacek in that company, though I don't know how I'd compare them with her. It's been a while since the primary aim of a leading lady in the movies was to fall in love. Her sexuality is more suggestive but, if anything, *less* aggressive than that of her 1930s and 1940s predecessors, and that may have something to do with the sort of currency she enjoys.

In her best roles she has had to survive a degree of objectification that no important actress in the days of unliberated heroines would have been made to endure. She has, in fact, starred through a hard period in our movies, bringing life to some roles that virtually establish emotional deadness as their reason for being. For this she deserves a special place in any moviegoer's affection. With luck that place will become more spacious as the actress inhabiting it continues to grow.

RICHARD DREYFUSS: FORCEFUL INTELLECT

CARL GOTTLIEB

Witnessing a visit from outer space in Close Encounters of the Third Kind.

A S RICHARD DREYFUSS accepted his 1978 Academy Award, he was unashamedly emotional, momentarily at a loss for words, and clearly flustered by the obligations of the moment. It's safe to assume that if he were acting the sequence in a movie, playing himself, he would've done it differently. Nevertheless, through the mediating and mysterious camera, we could still see that combination of rationality, passion, and ingenuous self-deprecation that informs Dreyfuss's art and defines his considerable charm.

Onscreen, Richard Dreyfuss recalls James Cagney. Besides being short and energetic, he has other Cag-

neyesque traits. Most important, I suppose, is the quality of intelligence that he projects — the illusion (perhaps even reality) that here is a character who thinks even as he speaks. When his speech exceeds rationality, it is only because his fast-moving mouth has not caught up with his even faster-racing brain; few other film stars have gut reactions that are so closely connected to the processes of reason.

Curiously enough, Richard is not an intellectual man. His college education is incomplete, and he can be surprisingly naive on certain issues. On the other hand, he is a voracious reader, and when a topic captures his attention, he can pursue an impressive bibliography in his sudden research. Like most facile minds, he is taken with epigrams and simple arguments that define issues in

---

CARL GOTTLIEB *wrote the shooting scripts for both* Jaws *and* Jaws II.

With Micheline Lanctot. The Apprenticeship of Duddy Kravitz.

Porno director in Inserts. *With Veronica Cartwright.*

vivid analogies; he is quickly seduced by superficial insights. This would be a fatal failing in a philosopher or scientist, but it is a surprising strength in an actor. Dreyfuss can easily grasp a complex problem, reduce its conflicts and ambiguities to a few broad generalities, and then set a course of action that enables him to deal specifically with those large assumptions. Dreyfuss rarely inhabits a character without knowing everything he thinks he needs to know for the role. This is the understanding that is the core of his self-confidence.

A large part of his approach is culturally derived; Dreyfuss is an American Jew with clearly defined ethnic roots. His is a tradition of intellectual inquiry, respect for learning, and intense involvement with morality and law. Besides a complement of New York socialists, lawyers, businessmen, and accountants, his family includes a tough, brawling labor organizer who helped found the Teamsters' Union on the West Coast. The lively family interaction inevitably involved Richard. Predictably, his first professional appearance was in *In Mama's House*, a Jewish family drama.

My own favorite performance from his early years is an episode of *Gunsmoke*. Entitled "The Golden Land," it is concerned with an Orthodox Jewish family of settlers on the frontier. Richard plays the impatient hotheaded son, complete with spectacles and yarmulke, who takes the law into his own hands after his pacifist family is shamed by presumably goyish cattle barons. There weren't many Orthodox Jewish characters on television then, and certainly not on *Gunsmoke,* but there was Dreyfuss, his youthful, alert face lit with self-righteous fire, eyes shining intelligently behind rimless glasses, a standout in the sagebrush. His agent Meyer Mishkin still has some of the enthusiastic fan mail from rabbis and synagogues, praising the show and Richard's part in it.

My recollections of Dreyfuss begin in 1966, just before the Haight-Ashbury flower-power explosion of psychedelic media hype. After a few years of stage-managing and interim directing at a successful improvisational revue, called *The Committee*, I had evolved into an improvisational actor, and was appearing nightly in *The Committee's* cabaret theater in San Francisco's North Beach.

We were frequently visited by various people from Los Angeles — whom we called "Sons of Famous Fathers" — Joey Bishop's son Larry; Carl Reiner's son Rob; David Arkin, distantly related to improvisational heavyweight Alan Arkin — and young Richard Dreyfuss, without any theatrical pedigree at all. Under Rob's agitated and enthusiastic direction, they had organized an improvisational revue based in Los Angeles called *The Session*.

Each member of *The Session* drew his nourishment from San Francisco's turbulent smorgasbord of psychoactive chemicals, nightly improvisation, and after-hours philosophy. Richard mastered the craft, but improvisation is only a tool to him, a part of his professional actor's training; it does not play a pivotal role in his life, and his onstage moments at *The Session* are largely unrecalled. The group itself was modestly successful (they got work), but disbanded without ever becoming a powerful act in nightclubs or cabarets. Yet, its influence on Richard is clearly there. Once an actor has improvised regularly for paying audiences in boozy clubs, there is no terror left in the unknown on stage. Whatever the moment, you know you are always capable of saying something — and Richard is rarely reticent, withdrawn, or inarticulate.

In the decade since 1968, Richard has stayed busy as an actor, working in Hollywood and in legitimate stage productions. Generally, because of his customary zeal

On the set of Close Encounters, *with François Truffaut.*

and intensity, he has found himself cast as a psychotic villain; often, because of his squeaky freshness, he has been the nerd or wimp, a comic foil to some presumably more wholesome teenage types. Most often, he has found himself in a succession of bits and occasional day-player parts that were purely utilitarian: a student in *The Graduate* (1967), passing moments in *The Young Runaways* (1968), on TV as a waiter in *That Girl* and minor bits in *The Mod Squad* — stuff like that. Rarely did he have a chance to display the characteristic Dreyfuss charm, energy, passion, and intelligence. Because of the necessities of earning a living as an actor, he often found himself miscast or appearing in a strangely conceived stage production; in these cases, it was simply a matter of craft, a carpenter building a closet into which he could stuff the skeleton of past performances. Everyone in the performing arts has memories of youthful follies and excesses, ghosts of better-to-be-forgotten lurking moments in old resumés and outdated press releases, ready to fall onto the floor in a clatter of dusty, embarrassing bones.

With *American Graffiti* (1973), Richard graduated from the demeaning television portrayals. In *Inserts*

Dreyfuss, Robert Shaw (L), and Roy Scheider fight shark in Jaws.

THE MAN BEHIND THE STAR

In Mama's House was a drama of social consciousness. Richard Dreyfuss was such a standout in his professional debut in that play that a prominent actor's agent, who was attending the show to see the performances of other clients, was moved to approach the sixteen-year-old Dreyfuss. That association continues to this day; Meyer Mishkin is still his representative. Dreyfuss has had no other agent during his entire career — and that is a singular loyalty in Hollywood.

By way of illustration, Dreyfuss was offered a script by a famous, flamboyant, and financially successful expatriate Italian producer, who, in face-to-face negotiations, assured Meyer Mishkin that his picture would make Richard Dreyfuss ''an international star.'' Meyer mildly countered that with the success of *Jaws,* which had drawn more worldwide admissions than any other film in history, Richard could already be considered an international star. The Italian demurred — the star of that picture was not Richard, it was the shark. Meyer tossed the script onto the conference table and said, ''Then get the shark to play the part.'' The negotiations concluded without Richard's involvement in the project.

Mishkin has a number of recollections of the early Dreyfuss performances, in a Los Angeles theater group called The Gallery Theater, and at Beverly Hills High School. ''It was like summer stock,'' he recalls, ''when you had a touring star supported by local kids and apprentices. Richard was always like that star — one of a kind.'' Mishkin declined to sign contracts with the sixteen-year-old actor, reasoning that being signed with a real Hollywood agent would prompt Richard to drop out of school altogether. Meyer represented him without a contract until Dreyfuss' graduation from high school, when they formalized their relationship with papers. Meyer's knowledge of his client has worked to Richard's benefit, sometimes without his knowledge.

When Richard consented to do *Jaws,* it was the result of a protracted waltz which I recalled and published in my book *The Jaws Log* in 1975. The turning point came during Richard's visit to Boston. He was in the midst of an exhilarating and debilitating promotional tour for *The Apprenticeship of Duddy Kravitz,* and I had telephoned him, asking him to come up and talk with us about the revisions and rewrites of the script he had previously rejected. Steven Spielberg and I both assured him the new version would be more to his liking; I recalled our prior experience together in improvisational theater. We were sure he'd be right for the part, and we felt certain I could write the part especially for his talents. Meanwhile, Meyer Mishkin offered Spielberg some insights into his bright, but headstrong client. His advice was simple: ''Pay for the trip to Boston. Whatever he wants. Make him feel like a big shot.'' Universal did: Richard got a free ride for himself and a couple of companions, and a role custom-tailored to his unique sensibilities. Nowadays, he expects, and deserves, that star treatment; in 1974 it was still enough of a novelty to catch his attention, and I'm sure that Mishkin was counting on that.

— C. G.

He won an Oscar for Herbert Ross' The Goodbye Girl.

(1976), *The Apprenticeship of Duddy Kravitz* (1974), *Jaws* (1975), and *The Goodbye Girl* (1977) he has demonstrated his prowess in roles that seem to be so closely matched to his personality that a generation of critics view him as a brash, cocky know-it-all, and a worshipful audience regards him as unfailingly articulate, animated, and opinionated. It is into this quicksand of preconception and assumption that Richard has delivered *The Big Fix* (1978), in which he plays an Adult, for the first time since becoming a star: Moses Wine, the private investigator, has children, alimony payments, and professional problems. He's also a Berkeley radical grown-up, a dope-smoking, politically conscious human who relates, with varying degrees of success, to women. Again, the character seems to follow the usual Dreyfuss persona, but there's a promise of more: moving moments of introspection, discovery, and filial affection that we have not seen before; qualities of character that quantify Dreyfuss' acting as art and suddenly expand the spectrum of emotions he is capable of discovering in himself, his characters, and his life's work.

APPENDIXES

FILMOGRAPHIES

To make the following filmographies accurate, much original research was done, and the most reputable reference sources were consulted. I was greatly aided by John Cocchi of *Boxoffice* magazine, Anthony Slide of the Academy of Motion Pictures Arts and Science Library, Judith M. Kass, and Jon Bloom. Films are listed in chronological order and directors are in parentheses. If a director appears more than once in a filmography, after the first mention, only the last name is shown.

ABBOTT AND COSTELLO

1940: One Night in the Tropics (A. Edward Sutherland)
1941: Buck Privates (Arthur Lubin)
In the Navy (Lubin)
Hold That Ghost (Lubin)
Keep 'em Flying (Lubin)
1942: Ride 'em Cowboy (Lubin)
Rio Rita (S. Sylvan Simon)
Pardon My Sarong (Erle C. Kenton)
Who Done It? (Kenton)
1943: It Ain't Hay (Kenton)
Hit the Ice (Charles Lamont)
1944: In Society (Jean Yarbrough)
Lost in a Harem (Charles Riesner)
1945: The Naughty Nineties (Yarbrough)
Abbott and Costello in Hollywood (S. Simon)
Here Come the Co-eds (Yarbrough)
1946: Little Giant (William A. Seiter)
The Time of Their Lives (Charles Barton)
1947: Buck Privates Come Home (Barton)
The Wistful Widow of Wagon Gap (Barton)
1948: The Noose Hangs High (Barton)
Abbott and Costello Meet Frankenstein (Barton)
Mexican Hayride (Barton)
Abbott and Costello Meet the Killer, Boris Karloff (Barton)
1949: Africa Screams (Barton)
1950: Abbott and Costello in the Foreign Legion (Lamont)
1951: Abbott and Costello Meet the Invisible Man (Barton)
Comin' Round the Mountain (Lamont)
1952: Jack and the Beanstalk (Yarbrough)
Lost in Alaska (Yarbrough)
Abbott and Costello Meet Captain Kidd (Lamont)
1953: Abbott and Costello Go to Mars (Lamont)
Abbott and Costello Meet Dr. Jekyll and Mr. Hyde (Lamont)
1955: Abbott and Costello Meet the Keystone Kops (Lamont)
Abbott and Costello Meet the Mummy (Lamont)
1956: Dance with Me, Henry (Barton)
Lou Costello alone:
1959: The 30-Foot Bride of Candy Rock (Sidney Miller)

WOODY ALLEN

1965: What's New, Pussycat? (Clive Donner)
1967: Casino Royale (John Huston, Ken Hughes, Robert Parrish, Joe McGrath, Val Guest)
What's Up, Tiger Lily? (Woody Allen)
1969: Take the Money and Run (W. Allen)
1971: Bananas (W. Allen)
1972: Everything You Always Wanted to Know About Sex (But Were Afraid to Ask) (W. Allen)
Play It Again, Sam (Herbert Ross)
1973: Sleeper (W. Allen)
1975: Love and Death (W. Allen)
1976: The Front (Martin Ritt)
1977: Annie Hall (W. Allen)
1978: Interiors (W. Allen, director only)
1979: Manhattan (W. Allen)

JULIE ANDREWS

1964: Mary Poppins (Robert Stevenson)
The Americanization of Emily (Arthur Hiller)
1965: The Sound of Music (Robert Wise)
1966: Torn Curtain (Alfred Hitchcock)
Hawaii (George Roy Hill)
1967: Thoroughly Modern Millie (G. R. Hill)
1968: Star! (Wise)
1970: Darling Lili (Blake Edwards)
1974: The Tamarind Seed (B. Edwards)

JEAN ARTHUR

1923: Cameo Kirby (John Ford)
1924: Biff Bang Buddy (Frank L. Ingraham)
Bringin' Home the Bacon (Richard Thorpe)
Travelin' Fast (unknown)
Fast and Fearless (Thorpe)
Thundering Romance (Thorpe)
1925: Hurricane Horseman (Robert Eddy)
Seven Chances (Buster Keaton)
Tearin' Loose (Thorpe)
The Fighting Smile (Jay Marchant)
A Man of Nerve (Louis Chaudet)
Thundering Through (Fred Bain)
The Drugstore Cowboy (Parke Frame)
1926: The Block Signal (Frank O'Connor)
Born to Battle (Robert De Lacy)
The Cowboy Cop (De Lacy)
Lightning Bill (Chaudet)
Twisted Triggers (Thorpe)
The College Boob (Harry Garson)
Under Fire (Clifford Elfelt)
Double Daring (Thorpe)
The Fighting Cheat (Thorpe)
1927: Horse Shoes (Clyde Bruckman)
The Broken Gate (James C. McKay)
Flying Luck (Herman Raymaker)
Husband Hunters (John G. Adolfi)
The Masked Menace (serial; Arch Heath)
The Poor Nut (Richard Wallace)
1928: Warming Up (Fred Newmeyer)
Wallflowers (Leo Meehan)
Brotherly Love (Charles Riesner)
Sins of the Fathers (Ludwig Berger)
1929: The Canary Murder Case (Malcolm St. Clair)
Stairs of Sand (Otto Brower)
The Greene Murder Case (Frank Tuttle)
The Saturday Night Kid (Edward Sutherland)
Halfway to Heaven (George Abbott)
The Mysterious Dr. Fu Manchu (Rowland V. Lee)
1930: Paramount on Parade (Dorothy Arzner, Brower, Edmund Goulding, Victor Heerman, Edwin Knopf, Rowland V. Lee, Ernst Lubitsch, Lothar Mendes, Victor Schertzinger, Sutherland, Tuttle)
Street of Chance (John Cromwell)
Young Eagles (William Wellman)
The Return of Dr. Fu Manchu (R. Lee)
Danger Lights (George B. Seitz)
The Silver Horde (George Archainbaud)
1931: The Gang Buster (Sutherland)

Virtuous Husband (Vin Moore)
The Lawyer's Secret (Louis Gasnier)
Ex-Bad Boy (Vin Moore)
1933: Get That Venus (Grover Lee)
The Past of Mary Holmes (Harlan Thompson)
1934: Whirlpool (Roy William Neill)
Most Precious Thing in Life (Lambert Hillyer)
The Defense Rests (Hillyer)
1935: The Whole Town's Talking (Ford)
Public Hero Number One (J. Walter Ruben)
Party Wire (Erle C. Kenton)
Diamond Jim (Sutherland)
The Public Menace (Kenton)
If You Could Only Cook (William Seiter)
1936: Mr. Deeds Goes to Town (Frank Capra)
The Ex-Mrs. Bradford (Stephen Roberts)
The Plainsman (Cecil B. DeMille)
Adventure in Manhattan (Edward Ludwig)
More Than a Secretary (Alfred E. Green)
1937: History Is Made at Night (Frank Borzage)
Easy Living (Mitchell Leisen)
1938: You Can't Take It with You (Capra)
1939: Only Angels Have Wings (Howard Hawks)
Mr. Smith Goes to Washington (Capra)
1940: Too Many Husbands (Wesley Ruggles)
Arizona (Ruggles)
1941: The Devil and Miss Jones (Sam Wood)
1942: The Talk of the Town (George Stevens)
1943: The More the Merrier (G. Stevens)
A Lady Takes a Chance (Seiter)
1944: The Impatient Years (Irving Cummings)
1948: A Foreign Affair (Billy Wilder)
1953: Shane (G. Stevens)

FRED ASTAIRE

1933: Dancing Lady (Robert Z. Leonard)
Flying Down to Rio (Thornton Freeland)
1934: The Gay Divorcee (Mark Sandrich)
1935: Roberta (William A. Seiter)
Top Hat (Sandrich)
1936: Follow the Fleet (Sandrich)
Swing Time (George Stevens)
1937: Shall We Dance (Sandrich)
A Damsel in Distress (G. Stevens)
1938: Carefree (Sandrich)
1939: The Story of Vernon and Irene Castle (H. C. Potter)
1940: Broadway Melody of 1940 (Norman Taurog)
Second Chorus (Potter)
1941: You'll Never Get Rich (Sidney Lanfield)
1942: Holiday Inn (Sandrich)
You Were Never Lovelier (Seiter)
1943: The Sky's the Limit (Edward H. Griffith)
1945: Yolanda and the Thief (Vincente Minnelli)
1946: Ziegfeld Follies (Minnelli)
Blue Skies (Stuart Heisler)
1948: Easter Parade (Charles Walters)
1949: The Barkleys of Broadway (Walters)
1950: Three Little Words (Richard Thorpe)
Let's Dance (Norman Z. McLeod)
1951: Royal Wedding (Stanley Donen)
1952: The Belle of New York (Walters)
1953: The Band Wagon (Minnelli)
1954: Deep in My Heart (Donen)

1955: Daddy Long Legs (Jean Negulesco)
1957: Funny Face (Donen)
Silk Stockings (Rouben Mamoulian)
1959: On the Beach (Stanley Kramer)
1961: The Pleasure of His Company (George Seaton)
1962: The Notorious Landlady (Richard Quine)
1968: Finian's Rainbow (Francis Ford Coppola)
1969: Midas Run (Alf Kjellin)
1974: The Towering Inferno (John Guillermin)
That's Entertainment! (Jack Haley, Jr.)
1976: The Amazing Dobermans (Byron Chudnow)
That's Entertainment, Part 2 (Gene Kelly)
1977: The Purple Taxi (Yves Boisset)

LAUREN BACALL

1944: To Have and Have Not (Howard Hawks)
1945: Confidential Agent (Herman Shumlin)
Two Guys from Milwaukee (David Butler)
1946: The Big Sleep (Hawks)
1947: Dark Passage (Delmer Daves)
1948: Key Largo (John Huston)
1950: Young Man with a Horn (Michael Curtiz)
Bright Leaf (Curtiz)
1953: How to Marry a Millionaire (Jean Negulesco)
1954: Woman's World (Negulesco)
1955: The Cobweb (Vincente Minnelli)
Blood Alley (William Wellman)
1956: Written on the Wind (Douglas Sirk)
1957: Designing Woman (Minnelli)
1958: The Gift of Love (Negulesco)
1960: Flame Over India (J. Lee Thompson)
1964: Shock Treatment (Denis Sanders)
Sex and the Single Girl (Richard Quine)
1966: Harper (Jack Smight)
1974: Murder on the Orient Express (Sidney Lumet)
1976: The Shootist (Don Siegel)

ANNE BANCROFT

1952: Don't Bother to Knock (Roy Baker)
1953: Treasure of the Golden Condor (Delmer Daves)
Tonight We Sing (Mitchell Leisen)
1954: Demetrius and the Gladiators (Daves)
The Raid (Hugo Fregonese)
The Kid from Left Field (Harmon Jones)
Gorilla at Large (H. Jones)
1955: The Last Frontier (Anthony Mann)
The Naked Street (Maxwell Shane)
A Life in the Balance (Harry Horner)
New York Confidential (Russell Rouse)
1956: Walk the Proud Land (Jesse Hibbs)
1957: The Girl in Black Stockings (Howard W. Koch)
Nightfall (Jacques Tourneur)
The Restless Breed (Allan Dwan)
1962: The Miracle Worker (Arthur Penn)
1964: The Pumpkin Eater (Jack Clayton)
1965: The Slender Thread (Sydney Pollack)
1966: Seven Women (John Ford)
1967: The Graduate (Mike Nichols)
1972: Young Winston (Richard Attenborough)
1974: The Prisoner of Second Avenue (Melvin Frank)
1976: The Hindenburg (Robert Wise)
Lipstick (Lamont Johnson)

Silent Movie (Mel Brooks)
1977: The Turning Point (Herbert Ross)

THEDA BARA

1915: A Fool There Was (Frank Powell)
Kreutzer Sonata (Herbert Brenon)
The Clemenceau Case (Brenon)
The Devil's Daughter (Powell)
Lady Audley's Secret (Marshall Farnum)
The Two Orphans (Brenon)
Sin (Brenon)
Carmen (Raoul Walsh)
The Galley Slave (J. Gordon Edwards)
1916: Destruction (Will S. Davis)
The Serpent (Walsh)
Gold and the Woman (James Vincent)
The Eternal Sappho (Bertram Bracken)
East Lynne (Bracken)
Under Two Flags (J. Edwards)
Her Double Life (J. Edwards)
Romeo and Juliet (J. Edwards)
The Vixen (J. Edwards)
1917: The Darling of Paris (J. Edwards)
The Tiger Woman (J. Edwards)
Her Greatest Love (J. Edwards)
Heart and Soul (J. Edwards)
Camille (J. Edwards)
Cleopatra (J. Edwards)
The Rose of Blood (J. Edwards)
1918: The Forbidden Path (J. Edwards)
Madame DuBarry (J. Edwards)
The Soul of Buddha (J. Edwards)
Under the Yoke (J. Edwards)
When a Woman Sins (J. Edwards)
Salome (J. Edwards)
1919: The She-Devil (J. Edwards)
The Light (J. Edwards)
When Men Desire (J. Edwards)
The Siren's Song (J. Edwards)
A Woman There Was (J. Edwards)
Kathleen Mavourneen (Charles Brabin)
La Belle Russe (Brabin)
The Lure of Ambition (Edmund Lawrence)
1925: The Unchastened Woman (James Young)
1926: Madame Mystery (short: Richard Wallace, Stan Laurel)

JOHN BARRYMORE

1914: An American Citizen (J. Searle Dawley)
The Man from Mexico (Thomas Heffron)
1915: Are You a Mason? (Heffron)
The Director (Heffron)
The Incorrigible Dukane (James Durkin)
1916: Nearly a King (Frederick Thompson)
The Lost Bridegroom (James Kirkwood)
The Red Widow (Durkin)
1917: Raffles, the Amateur Cracksman (George Irving)
1918: On the Quiet (Chester Whithey)
1919: Here Comes the Bride (John S. Robertson)
The Test of Honor (Robertson)
1920: Dr. Jekyll and Mr. Hyde (Robertson)
1921: The Lotus Eater (Marshall Neilan)
1922: Sherlock Holmes (Albert Parker)
1924: Beau Brummel (Harry Beaumont)
1926: The Sea Beast (Millard Webb)
Don Juan (Alan Crosland)
1927: When a Man Loves (Crosland)
The Beloved Rogue (Crosland)
1928: Tempest (Sam Taylor)
1929: Eternal Love (Ernst Lubitsch)
The Show of Shows (John Adolfi)
General Crack (Crosland)
1930: The Man from Blankley's (Alfred Green)
Moby Dick (Lloyd Bacon)
1931: Svengali (Archie Mayo)
The Mad Genius (Michael Curtiz)
1932: Arsène Lupin (Jack Conway)
Grand Hotel (Edmund Goulding)
State's Attorney (George Archainbaud)
A Bill of Divorcement (George Cukor)

Rasputin and the Empress (Richard Boleslawski)
1933: Topaze (Harry D'Arrast)
Reunion in Vienna (Sidney Franklin)
Dinner at Eight (Cukor)
Night Flight (Clarence Brown)
Counsellor–at–Law (William Wyler)
1934: Long Lost Father (Ernest Schoedsack)
Twentieth Century (Howard Hawks)
1936: Romeo and Juliet (Cukor)
1937: Maytime (Robert Z. Leonard)
Bulldog Drummond Comes Back (Louis King)
Night Club Scandal (Ralph Murphy)
Bulldog Drummond's Revenge (L. King)
True Confession (Wesley Ruggles)
1938: Romance in the Dark (H.C. Potter)
Bulldog Drummond's Peril (James Hogan)
Marie Antoinette (W.S. Van Dyke)
Spawn of the North (Henry Hathaway)
Hold That Co-ed (George Marshall)
1939: The Great Man Votes (Garson Kanin)
Midnight (Mitchell Leisen)
1940: The Great Profile (Walter Lang)
1941: The Invisible Woman (Edward Sutherland)
World Premiere (Ted Tetzlaff)
Playmates (David Butler)

WARREN BEATTY

1961: Splendor in the Grass (Elia Kazan)
The Roman Spring of Mrs. Stone (Jose Quintero)
1962: All Fall Down (John Frankenheimer)
1964: Lilith (Robert Rossen)
1965: Mickey One (Arthur Penn)
1966: Promise Her Anything (Arthur Hiller)
Kaleidoscope (Jack Smight)
1967: Bonnie and Clyde (Penn)
1970: The Only Game in Town (George Stevens)
1971: McCabe and Mrs. Miller (Robert Altman)
1972: $ (Dollars) (Richard Brooks)
1974: The Parallax View (Alan J. Pakula)
1975: Shampoo (Hal Ashby)
The Fortune (Mike Nichols)
1978: Heaven Can Wait (Warren Beatty, Buck Henry)

INGRID BERGMAN

1934: Munkbrogreven (Edvin Adolphson, Sigurd Vallen)
1935: Branningar (Ivar Johnasson)
Swedenhielms (Gustav Molander)
Valborgsmassoafton (Gustav Edgren)
1936: Pa Solsidan (Molander)
Intermezzo (Molander)
1937: Juninatten (Per Lindberg)
1938: Dollar (Molander)
En Kvinnas Ansikte (Molander)
Die Vier Gesellen (Carl Froelich)
1939: En Enda Natt (Molander)
Intermezzo: A Love Story (Gregory Ratoff)
1941: Adam Had Four Sons (Ratoff)
Rage in Heaven (W.S. Van Dyke)
Dr. Jekyll and Mr. Hyde (Victor Fleming)
1942: Casablanca (Michael Curtiz)
1943: For Whom the Bell Tolls (Sam Wood)
Swedes in America (documentary; Irving Lerner)
1944: Gaslight (George Cukor)
1945: The Bells of St. Mary's (Leo McCarey)
Spellbound (Alfred Hitchcock)
Saratoga Trunk (Sam Wood)
1946: Notorious (Hitchcock)
1948: Arch of Triumph (Lewis Milestone)
Joan of Arc (Victor Fleming)
1949: Under Capricorn (Hitchcock)
1950: Stromboli (Roberto Rossellini)
1951: Europa '51 (Rossellini)
1953: Siamo Donne (Rossellini)
1954: Viaggio in Italia (Rossellini)
1954: Joan of Arc at the Stake (Rossellini)
1955: Angst (Rossellini)

1956: Eléna et les Hommes (Jean Renoir)
Anastasia (Anatole Litvak)
1958: Indiscreet (Stanley Donen)
The Inn of the Sixth Happiness (Mark Robson)
1961: Goodbye Again (Litvak)
1964: The Visit (Bernhard Wicki)
1965: The Yellow Rolls-Royce (Anthony Asquith)
1967: Stimulantia (Molander)
1969: Cactus Flower (Gene Saks)
1970: A Walk in the Spring Rain (Guy Green)
1973: From the Mixed-Up Files of Mrs. Basil E. Frankweiler (Fielder Cook)
1974: Murder on the Orient Express (Sidney Lumet)
1976: A Matter of Time (Vincente Minnelli)
1978: Autumn Sonata (Ingmar Bergman)

JACQUELINE BISSET

1966: Cul de Sac (Roman Polanski)
1967: Casino Royale (John Huston, Ken Hughes, Robert Parrish, Joe McGrath, Val Guest)
Two for the Road (Stanley Donen)
1968: The Sweet Ride (Harvey Hart)
The Detective (Gordon Douglas)
Bullitt (Peter Yates)
1969: The First Time (James Neilson)
Secret World (Robert Freeman)
1970: Airport (George Seaton)
The Grasshopper (Jerry Paris)
1971: The Mephisto Waltz (Paul Wendkos)
Believe in Me (Stuart Hagmann)
1972: The Life and Times of Judge Roy Bean (Huston)
Stand Up and Be Counted (Jackie Cooper)
1973: Day for Night (François Truffaut)
The Thief Who Came to Dinner (Bud Yorkin)
1974: Murder on the Orient Express (Sidney Lumet)
Le Magnifique (Philippe de Broca)
The Spiral Staircase (Peter Collinson)
1976: St. Ives (J. Lee Thompson)
End of the Game (Maximilian Schell)
The Sunday Woman (Luigi Comenici)
1977: The Deep (J. L. Thompson)
1978: The Greek Tycoon (J. L. Thompson)
Secrets (Phillip Saville)
Who is Killing the Great Chefs of Europe (Ted Kotcheff)
1979: I Love you, I Love You Not (Armenia Balducci)

HUMPHREY BOGART

1930: Broadway's Like That (short; Murray Roth)
A Devil with Women (Irving Cummings)
Up the River (John Ford)
1931: Body and Soul (Alfred Santell)
Bad Sister (Hobart Henley)
Women of All Nations (Raoul Walsh)
A Holy Terror (Cummings)
1932: Love Affair (Thornton Freeland)
Big City Blues (Mervyn LeRoy)
Three on a Match (LeRoy)
1934: Midnight (Chester Erskine)
1936: The Petrified Forest (Archie Mayo)
Bullets or Ballots (William Keighley)
Two Against the World (William McGann)
China Clipper (Ray Enright)
Isle of Fury (Frank McDonald)
Black Legion (Mayo)
The Great O'Malley (William Dieterle)
1937: Marked Woman (Lloyd Bacon)
Kid Galahad (Michael Curtiz)
San Quentin (Bacon)
Dead End (William Wyler)
Stand-In (Tay Garnett)
1938: Swing Your Lady (Enright)
Crime School (Lewis Seiler)
Men Are Such Fools (Busby Berkeley)

The Amazing Dr. Clitterhouse (Anatole Litvak)
Racket Busters (Bacon)
Angels with Dirty Faces (Curtiz)
1939: King of the Underworld (Seiler)
The Oklahoma Kid (Bacon)
Dark Victory (Edmund Goulding)
You Can't Get Away with Murder (Seiler)
The Roaring Twenties (Walsh)
The Return of Dr. X (Vincent Sherman)
Invisible Stripes (Bacon)
1940: Virginia City (Curtiz)
It All Came True (Seiler)
Brother Orchid (Bacon)
They Drive by Night (Walsh)
1941: High Sierra (Walsh)
The Wagons Roll at Night (Enright)
The Maltese Falcon (John Huston)
1942: All Through the Night (V. Sherman)
The Big Shot (Seiler)
Across the Pacific (Huston)
Casablanca (Curtiz)
1943: Action in the North Atlantic (Bacon)
Thank Your Lucky Stars (David Butler)
Sahara (Zoltan Korda)
1944: Passage to Marseilles (Curtiz)
To Have and Have Not (Howard Hawks)
1945: Conflict (Curtis Bernhardt)
1946: The Big Sleep (Hawks)
1947: Dead Reckoning (John Cromwell)
The Two Mrs. Carrolls (Peter Godfrey)
Dark Passage (Delmer Daves)
1948: The Treasure of the Sierra Madre (Huston)
Key Largo (Huston)
1949: Knock on Any Door (Nicholas Ray)
Tokyo Joe (Stuart Heisler)
1950: Chain Lightning (Heisler)
In a Lonely Place (N. Ray)
1951: The Enforcer (Bretaigne Windust)
Sirocco (Bernhardt)
1952: The African Queen (Huston)
Deadline U.S.A. (Richard Brooks)
1953: Battle Circus (Brooks)
1954: Beat the Devil (Huston)
The Caine Mutiny (Edward Dmytryk)
Sabrina (Billy Wilder)
The Barefoot Contessa (Joseph L. Mankiewicz)
1955: We're No Angels (Curtiz)
The Left Hand of God (Dmytryk)
The Desperate Hours (Wyler)
1956: The Harder They Fall (Mark Robson)

CHARLES BOYER

1920: L'Homme du Large (Marcel L'Herbier)
1921: Chantelouve (Georges Monca, Rose Pansini)
1922: Le Grillon du Foyer (Jean Manoussi)
1923: L'Esclave (Monca, Pansini)
1927: La Ronde Infernale (Luitz-Morat)
1928: Le Capitaine Fracasse (Alberto Cavalcanti)
1929: La Bacarolle d'Amour (Henri Roussel)
Le Procès de Mary Dugan (Marcel de Sano)
1930: Big-House (Paul Fejos)
1931: The Magnificent Lie (Berthold Viertel)
Tumultes (Robert Siodmak)
1932: The Man from Yesterday (B. Viertel)
Red Headed Woman (Jack Conway)
F.P.I. Ne Répond Pas (Karl Hartl)
1933: Moi et l'Imperatrice (Friedrich Hollaender)
Heart Song (Hollaender)
L'Épervier (L'Herbier)
1934: Le Bonheur (L'Herbier)
La Bataille (Nicholas Farkas)
Liliom (Fritz Lang)
Caravan (Erik Charrell)
1935: Private Worlds (Gregory La Cava)
Break of Hearts (Philip Moeller)
Shanghai (James Flood)
1936: Mayerling (Anatole Litvak)
The Garden of Allah (Richard Boleslawski)

1937: History Is Made at Night (Frank Borzage)
Conquest (Clarence Brown)
Tovarich (Litvak)
L'Orage (Marc Allegret)
1938: Algiers (John Cromwell)
1939: Love Affair (Leo McCarey)
When Tomorrow Comes (John M. Stahl)
1940: All This and Heaven Too (Litvak)
1941: Back Street (Robert Stevenson)
Hold Back the Dawn (Mitchell Leisen)
Appointment for Love (William A. Seiter)
1942: Tales of Manhattan (Julien Duvivier)
1943: The Constant Nymph (Edmund Goulding)
The Heart of a Nation (Duvivier, as narrator)
Flesh and Fantasy (Duvivier)
1944: Gaslight (George Cukor)
Together Again (Charles Vidor)
1945: Confidential Agent (Herman Shumlin)
1946: Cluny Brown (Ernst Lubitsch)
1947: A Woman's Vengeance (Zoltan Korda)
1948: Arch of Triumph (Lewis Milestone)
1949: Bataille du Rail (documentary; Rene Clement, as narrator)
1951: The Thirteenth Letter (Otto Preminger)
The First Legion (Douglas Sirk)
1952: The Happy Time (Richard Fleischer)
1953: Thunder in the East (C. Vidor)
Madame de . . . (Max Ophuls)
1954: Nana (Christian-Jacque)
1955: La Fortuna de Essere Donna (Alessandro Blasetti)
The Cobweb (Vincente Minnelli)
1956: Paris-Palace Hotel (Henri Verneuil)
Around the World in Eighty Days (Michael Anderson)
1957: Une Parisienne (Michel Boisrond)
1958: Maxime (Verneuil)
The Buccaneer (Anthony Quinn)
1961: Fanny (Joshua Logan)
Julia du Bist Zauberhaft (Alfred Weidenmann)
1962: The Four Horsemen of the Apocalypse (Minnelli)
Les Demons de Minuit (Allegret, Charles Gerard)
1963: Love is a Ball (David Swift)
1965: A Very Special Favor (Michael Gordon)
1966: How to Steal a Million (William Wyler)
Is Paris Burning? (René Clement)
1967: Casino Royale (John Huston, Ken Hughes, Robert Parrish, Val Guest, Joe McGrath)
Barefoot in the Park (Gene Saks)
1968: The Day the Hot Line Got Hot (Etienne Perier)
1969: The April Fools (Stuart Rosenberg)
The Madwoman of Chaillot (Bryan Forbes)
1973: Lost Horizon (Charles Jarrott)
1974: Stavisky (Alain Resnais)
1976: A Matter of Time (Minnelli)

MARLON BRANDO

1950: The Men (Fred Zinnemann)
1951: A Streetcar Named Desire (Elia Kazan)
1952: Viva Zapata! (Kazan)
1953: Julius Caesar (Joseph L. Mankiewicz)
The Wild One (Laslo Benedek)
1954: On the Waterfront (Kazan)
Désirée (Henry Koster)
1955: Guys and Dolls (Mankiewicz)
1956: The Teahouse of the August Moon (Daniel Mann)
1957: Sayonara (Joshua Logan)
1958: The Young Lions (Edward Dmytryk)
1960: The Fugitive Kind (Sidney Lumet)
1961: One-Eyed Jacks (Marlon Brando)
1962: Mutiny on the Bounty (Lewis Milestone)
1963: The Ugly American (George Englund)
1964: Bedtime Story (Ralph Levy)
1965: Morituri (Bernhard Wicki)

1966: The Chase (Arthur Penn)
The Appaloosa (Sidney J. Furie)
1967: A Countess from Hong Kong (Charles Chaplin)
Reflections in a Golden Eye (John Huston)
1968: Candy (Christian Marquand)
1969: The Night of the Following Day (Hubert Cornfield)
1970: Burn! (Gillo Pontecorvo)
1972: The Nightcomers (Michael Winner)
The Godfather (Francis Ford Coppola)
Last Tango in Paris (Bernardo Bertolucci)
1976: The Missouri Breaks (Penn)
1978: Superman (Richard Donner)
1979: Apocalypse Now (Coppola)

JEFF BRIDGES

1970: Halls of Anger (Paul Bogart)
1971: The Last Picture Show (Peter Bogdanovich)
1972: Fat City (John Huston)
Bad Company (Robert Benton)
1973: The Last American Hero (Lamont Johnson)
Lolly-Madonna XXX (Richard Sarafian)
The Iceman Cometh (John Frankenheimer)
1974: Thunderbolt and Lightfoot (Michael Cimino)
1975: Rancho Deluxe (Frank Perry)
Hearts of the West (Howard Zieff)
1976: Stay Hungry (Bob Rafelson)
King Kong (John Guillermin)
1978: Somebody Killed Her Husband (L. Johnson)
Winter Kills (Bill Richert)

CHARLES BRONSON

1951: You're in the Navy Now (Henry Hathaway)
The People Against O'Hara (John Sturges)
The Mob (Robert Parrish)
1952: My Six Convicts (Hugo Fregonese)
Red Skies of Montana (Joseph M. Newman)
The Marrying Kind (George Cukor)
Pat and Mike (Cukor)
Diplomatic Courier (Hathaway)
Bloodhounds of Broadway (Harmon Jones)
1953: House of Wax (Andre de Toth)
Miss Sadie Thompson (Curtis Bernhardt)
Crime Wave (The City is Dark) (de Toth)
1954: Tennessee Champ (Fred M. Wilcox)
Riding Shotgun (de Toth)
Apache (Robert Aldrich)
Drum Beat (Delmer Daves)
Verz Cruz (Aldrich)
1955: Big House, U.S.A. (Howard W. Koch)
Target Zero (Jones)
1956: Jubal (Daves)
1957: Run of the Arrow (Sam Fuller)
1958: Showdown at Boot Hill (Gene Fowler, Jr.)
Machine Gun Kelly (Roger Corman)
Gang War (Fowler, Jr.)
When Hell Broke Loose (Kenneth G. Crane)
Ten North Frederick (Philip Dunne)
1959: Never So Few (J. Sturges)
1960: The Magnificent Seven (J. Sturges)
1961: Master of the World (William Witney)
A Thunder of Drums (Joseph Newman)
X-15 (Richard Donner)
1962: Kid Galahad (Phil Karlson)
1963: The Great Escape (J. Sturges)
Four for Texas (Aldrich)
1964: The Americanization of Emily (Arthur Hiller)
Guns of Diablo (Boris Sagal)
1965: The Sandpiper (Vincente Minnelli)
Battle of the Bulge (Ken Annakin)
1966: This Property Is Condemned (Sydney Pollack)
1967: The Dirty Dozen (Aldrich)
1968: Guns for San Sebastian (Henri Verneuil)

Villa Rides (Buzz Kulik)
Farewell Friend (Jean Herman)
1969: Once Upon a Time in the West (Sergio Leone)
Rider on the Rain (René Clement)
Twinky (Donner)
1970: You Can't Win 'em All (Peter Collinson)
Two Minds for Murder (Nicholas Gessner)
The Family (Sergio Solloman)
1971: Cold Sweat (Terence Young)
Red Sun (Young)
1972: Chato's Land (Michael Winner)
The Mechanic (Winner)
The Valachi Papers (Young)
1973: The Stone Killer (Winner)
Mr. Majestyk (Richard Fleischer)
1974: Death Wish (Winner)
1975: Break Out (Tom Gries)
Hard Times (Walter Hill)
1976: Breakheart Pass (Gries)
Chino (J. Sturges)
From Noon Till Three (Frank D. Gilroy)
St. Ives (J. Lee Thompson)
1977: The White Buffalo (Thompson)
Telefon (Don Siegel)
1978: Love and Bullets, Charlie (Stuart Rosenberg)

LOUISE BROOKS

1925: The Street of Forgotten Men (Herbert Brenon)
1926: The American Venus (Frank Tuttle)
A Social Celebrity (Malcolm St. Clair)
It's the Old Army Game (Edward Sutherland)
The Show-off (St. Clair)
Just Another Blonde (Alfred E. Santell)
Love 'em and Leave 'em (Tuttle)
1927: Evening Clothes (Luther Reed)
Rolled Stockings (Richard Rosson)
City Gone Wild (James Cruze)
Now We're in the Air (Frank B. Strayer)
1928: A Girl in Every Port (Howard Hawks)
Beggars of Life (William Wellman)
1929: The Canary Murder Case (St. Clair)
Pandora's Box (G. W. Pabst)
Diary of a Lost Girl (Pabst)
1930: Prix de Beauté (Augusto Genina)
1931: Windy Rides Goes Hollywood (Short; William Goodrich, Roscoe Arbuckle)
1931: It Pays to Advertise (Tuttle)
God's Gift to Women (Michael Curtiz)
1936: Empty Saddles (Lesley Selander)
1938: Overland Stage Raiders (George Sherman)

PHYLLIS BROOKS

1934: I've Been Around (Philip Cahn)
1935: McFadden's Flats (Ralph Murphy)
Another Face (Christy Cabanne)
To Beat the Band (Ben Stoloff)
Lady Tubbs (Alan Crosland)
1937: You Can't Have Everything (Norman Taurog)
Dangerously Yours (Malcolm St. Clair)
City Girl (Alfred Werker)
1938: In Old Chicago (Henry King)
Rebecca of Sunnybrook Farm (Allan Dwan)
Walking Down Broadway (Irving Cummings)
Little Miss Broadway (Cummings)
Straight, Place and Show (David Butler)
Up the River (Werker)
Charlie Chan in Honolulu (H. Bruce Humberstone)
1939: Charlie Chan in Reno (Norman Foster)
Slightly Honorable (Tay Garnett)
1940: The Flying Squad (Herbert Brenon)
1941: The Shanghai Gesture (Josef von Sternberg)
1943: Hi Ya Sailor (Jean Yarbrough)
Silver Spurs (Joseph Kane)
No Place for a Lady (James Hogan)
1944: Lady in the Dark (Mitchell Leisen)

Bring on the Girls (Sidney Lanfield)
Dangerous Passage (William Berke)
1945: The Unseen (Lewis B. Allen)
High Powered (Berke)

GENEVIEVE BUJOLD

1956: French Can-Can (Jean Renoir)
1966: La Guerre est Finie (Alain Resnais)
1967: The Adolescents (Gian Vittorio Baldi, Michel Brault, Jean Rouch)
King of Hearts (Philippe De Broca)
Le Voleur (Louis Malle)
1968: Isabel (Paul Almond)
1969: Anne of the Thousand Days (Charles Jarrott)
1970: Act of the Heart (Almond)
1972: Journey (Almond)
1974: Earthquake (Mark Robson)
1975: Kamouraska (Claude Jutra)
1976: Alex and the Gypsy (John Korty)
Swashbuckler (James Goldstone)
Obsession (Brian De Palma)
1977: Another Man, Another Chance (Claude Lelouch)
1978: Coma (Michael Crichton)
1979: Sherlock Holmes: Murder by Decree (Bob Clark)

RICHARD BURTON

1948: The Last Days of Dolwyn (Emlyn Williams)
1949: Now Barabbas Was a Robber (Gordon Parry)
1950: Waterfront (Michael Anderson)
1951: The Woman with No Name (Ladislas Vajda)
Green Grow the Rushes (Derek Twist)
1952: My Cousin Rachel (Henry Koster)
1953: The Robe (Koster)
The Desert Rats (Robert Wise)
1955: Prince of Players (Philip Dunne)
The Rains of Ranchipur (Jean Negulesco)
1956: Alexander the Great (Robert Rossen)
1957: Sea Wife (Bob McNaught)
1958: Bitter Victory (Nicholas Ray)
1959: Look Back in Anger (Tony Richardson)
1960: The Bramble Bush (Daniel Petrie)
Ice Palace (Vincent Sherman)
1962: The Longest Day (Ken Annakin, Andrew Marton, Bernhard Wicki)
1963: Cleopatra (Joseph L. Mankiewicz)
The V.I.P.s (Anthony Asquith)
1964: Becket (Peter Glenville)
The Night of the Iguana (John Huston)
1965: The Sandpiper (Vincente Minnelli)
The Spy Who Came in from the Cold (Martin Ritt)
1966: Who's Afraid of Virginia Woolf? (Mike Nichols)
1967: The Taming of the Shrew (Franco Zeffirelli)
The Comedians (Peter Glenville)
1968: Dr. Faustus (Richard Burton, Nevill Coghill)
Boom! (Joseph Losey)
Candy (Christian Marquand)
1969: Where Eagles Dare (Brian G. Hutton)
Staircase (Stanley Donen)
Anne of the Thousand Days (Charles Jarrott)
1971: Raid on Rommel (Henry Hathaway)
Villain (Michael Tuchner)
1972: The Assassination of Trotsky (Losey)
Hammersmith Is Out (Peter Ustinov)
Bluebeard (Edward Dmytryk)
1973: Under Milk Wood (Andrew Sinclair)
1974: The Journey (Vittorio De Sica)
Massacre in Rome (George P. Cosmatos)
The Klansman (Terence Young)
1977: Equus (Sidney Lumet)
The Exorcist II: The Heretic (John Boorman)
1978: The Medusa Touch (Jack Gold)
The Wild Geese (Andrew V. McLaglen)
1979: Boarding Party (McLaglen)
Absolution (Anthony Page)

JAMES CAGNEY

1930: Sinner's Holiday (John G. Adolfi)
Doorway to Hell (Archie Mayo)
1931: Other Men's Women (William Wellman)
The Millionaire (Adolfi)
The Public Enemy (Wellman)
Smart Money (Alfred E. Green)
Blonde Crazy (Roy Del Ruth)
1932: Taxi! (Del Ruth)
The Crowd Roars (Howard Hawks)
Winner Take All (Del Ruth)
1933: Hard to Handle (Mervyn LeRoy)
Picture Snatcher (Lloyd Bacon)
The Mayor of Hell (Mayo)
Footlight Parade (Bacon)
Lady Killer (Del Ruth)
1934: Jimmy the Gent (Michael Curtiz)
He was Her Man (Bacon)
Here Comes the Navy (Bacon)
The St. Louis Kid (Ray Enright)
1935: Devil Dogs of the Air (Bacon)
G-Men (William Keighley)
The Irish in Us (Bacon)
A Midsummer Night's Dream (Max Reinhardt, William Dieterle)
Frisco Kid (Bacon)
Ceiling Zero (Hawks)
1936: Great Guy (John G. Blystone)
1937: Something to Sing About (Victor Schertzinger)
1938: Boy Meets Girl (Bacon)
Angels with Dirty Faces (Curtiz)
1939: The Oklahoma Kid (Bacon)
Each Dawn I Die (Keighley)
The Roaring Twenties (Raoul Walsh)
1940: The Fighting 69th (Keighley)
Torrid Zone (Keighley)
City for Conquest (Anatole Litvak)
1941: The Strawberry Blonde (Walsh)
The Bride Came C.O.D. (Keighley)
1942: Captains of the Clouds (Curtiz)
Yankee Doodle Dandy (Curtiz)
1943: Johnny Come Lately (William K. Howard)
1945: Blood on the Sun (Frank Lloyd)
1946: 13 Rue Madeleine (Henry Hathaway)
1948: The Time of Your Life (H.C. Potter)
1949: White Heat (Walsh)
1950: West Point Story (Del Ruth)
Kiss Tomorrow Goodbye (Gordon Douglas)
1951: Come Fill the Cup (G. Douglas)
Starlift (Del Ruth)
1952: What Price Glory? (John Ford)
1953: A Lion Is in the Streets (Walsh)
1955: Run for Cover (Nicholas Ray)
Love Me or Leave Me (Charles Vidor)
Mister Roberts (Ford, LeRoy)
The Seven Little Foys (Melville Shavelson)
1956: Tribute to a Bad Man (Robert Wise)
These Wilder Years (Roy Rowland)
1957: Man of a Thousand Faces (Joseph Pevney)
Short Cut to Hell (James Cagney, director only)
1958: Never Steal Anything Small (Charles Lederer)
1959: Shake Hands with the Devil (Michael Anderson)
1960: The Gallant Hours (Robert Montgomery)
1961: One, Two, Three (Billy Wilder)

DAVID CARRADINE

1967: The Violent Ones (Fernando Lamas)
1969: The Good Guys and the Bad Guys (Burt Kennedy)
Young Billy Young (Kennedy)
Heaven with a Gun (Lee H. Katzin)
1970: The McMasters (Alf Kjellin)
Macho Callahan (Bernard L. Kowalski)
1972: Boxcar Bertha (Martin Scorsese)
1973: Mean Streets (Scorsese)
1975: Death Race 2000 (Paul Bartel)
You and Me (David Carradine)
1976: Cannonball (Bartel)
Bound for Glory (Hal Ashby)
1977: The Serpent's Egg (Ingmar Bergman)

Thunder and Lightning (Corey Allen)
1978: Deathsport (Henry Suso, Allan Arkush)
Gray Lady Down (David Greene)
The Moonbeam Rider (Steve Carver)
1979: Cloud Dancer (Barry Brown)

NANCY CARROLL

1927: Ladies Must Dress (Victor Heerman)
1928: Abie's Irish Rose (Victor Fleming)
Easy Come, Easy Go (Frank Tuttle)
Chicken à la King (Henry Lehrman)
The Water Hole (F. Richard Jones)
Manhattan Cocktail (Dorothy Arzner)
1929: The Shopworn Angel (Richard Wallace)
The Wolf of Wall Street (Rowland V. Lee)
Sin Sister (Charles Klein)
Close Harmony (John Cromwell, Edward Sutherland)
The Dance of Life (Sutherland)
Illusion (Lothar Mendes)
Sweetie (Frank Tuttle)
1930: Dangerous Paradise (William Wellman)
Honey (Wesley Ruggles)
Paramount on Parade (Arzner, Otto Brower, Edmund Goulding, Heerman, Edwin Knopf, R. Lee, Ernst Lubitsch, Mendes, Victor Schertzinger, Sutherland, Tuttle)
The Devil's Holiday (Goulding)
Follow Thru (Lawrence Schwab, Lloyd Corrigan)
Laughter (Harry D'Arrast)
1931: Stolen Heaven (George Abbott)
The Night Angel (Goulding)
Personal Maid (Monta Bell)
1932: Broken Lullaby (Lubitsch)
Wayward (Edward Sloman)
Scarlet Dawn (William Dieterle)
Hot Saturday (William A. Seiter)
Under Cover Man (James Flood)
1933: Child of Manhattan (Edward Buzzell)
The Woman Accused (Paul Sloane)
The Kiss Before the Mirror (James Whale)
I Love That Man (Harry Joe Brown)
1934: Springtime for Henry (Tuttle)
Transatlantic Merry-Go-Round (Benjamin Stoloff)
Jealousy (Roy William Neill)
1935: I'll Love You Always (Leo Bulgakov)
After the Dance (Bulgakov)
Atlantic Adventure (Albert S. Rogell)
1938: There Goes My Heart (Norman Z. McLeod)
That Certain Age (Edward Ludwig)

LON CHANEY, JR.

1932: Girl Crazy (William Seiter)
Bird of Paradise (King Vidor)
The Last Frontier (Serial; Spencer Bennet)
1933: Lucky Devils (Ralph Ince)
Scarlet River (Otto Brower)
Son of the Border (Lloyd Nosler)
The Three Musketeers (Serial; Armand L. Schaefer)
1934: Sixteen Fathoms Deep (Schaefer)
Girl O' My Dreams (Raymond McCarey)
The Life of Vergie Winters (Alfred Santell)
1935: Captain Hurricane (John Robertson)
Accent on Youth (Wesley Ruggles)
The Shadow of Silk Lennox (Ray Kirkwood)
Scream in the Night (Fred Newmeyer)
The Marriage Bargain (Albert Ray)
1936: The Singing Cowboy (Mack V. Wright)
Undersea Kingdom (B. Reeves Eason, Joseph Kane)
Ace Drummond (Serial; Ford Beebe, Cliff Smith)
Killer at Large (David Selman)
The Old Corral (Kane)
Rose Bowl (Charles Barton)
1937: Cheyenne Rides Again (Robert Hill)

Midnight Taxi (Eugene Forde)
Secret Agent X-9 (Serial; Beebe)
That I May Live (Allan Dwan)
Angel's Holiday (James Tinling)
Slave Ship (Tay Garnett)
Born Reckless (Malcolm St. Clair)
One Mile from Heaven (Dwan)
Wild and Woolly (Alfred Werker)
Thin Ice (Lanfield)
Wife, Doctor and Nurse (Walter Lang)
Life Begins at College (Seiter)
Charlie Chan on Broadway (E. Forde)
Second Honeymoon (W. Lang)
Love and Hisses (Lanfield)
Love Is News (Garnett)
City Girl (Werker)
1938: Happy Landing (Roy Del Ruth)
Sally, Irene and Mary (Seiter)
Walking Down Broadway (Norman Foster)
Mr. Moto's Gamble (Tinling)
Josette (Dwan)
Passport Husband (Tinling)
Alexander's Ragtime Band (Henry King)
Speed to Burn (Brower)
Straight, Place and Show (David Butler)
Road Demon (Brower)
1939: Jesse James (King)
Union Pacific (Cecil B. De Mille)
Frontier Marshal (Dwan)
Charlie Chan in the City of Darkness (Herbert Leeds)
Of Mice and Men (Lewis Milestone)
1940: One Million B.C. (Hal Roach; Hal Roach, Jr.)
Northwest Mounted Police (De Mille)
1941: Man Made Monster (George Waggner)
Too Many Blondes (Thornton Freeland)
Billy the Kid (David Miller)
San Antonio Rose (Charles Lamont)
Riders of Death Valley (Serial; Beebe, Ray Taylor)
Badlands of Dakota (Alfred Green)
The Wolf Man (Waggner)
1942: North to the Klondike (Erle C. Kenton)
Overland Mail (Serial; Beebe, John Rawlins)
The Ghost of Frankenstein (Kenton)
Keeping Fit (Short; Arthur Lubin)
The Mummy's Tomb (Harold Young)
1943: Eyes of the Underworld (Roy William Neill)
Frankenstein Meets the Wolf Man (Neill)
What We Are Fighting For (Serial; Kenton)
Frontier Badmen (Beebe)
Crazy House (Edward Cline)
Son of Dracula (Robert Siodmak)
1944: Calling Dr. Death (Reginald LeBorg)
Weird Woman (LeBorg)
Ghost Catchers (Cline)
Follow the Boys (Edward Sutherland)
Cobra Woman (R. Siodmak)
The Mummy's Ghost (LeBorg)
Dead Man's Eyes (LeBorg)
1945: Here Come the Co-eds (Jean Yarbrough)
House of Frankenstein (Kenton)
The Mummy's Curse (Leslie Goodwins)
The Frozen Ghost (Harold Young)
Strange Confession (John Hoffman)
The Daltons Ride Again (Ray Taylor)
House of Dracula (Kenton)
Pillow of Death (Wallace Fox)
1947: My Favorite Brunette (Elliott Nugent)
1948: Albuquerque (Peter Stewart)
Sixteen Fathoms Deep (Irving Allen)
Abbott and Costello Meet Frankenstein (Barton)
1949: There's a Girl in My Heart (Arthur Dreifuss)
Captain China (Lewis Foster)
1950: Once a Thief (W. Lee Wilder)

1951: Inside Straight (Gerald Mayer)
Only the Valiant (Gordon Douglas)
Behave Yourself! (George Beck)
Bride of the Gorilla (Curt Siodmak)
Flame of Araby (Lamont)
1952: The Bushwhackers (Rod Amateau)
Thief of Damascus (Will Jason)
High Noon (Fred Zinnemann)
Springfield Rifle (Andre De Toth)
The Black Castle (Nathan Juran)
The Battles of Chief Pontiac (Felix Feist)
1953: Raiders of the Seven Seas (Sidney Salkow)
Bandit Island (Serial; Robert Lippert)
A Lion Is in the Streets (Raoul Walsh)
1954: Jivaro (Edward Ludwig)
The Boy from Oklahoma (Michael Curtiz)
Casanova's Big Night (Norman Z. McLeod)
The Big Chase (Arthur Hilton)
Passion (Dwan)
The Black Pirates (Allen H. Miner)
1955: Big House U.S.A. (Howard W. Koch)
The Silver Star (Richard Bartlett)
Not as a Stranger (Stanley Kramer)
I Died a Thousand Times (Stuart Heisler)
The Indian Fighter (De Toth)
1956: Manfish (W. Lee Wilder)
The Black Sleep (LeBorg)
Along the Mohawk Trail (Sam Newfield)
The Redmen and the Renegades (Newfield)
The Pathfinder and the Mohican (Newfield)
The Indestructible Man (Jack Pollexfen)
Daniel Boone, Trail Blazer (Albert C. Gannaway, Ishmael Rodriquez)
Pardners (Taurog)
1957: The Cyclops (Bert I. Gordon)
1958: The Defiant Ones (Kramer)
Money, Women and Guns (Bartlett)
1959: The House of Terror (Gilberto Martinez Solares)
The Alligator People (Del Ruth)
Night of the Ghouls (Edward Wood)
1961: Rebellion in Cuba (Gannaway)
1962: The Devil's Messenger (Herbert Strock)
1963: The Haunted Palace (Roger Corman)
1964: Law of the Lawless (William F. Claxton)
Witchcraft (Don Sharp)
Stage to Thunder Rock (Claxton)
1965: Young Fury (Christian Nyby)
Black Spurs (R. G. Springsteen)
House of the Black Death (Harold Daniels)
Town Tamer (Lesley Selander)
1966: Apache Uprising (Springsteen)
Johnny Reno (Springsteen)
Night of the Beast (Daniels)
1967: Welcome to Hard Times (Burt Kennedy)
Hillbillys in a Haunted House (Yarbrough)
Dr. Terror's Gallery of Horror (David L. Hewitt)
The Far Out West (Joe Connelly)
1968: Buckskin (Michael Moore)
Cannibal (Jack Hill)
1969: A Stranger in Town (Earl J. Miller)
Fireball Jungle (G.B. Roberts)
1971: Dracula vs. Frankenstein (Al Adamson)
The Female Bunch (Adamson)

CHARLES CHAPLIN

Shorts:
1914: Making a Living (Henry Lehrman)
Kid Auto Races at Venice (Lehrman)
Mabel's Strange Predicament (Mack Sennett)
Between Showers (Lehrman)
A Film Johnnie (Sennett)
Tango Tangles (Sennett)
His Favorite Pastime (George Nichols)
Cruel, Cruel Love (Sennett)

The Star Boarder (Sennett)
Mabel at the Wheel (Sennett, Mabel Normand)
Twenty Minutes of Love (Sennett)
Caught in a Cabaret (Charles Chaplin, Normand)
Caught in the Rain (Chaplin)
A Busy Day (Chaplin)
The Fatal Mallet (Chaplin, Normand, Sennett)
Her Friend the Bandit (Chaplin, Normand)
The Knockout (Sennett)
Mabel's Busy Day (Chaplin, Normand)
Mabel's Married Life (Chaplin, Normand)
Laughing Gas (Chaplin)
The Property Man (Chaplin)
The Face on the Barroom Floor (Chaplin)
Recreation (Chaplin)
The Masquerader (Chaplin)
His New Profession (Chaplin)
The Rounders (Chaplin)
The New Janitor (Chaplin)
Those Love Pangs (Chaplin)
Dough and Dynamite (Chaplin)
Gentlemen of Nerve (Chaplin)
His Musical Career (Chaplin)
His Trysting Place (Chaplin)
Getting Acquainted (Chaplin)
His Prehistoric Past (Chaplin)
1915: His New Job (Chaplin)
A Night Out (Chaplin)
The Champion (Chaplin)
In the Park (Chaplin)
A Jitney Elopement (Chaplin)
The Tramp (Chaplin)
By the Sea (Chaplin)
Work (Chaplin)
A Woman (Chaplin)
The Bank (Chaplin)
A Night at the Show (Chaplin)
1916: Charlie Chaplin's Burlesque on Carmen (Chaplin)
Police (Chaplin)
The Fireman (Chaplin)
The Vagabond (Chaplin)
One A.M. (Chaplin)
The Count (Chaplin)
The Pawnshop (Chaplin)
Behind the Screen (Chaplin)
The Rink (Chaplin)
1917: Easy Street (Chaplin)
The Cure (Chaplin)
The Immigrant (Chaplin)
The Adventurer (Chaplin)
1918: Triple Trouble (Chaplin)
A Dog's Life (Chaplin)
Shoulder Arms (Chaplin)
1919: Sunnyside (Chaplin)
A Day's Pleasure (Chaplin)
1921: The Idle Class (Chaplin)
1922: Pay Day (Chaplin)
1923: The Pilgrim (Chaplin)
Features:
1914: Tillie's Punctured Romance (Sennett)
1921: The Kid (Chaplin)
1923: A Woman of Paris (Chaplin)
1923: The Gold Rush (Chaplin)
1928: The Circus (Chaplin)
1931: City Lights (Chaplin)
1936: Modern Times (Chaplin)
1940: The Great Dictator (Chaplin)
1947: Monsieur Verdoux (Chaplin, Robert Florey)
1952: Limelight (Chaplin)
1957: A King in New York)Chaplin)
1967: A Countess from Hong Kong (Chaplin)

MONTGOMERY CLIFT
1948: The Search (Fred Zinnemann)
Red River (Howard Hawks)
1949: The Heiress (William Wyler)
1950: The Big Lift (George Seaton)
1951: A Place in the Sun (George Stevens)
1953: I Confess (Alfred Hitchcock)
From Here to Eternity (Zinnemann)
1954: Indiscretion of an American Wife (Vittorio De Sica)
1957: Raintree County (Edward Dmytryk)
1958: The Young Lions (Dmytryk)
Lonelyhearts (Vincent J. Donehue)
1959: Suddenly, Last Summer (Joseph L. Mankiewicz)
1960: Wild River (Elia Kazan)

1961: The Misfits (John Huston)
Judgment at Nuremberg (Stanley Kramer)
1962: Freud (Huston)
1966: The Defector (Raoul Levy)

LEE J. COBB
1934: The Vanishing Shadow (Serial; Louis Friedlander)
1937: North of the Rio Grande (Nate Watt)
Ali Baba Goes to Town (David Butler)
Rustler's Valley (Watt)
1938: Danger on the Air (Otis Garrett)
1939: The Phantom Creeps (Serial; Ford Beebe, Saul A. Goodkind)
Golden Boy (Rouben Mamoulian)
1941: Men of Boys Town (Norman Taurog)
This Thing Called Love (Alexander Hall)
Paris Calling (Edwin L. Marin)
1943: Tonight We Raid Calais (John Brahm)
Buckskin Frontier (Lesley Selander)
The Moon Is Down (Irving Pichel)
The Song of Bernadette (Henry King)
1944: Winged Victory (George Cukor)
1946: Anna and the King of Siam (John Cromwell)
1947: Boomerang (Elia Kazan)
Johnny O'Clock (Robert Rossen)
Captain from Castile (King)
1948: Call Northside 777 (Henry Hathaway)
The Miracle of the Bells (Pichel)
The Luck of the Irish (Henry Koster)
1949: The Dark Past (Rudolph Mate)
Thieves' Highway (Jules Dassin)
1950: The Man Who Cheated Himself (Felix Feist)
1951: Sirocco (Curtis Bernhardt)
The Family Secret (Henry Levin)
1952: The Fighter (Herbert Kline)
1953: The Tall Texan (Elmo Williams)
1954: Yankee Pasha (Joseph Pevney)
Gorilla at Large (Harmon Jones)
On the Waterfront (Kazan)
Day of Triumph (Pichel, John Coyle)
1955: The Racers (Hathaway)
The Road to Denver (Joseph Kane)
The Left Hand of God (Edward Dmytryk)
1956: The Man in the Gray Flannel Suit (Nunnally Johnson)
Miami Expose (Fred Sears)
1957: Twelve Angry Men (Sidney Lumet)
The Garment Jungle (Vincent Sherman)
The Three Faces of Eve (N. Johnson)
1958: The Brothers Karamazov (Richard Brooks)
Man of the West (Anthony Mann)
Party Girl (Nicholas Ray)
1959: The Trap (Norman Panama)
Green Mansions (Mel Ferrer)
But Not for Me (Walter Lang)
1960: Exodus (Otto Preminger)
1962: The Four Horsemen of the Apocalypse (Vincente Minnelli)
How the West Was Won (Hathaway, John Ford, George Marshall)
1963: Come Blow Your Horn (Bud Yorkin)
1966: Our Man Flint (Daniel Mann)
1967: In Like Flint (Gordon Douglas)
1968: MacKenna's Gold (J. Lee Thompson)
Coogan's Bluff (Don Siegel)
The Day of the Owl (Damiano Damiani)
They Came to Rob Las Vegas (Antonio Isasi)
1970: The Liberation of L. B. Jones (William Wyler)
Macho Callahan (Bernard Kowalski)
1971: Lawman (Michael Winner)
1973: The Exorcist (William Friedkin)
The Man Who Loved Cat Dancing (Richard C. Sarafian)
1975: That Lucky Touch (Christopher Miles)

CLAUDETTE COLBERT
1927: For the Love of Mike (Frank Capra)
1929: The Hole in the Wall (Robert Florey)
The Lady Lies (Hobart Henley)
1930: The Big Pond (Henley)
Young Man of Manhattan (Monta Bell)
Manslaughter (George Abbott)
1931: Honor Among Lovers (Dorothy Arzner)
The Smiling Lieutenant (Ernst Lubitsch)
Secrets of a Secretary (Abbott)
His Woman (Edward Sloman)
1932: The Wiser Sex (Berthold Viertel)
Misleading Lady (Stuart Walker)
The Man from Yesterday (B. Viertel)
Phantom President (Norman Taurog)
The Sign of the Cross (Cecil B. De Mille)
1933: Tonight Is Ours (S. Walker)
I Cover the Waterfront (James Cruze)
Three-Cornered Moon (Elliott Nugent)
The Torch Singer (Alexander Hall)
1934: Four Frightened People (De Mille)
It Happened One Night (Capra)
Cleopatra (De Mille)
Imitation of Life (John M. Stahl)
1935: The Gilded Lily (Wesley Ruggles)
Private Worlds (Gregory La Cava)
She Married Her Boss (La Cava)
The Bride Comes Home (Ruggles)
1936: Under Two Flags (Frank Lloyd)
1937: Maid of Salem (Lloyd)
I Met Him in Paris (Ruggles)
Tovarich (Anatole Litvak)
1938: Bluebeard's Eighth Wife (Lubitsch)
1939: Zaza (Cukor)
Midnight (Mitchell Leisen)
It's a Wonderful World (W.S. Van Dyke)
Drums Along the Mohawk (John Ford)
1940: Boom Town (Jack Conway)
Arise, My Love (Leisen)
1941: Skylark (Mark Sandrich)
Remember the Day (Henry King)
1942: The Palm Beach Story (Preston Sturges)
1943: So Proudly We Hail (Sandrich)
No Time for Love (Leisen)
1944: Since You Went Away (John Cromwell)
1945: Practically Yours (Leisen)
Guest Wife (Sam Wood)
1946: Tomorrow Is Forever (Irving Pichel)
Without Reservations (Mervyn LeRoy)
The Secret Heart (Robert Z. Leonard)
1947: The Egg and I (Chester Erskine)
1948: Sleep, My Love (Douglas Sirk)
1949: Family Honeymoon (Claude Binyon)
Bride for Sale (William D. Russell)
1950: Three Came Home (Jean Negulesco)
The Secret Fury (Mel Ferrer)
1951: Thunder on the Hill (Sirk)
Let's Make It Legal (Richard Sale)
1952: Outpost in Malaya (Ken Annakin)
1954: Daughters of Destiny (Marcel Pagliero)
1955: Texas Lady (Tim Whelan)
1957: Royal Affairs in Versailles (Sacha Guitry)
1961: Parrish (Delmer Daves)

RONALD COLMAN
1919: The Toilers (Tom Watts)
A Daughter of Eve (Walter West)
Snow in the Desert (West)
1920: A Son of David (Hay Plumb)
Anna the Adventuress (Cecil Hepworth)
The Black Spider (William J. Humphrey)
1921: Handcuffs or Kisses (George Archainbaud)
1923: The Eternal City (George Fitzmaurice)
The White Sister (Henry King)

1924: Twenty Dollars a Week (Harmon F. Weight)
Tarnish (Fitzmaurice)
Romola (H. King)
1925: Her Night of Romance (Sidney Franklin)
A Thief in Paradise (Fitzmaurice)
His Supreme Moment (Fitzmaurice)
The Sporting Venus (Marshall Neilan)
Her Sister from Paris (Franklin)
The Dark Angle (Fitzmaurice)
Stella Dallas (H. King)
Lady Windermere's Fan (Ernst Lubitsch)
1926: Kiki (Clarence Brown)
Beau Geste (Herbert Brenon)
The Winning of Barbara Worth (H. King)
1927: The Night of Love (Fitzmaurice)
The Magic Flame (H. King)
1928: Two Lovers (Fred Niblo)
1929: The Rescue (Brenon)
Bulldog Drummond (F. Richard Jones)
Condemned (Wesley Ruggles)
1930: Raffles (Harry D'Arrast, Fitzmaurice)
The Devil to Pay (Fitzmaurice)
1931: The Unholy Garden (Fitzmaurice)
Arrowsmith (John Ford)
1932: Cynara (King Vidor)
1933: The Masquerader (Richard Wallace)
1934: Bulldog Drummond Strikes Back (Roy Del Ruth)
1935: Clive of India (Richard Boleslawski)
The Man Who Broke the Bank at Monte Carlo (Stephen Roberts)
A Tale of Two Cities (Jack Conway)
1936: Under Two Flags (Frank Lloyd)
1937: Lost Horizon (Frank Capra)
The Prisoner of Zenda (John Cromwell)
1938: If I Were King (F. Lloyd)
1939: The Light That Failed (William Wellman)
1940: Lucky Partners (Lewis Milestone)
1941: My Life With Caroline (Milestone)
1942: The Talk of the Town (George Stevens)
Random Harvest (Mervyn LeRoy)
1944: Kismet (William Dieterle)
1947: The Late George Apley (Joseph L. Mankiewicz)
A Double Life (George Cukor)
1950: Champagne for Caesar (Richard Whorf)
1956: Around the World in Eighty Days (Michael Anderson)
1957: The Story of Mankind (Irwin Allen)

SEAN CONNERY
1955: No Road Back (Montgomery Tully)
1957: Time Lock (Gerald Thomas)
Action of the Tiger (Terence Young)
Hell Drivers (Cy Enfield)
1958: Another Time, Another Place (Lewis Allen)
1959: Darby O'Gill and the Little People (Robert Stevenson)
Tarzan's Greatest Adventure (John Guillermin)
1960: The Frightened City (John Lemont)
1961: On the Fiddle (Cyril Frankel)
1962: The Longest Day (Ken Annakin, Andrew Marton, Bernhard Wicki)
1963: Dr. No (T. Young)
1964: From Russia With Love (T. Young)
A Woman of Straw (Basil Dearden)
Marnie (Alfred Hitchcock)
Goldfinger (Guy Hamilton)
1965: The Hill (Sidney Lumet)
Thunderball (T. Young)
1966: A Fine Madness (Irvin Kershner)
1967: You Only Live Twice (Lewis Gilbert)
1968: Shalako (Edward Dmytryk)
1970: The Molly Maguires (Martin Ritt)
1971: The Red Tent (Mikhail K. Kalatozov)
The Anderson Tapes (Lumet)
Diamonds Are Forever (Hamilton)
1972: The Offence (Lumet)
1974: Zardoz (John Boorman)
Murder on the Orient Express (Lumet)

1975: The Terrorists (Casper Wrede)
The Wind and the Lion (John Milius)
The Man Who Would Be King (John Huston)
1976: Robin and Marian (Richard Lester)
The Next Man (Richard Sarafian)
1978: The Great Train Robbery (Michael Crichton)
Meteor (Ronald Neame)

GARY COOPER

1926: The Winning of Barbara Worth (Henry King)
1927: It (Clarence Badger)
Children of Divorce (Frank Lloyd)
Arizona Bound (John Waters)
Wings (William Wellman)
Nevada (Waters)
The Last Outlaw (Arthur Rosson)
1928: Beau Sabreur (Waters)
The Legion of the Condemned (Wellman)
Doomsday (Rowland V. Lee)
Half a Bride (Gregory La Cava)
Lilac Time (George Fitzmaurice)
The First Kiss (R. Lee)
1929: The Shopworn Angle (Richard Wallace)
Wolf Song (Victor Fleming)
The Betrayal (Lewis Milestone)
The Virginian (Fleming)
1930: Only the Brave (Frank Tuttle)
Paramount on Parade (Dorothy Arzner, Otto Brower, Edmund Goulding, Victor Heerman, Edwin Knopf, R. Lee, Ernst Lubitsch, Lothar Mendes, Victor Schertzinger, Edward Sutherland, Tuttle)
The Texan (John Cromwell)
Seven Days' Leave (Wallace)
A Man from Wyoming (R. Lee)
The Spoilers (Edwin Carewe)
Morocco (Josef von Sternberg)
1931: Fighting Caravans (Brower, David Burton)
City Streets (Rouben Mamoulian)
I Take This Woman (Marion Gering)
His Woman (Edward Sloman)
1932: Make Me a Star (William Beaudine)
The Devil and the Deep (Gering)
If I Had a Million (James Cruze, H. Bruce Humberstone, Stephen Roberts, William A. Seiter, Lubitsch, Norman Taurog)
A Farewell to Arms (Frank Borzage)
1933: Today We Live (Howard Hawks)
One Sunday Afternoon (Roberts)
Design for Living (Lubitsch)
Alice in Wonderland (Norman Z. McLeod)
1934: Operator 13 (Richard Boleslawski)
Now and Forever (Henry Hathaway)
1935: The Wedding Night (King Vidor)
Lives of a Bengal Lancer (Hathaway)
Peter Ibbetson (Hathaway)
1936: Desire (Borzage)
Mr. Deeds Goes to Town (Frank Capra)
Hollywood Boulevard (Robert Florey)
The General Died at Dawn (Milestone)
The Plainsman (Cecil B. De Mille)
1937: Souls at Sea (Hathaway)
1938: The Adventures of Marco Polo (Archie Mayo)
Bluebeard's Eighth Wife (Lubitsch)
The Cowboy and the Lady (H. C. Potter)
1939: Beau Geste (Wellman)
The Real Glory (Hathaway)
1940: The Westerner (William Wyler)
Northwest Mounted Police (De Mille)
1941: Meet John Doe (Capra)
Sergeant York (Hawks)
Ball of Fire (Hawks)
1942: The Pride of the Yankees (Sam Wood)
1943: For Whom the Bell Tolls (Wood)
1944: The Story of Dr. Wassell (De Mille)
Casanova Brown (Wood)

1945: Along Came Jones (Stuart Heisler)
Saratoga Trunk (Wood)
1946: Cloak and Dagger (Fritz Lang)
1947: Unconquered (De Mille)
Variety Girl (George Marshall)
1948: Good Sam (Leo McCarey)
1949: The Fountainhead (K. Vidor)
It's a Great Feeling (David Butler)
Task Force (Delmer Daves)
1950: Bright Leaf (Michael Curtiz)
Dallas (Heisler)
1951: You're in the Navy Now (Hathaway)
Starlift (Roy Del Ruth)
It's a Big Country (Charles Vidor)
Distant Drums (Raoul Walsh)
1952: High Noon (Fred Zinnemann)
Springfield Rifle (Andre De Toth)
1953: Return to Paradise (Mark Robson)
Blowing Wind (Hugo Fregonese)
1954: Garden of Evil (Hathaway)
Vera Cruz (Robert Aldrich)
1955: The Court-Martial of Billy Mitchell (Otto Preminger)
1956: Friendly Persuasion (Wyler)
1957: Love in the Afternoon (Billy Wilder)
1958: Ten North Frederick (Philip Dunne)
Man of the West (Anthony Mann)
1959: The Hanging Tree (Daves)
Alias Jesse James (MacLeod)
They Came to Cordura (Robert Rossen)
The Wreck of the Mary Deare (Michael Anderson)
1961: The Naked Edge (Anderson)

BUSTER CRABBE

1930: Good News (Nick Grinde)
1932: That's My Boy (Roy William Neill)
The Most Dangerous Game (Irving Pichel, Ernest B. Shoedsack)
1933: King of the Jungle (H. Bruce Humberstone)
Man of the Forest (Henry Hathaway)
Tarzan the Fearless (Serial; Robert F. Hill)
To the Last Man (Hathaway)
The Sweetheart of Sigma Chi (Edwin L. Marin)
The Thundering Herd (Hathaway)
1934: Search for Beauty (Erle C. Kenton)
You're Telling Me (Kenton)
Badge of Honor (Spencer Bennet)
The Oil Raider (Bennet)
We're Rich Again (William A. Seiter)
She Had to Choose (Ralph Ceder)
1935: Hold 'em Yale (Sidney Lanfield)
The Wanderer of the Wasteland (Otto Lovering)
Nevada (Charles Barton)
1936: Drift Fence (Lovering)
Desert Gold (James Hogan)
Flash Gordon (Serial; Frederick Stephani)
The Arizona Raiders (Hogan)
Lady Be Careful (J. T. Reed)
Rose Bowl (Barton)
Arizona Mahoney (Hogan)
1937: Murder Goes to College (Charles Riesner)
King of Gamblers (Robert Florey)
Forlorn River (Barton)
Sophie Lang Goes West (Riesner)
Daughter of Shanghai (Florey)
Thrill of a Lifetime (George Archainbaud)
1938: Flash Gordon's Trip to Mars (Serial; Ford Beebe, Robert F. Hill)
Tip-off Girls (Louis King)
Hunted Men (L. King)
Red Barry (Serial; Beebe, Alan Jones)
Illegal Traffic (L. King)
1939: Buck Rogers (Serial; Beebe, Saul Goodking)
Unmarried (Kurt Neumann)
Million Dollar Legs (Grinde)
Colorado Sunset (George Sherman)
Call a Messenger (Arthur Lubin)
1940: Flash Gordon Conquers the Universe (Serial; Beebe, Ray Taylor)
Sailor's Lady (Allan Dwan)
1941: Jungle Man (Harry Fraser)

Billy the Kid Wanted (Sam Newfield)
Billy the Kid's Roundup (Newfield)
1942: Billy the Kid Trapped (Newfield)
Billy the Kid's Smoking Guns (Newfield)
Jungle Siren (Newfield)
Wildcat (Frank McDonald)
Law and Order (Newfield)
Mysterious Rider (Sherman Scott)
Sheriff of Sage Valley (Scott)
1943: The Kid Rides Again (Scott)
Queen of Broadway (Newfield)
Fugitive of the Plains (Newfield)
Western Cyclone (Newfield)
The Renegade (Newfield)
Cattle Stampede (Newfield)
Blazing Frontier (Newfield)
Devil Riders (Newfield)
The Drifter (Newfield)
1944: Nabonga (Newfield)
Frontier Outlaws (Newfield)
Thundering Gunslingers (Newfield)
Valley of Vengeance (Newfield)
The Contender (Newfield)
Fuzzy Settles Down (Newfield)
Rustlers' Hideout (Newfield)
Wild Horse Phantom (Newfield)
Oath of Vengeance (Newfield)
1945: His Brother's Ghost (Newfield)
Shadows of Death (Newfield)
Gangsters' Den (Newfield)
Stagecoach Outlaws (Newfield)
Border Badmen (Newfield)
Fighting Bill Carson (Newfield)
Prairie Rustlers (Newfield)
Lightning Raiders (Newfield)
1946: Ghost of Hidden Valley (Newfield)
Gentlemen with Guns (Newfield)
Prairie Badmen (Newfield)
Terrors on Horseback (Newfield)
Overland Riders (Newfield)
Outlaw of the Plains (Newfield)
Swamp Fire (William H. Pine)
1947: The Last of the Redmen (G. Sherman)
The Sea Hound (Serial; Walter B. Eason, Mack Wright)
1948: Caged Fury (William Berke)
1950: Captive Girl (Berke)
Pirates of the High Seas (Serial; Bennet, Thomas Carr)
1952: King of the Congo (Serial; Bennet, Wallace Grissell)
1956: Gun Brothers (Sidney Salkow)
1957: The Lawless Eighties (Joseph Kane)
1958: Badman's Country (Fred F. Sears)
1960: Gunfighters of Abilene (Edward L. Cahn)
1965: The Bounty Killer (Bennet)
Arizona Raiders (William Witney)
1971: The Comeback Trail (Harry Hurwitz)

JOAN CRAWFORD

1925: Pretty Ladies (Monta Bell)
Old Clothes (Eddie Cline)
The Only Thing (Jack Conway)
Sally, Irene and Mary (Edmund Goulding)
1926: The Boob (William Wellman)
Tramp, Tramp, Tramp (Harry Edwards)
Paris (Goulding)
1927: The Taxi Dancer (Harry Millarde)
Winners of the Wilderness (W.S. Van Dyke)
The Understanding Heart (Conway)
The Unknown (Tod Browning)
Twelve Miles Out (Conway)
Spring Fever (Edward Sedgwick)
1928: West Point (Sedgwick)
Rose Marie (Lucien Hubbard)
Across to Singapore (William Nigh)
The Law of the Range (Nigh)
Four Walls (Nigh)
Our Dancing Daughters (Harry Beaumont)
Dream of Love (Fred Niblo)
1929: The Duke Steps Out (James Cruze)
Our Modern Maidens (Conway)
Hollywood Revue of 1929 (Charles F. Riesner)
Untamed (Conway)
1930: Montana Moon (Malcolm St. Clair)
Our Blushing Brides (Beaumont)
Paid (Sam Wood)

1931: Dance, Fools, Dance (Beaumont)
Laughing Sinners (Beaumont)
This Modern Age (Nick Grinde)
Possessed (Clarence Brown)
1932: Letty Lynton (C. Brown)
Grand Hotel (Goulding)
Rain (Lewis Milestone)
1933: Today We Live (Howard Hawks)
Dancing Lady (Robert Z. Leonard)
1934: Sadie McKee (C. Brown)
Chained (C. Brown)
Forsaking All Others (Van Dyke)
1935: No More Ladies (Edward H. Griffith, George Cukor)
I Live My Life (Van Dyke)
1936: The Gorgeous Hussy (C. Brown)
Love on the Run (Van Dyke)
1937: The Last of Mrs. Cheyney (Richard Boleslawski)
The Bride Wore Red (Dorothy Arzner)
1938: Mannequin (Frank Borzage)
The Shining Hour (Borzage)
1939: The Ice Follies of 1939 (Reinhold Schunzel)
The Women (Cukor)
1940: Strange Cargo (Borzage)
Susan and God (Cukor)
1941: A Woman's Face (Cukor)
When Ladies Meet (R. Leonard)
1942: They All Kissed the Bride (Alexander Hall)
Reunion in France (Jules Dassin)
1943: Above Suspicion (Richard Thorpe)
1944: Hollywood Canteen (Delmer Daves)
1945: Mildred Pierce (Michael Curtiz)
1946: Humoresque (Jean Negulesco)
1947: Possessed (Curtis Bernhardt)
Daisy Kenyon (Otto Preminger)
1949: Flamingo Road (Curtiz)
It's a Great Feeling (David Butler)
1950: The Damned Don't Cry (Vincent Sherman)
Harriet Craig (V. Sherman)
1951: Goodbye My Fancy (V. Sherman)
1952: This Woman Is Dangerous (Felix Feist)
Sudden Fear (David Miller)
1953: Torch Song (Charles Walters)
1954: Johnny Guitar (Nicholas Ray)
1955: Female on the Beach (Joseph Pevney)
Queen Bee (Ranald MacDougall)
Autumn Leaves (Robert Aldrich)
1957: The Story of Esther Costello (David Miller)
1959: The Best of Everything (Negulesco)
1962: What Ever Happened to Baby Jane? (Aldrich)
1963: The Caretakers (Hall Bartlett)
1964: Strait Jacket (William Castle)
1965: I Saw What You Did (Castle)
1968: Berserk (Jim O'Connolly)
1970: Trog (Freddie Francis)

BING CROSBY

Prior to the following films, he appeared in several shorts for Mack Sennett.
1930: The King of Jazz (John Murray Anderson)
Check and Double Check (Melville Brown)
1931: Reaching for the Moon (Edmund Goulding)
Confessions of a Co-ed (David Burton, Dudley Murphy)
1932: The Big Broadcast (Frank Tuttle)
1933: College Humor (Wesley Ruggles)
Too Much Harmony (Edward Sutherland)
Going Hollywood (Raoul Walsh)
1934: We're Not Dressing (Norman Taurog)
She Loves Me Not (Elliott Nugent)
Here is My Heart (Tuttle)
1935: Mississippi (Sutherland)
Two for Tonight (Tuttle)
The Big Broadcast of 1936 (Taurog)
1936: Anything Goes (Lewis Milestone)
Rhythm on the Range (Taurog)
Pennies from Heaven (Norman Z. McLeod)
1937: Waikiki Wedding (Tuttle)
Double or Nothing (Theodore Reed)
1938: Doctor Rhythm (Tuttle)
Sing You Sinners (Ruggles)
1939: Paris Honeymoon (Tuttle)

East Side of Heaven (David Butler)
The Star Maker (Roy Del Ruth)
1940: Road to Singapore (Victor Schertzinger)
If I had My Way (Butler)
Rhythm on the River (Schertzinger)
1941: Road to Zanzibar (Schertzinger)
Birth of the Blues (Schertzinger)
1942: Holiday Inn (Mark Sandrich)
Road to Morocco (Butler)
Star Spangled Rhythm (George Marshall)
1943: Dixie (Sutherland)
1944: Going My Way (Leo McCarey)
Here Come the Waves (Sandrich)
1945: Out of this World (Hal Walker)
Duffy's Tavern (H. Walker)
The Bells of St. Mary's (Leo McCarey)
Road to Utopia (H. Walker)
1946: Blue Skies (Stuart Heisler)
1947: Welcome Stranger (Nugent)
Variety Girl (Marshall)
Road to Rio (McLeod)
1948: The Emperor Waltz (Billy Wilder)
1949: A Connecticut Yankee in King Arthur's Court (Tay Garnett)
Top o' the Morning (David Miller)
The Adventures of Ichabod and Mr. Toad (Cartoon; Jack Kinney, Clyde Geronimi, Jason Algar, as narrator)
1950: Riding High (Frank Capra)
Mr. Music (Richard Haydn)
1951: Here Comes the Groom (Capra)
1952: Just for You (Nugent)
The Greatest Show on Earth (Cecil B. De Mille)
Road to Bali (H. Walker)
1953: Little Boy Lost (George Seaton)
1954: White Christmas (Michael Curtiz)
The Country Girl (Seaton)
1956: Anything Goes (Robert Lewis)
High Society (Charles Walters)
1957: Man on Fire (Ranald MacDougall)
1959: Say One for Me (Frank Tashlin)
Allias Jesse James (McLeod)
1960: Let's Make Love (George Cukor)
High Time (Blake Edwards)
Pepe (George Sidney)
1962: Road to Hong Kong (Norman Panama)
1964: Robin and the Seven Hoods (Gordon Douglas)
1966: Cinerama's Russian Adventure (Leonid Kristy, Roman Karmen, Boris Dolin, Oleg Lebedev, Solomon Kogan, Vassily Katanian)
Stagecoach (Douglas)
1974: That's Entertainment! (Jack Haley Jr.)

BETTE DAVIS

1931: Bad Sister (Hobart Henley)
Seed (John M. Stahl)
Waterloo Bridge (James Whale)
Way Back Home (William A. Seiter)
1932: The Menace (Roy William Neill)
Hell's House (Howard Higgin)
The Man Who Played God (John Adolfi)
So Big (William Wellman)
The Rich Are Always With Us (Alfred E. Green)
The Dark Horse (A. Green)
Cabin in the Cotton (Michael Curtiz)
Three on a Match (Mervyn LeRoy)
1933: 20,000 Years in Sing Sing (Curtiz)
Parachute Jumper (A. Green)
The Working Man (Adolfi)
Ex-Lady (Robert Florey)
Bureau of Missing Persons (Roy Del Ruth)
1934: Fashions of 1934 (William Dieterle)
The Big Shakedown (John Francis Dillon)
Jimmy the Gent (Curtiz)
Fog Over Frisco (Dieterle)
Of Human Bondage (John Cromwell)
Housewife (A. Green)
1935: Bordertown (Archie Mayo)
The Girl from 10th Avenue (A. Green)

Front Page Woman (Curtiz)
Special Agent (William Keighley)
Dangerous (A. Green)
1936: The Petrified Forest (Mayo)
The Golden Arrow (A. Green)
Satan Met a Lady (Dieterle)
1937: Marked Woman (Lloyd Bacon)
Kid Galahad (Curtiz)
That Certain Woman (Edmund Goulding)
It's Love I'm After (Mayo)
1938: Jezebel (William Wyler)
The Sisters (Anatole Litvak)
1939: Dark Victory (Goulding)
Juarez (Dieterle)
The Old Maid (Goulding)
The Private Lives of Elizabeth and Essex (Curtiz)
1940: All This and Heaven Too (Litvak)
The Letter (Wyler)
1941: The Great Lie (Goulding)
The Bride Came C.O.D. (Keighley)
The Little Foxes (Wyler)
The Man Who Came to Dinner (Keighley)
1942: In This Our Life (John Huston)
Now, Voyager (Irving Rapper)
1943: Watch on the Rhine (Herman Shumlin)
Thank Your Lucky Stars (David Butler)
Old Acquaintance (Vincent Sherman)
1944: Mr. Skeffington (V. Sherman)
Hollywood Canteen (Delmer Daves)
1945: The Corn Is Green (Rapper)
1946: A Stolen Life (Curtis Bernhardt)
Deception (Rapper)
1948: Winter Meeting (Bretaigne Windust)
June Bride (Windust)
1949: Beyond the Forest (King Vidor)
1950: All About Eve (Joseph L. Mankiewicz)
1951: Payment on Demand (Bernhardt)
1952: Another Man's Poison (Rapper)
Phone Call from a Stranger (Jean Negulesco)
The Star (Stuart Heisler)
1955: The Virgin Queen (Henry Koster)
1956: Storm Center (Daniel Taradash)
The Catered Affair (Richard Brooks)
1959: John Paul Jones (John Farrow)
The Scapegoat (Robert Hamer)
1961: A Pocketful of Miracles (Frank Capra)
1962: What Ever Happened to Baby Jane? (Robert Aldrich)
1964: Dead Ringer (Paul Henreid)
The Empty Canvas (Damiano Damiani)
Where Love Has Gone (Edward Dmytryk)
Hush . . . Hush, Sweet Charlotte (Aldrich)
1965: The Nanny (Seth Holt)
1968: The Anniversary (Roy Ward Baker)
1971: Connecting Rooms (Franklin Gollings)
Bunny O'Hare (Gerd Oswald)
1972: Madame Sin (David Greene)
Lo Scopone Scientifico (Luigi Comencini)
1976: Burnt Offerings (Dan Curtis)
1978: Return from Witch Mountain (John Hough)
Death on the Nile (John Guillermin)

DORIS DAY

1948: Romance on the High Seas (Michael Curtiz)
1949: My Dream Is Yours (Curtiz)
It's a Great Feeling (David Butler)
1950: Young Man with a Horn (Curtiz)
Tea for Two (Butler)
The West Point Story (Roy Del Ruth)
1951: Storm Warning (Stuart Heisler)
Lullaby of Broadway (Butler)
On Moonlight Bay (Del Ruth)
Starlift (Del Ruth)
I'll See You in My Dreams (Curtiz)
1952: The Winning Team (Lewis Seiler)
April in Paris (Butler)
1953: By the Light of the Silvery Moon (Butler)

Calamity Jane (Butler)
1954: Lucky Me (Jack Donohue)
Young at Heart (Gordon Douglas)
1955: Love Me or Leave Me (Charles Vidor)
1956: The Man Who Knew Too Much (Alfred Hitchcock)
1957: Pajama Game (Stanley Donen)
1958: Teacher's Pet (George Seaton)
The Tunnel of Love (Gene Kelly)
1959: It Happened to Jane (Richard Quine)
Pillow Talk (Michael Gordon)
1960: Please Don't Eat the Daisies (Charles Walters)
Midnight Lace (David Miller)
1961: Lover Come Back (Delbert Mann)
1962: That Touch of Mink (D. Mann)
Billy Rose's Jumbo (Walters)
1963: The Thrill of It All (Norman Jewison)
Move Over, Darling (Michael Gordon)
1964: Send Me No Flowers (Jewison)
1965: Do Not Disturb (Ralph Levy)
1966: The Glass Bottom Boat (Frank Tashlin)
1967: Caprice (Tashlin)
1968: The Ballad of Josie (Andrew V. McLaglen)
Where Were You When the Lights Went Out? (Hy Averback)
With Six You Get Eggroll (Howard Morris)

JAMES DEAN

1951: Sailor Beware (Hal Walker)
Fixed Bayonets (Samuel Fuller)
1952: Has Anybody Seen My Gal? (Douglas Sirk)
1955: East of Eden (Elia Kazan)
Rebel Without a Cause (Nicholas Ray)
1956: Giant (George Stevens)

ROBERT DE NIRO

1968: Greetings (Brian De Palma)
1969: The Wedding Party (Wilford Leach, Cynthia Munroe, De Palma)
Bloody Mama (Roger Corman)
1970: Hi Mom (De Palma)
1971: Jennifer on My Mind (Noel Black)
Born to Win (Ivan Passer)
The Gang That Couldn't Shoot Straight (James Goldstone)
1973: Bang the Drum Slowly (John Hancock)
Mean Streets (Martin Scorsese)
1974: The Godfather, Part II (Francis Ford Coppola)
1976: Taxi Driver (Scorsese)
The Last Tycoon (Elia Kazan)
1977: New York, New York (Scorsese)
1900 (Bernardo Bertolucci)
1978: The Deer Hunter (Michael Cimino)
1979: Raging Bull (Scorsese)

MARLENE DIETRICH

1923: The Little Napoleon (Georg Jacoby)
Tragedy of Love (Joe May)
Man by the Roadside (William Dieterle)
1924: The Leap into Life (Johannes Guter)
1925: Joyless Street (G. W. Pabst)
1926: Manon Lescaut (Artur Robison)
A Modern DuBarry (Alexander Korda)
Madame Doesn't Want Children (Korda)
Heads Up, Charly! (Willi Wolff)
1927: The Imaginary Baron (Wolff)
His Greatest Bluff (Harry Piel)
Cafe Electric (Gustave Ucicky)
1928: Princess Olala (Robert Land)
1929: I Kiss Your Hand, Madame (Land)
The Woman One Longs For (Maurice Tourneur)
The Ship of Lost Souls (M. Tourneur)
Dangers of the Engagement Period (Fred Sauer)
1930: The Blue Angel (Josef von Sternberg)
Morocco (Sternberg)
1931: Dishonored (Sternberg)
1932: Shanghai Express (Sternberg)

Blonde Venus (Sternberg)
1933: Song of Songs (Rouben Mamoulian)
1934: The Scarlet Empress (Sternberg)
1935: The Devil Is a Woman (von Sternberg)
1936: Desire (Frank Borzage)
The Garden of Allah (Richard Boleslawski)
1937: Knight Without Armour (Jacques Feyder)
Angel (Ernst Lubitsch)
1939: Destry Rides Again (George Marshall)
1940: Seven Sinners (Tay Garnett)
1941: The Flame of New Orleans (René Clair)
Manpower (Raoul Walsh)
1942: The Lady Is Willing (Mitchell Leisen)
The Spoilers (Ray Enright)
Pittsburgh (Lewis Seiler)
1944: Follow the Boys (Edward Sutherland)
Kismet (Dieterle)
1946: Martin Roumagnac (George Lacombe)
1947: Golden Earrings (Leisen)
1948: A Foreign Affair (Billy Wilder)
1949: Jigsaw (Fletcher Markle)
1950: Stage Fright (Alfred Hitchcock)
1951: No Highway in the Sky (Henry Koster)
1952: Rancho Notorious (Fritz Lang)
1956: Around the World in Eighty Days (Michael Anderson)
1957: The Monte Carlo Story (Samuel A. Taylor)
Witness for the Prosecution (Wilder)
1958: Touch of Evil (Orson Welles)
1961: Judgment at Nuremburg (Stanley Kramer)
1962: The Black Fox (Louis C. Stoumen, as narrator)
1964: Paris When It Sizzles (Richard Quine)

KIRK DOUGLAS

1946: The Strange Love of Martha Ivers (Lewis Milestone)
1947: Out of the Past (Jacques Tourneur)
Mourning Becomes Electra (Dudley Nichols)
I Walk Alone (Byron Haskin)
1948: The Walls of Jericho (John M. Stahl)
My Dear Secretary (Charles Martin)
A Letter to Three Wives (Joseph L. Mankiewicz)
1949: Champion (Mark Robson)
1950: Young Man with a Horn (Michael Curtiz)
The Glass Menagerie (Irving Rapper)
1951: Ace in the Hole (Billy Wilder)
Along the Great Divide (Raoul Walsh)
Detective Story (Wyler)
1952: The Big Trees (Felix Feist)
The Big Sky (Howard Hawks)
The Bad and the Beautiful (Vincente Minnelli)
1953: The Story of Three Loves (Gottfried Reinhardt, Minnelli)
The Juggler (Edward Dmytryk)
Act of Love (Anatole Litvak)
1954: Ulysses (Mario Camerini)
20,000 Leagues Under the Sea (Richard Fleischer)
1955: The Racers (Henry Hathaway)
Man Without a Star (King Vidor)
The Indian Fighter (Andre De Toth)
1956: Lust for Life (Minnelli)
1957: Gunfight at the O.K. Corral (John Sturges)
Top Secret Affair (H. C. Potter)
Paths of Glory (Stanley Kubrick)
1958: The Vikings (Fleischer)
1959: Last Train from Gun Hill (J. Sturges)
The Devil's Disciple (Guy Hamilton)
1960: Strangers When We Meet (Richard Quine)
Spartacus (Kubrick)
1961: The Last Sunset (Robert Aldrich)
Town Without Pity (Reinhardt)

1962: Lonely Are the Brave (David Miller)
Two Weeks in Another Town (Minnelli)
1963: The Hook (George Seaton)
For Love or Money (Michael Gordon)
The List of Adrian Messenger (John Huston)
1964: Seven Days in May (John Frankenheimer)
1965: In Harm's Way (Otto Preminger)
The Heroes of Telemark (Anthony Mann)
1966: Cast a Giant Shadow (Melville Shavelson)
Is Paris Bruning? (René Clement)
1967: The Way West (Andrew V. McLaglen)
The War Wagon (Burt Kennedy)
1968: A Lovely Way to Die (David Lowell Rich)
The Brotherhood (Martin Ritt)
1969: The Arrangement (Elia Kazan)
1970: There Was a Crooked Man (Mankiewicz)
1971: A Gunfight (Lamont Johnson)
The Light at the End of the World (Kevin Billington)
Catch Me a Spy (Dick Clement)
1973: The Master Touch (Michele Lupo)
Scalawag (Kirk Douglas)
1975: Posse (Douglas)
Jacqueline Susann's Once Is Not Enough (Guy Green)
1978: The Fury (Brian De Palma)
The Chosen (Alberto DeMartino)

RICHARD DREYFUSS

1967: The Graduate (Mike Nichols)
1968: The Young Runaways (Arthur Dreifuss)
1969: Hello Down There (Jack Arnold)
1973: Dillinger (John Milius)
American Graffiti (George Lucas)
1974: The Apprenticeship of Duddy Kravitz (Ted Kotcheff)
1975: Jaws (Stephen Spielberg)
1976: Inserts (John Byrum)
1977: Close Encounters of the Third Kind (Lucas)
The Goodbye Girl (Herbert Ross)
1978: The Big Fix (Jeremy Paul Kagan)

FAYE DUNAWAY

1967: Hurry Sundown (Otto Preminger)
The Happening (Elliot Silverstein)
Bonnie and Clyde (Arthur Penn)
1968: The Thomas Crown Affair (Norman Jewison)
A Place for Lovers (Vittorio de Sica)
1969: The Arrangement (Elia Kazan)
The Extraordinary Seaman (John Frankenheimer)
1970: Little Big Man (Penn)
Puzzle of a Downfall Child (Jerry Schatzberg)
1971: Doc (Frank Perry)
The Deadly Trap (René Clement)
1973: Oklahoma Crude (Stanley Kramer)
1974: The Three Musketeers (Richard Lester)
Chinatown (Roman Polanski)
The Towering Inferno (John Guillermin)
1975: The Four Musketeers (Lester)
Three Days of the Condor (Syndey Pollack)
1976: Network (Sidney Lumet)
1978: Eyes of Laura Mars (Irvin Kershner)
1979: The Champ (Franco Zeffirelli)

IRENE DUNNE

1930: Leathernecking (Eddie Cline)
1931: Cimarron (Wesley Ruggles)
The Great Lover (Harry Beaumont)
Consolation Marriage (Paul Sloane)
Bachelor Apartment (Lowell Sherman)
1932: Back Street (John M. Stahl)
Symphony of Six Million (Gregory La Cava)
Thirteen Women (George Archainbaud)

1933: No Other Woman (J. Walter Ruben)
Secret of Madame Blanche (Charles Brabin)
The Silver Cord (John Cromwell)
Ann Vickers (Cromwell)
1934: If I Were Free (Cromwell)
This Man Is Mine (Cromwell)
Stingaree (William Wellman)
The Age of Innocence (Philip Moeller)
1935: Sweet Adeline (Mervyn LeRoy)
Roberta (William A. Seiter)
Magnificent Obsession (Stahl)
1936: Show Boat (James Whale)
Theodora Goes Wild (Richard Boleslawski)
1937: The Awful Truth (McCarey)
High, Wide and Handsome (Rouben Mamoulian)
1938: Joy of Living (Tay Garnett)
1939: Love Affair (Leo McCarey)
Invitation to Happiness (Ruggles)
When Tomorrow Comes (Stahl)
1940: My Favorite Wife (Garson Kanin)
1941: Penny Serenade (George Stevens)
Unfinished Business (La Cava)
1942: Lady in a Jam (La Cava)
1943: A Guy Named Joe (Victor Fleming)
1944: White Cliffs of Dover (Clarence Brown)
Together Again (Charles Vidor)
1945: Over Twenty-One (C. Vidor)
1946: Anna and the King of Siam (Cromwell)
1947: Life with Father (Michael Curtiz)
1948: I Remember Mama (G. Stevens)
1950: Never a Dull Moment (George Marshall)
The Mudlark (Jean Negulesco)
1952: It Grows on Trees (Arthur Lubin)

ROBERT DUVALL

1962: To Kill a Mockingbird (Robert Mulligan)
1964: Captain Newman, M.D. (David Miller)
1966: The Chase (Arthur Penn)
1968: Countdown (Robert Altman)
The Detective (Gordon Douglas)
Bullitt (Peter Yates)
1969: True Grit (Henry Hathaway)
The Rain People (Francis Ford Coppola)
1970: M*A*S*H (Altman)
The Revolutionary (Paul Williams)
1971: Lawman (Michael Winner)
THX 1138 (George Lucas)
1972: The Godfather (Coppola)
The Great Northfield, Minnesota Raid (Philip Kaufman)
Joe Kidd (John Sturges)
Tomorrow (Joseph Anthony)
1973: Badge 373 (Howard W. Koch)
Lady Ice (Tom Gries)
The Outfit (John Flynn)
1974: The Godfather, Part II (Coppola)
We're Not the Jet Set (Documentary; Robert Duvall, director only)
1975: The Killer Elite (Sam Peckinpah)
Breakout (Gries)
1976: The Seven-Per-Cent Solution (Herbert Ross)
Network (Sidney Lumet)
1977: The Eagle Has Landed (J. Sturges)
The Greatest (Gries)
1978: The Betsy (Daniel Petrie)
1979: Apocalype Now (Coppola)
The Great Santini (Louis John Carlino)

CLINT EASTWOOD

1955: Revenge of the Creature (Jack Arnold)
Francis in the Navy (Arthur Lubin)
Lady Godiva (Lubin)
Tarantula (Arnold)
1956: Never Say Goodbye (Jerry Hopper)
The First Traveling Saleslady (Lubin)
Star in the Dust (Charles Haas)
1957: Escapade in Japan (Lubin)
1958: Ambush at Cimarron Pass (Jodie Copelan)
Lafayette Escadrille (William Wellman)

1964: A Fistful of Dollars (Sergio Leone)
1966: For a Few Dollars More (Leone)
The Witches (Vittorio De Sica)
1967: The Good, the Bad, and the Ugly (Leone)
1968: Hang 'em High (Ted Post)
Coogan's Bluff (Don Siegel)
1969: Where Eagles Dare (Brian G. Hutton)
Paint Your Wagon (Joshua Logan)
1970: Kelly's Heroes (Hutton)
Two Mules for Sister Sara (Siegel)
1971: The Beguiled (Siegel)
Play Misty for Me (Clint Eastwood)
Dirty Harry (Siegel)
1972: Joe Kidd (John Sturges)
1973: Breezy (Eastwood, director only)
High Plains Drifter (Eastwood)
Magnum Force (Post)
1974: Thunderbolt and Lightfoot (Michael Cimino)
1975: The Eiger Sanction (Eastwood)
1976: The Outlaw Josey Wales (Eastwood)
The Enforcer (James Fargo)
1977: The Gauntlet (Eastwood)
1978: Every Which Way but Loose (Fargo)

DOUGLAS FAIRBANKS

1915: The Lamb (W. Christy Cabanne)
Double Trouble (Cabanne)
1916: His Picture in the Papers (John Emerson)
The Habit of Happiness (Allan Dwan)
The Good Bad Man (Dwan)
Reggie Mixes In (Cabanne)
Flirting with Fate (Cabanne)
The Mystery of the Leaping Fish (Emerson)
The Half Breed (Dwan)
Manhattan Madness (Dwan)
American Aristocracy (Lloyd Ingraham)
The Matrimaniac (Paul Powell)
The Americano (Emerson)
1917: In Again Out Again (Emerson)
Wild and Woolly (Emerson)
Down to Earth (Emerson)
The Man from Painted Post (Joseph Henabery)
Reaching for the Moon (Emerson)
1918: A Modern Musketeer (Dwan)
Headin' South (Arthur Rosson)
Mr. Fix-It (Dwan)
Say! Young Fellow (Henabery)
Bound in Morocco (Dwan)
He Comes Up Smiling (Dwan)
Arizona (Fairbanks)
1919: The Knickerbocker Buckaroo (Albert Parker)
His Majesty the American (Henabery)
When the Clouds Roll By (Victor Fleming)
1920: The Mollycoddle (Fleming)
The Mark of Zorro (Fred Niblo)
1921: The Nut (Ted Reed)
The Three Musketeers (Niblo)
1922: Robin Hood (Dwan)
1924: The Thief of Bagdad (Raoul Walsh)
1925: Don Q, Son of Zorro (Donald Crisp)
1926: The Black Pirate (Parker)
1927: The Gaucho (F. Richard Jones)
1929: The Iron Mask (Dwan)
The Taming of the Shrew (Sam Taylor)
1931: Reaching for the Moon (Edmund Goulding)
Around the World in 80 Minutes (Fleming, Fairbanks)
1932: Mr. Robinson Crusoe (Edward Sutherland)
1934: The Private Life of Don Juan (Alexander Korda)

W.C. FIELDS

1915: Pool Sharks (Short)
1924: Janice Meredith (E. Mason Hopper)
1925: Sally of the Sawdust (D. W. Griffith)
1926: That Royale Girl (Griffith)
It's the Old Army Game (Edward Sutherland)

So's Your Old Man (Gregory La Cava)
1927: The Potters (Fred Newmeyer)
Running Wild (La Cava)
Two Flaming Youths (John Waters)
1928: Tillie's Punctured Romance (Sutherland)
Fools for Luck (Charles F. Riesner)
1930: The Golf Specialist (Short; Monte Brice)
1931: Her Majesty Love (William Dieterle)
1932: Million Dollar Legs (Edward Cline)
If I Had a Million (James Cruze; H. Bruce Humberstone, Stephen Roberts, William A. Seiter, Ernst Lubitsch, Norman Taurog)
The Dentist (Short; Leslie Pearce)
1933: The Fatal Glass of Beer (Short; Clyde Bruckman)
The Pharmacist (Short; Arthur Ripley)
The Barber Shop (Short; Ripley)
International House (Sutherland)
Tillie and Gus (Francis Martin)
Alice in Wonderland (Norman Z. McLeod)
1934: Six of a Kind (Leo McCarey)
You're Telling Me (Erle C. Kenton)
The Old-Fashioned Way (William Beaudine)
Mrs. Wiggs of the Cabbage Patch (Taurog)
It's a Gift (McLeod)
1935: David Copperfield (George Cukor)
Mississippi (Sutherland)
The Man on the Flying Trapeze (Bruckman)
1936: Poppy (Sutherland)
1938: The Big Broadcast of 1938 (Mitchell Leisen)
1939: You Can't Cheat an Honest Man (George Marshall)
1940: My Little Chickadee (Cline)
The Bank Dick (Cline)
1941: Never Give a Sucker an Even Break (Cline)
1942: Tales of Manhattan (Julien Duvivier)
1944: Follow the Boys (Sutherland)
Song of the Open Road (S. Sylvan Simon)
Sensations of 1945 (Andrew L. Stone)

ERROL FLYNN

1932: Dr. H. Erbin's New Guinea Expedition (Documentary; Dr. H. Erbin)
1933: In the Wake of the Bounty (Charles Chauvel)
1934: Murder at Monte Carlo (Ralph Ince)
1935: The Case of the Curious Bride (Michael Curtiz)
Don't Bet on Blondes (Robert Florey)
Captain Blood (Curtiz)
1936: The Charge of the Light Brigade (Curtiz)
1937: The Green Light (Frank Borzage)
The Prince and the Pauper (William Keighley)
Another Dawn (William Dieterle)
The Perfect Specimen (Curtiz)
1938: The Adventures of Robin Hood (Curtiz, Keighley)
Four's a Crowd (Curtiz)
The Sisters (Anatole Litvak)
The Dawn Patrol (Edmund Goulding)
1939: Dodge City (Curtiz)
The Private Lives of Elizabeth and Essex (Curtiz)
1940: Virginia City (Curtiz)
The Sea Hawk (Curtiz)
Santa Fe Trail (Curtiz)
1941: Footsteps in the Dark (Lloyd Bacon)
Dive Bomber (Curtiz)
They Died with Their Boots On (Raoul Walsh)
1942: Desperate Journey (Walsh)
Gentleman Jim (Walsh)
1943: Edge of Darkness (Lewis Milestone)
Thank Your Lucky Stars (David Butler)
Northern Pursuit (Walsh)
1944: Uncertain Glory (Walsh)

1945: Objective, Burma! (Walsh)
San Antonio (Butler)
1946: Never Say Goodbye (James V. Kern)
1947: Cry Wolf (Peter Godfrey)
Escape Me Never (Godfrey)
Always Together (Frederick De Cordova)
1948: Silver River (Walsh)
The Adventures of Don Juan (Vincent Sherman)
1949: It's a Great Feeling (Butler)
That Forsyte Woman (Compton Bennett)
1950: Montana (Ray Enright)
Rocky Mountain (Keighley)
Kim (Victor Saville)
1951: The Adventures of Captain Fabian (William Marshall)
Hello God (Marshall)
1952: Cruise of the Zaca (Short; Errol Flynn, director, narrator)
Mara Maru (Gordon Douglas)
Against All Flags (George Sherman)
1953: The Master of Ballantrae (Keighley)
Crossed Swords (Milton Krims)
1954: Lilacs in the Spring (Herbert Wilcox)
The Warriors (Henry Levin)
1955: King's Rhapsody (Wilcox)
1956: Istanbul (Joseph Pevney)
1957: The Big Boodle (Richard Wilson)
The Sun Also Rises (Henry King)
1958: Too Much Too Soon (Art Napoleon)
The Roots of Heaven (John Huston)
1959: Cuban Rebel Girls (Barry Mahon)

HENRY FONDA

1935: The Farmer Takes a Wife (Victor Fleming)
Way Down East (Henry King)
I Dream Too Much (John Cromwell)
1936: Trail of the Lonesome Pine (Henry Hathaway)
The Moon's Our Home (William A. Seiter)
Spendthrift (Raoul Walsh)
1937: You Only Live Once (Fritz Lang)
Wings of the Morning (Harold Schuster)
Slim (Ray Enright)
That Certain Woman (Edmund Goulding)
1938: I Met My Love Again (Arthur Ripley)
Jezebel (William Wyler)
Blockade (William Dieterle)
Spawn of the North (Hathaway)
The Mad Miss Manton (Leigh Jason)
1939: Jesse James (H. King)
Let Us Live (John Brahm)
The Story of Alexander Graham Bell (Irving Cummings)
Young Mr. Lincoln (John Ford)
Drums Along the Mohawk (Ford)
1940: The Grapes of Wrath (Ford)
Lillian Russell (Cummings)
The Return of Frank James (F. Lang)
Chad Hanna (H. King)
1941: The Lady Eve (Preston Sturges)
Wild Geese Calling (Brahm)
You Belong to Me (Wesley Ruggles)
1942: The Male Animal (Elliott Nugent)
Rings on Her Fingers (Rouben Mamoulian)
Tales of Manhattan (Julien Duvivier)
The Magnificent Dope (Walter Lang)
The Big Street (Irving Reis)
1943: The Immortal Sergeant (John M. Stahl)
The Ox-Bow Incident (William Wellman)
1946: My Darling Clementine (Ford)
1947: The Long Night (Anatole Litvak)
The Fugitive (Ford)
Daisy Kenyon (Otto Preminger)
1948: On Our Merry Way (King Vidor, Leslie Fenton)
Fort Apache (Ford)
1955: Mister Roberts (Ford, Mervyn LeRoy)

1956: War and Peace (K. Vidor)
The Wrong Man (Alfred Hitchcock)
1957: Twelve Angry Men (Sidney Lumet)
The Tin Star (Anthony Mann)
1958: Stage Struck (Lumet)
1959: Warlock (Edward Dmytryk)
The Man Who Understood Women (Nunnally Johnson)
1962: Advise and Consent (Preminger)
The Longest Day (Ken Annakin, Andrew Marton, Bernhard Wicki)
1963: How the West Was Won (Ford, Hathaway, George Marshall)
Spencer's Mountain (Delmer Daves)
1964: The Best Man (Franklin Schaffner)
Fail Safe (Lumet)
The Dirty Game (Terence Young)
Sex and the Single Girl (Richard Quine)
1965: In Harm's Way (Preminger)
Battle of the Bulge (Annakin)
The Rounders (Burt Kennedy)
1966: A Big Hand for the Little Lady (Fielder Cook)
Welcome to Hard Times (Kennedy)
Firecreek (Vincent McEveety)
1968: Madigan (Don Siegel)
Yours, Mine and Ours (Melville Shavelson)
The Boston Strangler (Richard Fleischer)
1969: Once Upon a Time in the West (Sergio Leone)
1970: Too Late the Hero (Robert Aldrich)
The Cheyenne Social Club (Gene Kelly)
There Was a Crooked Man (Joseph L. Mankiewicz)
1971: Sometimes a Great Notion (Paul Newman)
1972: The Serpent (Henri Verneuil)
1973: Ash Wednesday (Larry Peerce)
My Name Is Nobody (Tonino Valerii)
1976: Midway (Jack Smight)
1977: Tentacles (Oliver Hellman)
Rollercoaster (James Goldstone)
1978: The Great Smokey Roadblock (John Leone)
Home to Stay (Delbert Mann)
The Swarm (Irwin Allen)
Fedora (Billy Wilder)
1979: Meteor (Ronald Neame)
Wanda Nevada (Peter Fonda)
City on Fire (Alvin Rakoff)

JANE FONDA

1960: Tall Story (Joshua Logan)
1962: Walk on the Wild Side (Edward Dmytryk)
The Chapman Report (George Cukor)
Period of Adjustment (George Roy Hill)
1963: In the Cool of the Day (Robert Stevens)
Jane (Documentary; Drew, Richard Leacock)
Sunday in New York (Peter Tewkesbury)
1964: Joy House (René Clement)
La Ronde (Roger Vadim)
1965: Cat Ballou (Elliot Silverstein)
1966: The Chase (Arthur Penn)
Any Wednesday (Robert Ellis Miller)
The Game Is Over (Vadim)
1967: Hurry Sundown (Otto Preminger)
Barefoot in the Park (Gene Saks)
Spirits of the Dead (Vadim, Louis Malle, Federico Fellini)
1968: Barbarella (Vadim)
1969: They Shoot Horses, Don't They? (Sydney Pollack)
1971: Klute (Alan J. Pakula)
1972: Steelyard Blues (Alan Myerson)
Tout Va Bien (Jean-Luc Godard)
Letter to Jane: Investigation of a Still (Documentary; Godard, Jean-Pierre Gorin)
F.T.A. (Documentary; Francine Parker)
1974: A Doll's House (Joseph Losey)
Vietnam Journey (Documentary; J. Fonda, Tom Hayden, Haskell Wexler)

1977: Fun with Dick and Jane (Ted Kotcheff)
Julia (Fred Zinnemann)
1978: Coming Home (Hal Ashby)
Comes a Horseman (Pakula)
1979: California Suite (Herbert Ross)
The China Syndrome (James Bridges)

JODIE FOSTER

1972: Napoleon and Samantha (Bernard McEveety)
Kansas City Bomber (Jerrold Freedman)
1973: Tom Sawyer (Don Taylor)
One Little Indian (McEveety)
1975: Alice Doesn't Live Here Anymore (Martin Scorsese)
1976: Taxi Driver (Scorsese)
Bugsy Malone (Alan Parker)
Echoes of Summer (D. Taylor)
1977: Freaky Friday (Gary Nelson)
The Little Girl Who Lives Down the Lane (Nicholas Gessner)
1978: Candleshoe (Norman Tokar)

CLARK GABLE

In addition to the titles listed below, he appeared as an extra in several silent films.
1924: Forbidden Paradise (Ernst Lubitsch)
White Man (Louis Gasnier)
1925: North Star (Paul Powell)
The Plastic Age (Wesley Ruggles)
1931: The Painted Desert (Howard Higgin)
The Easiest Way (Jack Conway)
Dance, Fools, Dance (Harry Beaumont)
The Finger Points (John Francis Dillon)
The Secret Six (George Hill)
Laughing Sinners (Beaumont)
A Free Soul (Clarence Brown)
Night Nurse (William Wellman)
Sporting Blood (Charles Brabin)
Susan Lenox—Her Fall and Rise (Robert Z. Leonard)
Possessed (C. Brown)
Hell Divers (G. Hill)
1932: Polly of the Circus (Alfred Santell)
Strange Interlude (Robert Z. Leonard)
Red Dust (Victor Fleming)
No Man of Her Own (Ruggles)
1933: The White Sister (Fleming)
Hold Your Man (Sam Wood)
Night Flight (C. Brown)
Dancing Lady (Leonard)
1934: It Happened One Night (Frank Capra)
Men in White (Richard Boleslawski)
Manhattan Melodrama (W. S. Van Dyke)
Chained (C. Brown)
Forsaking All Others (Van Dyke)
1935: After Office Hours (Leonard)
Call of the Wild (Wellman)
China Seas (Tay Garnett)
Mutiny on the Bounty (Frank Lloyd)
1936: Wife vs. Secretary (C. Brown)
San Francisco (Van Dyke)
Cain and Mabel (Lloyd Bacon)
Love on the Run (Van Dyke)
1937: Parnell (John M. Stahl)
Saratoga (Jack Conway)
1938: Test Pilot (Fleming)
Too Hot to Handle (Conway)
1939: Idiot's Delight (C. Brown)
Gone With the Wind (Fleming)
1940: Strange Cargo (Frank Borzage)
Boom Town (Conway)
Comrade X (King Vidor)
1941: They Met in Bombay (C. Brown)
Honky Tonk (Conway)
1942: Somewhere I'll Find You (Ruggles)
1945: Adventure (Fleming)
1947: The Hucksters (Conway)
1948: Homecoming (Mervyn LeRoy)
Command Decision (Sam Wood)
1949: Any Number Can Play (LeRoy)
1950: Key to the City (George Sidney)
To Please a Lady (C. Brown)
1951: Across the Wide Missouri (Wellman)
Callaway Went Thataway (Norman Panama, Melvin Frank)

1952: Lone Star (Vincent Sherman)
1953: Never Let Me Go (Delmer Daves)
Mogambo (John Ford)
1954: Betrayed (Gottfried Reinhardt)
1955: Soldier of Fortune (Edward Dmytryk)
The Tall Men (Raoul Walsh)
1956: The King and Four Queens (Walsh)
1957: Band of Angels (Walsh)
1958: Run Silent, Run Deep (Robert Wise)
Teacher's Pet (George Seaton)
1959: But Not for Me (Walter Lang)
1960: It Started in Naples (Melville Shavelson)
1961: The Misfits (John Huston)

GRETA GARBO

1921: How Not to Dress (Short; Captain Ragnar Ring)
1922: Our Daily Bread (Short; Ring)
1923: Peter the Tramp (Erik A. Petscher)
1924: Gosta Berlings Saga (Mauritz Stiller)
1925: Joyless Street (G. W. Pabst)
1926: The Torrent (Monta Bell)
The Temptress (Fred Niblo)
Flesh and the Devil (Clarence Brown)
1927: Love (Edmund Goulding)
1928: The Divine Woman (Victor Seastrom)
Wild Orchids (Sidney Franklin)
A Woman of Affairs (C. Brown)
The Mysterious Lady (Niblo)
1929: The Single Standard (John Robertson)
The Kiss (Jacques Feyder)
1930: Anna Christie (C. Brown)
Romance (C. Brown)
1931: Inspiration (C. Brown)
Susan Lenox — Her Fall and Rise (Robert Z. Leonard)
Mata Hari (George Fitzmaurice)
1932: Grand Hotel (Goulding)
As You Desire Me (Fitzmaurice)
1933: Queen Christina (Rouben Mamoulian)
1934: The Painted Veil (Richard Boleslawski)
Anna Karenina (C. Brown)
1936: Camille (George Cukor)
1937: Conquest (C. Brown)
1939: Ninotchka (Ernst Lubitsch)
1941: Two-Faced Woman (Cukor)

AVA GARDNER

1942: We Were Dancing (Robert Z. Leonard)
Joe Smith, American (Richard Thorpe)
This Time for Keeps (Charles Riesner)
Kid Glove Killer (Fred Zinnemann)
1943: Pilot No. 5 (George Sidney)
Hitler's Madman (Douglas Sirk)
Young Ideas (Jules Dassin)
Lost Angel (Roy Rowland)
1944: Swing Fever (Tim Whelan)
Three Men in White (Willis Goldbeck)
Maisie Goes to Reno (Harry Beaumont)
1945: She Went to the Races (Goldbeck)
1946: Whistle Stop (Leonide Moguy)
The Killers (Robert Siodmak)
1947: The Hucksters (Jack Conway)
Singapore (John Brahm)
1948: One Touch of Venus (William A. Seiter)
1949: The Bribe (R. Leonard)
The Great Sinner (R. Siodmak)
East Side, West Side (Mervyn LeRoy)
1951: My Forbidden Past (Robert Stevenson)
Pandora and the Flying Dutchman (Albert Lewin)
Show Boat (George Sidney)
1952: Lone Star (Vincent Sherman)
The Snows of Kilimanjaro (Henry King)
1953: Ride, Vaquero! (John Farrow)
The Band Wagon (Vincente Minnelli)

Mogambo (John Ford)
Knights of the Round Table (Thorpe)
1954: The Barefoot Contessa (Joseph Mankiewicz)
1956: Bhowani Junction (George Cukor)
1957: The Little Hut (Mark Robson)
The Sun Also Rises (H. King)
1959: The Naked Maja (Henry Koster)
On the Beach (Stanley Kramer)
1961: The Angel Wore Red (Nunnally Johnson)
1963: 55 Days at Peking (Nicholas Ray)
1964: Seven Days in May (John Frankenheimer)
The Night of the Iguana (John Huston)
1966: The Bible (Huston)
1969: Mayerling (Terence Young)
1972: The Life and Times of Judge Roy Bean (Huston)
The Devil's Widow (Roddy McDowall)
1974: Earthquake (Mark Robson)
1975: Permission to Kill (Cyril Frankel)
1976: The Bluebird (Cukor)
1977: The Sentinel (Michael Winner)
The Cassandra Crossing (George P. Cosmatos)
1979: City on Fire (Alvin Rakoff)

JOHN GARFIELD

1938: Four Daughters (Michael Curtiz)
1939: They Made Me a Criminal (Busby Berkeley)
Blackwell's Island (William McGann)
Juarez (William Dieterle)
Daughters Courageous (Curtiz)
Dust Be My Destiny (Lewis Seiler)
1940: Saturday's Children (Vincent Sherman)
Castle on the Hudson (Anatole Litvak)
Flowing Gold (Alfred Green)
East of the River (A. Green)
1941: The Sea Wolf (Curtiz)
Out of the Fog (Litvak)
Dangerously They Live (Robert Florey)
1942: Tortilla Flat (Victor Fleming)
1943: Air Force (Howard Hawks)
Destination Tokyo (Delmer Daves)
The Fallen Sparrow (Richard Wallace)
Thank Your Lucky Stars (David Butler)
1944: Hollywood Canteen (Daves)
Between Two Worlds (Edward A. Blatt)
1945: Pride of the Marines (Daves)
1946: The Postman Always Rings Twice (Tay Garnett)
Nobody Lives Forever (Jean Negulesco)
Humoresque (Negulesco)
1947: Body and Soul (Robert Rossen)
Gentleman's Agreement (Elia Kazan)
1948: Force of Evil (Abraham Polonsky)
1949: We Were Strangers (John Huston)
1950: Under My Skin (Negulesco)
The Difficult Years (Luigi Zampa, as narrator)
The Breaking Point (Curtiz)
1951: He Ran All the Way (John Berry)

JUDY GARLAND

1929: The Old Lady and the Shoe (Short)
1936: Every Sunday Afternoon (Short; Felix Feist)
Pigskin Parade (David Butler)
1937: Broadway Melody of 1938 (Roy Del Ruth)
Thoroughbreds Don't Cry (Alfred Green)
1938: Everybody Sing (Edwin L. Marin)
Listen, Darling (Marin)
Love Finds Andy Hardy (George Seitz)
1939: The Wizard of Oz (Mervyn LeRoy)
Babes in Arms (Busby Berkeley)
1940: Andy Hardy Meets Debutante (Seitz)
Strike Up the Band (Berkeley)

Little Nelly Kelly (Norman Taurog)
1941: Ziegfeld Girl (Robert Z. Leonard)
Life Begins for Andy Hardy (Seitz)
Babes on Broadway (Berkeley)
1942: For Me and My Gal (Berkeley)
1943: Presenting Arms (Taurog)
Girl Crazy (Taurog)
Thousands Cheer (George Sidney)
1944: Meet Me in St. Louis (Vincente Minnelli)
1945: The Clock (Minnelli)
1946: The Harvey Girls (Sidney)
Ziegfeld Girls (Minnelli)
Till the Clouds Roll By (Richard Whorf)
1948: The Pirate (Minnelli)
Easter Parade (Charles Walters)
Words and Music (Taurog)
1949: In the Good Old Summertime (R. Leonard)
1950: Summer Stock (Walters)
1954: A Star Is Born (George Cukor)
1961: Judgment at Nuremberg (Stanley Kramer)
1963: A Child Is Waiting (John Cassavetes)
I Could Go On Singing (Ronald Neame)

GREER GARSON

1939: Goodbye, Mr. Chips (Sam Wood)
Remember? (Norman J. McLeod)
1940: Pride and Prejudice (Robert Z. Leonard)
1941: Blossoms in the Dust (Mervyn LeRoy)
When Ladies Meet (R. Leonard)
1942: Mrs. Miniver (William Wyler)
Random Harvest (LeRoy)
1943: The Youngest Profession (Edward Buzzell)
Madame Curie (LeRoy)
1944: Mrs. Parkington (Tay Garnett)
1945: The Valley of Decision (Garnett)
Adventure (Victor Fleming)
1947: Desire Me (George Cukor)
1948: Julia Misbehaves (Jack Conway)
1949: That Forsyte Woman (Compton Bennett)
1950: The Miniver Story (H. C. Potter)
1951: The Law and the Lady (Edwin H. Knopf)
1953: Julius Caesar (Joseph L. Mankiewicz)
Scandal at Scourie (Jean Negulesco)
1954: Her Twelve Men (R. Leonard)
1955: Strange Lady in Town (LeRoy)
1960: Pepe (George Sidney)
Sunrise at Campobello (Vincent Donehue)
1966: The Singing Nun (Henry Koster)

LILLIAN GISH

1912: An Unseen Enemy (D. W. Griffith)
Two Daughters of Eve (Griffith)
In the Aisles of the Wild (Griffith)
The Musketeers of Pig Alley (Griffith)
The One She Loved (Griffith)
My Baby (Griffith)
Gold and Glitter (Griffith)
The New York Hat (Griffith)
The Burglar's Dilemma (Griffith)
A Cry for Help (Griffith)
1913: Oil and Water (Griffith)
The Unwelcome Guest (Griffith)
A Misunderstood Boy (Griffith)
The Left-Handed Man (Griffith)
The Lady and the Mouse (Griffith)
The House of Darkness (Griffith)
Just Gold (Griffith)
A Timely Interception (Griffith)
The Mothering Heart (Griffith)
During the Round Up (Griffith)
An Indian's Loyalty (Griffith)
A Woman in the Ultimate (Griffith)
A Modest Hero (Griffith)
So Runs the Way (Griffith)
The Madonna of the Storm (Griffith)
The Conscience of Hassan Bey (Griffith)
The Battle at Elderbush Gulch (Griffith)
Men and Muslin (Griffith)

Judith of Bethulia (Griffith)
1914: The Green Eyed Devil (James Kirkwood)
The Battle of the Sexes (Griffith)
Lord Chumley (Kirkwood)
The Hunchback (W. Christy Cabanne)
Silent Sandy (Kirkwood)
Men and Women (Kirkwood)
The Quicksands (Cabanne)
Man's Enemy (Frank Powell)
Home Sweet Home (Griffith)
The Wife (Paul Powell)
The Rebellion of Kitty Belle (Cabanne)
The Escape (Griffith)
The Angel of Contention (John G. O'Brien)
The Tear That Burned (O'Brien)
The Sisters (Cabanne)

1915: The Birth of a Nation (Griffith)
The Lost House (Cabanne)
Captain Macklin (O'Brien)
Enoch Arden (Cabanne)
The Lily and the Rose (P. Powell)
1916: Daphne and the Pirate (Cabanne)
Sold for Marriage (Cabanne)
An Innocent Magdalene (Allan Dwan)
Intolerance (Griffith)
Diane of the Follies (Cabanne)
Pathways of Life (Griffith)
Flirting with Fate (Cabanne)
The Children Pay (Lloyd Ingraham)
1917: The House Built Upon Sand (Ed Morrisey)
Souls Triumphant (O'Brien)
The Great Love (Griffith)
1918: Liberty Bond Short (Griffith)
The Greatest Thing in Life (Griffith)
Hearts of the World (Griffith)
1919: A Romance of Happy Valley (Griffith)
Broken Blossoms (Griffith)
True Heart Susie (Griffith)
The Greatest Question (Griffith)
1920: Remodeling Her Husband (Lillian Gish, director only)
Way Down East (Griffith)
1921: Orphans of the Storm (Griffith)
1923: The White Sister (Henry King)
1924: Romola (H. King)
1926: La Boheme (King Vidor)
The Scarlet Letter (Victor Seastrom)
1927: Annie Laurie (John S. Robertson)
1928: The Enemy (Fred Niblo)
The Wind (Seastrom)
1930: One Romantic Night (Paul L. Stein)
1933: His Double Life (Arthur Hopkins, William C. De Mille)
1942: The Comandos Strike at Dawn (John Farrow)
1943: Top Man (Charles Lamont)
1945: Miss Susie Slagle's (John Berry)
1946: Duel in the Sun (Vidor)
1949: Portrait of Jennie (William Dieterle)
1955: The Cobweb (Vincente Minnelli)
The Night of the Hunter (Charles Laughton)
1958: Orders to Kill (Anthony Asquith)
1960: The Unforgiven (John Huston)
1978: A Wedding (Robert Altman)

RUTH GORDON

1915: Camille (Albert Capellini)
1916: The Wheel of Life (unknown)
1940: Abe Lincoln in Illinois (John Cromwell)
Dr. Ehrlich's Magic Bullet (William Dieterle)
1941: Two-Faced Woman (George Cukor)
1942: Edge of Darkness (Lewis Milestone)
Action in the North Atlantic (Lloyd Bacon)
1965: Inside Daisy Clover (Robert Mulligan)
1966: Lord Love a Duck (George Axelrod)
1968: Rosemary's Baby (Roman Polanski)
1969: Whatever Happened to Aunt Alice? (Lee H. Katzin)
1970: Where's Poppa? (Carl Reiner)
1971: Harold and Maude (Hal Ashby)
1976: The Big Bus (Jim Frawley)
1978: Every Which Way but Loose (James Fargo)
1979: Boardwalk (Stephen Verona)

BETTY GRABLE

1930: Let's Go Places (Frank Strayer)
Whoopee (Thornton Freeland)
New Movietone Follies of 1930 (Benjamin Stoloff)
Palmy Days (Edward Sutherland)
1931: Kiki (Sam Taylor)
1932: Hold 'em Jail (Norman Taurog)
The Greeks Had a Word for Them (Lowell Sherman)
The Kid from Spain (Leo McCarey)
Probation (Richard Thorpe)
1933: Child of Manhattan (Edward Buzzell)
What Price Innocence? (Willard Mack)
Cavalcade (Frank Lloyd)
1934: The Gay Divorcee (Mark Sandrich)
Student Tour (Charles F. Riesner)
1935: Old Man Rhythm (Edward Ludwig)
The Nitwits (George Stevens)
Collegiate (Ralph Murphy)
1936: Follow the Fleet (Sandrich)
Pigskin Parade (David Butler)
Don't Turn 'em Loose (Stoloff)
1937: This Way Please (Robert Florey)
Thrill of a Lifetime (George Archainbaud)
1938: College Swing (Raoul Walsh)
Give Me a Sailor (Elliott Nugent)
Campus Confessions (Archainbaud)
1939: Million Dollar Legs (Eddie Cline)
Man About Town (Sandrich)
1940: Down Argentine Way (Irving Cummings)
Tin Pan Alley (Walter Lang)
Moon Over Miami (W. Lang)
1941: A Yank in the R.A.F. (Henry King)
I Wake Up Screaming (H. Bruce Humberstone)
1942: Song of the Islands (W. Lang)
Springtime in the Rockies (Cummings)
Footlight Serenade (Gregory Ratoff)
1943: Sweet Rosie O'Grady (Cummings)
Coney Island (W. Lang)
1944: Four Jills in a Jeep (William A. Seiter)
Pin-Up Girl (Humberstone)
1945: Diamond Horseshoe (George Seaton)
The Dolly Sisters (Cummings)
1947: The Shocking Miss Pilgrim (Seaton)
Mother Wore Tights (W. Lang)
1948: That Lady in Ermine (Ernst Lubitsch)
When My Baby Smiles at Me (W. Lang)
1949: The Beautiful Blonde from Bashful Bend (Preston Sturges)
1950: Wabash Avenue (Henry Koster)
My Blue Heaven (Koster)
1951: Call Me Mister (Lloyd Bacon)
Meet Me After the Show (Richard Sale)
1953: The Farmer Takes a Wife (Henry Levin)
How to Marry a Millionaire (Jean Negulesco)
1955: Three for the Show (H. C. Potter)
How to Be Very, Very Popular (Nunnally Johnson)

CARY GRANT

1932: This Is the Night (Frank Tuttle)
Sinners in the Sun (Alexander Hall)
Merrily We Go to Hell (Dorothy Arzner)
Devil and the Deep (Marion Gering)
Blonde Venus (Josef von Sternberg)
Hot Saturday (William A. Seiter)
Madame Butterfly (Gering)
1933: She Done Him Wrong (Lowell Sherman)
Woman Accused (Paul Sloane)
The Eagle and the Hawk (Stuart Walker)
Gambling Ship (Louis Gasnier, Max Marcin)
I'm No Angel (Wesley Ruggles)
Alice in Wonderland (Norman Z. McLeod)
1934: Thirty-Day Princess (Gering)
Born to Be Bad (L. Sherman)
Kiss and Make Up (Harlan Thompson)
Ladies Should Listen (Tuttle)

Enter, Madame (Elliott Nugent)
1935: Wings in the Dark (James Flood)
The Last Outpost (Charles Barton, Gasnier)
Sylvia Scarlett (George Cukor)
1936: Big Brown Eyes (Raoul Walsh)
Suzy (George Fitzmaurice)
Wedding Present (Richard Walker)
Romance and Riches (Alfred Zeisler)
1937: When You're in Love (Robert Riskin)
Toast of New York (Rowland V. Lee)
Topper (McLeod)
The Awful Truth (Leo McCarey)
1938: Bringing Up Baby (Howard Hawks)
Holiday (Cukor)
1939: Gunga Din (George Stevens)
Only Angels Have Wings (Hawks)
In Name Only (John Cromwell)
1940: His Girl Friday (Hawks)
My Favorite Wife (Garson Kanin)
The Howards of Virginia (Frank Lloyd)
The Philadelphia Story (Cukor)
1941: Penny Serenade (G. Stevens)
Suspicion (Alfred Hitchcock)
1942: Talk of the Town (G. Stevens)
Once Upon a Honeymoon (L. McCarey)
1943: Mr. Lucky (H. C. Potter)
Destination Tokyo (Delmer Daves)
1944: Once Upon a Time (A. Hall)
Arsenic and Old Lace (Frank Capra)
None but the Lonely Heart (Clifford Odets)
1947: The Bachelor and the Bobby-Soxer (Irving Reis)
The Bishop's Wife (Henry Koster)
1948: Mr. Blandings Builds His Dream House (Potter)
Every Girl Should be Married (Don Hartman)
1949: I Was a Male War Bride (Hawks)
1950: Crisis (Richard Brooks)
1951: People Will Talk (Joseph Mankiewicz)
1952: Room for One More (Norman Taurog)
Monkey Business (Hawks)
1953: Dream Wife (Sidney Sheldon)
1955: To Catch a Thief (Hitchcock)
1957: The Pride and the Passion (Stanley Kramer)
An Affair to Remember (L. McCarey)
Kiss Them for Me (Stanley Donen)
1958: Indiscreet (Donen)
Houseboat (Melville Shavelson)
1959: North by Northwest (Hitchcock)
Operation Petticoat (Blake Edwards)
1960: The Grass is Greener (Donen)
1962: That Touch of Mink (Delbert Mann)
1964: Charade (Donen)
Father Goose (Ralph Nelson)
1966: Walk, Don't Run (Charles Walters)

SYDNEY GREENSTREET

1941: The Maltese Falcon (John Huston)
They Died with Their Boots On (Raoul Walsh)
1942: Across the Pacific (Huston)
Casablanca (Michael Curtiz)
1943: Background to Danger (Walsh)
1944: Passage to Marseilles (Curtiz)
Between Two Worlds (Edward A. Blatt)
The Mask of Dimitrios (Jean Negulesco)
The Conspirators (Negulesco)
Hollywood Canteen (Delmer Daves)
1945: Pillow to Post (Vincent Sherman)
Conflict (Curtis Bernhardt)
Christmas in Connecticut (Peter Godfrey)
1946: Three Strangers (Negulesco)
Devotion (Bernhardt)
The Verdict (Don Siegel)
1947: That Way with Women (Frederick de Cordova)
The Hucksters (Jack Conway)
1948: Ruthless (Edgar G. Ulmer)
The Woman in White (Godfrey)
The Velvet Touch (John Gage)
1949: Flamingo Road (Curtiz)

It's a Great Feeling (David Butler)
Malaya (Richard Thorpe)

GENE HACKMAN

1964: Lilith (Robert Rossen)
1966: Hawaii (George Roy Hill)
1967: Bonnie and Clyde (Arthur Penn)
Banning (Ron Winston)
A Covenant with Death (Lamont Johnson)
First to Fight (Christian Nyby)
1968: The Split (Gordon Flemyng)
1969: Riot (Buzz Kulik)
The Gypsy Moths (John Frankenheimer)
Marooned (John Sturges)
Downhill Racer (Michael Ritchie)
1970: I Never Sang for My Father (Gilbert Cates)
1971: Doctors' Wives (George Schaefer)
Cisco Pike (Bill L. Norton)
The French Connection (William Friedkin)
The Hunting Party (Don Medford)
1972: Prime Cut (Ritchie)
The Poseidon Adventure (Ronald Neame)
1973: Scarecrow (Jerry Schatzberg)
1974: Zandy's Bride (Jan Troell)
The Conversation (Francis Ford Coppola)
Night Moves (Penn)
Young Frankenstein (Mel Brooks)
1975: Bite the Bullet (Richard Brooks)
French Connection II (Frankenheimer)
1977: The Domino Principle (Stanley Kramer)
March or Die (Dick Richards)
1978: Superman (Richard Donner)

JEAN HARLOW

1928: Moran of the Marines (Frank Strayer)
Weak but Willing (Short; Archie Mayo)
1929: Double Whoopee (Short; Lewis Foster)
The Unkissed Man (Leo McCarey)
Fugitives (William Beaudine)
Close Harmony (John Cromwell)
New York Nights (Lewis Milestone)
The Love Parade (Ernst Lubitsch)
Bacon Grabbers (Short; L. Foster)
The Saturday Night Kid (Edward Sutherland)
1930: Hell's Angels (Howard Hughes)
1931: City Lights (Charles Chaplin)
The Secret Six (George Hill)
Iron Man (Tod Browning)
The Public Enemy (William Wellman)
Goldie (Benjamin Stoloff)
Platinum Blonde (Frank Capra)
1932: Three Wise Girls (Beaudine)
Beast of the City (Charles Brabin)
Red Headed Woman (Jack Conway)
Red Dust (Victor Fleming)
1933: Dinner at Eight (George Cukor)
Hold Your Man (Sam Wood)
Bombshell (Fleming)
1934: The Girl from Missouri (Conway)
1935: Reckless (Fleming)
China Seas (Tay Garnett)
1936: Riffraff (Walter Ruben)
Wife vs. Secretary (Clarence Brown)
Suzy (George Fitzmaurice)
Libeled Lady (Conway)
1937: Personal Property (W. S. Van Dyke)
Saratoga (Conway)

WILLIAM S. HART

1913: The Fugitive (Reginald Barker)
1914: His Hour of Manhood (Thomas Ince)
Jim Cameron's Wife (Barker)
The Bargain (Barker)
The Passing of Two-Gun Hicks (William S. Hart)
The Scourge of the Desert (Barker)
1915: Mr. Silent Haskins (Barker)
The Sheriff's Streak of Yellow (Barker)

The Grudge (Barker)
In the Sagebrush Country (Barker)
The Rough Neck (Barker)
On the Night Stage (Barker)
The Taking of Luke McVane (Ralph Ince)
The Man from Nowhere (R. Ince)
Bad Buck of Santa Ynez (R. Ince)
The Darkening Trail (R. Ince)
The Ruse (Hart)
Cash Parrish's Pal (Hart)
The Conversion of Frosty Blake (Hart)
A Knight of the Trail (Hart)
The Tools of Providence (Hart)
Pinto Ben (Hart)
Grit (Hart)
Keno Bates, Liar (Hart)
The Disciple (Hart)
The Golden Claw (Barker)
Between Men (Barker)
1916: The Last Act (T. Ince)
Hell's Hinges (T. Ince)
The Primal Lure (Barker)
The Aryan (Barker)
Upholding the Law of the Sheriff (Barker)
The Captive God (Barker)
The Apostle of Vengeance (Barker)
The Patriot (Barker)
The Dawn Maker (Barker)
The Return of Draw Egan (Barker)
The Devil's Double (Barker)
1917: Truthful Tulliver (Barker)
The Gun Fighter (Barker)
Square Deal Man (Barker)
The Desert Man (Barker)
Wolf Lowry (Barker)
The Cold Deck (Barker)
The Silent Man (Hart)
1918: The Narrow Trail (Hart)
Wolves of the Rail (Hart)
Blue Blazes Rawden (Hart)
The Tiger Man (Hart)
Selfish Yates (Hart)
Shark Monroe (Hart)
Riddle Gawne (Hart)
The Border Wireless (Hart)
Branding Broadway (Hart)
1919: Breed of Men (Lambert Hillyer)
The Poppy Girl's Husband (Hart)
The Money Corral (Hillyer)
Square Deal Sanderson (Hillyer)
Wagon Tracks (Hillyer)
1919: John Petticoats (Hillyer)
1920: Sand! (Hillyer)
The Toll Gate (Hillyer)
The Cradle of Courage (Hillyer)
The Testing Block (Hillyer)
1921: O'Malley of the Mounted (Hillyer)
White Oak (Hillyer)
The Whistle (Hillyer)
Three Word Brand (Hillyer)
1922: Travelin' On (Hillyer)
1923: Hollywood (James Cruze)
Wild Bill Hickok (Clifford S. Smith)
1924: Singer Jim McKee (C. S. Smith)
1925: Tumbleweeds (Hart, King Baggott)

SUSAN HAYWARD

1938: Girls on Probation (William McGann)
1939: Our Leading Citizen (Alfred Santell)
Beau Geste (William Wellman)
$1000 a Touchdown (James Hogan)
1941: Adam Had Four Sons (Gregory Ratoff)
Sis Hopkins (Robert North)
Among the Living (Stuart Heisler)
1942: Reap the Wild Wind (Cecil B. De Mille)
The Forest Rangers (George Marshall)
I Married a Witch (René Clair)
Star-Spangled Rhythm (Marshall)
1943: Young and Willing (Edward H. Griffith)
Hit Parade of 1943 (Albert S. Rogell)
Jack London (Santell)
1944: The Fighting Seabees (Edward Ludwig)
The Hairy Ape (Santell)
And Now Tomorrow (Irving Pichel)
1946: Canyon Passage (Jacques Tourneur)

Deadline at Dawn (Harold Clurman)
1947: Smash-Up (Heisler)
They Won't Believe Me (Pichel)
The Lost Moment (Martin Gabel)
1948: Tap Roots (Marshall)
The Saxon Charm (Claude Binyon)
1949: House of Strangers (Joseph L. Mankiewicz)
Tulsa (Heisler)
My Foolish Heart (Mark Robson)
1951: Rawhide (Henry Hathaway)
I'd Climb the Highest Mountain (Henry King)
I Can Get It for You Wholesale (Michael Gordon)
David and Bathsheba (H. King)
1952: With a Song in My Heart (Walter Lang)
The Snows of Kilimanjaro (H. King)
The Lusty Men (Nicholas Ray)
1953: The President's Lady (Henry Levin)
White Witch Doctor (Hathaway)
1954: Demetrius and the Gladiators (Delmer Daves)
Garden of Evil (Edward Dmytryk)
1955: Untamed (H. King)
Soldier of Fortune (Dmytryk)
I'll Cry Tomorrow (Daniel Mann)
The Conqueror (Dick Powell)
1957: Top Secret Affair (H. C. Potter)
1958: I Want to Live! (Robert Wise)
1959: Thunder in the Sun (Russell Rouse)
Woman Obsessed (Hathaway)
1961: Marriage-Go-Round (W. Lang)
Ada (Daniel Mann)
Back Street (David Miller)
1962: I Thank a Fool (Robert Stevens)
1963: Stolen Hours (Daniel Petrie)
1964: Where Love Has Gone (Dmytryk)
1967: The Honey Pot (Mankiewicz)
Valley of the Dolls (Robson)
1972: The Revengers (Daniel Mann)

RITA HAYWORTH

1935: Under the Pampas Moon (James Tinling)
Charlie Chan in Egypt (Louis King)
Dante's Inferno (Harry Lachman)
Paddy O'Day (Lewis Seiler)
1936: Human Cargo (Allan Dwan)
Meet Nero Wolfe (Herbert Biberman)
Rebellion (Lynn Shores)
1937: Trouble in Texas (Robert N. Bradbury)
Old Louisiana (Irvin N. Willat)
Hit the Saddle (Mack V. Wright)
Criminals of the Air (C. C. Coleman, Jr.)
Girls Can Play (Lambert Hillyer)
The Shadow (Coleman)
The Game That Kills (D. Ross Lederman)
Paid to Dance (Coleman)
1938: Who Killed Gail Preston? (Leon Barsha)
There's Always a Woman (Alexander Hall)
Convicted (Barsha)
Juvenile Court (Lederman)
The Renegade Ranger (David Howard)
1939: Homicide Bureau (Coleman)
The Lone Wolf Spy Hunt (Peter Godfrey)
Special Inspector (Barsha)
Only Angels Have Wings (Howard Hawks)
1940: Music in My Heart (Joseph Santley)
Blondie on a Budget (Frank R. Strayer)
Susan and God (George Cukor)
The Lady in Question (Charles Vidor)
Angels Over Broadway (Ben Hecht, Lee Garmes)
1941: The Strawberry Blonde (Raoul Walsh)
Affectionately Yours (Lloyd Bacon)
Blood and Sand (Rouben Mamoulian)
You'll Never Get Rich (Sidney Lanfield)
1942: My Gal Sal (Irving Cummings)
Tales of Manhattan (Julien Duvivier)

You Were Never Lovelier (William A. Seiter)
1944: Cover Girl (C. Vidor)
1945: Tonight and Every Night (Victor Saville)
1946: Gilda (C. Vidor)
1947: Down to Earth (Hall)
1948: The Lady from Shanghai (Orson Welles)
The Loves of Carmen (C. Vidor)
1952: Affair in Trinidad (Vincent Sherman)
1953: Salome (William Dieterle)
Miss Sadie Thompson (Curtis Bernhardt)
1957: Fire Down Below (Robert Parrish)
Pal Joey (George Sidney)
1958: Separate Tables (Delbert Mann)
1959: They Came to Cordura (Robert Rossen)
1960: The Story on Page One (Clifford Odets)
1962: The Happy Thieves (George Marshall)
1964: Circus World (Henry Hathaway)
1966: The Money Trap (Burt Kennedy)
The Poppy Is Also a Flower (Terence Young)
1967: The Rover (T. Young)
1969: Sons of Satan (Duccio Tessari)
1971: Road to Salina (George Lautner)
The Naked Zoo (William Grefe)
1972: The Wrath of God (Ralph Nelson)
1976: Circle (Arthur Allan Seidelman)

KATHARINE HEPBURN

1932: A Bill of Divorcement (George Cukor)
1933: Christopher Strong (Dorothy Arzner)
Morning Glory (Lowell Sherman)
Little Women (Cukor)
1934: Spitfire (John Cromwell)
The Little Minister (Richard Wallace)
1935: Break of Hearts (Richard Moeller)
Alice Adams (George Stevens)
Sylvia Scarlett (Cukor)
1936: Mary of Scotland (John Ford)
A Woman Rebels (Mark Sandrich)
1937: Quality Street (G. Stevens)
Stage Door (Gregory La Cava)
1938: Bringing Up Baby (Howard Hawks)
Holiday (Cukor)
1940: The Philadelphia Story (Cukor)
1942: Woman of the Year (G. Stevens)
Keeper of the Flame (Cukor)
1943: Stage Door Canteen (Frank Borzage)
1944: Dragon Seed (Jack Conway, Harold S. Bucquet)
1945: Without Love (Bucquet)
1946: Undercurrent (Vincente Minnelli)
1947: The Sea of Grass (Elia Kazan)
Song of Love (Clarence Brown)
1948: State of the Union (Frank Capra)
1949: Adam's Rib (Cukor)
1951: The African Queen (John Huston)
1952: Pat and Mike (Cukor)
1955: Summertime (David Lean)
1956: The Rainmaker (Joseph Anthony)
The Iron Petticoat (Ralph Thomas)
1957: Desk Set (Walter Lang)
1959: Suddenly, Last Summer (Joseph L. Mankiewicz)
1962: Long Day's Journey Into Night (Sidney Lumet)
1967: Guess Who's Coming to Dinner? (Stanley Kramer)
1968: The Lion in Winter (Anthony Harvey)
1969: The Madwoman of Chaillot (Bryan Forbes)
1971: The Trojan Women (Michael Cacoyannis)
1973: A Delicate Balance (Tony Richardson)
1975: Rooster Cogburn (Stuart Millar)
1978: Olly Olly Oxen Free (Richard A. Colla)

JUDY HOLLIDAY

1944: Greenwich Village (Walter Lang)
Something for the Boys (Lewis Seiler)
Winged Victory (George Cukor)
1949: Adam's Rib (Cukor)
1950: Born Yesterday (Cukor)
1952: The Marrying Kind (Cukor)
1954: It Should Happen to You (Cukor)
Phffft! (Mark Robson)
1956: The Solid Gold Cadillac (Richard Quine)
Full of Life (Quine)
1960: Bells are Ringing (Vincente Minnelli)

BOB HOPE

1938: The Big Broadcast of 1938 (Mitchell Leisen)
College Swing (Raoul Walsh)
Give Me a Sailor (Elliott Nugent)
Thanks for the Memory (George Archainbaud)
1939: Never Say Die (Nugent)
Some Like It Hot (Archainbaud)
The Cat and the Canary (Nugent)
1940: Road to Singapore (Victor Schertzinger)
The Ghost Breakers (George Marshall)
1941: Road to Zanzibar (Schertzinger)
Caught in the Draft (David Butler)
Nothing But the Truth (Nugent)
Louisiana Purchase (Irving Cummings)
1942: My Favorite Blonde (Sidney Lanfield)
Road to Morocco (Butler)
Star-Spangled Rhythm (Marshall)
1943: They Got Me Covered (Butler)
Let's Face It (Lanfield)
1944: The Princess and the Pirate (Butler)
1945: Road to Utopia (Hal Walker)
1946: Monsieur Beaucaire (Marshall)
1947: My Favorite Brunette (Nugent)
Variety Girl (Marshall)
Where There's Life (Lanfield)
Road to Rio (Norman Z. McLeod)
1948: The Paleface (McLeod)
1949: Sorrowful Jones (Lansfield)
The Great Lover (Alexander Hall)
1950: Fancy Pants (Marshall)
1951: The Lemon Drop Kid (Lanfield)
My Favorite Spy (McLeod)
1952: Son of Paleface (Frank Tashlin)
Road to Bali (Walker)
1953: Off Limits (Marshall)
Here Come the Girls (Claude Binyon)
1954: Casanova's Big Night (McLeod)
1955: The Seven Little Foys (Melville Shavelson)
1956: That Certain Feeling (Norman Panama and Melvin Frank)
The Iron Petticoat (Ralph Thomas)
1957: Beau James (Shavelson)
1958: Paris Holiday (Gerd Oswald)
1959: Alias Jesse James (McLeod)
The Five Pennies (Shavelson)
1960: The Facts of Life (Frank)
1961: Bachelor in Paradise (Jack Arnold)
1962: Road to Hong Kong (Panama)
1963: Critic's Choice (Don Weis)
Call Me Bwana (Gordon Douglas)
1964: A Global Affair (Arnold)
1965: I'll Take Sweden (Frederick De Cordova)
1966: The Oscar (Russell Rouse)
Boy, Did I Get a Wrong Number! (Marshall)
1967: Eight on the Lam (Marshall)
1968: The Private Navy of Sgt. O'Farrell (Tashlin)
1969: How to Commit Marriage (Panama)
1972: Cancel My Reservation (Paul Bogart)

ROCK HUDSON

1948: Fighter Squadron (Raoul Walsh)
1949: Undertow (William Castle)
1950: I Was a Shoplifter (Charles Lamont)
One-Way Street (Hugo Fregonese)
Peggy (Frederick de Cordova)
Winchester .73 (Anthony Mann)
Shakedown (Joseph Pevney)
The Desert Hawk (de Cordova)
1951: Double Crossbones (Charles Barton)
Tomahawk (George Sherman)
The Fat Man (Castle)
Air Cadet (Pevney)
Iron Man (Pevney)
Bright Victory (Mark Robson)
1952: Here Come the Nelsons (de Cordova)
Bend of the River (A. Mann)
Has Anybody Seen My Gal? (Douglas Sirk)
Scarlet Angel (Sidney Salkow)
Horizons West (Budd Boetticher)
The Lawless Breed (Walsh)
1953: Seminole (Boetticher)
Sea Devils (Walsh)
Golden Blade (Nathan Juran)
Back to God's Country (Pevney)
Gun Fury (Walsh)
1954: Taza, Son of Cochise (Sirk)
Magnificent Obsession (Sirk)
Bengal Brigade (Laslo Benedek)
1955: Captain Lightfoot (Sirk)
One Desire (Jerry Hopper)
All That Heaven Allows (Sirk)
1956: Never Say Goodbye (J. Hopper)
Giant (George Stevens)
Written on the Wind (Sirk)
Battle Hymn (Sirk)
1957: Something of Value (Richard Brooks)
The Tarnished Angels (Sirk)
A Farewell to Arms (Charles Vidor)
1958: Twilight of the Gods (Pevney)
1959: This Earth is Mine (Henry King)
Pillow Talk (Michael Gordon)
1961: The Last Sunset (Robert Aldrich)
Come September (Robert Mulligan)
Lover, Come Back (William A. Seiter)
1962: The Spiral Road (Mulligan)
1963: A Gathering of Eagles (Delbert Mann)
Marilyn (Documentary; as narrator)
1964: Man's Favorite Sport? (Howard Hawks)
Send Me No Flowers (Norman Jewison)
1965: A Very Special Favor (Gordon)
1966: Blindfold (Philip Dunne)
Seconds (John Frankenheimer)
1967: Tobruk (Arthur Hiller)
1968: Ice Station Zebra (John Sturges)
1969: A Fine Pair (Francesco Maselli)
The Undefeated (Andrew V. McLaglen)
1970: Darling Lili (Blake Edwards)
Hornet's Nest (Phil Karlson)
1971: Pretty Maids All in a Row (Roger Vadim)
1973: Showdown (George Seaton)
1976: Embryo (Ralph Nelson)
1978: Avalanche (Corey Allen)

AL JOLSON

1926: Vitaphone (Short)
1927: The Jazz Singer (Alan Crosland)
1928: The Singing Fool (Lloyd Bacon)
1929: Sonny Boy (Archie Mayo)
Say It with Songs (Bacon)
1930: Mammy (Michael Curtiz)
Big Boy (Crosland)
1933: Hallelujah, I'm a Bum (Lewis Milestone)
1934: Wonder Bar (Bacon)
1935: Go into Your Dance (Mayo)
1936: The Singing Kid (William Keighley)
1939: Rose of Washington Square (Gregory Ratoff)
Swanee River (Sidney Lanfield)
1945: Rhapsody in Blue (Irving Rapper)
1946: The Jolson Story (Alfred E. Green; sound track only)
1949: Jolson Sings Again (Henry Levin; sound track only)

JENNIFER JONES

1939: New Frontier (George Sherman)
Dick Tracy's G-Men (Serial; William Witney, John English)
1943: The Song of Bernadette (Henry King)
1944: Since You Went Away (John Cromwell)
1945: Love Letters (William Dieterle)
1946: Cluny Brown (Ernst Lubitsch)
Duel in the Sun (King Vidor)
1948: Portrait of Jennie (Dieterle)
1949: We Were Strangers (John Huston)
Madame Bovary (Vincente Minnelli)
1950: Gone to Earth (Michael Powell)
1952: Carrie (William Wyler)
Ruby Gentry (K. Vidor)
1954: Beat the Devil (Huston)
Indiscretion of an American Wife (Vittorio De Sica)
1955: Love is a Many Splendored Thing (H. King)
Good Morning, Miss Dove (Henry Koster)
1956: The Man in the Gray Flannel Suit (Nunnally Johnson)
1957: The Barretts of Wimpole Street (Sidney Franklin)
A Farewell to Arms (Charles Vidor)
1962: Tender Is the Night (H. King)
1966: The Idol (Daniel Petrie)
1969: Angel, Angel, Down We Go (Robert Thom)
1974: The Towering Inferno (John Guillermin)

BORIS KARLOFF

1916: The Dumb Girl of Portici (Lois Wilson)
1925: Forbidden Cargo (Tom Buckingham)
1927: Two Arabian Knights (Lewis Milestone)
1928: The Burning Wind (Henry MacRae)
1929: Two Arabian Nights (Milestone)
The Fatal Warning (Serial; Richard Thorpe)
King of the Kongo (Serial; R. Thorpe)
1931: The Criminal Code (Howard Hawks)
Five Star Final (Mervyn LeRoy)
Frankenstein (James Whale)
1932: The Miracle Man (Norman McLeod)
The Mummy (Karl Freund)
The Mask of Fu Manchu (Charles Brabin)
Scarface (Hawks)
The Old Dark House (Whale)
1933: The Ghoul (T. Hayes Hunter)
1934: The Black Cat (Edgar G. Ulmer)
The House of Rothschild (Alfred Werker)
The Lost Patrol (John Ford)
1935: The Black Room (Roy William Neill)
The Raven (Louis Friedlander)
The Man Who Changed His Mind (Robert Stevenson)
Bride of Frankenstein (Whale)
1936: Charlie Chan at the Opera (H. Bruce Humberstone)
Juggernaut (Henry Edwards)
The Walking Dead (Michael Curtiz)
The Invisible Ray (Lambert Hillyer)
1937: Night Key (Lloyd Corrigan)
Without Warning (William Nigh)
1938: Mr. Wong Detective (Nigh)
1939: Devil's Island (William Clemens)
The Son of Frankenstein (Rowland V. Lee)
Mr. Wong in Chinatown (Nigh)
The Man They Couldn't Hang (Nick Grinde)
Tower of London (R. Lee)
1949: The Man with Nine Lives (Grinde)
You'll Find Out (David Butler)
Before I Hang (R. Lee)
1941: The Devil Commands (Edward Dmytryk)
1942: The Boogie Man Will Get You (Lew Landers)
1944: The Climax (George Waggner)
1945: The Body Snatcher (Robert Wise)
Isle of the Dead (Mark Robson)
House of Frankenstein (Erle C. Kenton)
1947: Unconquered (Cecil B. De Mille)
The Secret Life of Walter Mitty (McLeod)
1948: Tap Roots (George Marshall)
Lured (Douglas Sirk)
1949: Bud Abbott and Lou Costello Meet the Killer, Boris Karloff (Charles Barton)

1951: The Strange Door (Joseph Pevney)
1952: The Black Castle (Nathan Juran)
1953: Colonel March Investigates (Cyril Endfield)
Il Monstro Dell'Isola (Roberto Montero)
1955: Sabaka (Arthur Lubin)
1957: Voodoo Island (Reginald LeBorg)
The Juggler of Our Lady (Cartoon Paul Terry, as narrator)
1958: Frankenstein 1970 (Howard W. Koch)
Grip of the Strangler (Robert Day)
1963: The Raven (Roger Corman)
The Terror (Corman)
A Comedy of Terrors (Jacques Tourneur)
Black Sabbath (Mario Bava)
1965: Die, Monster, Die (Daniel Haller)
1966: Ghost in the Invisible Bikini (Don Weis)
1967: The Sorcerers (Michael Reeves)
The Venetian Affair (Jerry Thorpe)
Mondo Balordo (Robert Bianchi Montero)
1968: Targets (Peter Bogdanovich)
1969: Cauldron of Blood (Santos Alcocer)
1970: The Crimson Cult (Vernon Sewell)
1971: Snake People (Jack Hill, Juan Ibanez)
The Incredible Invasion (Hill, Ibanez)

BUSTER KEATON

Shorts:
1917: The Butcher Boy (Roscoe Arbuckle)
A Reckless Romeo (Arbuckle)
Rough House (Arbuckle)
His Wedding Night (Arbuckle)
Oh, Doctor (Arbuckle)
Coney Island (Arbuckle)
1918: Out West (Arbuckle)
The Bell Boy (Arbuckle)
Moonshine (Arbukcle)
Goodnight Nurse (Arbuckle)
The Cook (Arbuckle)
1919: A Desert Hero (Arbuckle)
Back Stage (Arbuckle)
The Hayseed (Arbuckle)
The Garage (Arbuckle)
1920: The High Sign (Buster Keaton, Eddie Cline)
One Week (Keaton, Cline)
Convict 13 (Keaton, Cline)
The Scarecrow (Keaton, Cline)
Neighbors (Keaton, Cline)
1921: The Haunted House (Keaton, Cline)
Hard Luck (Keaton, Cline)
The Playhouse (Keaton, Cline)
The Boat (Keaton, Cline)
The Paleface (Keaton, Cline)
1922: Cops (Keaton, Cline)
My Wife's Relations (Keaton, Cline)
The Blacksmith (Keaton, Malcolm St. Clair)
The Frozen North (Keaton, Cline)
Day Dreams (Keaton, Cline)
The Electric House (Keaton, Cline)
1923: The Balloonatic (Keaton, Cline)
The Love Nest (Keaton)
1934: Alley Oop (Charles Lamont)
The Gold Ghost (Lamont)
1935: Palooka from Paducah (Lamont)
Tars and Stripes (Lamont)
Hayseed Romance (Lamont)
The E-Flat Man (Lamont)
One Run Elmer (Lamont)
The Timid Young Man (Mack Sennett)
1936: Three on a Limb (Lamont)
Grand Slam Opera (Lamont)
Blue Blazes (Raymond Kane)
Mixed Magic (Kane)
1937: Ditto (Lamont)
Jail Bait (Lamont)
Love Nest on Wheels (Lamont)
1939: Mooching Through Georgia (Jules White)
Pest from the West (Del Lord)
Nothing but Pleasure (White)
1940: Pardon My Berth Marks (White)
Taming of the Snood (White)
1941: So You Won't Squawk (Lord)
His Ex Marks the Spot (Lord)
General Nuisance (Lord)
She's Oil Mine (Lord)

1952: Un Duela Mort (Pierre Blondy)
1965: The Railroader (Gerald Potterton)
Keaton Rides Again (John Spotton)
Film (Alan Schneider)
1966: The Scribe (John Sebert)
Features:
1920: The Saphead (Herbert Blache)
1923: The Three Ages (Keaton, Cline)
Our Hospitality (Keaton, John Blystone)
1924: Sherlock Junior (Keaton)
The Navigator (Keaton, Donald Crisp)
1925: Seven Chances (Keaton)
Go West (Keaton, Lex Neal)
1926: Battling Butler (Keaton)
The General (Keaton, Clyde Bruckman)
1927: College (James W. Horne)
Steamboat Bill Jr. (Charles F. Riesner)
1928: The Cameraman (Edward Sedgwick)
Spite Marriage (Sedgwick)
1929: Hollywood Revue of 1929 (Riesner)
1930: Free and Easy (Sedgwick)
Doughboys (Sedgwick)
1931: Sidewalks of New York (White, Zion Myers)
Parlor, Bedroom and Bath (Sedgwick)
1932: Speak Easily (Sedgwick)
The Passionate Plumber (Sedgwick)
1933: What, No Beer? (Sedgwick)
1939: Hollywood Cavalcade (Irving Cummings, St. Clair)
The Jones Family in Hollywood (St. Clair)
The Jones Family in Quick Millions (St. Clair)
1940: The Villain Still Pursued Her (Cline)
L'il Abner (Albert S. Rogell)
1943: Forever and a Day (René Clair, Edmund Goulding, Cedric Hardwicke, Frank Lloyd, Victor Saville, Robert Stevenson, Herbert Wilcox)
1944: San Diego, I Love You (Reginald LeBorg)
1945: That's the Spirit (Lamont)
That Night with You (William Seiter)
1946: El Moderno Barba Azul (Jaime Salvador)
God's Country (Robert Tansey)
1949: You're My Everything (Walter Lang)
In the Good Old Summertime (Robert Z. Leonard)
The Lovable Cheat (Richard Oswald)
1950: Sunset Boulevard (Billy Wilder)
1952: Limelight (Charles Chaplin)
The Awakening (unknown)
1956: Around the World in 80 Days (Michael Anderson)
1960: The Adventures of Huckleberry Finn (Michael Curtiz)
1963: It's a Mad, Mad, Mad, Mad World (Stanley Kramer)
The Triumph of Lester Snapwell (James Calhoun)
1965: Pajama Party (Don Weis)
Beach Blanket Bingo (William Asher)
How to Stuff a Wild Bikini (Asher)
Due Marines e uno Generale (Luigi Scattini)
1966: A Funny Thing Happened on the Way to the Forum (Richard Lester)

DIANE KEATON

1970: Lovers and Other Strangers (Cy Howard)
1972: The Godfather (Francis Ford Coppola)
Play It Again, Sam (Herbert Ross)
1974: Sleeper (Woody Allen)
The Godfather, Part II (Coppola)
1975: Love and Death (W. Allen)
1976: Harry and Walter Go to New York (Mark Rydell)
I Will, I Will . . . for Now (Norman Panama)

1977: Annie Hall (W. Allen)
Looking for Mr. Goodbar (Richard Brooks)
1978: Interiors (W. Allen)
1979: Manhattan (W. Allen)

GENE KELLY

1942: For Me and My Gal (Busby Berkeley)
1943: Pilot No. 5 (George Sidney)
DuBarry Was a Lady (Roy Del Ruth)
Thousands Cheer (Sidney)
The Cross of Lorraine (Tay Garnett)
1944: Cover Girl (Charles Vidor)
Christmas Holiday (Robert Siodmak)
1945: Anchors Aweigh (Sidney)
1946: Ziegfeld Follies (Vincente Minnelli)
1947: Living in a Big Way (Gregory La Cava)
1948: The Pirate (Minnelli)
The Three Musketeers (Sidney)
Words and Music (Norman Taurog)
1949: Take Me Out to the Ball Game (Berkeley)
On the Town (Stanley Donen, Gene Kelly)
1950: Black Hand (Richard Thorpe)
Summer Stock (Charles Walters)
1951: It's a Big Country (C. Vidor)
An American in Paris (Minnelli)
1952: Singin' in the Rain (Donen, Kelly)
Love Is Better Than Ever (Donen)
1953: The Devil Makes Three (Andrew Marton)
1954: Brigadoon (Minnelli)
Seagulls Over Sorrento (John and Roy Boulting)
Deep in My Heart (Donen)
1955: It's Always Fair Weather (Donen)
1956: Invitation to the Dance (Kelly)
1957: The Happy Road (Kelly)
Les Girls (George Cukor)
1958: Marjorie Morningstar (Irving Rapper)
The Tunnel of Love (Kelly, director only)
1960: Inherit the Wind (Stanley Kramer)
Let's Make Love (Cukor)
1963: Gigot (Kelly, director only)
1964: What a Way to Go! (J. Lee Thompson)
1967: The Young Girls of Rochefort (Jacques Demy)
A Guide for the Married Man (Kelly, director only)
1969: Hello, Dolly! (Kelly, director only)
1970: The Cheyenne Social Club (Kelly, director only)
1973: Forty Carats (Milton Katselas)
1974: That's Entertainment! (Jack Haley, Jr.)
1976: That's Entertainment, Part 2 (Kelly)
1977: Viva Knievel! (Gordon Douglas)

GRACE KELLY

1951: Fourteen Hours (Henry Hathaway)
1952: High Noon (Fred Zinnemann)
1953: Mogambo (John Ford)
1954: Dial M for Murder (Alfred Hitchcock)
Rear Window (Hitchcock)
Green Fire (Andrew Marton)
The Country Girl (George Seaton)
1955: The Bridges at Toko-Ri (Mark Robson)
To Catch a Thief (Hitchcock)
1956: The Swan (Charles Vidor)
High Society (Charles Walters)

ALAN LADD

1936: Pigskin Parade (David Butler)
1937: Last Train from Madrid (James Hogan)
Souls at Sea (Henry Hathaway)
Hold 'em Navy (Kurt Neumann)
1938: The Goldwyn Follies (George Marshall)
Come on Leathernecks (James Cruze)
1939: The Green Hornet (Serial; Ford Beebe, Ray Taylor)

Rulers of the Sea (Frank Lloyd)
Beasts of Berlin (Sherman Drew)
1940: Light of Western States (Lesley Selander)
Gangs of Chicago (Arthur Lubin)
In Old Missouri (Frank McDonald)
Those Were the Days (J. Theodore Ried)
Captain Caution (Richard Wallace)
Wildcat Bus (Frank Woodruff)
Meet the Missus (Malcolm St. Clair)
Her First Romance (Edward Dmytryk)
1941: Great Guns (Monty Banks)
Citizen Kane (Orson Welles)
Cadet Girl (Ray McCarey)
Petticoat Politics (Erle C. Kenton)
The Black Cat (Albert S. Rogell)
The Reluctant Dragon (Alfred Werker)
Paper Bullets (Phil Rosen)
1942: Joan of Paris (Robert Stevenson)
This Gun for Hire (Frank Tuttle)
The Glass Key (Stuart Heisler)
Lucky Jordan (Marshall)
Star Spangled Rhythm (Marshall)
1943: China (John Farrow)
1944: And Now Tomorrow (Irving Pichel)
1945: Salty O'Rourke (Raoul Walsh)
Duffy's Tavern (Hal Walker)
1946: The Blue Dahlia (Marshall)
O.S.S. (Pichel)
Two Years Before the Mast (Farrow)
1947: Calcutta (Farrow)
Variety Girl (Marshall)
Wild Harvest (Tay Garnett)
1948: Saigon (Leslie Fenton)
Beyond Glory (Farrow)
Whispering Smith (Fenton)
1949: The Great Gatsby (Elliott Nugent)
Chicago Deadline (Lewis Allen)
1950: Branded (Rudolph Mate)
Captain Carey, U.S.A. (Mitchell Leisen)
1951: Appointment with Danger (L. Allen)
Red Mountain (William Dieterle)
1952: The Iron Mistress (Gordon Douglas)
1953: Thunder in the East (Charles Vidor)
Desert Legion (Joseph Pevney)
Shane (George Stevens)
Botany Bay (Farrow)
1954: Paratrooper (Terence Young)
Saskatchewan (Walsh)
Hell Below Zero (Mark Robson)
The Black Knight (Garnett)
Drum Beat (Delmer Daves)
1955: The McConnell Story (G. Douglas)
Hell on Frisco Bay (Tuttle)
1956: Santiago (G. Douglas)
1957: The Big Land (G. Douglas)
Boy on a Dolphin (Jean Negulesco)
1958: The Deep Six (Mate)
The Proud Rebel (Michael Curtiz)
The Badlanders (Daves)
1959: The Man in the Net (Curtiz)
1960: Guns of the Timberland (Robert D. Webb)
All the Young Men (Hall Bartlett)
One Foot in Hell (James B. Clark)
1961: Duel of Champions (T. Young)
1962: 13 West Street (Philip Leacock)
1964: The Carpetbaggers (Dmytryk)

CHARLES LAUGHTON

1928: Daydreams (Short; Ivor Montagu)
Bluebottles (Short; Montagu)
Frankie and Johnnie (Short; Montagu)
1929: Piccadilly (E. A. Dupont)
1930: Wolves (Albert De Courville)
1931: Down River (Peter Godfrey)
1932: The Old Dark House (James Whale)
The Devil and the Deep (Marion Gering)
Payment Deferred (Lothar Mendes)
The Sign of the Cross (Cecil B. De Mille)
If I Had a Million (Ernst Lubitsch, Norman Taurog, Stephen Roberts, Norman Z. McLeod, James Cruze, William A. Seiter, H. Bruce Humberstone)
1933: Island of Lost Souls (Erle C. Kenton)

The Private Life of Henry VIII
(Alexander Korda)
White Woman (Stuart Walker)
1934: The Barretts of Wimpole Street
(Sidney Franklin)
1935: Ruggles of Red Gap (Leo McCarey)
Les Miserables (Richard
Boleslawski)
Mutiny on the Bounty (Frank Lloyd)
1936: Rembrandt (A. Korda)
I, Claudius (incomplete; Josef von
Sternberg)
1938: The Beachcomber (Erich Pommer)
St. Martin's Lane (Tim Whelan)
1939: Jamaica Inn (Alfred Hitchcock)
The Hunchback of Notre Dame
(William Dieterle)
1940: They Knew What They Wanted
(Garson Kanin)
1941: It Started with Eve (Henry Koster)
1942: The Tuttles of Tahiti (Charles
Vidor)
Tales of Manhattan (Julien
Duvivier)
Stand by for Action (Robert Z.
Leonard)
1943: Forever and a Day (René Clair,
Edmund Goulding, Cedric
Hardwicke, Lloyd, Victor
Saville, Robert Stevenson,
Herbert Wilcox)
This Land Is Mine (Jean Renoir)
The Man from Down Under (R.
Leonard)
1944: The Canterville Ghost (Jules
Dassin)
The Suspect (Robert Siodmak)
1945: Captain Kidd (Rowland V. Lee)
1946: Because of Him (Richard Wallace)
1948: The Paradine Case (Hitchcock)
On Our Merry Way (King Vidor,
Leslie Fenton)
The Big Clock (John Farrow)
Arch of Triumph (Lewis Milestone)
The Girl from Manhattan (Alfred E.
Green)
1949: The Bribe (R. Leonard)
The Man on the Eiffel Tower
(Burgess Meredith)
1951: The Blue Veil (Curtis Bernhardt)
The Strange Door (Joseph Pevney)
1952: O'Henry's Full House (Koster)
Abbott and Costello Meet Captain
Kidd (Charles Lamont)
1953: Salome (William Dieterle)
Young Bess (George Sidney)
1954: Hobson's Choice (David Lean)
1955: The Night of the Hunter (Charles
Laughton, director only)
1957: Witness for the Prosecution (Billy
Wilder)
1960: Under the Flags (Duilio Coletti)
Spartacus (Stanley Kubrick)
1962: Advise and Consent (Otto
Preminger)

LAUREL AND HARDY

Shorts:
1917: Lucky Dog (Jesse Robbins)
1926: Forty-Five Minutes from
Hollywood (Hal Roach)
1927: Duck Soup (Roach)
Slipping Wives (Fred Guiol)
Love 'em and Weep (Guiol)
Why Girls Love Sailors (Guiol)
With Love and Hisses (Guiol)
Sailors, Beware! (Hal Yates)
Do Detectives Think? (Guiol)
Flying Elephants (Frank Butler)
Sugar Daddies (Guiol)
The Call of the Cuckoo (Clyde
Bruckman)
The Second Hundred Years (Guiol)
Hats Off (Leo McCarey, Yates)
Putting Pants on Philip (Bruckman)
The Battle of the Century
(Bruckman, L. McCarey)
1928: Leave 'em Laughing (Bruckman, L.
McCarey)
The Finishing Touch (Bruckman, L.
McCarey)
From Soup to Nuts (E. Livingston,
Edgar Kennedy)
You're Darn Tootin' (Kennedy)
Their Purple Moment (James
Parrott, L. McCarey)

Should Married Men Go Home?
(Parrott, L. McCarey)
Early to Bed (Emmett Flynn)
Two Tars (Parrott)
Habeus Corpus (L. McCarey)
We Faw Down (L. McCarey)
1929: Liberty (L. McCarey)
Wrong Again (L. McCarey)
Big Business (James Horne)
That's My Wife (Lloyd French)
Double Whoopee (Lewis Foster)
Unaccustomed As We Are (L.
Foster)
Berth Marks (L. Foster)
Men O'War (L. Foster)
A Perfect Day (Parrott)
They Go Boom (Parrott)
Bacon Grabbers (L. Foster)
The Hoosegow (L. Foster)
Angora Love (L. Foster)
1930: Night Owls (Parrott)
Blotto (Parrott)
Brats (Parrott)
Below Zero (Parrott)
Hog Wild (Parrott)
The Laurel-Hardy Murder Case
(Parrott)
Another Fine Mess (Parrott)
Be Big (Parrott)
1931: Chickens Come Home (Horne)
Laughing Gravy (Horne)
Our Wife (Horne)
Come Clean (Horne)
One Good Turn (Horne)
Beau Hunks (Horne)
Helpmates (Parrott)
1932: Any Old Port (Horne)
The Music Box (Parrott)
The Chimp (Parrott)
County Hospital (Parrott)
Scram (Raymond McCarey)
Their First Mistake (George
Marshall)
The Slippery Pearls (A Masquers
Club Comedy)
1933: Towed in a Hole (Marshall)
Twice Two (Parrott)
Me and My Pal (Charles Rogers,
French)
The Midnight Patrol (French)
Busy Bodies (French)
Wild Poses (Robert McGowan)
Dirty Work (French)
1934: Oliver the Eighth (French)
Going Bye Bye (Rogers)
Them Thar Hills (Rogers)
1935: Tit for Tat (Rogers)
The Fixer-Uppers (Rogers)
Thicker Than Water (Horne)
1936: On the Wrong Trek (Parrott, Harold
Law)
1937: The Flying Deuces (Edward
Sutherland)
Tree in a Test Tube (U.S.
Government)

Features:
1929: The Hollywood Revue of 1929
(Charles F. Riesner)
1930: The Rogue Song (Lionel
Barrymore)
1931: Pardon Us (Parrott)
1932: Pack Up Your Troubles (Marshall,
McCarey)
1933: The Devil's Brother (Roach,
Rogers)
The Sons of the Desert (William A.
Seiter)
1934: Hollywood Party (Richard
Boleslawski)
Babes in Toyland — March of the
Wooden Soldiers (Gus Meins,
Rogers)
1935: Bonnie Scotland (Horne)
1936: The Bohemian Girl (Horne, Rogers)
Our Relations (Harry Lachman)
1937: Way Out West (Horne)
Pick a Star (Edward Sedgwick)
1938: Swiss Miss (John Blystone)
1940: A Chump at Oxford (Alfred
Goulding)
Saps at Sea (Gordon Douglas)
1941: Great Guns (Monty Banks)
1942: A-Hunting We Will Go (Alfred
Werker)
1943: Air Raid Wardens (Sedgwick)
Jitterbugs (Malcolm St. Clair)
The Dancing Masters (St. Clair)

1944: The Big Noise (St. Clair)
Nothing but Trouble (Sam Taylor)
1945: The Bullfighters (St. Clair)
1951: Atoll K. (John Berry, Leo Joannon)

BRUCE LEE

Bruce Lee made many films as a child
actor in Hong Kong; including *Birth of a
Man* and *My Son a Chang.*

His American titles:
1969: Marlowe (Paul Bogart)
1972: Fists of Fury (Lo Wei)
The Chinese Connection (Lo Wei)
1973: Enter the Dragon (Robert Clouse)
Return of the Dragon (Bruce Lee)
1974: Game of Death (Lee)
Bruce Lee: The Man and the Legend
(Documentary)

VIVIEN LEIGH

1934: Things Are Looking Up (Albert de
Courville)
1935: The Village Squire (Reginald
Denham)
Gentleman's Agreement (George
Pearson)
Look Up and Laugh (Basil Dean)
1937: Fire Over England (William K.
Howard)
Dark Journey (Victor Saville)
Storm in a Teacup (Saville)
1938: A Yank at Oxford (Jack Conway)
St. Martin's Lane (Tim Whelan)
1939: Gone With the Wind (Victor
Fleming)
1940: Waterloo Bridge (Mervyn LeRoy)
21 Days Together (Dean)
1941: That Hamilton Woman (Alexander
Korda)
1946: Caesar and Cleopatra (Gabriel
Pascal)
1948: Anna Karenina (Julien Duvivier)
1951: A Streetcar Named Desire (Elia
Kazan)
1955: The Deep Blue Sea (Anatole Litvak)
1961: The Roman Spring of Mrs. Stone
(Jose Quintero)
1965: Ship of Fools (Stanley Kramer)

JACK LEMMON

1954: It Should Happen to You (George
Cukor)
Phffft! (Mark Robson)
1955: Three for the Show (H. C. Potter)
Mister Roberts (John Ford, Mervyn
LeRoy)
My Sister Eileen (Richard Quine)
1956: You Can't Run Away from It (Dick
Powell)
1957: Fire Down Below (Robert Parrish)
Operation Mad Ball (Quine)
1958: Cowboy (Delmer Daves)
Bell, Book and Candle (Quine)
1959: Some Like It Hot (Billy Wilder)
It Happened to Jane (Quine)
1960: The Apartment (B. Wilder)
Pepe (George Sidney)
1961: The Wackiest Ship in the Army
(Richard Murphy)
1962: Stowaway in the Sky (Albert
Lamorisse, as narrator)
The Notorious Landlady (Quine)
Days of Wine and Roses (Blake
Edwards)
1963: Irma La Douce (B. Wilder)
Under the Yum-Yum Tree (David
Swift)
1964: Good Neighbor Sam (Swift)
1965: How to Murder Your Wife (Quine)
The Great Race (Edwards)
1966: The Fortune Cookie (B. Wilder)
1967: Luv (Clive Donner)
1968: The Odd Couple (Gene Saks)
1969: The April Fools (Stuart Rosenberg)
1970: The Out-of-Towners (Arthur Hiller)
1971: Kotch (Jack Lemmon)
1972: The War Between Men and Women
(Melville Shavelson)
Avanti! (B. Wilder)
1973: Save the Tiger (John Avildsen)
1974: The Front Page (B. Wilder)
1976: Alex and the Gypsy (John Korty)
1977: Airport '77 (Jerry Jameson)
1979: The China Syndrome (James
Bridges)

JERRY LEWIS

With Dean Martin:
1949: My Friend Irma (George Marshall)
1950: My Friend Irma Goes West (Hal
Walker)
1951: At War with the Army (H. Walker)
That's My Boy (H. Walker)
1952: Sailor Beware (H. Walker)
Jumping Jacks (Norman Taurog)
1953: The Stooge (Taurog)
Scared Stiff (Marshall)
The Caddy (Taurog)
Money from Home (Marshall)
1954: Living it Up (Taurog)
Three Ring Circus (Joseph Peveny)
1955: You're Never Too Young (Taurog)
Artists and Models (Frank Tashlin)
1956: Pardners (Taurog)
Hollywood or Bust (Tashlin)

Alone:
1957: The Delicate Delinquent (Don
McGuire)
The Sad Sack (Marshall)
1958: Rock-A-Bye Baby (Tashlin)
1958: The Geisha Boy (Tashlin)
1959: Don't Give Up the Ship (Taurog)
1960: Visit to a Small Planet (Taurog)
The Bellboy (Jerry Lewis)
Cinderfella (Tashlin)
1961: The Errand Boy (Lewis)
1962: It's Only Money (Tashlin)
1963: The Nutty Professor (Lewis)
Who's Minding the Store (Tashlin)
1964: The Patsy (Lewis)
The Disorderly Orderly (Tashlin)
1965: The Family Jewels (Lewis)
Boeing Boeing (John Rich)
1966: Three on a Couch (Lewis)
Way Way Out (Gordon Douglas)
1967: The Big Mouth (Lewis)
1968: Don't Raise the Bridge, Lower the
Water (Jerry Paris)
1970: One More Time (Lewis, director
only)
1971: Which Way to the Front? (Lewis)

Unreleased:
The Day the Clown Cried (Lewis)

HAROLD LLOYD

Shorts:
According to *Films in Review,* Harold
Lloyd made 64 Lonesome Luke one-reel
films between 1916 and 1917. The films
were never copyrighted and the
negatives were not preserved, so the
titles as well as the films themselves
have been lost. The following list begins
with the Lloyd films which were
copyrighted. These shorts were directed
by either Hal Roach, Alf Goulding, or
Lloyd himself.
1917: Lonesome Luke on Tin Can Alley
Lonesome Luke's Honeymoon
Lonesome Luke's Lively Life
Lonesome Luke, Plumber
Lonesome Luke in Stop! Luke!
Listen!
Lonesome Luke, Messenger
Lonesome Luke, Mechanic
Lonesome Luke's Wild Women
Lonesome Luke Loses Patients
Over the Fence
Pinched
Lonesome Luke in Birds of a
Feather
Bliss
Lonesome Luke from London to
Laramie
Rainbow Island
The Flirt
Lonesome Luke in Love, Laughs
and Lather
Lonesome Luke in Clubs are
Trumps
All Aboard
Lonesome Luke in We Never Sleep
Move On
By the Sad Sea Waves
The Tip
Bashful
1918: Take a Chance
The Non-Stop Kid
That's Him
She Loves Me Not
The Lamb

Look Out Below
The Big Idea
Here Comes the Girls
On the Jump
On the Fire
Hey There
Hit Him Again
Beat It
Next Aisle Over
An Ozark Romance
Bride and Groom
Pipe the Whiskers
Follow the Crowd
Swing Your Partner
Why Pick on Me?
Ask Father
Nothing but Trouble
Wanted — 5,000
Going! Going! Gone!
A Gasoline Wedding
The City Slicker
Are Crooks Dishonest?
Beach Nuts
Blood Will Tell
Check Your Baggage
Cleopatsy
Do Husbands Deceive?
An Enemy of Soap
Fireman, Save My Child
The Furniture Movers
The Great Water Peril
Hello Teacher
His Busy Day
Hustling for Health
Just Rambling Along
Kicked Out
Look Pleasant Please
Let's Go
Kicking the Germ Out of Germany
Love's Young Scream
Nipped in the Bud
No Place Like Jail
Ring Up the Curtain
Somewhere in Turkey
Two Gun Gussie
It's a Wild Life
Hear 'em Rave
Two Scrambled
Bees in His Bonnet
Sic 'em Towser
Step Lively
1919: Before Breakfast
Billy Blazes, Esq.
Be My Wife
Just Neighbors
A Jazzed Honeymoon
Spring Fever
Back to the Woods
Count Your Change
Crack Your Heels
The Dutiful Dub
He Leads, Others Follow
Hoot Mon
Just Dropped In
The Marathon
Swat the Crook
Off the Trolley
St. Senor
Pay Your Dues
Never Touched Me
Chop Suey & Co.
The Rajah
As the Old Stage Door
His Only Father
I'm on My Way
Don't Shove
Soft Money
Young Mr. Jazz
A Sammy in Siberia
Pistols for Breakfast
Count the Votes
Bumping into Broadway
Captain Kidd's Kids
From Hand to Mouth
His Royal Slyness
1920: Haunted Spooks
An Eastern Westerner
High and Dizzy
Get Out and Get Under
Number, Please
1921: Now or Never
Among Those Present
I Do
Never Weaken
Features:
1921: A Sailor-Made Man (Fred
    Newmeyer)

1922: Grandma's Boy (Newmeyer)
    Dr. Jack (Newmeyer)
1923: Safety Last (Newmeyer, Sam
    Taylor)
    Why Worry? (Newmeyer, S.
    Taylor)
1924: Hot Water (Newmeyer, S. Taylor)
1925: The Freshman (Newmeyer, S.
    Taylor)
1926: For Heaven's Sake (S. Taylor)
1927: The Kid Brother (Ted Wilde)
1929: Welcome Danger (Clyde
    Bruckman)
1930: Feet First (Bruckman)
1932: Movie Crazy (Bruckman)
1934: The Cat's Paw (S. Taylor)
1936: The Milky Way (Leo McCarey)
1938: Professor Beware (Elliott Nugent)
1947: Mad Wednesday (Preston Sturges)

CAROLE LOMBARD

1921: A Perfect Crime (Allan Dwan)
1925: Hearts and Spurs (W.S. Van Dyke)
    Durand of the Badlands (Lynn
    Reynolds)
    Marriage in Transit (Roy William
    Neill)
1928: Me, Gangster (Raoul Walsh)
    The Divine Sinner (Scott Pembroke)
    Power (Howard Higgin)
    Show Folks (Paul L. Stein)
1929: Ned McCobb's Daughter (William
    J. Cowan)
    High Voltage (Higgin)
    Big News (Gregory La Cava)
    The Racketeer (Higgin)
1930: The Arizona Kid (Alfred Santell)
    Safety in Numbers (Victor
    Schertzinger)
    Fast and Loose (Fred Newmeyer)
1931: It Pays to Advertise (Frank Tuttle)
    Man of the World (Richard
    Wallace)
    Ladies' Man (Lothar Mendes)
    Up Pops the Devil (Edward
    Sutherland)
    I Take This Woman (Marion
    Gering)
1932: No One Man (Lloyd Corrigan)
    Sinners in the Sun (Alexander Hall)
    Virtue (Edward Buzzell)
    No More Orchids (Walter Lang)
    No Man of Her Own (Wesley
    Ruggles)
1933: From Hell to Heaven (Erle C.
    Kenton)
    Supernatural (Victor Halperin)
    The Eagle and the Hawk (Stuart
    Walker)
    Brief Moment (David Burton)
    White Woman (Walker)
1934: Bolero (Ruggles)
    We're Not Dressing (Norman
    Taurog)
    Twentieth Century (Howard Hawks)
    Now and Forever (Henry Hathaway)
    Lady by Choice (D. Burton)
    The Gay Bride (Jack Conway)
1935: Rumba (Gering)
    Hands Across the Table (Mitchell
    Leisen)
1936: Love Before Breakfast (W. Lang)
    The Princess Comes Across
    (William K. Howard)
    My Man Godfrey (La Cava)
1937: Swing High, Swing Low (Leisen)
    Nothing Sacred (William Wellman)
    The Confession (Ruggles)
1938: Fools for Scandal (Mervyn LeRoy)
    Made for Each Other (John
    Cromwell)
    In Name Only (Cromwell)
1940: Vigil in the Night (George Stevens)
    They Knew What They Wanted
    (Garson Kanin)
1941: Mr. and Mrs. Smith (Alfred
    Hitchcock)
1942: To Be or Not To Be (Ernst Lubitsch)

PETER LORRE

1929: Fruhlings Erwachen (Richard
    Oswald)
1931: Die Koffer des Herrn O.F. (Alexis
    Granovsky)

M (Fritz Lang)
    Bomben auf Monte Carlo (Hanns
    Schwarz)
1932: F.P.1 Antwortet Nicht (Karl Hartl)
    Schuss im Morgengrauen (Alfred
    Zeisler)
    Der Weisse Damon (Kurt Gerron)
    Funf von der Jazzband (Erich Engel)
1933: Was Frauen Traumen (Geza von
    Bolvary)
    Unsichtbare Gegner (Rudolf
    Katscher)
    De Haut en Bas (G.W. Pabst, voice
    only)
1934: The Man Who Knew Too Much
    (Alfred Hitchcock)
1935: Mad Love (Karl Freund)
    Crime and Punishment (Josef von
    Sternberg)
1936: Secret Agent (Hitchcock)
    Crack-Up (Malcolm St. Clair)
1937: Nancy Steele Is Missing (George
    Marshall)
    Lancer Spy (Gregory Ratoff)
    Think Fast, Mr. Moto (Norman
    Foster)
    Thank You, Mr. Moto (Foster)
1938: Mr. Moto's Gamble (James Tinling)
    Mr. Moto Takes a Chance (Foster)
    I'll Give a Million (Walter Lang)
    Mysterious Mr. Moto (Foster)
1939: Mr. Moto's Last Warning (Foster)
    Mr. Moto Takes a Vacation (Foster)
    Mr. Moto in Danger Island (Herbert
    I. Leeds)
1940: Stranger on the Third Floor (Boris
    Ingster)
    I Was an Adventuress (Ratoff)
    You'll Find Out (David Butler)
    Strange Cargo (Frank Borzage)
1941: The Maltese Falcon (John Huston)
    All Through the Night (Vincent
    Sherman)
    The Face Behind the Mask (Robert
    Florey)
    Mr. District Attorney (William
    Morgan)
    They Met in Bombay (Clarence
    Brown)
1942: Casablanca (Michael Curtiz)
    The Boogie Man Will Get You
    (Lew Landers)
    Invisible Agent (Edwin L. Marin)
1943: The Constant Nymph (Edmund
    Goulding)
    Background to Danger (Raoul
    Walsh)
    Cross of Lorraine (Tay Garnett)
1944: The Conspirators (Jean Negulesco)
    Arsenic and Old Lace (Frank Capra)
    Passage to Marseilles (Curtiz)
    Hollywood Canteen (Delmer Daves)
    The Mask of Dimitrios (Negulesco)
1945: Confidential Agent (Herman
    Shumlin)
    Hotel Berlin (Peter Godfrey)
1946: Three Strangers (Negulesco)
    The Verdict (Don Siegel)
    The Beast with Five Fingers
    (Florey)
    The Chase (Arthur Ripley)
    Black Angel (Roy William Neill)
1947: My Favorite Brunette (Elliott
    Nugent)
1948: Casbah (John Berry)
1949: Rope of Sand (William Dieterle)
1950: Quicksand (Irving Pichel)
1951: The Lost One (Peter Lorre)
    Double Confession (Harry
    Reynolds)
1954: Beat the Devil (Huston)
    20,000 Leagues Under the Sea
    (Richard Fleischer)
1956: Congo Crossing (Joseph Pevney)
    Around the World in 80 Days
    (Michael Anderson)
1957: The Buster Keaton Story (Sidney
    Sheldon)
    Hell Ship Mutiny (Lee Sholem,
    Elmo Williams)
    The Story of Mankind (Irwin Allen)
    The Sad Sack (George Marshall)
    Silk Stockings (Rouben Mamoulian)
1959: The Big Circus (Joseph Newman)
    Scent of Mystery (Jack Cardiff)
1961: Voyage to the Bottom of the Sea (I.
    Allen)

1962: Tales of Terror (Roger Corman)
    Five Weeks in a Balloon (I. Allen)
1963: The Raven (Corman)
    Comedy of Terrors (Jacques
    Tourneur)
1964: The Patsy (Jerry Lewis)

MYRNA LOY

1925: Pretty Ladies (Monta Bell)
    Satan in Sables (James Flood)
    Sporting Life (Maurice Tourneur)
    Ben-Hur (Fred Niblo)
1926: The Caveman (Roy Del Ruth)
    The Love Toy (Erle C. Kenton)
    The Gilded Highway (J. Stuart
    Blackton)
    Why Girls Go Back Home (Flood)
    The Exquisite Sinner (Josef von
    Sternberg)
    Don Juan (Alan Crosland)
    Across the Pacific (Del Ruth)
    The Millionaires (Herman C.
    Raymaker)
1927: Finger Prints (Lloyd Bacon)
    When a Man Loves (Crosland)
    Bitter Apples (Harry Hoyt)
    The Climbers (Paul Stein)
    Simple Sis (Raymaker)
    Heart of Maryland (Bacon)
    A Sailor's Sweetheart (Bacon)
    The Jazz Singer (Crosland)
    The Girl from Chicago (Enright)
    If I Were Single (Del Ruth)
    Ham and Eggs at the Front (Del
    Ruth)
1928: Beware of Married Men (Archie
    Mayo)
    What Price Beauty (Thomas
    Buckingham)
    Fancy Baggage (John Adolfi)
    Turn Back the Hours (Howard
    Bretherton)
    Crimson City (Mayo)
    Pay As You Enter (Adolfi)
    State Street Sadie (Mayo)
    The Midnight Taxi (Adolfi)
    Noah's Ark (Michael Curtiz)
1929: The Desert Song (Del Ruth)
    The Black Watch (John Ford)
    The Squall (Alexander Korda)
    Hardboiled Rose (Harmon Weight)
    Evidence (Adolfi)
    The Show of Shows (Adolfi)
1930: The Great Divide (Reginald Barker)
    Jazz Cinderella (Scott Pembroke)
    Cameo Kirby (Irving Cummings)
    Isle of Escape (Bretherton)
    Under a Texas Moon (Curtiz)
    Cock O' the Walk (Walter Lang)
    Bride of the Regiment (John Francis
    Dillon)
    Last of the Duanes (Alfred Werker)
    The Truth About Youth (William A.
    Seiter)
    Renegades (Victor Fleming)
    Rogue of the Rio Grande (Spencer
    Bennet)
    The Devil to Pay (George
    Fitzmaurice)
1931: The Naughty Flirt (Edward Cline)
    Body and Soul (Alfred Santell)
    A Connecticut Yankee (David
    Butler)
    Hush Money (Sidney Lanfield)
    Transatlantic (William K. Howard)
    Rebound (Edward H. Griffith)
    Skyline (Sam Taylor)
    Consolation Marriage (Paul Sloane)
    Arrowsmith (Ford)
1932: Emma (Clarence Brown)
    The Wet Parade (Fleming)
    Vanity Fair (Chester Franklin)
    The Woman in Room 13 (Henry
    King)
    New Morals for Old (Charles
    Brabin)
    Love Me Tonight (Rouben
    Mamoulian)
    Thirteen Women (George
    Archainbaud)
    The Mask of Fu Manchu (Brabin)
    The Animal Kingdom (Griffith)
1933: Topaze (Harry D'Arrast)
    The Barbarian (Sam Wood)
    The Prizefighter and the Lady (W.
    S. Van Dyke)

When Ladies Meet (Harry Beaumont)
Penthouse (Van Dyke)
Night Flight (C. Brown)
1934: Men in White (Richard Boleslawski)
Manhattan Melodrama (Van Dyke)
The Thin Man (Van Dyke)
Stamboul Quest (Wood)
Evelyn Prentice (Howard)
Broadway Bill (Frank Capra)
1935: Wings in the Dark (Flood)
Whipsaw (Wood)
1936: Wife vs. Secretary (C. Brown)
The Great Ziegfeld (Robert Z. Leonard)
To Mary — With Love (John Cromwell)
Libeled Lady (Jack Conway)
After the Thin Man (Van Dyke)
1937: Parnell (John M. Stahl)
Double Wedding (Richard Thorpe)
1938: Man-Proof (Thorpe)
Test Pilot (Fleming)
Too Hot to Handle (Conway)
1939: Lucky Night (Norman Taurog)
The Rains Came (C. Brown)
Another Thin Man (Van Dyke)
1940: I Love You Again (Van Dyke)
Third Finger, Left Hand (E. Leonard)
1941: Love Crazy (Conway)
Shadow of the Thin Man (Van Dyke)
1944: The Thin Man Goes Home (Thorpe)
1946: So Goes My Love (Frank Ryan)
The Best Years of Our Lives (William Wyler)
1947: The Bachelor and the Bobby-Soxer (Irving Reis)
Song of the Thin Man (Edward Buzzell)
The Senator Was Indiscreet (George S. Kaufman)
1948: Mr. Blandings Builds His Dream House (Lewis Milestone)
1949: The Red Pony (Milestone)
1950: Cheaper by the Dozen (W. Lang)
If This Be Sin (Gregory Ratoff)
1952: Bells on Their Toes (Henry Levin)
1956: The Ambassador's Daughter (Norman Krasna)
1958: Lonelyhearts (Vincent J. Donehue)
1960: Midnight Lace (David Miller)
From the Terrace (Mark Robson)
1969: The April Fools (Stuart Rosenberg)
1974: Airport 1975 (Jack Smight)
1978: The End (Burt Reynolds)

SHIRLEY MacLAINE

1955: The Trouble with Harry (Alfred Hitchcock)
Artists and Models (Frank Tashlin)
1956: Around the World in 80 Days (Michael Anderson)
1958: The Sheepman (George Marshall)
The Matchmaker (Joseph Anthony)
Hot Spell (Daniel Mann)
1959: Some Came Running (Vincente Minnelli)
Ask Any Girl (Charles Walters)
Career (Walter Lang)
1960: Can-Can (W. Lang)
The Apartment (Billy Wilder)
1961: All in a Night's Work (Anthony)
Two Loves (Walters)
1962: The Children's Hour (William Wyler)
My Geisha (Jack Cardiff)
Two for the Seesaw (Robert Wise)
1963: Irma La Douce (B. Wilder)
1964: What a Way to Go (J. Lee Thompson)
John Goldfarb, Please Come Home (J. L. Thompson)
1965: The Yellow Rolls-Royce (Anthony Asquith)
1966: Gambit (Ronald Neame)
1967: Woman Times Seven (Vittorio De Sica)
1968: The Bliss of Mrs. Blossom (Joseph McGrath)
1969: Sweet Charity (Bob Fosse)
1970: Two Mules for Sister Sara (Don Siegel)

1971: Desperate Characters (Frank D. Gilroy)
1972: The Possession of Joel Delaney (Waris Hussein)
1974: The Other Half of the Sky: A China Memoir (Documentary; Shirley MacLaine, Claudia Weill)
1977: The Turning Point (Herbert Ross)

FREDRIC MARCH

1929: The Dummy (Robert Milton)
The Wild Party (Dorothy Arzner)
The Studio Murder Mystery (Frank Tuttle)
Jealousy (Jean de Limur)
Paris Bound (Edward H. Griffith)
Footlights and Fools (William A. Seiter)
The Marriage Playground (Lothar Mendes)
1930: Sarah and Son (Arzner)
Ladies Love Brutes (Rowland V. Lee)
True to the Navy (Tuttle)
Manslaughter (George Abbott)
Laughter (Harry D'Arrast)
The Royal Family of Broadway (George Cukor, Cyril Gardner)
Paramount on Parade (Arzner, Otto Brower, Edmund Goulding, Victor Heerman, Edwin Knopf, R. V. Lee, Ernst Lubitsch, Mendes, Victor Schertzinger, Edward Sutherland, Tuttle)
1931: Honor Among Lovers (Arzner)
The Night Angel (Goulding)
My Sin (Abbott)
1932: Dr. Jekyll and Mr. Hyde (Rouben Mamoulian)
Strangers in Love (Mendes)
Merrily We Go to Hell (Arzner)
Smilin' Through (Sidney Franklin)
The Sign of the Cross (Cecil B. De Mille)
1933: Tonight Is Ours (Stuart Walker)
The Eagle and the Hawk (S. Walker)
Design for Living (Lubitsch)
1934: All of Me (James Flood)
Death Takes a Holiday (Mitchell Leisen)
Good Dame (Marion Gering)
The Affairs of Cellini (Gregory La Cava)
The Barretts of Wimpole Street (Franklin)
We Live Again (Mamoulian)
1935: Les Miserables (Richard Boleslawski)
Anna Karenina (Clarence Brown)
The Dark Angel (Franklin)
1936: Mary of Scotland (John Ford)
The Road to Glory (Howard Hawks)
Anthony Adverse (Mervyn LeRoy)
1937: A Star Is Born (William Wellman)
Nothing Sacred (Wellman)
1938: The Buccaneer (De Mille)
There Goes My Heart (Norman Z. McLeod)
1939: Trade Winds (Tay Garnett)
1940: Susan and God (Cukor)
Victory (John Cromwell)
1941: So Ends Our Night (Cromwell)
One Foot in Heaven (Irving Rapper)
1942: Bedtime Story (Alexander Hall)
I Married a Witch (Rene Clair)
1944: The Adventures of Mark Twain (Rapper)
Tomorrow the World (Leslie Fenton)
1946: The Best Years of Our Lives (William Wyler)
1948: Another Part of the Forest (Michael Gordon)
Live Today for Tomorrow (Gordon)
1949: Christopher Columbus (David MacDonald)
1951: Death of a Salesman (Laslo Benedek)
1952: It's a Big Country (Charles Vidor, Richard Thorpe, John Sturges, Don Hartman, Don Weis, C. Brown, Wellman)
1953: Man on a Tightrope (Elia Kazan)
1954: Executive Suite (Robert Wise)

1955: The Bridges At Toko-Ri (Mark Robson)
The Desperate Hours (Wyler)
1956: Alexander the Great (Robert Rossen)
The Man in the Gray Flannel Suit (Nunnally Johnson)
1959: Middle of the Night (Delbert Mann)
1960: Inherit the Wind (Stanley Kramer)
1961: The Young Doctors (Phil Karlson)
1963: The Condemned of Altona (Vittorio De Sica)
1964: Seven Days in May (John Frankenheimer)
1967: Hombre (Martin Ritt)
1969: . . . tick . . . tick . . . tick (Ralph Nelson)
1973: The Iceman Cometh (Frankenheimer)

LEE MARVIN

1951: You're in the Navy Now (Henry Hathaway)
1952: We're Not Married (Edmund Goulding)
Duel at Silver Creek (Don Siegel)
Hangman's Knot (Roy Huggins)
Diplomatic Courier (Hathaway)
Eight Iron Men (Edward Dmytryk)
1953: Down Among the Sheltering Palms (Goulding)
The Stranger Wore a Gun (Andre De Toth)
Seminole (Budd Boetticher)
Gun Fury (Raoul Walsh)
The Big Heat (Fritz Lang)
The Wild One (Laslo Benedek)
1954: Gorilla at Large (Harmon Jones)
The Caine Mutiny (Dmytryk)
The Raid (Hugo Fregonese)
Bad Day at Black Rock (John Sturges)
1955: A Life in the Balance (Harry Horner)
Violent Saturday (Richard Fleischer)
Not as a Stranger (Stanley Kramer)
Pete Kelly's Blues (Jack Webb)
I Died a Thousand Times (Stuart Heisler)
Shack Out on 101 (Edward Dein)
1956: Seven Men from Now (Boetticher)
Attack! (Robert Aldrich)
Pillars of the Sky (George Marshall)
The Rack (Arnold Laven)
1957: Raintree County (Dmytryk)
1958: The Missouri Traveller (Jerry Hopper)
1961: The Comancheros (Michael Curtiz)
1962: The Man Who Shot Liberty Valance (John Ford)
1963: Donovan's Reef (Ford)
1964: The Killers (Siegel)
1965: Cat Ballou (Elliot Silverstein)
Ship of Fools (Kramer)
1966: The Professionals (Richard Brooks)
1967: The Dirty Dozen (Aldrich)
Point Blank (John Boorman)
The London Scene (Peter Whitehead)
1968: Hell in the Pacific (Boorman)
Sergeant Ryker (Buzz Kulik)
1969: Paint Your Wagon (Joshua Logan)
1970: Monte Walsh (William Fraker)
1972: Prime Cut (Michael Ritchie)
1973: The Emperor of the North Pole (Aldrich)
The Iceman Cometh (John Frankenheimer)
1974: The Spikes Gang (Fleischer)
The Klansman (Terence Young)
1976: Shout at the Devil (Peter Hunt)
1978: Avalanche Express (Mark Robson)
1979: The Big Red One (Sam Fuller)

THE MARX BROTHERS

1929: The Cocoanuts (Robert Florey, Joseph Santley)
1930: Animal Crackers (Victor Heerman)
1931: Monkey Business (Norman Z. McLeod)
1932: Horse Feathers (McLeod)
1933: Duck Soup (Leo McCarey)
1935: A Night at the Opera (Sam Wood)
1937: A Day at the Races (Wood)

1938: Room Service (William A. Seiter)
1939: At the Circus (Edward Buzzell)
1940: Go West (Buzzell)
1941: The Big Store (Charles Riesner)
1946: A Night in Casablanca (Archie Mayo)
1949: Love HapyY (David Miller)
1957: The Story of Mankind (Irwin Allen)
Groucho alone:
1947: Copacabana (Alfred E. Green)
1950: Mr. Music (Richard Haydn)
1951: Double Dynamite (Irving Cummings)
1952: A Girl in Every Port (Chester Erskine)
1969: Skidoo (Otto Preminger)

JOEL McCREA

1927: The Fair Co-ed (Sam Wood)
1929: The Jazz Age (Lynn Shores)
The Single Standard (John S. Robertson)
So This Is College (Wood)
Dynamite (Cecil B. De Mille)
1930: The Silver Horde (George Archainbaud)
Lightnin' (Henry King)
1931: Once a Sinner (Guthrie McClintic)
Kept Husbands (Lloyd Bacon)
Born to Love (Paul Stein)
Girls About Town (George Cukor)
1932: Business and Pleasure (David Butler)
The Lost Squadron (Archainbaud)
Bird of Paradise (Vidor)
The Most Dangerous Game (Irving Pichel, Ernest B. Schoedsack)
Rockabye (Cukor)
The Sport Parade (Dudley Murphy)
1933: The Silver Cord (John Cromwell)
Bed of Roses (Gregory La Cava)
One Man's Journey (Robertson)
Chance at Heaven (William A. Seiter)
1934: Gambling Lady (Archie Mayo)
Half a Sinner (Kurt Neumann)
Richest Girl in the World (W. A. Seiter)
1935: Private Worlds (La Cava)
Our Little Girl (Robertson)
Woman Wanted (George B. Seiter)
Barbary Coast (Howard Hawks)
Splendor (Elliott Nugent)
1936: These Three (William Wyler)
Two in a Crowd (Alfred E. Green)
Adventure in Manhattan (Edward Ludwig)
Come and Get It (Wyler, Hawks)
Banjo on My Knee (Cromwell)
1937: Internes Can't Take Money (Alfred Santell)
Wells Fargo (Frank Lloyd)
Woman Chases Man (John G. Blystone)
Dead End (Wyler)
1938: Three Blind Mice (W. A. Seiter)
Youth Takes a Fling (Mayo)
1939: Union Pacific (De Mille)
They Shall Have Music (Mayo)
Espionage Agent (Bacon)
1940: He Married His Wife (Roy Del Ruth)
The Primrose Path (La Cava)
Foreign Correspondent (Alfred Hitchcock)
1941: Reaching for the Sun (William Wellman)
Sullivan's Travels (Preston Sturges)
1942: The Great Man's Lady (Wellman)
The Palm Beach Story (P. Sturges)
1943: The More the Merrier (George Stevens)
1944: Buffalo Bill (Wellman)
The Great Moment (P. Sturges)
1945: The Unseen (Lewis Allen)
1946: The Virginian (Victor Fleming)
1947: Ramrod (Andre De Toth)
1948: Four Faces West (A. Green)
1949: South of St. Louis (Ray Enright)
Colorado Territory (Raoul Walsh)
1950: Stars in My Crown (Jacques Tourneur)
The Outriders (Roy Rowland)
Saddle Tramp (Hugo Fregonese)
Frenchie (Louis King)
1951: The Hollywood Story (William Castle)

Cattle Drive (Neumann)
1952: The San Francisco Story (Robert Parrish)
1953: Lone Hand (George Sherman)
Shoot First (Parrish)
1954: Black Horse Canyon (Jesse Hibbs)
Border River (Sherman)
1955: Stranger on Horseback (J. Tourneur)
Wichita (J. Tourneur)
1956: The First Texan (Byron Haskin)
1957: The Oklahoman (Lyon)
Trooper Hook (Charles Marquis Warren)
Gunsight Ridge (Francis D. Lyon)
The Tall Stranger (Thomas Carr)
1958: Cattle Empire (Warren)
Fort Massacre (Joseph M. Newman)
1959: The Gunfight at Dodge City (Newman)
1962: Ride the High Country (Sam Peckinpah)
1970: Cry Blood, Apache (Jack Starrett)
Sioux Nation (Documentary)
1974: The Great American Cowboy (Documentary; as narrator)
1976: Mustang Country (John C. Champion)

STEVE McQUEEN

1958: Never Love a Stranger (Robert Stevens)
The Blob (Irwin S. Yeaworth, Jr.)
1959: The Great St. Louis Bank Robbery (John Stix, Charles Guggenheim)
Never So Few (John Sturges)
1960: The Magnificent Seven (J. Sturges)
1961: The Honeymoon Machine (Richard Thorpe)
1962: Hell Is for Heroes (Don Siegel)
The War Lover (Philip Leacock)
1963: The Great Escape (J. Sturges)
Love with the Proper Stranger (Robert Mulligan)
Soldier in the Rain (Ralph Nelson)
1965: Baby the Rain Must Fall (Mulligan)
The Cincinnati Kid (Norman Jewison)
1966: Nevada Smith (Henry Hathaway)
The Sand Pebbles (Robert Wise)
1968: The Thomas Crown Affair (Jewison)
Bullitt (Peter Yates)
1969: The Reivers (Mark Rydell)
1971: Le Mans (John Frankenheimer)
On Any Sunday (Bruce Brown)
1972: Junior Bonner (Sam Peckinpah)
The Getaway (Peckinpah)
1973: Papillon (Franklin J. Schaffner)
1974: The Towering Inferno (John Guillermin)
1978: An Enemy of the People (George Schaefer)

ROBERT MITCHUM

1943: Hoppy Serves a Writ (George Archainbaud)
The Leather Burners (Joseph Henabery)
Border Patrol (Lesley Selander)
Follow the Band (Jean Yarbrough)
Colt Comrades (Selander)
The Human Comedy (Clarence Brown)
We've Never Been Licked (John Rawlins)
Beyond the Last Frontier (Howard Bretherton)
Bar 20 (Selander)
Doughboys in Ireland (Lew Landers)
Corvette K-225 (Richard Rosson)
The Lone Star Trail (Ray Taylor)
False Colors (Archainbaud)
The Dancing Masters (Malcom St. Clair)
Rider of the Deadline (Selander)
Gung Ho! (Ray Enright)
1944: Johnny Doesn't Live Here Anymore (Joe May)
When Strangers Marry (William Castle)
The Girl Rush (Gordon Douglas)
Thirty Seconds Over Tokyo (Mervyn LeRoy)
Nevada (Edward Killy)

1945: West of the Pecos (Killy)
The Story of G.I. Joe (William Wellman)
1946: Till the End of Time (Edward Dmytryk)
Undercurrent (Vincente Minnelli)
The Locket (John Brahm)
1947: Pursued (Raoul Walsh)
Crossfire (Dmytryk)
Desire Me (George Cukor)
Out of the Past (Jacques Tourneur)
1948: Rachel and the Stranger (Norman Foster)
Blood on the Moon (Robert Wise)
1949: The Red Pony (Lewis Milestone)
The Big Steal (Don Siegel)
Holiday Affair (Don Hartman)
1950: Where Danger Lives (John Farrow)
1951: My Forbidden Past (Robert Stevenson)
His Kind of Woman (Farrow)
The Racket (John Cromwell)
1952: Macao (Josef von Sternberg)
One Minute to Zero (Tay Garnett)
The Lusty Men (Nicholas Ray)
Angel Face (Otto Preminger)
1954: White Witch Doctor (Henry Hathaway)
Second Chance (Rudolph Mate)
1954: She Couldn't Say No (Lloyd Bacon)
River of No Return (Preminger)
Track of the Cat (Wellman)
1955: Not as a Stranger (Stanley Kramer)
The Night of the Hunter (Charles Laughton)
Man with the Gun (Richard Wilson)
1956: Foreign Intrigue (Sheldon Reynolds)
Bandido (Richard Fleischer)
1957: Heaven Knows, Mr. Allison (John Huston)
Fire Down Below (Robert Parrish)
The Enemy Below (Dick Powell)
1958: Thunder Road (Arthur Ripley)
The Hunters (D. Powell)
1959: The Angry Hills (Robert Aldrich)
The Wonderful Country (Parrish)
1960: Home from the Hill (Minnelli)
The Night Fighters (Garnett)
The Grass Is Greener (Stanley Donen)
The Sundowners (Fred Zinnemann)
1961: The Last Time I Saw Archie (Jack Webb)
1962: Cape Fear (J. Lee Thompson)
The Longest Day (Andrew Marton, Ken Annakin, Bernhard Wicki)
Two for the Seesaw (Wise)
1963: The List of Adrian Messenger (Huston)
Rampage (Phil Karlson)
1964: Man in the Middle (Guy Hamilton)
What a Way to Go! (J. L. Thompson)
1965: Mister Moses (Ronald Neame)
1967: The Way West (Andrew V. McLaglen)
El Dorado (Howard Hawks)
Anzio (Dmytryk)
1968: Villa Rides (Buzz Kulik)
Five Card Stud (Hathaway)
Secret Ceremony (Joseph Losey)
1969: Young Billy Young (Burt Kennedy)
The Good Guys and the Bad Guys (Kennedy)
1970: Ryan's Daughter (David Lean)
1972: Going Home (Herbert B. Leonard)
The Wrath of God (Ralph Nelson)
1973: The Friends of Eddie Coyle (Peter Yates)
1975: The Yazuka (Sydney Pollack)
Farewell, My Lovely (Dick Richards)
The Last Tycoon (Elia Kazan)
1978: The Big Sleep (Michael Winner)
Amsterdam Kill (Robert Clouse)
Matilda (Daniel Mann)

MARILYN MONROE

1947: Dangerous Years (Arthur Pierson)
1948: Scudda Hoo! Scudda Hay! (Hugh Herbert)
1949: Ladies of the Chorus (Phil Karlson)
Love Happy (David Miller)
1950: A Ticket to Tomahawk (Richard Sale)

The Asphalt Jungle (John Huston)
All About Eve (Joseph L. Mankiewicz)
The Fireball (Tay Garnett)
Right Cross (John Sturges)
Hometown Story (Pierson)
As Young As You Feel (Harmon Jones)
Love Nest (Joseph Newman)
Let's Make It Legal (Sale)
1952: Clash by Night (Fritz Lang)
Don't Bother to Knock (Roy Baker)
Monkey Business (Howard Hawks)
O. Henry's Full House (Henry Koster)
1953: Niagara (Henry Hathaway)
Gentlemen Prefer Blondes (Hawks)
How to Marry a Millionaire (Jean Negulesco)
1954: River of No Return (Otto Preminger)
There's No Business Like Show Business (Walter Lang)
1955: The Seven Year Itch (Billy Wilder)
1956: Bus Stop (Joshua Logan)
1957: The Prince and the Showgirl (Laurence Olivier)
1959: Some Like It Hot (B. Wilder)
1960: Let's Make Love (George Cukor)
1961: The Misfits (Huston)

MICHAEL MORIARTY

1971: Glory Boy (Edwin L. Sherin)
1972: Hickey and Boggs (Robert Culp)
1973: The Last Detail (Hal Ashby)
Bang the Drum Slowly (John Hancock)
1974: Shoot It:Black, Shoot It:Blue (Dennis McGuire)
1975: Report to the Commissioner (Milton Katselas)
1978: Who'll Stop the Rain? (Karel Reisz)

MICKEY MOUSE

All Mickey Mouse cartoons were produced by Walt Disney. All but *Fantasia* (1940) are shorts.
1928/29: Steamboat Willie
Gallopin' Gaucho
Plane Crazy
Barn Dance
The Opry House
When the Cat's Away
Barnyard Battle
The Plow Boy
The Karnival Kid
Mickey's Follies
El Terrible Toreador
Mickey's Choo Choo
The Jazz Fool
Haunted House
Wild Waves
1930: Just Mickey
The Barnyard Concert
Cactus Kid
Fire Fighters
The Shindig
The Chain Gang
Gorilla Mystery
The Picnic
Pioneer Days
1931: Birthday Party
Traffic Troubles
The Castaway
The Moose Hunt
Delivery Boy
Mickey Steps Out
Blue Rhythm
Fishin' Around
Barnyard Broadcast
Beach Party
Mickey Cuts Up
Mickey's Orphans
1932: Duck Hunt
Grocery Boy
Mad Dog
Barnyard Olympics
Mickey's Revue
Musical Farmer
Mickey in Arabia
Mickey's Nightmare
Trader Mickey
The Whoopee Party
Touchdown Mickey
The Wayward Canary

The Klondike Kid
Mickey's Good Deed
1933: Building a Building
The Mad Doctor
Mickey's Pal Pluto
Mickey's Mellerdrammer
Ye Olden Days
The Mail Pilot
Mickey's Mechanical Man
Mickey's Gala Premiere
Puppy Love
The Steeplechase
The Pet Store
Giant Land
1934: Shanghaied
Camping Out
Playful Pluto
Gulliver Mickey
Mickey' Steamroller
Orphans' Benefit
Mickey Plays Papa
The Dog-Napper
Two-Gun Mickey
1935: Mickey's Man Friday
The Band Concert
Mickey's Service Station
Mickey's Kangaroo
Mickey's Garden
Mickey's Fire Brigade
Pluto's Judgment Day
On Ice
1936: Mickey's Polo Team
Orphans Picnic
Mickey's Grand Opera
Thru the Mirror
Moving Day
Mickey's Rival
Donald and Pluto
Mickey's Elephant
Mother Pluto
1937: The Worm Turns
Don Donald
Magician Mickey
Moose Hunters
Mickey's Amateurs
Modern Inventions
Hawaiian Holiday
Clock Cleaners
The Old Mill
Lonesome Ghosts
1938: Boat Builders
Mickey's Trailer
The Whalers
Mickey's Parrot
The Brave Little Tailor
1939: Society Dog Show
The Pointer
1940: Tugboat Mickey
Mr. Mouse Takes a Trip
Fantasia ("The Sorcerer's Apprentice" sequence)
1941: The Little Whirlwind
Nifty Nineties
Orphans' Benefit
1942: Mickey's Birthday Party
Symphony Hour
1947: Mickey's Delayed Date
1948: Mickey Down Under
Mickey and the Seal
1951: R'coon Dawg
1952: Pluto's Christmas Tree
1953: The Simple Things

PAUL NEWMAN

1954: The Silver Chalice (Victor Saville)
1956: Somebody Up There Likes Me (Robert Wise)
The Rack (Arnold Laven)
1957: The Helen Morgan Story (Michael Curtiz)
Until They Sail (Wise)
1958: The Long Hot Summer (Martin Ritt)
The Left-Handed Gun (Arthur Penn)
Cat on a Hot Tin Roof (Richard Brooks)
Rally 'Round the Flag, Boys! (Leo McCarey)
1959: The Young Philadelphians (Vincent Sherman)
1960: From the Terrace (Mark Robson)
Exodus (Otto Preminger)
1961: The Hustler (Ritt)
Paris Blues (Ritt)
1962: Sweet Bird of Youth (R. Brooks)
Adventures of a Young Man (R. Brooks)

1963: Hud (Ritt)
A New Kind of Love (Melville Shavelson)
The Prize (Robson)
1964: What a Way to Go! (J. Lee Thompson)
The Outrage (Ritt)
1965: Lady L (Peter Ustinov)
1966: Harper (Jack Smight)
Torn Curtain (Alfred Hitchcock)
1967: Hombre (Ritt)
Cool Hand Luke (Stuart Rosenberg)
1968: The Secret War of Harry Frigg (Smight)
Rachel, Rachel (Paul Newman, director only)
1969: Winning (James Goldstone)
Butch Cassidy and the Sundance Kid (George Roy Hill)
1970: WUSA (Rosenberg)
1971: Sometimes a Great Notion (P. Newman)
1972: Pocket Money (Rosenberg)
The Life and Times of Judge Roy Bean (John Huston)
The Effect of Gamma Rays on Man-in-the-Moon Marigolds (P. Newman, director only)
1973: The Mackintosh Man (Huston)
The Sting (G.R. Hill)
1974: The Towering Inferno (John Guilermin, Irwin Allen)
1975: The Drowning Pool (Rosenberg)
1976: Buffalo Bill and the Indians (Robert Altman)
1977: Slap Shot (G. R. Hill)
1978: Quintet (Altman)

JACK NICHOLSON

1958: Crybaby Killer (Jus Addis)
1960: The Little Shop of Horrors (Roger Corman)
Too Soon to Love (Richard Rush)
The Wild Ride (Harvey Berman)
Studs Lonigan (Irving Lerner)
1962: The Broken Land (John Bushelman)
1963: The Raven (Corman)
The Terror (Corman)
Thunder Island (Jack Leewood)
1964: Ensign Pulver (Joshua Logan)
Back Door to Hell (Monte Hellman)
1967: The Shooting (Hellman)
Ride the Whirlwind (Hellman)
Hells Angels on Wheels (Rush)
The Trip (Corman)
The St. Valentine's Day Massacre (Corman)
1968: Flight to Fury (Hellman)
Psych-Out (Rush)
Head (Bob Rafelson)
1969: Easy Rider (Dennis Hopper)
1970: On a Clear Day You Can See Forever (Vincente Minnelli)
Five Easy Pieces (Rafelson)
1971: Drive, He Said (Jack Nicholson, director only)
Carnal Knowledge (Mike Nichols)
1972: The King of Marvin Gardens (Rafelson)
1973: The Last Detail (Hal Ashby)
1974: Chinatown (Roman Polanski)
1975: Tommy (Ken Russell)
The Passenger (Michelangelo Antonioni)
The Fortune (Nichols)
One Flew Over the Cuckoo's Nest (Milos Forman)
1976: The Missouri Breaks (Arthur Penn)
1978: Goin' South (Nicholson)
1979: The Shining (Stanley Kubrick)

KIM NOVAK

1954: The French Line (Lloyd Bacon)
Pushover (Richard Quine)
Phffft! (Mark Robson)
1955: Five Against the House (Phil Karlson)
Son of Sinbad (Ted Tetzlaff)
The Man with the Golden Arm (Otto Preminger)
1956: Picnic (Joshua Logan)
The Eddy Duchin Story (George Sidney)
1957: Jeanne Eagels (Sidney)

Pal Joey (Sidney)
1958: Vertigo (Alfred Hitchcock)
Bell, Book and Candle (Quine)
1959: Middle of the Night (Delbert Mann)
1960: Strangers When We Meet (Quine)
Pepe (Sidney)
1962: Boys' Night Out (Michael Gordon)
The Notorious Landlady (Quine)
1964: Of Human Bondage (Ken Hughes)
Kiss Me, Stupid (Billy Wilder)
1965: The Amorous Adventures of Moll Flanders (Terence Young)
1968: The Legend of Lylah Clare (Robert Aldrich)
1969: The Great Bank Robbery (Hy Averback)
1973: Tales That Witness Madness (Freddie Francis)
1974: The Celebrity Art Portfolio (Short; Richard D'Anjolell)
1977: The White Buffalo (J. Lee Thompson)

MAUREEN O'HARA

1938: My Irish Molly (Alex Bryce)
Rocking the Moon Around (Walter Forde)
1939: The Hunchback of Notre Dame (William Dieterle)
Jamaica Inn (Alfred Hitchcock)
1940: A Bill of Divorcement (John Farrow)
Dance, Girl, Dance (Dorothy Arzner)
1941: They Met in Argentina (Leslie Goodwins)
How Green Was My Valley (John Ford)
1942: To the Shores of Tripoli (H. Bruce Humberstone)
Ten Gentlemen from West Point (Henry Hathaway)
The Black Swan (Henry King)
1943: The Immortal Sergeant (John M. Stahl)
This Land Is Mine (Jean Renoir)
The Fallen Sparrow (Richard Wallace)
1944: Buffalo Bill (William Wellman)
1945: The Spanish Main (Frank Borzage)
1946: Sentimental Journey (Walter Lang)
Do You Love Me? (Gregory Ratoff)
1947: Sinbad the Sailor (Wallace)
The Foxes of Harrow (Stahl)
The Homestretch (Humberstone)
Miracle on 34th Street (George Seaton)
1948: Sitting Pretty (W. Lang)
The Forbidden Street (Jean Negulesco)
A Woman's Secret (Nicholas Ray)
Father Was a Fullback (Stahl)
Bagdad (Charles Lamont)
1950: Comanche Territory (G. Sherman)
Tripoli (Will Price)
Rio Grande (Ford)
1951: Flame of Araby (Lamont)
1952: At Sword's Point (Lewis Allen)
Kangaroo (Lewis Milestone)
The Quiet Man (Ford)
Against All Flags (G. Sherman)
Redhead from Wyoming (Lee Sholem)
1953: War Arrow (G. Sherman)
1954: Fire Over Africa (Richard Sale)
1955: The Long Gray Line (Ford)
The Magnificent Matador (Budd Boetticher)
Lady Godiva (Arthur Lubin)
1956: Lisbon (Ray Milland)
Everything but the Truth (Jerry Hopper)
1957: Wings of Eagles (Ford)
1960: Our Man in Havana (Carol Reed)
1961: The Parent Trap (David Swift)
The Deadly Companions (Sam Peckinpah)
1962: Mr. Hobbs Takes a Vacation (Henry Koster)
1963: Spencer's Mountain (Delmer Daves)
McLintock! (Andrew V. McLaglen)
1965: The Battle of the Villa Florita (Daves)
1966: The Rare Breed (McLaglen)

1970: How Do I Love Thee? (Michael Gordon)
1971: Big Jake (G. Sherman)

LAURENCE OLIVIER

1930: Too Many Crooks (George King)
The Temporary Widow (Gustav Ucicky)
1931: Potiphar's Wife (Maurice Elvey)
The Yellow Ticket (Raoul Walsh)
Friends and Lovers (Victor Schertzinger)
1932: Westward Passagae (Robert Milton)
1933: Perfect Understanding (Cyril Gardner)
No Funny Business (John Stafford, Victor Hanbury)
1935: Conquest of the Air (John Monk Saunders)
Moscow Nights (Anthony Asquith)
1936: As You Like It (Paul Czinner)
1937: Fire Over England (William K. Howard)
1938: The Divorce of Lady X (Tim Whelan)
1939: Q Planes (Whelan)
Wuthering Heights (William Wyler)
21 Days Together (Basil Dean)
1940: Rebecca (Alfred Hitchcock)
Pride and Prejudice (Robert Z. Leonard)
1941: That Hamilton Woman (Alexander Korda)
49th Parallel (Michael Powell)
1943: The Demi Paradise (Asquith)
1944: Henry V (Laurence Olivier)
1948: Hamlet (Olivier)
1951: The Magic Box (John Boulting)
1952: Carrie (Wyler)
1953: The Beggars Opera (Peter Brook)
1955: Richard III (Olivier)
1957: The Prince and the Showgirl (Olivier)
1959: The Devil's Disciple (Guy Hamilton)
1960: The Entertainer (Tony Richardson)
Spartacus (Stanley Kubrick)
1962: Term of Trial (Peter Glenville)
1965: Bunny Lake Is Missing (Otto Preminger)
Othello (Stuart Burge)
1966: Khartoum (Basil Dearden)
1968: The Dance of Death (David Giles)
The Shoes of the Fisherman (Michael Anderson)
1969: David Copperfield (Delbert Mann)
The Battle of Britain (Hamilton)
Oh! What a Lovely War (Richard Attenborough)
1970: Three Sisters (Olivier)
1971: Nicholas and Alexander (Franklin J. Schaffner)
1972: Lady Caroline Lamb (Robert Bolt)
Sleuth (Joseph L. Mankiewicz)
1976: The Seven-Per-Cent Solution (Herbert Ross)
Marathon Man (John Schlesinger)
1978: The Betsy (Daniel Petrie)
The Boys from Brazil (Schaffner)
1979: A Little Romance (George Roy Hill)

PETER O'TOOLE

1959: Kidnapped (Robert Stevenson)
The Savage Innocents (Nicholas Ray)
1960: The Day They Robbed the Bank of England (John Guillermin)
1962: Lawrence of Arabia (David Lean)
1964: Becket (Peter Glenville)
1965: Lord Jim (Richard Brooks)
What's New, Pussycat? (Clive Donner)
1966: How to Steal a Million (William Wyler)
The Night of the Generals (Anatole Litvak)
The Bible (John Huston)
1967: Great Catherine (Gordon Flemyng)
1968: The Lion in Winter (Anthony Harvey)
1969: Goodbye, Mr. Chips (Herbert Ross)
1970: Country Dance (J. Lee Thompson)
Murphy's War (Peter Yates)
1971: Under Milk Wood (Andrew Sinclair)

The Ruling Class (Peter Medak)
1972: Man of La Mancha (Arthur Hiller)
1975: Rosebud (Hiller)
Man Friday (Jack Gold)
Foxtrot (Arturo Ripstein)
1976: Gore Vidal's Caligula (Giovanni Tinto Brass)
1978: The Stunt Man (Richard Rush)
Power Play (Martyn Burke)
1979: Zulu Dawn (Douglas Hickox)

LARRY PARKS

1941: Mystery Ship (Lew Landers)
Harmon of Michigan (Charles J. Barton)
Three Girls About Town (Leigh Jason)
You Belong to Me (Wesley Ruggles)
Sing for Your Supper (Barton)
Honolulu Lu (Barton)
1942: Harvard, Here I Come (Landers)
Blondie Goes to College (Frank R. Strayer)
Canal Zone (Landers)
Flight Lieutenant (Sidney Salkow)
Submarine Raider (Landers)
Atlantic Convoy (Landers)
Hello, Annapolis (Barton)
You Were Never Lovelier (William A. Seiter)
The Boogie Man Will Get You (Landers)
A Man's World (Barton)
North of the Rockies (Lambert Hillyer)
They All Kissed the Bride (Alexander Hall)
Alias Boston Blackie (Landers)
1943: Reveille with Beverly (Barton)
Destroyer (W. A. Seiter)
First Comes Courage (Dorothy Arzner)
Is Everybody Happy? (Barton)
Redhead from Manhattan (Landers)
Power of the Press (Landers)
Deerslayer (Landers)
1944: Stars on Parade (Landers)
The Racket Man (D. Ross Lederman)
The Black Parachute (Landers)
Sergeant Mike (Henry Levin)
She's a Sweetheart (Del Lord)
1945: Counterattack (Zoltan Korda)
1946: The Jolson Story (Alfred E. Green)
Renegades (George Sherman)
1947: Down to Earth (A. Hall)
The Swordsman (Joseph H. Lewis)
Her Husband's Affairs (S. Sylvan Simon)
1948: The Gallant Blade (Levin)
1949: Jolson Sings Again (Levin)
1950: Emergency Wedding (Edward Buzzell)
1952: Love Is Better Than Ever (Stanley Donen)
1955: Crossup (John Gilling)
1962: Freud (John Huston)

GREGORY PECK

1944: Days of Glory (Jacques Tourneur)
The Keys of the Kingdom (John M. Stahl)
1945: The Valley of Decision (Tay Garnett)
Spellbound (Alfred Hitchcock)
1946: The Yearling (Clarence Brown)
Duel in the Sun (King Vidor)
1947: The Macomber Affair (Zoltan Korda)
Gentleman's Agreement (Elia Kazan)
The Paradine Case (Hitchcock)
1948: Yellow Sky (William A. Wellman)
1949: The Great Sinner (Robert Siodmak)
Twelve O'Clock High (Henry King)
1950: The Gunfighter (H. King)
1951: Captain Horatio Hornblower (Raoul Walsh)
Only the Valiant (Gordon Douglas)
David and Bathsheba (H. King)
1952: The World in His Arms (Walsh)
The Snows of Kilimanjaro (H. King)
1953: Roman Holiday (William Wyler)

1954: Night People (Nunnally Johnson)
Man With a Million (Ronald Neame)
1955: The Purple Plain (Robert Parrish)
1956: The Man in the Gray Flannel Suit (Johnson)
Moby Dick (John Huston)
1957: Designing Woman (Vincente Minnelli)
1958: The Bravados (H. King)
The Big Country (Wyler)
1959: Pork Chop Hill (Lewis Milestone)
Beloved Infidel (H. King)
On the Beach (Stanley Kramer)
1961: The Guns of Navarone (J. Lee Thompson)
1962: Cape Fear (J. L. Thompson)
To Kill a Mockingbird (Robert Mulligan)
1963: How the West Was Won (John Ford, George Marshall, Henry Hathaway)
1964: Behold a Pale Horse (Fred Zinnemann)
Captain Newman, M.D. (David Miller, Robert D. Webb)
1965: Mirage (Edward Dmytryk)
1966: John F. Kennedy: Years of Lightning, Day of Drums (Documentary; Bruce Herschensohn, as narrator)
Arabesque (Stanley Donen)
1968: The Stalking Moon (Mulligan)
1969: Mackenna's Gold (J. L. Thompson)
The Chairman (J. L. Thompson)
Marooned (John Sturges)
1970: I Walk the Line (John Frankenheimer)
1971: Shoot Out (Hathaway)
1974: Billy Two Hats (Ted Kotcheff)
1976: The Omen (Richard Donner)
1977: MacArthur (Joseph Sargent)
1978: Boys from Brazil (Franklin J. Schaffner)

MARY PICKFORD

1909: The Violin Maker of Cremona (D. W. Griffith)
The Lonely Villa (Griffith)
Her First Biscuit (Griffith)
The Way of a Man (Griffith)
Sweet and Twenty (Griffith)
They Would Elope (Griffith)
His Wife's Visitors (Griffith)
The Indian Runner's Romance (Griffith)
In Old Kentucky (Griffith)
Pippa Passes (Griffith)
The Little Teacher (Griffith)
To Save Her Soul (Griffith)
1776 or, the Hessian Renegades (Griffith)
Getting Even (Griffith)
The Awakening (Griffith)
1910: The Englishman and the Girl (Griffith)
The Thread of Destiny (Griffith)
A Romance of the Western Hills (Griffith)
Ramona (Griffith)
The Face at the Window (Griffith)
What the Daisy Said (Griffith)
The Call to Arms (Griffith)
An Arcadian Maid (Griffith)
The Sorrows of the Unfaithful (Griffith)
Wilful Peggy (Griffith)
A Rich Revenge (Griffith)
A Lucky Toothache (Mack Sennett)
The Masher (Sennett)
Simple Charity (Griffith)
White Rose (Griffith)
1911: The Italian Barber (Griffith)
A Decree of Destiny (Griffith)
Their First Misunderstanding (Thomas H. Ince)
The Dream (T. Ince)
Maid or Man (T. Ince)
Her Darkest Hour (T. Ince)
Artful Kate (T. Ince)
A Manly Man (T. Ince)
The Fisher Maid (T. Ince)
In Old Madrid (T. Ince)
For Her Brother's Sake (T. Ince)
Her Awakening (Griffith)
The Courting of Mary (George Loane Tucker)

1912: The Mender of Nets (Griffith)
The Old Actor (Griffith)
A Lodging for the Night (Griffith)
A Beast at Bay (Griffith)
So Near Yet So Far (Griffith)
My Baby (Griffith)
Home Folks (Griffith)
Lena and the Geese (Griffith)
A Pueblo Legend (Griffith)
Friends (Griffith)
A Feud in the Kentucky Hills (Griffith)
The Female of the Species (Griffith)
Just Like a Woman (Griffith)
Jola's Promise (Griffith)
The New York Hat (Griffith)
The Informer (Griffith)
1913: The Unwelcome Guest (Griffith)
In the Bishop's Carriage (Edwin S. Porter)
Caprice (J. Searle Dawley)
1914: A Good Little Devil (Dawley)
Hearts Adrift (E. Porter)
Tess of the Storm Country (E. Porter)
The Eagle's Mate (James Kirkwood)
Such a Little Queen (Porter, Hugh Ford)
Behind the Scenes (James Kirkwood)
Cinderella (Kirkwood)
1915: Mistress Nell (Kirkwood)
Fanchon the Cricket (Tucker)
The Dawn of a Tomorrow (Kirkwood)
Little Pal (Marshall Neilan)
Esmeralda (Kirkwood)
The Girl of Yesterday (Allan Dwan)
Madame Butterfly (David Belasco)
1916: The Foundling (John O'Brien)
Poor Little Peppina (Sidney Olcott)
Hulda from Holland (John O'Brien)
The Eternal Grind (Maurice Tourneur)
Less Than the Dust (John Emerson)
1917: The Pride of the Clan (M. Tourneur)
A Poor Little Rich Girl (M. Tourneur)
A Romance of the Redwoods (Cecil B. De Mille)
The Little American (De Mille)
Rebecca of Sunnybrook Farm (Neilan)
The Little Princess (Neilan)
Molly Entangled (Robert Thornby)
1918: Stella Maris (Neilan)
Amarilly of Clothesline Alley (Neilan)
M'liss (Neilan)
How Could You, Jean? (William D. Taylor)
Johanna Enlists (W. Taylor)
1919: Captain Kidd, Jr. (W. Taylor)
Daddy Long Legs (Neilan)
The Hoodlum (Sidney Franklin)
Heart O' the Hills (Franklin)
1920: Pollyanna (Paul Powell)
Suds (Jack Dillon)
1921: The Love Light (Frances Marion)
Through the Back Door (Alfred E. Green, Jack Pickford)
Little Lord Fauntleroy (A. Green)
1922: Tess of the Storm Country (John S. Robertson)
1923: Rosita (Ernst Lubitsch)
1924: Dorothy Vernon of Haddon Hall (Neilan)
1925: Little Annie Rooney (William Beaudine)
1926: Sparrows (Beaudine)
1927: My Best Girl (Sam Taylor)
1929: Coquette (S. Taylor)
The Taming of the Shrew (S. Taylor)
1931: Kiki (S. Taylor)
1933: Secrets (Frank Borzage)

DICK POWELL

1932: Blessed Event (Roy Del Ruth)
Too Busy to Work (John Blystone)
1933: The King's Vacation (John Adolfi)
42nd Street (Lloyd Bacon)
Gold Diggers of 1933 (Mervyn LeRoy)
Footlight Parade (Bacon)
College Coach (William Wellman)
Convention City (Archie Mayo)
1934: Dames (Ray Enright, Busby Berkeley)
Wonder Bar (Bacon)
Twenty Million Sweethearts (Enright)
Happiness Ahead (LeRoy)
Flirtation Walk (Frank Borzage)
1935: Gold Diggers of 1935 (Berkeley)
Page Miss Glory (LeRoy)
Broadway Gondolier (Bacon)
A Midsummer Night's Dream (Max Reinhardt, William Dieterle)
Shipmates Forever (Borzage)
Thanks a Million (Del Ruth)
1936: Colleen (Alfred E. Green)
Hearts Divided (Borzage)
Stage Struck (Berkeley)
Gold Diggers of 1937 (Berkeley)
1937: On the Avenue (Del Ruth)
The Singing Marine (Enright)
Varsity Show (Berkeley)
Hollywood Hotel (Berkeley)
1938: Cowboy from Brooklyn (Bacon)
Hard to Get (Enright)
Going Places (Enright)
1939: Naughty but Nice (Enright)
1940: Christmas in July (Preston Sturges)
I Want a Divorce (Ralph Murphy)
1941: Model Wife (Leigh Jason)
In the Navy (Arthur Lubin)
1942: Star Spangled Rhythm (George Marshall)
Happy Go Lucky (Curtis Bernhardt)
1943: True to Life (Marshall)
Riding High (Marshall)
1944: It Happened Tomorrow (Rene Clair)
Meet the People (Charles F. Riesner)
Murder My Sweet (Edward Dmytryk)
1945: Cornered (Dmytryk)
1947: Johnny O'Clock (Robert Rossen)
1948: To the Ends of the Earth (Robert Stevenson)
Pitfall (Andre De Toth)
Station West (Sidney Lanfield)
Rogue's Regiment (Robert Florey)
1949: Mrs. Mike (Louis King)
1950: The Reformer and the Redhead (Norman Panama)
Right Cross (John Sturges)
1951: Cry Danger (Robert Parrish)
The Tall Target (Anthony Mann)
You Never Can Tell (Lou Breslow)
1952: The Bad and the Beautiful (Vincente Minnelli)
1953: Split Second (Dick Powell, director only)
1954: Susan Slept Here (Frank Tashlin)
1955: The Conqueror (D. Powell, director only)
1956: You Can't Run Away from It (D. Powell, director only)
1957: The Enemy Below (D. Powell, director only)
1958: The Hunters (D. Powell, director only)

ELVIS PRESLEY

1956: Love Me Tender (Robert D. Webb)
1957: Loving You (Hal Kanter)
Jailhouse Rock (Richard Thorpe)
1958: King Creole (Michael Curtiz)
1960: G.I. Blues (Norman Taurog)
Flaming Star (Don Siegel)
1961: Wild in the Country (Philip Dunne)
Blue Hawaii (Taurog)
1962: Girls! Girls! Girls! (Taurog)
Follow That Dream (Gordon Douglas)
Kid Galahad (Phil Karlson)
It Happened at the World's Fair (Taurog)
1963: Fun in Acapulco (R. Thorpe)
1964: Kissin' Cousins (Gene Nelson)
Viva Las Vegas (George Sidney)
Roustabout (John Rich)
1965: Girl Happy (Boris Sagal)
Tickle Me (Taurog)
Harum Scarum (Nelson)
1966: Frankie and Johnny (Frederick de Cordova)

Paradise, Hawaiian Style (Michael Moore)
Spinout (Taurog)
1967: Easy Come, Easy Go (Rich)
Double Trouble (Taurog)
Clambake (Arthur H. Nadel)
1968: Stay Away Joe (Peter Tewksbury)
Speedway (Taurog)
Live a Little, Love a Little (Taurog)
1969: Charro! (Charles Marquis Warren)
The Chautauqua (Tewksbury)
Change of Habit (William Graham)
1970: Elvis — That's the Way It Is (Documentary; Denis Sanders)
1973: Elvis on Tour (Documentary; Robert Abel, Pierre Adige)

CLAUDE RAINS

1933: The Invisible Man (James Whale)
1934: Crime Without Passion (Ben Hecht, Charles MacArthur, Lee Garmes)
The Man Who Reclaimed His Head (Edward Ludwig)
1935: The Clairvoyant (Maurice Elvey)
The Mystery of Edwin Drood (Stuart Walker)
The Last Outpost (Charles T. Barton)
1936: Anthony Adverse (Mervyn LeRoy)
Hearts Divided (Frank Borzage)
Stolen Holiday (Michael Curtiz)
1937: The Prince and the Pauper (William Keighley)
They Won't Forget (LeRoy)
1938: Gold Is Where You Find It (Curtiz)
The Adventures of Robin Hood (Curtiz, Keighley)
White Banners (Edmund Goulding)
Four Daughters (Curtiz)
1939: They Made Me a Criminal (Busby Berkeley)
Juarez (William Dieterle)
Sons of Liberty (Short; Curtiz)
Daughters Courageous (Curtiz)
Mr. Smith Goes to Washington (Frank Capra)
Four Wives (Curtiz)
1940: Saturday's Children (Vincent Sherman)
The Sea Hawk (Curtiz)
The Lady with Red Hair (Curtis Bernhardt)
1941: Four Mothers (Keighley)
Here Comes Mr. Jordan (Alexander Hall)
The Wolf Man (George Waggner)
Kings Row (Sam Wood)
1942: Moontide (Archie Mayo)
Now, Voyager (Irving Rapper)
Casablanca (Curtiz)
1943: Phantom of the Opera (Arthur Lubin)
Forever and a Day (René Clair, Goulding, Cedric Hardwicke, Frank Lloyd, Victor Saville, Robert Stevenson, Herbert Wilcox)
1944: Passage to Marseilles (Curtiz)
Mr. Skeffington (V. Sherman)
1945: This Love of Ours (Dieterle)
Caesar and Cleopatra (Gabriel Pascal)
1946: Angel on My Shoulder (Mayo)
Notorious (Alfred Hitchcock)
Deception (Rapper)
1947: The Unsuspected (Curtiz)
Strange Holiday (Arch Oboler)
1949: One Woman's Story (David Lean)
Rope of Sand (Dieterle)
Song of Surrender (Mitchell Leisen)
1950: The White Tower (Ted Tetzlaff)
Where Danger Lives (John Farrow)
1951: Sealed Cargo (Alfred Werker)
1953: The Paris Express (Harold French)
1956: Lisbon (Ray Milland)
1959: This Earth Is Mine (Henry King)
1960: The Lost World (Irwin Allen)
1961: Battle of the Worlds (Anthony Dawson)
1962: Lawrence of Arabia (Lean)
1963: Twilight of Honor (Boris Sagal)

ROBERT REDFORD

1962: War Hunt (Denis Sanders)
1965: Situation Hopeless, But Not Serious (Gottfried Reinhardt)

Inside Daisy Clover (Robert
    Mulligan)
1966: The Chase (Arthur Penn)
    This Property Is Condemned
    (Sydney Pollack)
1967: Barefoot in the Park (Gene Saks)
1969: Butch Cassidy and the Sundance
    Kid (George Roy Hill)
    Downhill Racer (Michael Ritchie)
    Tell Them Willie Boy Is Here
    (Abraham Polonsky)
1970: Little Fauss and Big Halsy (Sidney
    J. Furie)
1972: The Hot Rock (Peter Yates)
    The Candidate (Ritchie)
    Jeremiah Johnson (Pollack)
1973: The Way We Were (Pollack)
    The Sting (G.R. Hill)
1974: The Great Gatsby (Jack Clayton)
1975: The Great Waldo Pepper (G.R. Hill)
    Three Days of the Condor (Pollack)
1976: All the President's Men (Alan J.
    Pakula)
1977: A Bridge Too Far (Richard
    Attenborough)
1978: Electric Horseman (Pollack)

BURT REYNOLDS

1961: Angel Baby (Paul Wendkos)
    Armored Command (Byron Haskin)
1965: Operation C.I.A. (Christian Nyby)
1967: Navajo Joe (Sergio Corbucci)
1968: Shark (Sam Fuller)
    Impasse (Richard Benedict)
    Fade In (Alan Smithee)
1969: Sam Whiskey (Arnold Laven)
    100 Rifles (Tom Gries)
1970: Skullduggery (Gordon Douglas)
1972: Fuzz (Richard Colla)
    Deliverance (John Boorman)
    Shamus (Buzz Kulik)
    Everything You Always Wanted to
    Know About Sex (But Were
    Afraid to Ask) (Woody Allen)
1973: White Lightning (Joseph Sargent)
    The Man Who Loved Cat Dancing
    (Richard Sarafian)
1974: The Longest Yard (Robert Aldrich)
1975: W.W. and the Dixie Dancekings
    (John Avildsen)
    At Long Last Love (Peter
    Bogdanovich)
    Hustle (Aldrich)
    Lucky Lady (Stanley Donen)
1976: Gator (Burt Reynolds)
    Nickelodeon (Bogdanovich)
    Silent Movie (Mel Brooks)
1977: Smokey and the Bandit (Hal
    Needham)
    Semi-Tough (Michael Ritchie)
1978: The End (Reynolds)
    Hooper (Needham)

ROAD RUNNER/WILE E. COYOTE

Chuck Jones directed all this team's
cartoons from their debut in 1948 until
1962. Subsequent cartoons were directed
by various people, including Robert
McKimson and Rudy Larriva. (Wile E.
has also appeared in cartoons with Bugs
Bunny and Sam the Sheepdog.) Titles of
Road Runner/Wile E. Coyote cartoons
include:
1948: Fast and Furry-ous
1951: Beep, Beep
1955: Gee Wiz-z-z-z
1959: Wild About Hurry
1960: Hopalong Casualty
    Lickety Splat
1962: Zoom at the Top
1964: To Beep or Not to Beep
1965: Run Run Sweet Road Runner

PAUL ROBESON

1933: The Emperor Jones (Dudley
    Murphy)
1935: Sanders of the River (Zoltan Korda)
1936: Show Boat (James Whale)
    Song of Freedom (J. Elder Willis)
1937: Dark Sands of Jericho (Thornton
    Freeland)
    King Solomon's Mines (Robert
    Stevenson)
    Big Fella (Willis)
1940: The Proud Valley (Pen Tennyson)

1942: Native Land (Paul Strand)
    Tales of Manhattan (Julien
    Duvivier)
1954–Il Canto dei Grandi Fiumi (Joris
55:    Ivens)

EDWARD G. ROBINSON

1923: The Bright Shawl (John J.
    Robertson)
1929: The Hole in the Wall (Robert
    Florey)
1930: A Lady to Love (Victor Seastrom)
    Night Ride (Robertson)
    Outside the Law (Tod Browning)
    East is West (Monta Bell)
    The Widow from Chicago (Edward
    Cline)
    Little Caesar (Mervyn LeRoy)
1931: Smart Money (Alfred E. Green)
    Five Star Final (LeRoy)
1932: The Hatchet Man (William
    Wellman)
    Two Seconds (LeRoy)
    Tiger Shark (Howard Hawks)
    Silver Dollar (A. Green)
1933: The Little Giant (Roy Del Ruth)
    I Loved a Woman (A. Green)
1934: Dark Hazard (A. Green)
    The Man with Two Faces (Archie
    Mayo)
1935: The Whole Town's Talking (John
    Ford)
    Barbary Coast (Hawks)
1936: Bullets or Ballots (William
    Keighley)
1937: Thunder in the City (Marion Gering)
    Kid Galahad (Michael Curtiz)
    The Last Gangster (Edward
    Ludwig)
1938: A Slight Case of Murder (Lloyd
    Bacon)
    The Amazing Dr. Clitterhouse
    (Anatole Litvak)
    I Am the Law (Alexander Hall)
1939: Confessions of a Nazi Spy (Litvak)
    Blackmail (H.C. Potter)
1940: Dr. Ehrlich's Magic Bullet (William
    Dieterle)
    Brother Orchid (Bacon)
    A Dispatch from Reuters (Dieterle)
1941: The Sea Wolf (Curtiz)
    Manpower (Raoul Walsh)
    Unholy Partners (LeRoy)
1942: Larceny Inc. (Bacon)
    Tales of Manhattan (Julien
    Duvivier)
1943: Destroyer (William A. Seiter)
    Flesh and Fantasy (Duvivier)
1944: Tampico (Lothar Mendes)
    Mr. Winkle Goes to War (A. Green)
    Double Indemnity (Billy Wilder)
    The Woman in the Window (Fritz
    Lang)
1945: Our Vines Have Tender Grapes
    (Roy Rowland)
    Scarlet Street (F. Lang)
    Journey Together (John Boulting)
1946: The Stranger (Orson Welles)
1947: The Red House (Delmer Daves)
1948: All My Sons (Irving Reis)
    Key Largo (John Huston)
    Night Has a Thousand Eyes (John
    Farrow)
1949: House of Strangers (Joseph L.
    Mankiewicz)
    It's a Great Feeling (David Butler)
1950: My Daughter Joy (Gregory Ratoff)
1952: Actors and Sin (Ben Hecht)
1953: Vice Squad (Arnold Laven)
    Big Leaguer (Robert Aldrich)
    The Glass Web (Jack Arnold)
1954: Black Tuesday (Hugo Fregonese)
1955: The Violent Men (Rudolph Mate)
    Tight Spot (Phil Karlson)
    A Bullet for Joey (Lewis Allen)
    Illegal (L. Allen)
1956: Hell on Frisco Bay (Frank Tuttle)
    Nightmare (Maxwell Shane)
    The Ten Commandments (Cecil B.
    De Mille)
1959: A Hole in the Head (Frank Capra)
1960: Pepe (George Sidney)
1962: My Geisha (Jack Cardiff)
    Two Weeks in Another Town
    (Vincente Minnelli)
1963: The Prize (Mark Robson)
1964: Good Neighbor Sam (David Swift)

Robin and the Seven Hoods
    (Gordon Douglas)
    The Outrage (Martin Ritt)
    Cheyenne Autumn (Ford)
1965: A Boy Ten Feet Tall (Alexander
    Mackendrick)
    The Cincinnati Kid (Norman
    Jewison)
1968: The Blonde From Peking (Nicolas
    Gessner)
    The Biggest Bundle of Them All
    (Ken Annakin)
    Ad Ogni Costo (Giuliano Montaldo)
    Uno Scacco Tutto Matto (Robert
    Fiz)
    Operation St. Peter's (Lucio Fulci)
    Never a Dull Moment (Jerry Paris)
1969: MacKenna's Gold (J. Lee
    Thompson)
1970: Song of Norway (Andrew L. Stone)
1973: Soylent Green (Richard Fleischer)

GINGER ROGERS

1930: Young Man of Manhattan (Monta
    Bell)
    Queen High (Fred Newmeyer)
    The Sap From Syracuse (Edward
    Sutherland)
    Follow the Leader (Norman Taurog)
1931: Honor Among Lovers (Dorothy
    Arzner)
    The Tip Off (Albert Rogell)
    Suicide Fleet (Rogell)
1932: Carnival Boat (Rogell)
    The Tenderfoot (Ray Enright)
    The Thirteenth Guest (Albert Ray)
    Hat Check Girl (Sidney Lanfield)
    You Said a Mouthful (Lloyd Bacon)
1933: 42nd Street (Lloyd Bacon)
    Broadway Bad (Lanfield)
    Gold Diggers of 1933 (Mervyn
    LeRoy)
    Professional Sweetheart (William
    A. Seiter)
    A Shriek in the Night (A. Ray)
    Don't Bet on Love (Murray Roth)
    Sitting Pretty (Harry Joe Brown)
    Flying Down to Rio (Thornton
    Freeland)
    Chance at Heaven (Seiter)
1934: Rafter Romance (Seiter)
    Finishing School (Wanda Tuchock,
    George Nicholls)
    Twenty Million Sweethearts
    (Enright)
    Change of Heart (John G. Blystone)
    Upper World (Roy Del Ruth)
    The Gay Divorcee (Mark Sandrich)
    Romance in Manhattan (Stephen
    Roberts)
1935: Roberta (Seiter)
    Star of Midnight (Roberts)
    Top Hat (Sandrich)
    In Person (Seiter)
1936: Follow the Fleet (Sandrich)
    Swing Time (George Stevens)
1937: Shall We Dance (Sandrich)
    Stage Door (Gregory La Cava)
1938: Having Wonderful Time (Alfred
    Santell)
    Vivacious Lady (G. Stevens)
    Carefree (Sandrich)
1939: The Story of Vernon and Irene
    Castle (H.C. Potter)
    Bachelor Mother (Garson Kanin)
    Fifth Avenue Girl (La Cava)
1940: The Primrose Path (La Cava)
    Lucky Partners (Lewis Milestone)
    Kitty Foyle (Sam Wood)
1941: Tom, Dick and Harry (Kanin)
1942: Roxie Hart (William Wellman)
    Tales of Manhattan (Julien
    Duvivier)
    The Major and the Minor (Billy
    Wilder)
    Once Upon a Honeymoon (Leo
    McCarey)
1943: Tender Comrade (Edward Dmytryk)
1944: Lady in the Dark (Mitchell Leisen)
    I'll Be Seeing You (William
    Dieterle)
1945: Weekend at the Waldorf (Robert Z.
    Leonard)
1946: Heartbeat (Wood)
    The Magnificent Doll (Frank
    Borzage)

1947: It Had to Be You (Don Hartman,
    Rudolph Maté)
1949: The Barkleys of Broadway (Charles
    Walters)
1950: Perfect Strangers (Bretaigne
    Windust)
    Storm Warning (Stuart Heisler)
1951: The Groom Wore Spurs (Richard
    Whorf)
1952: We're Not Married (Edmund
    Goulding)
    Monkey Business (Howard Hawks)
    Dreamboat (Claude Binyon)
1953: Forever Female (Irving Rapper)
1954: Black Widow (Nunnally Johnson)
    Twist of Fate (David Miller)
1955: Tight Spot (Phil Karlson)
1956: The First Traveling Saleslady
    (Arthur Lubin)
    Teenage Rebel (Goulding)
1957: Oh Men! Oh Women! (N. Johnson)
1964: The Confession (Dieterle)
1965: Harlow (Alex Segal)

MICKEY ROONEY

Between 1927–34, he made many
"Mickey McGuire" shorts directed by Al
Herman, E.T. Montgomery and J.A.
Duffy.
1926: Not to Be Trusted (Short; Thomas
    Buckingham)
1927: Orchids and Ermine (Alfred Santell)
1930: The King (Short; James W. Horne,
    Charles Rogers)
1932: Fast Companions (Kurt Neumann)
    My Pal the King (Neumann)
1933: Broadway to Hollywood (Willard
    Mack)
    The World Changes (Mervyn
    LeRoy)
    The Life of Jimmy Dolan (Archie
    Mayo)
    The Chief (Charles F. Riesner)
    The Big Cage (Neumann)
1934: Beloved (Victor Schertzinger)
    Death on the Diamond (Edgar
    Sedgwick)
    Half a Sinner (Neumann)
    Blind Date (Roy William Neill)
    Manhattan Melodrama (W.S. Van
    Dyke)
    Hide-Out (Van Dyke)
    Chained (Clarence Brown)
1935: The County Chairman (John
    Blystone)
    A Midsummer Night's Dream (Max
    Reinhardt, William Dieterle)
    The Healer (Reginald Barker)
    Ah, Wilderness! (C. Brown)
    Riff Raff (J. Walter Ruben)
1936: Little Lord Fauntleroy (John
    Cromwell)
    The Devil is a Sissy (Van Dyke)
    Down the Stretch (William
    Clemens)
1937: A Family Affair (George B. Seitz)
    Captains Courageous (Victor
    Fleming)
    Live, Love and Learn (George
    Fitzmaurice)
    Thoroughbreds Don't Cry (Alfred
    E. Geeen)
    You're Only Young Once (Seitz)
    Slave Ship (Tay Garnett)
    The Hoosier Schoolboy (William
    Nigh)
1938: Love Is a Headache (Richard
    Thorpe)
    Judge Hardy's Children (Seitz)
    Hold That Kiss (Edwin L. Marin)
    Lord Jeff (Sam Wood)
    Love Finds Andy Hardy (Seitz)
    Boys' Town (Norman Taurog)
    Stablemates (Wood)
    Out West with the Hardys (Seitz)
1939: The Adventures of Huckleberry
    Finn (Richard Thorpe)
    Andy Hardy Gets Spring Fever
    (Van Dyke)
    Babes in Arms (Busby Berkeley)
    Young Tom Edison (Taurog)
    Judge Hardy and Son (Seitz)
1940: Andy Hardy Meets Debutante
    (Seitz)

Strike Up the Band (Berkeley)
1941: Andy Hardy's Private Secretary (Seitz)
Men of Boys' Town (Taurog)
Life Begins for Andy Hardy (Seitz)
Babes on Broadway (Berkeley)
1942: The Courtship of Andy Hardy (Seitz)
A Yank at Eton (Taurog)
Andy Hardy's Double Life (Seitz)
1943: The Human Comedy (C. Brown)
Girl Crazy (Taurog)
1944: Thousands Cheer (George Sidney)
Andy Hardy's Blonde Trouble (Seitz)
National Velvet (C. Brown)
1946: Ziegfeld Follies (Vincente Minnelli)
Love Laughs at Andy Hardy (Willis Goldbeck)
1947: Killer McCoy (Roy Rowland)
1948: Summer Holiday (Rouben Mamoulian)
Words and Music (Taurog)
1949: The Big Wheel (Edward Ludwig)
1950: He's a Cockeyed Wonder (Peter Godfrey)
Quicksand (Irving Pichel)
The Fireball (Garnett)
1951: My Outlaw Brother (Elliott Nugent)
The Strip (Leslie Kardos)
1952: Sound Off (Richard Quine)
1953: Off Limits (George Marshall)
All Ashore (Quine)
A Slight Case of Larceny (Don Weis)
1954: Drive a Crooked Road (Quine)
The Atomic Kid (Leslie H. Martinson)
1955: The Bridges at Toko-Ri (Mark Robson)
The Twinkle in God's Eye (George Blair)
1956: The Bold and the Brave (Lewis R. Foster)
Francis in the Haunted House (Charles Lamont)
Magnificent Roughnecks (Sherman A. Rose)
1957: Operation Mad Ball (Quine)
Baby Face Nelson (Don Siegel)
1958: A Nice Little Bank That Should Be Robbed (Henry Levin)
Andy Hardy Comes Home (Howard W. Koch)
The Last Mile (H.W. Koch)
1959: The Big Operator (Charles Haas)
1960: Platinum High School (Haas)
The Private Lives of Adam and Eve (Albert Zugsmith)
1961: Breakfast at Tiffany's (Blake Edwards)
King of the Roaring Twenties (Joseph Newman)
Everything's Ducky (Don Taylor)
1962: Requiem for a Heavyweight (Ralph Nelson)
1963: It's a Mad, Mad, Mad, Mad World (Stanley Kramer)
1964: The Secret Invasion (Roger Corman)
1965: How to Stuff a Wild Bikini (William Asher)
1966: Ambush Bay (Ron Winston)
1968: The Devil in Love (Ettore Scola)
Skidoo (Otto Preminger)
1969: The Comic (Carl Reiner)
The Extraordinary Seaman (John Frankenheimer)
1970: The Cockeyed Cowboys of Calico County (Tony Leader)
Hollywood Blue (Bill Osco)
1971: B.J. Lange Presents (Yabo Yablonsky)
1972: Richard (Lorees Yerby, Harry Hurwitz)
Pulp (Michael Hodges)
1973: The Godmothers (William Grefe)
1974: Journey Back to Oz (Hal Sutherland)
That's Entertainment! (Jack Haley, Jr.)
1975: Find the Lady (John Trent)
Bon Baisers de Hong Kong (Yvan Chiffre)
1977: The Domino Principle (Kramer)
Rachel's Man (Moshe Mizrahi)
Pete's Dragon (Don Chaffey)

1978: The Magic of Lassie (Chaffey)
1979: The Black Stallion (Carroll Ballard)

GEORGE C. SCOTT

1959: The Hanging Tree (Delmer Daves)
Anatomy of A Murder (Otto Preminger)
1960: The Hustler (Robert Rossen)
1963: The List of Adrian Messenger (John Huston)
1964: Dr. Strangelove (Stanley Kubrick)
The Yellow Rolls-Royce (Anthony Asquith)
1966: The Bible (Huston)
Not with My Wife You Don't (Norman Panama)
1967: The Flim Flam Man (Irvin Kershner)
1968: Petulia (Richard Lester)
1970: Patton (Franklin J. Schaffner)
1971: The Last Run (Richard Fleischer)
The Hospital (Arthur Hiller)
1972: They Might Be Giants (Anthony Harvey)
The New Centurions (Fleischer)
1973: Oklahoma Crude (Stanley Kramer)
The Day of the Dolphin (Mike Nichols)
Rage (George C. Scott)
1974: The Savage Is Loose (Scott)
Bank Shot (Gower Champion)
1975: The Hindenburg (Robert Wise)
1977: Islands in the Stream (Schaffner)
The Prince and the Pauper (Fleischer)
1979: Movie Movie (Stanley Donen)
Hardcore (Paul Schrader)

SYLVIA SIDNEY

1929: Thru Different Eyes (John Blystone)
1931: City Streets (Rouben Mamoulian)
Confessions of a Co-ed (David Burton, Dudley Murphy)
An American Tragedy (Josef von Sternberg)
Street Scene (King Vidor)
Ladies of the Big House (Marion Gering)
1932: The Miracle Man (Norman Z. McLeod)
Merrily We Go to Hell (Dorothy Arzner)
Madame Butterfly (Gering)
1933: Pick Up (Gering)
Jennie Gerhardt (Gering)
1934: Good Dame (Gering)
Thirty Day Princess (Gering)
Behold My Wife! (Mitchell Leisen)
1935: Accent on Youth (Wesley Ruggles)
Mary Burns, Fugitive (William K. Howard)
1936: Trail of the Lonesome Pine (Henry Hathaway)
Fury (Fritz Lang)
1937: You Only Live Once (F. Lang)
Dead End (William Wyler)
Sabotage (Alfred Hitchcock)
1938: You and Me (F. Lang)
1939: One Third of a Nation (Dudley Murphy)
1941: The Wagons Roll at Night (Ray Enright)
1945: Blood on the Sun (Frank Lloyd)
1946: The Searching Wind (William Dieterle)
Mr. Ace (Edwin L. Marin)
1947: Love from a Stranger (Richard Whorf)
1952: Les Miserables (Lewis Milestone)
1955: Violent Saturday (Richard Fleischer)
1956: Behind the High Wall (Abner Biberman)
1973: Summer Wishes, Winter Dreams (Gilbert Cates)
1977: I Never Promised You a Rose Garden (Anthony Page)
Demon (Larry Cohen)
1978: Damien — Omen II (Don Taylor)

SISSY SPACEK

1972: Prime Cut (Michael Ritchie)
Ginger in the Morning (Gordon Wiles)
1973: Badlands (Terrence Malick)
1976: Carrie (Brian De Palma)

1977: Welcome to L.A. (Alan Rudolph)
3 Women (Robert Altman)
1979: Heart Beat (John Byrum)
Coal Miner's Daughter (unknown)

BARBARA STANWYCK

1927: Broadway Nights (Joseph C. Boyle)
1929: The Locked Door (George Fitzmaurice)
Mexicali Rose (Erle C. Kenton)
1930: Ladies of Leisure (Frank Capra)
1931: Illicit (Archie Mayo)
Ten Cents a Dance (Lionel Barrymore)
Night Nurse (William Wellman)
The Miracle Woman (Capra)
1932: Forbidden (Capra)
Shopworn (Nicholas Grinde)
So Big (Wellman)
The Purchase Price (Wellman)
1933: The Bitter Tea of General Yen (Capra)
Ladies They Talk About (Howard Bretherton, William Keighley)
Baby Face (Alfred E. Green)
Ever in My Heart (Archie Mayo)
1934: Gambling Lady (Mayo)
A Lost Lady (A. Green)
The Secret Bride (William Dieterle)
1935: The Woman in Red (Robert Florey)
Red Salute (Sidney Lanfield)
Annie Oakley (George Stevens)
1936: A Message to Garcia (George Marshall)
The Bride Walks Out (Leigh Jason)
His Brother's Wife (W.S. Van Dyke)
Banjo on My Knee (John Cromwell)
The Plough and the Stars (John Ford)
Internes Can't Take Money (Alfred Santell)
This Is My Affair (William A. Seiter)
Stella Dallas (King Vidor)
Breakfast for Two (Alfred Santell)
1938: Always Goodbye (Lanfield)
The Mad Miss Manton (Jason)
1939: Union Pacific (Cecil B. De Mille)
Golden Boy (Rouben Mamoulian)
1940: Remember the Night (Mitchell Leisen)
1941: The Lady Eve (Preston Sturges)
Meet John Doe (Capra)
You Belong to Me (Wesley Ruggles)
Ball of Fire (Howard Hawks)
1942: The Great Man's Lady (Wellman)
The Gay Sisters (Irving Rapper)
1943: Lady of Burlesque (Wellman)
Flesh and Fantasy (Julien Duvivier)
1944: Double Indemnity (Billy Wilder)
Hollywood Canteen (Delmer Daves)
1945: Christmas in Connecticut (Peter Godfrey)
1946: My Reputation (Curtis Bernhardt)
The Bride Wore Boots (Irving Pichel)
The Strange Love of Martha Ivers (Lewis Milestone)
California (John Farrow)
1947: The Two Mrs. Carrolls (Godfrey)
The Other Love (Andre De Toth)
Cry Wolf (Godfrey)
Variety Girl (Marshall)
1948: B. F.'s Daughter (Robert Z. Leonard)
Sorry, Wrong Number (Anatole Litvak)
1949: The Lady Gambles (Michael Gordon)
East Side, West Side (Mervyn LeRoy)
Thelma Jordan (Robert Siodmak)
1950: No Man of Her Own (Leisen)
The Furies (Anthony Mann)
To Please a Lady (Clarence Brown)
1951: The Man with a Cloak (Fletcher Markle)
1952: Clash by Night (Fritz Lang)
1953: Jeopardy (John Sturges)
Titanic (Jean Negulesco)
All I Desire (Douglas Sirk)
The Moonlighter (Roy Rowland)
Blowing Wild (Hugo Fregonse)
1954: Witness to Murder (Rowland)

Executive Suite (Robert Wise)
Cattle Queen of Montana (Allan Dwan)
1955: The Violent Men (Rudolph Maté)
Escape to Burma (Dwan)
1956: There's Always Tomorrow (Sirk)
The Maverick Queen (Joseph Kane)
These Wilder Years (Rowland)
1957: Crime of Passion (Gerd Oswald)
Trooper Hook (Charles Marquis Warren)
Forty Guns (Sam Fuller)
1962: Walk on the Wild Side (Edward Dmytryk)
1964: Roustabout (John Rich)
1965: The Night Walker (William Castle)

BARBARA STEELE

In addition to the titles listed below, she has appeared in numerous European films with no American distribution.

1958: Bachelor of Hearts (Wolf Rilla)
Sapphire (Basil Deardon)
1959: The Thirty-Nine Steps (Ralph Thomas)
Upstairs and Downstairs (R. Thomas)
1960: Your Money or Your Wife (Anthony Simmons)
1961: Black Sunday (Mario Bava)
The Pit and the Pendulum (Roger Corman)
1962: The Horrible Secret of Dr. Hitchcock (Ricardo Freda)
A Sentimental Attempt (unknown)
1963: 8½ (Federico Fellini)
The Hours of Love (Luciano Sakc)
The Dance Macabre (Antonio Margheriti)
1964: The Spectre (Freda)
The Long Hair of Death (Margheriti)
1965: Revenge of the Blood Beast (Michael Reeves)
White Voices (Pasquale Festa Campinile, Massimo Franciosa)
The Faceless Monster (Mario Caiano)
1967: Young Törless (Volker Schlondorff)
1968: The Crimson Cult (Vernon Sewell)
1974: Caged Heat (Jonathan Demme)
1976: They Came from Within (David Cronenberg)
1977: I Never Promised You a Rose Garden (Anthony Page)
1978: Pretty Baby (Louis Malle)
Piranha (Joe Dante)

JAMES STEWART

1935: The Murder Man (Tim Whelan)
1936: Rose Marie (W.S. Van Dyke)
Next Time We Love (Edward H. Griffith)
Wife vs Secretary (Clarence Brown)
Small Town Girl (William Wellman)
Speed (Edwin L. Marin)
The Gorgeous Hussy (C. Brown)
Born to Dance (Roy Del Ruth)
After the Thin Man (Van Dyke)
1937: Seventh Heaven (Henry King)
The Last Gangster (Edward Ludwig)
Navy Blue and Gold (Sam Wood)
1938: Of Human Hearts (C. Brown)
Vivacious Lady (George Stevens)
Shopworn Angel (H.C. Potter)
You Can't Take It with You (Frank Capra)
1939: Made for Each Other (John Cromwell)
Ice Follies of 1939 (Reinhold Schunzel)
It's a Wonderful World (Van Dyke)
Mr. Smith Goes to Washington (Capra)
Destry Rides Again (George Marshall)
1940: The Shop Around the Corner (Ernst Lubitsch)
The Mortal Storm (Frank Borzage)
No Time for Comedy (William Keighley)
The Philadelphia Story (George Cukor)
1941: Come Live with Me (C. Brown)

Pot O' Gold (Marshall)
Ziegfeld Girl (Robert Z. Leonard)
1946: It's a Wonderful Life (Capra)
1947: Magic Town (Wellman)
1948: Call Northside 777 (Henry Hathaway)
On Our Merry Way (King Vidor, Leslie Fenton)
Rope (Alfred Hitchcock)
1949: You Gotta Stay Happy (Potter)
The Stratton Story (Wood)
Malaya (Richard Thorpe)
1950: Winchester 73 (Anthony Mann)
Broken Arrow (Delmer Daves)
The Jackpot (Walter Lang)
Harvey (Henry Koster)
1951: No Highway in the Sky (Koster)
1952: The Greatest Show On Earth (Cecil B. De Mille)
Bend of the River (A. Mann)
Carbine Williams (Thorpe)
1953: The Naked Spur (A. Mann)
Thunder Bay (A. Mann)
1954: The Glenn Miller Story (A. Mann)
Rear Window (Hitchcock)
1955: The Far Country (A. Mann)
Strategic Air Command (A. Mann)
The Man from Laramie (A. Mann)
1956: The Man Who Knew Too Much (Hitchcock)
1957: The Spirit of St. Louis (Billy Wilder)
Night Passage (James Neilson)
1958: Vertigo (Hitchcock)
Bell, Book and Candle (Richard Quine)
1959: Anatomy of a Murder (Otto Preminger)
The FBI Story (Mervyn LeRoy)
1960: The Mountain Road (Daniel Mann)
1961: Two Rode Together (John Ford)
X-15 (Richard D. Donner, as narrator)
1962: The Man Who Shot Liberty Valance (Ford)
Mr. Hobbs Takes a Vacation (Koster)
How the West Was Won (Ford, Marshall, Hathaway)
1963: Take Her, She's Mine (Koster)
1964: Cheyenne Autumn (Ford)
1965: Dear Brigitte (Koster)
Shenandoah (Andrew V. McLaglen)
1966: The Flight of the Phoenix (Robert Aldrich)
The Rare Breed (McLaglen)
1968: Firecreek (Vincent McEveety)
Bandolero! (McLaglen)
1970: The Cheyenne Social Club (Gene Kelly)
1971: Fools' Parade (McLaglen)
1974: That's Entertainment! (Jack Haley, Jr.)
1976: The Shootist (Don Siegel)
1977: Airport '77 (Jerry Jameson)
1978: The Big Sleep (Michael Winner)
The Magic of Lassie (Don Chaffey)

BARBRA STREISAND

1968: Funny Girl (William Wyler)
1969: Hello, Dolly! (Gene Kelly)
1970: On a Clear Day You Can See Forever (Vincente Minnelli)
The Owl and the Pussycat (Herbert Ross)
1972: What's Up, Doc? (Peter Bogdanovich)
Up the Sandbox (Irvin Kershner)
1973: The Way We Were (Sydney Pollack)
1974: For Pete's Sake (Peter Yates)
1975: Funny Lady (Ross)
1976: A Star Is Born (Frank Pierson)
1979: Main Event (Howard Zieff)

GLORIA SWANSON

Shorts:
1915: The Fable of Elvira and Farina and the Meal Ticket (R. F. Baker)
Sweetie Goes to College (Serial; Baker)
The Romance of an American Duchess (unknown)
The Broken Pledge (unknown)
1916: A Dash of Courage (Charles Parrott)

Hearts & Sparks (Parrott)
A Social Club (Clarence Badger)
The Danger Girl (Edward Dillon)
Love on Skates (unknown)
Haystacks and Steeples (Badger)
The Nick of Time Baby (Badger)
1917: Teddy at the Throttle (Badger)
Baseball Madness (Billy Mason)
Dangers of a Bride (Robert Kerr, Ferris Hartman)
The Sultan's Wife
A Pullman Bride (Badger)
Features:
1918: Society for Sale (Frank Borzage)
Her Decision (Jack Conway)
You Can't Believe Everything (Conway)
Everywoman's Husband (Gilbert P. Hamilton)
Shifting Sands (Albert Parker)
Station Content (Arthur Hoyt)
Secret Code (Parker)
Wife of Country (Mason Hopper)
1919: Don't Change Your Husband (Cecil B. De Mille)
For Better, for Worse (De Mille)
Male and Female (De Mille)
1920: Why Change Your Wife (De Mille)
Something to Think About (De Mille)
The Great Moment (Sam Wood)
1921: The Affairs of Anatol (De Mille)
Under the Lash (Wood)
Don't Tell Everything (Wood)
1922: Her Husband's Trademark (Wood)
Beyond the Rocks (Wood)
Her Gilded Cage (Wood)
The Impossible Mrs. Bellew (Wood)
1923: My American Wife (Wood)
Prodigal Daughters (Wood)
Bluebeard's Eighth Wife (Wood)
Zaza (Allan Dwan)
1924: The Humming Bird (Sidney Olcott)
A Society Scandal (Dwan)
Manhandled (Dwan)
Her Love Story (Dwan)
Wages of Virtue (Dwan)
1925: Madame Sans-Gene (Leonce Perret)
The Coast of Folly (Dwan)
Stage Struck (Dwan)
1926: Untamed Lady (Frank Tuttle)
Fine Manners (Richard Rosson)
1927: The Loves of Sunya (Parker)
1928: Sadie Thompson (Raoul Walsh)
1929: Queen Kelly (Erich von Stroheim)
The Trespasser (Edmund Goulding)
1930: What a Widow (Dwan)
1931: Indiscreet (L. McCarey)
Tonight or Never (Mervyn LeRoy)
1933: Perfect Understanding (Cyril Gardner)
1934: Music in the Air (Joe May)
1941: Father Takes a Wife (Jack Hively)
1950: Sunset Boulevard (Billy Wilder)
1952: Three for Bedroom C (Milton H. Bren)
1958: Mio Figlio Nerone (Steno)
1974: Airport 1975 (Jack Smight)

ELIZABETH TAYLOR

1942: There's One Born Every Minute (Harold Young)
1943: Lassie Come Home (Fred M. Wilcox)
1944: Jane Eyre (Robert Stevenson)
White Cliffs of Dover (Clarence Brown)
National Velvet (C. Brown)
1946: Courage of Lassie (F. Wilcox)
1947: Cynthia (Robert Z. Leonard)
Life with Father (Michael Curtiz)
1948: A Date with Judy (Richard Thorpe)
Julia Misbehaves (Jack Conway)
1949: Little Women (Mervyn LeRoy)
Conspirator (Victor Saville)
1950: The Big Hangover (Norman Krasna)
Father of the Bride (Vincente Minnelli)
1951: A Place in the Sun (George Stevens)
Father's Little Dividend (Minnelli)
1952: Love is Better Than Ever (Stanley Donen)
Ivanhoe (R. Thorpe)
1953: The Girl Who Had Everything (R. Thorpe)

1954: Rhapsody (Charles Vidor)
Elephant Walk (William Dieterle)
Beau Brummel (Curtis Bernhardt)
The Last Time I Saw Paris (Richard Brooks)
1956: Giant (G. Stevens)
1957: Raintree County (Edward Dmytryk)
1958: Cat on a Hot Tin Roof (Brooks)
1959: Suddenly, Last Summer (Joseph L. Mankiewicz)
1960: Butterfield 8 (Daniel Mann)
1963: Cleopatra (Mankiewicz)
The V.I.P.S (Anthony Asquith)
1965: The Sandpiper (Minnelli)
1966: Who's Afraid of Virginia Woolf? (Mike Nichols)
1967: The Taming of the Shrew (Franco Zeffirelli)
Reflections in a Golden Eye (John Huston)
The Comedians (Peter Glenville)
1968: Doctor Faustus (Richard Burton, Nevill Coghill)
Secret Ceremony (Joseph Losey)
Boom! (Losey)
1970: The Only Game in Town (G. Stevens)
1971: Under Milk Wood (Andrew Sinclair)
1972: X, Y and Zee (Brian G. Hutton)
Hammersmith Is Out (Peter Ustinov)
1973: Night Watch (Hutton)
Ash Wednesday (Larry Peerce)
The Driver's Seat (Giuseppe Patroni Griffi)
1974: That's Entertainment! (Jack Haley, Jr.)
1976: The Blue Bird (George Cukor)
1977: A Little Night Music (Hal Prince)
1978: Winter Kills (Bill Richert)

SHIRLEY TEMPLE

1932: War Babies (Short; Charles Lamont)
The Runt Page (Short; Lamont)
The Pie-Covered Wagon (Short; Lamont)
Glad Rags to Riches (Short; Lamont)
Red-Haired Alibi (Christy Cabanne)
1933: Kid's Last Fight (Short; Lamont)
Kid 'n' Hollywood (Short; Lamont)
Polly-Tix in Washington (Short; Lamont)
Kid 'n' Africa (Short; Lamont)
Merrily Yours (Short; Lamont)
Dora's Dunkin' Donuts (Short; Lamont)
To the Last Man (Henry Hathaway)
Out All Night (Sam Taylor)
1934: Pardon My Pups (Short; Lamont)
Managed Money (Short; Lamont)
New Deal Rhythm (Short; unknown)
Carolina (Henry King)
Mandalay (Michael Curtiz)
Stand Up and Cheer (Hamilton MacFadden)
Now I'll Tell (Edwin Burke)
Change of Heart (John Blystone)
Little Miss Marker (Alexander Hall)
Baby, Take a Bow (Harry Lachman)
Now and Forever (Hathaway)
Bright Eyes (David Butler)
1935: The Little Colonel (Butler)
Our Little Girl (John Robertson)
Curly Top (Irving Cummings)
The Littlest Rebel (Butler)
1936: Captain January (Butler)
Poor Little Rich Girl (Cummings)
Dimples (William A. Seiter)
Stowaway (Seiter)
1937: Wee Willie Winkie (John Ford)
Heidi (Allan Dwan)
1938: Rebecca of Sunnybrook Farm (Dwan)
Little Miss Broadway (Cummings)
Just Around the Corner (Cummings)
1939: The Little Princess (Walter Lang)
Susannah of the Mounties (Seiter)
1940: The Blue Bird (W. Lang)
Young People (Dwan)
1941: Kathleen (Harold S. Bucquet)
1942: Miss Annie Rooney (Edwin L. Marin)

1944: Since You Went Away (John Cromwell)
I'll Be Seeing You (William Dieterle)
1945: Kiss and Tell (Richard Wallace)
1947: Honeymoon (William Keighley)
The Bachelor and the Bobby-Soxer (Irving Reis)
That Hagen Girl (Peter Godfrey)
1948: Fort Apache (Ford)
1949: Mr. Belvedere Goes to College (Eliott Nugent)
Adventure in Baltimore (Wallace)
The Story of Seabiscuit (Butler)
A Kiss for Corliss (Wallace)

THE THREE STOOGES

Shorts:
1934: Plane Nuts (Jack Cummings)
Woman Haters (Archie Gottler)
Punch Drunks (Lou Breslow)
Men in Black (Raymond McCarey)
Three Little Pigskins (R. McCarey)
Horses' Collars (Clyde Bruckman)
Pop Goes the Easel (Del Lord)
Uncivil Warriors (Lord)
Pardon My Scotch (Lord)
Hoi Polloi (Lord)
Three Little Beers (Lord)
1936: Anis Is in the Pantry (Preston Black)
Movie Maniacs (Lord)
Half Shot Shooters (Black)
Disorder in the Court (Black)
A Pain in the Pullman (Black)
False Alarms (Lord)
Whoops I'm an Indian (Lord)
Slippery Silks (Black)
1937: Grips, Grunts and Groans (Black)
Dizzy Doctors (Lord)
Three Dumb Clucks (Lord)
Back to the Woods (Black)
Goofs and Saddles (Lord)
Cash and Carry (Lord)
Playing the Ponies (Charles Lamont)
The Sitter Downers (Lord)
1938: Termites of 1938 (Lord)
Wee Wee Monsieur (Lord)
Tassels in the Air (Charley Chase)
Healthy, Wealthy and Dumb (Lord)
Three Missing Links (Jules White)
Violent Is the Word for Curly (Chase)
Mutts to You (Chase)
Flat Foot Stooges (Chase)
Three Little Sew and Sews (Lord)
We Want Our Mummy (Lord)
1939: Yes, We Have No Bonanza (Lord)
A Ducking They Did Go (Lord)
Saved By the Belle (Chase)
Calling All Curs (Jules White)
Oily To Bed and Oily To Rise (White)
Three Sappy People (White)
1940: You Natzy Spy! (Jules White)
Rockin Through the Rockies (White)
A Plumbing We Will Go (Lord)
Nutty but Nice (White)
How High Is Up (Lord)
From Nurse to Worse (White)
No Census, No Feeling (Lord)
Cuckoo Cavaliers (White)
1941: Boobs in Arms (White)
So Long, Mr. Chumps (White)
Dutiful But Dumb (Lord)
All the World's a Stooge (Lord)
I'll Never Heil Again (White)
Time Out for Rhythm (Sidney Salkow)
An Ache in Every Stake (Lord)
In the Sweet Pie and Pie (White)
Some More of Samoa (Lord)
Loco Boy Makes Good (White)
1942: Cactus Makes Perfect (Lord)
What's the Matador? (White)
Matri-Phony (Harry Edwards)
Three Smart Saps (White)
Even as IOU (Lord)
Sock-A-Bye Baby (White)
They Stooge to Conga (Lord)
Dizzy Detectives (White)
Back from the Front (White)
Three Little Twerps (Harry Edwards)
1943: Higher Than a Kite (Lord)
Spook Louder (Lord)

I Can Hardly Wait (White)
Dizzy Pilots (White)
Phony Express (Lord)
A Gem of a Jam (Lord)
1944: Crash Goes the Hash (White)
Busy Buddies (Lord)
The Yoke's on Me (White)
Idle Roomers (Lord)
Gents Without Cents (White)
No Dough Boys (White)
1945: Three Pests in a Mess (Lord)
Booby Dupes (Lord)
Idiots Deluxe (White)
If a Body Meets a Body (White)
Micro-Phonies (Edward Bernds)
1946: Beer Barrel Polecats (White)
A Bird in the Head (Bernds)
Uncivil War Birds (White)
Three Troubledoers (Bernds)
Monkey Businessmen (Bernds)
Three Loan Wolves (White)
GI Wanna Go Home (White)
Rhythm and Week (White)
Three Little Pirates (Bernds)
1947: Half-Wit's Holiday (White)
Fright Night (Bernds)
Out West (Bernds)
Hold That Lion (White)
Brideless Groom (Bernds)
Sing a Song of Six Pants (White)
All Gummed Up (White)
1948: Shivering Sherlocks (Lord)
Pardon My Clutch (Bernds)
Squareheads of the Round Table (Bernds)
Fiddlers Three (White)
Hot Scots (Bernds)
I'm a Monkey's Uncle (White)
Mummy's Dummies (Bernds)
Crime on Their Hands (Bernds)
1949: The Ghost Talks (White)
Who Done It? (Bernds)
Hocus Pocus (White)
Feulin' Around (Bernds)
Heavenly Daze (White)
Malice in the Palace (White)
Vagabond Loafers (Bernds)
Dunked in the Deep (White)
1950: Punchy Cowpunchers (Hugh McCollum)
Dopey Dicks (McCollum)
Self-Made Maids (McCullum)
Hugs and Mugs (White)
Love at First Bite (White)
Three Hams on Rye (White)
Studio Stoops (White)
Slap-Happy Sleuths (McCollum)
A Snitch in Time (White)
1951: Three Arabian Nuts (Bernds)
Baby Sitters' Jitters (White)
Don't Throw That Kite (White)
Scrambled Brains (White)
Merry Mavericks (Bernds)
The Tooth Will Out (Bernds)
Hula La La (McCollum)
The Pest Man Wins (White)
A Missed Fortune (White)
1952: Listen Judge (McCollum)
Corny Casanovas (White)
He Cooked His Goose (White)
Gents in a Jam (Bernds)
Three Dark Horses (White)
Cockoo on a Choo Choo (White)
1953: Booty and the Beast (White)
Up in Daisy's Penthouse (White)
Loose Loot (White)
Tricky Dicks (White)
Spooks (White)
Pardon My Backfire (White)
Rip. Sew. And Stitch (White)
Bubble Trouble (White)
Goof on the Roof (White)
1954: Income Tax Sappy (White)
Musty Musketeers (White)
Pals and Gals (White)
Knutzy Knights (White)
Shot in the Frontier (White)
Scotched in Scotland (White)
1955: Fling in the Ring (White)
Of Cash and Hash (White)
Gypped in the Penthouse (White)
Bedlam in Paradise (White)
Stone Age Romeos (White)
Wham-Bam-Slam (White)
Hot Ice (White)
Blunder Boys (White)
1956: Husbands Beware (White)

Creeps (White)
Flagpole Jitters (White)
For Crimin' Out Loud (White)
Rumpus in the Harem (White)
Hot Stuff (White)
Scheming Schemers (White)
Commotion on the Ocean (White)
1957: Hoofs and Goofs (White)
Muscle Up a Little Closer (White)
A Merry Mix-Up (White)
Space Ship Sappy (White)
Guns A-Poppin' (White)
Horsing Around (White)
Rusty Romeos (White)
Outer Space Jitters (White)
1958: Quiz Whiz (White)
Fifi Blows Her Top (White)
Flying Saucer Daffy (White)
Pies and Guys (White)
Sweet and Hot (White)
Oil's Well That Ends Well (White)
1959: Triple Crossing (White)
Sappy Bull Fighters (White)
Features:
1930: Soup to Nuts (Benjamin Stoloff)
1933: Turn Back the Clock (Edgar Selwyn)
Meet the Baron (Walter Lang)
Dancing Lady (Robert Z. Leonard)
1934: Fugitive Lovers (Richard Boleslawski)
Hollywood Party (Boleslawski)
The Captain Hates the Sea (Lewis Milestone)
1938: Start Cheering (Albert S. Rogell)
1941: Time Out for Rhythm (Sidney Salkow)
1942: My Sister Eileen (Alexander Hall)
1945: Rockin' in the Rockies (Vernon Keays)
1946: Swing Parade of 1946 (Phil Karlson)
1951: Gold Raiders (Bernds)
1959: Have Rocket, Will Travel (David Lowell Rich)
1960: Three Stooges Scrapbook (Sidney Miller)
Stop! Look! and Laugh! (White, compilation)
1961: Snow White and the Three Stooges (W. Lang)
1962: The Three Stooges Meet Hercules (Bernds)
The Three Stooges in Orbit (Bernds)
1963: The Three Stooges Go Around the World in a Daze (Norman Maurer)
It's a Mad, Mad, Mad, Mad World (Stanley Kramer)
Four for Texas (Robert Aldrich)
1965: The Outlaws Is Coming! (Maurer)

SPENCER TRACY

1930: Up the River (John Ford)
1931: Quick Millions (Rowland Brown)
Six Cylinder Love (Thornton Freeland)
Goldie (Benjamin Stoloff)
1932: She Wanted a Millionaire (John Blystone)
Sky Devils (Edward Sutherland)
Disorderly Conduct (John W. Considine, Jr.)
Young America (Frank Borzage)
Society Girl (Sidney Lanfield)
The Painted Woman (Blystone)
Me and My Gal (Raoul Walsh)
1933: 20,000 Years in Sing Sing (Michael Curtiz)
The Face in the Sky (Harry Lachman)
The Power and the Glory (William K. Howard)
Shanghai Madness (Blystone)
The Mad Game (Irving Cummings)
Man's Castle (Borzage)
1934: The Show-Off (Charles F. Riesner)
Bottoms Up (David Butler)
Looking for Trouble (William Wellman)
Now I'll Tell (Edwin Burke)
Marie Galante (Henry King)
1935: It's a Small World (Cummings)
Dante's Inferno (Lachman)
The Murder Man (Tim Whelan)
Whipsaw (Sam Wood)
1936: Fury (Fritz Lang)

San Francisco (W. S. Van Dyke)
Libeled Lady (Jack Conway)
1937: They Gave Him a Gun (Van Dyke)
Captains Courageous (Victor Fleming)
The Big City (Borzage)
1938: Mannequin (Borzage)
Test Pilot (Fleming)
Boys' Town (Norman Taurog)
1939: Stanley and Livingstone (H. King)
1940: I Take This Woman (Van Dyke)
Northwest Passage (King Vidor)
Edison, the Man (Clarence Brown)
Boom Town (Conway)
1941: Men of Boys' Town (Taurog)
Dr. Jekyll and Mr. Hyde (Fleming)
1942: Woman of the Year (George Stevens)
Tortilla Flat (Fleming)
Keeper of the Flame (George Cukor)
1943: A Guy Named Joe (Fleming)
1944: The Seventh Cross (Fred Zinnemann)
Thirty Seconds Over Tokyo (Mervyn LeRoy)
1945: Without Love (Harold S. Bucquet)
1947: The Sea of Grass (Elia Kazan)
Cass Timberlane (George Sidney)
1948: State of the Union (Frank Capra)
1949: Edward, My Son (Cukor)
Adam's Rib (Cukor)
Malaya (Richard Thorpe)
1950: Father of the Bride (Vincente Minnelli)
1951: Father's Little Dividend (Minnelli)
The People Against O'Hara (John Sturges)
1952: Pat and Mike (Cukor)
Plymouth Adventure (C. Brown)
1953: The Actress (Cukor)
1954: Broken Lance (Edward Dmytryk)
Bad Day at Black Rock (J. Sturges)
1956: The Mountain (Dmytryk)
1957: Desk Set (Walter Lang)
1958: The Old Man and the Sea (J. Sturges)
The Last Hurrah (Ford)
1960: Inherit the Wind (Stanley Kramer)
1961: The Devil at 4 O'Clock (LeRoy)
Judgment at Nuremberg (Kramer)
1963: How the West Was Won (Henry Hathaway, Ford, George Marshall)
It's a Mad, Mad, Mad, Mad World (Kramer)
1967: Guess Who's Coming to Dinner? (Kramer)

RUDOLPH VALENTINO

1914: My Official Wife (James Young)
1916: Patria (Serial; Leopold and Theodore Wharton, Jacques Jaccard)
1918: Alimony (Emmett J. Flynn)
A Society Sensation (Paul Powell)
All Night (P. Powell)
1919: The Delicious Little Devil (Robert Z. Leonard)
A Rogue's Romance (J. Young)
The Homebreaker (Victor Schertzinger)
Virtuous Sinners (Flynn)
The Big Little Person (R. Z. Leonard)
Out of Luck (Elmer Clifton)
Eyes of Youth (Albert Parker)
1920: The Married Virgin (Joseph Maxwell)
An Adventuress (Fred J. Balshofer)
The Cheater (Henry Otto)
Passion's Playground (J. A. Barry)
Once to Every Woman (Allen J. Holubar)
Stolen Moments (James Vincent)
The Wonderful Chance (George Archainbaud)
1921: The Four Horsemen of the Apocalyspe (Rex Ingram)
Uncharted Seas (Wesley Ruggles)
The Conquering Power (Ingram)
Camille (Ray C. Smallwood)
The Sheik (George Melford)
Moran of the Lady Letty (Melford)
1922: Beyond the Rocks (Sam Wood)
Blood and Sand (Fred Niblo)
The Young Rajah (Philip Rosen)

1924: Monsieur Beaucaire (Sidney Olcott)
A Sainted Devil (Joseph Henabery)
1925: Cobra (Henabery)
The Eagle (Clarence Brown)
1926: Son of the Sheik (George Fitzmaurice)

JON VOIGHT

1967: The Hour of the Gun (John Sturges)
1968: Fearless Frank (Philip Kaufman)
1969: Out of It (Paul Williams)
Midnight Cowboy (John Schlesinger)
1970: The Revolutionary (P. Williams)
Catch 22 (Mike Nichols)
1972: Deliverance (John Boorman)
1973: The All American Boy (Charles Erdman)
1974: Conrack (Martin Ritt)
The Odessa File (Ronald Neame)
1976: End of the Game (Maximilian Schell)
1978: Coming Home (Hal Ashby)
1979: The Champ (Franco Zeffirelli)

ROBERT WALKER

1939: Winter Carnival (Charles F. Riesner)
These Glamour Girls (S. Sylvan Simon)
Dancing Co-ed (Simon)
1943: Bataan (Tay Garnett)
Madame Curie (Mervyn LeRoy)
1944: See Here, Private Hargrove (Wesley Ruggles)
Since You Went Away (John Cromwell)
Thirty Seconds Over Tokyo (LeRoy)
1945: The Clock (Vincente Minnelli)
Her Highness and the Bellboy (Richard Thorpe)
What Next, Corporal Hargrove? (R. Thorpe)
The Sailor Takes a Wife (Richard Whorf)
1946: Till the Clouds Roll By (Whorf)
1947: The Sea of Grass (Elia Kazan)
The Beginning or the End (Norman Taurog)
Song of Love (Clarence Brown)
1948: One Touch of Venus (William A. Seiter)
1950: Please Believe Me (Taurog)
The Skipper Surprised His Wife (Elliott Nugent)
1951: Strangers on a Train (Alfred Hitchcock)
Vengeance Valley (R. Thorpe)
1952: My Son John (Leo McCarey)

JOHN WAYNE

1927: The Drop Kick (Millard Webb)
1928: Hangman's House (John Ford)
1929: Words and Music (James Tinling)
Salute (Ford)
1930: Men Without Women (Ford)
A Rough Romance (A. F. Erickson)
Cheer Up and Smile (Sidney Lanfield)
The Big Trail (Raoul Walsh)
1931: Girls Demand Excitement (Seymour Felix)
Three Girls Lost (Lanfield)
Men Are Like That (George Seitz)
The Deceiver (Louis King)
Range Feud (D. Ross Lederman)
Maker of Men (Edward Sedgwick)
1932: Shadow of the Eagle (serial; Ford Beebe)
Texas Cyclone (Lederman)
Two Fisted Law (Lederman)
Lady and Gent (Stephen Roberts)
The Hurricane Express (Serial; Armand Schaefer, J. P. McGowan)
The Hollywood Handicap (Short; Charles Lamont)
Ride Him Cowboy (Fred Allen)
The Big Stampede (Terry Wright)
Haunted Gold (Mack V. Wright)
1933: The Telegraph Trail (Wright)
The Three Musketeers (Serial; Colbert Clark)
Central Airport (William Wellman)

Somewhere in Sonora (M. Wright)
His Private Secretary (Philip H. Whitman)
The Life of Jimmy Dolan (Archie Mayo)
Baby Face (Alfred E. Green)
The Man from Monterey (M. Wright)
Riders of Destiny (Robert N. Bradbury)
College Coach (Wellman)
Sagebrush Trail (Schaefer)
1934: West of the Divide (Bradbury)
The Lucky Texan (Bradbury)
Blue Steel (Bradbury)
Man from Utah (Bradbury)
Randy Rides Alone (Harry Fraser)
The Star Packer (Bradbury)
The Trail Beyond (Bradbury)
The Lawless Frontier (Bradbury)
'Neath Arizona Skies (Fraser)
1935: Texas Terror (Bradbury)
Rainbow Valley (Bradbury)
The Desert Trail (Cullen Lewis)
The Dawn Rider (Bradbury)
Paradise Canyon (Carl Pierson)
Westward Ho (Bradbury)
The New Frontier (C. Pierson)
The Lawless Range (Bradbury)
1936: The Oregon Trail (Scott Pembroke)
The Lawless Nineties (Joseph Kane)
King of the Pecos (Kane)
The Lonely Trail (Kane)
Winds of the Wasteland (M. Wright)
The Sea Spoilers (Frank Strayer)
Conflict (David Howard)
1937: California Straight Ahead (Arthur Lubin)
I Cover the War (Lubin)
Idol of the Crowds (Lubin)
Adventure's End (Lubin)
Born to the West (Charles T. Barton)
1938: Pals of the Saddle (George Sherman)
Overland Stage Raiders (G. Sherman)
Santa Fe Stampede (G. Sherman)
Red River Range (G. Sherman)
1939: Stagecoach (Ford)
The Night Riders (G. Sherman)
Three Texas Steers (G. Sherman)
Wyoming Outlaw (G. Sherman)
New Frontier (G. Sherman)
Allegheny Uprising (William A. Seiter)
1940: Dark Command (Walsh)
Three Faces West (Bernard Vorhaus)
The Long Voyage Home (Ford)
Seven Sinners (Tay Garnett)
1941: A Man Betrayed (John H. Auer)
Lady from Louisiana (Vorhaus)
The Shepherd of the Hills (Henry Hathaway)
1942: Lady of the Night (Leigh Jason)
Reap the Wild Wind (Cecil B. De Mille)
The Spoilers (Ray Enright)
In Old California (William McGann)
Flying Tigers (David Miller)
Reunion in France (Jules Dassin)
Pittsburgh (Lewis Seiler)
1943: A Lady Takes a Chance (Seiter)
In Old Oklahoma (Albert S. Rogell)
1944: The Fighting Seabees (Edward Ludwig)
Tall in the Saddle (Edwin L. Marin)
1945: Flame of Barbary Coast (Kane)
Back to Bataan (Edward Dmytryk)
They Were Expendable (Ford)
Dakota (Kane)
1946: Without Reservations (Mervyn LeRoy)
1947: Angel and the Badman (James Edward Grant)
Tycoon (Richard Wallace)
1948: Fort Apache (Ford)
Red River (Howard Hawks)
Three Godfathers (Ford)
Wake of the Red Witch (Ludwig)
1949: The Fighting Kentuckian (George Waggner)
She Wore a Yellow Ribbon (Ford)
Sands of Iwo Jima (Allan Dwan)

1950: Rio Grande (Ford)
1951: Operation Pacific (G. Waggner)
Flying Leathernecks (Nicholas Ray)
1952: The Quiet Man (Ford)
Big Jim McLain (Ludwig)
1953: Trouble Along the Way (Michael Curtiz)
Island in the Sky (Wellman)
Hondo (John Farrow)
1954: The High and the Mighty (Wellman)
1955: The Sea Chase (Farrow)
Blood Alley (Wellman)
The Conqueror (Dick Powell)
1956: The Searchers (Ford)
1957: The Wings of Eagles (Ford)
Jet Pilot (Josef von Sternberg)
Legend of the Lost (Hathaway)
1958: I Married a Woman (Hal Kanter)
The Barbarian and the Geisha (John Huston)
1959: Rio Bravo (Hawks)
The Horse Soldiers (Ford)
1960: The Alamo (John Wayne)
North to Alaska (Hathaway)
1961: The Comancheros (Curtiz)
1962: The Man Who Shot Liberty Valance (Ford)
Hatari! (Hawks)
1963: The Longest Day (Ken Annakin, Andrew Marton, Bernard Wicki)
How the West Was Won (Ford, George Marshall, Hathaway)
Donovan's Reef (Ford)
McLintock! (Andrew V. McLaglen)
1964: Circus World (Hathaway)
1965: The Greatest Story Ever Told (George Stevens)
In Harm's Way (Otto Preminger)
The Sons of Katie Elder (Hathaway)
1960: Cast a Giant Shadow (Melville Shavelson)
1967: The War Wagon (Burt Kennedy)
El Dorado (Hawks)
1968: The Green Berets (Wayne)
1969: Hellfighters (McLaglen)
True Grit (Hathaway)
The Undefeated (McLaglen)
1970: Chisum (McLaglen)
Rio Lobo (Hawks)
1971: Big Jake (McLaglen)
1972: The Cowboys (Mark Rydell)
1973: The Train Robbers (Kennedy)
Cahill: United States Marshal (McLaglen)
1974: McQ (John Sturges)
1975: Brannigan (Douglas Hickox)
Rooster Cogburn (Stuart Millar)
1976: The Shootist (Don Siegel)

CLIFTON WEBB

1920: Polly with a Past (Maxwell Karger)
1925: The Heart of a Siren (Phil Rosen)
New Toys (John S. Robertson)
1944: Laura (Otto Preminger)
1946: The Dark Corner (Henry Hathaway)
The Razor's Edge (Edmund Goulding)
1948: Sitting Pretty (Walter Lang)
1949: Mr. Belvedere Goes to College (Elliott Nugent)
1950: Cheaper by the Dozen (W. Lang)
For Heaven's Sake (George Seaton)
1951: Mr. Belvedere Rings the Bell (Henry Koster)
Elopement (Koster)
1952: Dreamboat (Claude Binyon)
Stars and Stripes Forever (Koster)
1953: Titanic (Jean Negulesco)
Mister Scoutmaster (Henry Levin)
1954: Three Coins in the Fountain (Negulesco)
Woman's World (Negulesco)
1956: The Man Who Never Was (Ronald Neame)
1957: Boy on a Dolphin (Negulesco)
1958: The Remarkable Mr. Pennypacker (Levin)
1959: Holiday for Lovers (Levin)
1962: Satan Never Sleeps (Leo McCarey)

RAQUEL WELCH

1964: Roustabout (John Rich)
A House Is Not a Home (Russell Rouse)
1965: A Swingin' Summer (Robert H. Sparr)

1966: Fantastic Voyage (Richard Fleischer)
One Million Years B.C. (Don Chaffey)
Shoot Loud, Louder . . . I Don't Understand (Eduardo De Filippo)
1967: The Queens (Luciano Salce, Mario Monicelli, Mauro Bolognini, Antonio Pietrangeli)
Fathom (Leslie H. Martinson)
Bedazzled (Stanley Donen)
The Oldest Profession (Franco Indonna, Bolognini, Philippe de Broca, Michel Pfleghar, Claude Autant-Lara, Jean-Luc Godard)
1968: Bandolero (Andrew V. McLaglen)
Lady in Cement (Gordon Douglas)
1969: 100 Rifles (Tom Gries)
Myra Breckinridge (Michael Sarne)
Flare Up (James Neilson)
1971: Hannie Caulder (Burt Kennedy)
1972: Kansas City Bomber (Jerrold Freedman)
Fuzz (Richard A. Colla)
Bluebeard (Edward Dmytryk)
1973: The Last of Sheila (Herbert Ross)
1974: The Three Musketeers (Richard Lester)
1975: The Four Musketeers (Lester)
The Wild Party (James Ivory)
1976: Mother, Jugs and Speed (Peter Yates)
1977: The Prince and the Pauper (Richard Fleischer)
1978: Restless (George P. Cosmatos)

ORSON WELLES

1940: Swiss Family Robinson (Edward Ludwig, as narrator)
1941: Citizen Kane (Orson Welles)
1942: The Magnificent Ambersons (Welles, director only)
Journey into Fear (Norman Foster, Welles)
1944: Jane Eyre (Robert Stevenson)
Follow the Boys (Edward Sutherland)
1946: Tomorrow Is Forever (Irving Pichel)
The Stranger (Welles)
Duel in the Sun (King Vidor)
1948: The Lady from Shanghai (Welles)
MacBeth (Welles)
1949: Black Magic (Gregory Ratoff)
Prince of Foxes (Henry King)
The Third Man (Carol Reed)
1950: The Black Rose (Henry Hathaway)
1952: Othello (Welles)
1953: Trent's Last Case (Herbert Wilcox)
Si Versailles M'etait Conté (Sacha Guitry)
L'Uomo, La Bestia e la Virtù (Stefano Vanzina)
1954: Napoleon (Guitry)
Three Cases of Murder (George More O'Ferrall)
Trouble in the Glen (Hal Wilcox)
1955: Mr. Arkadin (Welles)
Don Quixote (Welles)
1956: Moby Dick (John Huston)
1957: Man in the Shadow (Jack Arnold)
1958: The Long Hot Summer (Martin Ritt)
Touch of Evil (Welles)
The Roots of Heaven (Huston)
The Vikings (Richard Fleischer, as narrator)
1959: Compulsion (Fleischer)
David e Golia (Richard Pottier, Ferdinando Baldi)
Ferry to Hong Kong (Lewis Gilbert)
1960: Austerlitz (Abel Gance)
Crack in the Mirror (Fleischer)
The Tartars (Richard Thorpe)
1961: King of Kings (Nicholas Ray, as narrator)
Lafayette (Jean Dréville)
1962: The Trial (Welles)
Rogopag (Pier Paolo Pasolini)
1964: La Fabuleuse Aventure de Marco Polo (Denys de la Patellière, Noël Howard)
1965: Treasure Island (incomplete; Jesús Franco)
1966: Is Paris Burning? (René Clement)
Chimes at Midnight (Welles)
A Man for All Seasons (Fred Zinnemann)

1967: The Sailor from Gibraltar (Tony Richardson)
The Immortal Story (Welles)
Casino Royale (Huston, Ken Hughes, Robert Parrish, Joseph McGrath, Val Guest)
I'll Never Forget What's 'is Name (Michael Winner)
Oedipus the King (Philip Saville)
1968: House of Cards (John Guillermin)
The Southern Star (Sidney Hayers)
1969: The Battle of the River Neretva (Veljko Bulajic)
Michael the Brave (Sergiu Nicolaescu)
Tepepa (Giulio Petroni)
1970: Twelve Plus One (Nicolas Gessner)
The Kremlin Letter (Huston)
Start the Revolution Without Me (Bud Yorkin)
Catch-22 (Mike Nichols)
Waterloo (Sergei Bondarchuk)
The Deep (Welles)
Upon This Rock (Harry Rasky)
1971: A Safe Place (Henry Jaglom)
1972: Necromancy (Bert Gordon)
Get to Know Your Rabbit (Brian De Palma)
La Décade Prodigieuse (Claude Chabrol)
The Canterbury Tales (Pasolini)
To Kill a Stranger (Peter Collinson)
Treasure Island (John Hough)
1973: F For Fake (Welles)
1975: Bugs Bunny Superstar (Larry Jackson, as narrator)
1976: Voyage of the Damned (Stuart Rosenberg)
1977: The Challenge (Herbert Kline, narrator only)
1978: The Late Great Planet Earth (Rolf Forsberg)
1979: The Muppet Movie (James Frawley)

MAE WEST

1932: Night After Night (Archie Mayo)
1933: She Done Him Wrong (Lowell Sherman)
I'm No Angel (Wesley Ruggles)
1934: Belle of the Nineties (Leo McCarey)
1935: Goin' to Town (Alexander Hall)
1936: Klondike Annie (Raoul Walsh)
Go West Young Man (Henry Hathaway)
1938: Every Day's a Holiday (Edward Sutherland)
1940: My Little Chickadee (Eddie Cline)
1943: The Heat's On (Gregory Ratoff)
1970: Myra Breckinridge (Michael Sarne)
1978: Sextette (Ken Hughes)

JOANNE WOODWARD

1955: Count Three and Pray (George Sherman)
1956: A Kiss Before Dying (Gerd Oswald)
1957: The Three Faces of Eve (Nunnally Johnson)
No Down Payment (Martin Ritt)
1958: The Long, Hot Summer (Ritt)
Rally 'Round the Flag, Boys! (Leo McCarey)
1959: The Sound and the Fury (Ritt)
The Fugitive Kind (Sidney Lumet)
1960: From the Terrace (Mark Robson)
1961: Paris Blues (Ritt)
1963: The Stripper (Franklin J. Schaffner)
A New Kind of Love (Melville Shavelson)
1965: Signpost to Murder (George Englund)
1966: A Big Hand for a Little Lady (Fielder Cook)
A Fine Madness (Irvin Kershner)
1968: Rachel, Rachel (Paul Newman)
1969: Winning (James Goldstone)
1970: WUSA (Stuart Rosenberg)
1971: They Might Be Giants (Anthony Harvey)
1972: The Effect of Gamma Rays on Man-in-the-Moon Marigolds (P. Newman)
1973: Summer Wishes, Winter Dreams (Gilbert Cates)
1975: The Drowning Pool (Rosenberg)
1978: The End (Burt Reynolds)

INDEX TO
MOVIE TITLES

T

Thrill of it All, The, 82, 82, 254
Thunderball, 252
Thunderbolt and Lightfoot, 526
Thunder Road, 261
Tiger Woman, The, 124
Time of Their Lives, The, 38
Timetable, 510
Titanic, 352
To be Or Not To Be, 33
Toby Tyler, 38
To Catch a Thief, 389, 394, 395
To Each His Own, 371
Together Again, 155
To Have and Have Not, 224, 225, 468, 469
To Kill a Mockingbird, 362, 375, 473, 474
Tom, Dick, and Harry, 114
Tom Jones, 183
Tomorrow, 362, 363
Tom Sawyer, 206
Tonight or Never, 489
Too Much Too Soon, 159
Topaze, 93, 95
Top Hat, 66, 67
Torn Curtain, 62, 69, 399
Torrent, The, 215
Tortilla Flat, 516
Torture Garden, The, 7
To the Ends of the Earth, 453
Touch of Class, A, 376
Touch of Evil, 257, 258–59
Tovarich, 156
Towering Inferno, The, 546
Trail of the Lonesome Pine, 96, 447
Treasure Island, 502
Treasure of the Sierra Madre, 222, 224
Trespasser, The, 489
Trooper Hook, 440
Trudy, 458
True Grit, 375
Tugboat Annie, 247
Tumbleweeds, 98
Turning Point, The, 87, 275, 479, 480
Turn of the Screw, The, 300
Twelve Angry Men, 347, 534
Twelve O'Clock High, 473
Twentieth Century, 93, 95
20,000 Leagues Under the Sea, 404
Two-Faced Woman, 214, 216
Two for the Seesaw, 273, 460
Two Loves, 273
Two Rode Together, 541
2001: A Space Odyssey, 219
Two Weeks in Another Town, 405
Two Women, 375

U

Uncle Harry, 157
Under Two Flags, 123, 380
Unholy Three, The, 336, 339, 340–41
Union Pacific, 440
Unsuspected, The, 344
Untamed, 494
Untamed Youth, 157
Until They Sail, 268

V

Valley of Decision, The, 248, 472
Verdict, The, 350
Verna the USO Girl, 561–62
Vertigo, 181, 182, 540–41
Very Thought of You, The, 523, 524
View From Pompey's Head, The, 118
Vigil in the Night, 32
Vikings, The, 404
Vivacious, 68
Viva Las Vegas, 84
Vivien Leigh, 313
Vixen, The, 124
Voyage to the Bottom of the Sea, 333

W

Wabash Avenue, 250
Wait Till the Sun Shines Nellie, 99
Walk in the Sun, A, 41
Walk on the Wild Side, 284
War Arrow, 458
War Hunt, 288
War Lover, The, 276–78
Watch on the Rhine, 370, 525
Waterloo Bridge, 144, 314, 316
Way Down East, 487–88
Way of All Flesh, The, 369
Way We Were, The, 88–89, 253, 287–88, 289
Wee Willie Winkie, 248
Weird Woman, 339
Welcome Stranger, 249
Welcome to L.A., 561
Wells Fargo, 438
We're Not the Jet Set, 363
Westerner, The, 500
West of Zanzibar, 339
West Side Story, 74, 460
Westworld, 408
What a Way to Go!, 270, 275
Whatever Happened to Aunt Alice?, 116
Whatever Happened to Baby Jane? 300, 494, 525
What Makes Sammy Run?, 309
What's the Matter With Helen?, 329
What's Up, Doc?, 90, 254
Wheeler Dealers, The, 358
When My Baby Smiles, 249
Where Eagles Dare, 415
Where It's At, 114
Where's Poppa?, 114, 116
Where There's Life, 34
White Buffalo, The, 418
White Heat, 513
White Lightning, 199
White Sister, The, 379
Who Done It?, 248
Whole Town's Talking, The, 432
Who'll Stop the Rain?, 552
Who's Afraid of Virginia Woolf?, 187–88, 375
Who Slew Auntie Roo?, 329
Wife vs. Secretary, 436

Wild Heart, The, 170
Wild One, The, 265
Wild Orchids, 213
Wild Party, The, 194–97
Wild River, 232
William Tell, 159–60
Will Penny, 96
Winchester 73, 539
Wind Across the Everglades, 309
Wings, 483
Wings of Eagles, 505
Winner of the Wilderness, 496
Wistful Widow of Wagon Gap, The, 38
Without Love, 519
With Six You Get Eggroll, 78
Witness for the Prosecution, 326
Wizard of Oz, The, 27, 144, 310
Wolf Man, The, 337, 339
Woman in White, The, 349
Woman of Affairs, A, 215
Woman of the Year, 519
Woman Rebels, A, 99
Women in Love, 375
Wonderful Choice, The, 131
Wonderful World of the Brothers Grimm, The, 351
World Premiere, 95
Words and Music, 75, 302, 456
Written on the Wind, 178–79, 257, 470
WUSA, 252, 270
W. W. and the Dixie Dancekings, 201

Y

Yankee Doodle Dandy, 371
Yank in the R.A.F., A, 165
Yearling, The, 472
Years Ago, 103
You and Me, 447
You Can't Cheat an Honest Man, 19
You Can't Take It With You, 434
You'll Never Get Rich, 71, 169
Young Abe Lincoln, 534
Young Lions, The, 232, 266
Young Man With a Horn, 404
Young Mr. Lincoln, 532, 534
Young Philadelphians, The, 342
Young Rajah, The, 131
Young Runaways, The 565
Young Torless, 240
You Only Live Once, 447

Z

Zandy's Bride, 366
Zardov, 290, 410, 411
Ziegfeld Girl, 311
Ziegfeld Follies, 72–73

INDEX